Kahur

Nelson

NELSON

Blenheim

Vernon
Lagoon

Westport

L Grassmere

Cape
Campbell

Cape Foulwind

L Rotoroa

MARLBOROUGH

Punakaiki

Paparoa Ra

L Rotoiti

Lewis
Pass

Seaward Kaikoura Ra

Greymouth

Kaikoura

L Sumner

WEST
COAST

Arthur's
Pass

Motunau I

Ashley Estuary

Okarito Lagoon

Southern

Avon-Heathcote
Estuary

Christchurch

Alps

CANTERBURY

Banks
Peninsula

Open Bay Is

L Tekapo

Lake
Ellesmere

Jackson Head

Haast

L Pukaki

MACKENZIE
BASIN

Washdyke Lagoon

Wainono Lagoon

Milford Sound

L Wanaka

Waitaki River

Queenstown

Oamaru

L Wakatipu

Moeraki Point

Te Anau

OTAGO

L Te Anau

FIORDLAND

Taiaroa Head

Breaksea I

L Manapouri

Otago Peninsula

Resolution
I

SOUTHLAND

Dunedin

Puysegur
Point

Catlins

Invercargill

Solander Is

Muttonbird Is

Codfish I

Stewart
Island

Muttonbird Is

The
FIELD GUIDE
to the
BIRDS
of
NEW ZEALAND

The
FIELD GUIDE
to the
BIRDS
of
NEW ZEALAND

Barrie D. Heather
&
Hugh A. Robertson

Illustrated by Derek J. Onley

VIKING

To Rosemary & Lea

VIKING

Penguin Books (NZ) Ltd, cnr Rosedale and Airborne Roads, Albany,
Auckland 1310, New Zealand
Penguin Books Ltd, 27 Wrights Lane, London W8 5TZ, England
Penguin USA, 375 Hudson Street, New York, NY 10014, United States
Penguin Books Australia Ltd, 487 Maroondah Highway, Ringwood, Australia 3134
Penguin Books Canada Ltd, 10 Alcorn Avenue, Toronto, Ontario, Canada M4V 3B2
Penguin Books (South Africa) Pty Ltd, 5 Watkins Street, Denver Ext 4, 2094, South Africa
Penguin Books India (P) Ltd, 11, Community Centre, Panchsheel Park, New Delhi 110 017, India

Penguin Books Ltd, Registered Offices: Harmondsworth, Middlesex, England

First published in 1996
This edition published 2005

1 3 5 7 9 10 8 6 4 2

Designed by Richard King
Typeset by Egan-Reid Ltd, Auckland
Endpaper maps by Chris Edkins
Printed in Hong Kong

ISBN 0 14 302040 4

www.penguin.com

CONTENTS

Foreword 7

Introduction 8

IDENTIFICATION GUIDE
Plates, facing text and maps 18

HANDBOOK
Kiwi: Apterygidae 167
Grebes: Podicipedidae 171
Albatrosses: Diomedeidae 175
Shearwaters, Fulmars, Prions
     and Petrels: Procellariidae . . . 184
Storm Petrels: Oceanitidae 220
Penguins: Spheniscidae 225
Tropicbirds: Phaethontidae 236
Pelicans: Pelecanidae 237
Gannets and Boobies: Sulidae . . 237
Shags: Phalacrocoracidae 240
Darters: Anhingidae 248
Frigatebirds: Fregatidae 249
Herons, Egrets and
     Bitterns: Ardeidae 250
Ibises and Spoonbills:
     Threskiornithidae 256
Waterfowl: Anatidae 258
Raptors: Accipitridae
     and Falconidae 274
Gamebirds: Phasianidae 279
Rails, Gallinules and
     Coots: Rallidae 283

Cranes: Gruidae 292
Painted Snipe: Rostratulidae 292
Oystercatchers:
     Haematopodidae 293
Stilts and Avocets:
     Recurvirostridae 297
Pratincoles and
     Coursers: Glareolidae 299
Plovers, Dotterels and
     Lapwings: Charadriidae 300
Snipe, Sandpipers, Godwits
     and Curlews: Scolopacidae . . 312
Phalaropes: Phalaropodidae 326
Skuas: Stercorariidae 327
Gulls, Terns and
     Noddies: Laridae 332
Pigeons and Doves:
     Columbidae 348
Cockatoos and Parrots:
     Cacatuidae and Psittacidae 352
Cuckoos: Cuculidae 361
Typical Owls: Strigidae 365
Barn Owls: Tytonidae 367
Swifts: Apodidae 368
Kingfishers: Alcedinidae 369
Rollers: Coraciidae 371
New Zealand
     Wrens: Acanthisittidae 371
Larks: Alaudidae 375

Swallows and
    Martins: Hirundinidae *376*
Pipits: Motacillidae *379*
Cuckoo-shrikes and
    Trillers: Campephagidae *380*
Bulbuls: Pycnonotidae *381*
Accentors: Prunellidae *382*
Thrushes: Muscicapidae *383*
Old World Warblers: Sylviidae . *386*
Whistlers and
    allies: Pachycephalidae *387*
Australasian Warblers:
    Acanthizidae *391*
Monarch Flycatchers:
    Monarchidae *393*
Australasian Robins:
    Eopsaltriidae *395*
White-eyes: Zosteropidae *400*
Honeyeaters: Meliphagidae *402*

Buntings, Cardinals and
    Tanagers: Emberizidae *406*
Finches: Fringillidae *408*
Sparrows and
    Weavers: Ploceidae *412*
Starlings and
    Mynas: Sturnidae *413*
Wattlebirds: Callaeidae *416*
Woodswallows: Artamidae *420*
Bell Magpies: Cracticidae *421*
Birds-of-Paradise, Bowerbirds
    and Piopio: Paradisaeidae . . . *422*
Crows and Jays: Corvidae *423*

Addendum *424*

Where to see birds in *428*
    New Zealand

Index *434*

FOREWORD

The development of the field guide has been the key to the advance of recreational bird-watching and has contributed to many essential aspects of scientific ornithology; in turn, other disciplines – plant life, mammals, invertebrates – have produced their field guides. But the lead given by birdwatchers and ornithologists in this field of practical natural history remains unchallenged.

Our first New Zealand bird guide – with which my own association with the then-burgeoning art of the field guide as pioneered by Roger Tory Peterson began – appeared in 1966. Dr D. L. Serventy, in introducing a later Australian bird field guide, said: 'The virtue of a field guide is that it contains all the information necessary, in pictures and text, to *identify* a bird. But no more. Authors should resist the temptation to include extra data.'

Our 1966 *Field Guide* strayed from Dom Serventy's somewhat uncompromising formula. But we felt that – especially with respect to our comparatively few native passerines – a little extra information on life history and other aspects would not go amiss and would, in fact, probably serve to stimulate the observer. The 1966 *Field Guide*, in its numerous editions and, later, improved plates succeeded beyond our expectations and has surely fulfilled its aim of being a usable and practical guide.

A new guide to New Zealand birds is now timely. First, the art of the field guide – that essential blend of illustrations and information – has steadily reached greater perfection: new methods have been produced by bird artists to enable species to be compared at rest and in flight, and new standards of typography and book design aimed at ease of identification have been achieved. Then there is all the new material – as Dick Sibson said in his editorial Preface to the 1966 *Field Guide*, the decision to produce such a book was timely, for 'the last few decades have been exciting'. This is ever truer for the present stage!

In the 30 years since 1966 there has been much discussion on the reliability of important field characters and much rigorous checking of plumage and behavioural characteristics. Together with a wealth of new information, this has led inevitably to the decision to produce a completely new *Field Guide*. In Derek Onley, a keen amateur ornithologist, an artist has been found capable of translating the now impressive art of bird illustration into the needs of a modern field guide.

I would like to take this opportunity of congratulating both authors on their mastery of the technique required in condensing and expressing field information: the facing-page text is utility natural history writing at its best. The main text provides an excellent summary of what is known of each species and should satisfy the inquiring minds of field naturalists and professional ornithologists alike. In particular, I know how much thought and inspiration the authors have contributed towards developing the idea of this new field guide, and how much sheer hard work goes into writing such a guide.

Dr Hugh Robertson belongs to the new school of ornithologist, coupling a strong scientific training and career in ornithology with a love of birdwatching.

Like every New Zealand author of ornithological material, I was deeply indebted to Barrie Heather for his editorial skill during his period as voluntary editor of *Notornis*, and have benefited from his high standards of accuracy and scientific expression: he can be justly proud of this book and of having done so much to launch New Zealand ornithology on its latest phase.

E. G. Turbott, 1996

Past President
Ornithological Society of New Zealand

INTRODUCTION

The Field Guide to the Birds of New Zealand aims to help you to identify wild birds seen anywhere in the New Zealand region, and also follows its predecessor, *A Field Guide to the Birds of New Zealand* (and subsequent editions) by Falla, Sibson & Turbott in providing the reader with a brief and informative summary of what is known about the birds of New Zealand.

History

The Council of the Ornithological Society of New Zealand in 1959 asked Robert Falla, Dick Sibson and Graham Turbott to collaborate in compiling a practical field guide to the birds in the New Zealand region.

The first edition, with 18 colour plates by Chlöe Talbot Kelly, was published in 1966 and revised in 1970. In 1978, a further revision of the text was made and a new edition was published with 48 colour plates by Elaine Power.

These various editions have served as the 'bible' for several generations of birdwatchers in New Zealand, not only as a practical guide for identifying birds, but as a ready source of information on the distribution and habits of New Zealand birds.

The first edition of *The Field Guide to the Birds of New Zealand* was published in 1996. With our publishers, we decided to base its general layout on the very popular *Field Guide to the Birds of Australia* by Simpson & Day, and to produce the New Zealand book as a sister edition. New Zealand and overseas birdwatchers whom we consulted wanted the colour plates grouped together in a handy identification section, and also wanted distribution maps added as a new feature. There was a clear call for us to also retain the type of informative text available in the earlier Falla, Sibson & Turbott guide.

Derek Onley, a respected New Zealand ornithologist, painted 74 new colour plates depicting all 328 species, and most subspecies, of birds recorded in the New Zealand region up to 1995.

Since 1978, much new information on the distribution and biology of New Zealand birds has become available through publication of *The Atlas of Bird Distribution in New Zealand* in 1985, the *Checklist of the Birds of New Zealand* in 1990, *The Handbook to the Birds of Australia, New Zealand and Antarctica*, and about 8000 pages of *Notornis*, the journal of the Ornithological Society of New Zealand. This meant that much of the original material had become so dated that we had to write the text afresh, although we retained some of the pithy lines or gems from the previous field guides. The growth of interest in conservation since the 1970s prompted us to add a section on conservation management for appropriate species, and we added a section of more detailed information to aid the identification of ages and sexes of some particular groups of birds. The first edition of *The Field Guide* included 20 species added to the New Zealand list between 1978 and 1995 as a result of recent records and some taxonomic changes. The second edition included an addendum, with text for six new species seen in New Zealand between 1994 and 1998, and this edition adds a further five species seen recently.

Scope

For the purposes of this guide, the New Zealand region includes only New Zealand territory, from the Kermadec Islands at latitude 29°S to the Ross Dependency in Antarctica. Missing from the previous 'field guide' is Macquarie Island (latitude 55°S), which, although closest to New Zealand subantarctic islands, is actually part of Australia and is covered in recent editions of Simpson & Day. We have included all species accepted on the New Zealand list between 1900 and 2005. We have therefore excluded records of vagrants seen in the 1800s, and of native birds that became extinct before 1900. We have included a specific plate that depicts those species that have probably become extinct during the 1900s in the slim hope that a few birds may survive somewhere; this plate also serves as a reminder of what we have recently lost from our New Zealand heritage.

Layout

The first section of the book is an identification guide; on the page opposite the colour plate is a distribution map for those species breeding in New Zealand, and sufficient plumage and behavioural details that should help identify the species, sex and/ or age of the bird you see in the field.

The distribution maps show where species breeding in New Zealand may be found in suitable habitat; maps for vagrants, stragglers and non-native seabirds, and for migratory waders (which can turn up in any estuary around the coast) are not necessary for identification purposes, and so this information is instead given in the second part of the book. Most of the information in the maps comes from *The Atlas of Bird Distribution in New Zealand*, updated from our own knowledge or from advice from ornithologists around New Zealand.

The plates are arranged roughly in the standard taxonomic order, but where two similar-looking species are not closely related, they are shown together on the same plate. Two exceptions to this rule are a plate devoted to rare Australian vagrants, and the final plate, which depicts a variety of species believed to have become extinct in the 1900s.

The second part of the book gives more details on the distribution and ecology of each species, but does not attempt to present a full coverage of all that is known for each species, which the impressive seven-volume *Handbook of Australian, New Zealand and Antarctic Birds* is doing. Those species that

breed in New Zealand receive a full treatment under the headings: Other Names, Size, Geographical variation, Distribution, Population, Conservation, Breeding, Behaviour, Feeding, In the hand (optional) and Reading.

The final section of the book is an introduction to 12 easily accessible birdwatching sites around New Zealand. A visit to these sites will allow you to see or hear a wide variety of native birds, often in spectacular or interesting settings. Many native species can be seen almost anywhere and so they are not included in the lists of notable native species you are likely to see at each site.

Treatment

The scientific world is in a state of transition between two different methods of ordering or listing the names of species. Scientific checklists and field guides have followed a consistent taxonomic ordering of species with groups that are thought to be closely related being placed alongside one another; however, new genetic techniques based on analysis of DNA and allozymes of different species indicate that we may soon have to completely rearrange the taxonomic ordering system. In the meantime, we have decided to follow the order and scientific names given in the *Checklist of the Birds of New Zealand*, with some very minor variations that are based on recently published work on the separation or amalgamation of subspecies.

Scientific names follow a standard format throughout the world and are traditionally given in italics with the genus listed first, the species name second, and the subspecific name (if required) third. For example, the full scientific name for the Red-billed Gull is *Larus novaehollandiae scopulinus*. The word *Larus* refers to the genus, a group of related species (the Black-billed Gull and Black-backed Gull also belong to this group of gulls, although not all 'gulls' around the world do). The word *novaehollandiae* distinguishes this particular species, and forms a unique combination with the word *Larus* to identify the species wherever it occurs in the world. Some species can be further divided into geographically distinct forms, called subspecies or races; these are distinguished by a third name; in this case, *scopulinus* refers to the form breeding in New Zealand, which are slightly, but consistently, different from those breeding in Australia (*novaehollandiae*). This subspecies in Australia is called the 'nominate' subspecies, as it has the same subspecific name as the species name, which indicates that a bird of this form was used to originally describe the species as being different from other gulls.

There is an international move to standardise the popular or common names of birds, as well as the already-accepted standardised scientific name. This move is prompted mainly by people who list all the species they have seen (variously known as listers, tickers or twitchers) who want to know if they can add a tick to their 'world list' if they see a Red-billed Gull in New Zealand, having seen a Silver Gull in Australia – they can't because they belong to the same species. We have resisted attempts to internationalise the common names used in New Zealand, because calling our Red-billed Gulls 'Silver Gulls' would add confusion, as our endemic Black-billed Gull is more silver-coloured than the Red-billed Gull!

Some species in New Zealand are known to everyone by their Maori name, e.g. Tui, Takahe, and we resist the loss of part of our heritage by imposing artificial labels on New Zealand birds. We have given the most widely accepted Maori name(s), but not all, as some species (e.g. Stitchbird) have up to seven recorded geographical variations of their Maori names. We have also followed Maori (and quickly becoming New Zealand) useage by not adding 's' to plurals; so we have one Takahe and three Tui. Again, we have followed the common names given in the *Checklist*, except that we have dropped a few confusing prefixes not in common use here, and have used our own personal preferences where a choice is available (e.g. Dunnock rather than the more confusing Hedge Sparrow, given that they are not closely related to the 'true' sparrows).

Instead of just giving body length from the tip of the bill to the tip of the tail, in the 'Size' sections we have also tried to give an impression of the size of the bird by presenting the weight. Where males and females differ appreciably in size, these are given separately. The weights are only approximate, since weights of birds are highly variable, depending on such things as time of year, the time of day (up to 10% difference between dawn and dusk weights of some passerines), stage in the breeding cycle (e.g. a 20% weight loss between the start and end of incubation in male kiwi, and similar declines during incubation shifts of some seabirds), and weights can be inflated when a bird is preparing for laying, moulting or migration.

We briefly review the geographical variation within each species. It is beyond the scope of this book to give all the information to allow identification to the subspecies level for all species.

For most landbirds breeding in New Zealand, there is no significant seasonal change in distribution, as the equable climate of New Zealand means that there is no need for major migration, although there is some evidence of vertical migration, local movements and some movement across Cook Strait, and the two native cuckoos migrate to the tropical Pacific. Inland breeding waders, terns and gulls show the most obvious migration within New Zealand; Banded Dotterels, Gannets, White-fronted Terns and some other seabirds visit Australia outside the breeding season, while many waders, terns and seabirds undertake major trans-equatorial migration, and some seabirds have a circumpolar movement pattern between breeding seasons. Much of the information on the movements of birds comes from banding (ringing) studies and, more recently, from radio-tracking or satellite-tracking research. If you find a dead banded bird it is important that you send the band to the address shown on the band. If you see or catch a live banded bird, please send band details, including colour-band combinations on each leg (the left leg is the birds' left leg), to The Banding Office, Department of Conservation, P.O. Box 10-420, Wellington.

In the 'Distribution' sections, we explain in more detail the breeding distribution, historical changes since human settlement, as shown in sub-fossil, midden or historical evidence, discuss seasonal movements and habitat use of birds, summarise the geographical and seasonal patterns of beach-wrecked seabirds, main sites used by waterfowl and waders, and give details on the records of vagrants and stragglers from published papers in *Notornis*, from files of the Rare Birds Committee of the Ornithological Society, and from from the annual 'Classified Summarised Notes' section of *Notornis*.

Many people want to know how many birds there are of a particular species. This information is now becoming available for many threatened species that are being studied or managed intensively, for some seabird populations where it is possible to make reasonably accurate counts of birds at breeding colonies, and the Ornithological Society's 'National Wader Census' from 1983 to 1994 has provided excellent information on the numbers of waders using estuaries or lake shores in winter and summer. For common landbird species, population estimates are not possible at this stage and so we have simply used subjective terms to describe the populations.

New Zealand is regarded as one of the world leaders in bird conservation; first, through the work of the Wildlife Service of the Department of Internal Affairs, and since 1987 through the Department of Conservation. Much of this innovative management work has relied heavily on preparatory work undertaken in research sections of government departments and universities, and by amateur ornithologists, especially members of the Ornithological Society of New Zealand. Many amateurs have volunteered their time to give practical field assistance to conservation programmes, perhaps best exemplified by the Chatham Island Taiko expeditions organised by David Crockett that led to the rediscovery of the species in 1978. Other organisations such as Ducks Unlimited, Royal Forest and Bird Protection Society and the Miranda Naturalists' Trust have helped with specific programmes.

Almost all of our native birds are fully protected, as are migrants, vagrants, stragglers and visitors. In the 'Conservation' sections, we have given a brief outline of conservation problems for many native species and outlined the management undertaken or planned for those species. Somewhat loosely, we have also included under this heading the harvest and management of gamebirds and the impact of some bird pests.

The information on breeding has been gleaned from a variety of sources, especially the Nest Record Scheme of the Ornithological Society, which holds details of the breeding biology of about 150 species on over 25,000 cards. There is still much to be learnt about the basic breeding biology of even moderately common species, and for most species there are insufficient data to investigate geographical patterns of timing of breeding, clutch size, incubation and fledging periods, and productivity. Within these sections we also present what little information is known on the age at first breeding.

Because a common question is 'How long does Species X live?', we have given what information we could find on adult survivorship and life expectancy, and the Banding Office of the Department of Conservation has kindly provided information on the longest elapsed time between banding and recovery for a number of species – other similar data have been gleaned from published material on overseas studies.

In general, birds in New Zealand have relatively small clutch sizes, long incubation and fledging periods, and seem exceptionally long-lived compared with the same or similar-sized species in the Northern Hemisphere.

The 'Behaviour' sections have tended to be catch-alls for interesting snippets on whether the bird forms flocks at certain times of the year, how it relates to its mate and other birds in the breeding and non-breeding seasons, and how it relates to humans. These sections include descriptions of the main of songs, calls and displays. In New Zealand, there are very few species that look so similar that calls are needed to clinch the identification, but there are many cryptic or nocturnal species that can be identified reliably from call alone.

The rapidly growing body of knowledge on the foods and feeding behaviour of New Zealand birds is summarised in the 'Feeding' sections. Many specific studies have been undertaken, but a number of incidental observations have been included in the 'Classified Summarised Notes' section of *Notornis*.

The sections entitled 'In the hand' are intended to help identify species or subspecies of seabirds and to identify the ages and sexes of some landbirds. These accounts are aimed more at the specialist ornithologist than the general reader. The seabird section is particularly aimed at Ornithological Society beach-patrollers who record the species and numbers of seabirds found dead on beaches as a means of monitoring the status of populations, searching for banded birds, and providing suitable material for museum skins for further study or display purposes. Many seabird species are similar, and beach-wrecked specimens not only smell horrible but generally do not look like the live birds depicted in the plates, and so accurate identification often relies on measurements, colours and shape of bill, wing, tail and legs.

Coverage of landbirds is aimed largely at researchers who want to determine the age and sex of birds caught so that they can distinguish different parts of the population, which may behave, breed or survive differently. Information on introduced passerines is mainly from the Central Passerine Banding Group.

At the foot of most species accounts is a 'Reading' list of books, scientific papers (often quite readable) or university theses that contain further information about the particular species; this is in addition to the following list of more general books that cover many species, particular groups of birds, or birds from specific geographical areas. The 'Reading' sections are a form of acknowledgement to those who have gathered much of the original information that we have compiled to make this book. All the references given should be available to the reader to borrow through the interloan service at any public library in New Zealand.

Standard References

The following books provide information on the birds that are found in the New Zealand region. They have been the source of much information used to compile this field guide, and all are recommended for any private or public library collection.

Bull, P.C., Gaze, P.D. & Robertson, C.J.R. 1985. *The Atlas of Bird Distribution in New Zealand*. Wellington: OSNZ. Ornithological Society of New Zealand.

Chambers, S. 1989. *Birds of New Zealand: locality guide*. Hamilton: Arun.

Coates, B.J. 1985. *The Birds of Papua New Guinea*. Vols 1 & 2. Alderley: Dove.

Falla, R.A., Sibson, R.B. & Turbott, E.G. 1979. *The New Guide to the Birds of New Zealand and Outlying Islands*. Auckland: Collins.

Fleming, C.A. 1982. *George Edward Lodge: the unpublished New Zealand bird paintings*. Wellington: Nova Pacifica.

Gaze, P.D. 1994. *Rare and Endangered New Zealand Birds*. Christchurch: Canterbury University Press.

Gill, B. & Martinson, P. 1991. *New Zealand's Extinct Birds*. Auckland: Random Century.

Harrison, P. 1988. *Seabirds: an identification guide*. London: Christopher Helm.

Hayman, P., Marchant, J. & Prater, T. 1986. *Shorebirds: an identification guide to the waders of the world*. Beckenham: Croom Helm.

Higgins, P. & Davies, S. (eds). 1996. *The Handbook of Australian, New Zealand and Antarctic Birds*. Vol. 3. Melbourne: OUP.

Jonnson, L. 1992. *Birds of Europe, with North Africa and the Middle East*. London: Christopher Helm.

Lane, B.A. 1987. *Shorebirds in Australia*. Melbourne: Nelson.

Maclean, G. L. 1993. *Roberts' Birds of Southern Africa*. London: New Holland.

Madge, S. & Burn, H. 1988. *Wildfowl: an identification guide to the ducks, geese and swans of the world*. London: Christopher Helm.

Marchant, S. & Higgins, P. (eds). 1990. *Handbook of Australian,New Zealand and Antarctic Birds.* Vol. 1. Melbourne: OUP.

Marchant, S. & Higgins, P. (eds). 1993. *Handbook of Australian, New Zealand and Antarctic Birds.* Vol. 2. Melbourne: OUP.

Oliver, W.R.B. 1955. *New Zealand Birds.* Wellington: Reed.

Perrins, C.M. & Middleton, A.L.A. 1985. *The Encyclopaedia of Birds.* London: George Allen & Unwin.

Pizzey, G. 1980. *A Field Guide to the Birds of Australia.* Sydney: Collins.

Pratt, H.D.; Bruner, P.L. & Berrett, D.G. 1987. *A Field Guide to the Birds of Hawaii and the Tropical Pacific.* Princeton: Princeton University Press.

Pringle, J.D. 1985. *Waterbirds.* Sydney: Angus & Robertson.

Pringle, J.D. 1986. *The Shorebirds of Australia.* Sydney: Angus & Robertson.

Robertson, C.J.R. (ed.) 1985. *Reader's Digest Complete Book of New Zealand Birds.* Sydney: Reader's Digest.

Serventy, D.L., Serventy, V. & Warham, J. 1971. *The Handbook of Australian Seabirds.* Sydney: Reed.

Simpson, K. & Day, N. 1993. *Field Guide to the Birds of Australia.* Melbourne: Viking O'Neil.

Sinclair, I., Hockey, P. & Tarboton, W. 1993. *Illustrated Guide to the Birds of Southern Africa.* London: New Holland.

Soper, M.F. 1984. *Birds of New Zealand and Outlying Islands.* Christchurch: Whitcoulls.

Svensson, L. 1992. *Identification Guide to European Passerines.* Stockholm: Lars Svensson.

Turbott, E.G. 1967. *Buller's Birds of New Zealand.* Chistchurch: Whitcombe & Tombs.

Turbott, E.G. 1990. *Checklist of the Birds of New Zealand and the Ross Dependency, Antarctica.* Auckland: Random Century.

Acknowledgements

It would have been impossible to compile a book of this nature without considerable help from many others. We are extremely grateful for the time and efforts of the following people who have either refereed texts, provided unpublished data, commented constuctively on artwork, or allowed free access to museum collections:

Hilary Aikman, Maida Barlow, Sandy Bartle, Kevin Bartram, Phil Battley, Brian Bell, Peter Bull, Isabel Castro-Udy, George Chance, Mick Clout, Rogan Colbourne, Rod Cossee, Les Cristidis, David Crockett, John Darby, Rose Delany, Peter Dilks, John Dowding, Graeme Elliott, Mike Fitzgerald, Ian Flux, Robin Fordham, John Gibb, Brian Gill, Lou Gurr, Don Hadden, Jenny Hawkins, Rod Hay, Allan Hemmings, Peter Higgins, Noel Hyde, Mike Imber, John Innes, Ian Jamieson, Paddy Latham, Linda Lawrence, John Lyall, Tim Lovegrove, Gabor Lovei, Ian McLean, John McLennan, Don Merton, Pat Miller, Colin Miskelly, Geoff Moon, Jim Moore, Peter Moore, Ron Moorhouse, Rory O'Brien, Colin O'Donnell, Richard Parrish, Ray Pierce, Mary Powlesland, Ralph Powlesland, Murray Potter, Gwenda Pulham, Gretchen Rasch, Christine Reed, Adrian Riegen, Christopher Robertson, Lea Robertson, Danny Rogers, Paul Sagar, Ed Saul, Peter Schweigman, Ken Simpson, Hamish Spencer, John Squire, Jean-Claude Stahl, Andrew Styche, Roger Sutton, Graeme Taylor, Jack Taylor, Rowley Taylor, Alan Tennyson, Geoff Tunnicliffe, Dick Veitch, Roy Weston, Murray Williams, Pete Wilson, Keith Woodley, Euan Young.

Ken Simpson, Ray Richards, David Medway and Geoff Walker helped to get this book off the ground, and Richard King and Kate Stone designed and edited the first edition, and Louise Armstrong edited this edition. Chris Edkins drew the endpaper maps for this edition.

To all, a big thank you!

Ornithological Society of New Zealand

The OSNZ has supported the production of this field guide by commissioning Derek Onley to paint the 74 colour plates plus the black and white illustrations; like the authors of the earlier *Field Guide*, the authors are donating royalties from sales of this book to the Society to support further bird study.

The object of the OSNZ, which was

founded in 1939, is to encourage, organise and carry out ornithological field work on a national scale. No special qualifications are needed for membership, except for an interest in the study of the habits and distribution of birds.

Because members are scattered throughout New Zealand, the Society operates chiefly by organising co-operative investigations, encouraging individual projects, and by issuing publications such as the quarterly scientific journal *Notornis* and accompanying newsletter, *Southern Bird.*

An ornithological library containing many of the world's leading ornithological journals is maintained at the Auckland Institute and Museum. The main field activities include collection of nesting records and of data on storm-killed seabirds, special inquiries on the status of birds common and rare, and studies of the movements of birds throughout the country.

Further information about the OSNZ can be obtained from the Secretary, P.O. Box 12397, Wellington.

Glossary

Australasia: the region including Australia, eastern Indonesia, New Guinea, the southwestern Pacific and NZ

axillaries: feathers of the 'armpit' where the underwing joins the body

banding: marking of birds with a uniquely numbered metal band (ring) on the leg, often with a combination of coloured plastic bands to allow recognition of individuals or an age/sex class without the need to recapture the birds

carpal bar: a dark band at the bend of the folded wing, particularly noticeable in some immature terns

caruncles: fleshy growths on the facial skin of some shags near the nostrils

cere: fleshy covering of the upper bill of certain birds, e.g. hawks, parrots, pigeons; often brightly coloured

cline: a gradual change from one end of a bird's range to the other, usually of size or colour

coverts: feathers that cover the bases of the main wing feathers and tail feathers

culmen: the ridge along the whole length or top of the upper mandible

dimorphic: species with two forms or phases, usually of plumage or size, e.g. raptors, Stewart Island Shag, Stitchbird

eclipse: dull plumage assumed by males of, especially, ducks after breeding; they become very like females and immatures

endangered: likely to become extinct if not managed carefully

endemic: natural range is in a certain country and nowhere else, e.g. Kiwi and Kakapo are found in NZ only

feral: living wild after domestication

filoplumes: simple threadlike white plumes; appear in breeding plumage of some seabirds and shags

fledge: fully feathered; able to fly (fledgling)

flight feathers: the primaries, secondaries and tertials of the wings (remiges) and the main feathers of the tail (rectrices)

front: the forehead between the base of the upper bill and the crown, e.g. White-fronted Tern

frontal shield: horny shield on the forehead, taking the place of feathers, e.g. Pukeko

gape: fleshy skin at the sides of the base of the bill

gregarious: living together in flocks or in colonies

gular sac or pouch: the elastic naked skin of the throat that can be filled with food (pelicans) or air (frigatebirds)

holarctic: includes all the Arctic region

immature: stages of plumage between the first moult and the breeding plumage (= subadult)

introduced: a bird brought to NZ by people, not by its own efforts

invertebrates: animals without a backbone, with an external skeleton, e.g. crustaceans, insects, spiders

juvenile: birds in their first plumage after replacing natal down (US = juvenal)

lobes: folds of skin on the toes, extending out for swimming and closing when feet are drawn back, e.g. grebes and coot; the equivalent of webs in ducks

maimai: duckshooting hide or blind

mandibles: the upper and lower parts of a bird's bill

mantle: the upper back

midden: the remains (often bones, shell and charcoal) of Maori feasting, showing that a species used to be locally present

migrant: a species that moves annually and seasonally between breeding and non-breeding areas, either within NZ, e.g. Wrybill, or to other countries, e.g. Bar-tailed Godwit. Includes species which reach NZ each year, even if in small numbers, e.g. Pectoral Sandpiper

mollusc: an invertebrate with a shell as a skeleton; varies from shellfish to squid in water, to snails on land

monogamous: having only one mate (cf. polygamous)

moult: the annual, or more periodic, replacement of all feathers; because feathers are soft they fray and lose their effectiveness in flight, insulation and waterproofing

mustelid: a group of mammalian predators (ferrets, stoats and weasels) introduced to NZ in the late 1800s in a vain attempt to control rabbits

nape: the back of a bird's neck

native: birds that are naturally found in a country, e.g. Tui and Fantail, or are self-introduced, e.g. the Welcome Swallow

nearctic: belonging to the arctic zone of North America

palaearctic: belonging to the arctic zone of Europe and Asia

pakihi: open boggy wetlands with a mix of rushes and shrubs

pelagic: of the ocean; feeding far out to sea

possum: the brush-tailed possum *Trichosurus vulpecula* is a browsing marsupial introduced to NZ from Australia

predator: an animal that takes birds or their eggs and chicks

protrusible tongue: can be extended to reach into flowers for nectar

raptor: a bird of prey

rat, ship: *Rattus rattus*, the 'black rat' or 'roof rat'; climbs well and so it is the most dangerous predatory rat

rat, Pacific: *R. exulans*, (kiore); a predator that arrived with Maori, and takes eggs and chicks; common on many offshore islands, but now rare on the NZ mainland

rat, Norway: *R. norvegicus*, the 'brown rat'; climbs less readily than ship rat

regurgitate: bring back into the mouth food that has been swallowed and digested

scapulars: feathers that lie along upper shoulder of the wing, sometimes distinctively coloured, e.g. Black-fronted Dotterel

scrape: a shallow depression in the ground or in low vegetation to serve as a nest

species: distinct forms of birds which would not normally interbreed if they lived together

speculum: iridescent patch on the upperwing secondary feathers of ducks

straggler: a bird that follows its normal migratory path but goes too far or strays off course

subfossil: bones too young to be a true fossil, e.g. in sand dunes or caves

subspecies: a geographical race of a species that has some consistent differences from others of the species

taxonomy: the system of classifying birds (and other organisms) to reflect their natural relationships

threatened: species that are in low numbers or declining in number and/or range and that require management or intervention to ensure their survival

vagrant: a wanderer; a bird having turned up unexpectedly in an unusual direction, having strayed there by mistake or, having been caught up in a severe storm, is blown well off course, whereas a straggler is in about the right direction but has gone further than usual

vestigial: a non-functional remnant of something other birds have, e.g. tail of grebes, wings of kiwi

visitor: species which disperse from mating areas and some reach NZ every year, e.g. Thin-billed Prion

wattles: colourful fleshy drupes on either side of the gape in Saddleback, Kokako and Huia

wingbar: a band of contrast, usually white, on the upperwing in flight, often formed by the coloured tips of the wing-coverts

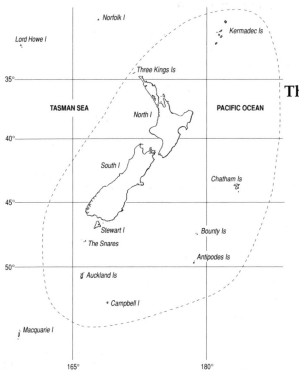

The New Zealand region

Norfolk I

Lord Howe I

Kermadec Is

Three Kings Is

35°

TASMAN SEA

North I

PACIFIC OCEAN

40°

South I

45°

Chatham Is

Stewart I

Bounty Is

The Snares

Antipodes Is

50°

Auckland Is

Campbell I

Macquarie I

165°   180°

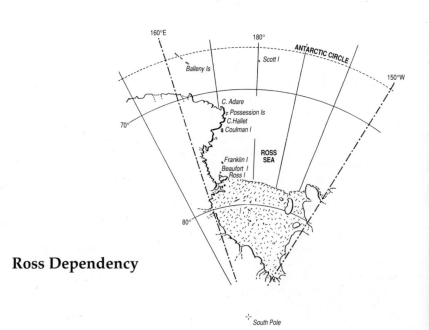

160°E   180°   ANTARCTIC CIRCLE

Balleny Is   Scott I

150°W

C. Adare

Possession Is

70°   C. Hallet

Coulman I

ROSS
SEA

Franklin I

Beaufort I

Ross I

Ross Dependency

80°

South Pole

16

Parts of a bird

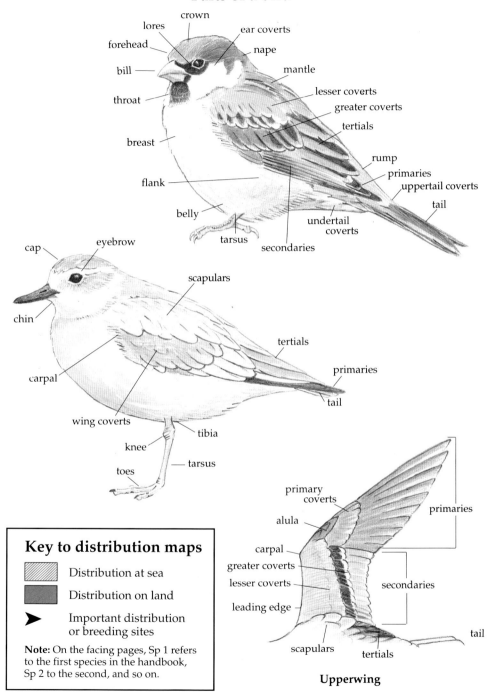

crown
lores
ear coverts
forehead
nape
bill
mantle
throat
lesser coverts
greater coverts
tertials
breast
rump
flank
primaries
uppertail coverts
belly
tail
tarsus
undertail coverts
secondaries

cap
eyebrow
scapulars
chin
tertials
primaries
carpal
tail
wing coverts
tibia
knee
toes
tarsus

primary coverts
alula
primaries
carpal
greater coverts
lesser coverts
secondaries
leading edge
tail
scapulars
tertials

Upperwing

Key to distribution maps

Distribution at sea

Distribution on land

➤ Important distribution or breeding sites

Note: On the facing pages, Sp 1 refers to the first species in the handbook, Sp 2 to the second, and so on.

Plate 1 **KIWI**

Small group of distinctive flightless and generally nocturnal birds. More often heard than seen; most vocal in the first two hours of darkness. Males smaller and have loud shrill clear ascending whistle; females deeper hoarse whistle, often given in response to male call; calls repeated 10–25 times. Large cone-shaped birds with small head and long bill with nostrils near tip; minute remnant wings and no tail; coarse loose feathers; strong legs and toes with long claws. Slow lumbering gait, but can run fast. In native forests, scrub, rough tussock grassland and in some exotic forests; from sea level to subalpine. Kiwi snuffle as they explore for food on ground. Feed on invertebrates (especially worms, bugs, beetles and spiders) and fallen fruits, from surface and by probing up to 10 cm into soil. Lay 1–2 huge white eggs in a burrow, hollow log or under dense vegetation. Very long incubation – by the male only in Little Spotted Kiwi and Brown Kiwi in the North Island, but by male and female in Great Spotted Kiwi and Brown Kiwi in the South Island, and by the pair plus helpers in Brown Kiwi on Stewart Island. Chicks hatch fully feathered, like miniature adults, and are mobile within a week but return to the nest each day for several weeks or even years.

BROWN KIWI (Rowi – Okarito, Tokoeka – Fiordland and Stewart Island)
Apteryx australis **Uncommon endemic**

40 cm; ♂ 2.2 kg, ♀ 2.8 kg. Dark greyish brown *streaked lengthways* reddish brown; *long* ivory bill. Male has shrill clear (or slightly warbling) ascending and then descending whistle; female has lower-pitched, hoarse cry. **Habitat:** Native forest, scrub, exotic forest (especially in Northland, Coromandel and Taranaki), rough farmland and tussockland (subalpine and dunes). Most common in Northland and on Stewart Island; small distinctive populations at Okarito (60–100 birds) and near Haast (200–300 birds). **Breeding:** Jun–Mar. **[Sp 1]**

GREAT SPOTTED KIWI (Roroa, Roa) *Apteryx haastii* **Uncommon endemic**

45 cm; ♂ 2.4 kg, ♀ 3.3 kg. Largest kiwi. Light brownish grey tinged with chestnut, mottled or banded *horizontally* with white; massive ivory bill; legs dark brown; claws vary from horn to black. Juvenile has proportionately longer bill and darker legs than similar Little Spotted Kiwi. Male very loud shrill warbling whistle; female slower and lower-pitched ascending warble; calls more powerful and slower than Little Spotted Kiwi. **Habitat:** Native forest, scrub, pakihi wetlands and tussock grassland from sea level to subalpine, but distribution patchy. Strongholds in north-western Nelson, Paparoa Ranges and between Lake Sumner and Arthur's Pass. **Breeding:** Jul–Dec. **[Sp 3]**

LITTLE SPOTTED KIWI (Kiwi-pukupuku) *Apteryx owenii* **Rare endemic**

30 cm; ♂ 1150 g, ♀ 1325 g. Smallest kiwi. Brownish grey finely mottled or banded *horizontally* with white; long ivory bill; pale legs and claws. Male high-pitched ascending whistle; female lower and more tremulous; call rate faster and higher pitched than other kiwi, especially the female. **Habitat:** Native forest, scrub and grassland on a few offshore islands: c. 1,000 on Kapiti I, small populations have been established on Hen, Tiritiri Matangi, Red Mercury and Long (Marlborough) Is, and at Karori Sanctuary, Wellington. Some may persist in Westland or Fiordland. **Breeding:** Sep–Feb. **[Sp 2]**

BROWN KIWI

GREAT SPOTTED KIWI

LITTLE SPOTTED KIWI

Plate 2 # GREBES

Freshwater diving birds with a distinctive silhouette – dumpy body, low to the water, with rounded rear end because of no visible tail; bill pointed; head held erect. Sexes alike. They feed underwater, propelled by special lobed feet. As their legs are set well back, they are awkward on land and seldom venture onto it. Patter across the water when disturbed or during displays, but can fly well at night. Gather in loose flocks in autumn and winter. Silent. Nests are bulky floating structures, often attached to emergent or overhanging vegetation. Lay 2–4 chalky white eggs, staining to brown; covered whenever the adult leaves the nest. Chicks are carried on an adult's back when very small. Young have striped heads, through to the age of independence.

AUSTRALASIAN CRESTED GREBE (Puteketeke) *Podiceps cristatus*
Uncommon native

50 cm, 1100 g. A large long-necked grebe with a dagger-like bill and a prominent double crest and ruff. Swims with its slender white neck held erect, head horizontal. Brilliant white foreneck and chest visible when head lowered at rest. Adult plumage similar all year. Juveniles retain stripes on head until independent. Immature lacks ruff and has only a small crest, making it look like an immature Pied Shag. In flight, long thin body and prominent white panels on front and back of dark upperwing. Dives smoothly without splash. **Habitat:** Large open lakes of inland South I. Usually in pairs but gather on some Canterbury lakes in winter. A rare vagrant to North I. **Breeding:** Sep–Feb. **[Sp 4]**

NEW ZEALAND DABCHICK (Weweia) *Poliocephalus rufopectus*
Uncommon endemic

29 cm, 250 g. A small dark grebe with a dumpy body, slim neck, small head, short bill and tiny, fluffy white tail. *Blackish head, finely streaked with silver feathers; prominent yellow eye; rusty chestnut foreneck and breast.* After breeding, plumage paler and nondescript. After several months, juveniles look like adults. Dives frequently, often smoothly but sometimes after a leap. When alarmed, swims quietly away on or under the water, or skitters across the water, its rapidly beating wings hitting the surface. **Habitat:** Sheltered parts of lakes, farm ponds and, in winter, sewage oxidation ponds. Locally common in North I; a rare vagrant to South I. **Breeding:** Jun–Mar. **[Sp 5]**

HOARY-HEADED GREBE *Poliocephalus poliocephalus*   Rare Australian vagrant

28 cm, 250 g. Similar to NZ Dabchick in size and habits; *much paler and slimmer* than other small grebes. Breeding adult dark grey above, breast pale buff, *head prominently streaked silver* (hoary), eye not contrasting; bill tipped white. Non-breeding adult *pale grey with contrasting grey-brown cap to below eye* and extending as a dark stripe from the crown down the hindneck; bill pinkish. Regularly swims with thin neck held erect. **Habitat:** Lakes and farm ponds. **[Sp 6]**

AUSTRALASIAN LITTLE GREBE *Tachybaptus novaehollandiae*   Rare native

25 cm, 220 g. The smallest grebe in NZ. Breeding adult has black head with contrasting yellow eye, *a yellow patch of skin between eye and bill*, and broad band of rich chestnut on sides of neck. Non-breeding adult and immature lack head and neck colours, the skin patch becomes whitish and hard to see, but upperparts remain dark brown; *pale cheeks and foreneck contrast with dark brown cap to level of eye*. Dives frequently. Wary; when disturbed, dives and may lurk in vegetation, often with only its head above water. **Habitat:** Lakes and farm ponds. **[Sp 7]**

AUSTRALASIAN CRESTED GREBE

juv

NEW ZEALAND DABCHICK

imm/non-breeding

HOARY-HEADED GREBE

breeding

non-breeding

AUSTRALASIAN LITTLE GREBE

breeding

non-breeding

Huge ('albatrosses') or very large ('mollymawks') seabirds with long narrow wings and short tail. Long heavy hooked bill covered with horny plates, nostrils in small tubes on the sides near the base. Most are dark above and mainly white below. Pattern of upperwing, under-wing, head and bill are distinctive. In flight, soar gracefully on stiffly held wings, and only rarely flap. Clumsy on ground; legs and webbed feet set well back. Generally oceanic; occasionally seen near land. Many follow ships or gather around fishing boats. Silent at sea except when fighting over food. Loud bleats, croaks, whines and cackles at breeding colonies, and elaborate displays accompanied by bill-clapping and calls. Lay 1 large white egg in shallow bowl or on top of pedestal constructed of vegetation and mud. Long incubation period and extremely long fledging period (7–11 months for full breeding cycle). Sexes alike but males larger. Juveniles generally distinctive for several years.

ROYAL ALBATROSS (Toroa)   *Diomedea epomophora*   Locally common endemic

115 cm, 9 kg. Two races distinguished by size and amount of black on upperwings. Like the palest adult Wandering Albatrosses but with no distinctive juvenile plum-age, wings normally black above or with white on the leading edge of the inner upperwing, and tail usually white; bill massive (170 x 65 mm), light pink with creamy tip and *with black cutting edge to upper mandible*. Juvenile has white body except for heavy black flecking on the back, flanks, crown and tail; upperwings black (Northern race *sanfordi*) or mainly black with small patches of white at base of leading edge and in centre of inner wing, becoming increasingly white from the leading edge backwards (Southern race *epomophora*). Adult has completely white body; upper-wings black (Northern race) or black with white patches extending backwards from leading edge (Southern race); underwings white with black tip and thin black trailing edge. Legs and feet pinkish to bluish white. **Habitat:** Northern race breeds at Taiaroa Head (Dunedin) and Sisters and Forty Fours Is (Chathams); Southern race breeds Campbell and Auckland Is. Ranges widely circumpolar through the southern oceans, and most often seen in NZ coastal waters in winter, except off Taiaroa Head. **Breeding:** All year; eggs laid Oct–Dec; young fledge c. 11 months later. **[Sp 9]**

WANDERING ALBATROSS   *Diomedea exulans*   Uncommon native

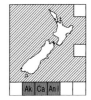

115 cm, 6.5 kg. Variable plumages, according to age and race. Some pale adults are like Royal Albatross, but all have a huge bill (160 x 55 mm), light pink with creamy tip and with *no black on cutting edges*; leading edge of inner upperwing usually black or mottled black in all but the whitest birds (which have much more extensive white on upperwings than the whitest Royal); tail usually black-tipped. Juvenile initially *uniformly dark brown, except for white face and dark-tipped white underwings* (A). Over the next 10–15 years, the plumage whitens, initially on the belly (B), then from the back onto the upperwings, and outwards from a central patch on the upperwing, following the progression from C to F in the whitest NZ breeding birds; however, birds breed in the NZ region in all forms from C through to F. Those birds in phase G, with white leading edge to upperwing, are of the larger race *chionoptera* (Snowy Albatross), which breeds outside the NZ region. Underwings white with black tip and thin black trailing edge. Legs and feet pinkish to brownish grey. **Habitat:** Breeds circumpolar subantarctic; in NZ region, breeds at Antipodes, Campbell and Auckland Is. Ranges widely through the southern oceans and most often seen in NZ coastal waters in winter. **Breeding:** All year; eggs laid Jan–Mar, young fledge c. 11 months later. **[Sp 8]**

Southern

Northern

juv Northern

ROYAL
ALBATROSS

A
juv

B

WANDERING
ALBATROSS

C

D

E

F

G

Plate 4   **ALBATROSSES**

SHY MOLLYMAWK   *Diomedea cauta*   **Common native**

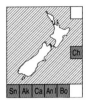

90 cm, 4 kg. Three subspecies breed in NZ region, separated by size, plumage and bill colours. All have diagnostic *white underwing with very narrow black borders and a small black triangular notch at base of the leading edge.* Larger and longer-winged than other mollymawks. Adult NZ White-capped Mollymawk (*steadi*) has white head and neck, small black patch from eye to bill shading to very faint grey wash on cheeks; mantle grey-brown merging into grey-black back and upperwings; rump white, tail grey-black, underparts white; *tips of underwing white with thin black edging*: bill (133 mm) pale bluish horn with yellowish top to bill, especially at base and tip; legs and feet pale blue-grey. Salvin's Mollymawk (*salvini*) smaller; crown pale grey, more extensive light grey on face, throat, hindneck and mantle; *tips of underwing black*; sides of bill (128 mm) grey-green, with paler top and bottom, and dark spot at tip of lower bill. Chatham I Mollymawk (*eremita*) is smallest and darkest race; crown pale grey; face, throat, hindneck and mantle dark grey; tips of underwings black; bill (120 mm) *yellow with dark spot at tip of lower mandible*. Immatures of all subspecies have more extensive grey areas; underwing patterns are similar to that in adults; *bill bluish grey with black tips to both mandibles*. **Habitat:** Breeds subantarctic, mainly in NZ region; at Auckland and Antipodes Is (*steadi*), Bounty Is and The Snares (*salvini*), Pyramid Rock, Chathams (*eremita*). Races *steadi* and *salvini* range widely through southern oceans and often to NZ coastal waters, especially around boats; *eremita* is rarely seen away from Chathams but reported off eastern S America and sometimes beach-wrecked on NZ mainland. **Breeding:** Nov–Aug (*steadi*), Sep–Apr (*salvini* and *eremita*).   **[Sp 11]**

YELLOW-NOSED MOLLYMAWK   *Diomedea chlororhynchos*   **Uncommon visitor**

75 cm, 2.5 kg. Small slender mollymawk. Adult has white head with small dark eye patch, sometimes with grey cheeks; neck, underparts and rump white; back, upperwings and tail black; underwings white with black tips and thin clear-cut black margins, wider on leading than trailing edge. *Bill slender (117 mm), black with yellow ridge deepening to reddish orange at the tip*. Immature similar but eye patch smaller; hindneck is washed grey; leading margin of underwing is broader and less clear-cut; *bill completely black*. **Habitat:** Breeds on islands in South Atlantic and South Indian Oceans. Ranges widely through warm subantarctic and subtropical waters, and a few regularly reach the Tasman Sea, Hauraki Gulf and Bay of Plenty, mostly in winter.   **[Sp 13]**

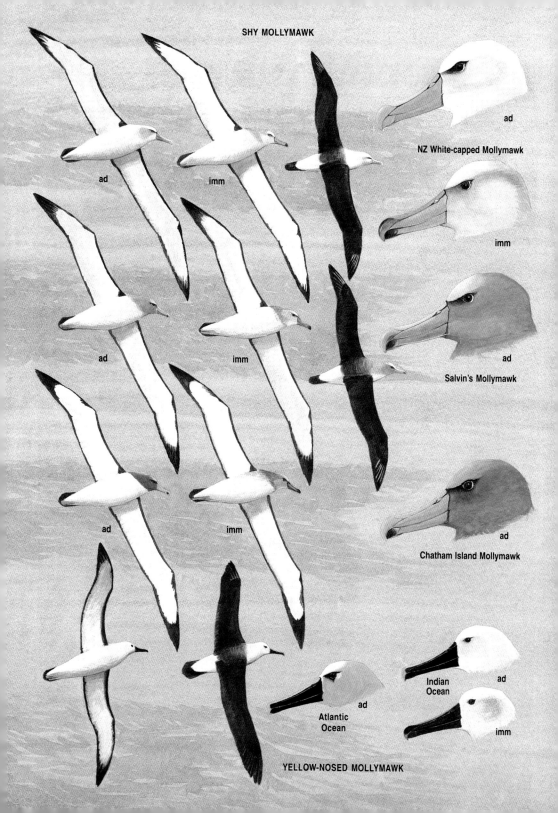

SHY MOLLYMAWK

ad

NZ White-capped Mollymawk

imm

Salvin's Mollymawk

Chatham Island Mollymawk

Atlantic
Ocean

ad

Indian
Ocean

ad

imm

YELLOW-NOSED MOLLYMAWK

Plate 5   **ALBATROSSES**

BLACK-BROWED MOLLYMAWK   *Diomedea melanophrys*   Common native

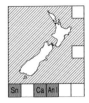

90 cm, 3 kg. Two subspecies in NZ region, separated by size, plumage and eye colour. Adult NZ Black-browed Mollymawk (*impavida*) has *whole body white except for heavy black triangle around eye* giving frowning appearance, blackish-grey back connecting black upperwings, and dark grey tail; underwings white with *broad black edges*, wider on the leading edge especially on the inner part of the wing; some have extensive dark streaking in armpits, almost connecting front to back; bill (110 mm) yellow with orange tip; *eye honey-coloured*; legs and feet pale bluish white. Subantarctic Black-browed Mollymawk (*melanophrys*) similar, but eyebrow smaller; underwings have less extensive, although still broad, black edges; bill (118 mm) heavier; *eye dark brown*. Immature NZ Black-browed Mollymawk like adult except eyebrow smaller; greyish wash on crown and hindneck; *underwings almost completely black*; bill greyish green with dark tip, turning yellow with a dark tip in older birds; eye white. Immature Subantarctic Black-browed Mollymawk similar, but eyebrow smaller; grey wash extends as a collar onto chest; eye dark brown. **Habitat:** NZ Black-browed Mollymawk breeds only at Campbell I; Subantarctic Black-browed Mollymawk breeds circumpolar subantarctic, including Bollons I (Antipodes), Western Chain (The Snares) and Campbell I. Ranges widely through southern oceans and into subtropical waters. Often seen off NZ coast or behind boats, especially in winter. **Breeding:** Sep–Apr.   **[Sp 10]**

GREY-HEADED MOLLYMAWK   *Diomedea chrysostoma*   Locally common native

80 cm, 3.25 kg. Adult has *light grey head, throat, neck and mantle*, paler on forehead; dark grey patch around and ahead of eye, small but prominent white mark just behind eye; sharp margin on chest to white underparts, white rump, grey tail. Upperwings and back dark grey; underwings *white with broad black leading edge and narrow black trailing edge. Bill (113 mm) black with rich yellow along ridge and along bottom edge*, shading to rosy pink at tip; legs and feet greyish white. Immature similar, but initial darker grey on head wears to very pale on forehead and cheeks in some birds; underwings black or with narrow greyish or white central stripe. Bill dark grey, darker tip changing to dull yellow with age. **Habitat:** Breeds circumpolar subantarctic; in NZ region, only at Campbell I. Ranges widely through southern oceans, and a few visit NZ coastal waters, especially in winter. **Breeding:** Sep–May.   **[Sp 12]**

BULLER'S MOLLYMAWK   *Diomedea bulleri*   Common endemic

80 cm, 3 kg. Two subspecies in NZ region, separated by bill size and head plumage. Adult Southern Buller's Mollymawk (*bulleri*) has *silvery-white forehead*, contrasting light grey crown, black patch around and ahead of eye, small white crescent behind to below eye; neck, hindneck and throat grey, with sharp margin on chest from white underparts; rump white, tail grey. Upperwings and back dark grey; underwings *white with clear-cut broad black leading edge and very narrow black trailing edge*. Bill (118 x 27 mm) black with golden yellow along ridge and tip and along bottom edge; legs and feet pale bluish grey to grey-mauve. Northern Buller's Mollymawk (*platei*) similar but *forehead silvery grey*; darker grey on head and throat. Bill more robust (120 x 31 mm); feet darker. Immature like adult except whole head dark grey and bill brownish horn with darker tip. **Habitat:** Southern Buller's breeds The Snares and Solander Is; Northern Buller's breeds Three Kings and Chatham Is. Commonly seen off NZ coast or behind boats and trawlers offshore during breeding. An unknown proportion of the population disperses to eastern Pacific after breeding. **Breeding:** Jan–Oct (Southern), Oct–Jun (Northern).   **[Sp 14]**

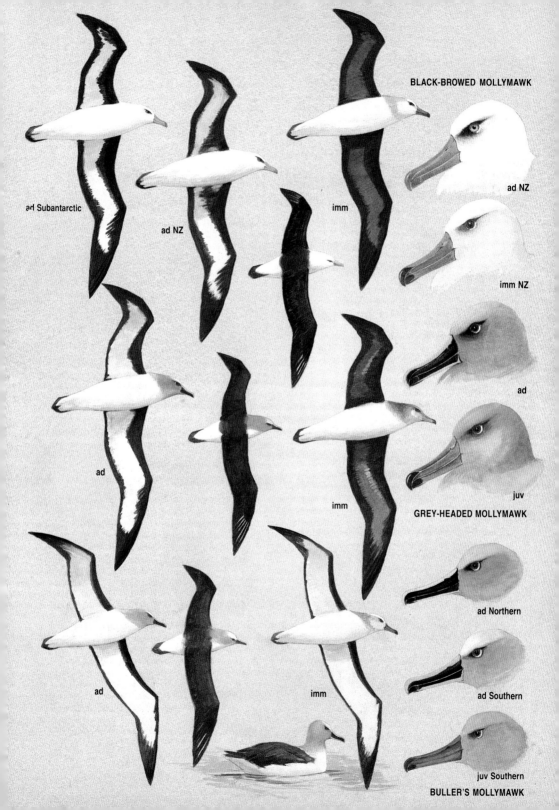

BLACK-BROWED MOLLYMAWK

ad Subantarctic

ad NZ

imm

ad NZ

imm NZ

ad

imm

ad

imm

juv

GREY-HEADED MOLLYMAWK

ad Northern

ad

imm

ad Southern

juv Southern

BULLER'S MOLLYMAWK

Plate 6

SOOTY ALBATROSSES and GIANT PETRELS

Sooty albatrosses are slender sooty brown and grey birds with black bill, long narrow wings and very long pointed tail.

LIGHT-MANTLED SOOTY ALBATROSS   *Phoebetria palpebrata*   Uncommon native

80 cm, 2.75 kg. Adult has sooty-brown head, throat and wings; *ash-grey back from nape to rump,* pale brownish-grey underparts. Bill (105 mm) slender, black with blue line along lower bill; legs and feet pale grey-flesh. Juvenile similar, but brown scalloping on neck and upper back, grey eye-ring and greyish-yellow line along lower bill. **Habitat:** Breeds circumpolar subantarctic; in NZ region, at Antipodes, Auckland and Campbell Is. Ranges widely at sea, and a few reach NZ waters or are beachwrecked, mainly in winter. **Breeding:** Oct–May.   **[Sp 15]**

SOOTY ALBATROSS   *Phoebetria fusca*   Rare vagrant

80 cm, 2.5 kg. Adult is entirely sooty brown except slightly darker on head and wings, white eye-ring, and pale shafts to primaries and tail. Bill (112 mm) slender, black with yellow line along lower bill; legs and feet pale grey-flesh. Juvenile similar but buff scalloping on collar and sides of neck; ash-grey nape, grey eye-ring and grey line along lower bill. **Habitat:** Breeds subantarctic and subtropical Atlantic and Indian Oceans. Recorded a few times in NZ waters.   **[Sp 16]**

The two giant petrels are very similar robust brown-to-white (rare) fulmarine petrels with short wings and tail. Massive pale bill with prominent nasal tubes. Flight laboured with burst of flapping interspersed with long glides and wheeling, not soaring. On land, mobile and can stand upright. Oceanic and coastal. Frequently follow ships and trawlers. Silent at sea except when fighting for food. Loud calls at colonies. Lay 1 large white egg in low cup-shaped bowl. Long incubation and fledging periods. Sexes alike but male larger; juveniles darker.

NORTHERN GIANT PETREL (Nelly)   *Macronectes halli*   Common native

90 cm, 4.5 kg. Similar to dark phase Southern Giant Petrel, but *bill pinkish-yellow horn tipped brownish,* and face darker. Adult has greyish-brown body with paler forehead, sides of face and chin, sometimes white on chin and around base of bill. Bill robust (90–105 mm); eye grey to off-white. No white phase. Juvenile all dark sooty brown, fading to grey-brown with age; eye usually grey. **Habitat:** Breeds circumpolar subantarctic; in NZ region, at Chathams, Port Pegasus (Stewart I), Antipodes, Auckland and Campbell Is. Ranges widely through southern oceans and often seen in NZ waters, especially Cook Strait. **Breeding:** Aug–Feb.   **[Sp 42]**

SOUTHERN GIANT PETREL (Nelly)   *Macronectes giganteus*   Common visitor

90 cm, 4.5 kg. Variable plumages; dark adults and juveniles are almost identical to Northern Giant Petrel except *bill yellowish horn, tipped green,* and face paler. Adult (dark phase) has white head, flecked brown, merging into greyish-brown body, wings and tail; often shows thin white leading edge to innerwings. Bill robust (90–105 mm); eye brown to grey. Juvenile all dark sooty brown, fading to grey-brown with age; eye generally brown. Adult and juvenile (white phase) completely white except for scattered flecks of brown. **Habitat:** Breeds circumpolar subantarctic and around Antarctic coast; in NZ region, recorded breeding once at Cape Crozier, Antarctica. Ranges widely through southern oceans, and juveniles common in NZ waters, especially in winter and spring; a few adults reach NZ. **Breeding:** Sep–Apr.   **[Sp 41]**

LIGHT-MANTLED
SOOTY ALBATROSS

imm

SOOTY ALBATROSS

worn
plumage

juv

NORTHERN
GIANT PETREL

SOUTHERN
GIANT PETREL

juv

Plate 7   **SHEARWATERS**

Medium to large seabirds with long slender bill and nostrils encased in a short flattened tube. Sexes and ages alike; most are dark above and mainly white below, but some are all dark. Many species form large feeding flocks. Usually fly close to the surface, often with a series of rapid wingbeats followed by a glide, but in windy conditions can wheel high on stiffly held wings. Clumsy on ground; legs and webbed feet set well back. Range from coastal to oceanic. Some species are highly migratory. Most species very vocal at breeding colonies at night. Lay 1 large white egg, usually deep in a burrow. Long incubation and fledging periods.

BULLER'S SHEARWATER   *Puffinus bulleri*   Common endemic

46 cm, 425 g. Head and hindneck blackish brown; *back and upperwings frosty grey with bold dark M across wings, lower back and rump*; uppertail light grey with broad black tip to long wedge-shaped tail; sharp line of demarcation from white underparts and underwing. Bill long and slender (41 x 12 mm), bluish grey with darker tip; legs and feet pink with dark outer toes and outer edge of tarsus. **Habitat:** Breeds only at Poor Knights Is. Ranges widely around NZ coast and migrates to northern and eastern Pacific. **Breeding:** Nov–May.   **[Sp 21]**

WEDGE-TAILED SHEARWATER   *Puffinus pacificus*   Locally common native

46 cm, 450 g. Variable plumages but always with *broad wings and long wedge-shaped tail*. Rare pale phase has head, hindneck and upperparts dark brown with a sharp line of demarcation from white chin and throat; underparts mainly white but variably mottled brown on sides of breast, flanks and undertail; underwing white with dark borders and tip, mottled brownish grey on underwing coverts. Bill compressed (38 x 13 mm), slate grey; legs and feet pale flesh. See Plate 8 for dark phase. **Habitat:** Subtropical and tropical Pacific and Indian Oceans. Breeds on Kermadec Is and rarely reaches NZ mainland. **Breeding:** Dec–Jun.   **[Sp 20]**

Grey Petrel (see Plate 10)   **[Sp 31]**

PINK-FOOTED SHEARWATER   *Puffinus creatopus*   Rare subtropical vagrant

48 cm, 900 g. Head, hindneck and upperparts greyish brown; chin, throat and underparts mainly white, but some have greyish brown on chin, throat and flanks; underwings whitish with varying grey and white mottling. Bill heavy (42 mm), pinkish with a dark tip; legs and feet pink. **Habitat:** Breeds off Chile. Migrates to eastern N Pacific. A few have reached NZ waters, off east coast South I.   **[Sp 18]**

CORY'S SHEARWATER   *Calonectris diomedea*   Rare Atlantic vagrant

46 cm, 900 g. Head, hindneck and upperparts greyish brown; chin, throat and underparts white, without clear line of demarcation. *Underwing white*, with narrow dark margins and tips. *Bill large (57 x 21 mm), dull yellow with darker tip*; legs and feet fleshy pink, stained brown on outer toe and outer surface of tarsus. **Habitat:** Breeds N Atlantic and Mediterranean. Migrates to S Atlantic and S Indian Oceans. One NZ record: Foxton Beach, January 1934.   **[Sp 17]**

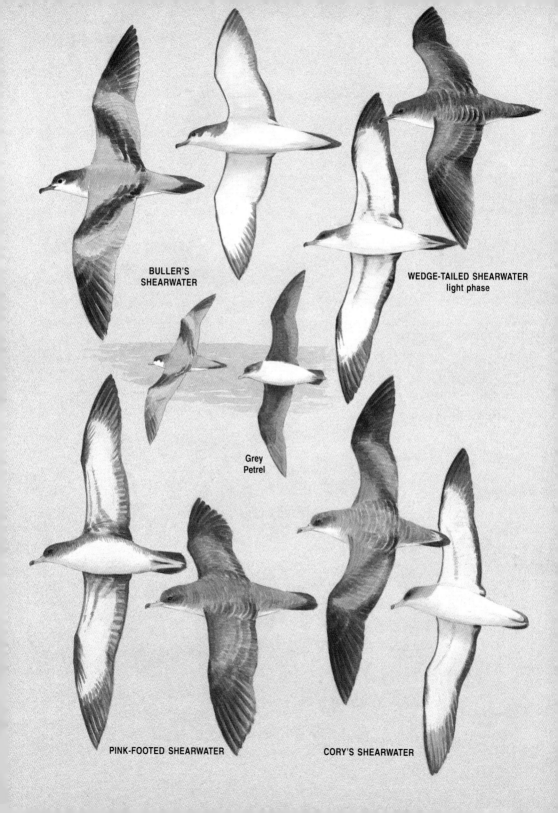

BULLER'S
SHEARWATER

WEDGE-TAILED SHEARWATER
light phase

Grey
Petrel

PINK-FOOTED SHEARWATER

CORY'S SHEARWATER

Plate 8 **SHEARWATERS**

SOOTY SHEARWATER (Titi, Muttonbird) *Puffinus griseus*   **Abundant native**

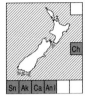

44 cm, 800 g. Sooty-brown upperparts, slightly greyer underparts with *silvery-grey flash on underwings*. Wings long and narrow, tail short and rounded. Bill long and slender (42 x 13 mm), dark grey; feet dark lilac with brown markings on the outer side. Main call a series of hoarse moans: 'oo-oo-ah', getting louder and faster each time. **Habitat:** Breeds mainly around NZ, on islands and mainland headlands from Three Kings to Campbell Is, but also southern Australia, Macquarie I and southern S America. Main NZ colonies are at The Snares, islands off Stewart Island and in Foveaux Strait, and Chatham Is. NZ birds migrate to N Pacific, many becoming beach-wrecked in Apr–May and Oct–Dec. **Breeding:** Nov–May.   **[Sp 22]**

SHORT-TAILED SHEARWATER *Puffinus tenuirostris*   **Common Australian migrant**

42 cm, 550 g. Like small Sooty Shearwater but shorter-billed (32 x 11 mm) and *underwings are normally dull grey and do not flash prominently*. Feet dark lilac with brown markings on the outer side. **Habitat:** Breeds southern Australia, especially on islands in Bass Strait. Migrates to N Pacific, but some pass through NZ waters on the outward and return journeys, and are often beach-wrecked around May and October.   **[Sp 23]**

WEDGE-TAILED SHEARWATER *Puffinus pacificus*   **Locally common native**

46 cm, 450 g. Variable plumages but always with *broad wings and long wedge-shaped tail*. Common dark phase all blackish brown except for slightly paler but *nonreflective* centres to underwing. Bill compressed (38 x 13 mm), slate grey; legs and feet pale flesh. See Plate 7 for pale phase. Main ground call a wailing moan: 'ka-whooo-ahh'. **Habitat:** Subtropical and tropical Pacific and Indian Oceans. Breeds on Kermadec Is and rarely reaches NZ mainland. **Breeding:** Dec–Jun.   **[Sp 20]**

CHRISTMAS ISLAND SHEARWATER *Puffinus nativitatis*   **Rare tropical vagrant**

38 cm, 350 g. Completely sooty brown. Like Sooty Shearwater and Short-tailed Shearwater but much smaller; *dark brown underwing* and longer slightly wedge-shaped tail. Bill long and slender (40 x 10 mm), black; *feet dark brown.* **Habitat:** Breeds tropical and subtropical mid-Pacific Ocean. Two NZ records: Dargaville Beach, February 1976; Curtis I (Kermadecs) November 1989.   **[Sp 24]**

FLESH-FOOTED SHEARWATER *Puffinus carneipes*   **Common native**

44 cm, 600 g. Large, bulky chocolate-brown shearwater with *pale bill (42 x 13 mm), darker at tip, and flesh-pink legs and feet.* Main call a series of high-pitched moans, resembling sound of cats fighting. **Habitat:** Breeds in western Indian Ocean, southern Australia, Lord Howe I, northern NZ and in Cook Strait. Main NZ colonies at Hen and Chickens, Mercury group, Karewa I, Saddleback I (near New Plymouth), and Trio and Titi Is (Cook Strait). Ranges through coastal waters of North I, occasionally south to Foveaux Strait in the west and Banks Peninsula to Chathams in the east. Migrates to N Pacific. **Breeding:** Nov–May.   **[Sp 19]**

SOOTY SHEARWATER

SHORT-TAILED SHEARWATER

WEDGE-TAILED
SHEARWATER
dark phase

FLESH-FOOTED
SHEARWATER

CHRISTMAS ISLAND
SHEARWATER

Plate 9   SHEARWATERS and DIVING PETRELS

FLUTTERING SHEARWATER (Pahaka)   *Puffinus gavia*   **Abundant endemic**

33 cm, 300 g. Head to below eye, upperparts and thigh patch dark greyish brown *merging into* white underparts and flank patch; faintly mottled partial collar; *underwings white* with brownish borders and dusky-grey armpits. Bill fine (33 x 9 mm). Like Hutton's Shearwater at sea but smaller; *paler underwings*. In hand, *sides of undertail coverts white*. Main call at colony a rapid staccato 'ka-how ka-how ka-how ka-how kehek kehek kehek kehek-errr'. **Habitat:** Breeds on many islands around North I and Cook Strait. Flocks common in coastal waters and harbours; some, especially juveniles, visit Australian waters in non-breeding season. **Breeding:** Sep–Feb.   **[Sp 26]**

HUTTON'S SHEARWATER   *Puffinus huttoni*   **Locally common endemic**

36 cm, 350 g. Head to below eye, upperparts and thigh patch blackish brown *merging into* white underparts and flank patch; faintly mottled broad collar; *underwings centred off-white with indistinct broad brownish borders and extensive dusky-grey armpits*. Bill (37 x 9 mm). Like Fluttering Shearwater at sea but larger; *darker underwings*. In hand, *sides of undertail coverts brown*. Main colony call 'ko-uw ko-uw ko-uw ko-uw, kee kee kee kee – aaah'. **Habitat:** Breeds only in Seaward Kaikoura Range. In NZ waters, mainly off east coast South I and in Cook Strait but migrates to Australian waters in winter. **Breeding:** Oct–Apr.   **[Sp 27]**

MANX SHEARWATER   *Puffinus puffinus*   **Rare Atlantic vagrant**

36 cm, 450 g. Head to below eye, and upperparts dark brownish black, *sharply demarcated* from white underparts; notch of white on upper neck. *Underwings, including armpits, white with sharply defined black edges and tips*. Bill slender (35 x 8 mm). **Habitat:** Breeds N Atlantic. Two NZ records.   **[Sp 25]**

LITTLE SHEARWATER   *Puffinus assimilis*   **Common native**

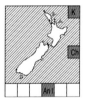

30 cm, 200 g. Head to *above eye*, and upperparts dark bluish black; eyebrow, face and underparts white; underwing white except for thin black border on trailing edge. Bill slender (25 x 8 mm), dull lead blue with black ridge and tip; *legs and feet pale blue* with fleshy webs. **Habitat:** Breeds widely in Atlantic and southern oceans. Main NZ colonies at Kermadecs, off Northland, Mercury Is, Chathams and Antipodes. Mostly sedentary but rarely seen in coastal waters. **Breeding:** Jul–Jan.   **[Sp 28]**

Diving petrels are small stocky seabirds with short broad wings, short wide bill and paired nostrils opening upwards; blue legs. Sexes alike. Fast whirring flight close to the surface. Generally coastal. Do not follow ships or trawlers. Noisy at night over and at breeding colonies.

COMMON DIVING PETREL (Kuaka)   *Pelecanoides urinatrix*   **Abundant native**

20 cm, 130 g. Upperparts black; sides of face, neck and throat mottled grey; underparts white but underwings smoky grey. Bill stubby (16 x 8 mm), black; blue legs and feet. Like South Georgian Diving Petrel at sea but underwing darker. In hand, underwing coverts greyish brown, inner webs of *3 outer primaries dusky brown, and septal process near base of nostril*. **Habitat:** Breeds circumpolar subantarctic. Main NZ sites off eastern North I, Cook and Foveaux Straits, Chatham Is, The Snares, Antipodes and Auckland Is. **Breeding:** Aug–Feb.   **[Sp 29]**

SOUTH GEORGIAN DIVING PETREL   *Pelecanoides georgicus*   **Rare native**

18 cm, 120 g. Like Common Diving Petrel at sea, but underwing usually paler. In hand, underwing coverts white, inner webs of *3 outer primaries white or pale grey, septal process in bill near centre of nostril*. **Habitat:** Breeds circumpolar subantarctic; in NZ region, only on Codfish I, off Stewart I. **Breeding:** Nov–Mar.   **[Sp 30]**

FLUTTERING
SHEARWATER

HUTTON'S
SHEARWATER

MANX
SHEARWATER

LITTLE SHEARWATER

Subantarctic

COMMON DIVING PETREL

SOUTH GEORGIAN DIVING PETREL

Plate 10

PROCELLARIA PETRELS

Large heavy-bodied seabirds with robust pale and well-hooked bill; prominent nostrils encased in a tube. Sexes and ages alike. In flight, long glides on stiffly held wings with occasional wingbeats. When windy, soar and wheel in huge arcs. Dive into sea and swim underwater with wings. Generally oceanic; rarely seen near land. Most follow ships and fishing boats. Clumsy on ground; legs and webbed feet set well back. Generally silent over breeding grounds at night, but loud calls and clacks from ground and burrows. Lay 1 large white egg, usually deep in a burrow. Long incubation and fledging periods.

Flesh-footed Shearwater (see Plate 8)   **[Sp 19]**

WHITE-CHINNED PETREL (Shoemaker)   *Procellaria aequinoctialis*
Uncommon native

55 cm, 1250 g. Entirely dark blackish brown except for a *variable amount of white feathering on chin*. Bill (52 x 21 mm) yellowish horn, *without dark tip*, but dark nostrils and lines between plates; legs and feet black. Sometimes follows ships and fishing boats. **Habitat:** Breeds circumpolar subantarctic, including Antipodes, Auckland and Campbell Is. Occasionally seen near mainland NZ but mainly ranges to the south and east. **Breeding:** Nov–May.   **[Sp 34]**

WESTLAND PETREL   *Procellaria westlandica*   **Uncommon endemic**

48 cm, 1100 g. Entirely dark blackish brown. Bill (49 x 20 mm) yellowish horn *with dark tip* and black between the plates; legs and feet black. Like Black Petrel but larger. Often follows ships and fishing boats. **Habitat:** Breeds in the forested coastal foothills of the Paparoa Range between Barrytown and Punakaiki, West Coast. In breeding season, seen mainly off east coast from East Cape to Banks Peninsula, Cook Strait and off west coast from Fiordland to Taranaki, but ranges west to Australia. Migrates to central or eastern S Pacific, Dec–Mar. **Breeding:** May–Dec.   **[Sp 33]**

BLACK PETREL (Taiko)   *Procellaria parkinsoni*   **Uncommon endemic**

46 cm, 700 g. Entirely dark blackish brown. Bill (41 x 15 mm) bluish yellow *with dark tip* and black between the plates; legs and feet black. Like Westland Petrel but smaller. Often follows ships and fishing boats. **Habitat:** Breeds only on Little Barrier and Great Barrier Is; formerly on inland ranges of the mainland. In breeding season, seen mainly around North I and west to Australia. Migrates to eastern tropical Pacific, Jul–Oct. **Breeding:** Nov–Jun.   **[Sp 32]**

GREY PETREL (Pediunker)   *Procellaria cinerea*   **Uncommon native**

48 cm, 1000 g. Head and sides of face to below eye dark grey; upperparts ashy grey, darker on tail and wings, *merging* into white underparts without any strongly defined line; *dark grey underwings and undertail* separate it from large grey and white shearwaters (see Plate 7). Bill stout (47 x 17 mm), greenish flesh with black between plates and on nostrils; legs and feet greyish flesh, darker on outside, yellowish webs. Distinctive albatross-like gliding with rapid duck-like wingbeats. Regularly follows ships and fishing boats. **Habitat:** Breeds circumpolar subantarctic; in NZ region, at Antipodes and Campbell Is. Rarely seen near NZ mainland. **Breeding:** Feb–Nov.   **[Sp 31]**

Flesh-footed
Shearwater

WHITE-CHINNED PETREL

WESTLAND PETREL

BLACK PETREL

GREY PETREL

Plate 11 FULMARINE PETRELS and BLUE PETREL

A diverse group of distinctive medium to large seabirds. Sexes alike. Most breed at high latitudes and lay 1 white egg, mostly in a scrape on ledges, in crevices or rockfalls; the exceptions being giant petrels (Plate 6), which lay in a cupped mound, and Kerguelen Petrels (Plate 15), which nest in a burrow.

ANTARCTIC PETREL *Thalassoica antarctica* Locally common native

45 cm, 650 g. Head, neck, back and rump dark brown; *upperwings dark brown with broad white trailing edge and inner part of primaries*; tail white, tipped brown; underparts white; underwing with black leading edge and thin border. Bill dark olive brown (black in juvenile); legs and feet greyish flesh. **Habitat:** Breeds circumpolar Antarctica, sometimes well inland; in NZ region, at Rockefeller Mts, Scott I and possibly Balleny Is. Ranges through Antarctic waters; especially common in Ross Sea sector. In winter, few reach NZ mainland waters but sometimes present in moderate numbers. **Breeding:** Nov–Mar. **[Sp 39]**

ANTARCTIC FULMAR *Fulmarus glacialoides* Locally common native

50 cm, 800 g. Head, neck and underparts white; mantle, back, rump and tail pearly grey; *upperwings pearly grey with darker grey trailing edge, and primaries black with large white patch near wingtip*. Bill strong (45 mm), pinkish horn with blue tinge on nasal tubes, and black tip; legs and feet pinkish blue. Appears large-headed; glides on stiff wings. **Habitat:** Breeds circumpolar on coast of Antarctica and subantarctic islands of Atlantic Ocean; in NZ region, at Balleny Is. Ranges widely in southern oceans, and a few visit NZ waters in winter and spring, but sometimes many are beach-wrecked in spring. **Breeding:** Dec–Apr. **[Sp 40]**

CAPE PIGEON *Daption capense* Common native

40 cm, 450 g. Head, neck and mantle black; lower back, base of upperwing and rump white, heavily chequered with black; outer upperwing black with broad white patches near body and beyond bend of wing; white tail is flecked black and broadly tipped black; underparts white; underwings white with black leading edge and thin borders. Bill stout (30 x 15 mm), black; legs and feet black. Snares Cape Pigeon (*australe*) has less white on upperparts than Southern Cape Pigeon (*capense*). Often follows ships and gathers around fishing boats. **Habitat:** Breeds circumpolar subantarctic and coast of Antarctica; in NZ region, as far north as The Snares and Chathams. Ranges widely through southern oceans and common off NZ mainland, especially in winter. **Breeding:** Nov–Apr. **[Sp 38]**

BLUE PETREL *Halobaena caerulea* Uncommon subantarctic visitor

29 cm, 200 g. Head bluish black; upperparts and side of neck pale blue, with dark M-shaped mark from wingtip to wingtip, broken only on lower back; *tail distinctively tipped white*. Bill narrow (27 x 11 mm), bluish black; legs and feet blue with flesh webs. At sea, looks like a prion (see Plate 12), but white-tipped tail distinctive and flight faster and wheeling. Rarely follows ships. **Habitat:** Breeds circumpolar subantarctic; nearest colony to NZ is on Macquarie I. Uncommon winter and spring visitor to waters around NZ mainland but sometimes beach-wrecked in moderate numbers. **[Sp 49]**

SNOW PETREL *Pagodroma nivea* Locally common native

35 cm, 325 g. *All white.* Bill narrow (22 x 11 mm), black; legs and feet black. Flight erratic with short, rapid wingbeats. **Habitat:** Breeds circumpolar coast of Antarctica; in NZ region, at Balleny Is (Greater Snow Petrel *nivea*) and around Ross Sea (Lesser Snow Petrel *minor*). Ranges through southern oceans but never confirmed as far north as NZ mainland. **Breeding:** Nov–Apr. **[Sp 37]**

ANTARCTIC PETREL

ANTARCTIC FULMAR

CAPE PIGEON

Snares

Southern

BLUE PETREL

SNOW PETREL

Plate 12

PRIONS

Small seabirds with blue-grey upperparts with black M across upperwings and lower back, white underparts, black-tipped tail, and blue legs and feet. Bill has comb-like lamellae on inside. Sexes and ages alike. Species separated by size, bill structure, face colours and extent of black on tail. Flight fast, buoyant and erratic; usually stay close to the surface. Feed near surface by plunging or dipping. Generally oceanic. Do not follow ships or fishing boats. Noisy at night at breeding colonies, with harsh cooing and cackling calls in air or on ground.

FAIRY PRION (Titi Wainui)   *Pachyptila turtur*   **Abundant native**

25 cm, 125 g. Upperparts blue-grey; faint white eyebrow; bold black M across wings; *tail broadly tipped black, including tips of uppertail coverts.* Bill (22 x 11 mm) blue with large nail. **Habitat:** Breeds circumpolar subantarctic, including many islands around NZ, especially Poor Knights, Cook Strait, Motunau I, Foveaux Strait, The Snares and Chathams. Abundant in coastal waters near breeding colonies, and the most common beach-wrecked bird. Ranges through Tasman Sea and east of NZ. **Breeding:** Nov–Feb. **[Sp 43]**

FULMAR PRION   *Pachyptila crassirostris*   **Locally common native**

26 cm, 140 g. Like Fairy Prion but slightly larger and paler. Bill (23 x 11 mm) deeper and with very large nail. **Habitat:** Breeds subantarctic at Heard I (S Indian Ocean), Chathams (Pyramid, Forty Fours), Bounty, The Snares and Auckland Is. Probably mainly sedentary but occasionally reaches NZ coast. **Breeding:** Nov–Feb. **[Sp 44]**

BROAD-BILLED PRION (Parara)   *Pachyptila vittata*   **Common native**

28 cm, 200 g. Upperparts blue-grey; black M across wings; dark face with clear white eyebrow; *very narrow black tip to tail.* Bill very broad (34 x 20 mm), *iron-grey.* **Habitat:** Breeds S Atlantic and around southern NZ; main colonies are in Fiordland, Foveaux Strait, off Stewart I, The Snares and Chathams. Ranges around NZ coast and rarely to Australia. **Breeding:** Aug–Jan.   **[Sp 48]**

THIN-BILLED PRION   *Pachyptila belcheri*   **Common visitor**

26 cm, 145 g. *Upperparts pale blue-grey; indistinct blackish M across wings; very pale face with prominent white eyebrow; very narrow black tip to tail.* Bill slender (25 x 11 mm) with weak hook. **Habitat:** Breeds subantarctic S America, Falklands and Indian Ocean. Ranges through southern oceans in winter and spring, regularly reaching NZ.   **[Sp 45]**

SALVIN'S PRION   *Pachyptila salvini*   **Common visitor**

27 cm, 170 g. Upperparts blue-grey, *slightly darker on the head;* blackish M across wings; *narrow black tip to tail.* Bill stout (30 x 16 mm), bluish. Like Antarctic Prion, but in the hand, bill larger and *lamellae visible* at base of closed bill. **Habitat:** Breeds in subantarctic Indian Ocean. Regular visitor to NZ seas in winter and spring.   **[Sp 47]**

ANTARCTIC PRION   *Pachyptila desolata*   **Locally common native**

26 cm, 150 g. Like Salvin's Prion, but in the hand, bill smaller (27 x 14 mm) and *lamellae not visible* at the base of the closed bill. **Habitat:** Breeds widely in subantarctic and antarctic zones; in NZ region, many breed at Auckland Is and a few nest at Scott Is, Ross Sea. Regular visitor to seas off NZ mainland, mainly in winter and spring. **Breeding:** Dec–Mar.   **[Sp 46]**

Blue Petrel (see Plate 11)   **[Sp 49]**

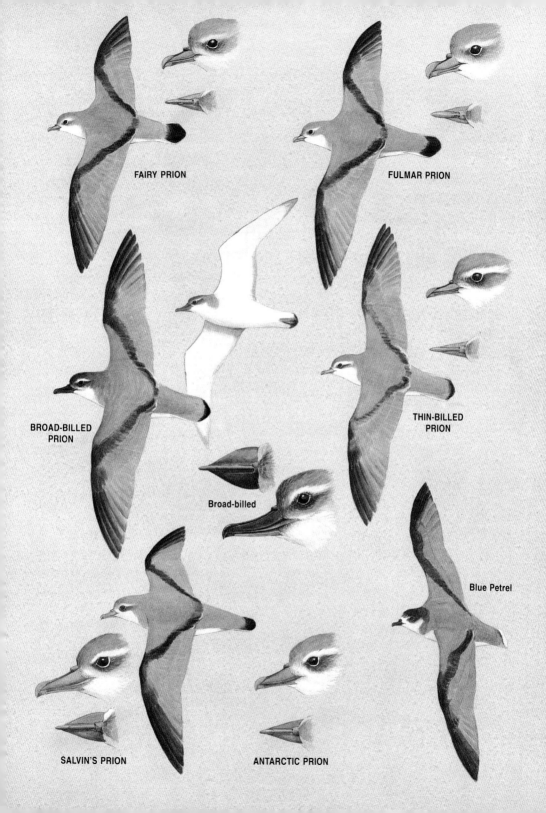

FAIRY PRION

FULMAR PRION

BROAD-BILLED
PRION

THIN-BILLED
PRION

Broad-billed

Blue Petrel

SALVIN'S PRION

ANTARCTIC PRION

Plate 13   GADFLY PETRELS

Medium to large seabirds with mostly short deep and heavily hooked bill, nostrils encased in a tube, joined at the base of the bill. Most are dark above and mainly white below. Sexes and ages alike; males slightly larger. Underwing patterns are often distinctive. In flight, long narrow wings held stiffly and appear graceful as they glide and wheel in huge arcs. Generally oceanic; rarely seen near land. Many species highly migratory. Many species give high-pitched repetitive calls over breeding grounds at night. Lay 1 large egg, usually deep in a burrow. Long incubation and fledging periods.

COOK'S PETREL (Titi) *Pterodroma cookii*   Uncommon endemic

29 cm, 200 g. Forehead white, scaled grey on forecrown; dark eye patch; crown and upperparts pale grey with dark M across wings. Underparts and underwings white except mottled black patch at bend of wing extending towards tip and as short diagonal line a short way towards body. Bill long and fine (28 x 10 mm), black; legs and feet bluish with yellowish base of webs, dark toes and ends to webs. **Habitat**: Breeds Little Barrier, Great Barrier and Codfish Is. Migrates to eastern Pacific, from California to Chile. **Breeding:** Oct–May.   **[Sp 53]**

PYCROFT'S PETREL *Pterodroma pycrofti*   Rare endemic

28 cm, 160 g. Forehead and forecrown white scaled with grey; crown, hindneck and sides of face to under eye medium grey *(paler than Stejneger's Petrel but darker than Cook's Petrel); upperparts medium grey* with dark M across wings. Underparts and underwings white except for mottled black patch at bend of wing extending towards tip and as short diagonal line a short way towards body. Bill short and fine (24 x 9 mm), black; legs and feet bluish with darker toes and ends to webs. **Habitat:** Breeds northeastern NZ; main colonies at Mercury, Hen and Chickens, and Poor Knights Is. Occasionally beach-wrecked, mainly in northern NZ in summer and autumn. Migrates to central N Pacific. **Breeding:** Nov–Apr.   **[Sp 51]**

GOULD'S PETREL *Pterodroma leucoptera*   Uncommon subtropical visitor

29 cm, 175 g. Forehead white; *black crown, sides of face, nape and sides of neck to wing*; rest of upperparts grey with darker M across wings. Underparts and underwings white except for black patch at bend of wing extending towards tip and as thick diagonal bar well towards body. Bill short and fine (24 x 10 mm), black; legs and feet bluish with dark toes and ends to webs. **Habitat:** Breeds Cabbage Tree I (NSW) and New Caledonia. The latter birds range through Tasman Sea and to NZ waters. Migrates to eastern tropical Pacific.   **[Sp 52]**

STEJNEGER'S PETREL *Pterodroma longirostris*   Rare subtropical vagrant

28 cm, 150 g. Like Gould's Petrel except smaller and black cap is reduced with *white on forecrown; grey neck and sides of neck*; diagonal bar on underwing less prominent. **Habitat:** Breeds at Mas-a-fuera, Juan Fernandez group, off Chile. Migrates to subtropical N Pacific. Vagrants occasionally reach NZ in summer.
[Sp 50]

Black-winged Petrel (see Plate 14)   **[Sp 54]**

COOK'S PETREL

PYCROFT'S PETREL

STEJNEGER'S
PETREL

GOULD'S PETREL

Black-winged Petrel

Plate 14

GADFLY PETRELS

WHITE-NAPED PETREL *Pterodroma cervicalis*   Uncommon endemic

43 cm, 450 g. Forehead white; blackish cap on crown, nape and sides of face to below eye; *broad white collar across hindneck*; upperparts frosty grey with broad black M across wings; small grey tab in front of wings. Underparts and underwing white except for black patch at bend of wing extending towards tip and diagonally towards body. Bill sturdy (37 x 16 mm), black; feet and legs fleshy pink with black toes and ends of webs. **Habitat:** Breeds Macauley I, Kermadecs. Migrates to subtropical N Pacific, mainly in the west. A few vagrants reach waters off mainland NZ. **Breeding:** Dec–Jun.   **[Sp 57]**

JUAN FERNANDEZ PETREL *Pterodroma externa*   Rare subtropical vagrant

43 cm, 500 g. Like White-naped Petrel except hindneck grey, cap is paler and underwings have only a short black tab extending from bend of wing towards body. **Habitat:** Breeds Mas-a-fuera, Juan Fernandez group, off Chile. Migrates to subtropical N Pacific. A few vagrants reach NZ waters.   **[Sp 58]**

MOTTLED PETREL (Korure) *Pterodroma inexpectata*   Common endemic

34 cm, 325 g. *Face white, heavily mottled grey*; upperparts dark frosty grey, with darker M across wings; dark eye patch; *underparts white except grey patch on the lower breast and belly*. Underwing white with broad black diagonal band from bend of wing to near body. Bill small (27 x 12 mm), black; legs and feet fleshy pink with black toes and ends of webs. **Habitat:** Breeds Fiordland, Codfish I and other islands off Stewart I, and at The Snares. Ranges to pack ice, around NZ mainland and to Chathams in breeding season. Migrates to N Pacific. **Breeding:** Dec–Jun.   **[Sp 56]**

BLACK-WINGED PETREL *Pterodroma nigripennis*   Common native

30 cm, 175 g. Forehead white, mottled on forecrown; dark patch below eye; crown, sides of neck and upperparts pale grey; upperwings grey with darker M across wings. Underparts and underwings white except for dark outer half to primaries, dark trailing edge and *black diagonal band from bend of wing to near body*. Bill short and stubby (24 x 11 mm), black; legs and feet fleshy pink with dark toes and ends to webs. **Habitat:** Breeds subtropical S Pacific, including Kermadecs, Three Kings, East, Portland and Chatham Is. Seen prospecting over headlands on northern NZ coast. Migrates to N Pacific. **Breeding:** Dec–Jun.   **[Sp 54]**

CHATHAM PETREL *Pterodroma axillaris*   Rare endemic

30 cm, 200 g. Like Black-winged Petrel, but underwing has only tips of primaries dark, narrow dark trailing edge, but *black diagonal bar reaches to black base of underwing*. **Habitat:** Breeds only at South East I, Chathams. **Breeding:** Dec–Jun.   **[Sp 55]**

WHITE-NAPED PETREL

JUAN FERNANDEZ
PETREL

MOTTLED
PETREL

BLACK-WINGED PETREL

CHATHAM PETREL

Plate 15

GADFLY PETRELS

WHITE-HEADED PETREL *Pterodroma lessonii* Locally common native

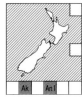

43 cm, 600 g. *Head mainly white with dark eye patch* and very faintly grey on crown and hindneck; pale grey on back and tail; upperwings greyish brown with indistinct M joining across lower back; *underwings dark grey, undertail white*. Bill stout (37 x 15 mm), black; legs and feet fleshy pink with brown on outer toe, joints of toes and ends of webs. Flight strong and rapid, wheeling and swooping in high arcs. Rarely follows ships. **Habitat:** Breeds subantarctic in Indian Ocean and Macquarie I; in NZ region, at Antipodes and Auckland Is. Ranges through southern oceans between pack ice and about 34°S in winter. Regularly recorded beach-wrecked on west coast of North I. **Breeding:** Nov–May. [Sp 64]

KERGUELEN PETREL *Lugensa brevirostris* Uncommon subantarctic visitor

33 cm, 350 g. Almost uniformly *dark frosty grey*, with slight mottling on forehead, chin and sometimes flanks; underwings silvery grey. *Bill short and narrow* (26 x 10 mm), black; looks small compared to large head. Legs and feet purplish flesh, darker on outsides. Flight extremely fast. **Habitat:** Breeds subantarctic in Atlantic and Indian Oceans. Ranges eastwards and can be quite common in the Tasman Sea some years in winter and early spring, when sometimes wrecked on west coast NZ beaches. [Sp 36]

PROVIDENCE PETREL *Pterodroma solandri* Rare subtropical vagrant

40 cm, 500 g. Brown head, mottled white on face and forehead and dark patch in front of eye; upperparts steely grey, contrasting with browner wings and tail; underparts greyish brown; underwings dark grey with distinctive *white patch at the base of dark primaries*. Bill stout (35 x 15 mm), black; legs and feet dark grey. **Habitat:** Breeds in winter at Lord Howe and Philip Is; formerly also at Norfolk I. Migrates to N Pacific. A few beach-wrecked birds recorded in NZ. [Sp 61]

GREY-FACED PETREL (Oi) *Pterodroma macroptera* Common native

41 cm, 550 g. *Entire plumage blackish brown except pale grey forehead, sides of face, chin and throat*. Bill stout (36 x 14 mm), black; legs and feet black. Long narrow wings. Flight strong and rapid, wheeling and swooping in big arcs. Aerial chases at dusk or after dark over breeding colonies often accompanied by 'o-hi' or 'o-hoe' calls. Many calls also from birds on ground or in burrows, especially a loud 'or-wik' and 'si-si-si'. **Habitat:** Breeds circumpolar subantarctic and southern temperate; in NZ, on many northern offshore islands and some mainland cliffs and headlands, within the triangle Cape Egmont to Three Kings Is to Gisborne. **Breeding:** Jun–Jan. [Sp 62]

KERMADEC PETREL *Pterodroma neglecta* Locally common native

38 cm, 500 g. Variable plumages. Dark phase is uniformly brownish black except for *obvious white bases to the primaries on underwing*, and white inner webs and shafts of primaries sometimes visible on upperwing. Bill (30 x 13 mm) black; feet and legs variable from black to pale flesh with dark tips to webs. See Plate 16 for other phases. **Habitat:** Breeds subtropical S Pacific, including Kermadec Is. Migrates to tropical Pacific. Vagrants occasionally reach NZ mainland. **Breeding:** Oct–May. [Sp 60]

WHITE-HEADED PETREL

KERGUELEN PETREL

PROVIDENCE PETREL

GREY-FACED PETREL

KERMADEC PETREL
dark phase

Plate 16

GADFLY PETRELS

SOFT-PLUMAGED PETREL *Pterodroma mollis* Uncommon native

34 cm, 300 g. Head including patch below and behind eye greyish brown; forehead scaled white; eyebrow, chin, sides of neck and throat white. Upperparts slaty grey with a broad blackish band across wing coverts; underparts white except for a *narrow grey band completely or partially across the chest; underwing grey*. Bill stout (35 x 12 mm), black; feet and legs pinkish with dark outer toe and tips to webs. **Habitat:** Breeds subantarctic in Atlantic and Indian Oceans, and at Antipodes Is. Ranges through southern oceans but not common in S Pacific, although increasing numbers seen off southern and eastern coasts of NZ since 1970s. **Breeding:** Dec–May. **[Sp 65]**

CHATHAM ISLAND TAIKO (Magenta Petrel) *Pterodroma magentae* Rare endemic

38 cm, 475 g. Head, neck, upper breast and upperparts uniformly dark sooty grey except for variable greyish scalloping on forehead and grey chin; lower breast, underparts and undertail white; underwing sooty grey. Bill robust (32 x 16 mm), black; legs and feet pink with dark outer toe and tips to webs. **Habitat:** Breeds in forests of southern Chatham I. Assumed to migrate into subtropical Pacific. **Breeding:** Nov–May. **[Sp 63]**

PHOENIX PETREL *Pterodroma alba* Rare tropical vagrant

35 cm, 275 g. Head, upperparts and upper breast uniform sooty brown; *chin and upper throat white*; breast, belly and undertail white except for narrow dark rim around tip of long tail; underwings sooty brown except for *thin white band just back from leading edge from body to bend of wing*. Bill slight (28 x 11 mm), black; legs and feet pink with dark outer toe and tips to webs. **Habitat:** Breeds tropical and subtropical Pacific; possibly formerly on Kermadec Is, where twice recorded. **[Sp 59]**

TAHITI PETREL *Pseudobulweria rostrata* Rare tropical vagrant

38 cm, 400 g. Head, upperparts, chin, throat and upper breast uniform sooty brown; lower breast, belly and undertail white, except for *broad dark tip to long pointed tail*; underwings *uniformly* sooty brown. Bill massive (37 x 17 mm), black; legs mainly pink, feet mainly dark. **Habitat:** Breeds tropical and subtropical Pacific. One NZ specimen: Dargaville Beach, June 1988; but others seen in Bay of Plenty in winter 1988. **[Sp 35]**

KERMADEC PETREL *Pterodroma neglecta* Locally common native

38 cm, 500 g. Variable plumages. Pale phase has head, neck and body white to pale ashy grey with flecks of grey or brown; upperwing brownish black except white inner webs and shaft of primaries sometimes visible; underwing dark greyish brown with *obvious white bases to the primaries*. Intermediate phase similar but has variable amounts of brown on head, upperparts, upper breast and undertail. See Plate 15 for dark phase. Bill (30 x 13 mm) black; feet and legs variable from black to pale flesh with dark tips to webs. **Habitat:** Breeds subtropical S Pacific, including Kermadec Is. Migrates to tropical Pacific. Vagrants occasionally reach NZ mainland. **Breeding:** Oct–May. **[Sp 60]**

SOFT-PLUMAGED PETREL

CHATHAM ISLAND
TAIKO

KERMADEC
PETREL
light phase

PHOENIX PETREL

KERMADEC
PETREL
intermediate phase

TAHITI PETREL

Plate 17

STORM PETRELS

Very small dainty seabirds with broad rounded wings, short bill with a prominent nostril with a single opening, and very long legs. Mostly black or grey upperparts except for rump. Sexes and ages alike. Fly close to the surface, erratically with short glides or hops. Pick up food while hovering or pattering on the water. Oceanic; rarely follow boats. Most silent at night over colonies, but give coos, churrs or whistles from burrows or the ground.

WILSON'S STORM PETREL *Oceanites oceanicus* Locally common native

18 cm, 35 g. *Brownish black* with faint diagonal grey-brown bar on upperwing from bend of wing to body; prominent *unmarked white rump; square tail.* Yellow-webbed feet project beyond tail. **Habitat:** Breeds subantarctic and Antarctica, including several colonies in the Ross Sea Sector. Migrates to Northern Hemisphere but occasionally seen in NZ waters, mainly Nov–Dec and Mar–May. **Breeding:** Dec–Apr. **[Sp 67]**

LEACH'S STORM PETREL *Oceanodroma leucorhoa* Rare straggler

20 cm, 45 g. *All blackish brown* except head darker, clear diagonal grey-brown bar on upperwing from bend of wing to body, *white rump with a dark central line; forked tail.* **Habitat:** Breeds N Pacific and N Atlantic. Migrates to tropics, but a few reach NZ waters. **[Sp 66]**

GREY-BACKED STORM PETREL *Oceanites nereis* Locally common native

18 cm, 35 g. Head, neck, throat and upper breast greyish black, rest of underparts white; back, upperwings and tail ashy grey, with black tips to wings and square tail. **Habitat:** Breeds circumpolar subantarctic; in NZ region, at Chathams, Antipodes, Auckland and Campbell Is. Mainly sedentary but ranges to 30°S in NZ seas, though rarely seen near mainland coast. **Breeding:** Sep–Mar. **[Sp 68]**

WHITE-FACED STORM PETREL (Takahikare-moana) *Pelagodroma marina*
Common native

20 cm, 45 g. *Forehead, eyebrow and underparts white;* crown, nape and patch through eye dark grey brown; back and upperwing brownish grey, contrasting with pale grey (NZ subspecies) or white (Kermadec subspecies) rump; slightly forked black tail. **Habitat:** Breeds temperate and subtropical Atlantic and around Australia and NZ; main NZ colonies in Hauraki Gulf, Bay of Plenty, Motunau I, around Stewart and Auckland Is and Chathams. Disperses widely after breeding and rarely seen in NZ coastal waters. **Breeding:** Oct–Mar. **[Sp 69]**

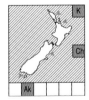

BLACK-BELLIED STORM PETREL *Fregetta tropica* Locally common native

20 cm, 55 g. Variable; some almost identical to White-bellied Storm Petrel, but *feet project well beyond tail.* Typically has black upperparts except broad *white rump,* grey chin and *variable black line down centre of white belly* connecting black breast and undertail. A few have all white belly. **Habitat:** Breeds circumpolar subantarctic, including Antipodes and Auckland Is. Ranges widely and migrates to tropics in winter. **Breeding:** Dec–Apr. **[Sp 70]**

WHITE-BELLIED STORM PETREL *Fregetta grallaria* Rare native

20 cm, 50 g. Variable plumages; some like a few Black-bellied Storm Petrels, but *feet level with tip of tail.* Typically has black upperparts, mantle feathers often white-tipped; *rump white;* black chin, throat and breast contrasts with *white belly;* black undertail. Some have smudgy, not white, underwings. **Habitat:** Breeds subtropics, including Kermadecs. Ranges widely at sea but rarely seen off NZ coast. **Breeding:** Jan–Jun. **[Sp 71]**

WILSON'S
STORM PETREL

LEACH'S
STORM PETREL

GREY-BACKED
STORM PETREL

WHITE-FACED
STORM PETREL

BLACK-BELLIED STORM PETREL

WHITE-BELLIED STORM PETREL

Plate 18   PENGUINS

Flightless stocky seabirds with dark upperparts and white underparts. Wings modified into flippers. Robust bill. Short stout legs with webbed feet. Dense short and flattened feathers in adults; thick down in chicks. Swim low in the water, with head and upper back (occasionally tail) visible; some porpoise when swimming fast. Feed at sea by diving. On land, walk upright with waddling gait or short hops with flippers used to maintain balance. Toboggan on ice and mud. Visit land to breed and to moult. During the 2–6-week moult, birds look ragged while all feathers are replaced rapidly; birds fast and are unable to swim. Breed solitarily in burrows or under vegetation, or in large dense colonies on the surface. Lay 1–2 white eggs.

KING PENGUIN *Aptenodytes patagonicus*   Uncommon subantarctic visitor

90 cm, 13 kg. Glossy black head and sides of face; *golden-orange comma-shaped wedge behind eye* tapering towards orange upper breast; silver-grey nape, shading to blue-grey on back and darker margin on flanks; rest of underparts white. Bill long and decurved at tip; broad tapering panel of orange-pink at base of lower mandible. Juvenile similar but much paler yellow, bill patch small and pink, and *dark chin and throat*. **Habitat:** Breeds circumpolar in subantarctic; nearest colony to NZ at Macquarie I. Ranges south to pack ice; regularly seen at NZ subantarctic islands in summer and autumn, but only vagrants reach NZ mainland.   **[Sp 73]**

EMPEROR PENGUIN *Aptenodytes forsteri*   Uncommon native

115 cm, 30 kg. Head, chin and throat blackish blue; *orange patch extending downward from behind eye towards the back*, connected to lemon-yellow upper breast; upperparts bluish grey with darker border along flanks; underparts white. Bill long and decurved towards tip; tapering panel of lilac-pink at base of lower mandible. Juvenile lacks yellow and has *white chin and throat*. **Habitat:** Breeds circumpolar in large colonies around Antarctica, including Ross Dependency. Rare vagrants reach NZ mainland. **Breeding:** Apr–Jan.   **[Sp 72]**

MAGELLANIC PENGUIN *Spheniscus magellanicus*   Rare South American vagrant

70 cm, 3.5 kg. Upperparts blue-black; wide white crescent from above bill, behind eye to upper breast separates crown and nape from black face and chin; two black bands cross upper breast, the narrower lower one horseshoe-shaped, turning down sides of belly to near feet. Juvenile has less clearly marked face pattern and a smudgy breast band. **Habitat:** Breeds on coast of S America. Rare vagrant to NZ.
                                                                   [Sp 84]

GENTOO PENGUIN *Pygoscelis papua*   Rare subantarctic vagrant

75 cm, 5.5 kg. Upperparts, chin and throat dark slate grey; *white triangle above each eye, connected by thin white line over top of head*; scattered white spots on head and neck; underparts white. Bill black with sides orange (male) or pinkish orange (female). Juvenile similar, but throat pale and patches over eye do not connect over crown. **Habitat:** Breeds circumpolar subantarctic and Antarctica; nearest colony to NZ at Macquarie I. Vagrants reach NZ subantarctic islands and occasionally NZ mainland.   **[Sp 75]**

juv

KING PENGUIN

juv

EMPEROR PENGUIN

MAGELLANIC PENGUIN

moulting

GENTOO PENGUIN

Plate 19   **PENGUINS**

YELLOW-EYED PENGUIN (Hoiho)   *Megadyptes antipodes*   Uncommon endemic

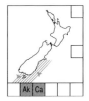

65 cm, 5.4 kg. Upperparts slaty grey; *forehead, crown and sides of face pale golden yellow* with black feather shafts; eye yellow. Adult has *band of yellow feathers starting at eye and encircling back of head.* Juvenile has greyer head and lacks yellow band. **Habitat:** Breeds and moults around southeastern South I, Foveaux Strait, Stewart, Codfish, Campbell and Auckland Is. Mainly sedentary, but some disperse northwards to Cook Strait, occasionally further. **Breeding:** Sep–Mar.   **[Sp 74]**

ADÉLIE PENGUIN   *Pygoscelis adeliae*   Locally common native

70 cm, 5 kg. Black head, face, chin and upperparts, except conspicuous *white eye-ring*; underparts white; *no crest.* Juvenile similar but has white chin and sides to face to just below the eye. **Habitat:** Breeds circumpolar in large colonies in Antarctica, including Ross Dependency. Rare vagrants reach NZ mainland. **Breeding:** Nov–Feb.   **[Sp 76]**

CHINSTRAP PENGUIN   *Pygoscelis antarctica*   Rare native

75 cm, 5.5 kg. Black upperparts; sides of face from above eye, chin and underparts white, except for a *narrow black band extending diagonally across face* from behind eye to under throat. Juvenile has dusky face above facial band. **Habitat:** Breeds Antarctica from Antarctic Peninsula eastwards to Ross Dependency. Rare vagrants reach NZ mainland. **Breeding:** Nov–Mar.   **[Sp 77]**

BLUE PENGUIN (Korora)   *Eudyptula minor*   Common native

40 cm, 1100 g. Smallest penguin. *Slate-blue upperparts* and sides of face to near eye, white below; lacks crest or distinctive face markings. Juvenile has a brighter blue back. White-flippered phase, of Canterbury, has more white on upperside of flipper. Often noisy on land at night; utters loud screams, wails, trumpeting and deep growls. **Habitat:** Breeds on rocky coasts and islands throughout NZ, but nest can be several hundred metres inland. When breeding, comes ashore at dusk and departs at dawn. Moults in burrows, under rock piles or in dense vegetation; often surrounded by piles of moulted feathers. Often seen in coastal waters. **Breeding:** Aug–Mar.   **[Sp 78]**

YELLOW-EYED PENGUIN

moulting

juv

juv

ADÉLIE PENGUIN

juv

BLUE PENGUIN

CHINSTRAP PENGUIN

white-flippered phase

Plate 20 **PENGUINS**

FIORDLAND CRESTED PENGUIN (Tawaki) *Eudyptes pachyrhynchus*
Rare endemic

60 cm, 4 kg. Upperparts dark bluish grey, darker on head; sides of face, chin and throat dark slaty grey; broad yellow eyebrow stripe that *splays out and droops* down neck; most have *3–6 whitish stripes on cheeks*. Little black on tip of underflipper. Moderately large orange bill with *no bare skin at base*. Juvenile has thin eyebrow, and whitish chin and throat. **Habitat:** Breeds and moults in dense coastal forest or in caves on rocky shores of southern NZ, mainly S Westland, Fiordland and Codfish I. During breeding, stays close to shore over continental shelf. Stragglers recorded around NZ coast and subantarctic islands. **Breeding:** Jul–Dec.   [Sp 81]

SNARES CRESTED PENGUIN *Eudyptes robustus*   **Locally common endemic**

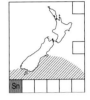

60 cm, 3 kg. Head, throat and upperparts dark blue-black; underparts white. *Thin bright yellow eyebrow stripe forms *bushy drooping crest* behind eye. *Prominent pink skin at base of heavy* reddish-brown bill. Solid black tip to underflipper. Juvenile has smaller and creamy crest, darker bill and mottled whitish throat. **Habitat:** Breeds only at The Snares. Straggles to other subantarctic islands and mainland NZ. **Breeding:** Sep–Feb.   [Sp 82]

ERECT-CRESTED PENGUIN *Eudyptes sclateri*   **Locally common endemic**

60 cm, 4.5 kg. Forehead, sides of face, chin and throat jet black; crown and upperparts very dark bluish black; underparts white. *Broad* bright yellow eyebrow stripe rises at a *steep angle over eye to form a short brush-like erectile crest* on each side of crown. Whitish skin at base of slender reddish-brown bill. Solid black tip to underflipper, extending well along leading edge. Juvenile has smaller and creamy crest, and throat mottled grey and white. **Habitat:** Breeds NZ subantarctic; main colonies at Bounty and Antipodes Is. After breeding, disperses widely; a few moult each autumn on NZ mainland coast, and regularly seen off NZ mainland in winter. **Breeding:** Oct–Feb.   [Sp 83]

ROCKHOPPER PENGUIN *Eudyptes chrysocome*   **Locally common native**

55 cm, 2.8 kg. Smallest crested penguin and has much smaller bill. Upperparts slate, darker on head, sides of face and chin. *Thin golden-yellow eyebrow stripe from either side of forehead* extending to splay at crown; some droop towards neck, others forming a *plume at edge of crest on hindcrown*. Juvenile similar but shorter crest, eyebrow stripe less well developed, and chin and throat streaked with ashy white. Size of crest, colour of bare skin at base of bill and pattern of black at underside tip of flipper used to separate subspecies. **Habitat:** Breeds circumpolar subantarctic; in NZ region, at Campbell, Auckland and Antipodes Is, often near or with Erect-crested Penguins. Stragglers reach The Snares, Chathams and NZ mainland. **Breeding:** Oct–Mar.
[Sp 79]

MACARONI PENGUIN *Eudyptes chrysolophus*   **Rare subantarctic straggler**

70 cm, 4.5 kg. Largest crested penguin. Upperparts black; sides of face, chin and throat black in Macaroni form, but grey or white in Royal form. Both have *massive red-brown bill* with fleshy gape; yellow, golden orange and black *plumes starting from centre of forehead*. Juvenile has smaller tuft-like plumes. **Habitat:** Breeds Antarctica and subantarctic of S Atlantic and Indian Oceans (Macaroni) and at Macquarie I (Royal). Occasionally reaches NZ sector of Antarctica, NZ subantarctic islands and, rarely, the NZ mainland.
[Sp 80]

FIORDLAND CRESTED PENGUIN

SNARES CRESTED PENGUIN

juv

Eastern

Moseley's

ROCKHOPPER PENGUIN

ERECT-CRESTED
PENGUIN

Macaroni

Royal

MACARONI PENGUIN

Plate 21

TROPICBIRDS and FRIGATEBIRDS

Tropicbirds are medium-sized, white, rather tern-like seabirds mostly confined to the tropics. Distinguished from terns by their wedge-shaped tail. Sexes alike. Adults have 2 long central tail-streamers. Juveniles have black barring above and lack tail streamers. Their flight is distinctive; direct with strong steady wingbeats about 30 m above the sea. Over land, they ride the updraughts along cliffs and hills. At sea, they plunge-dive for fish and squid.

RED-TAILED TROPICBIRD (Amokura) *Phaethon rubricauda* Rare tropical native

46 cm, (+ up to 40 cm for tail streamers), 800 g. Adult white with *black feather-shafts* on primaries, tertials and tail; black mark through eye. Tern-like *bright red bill*; tail streamers *red* but often difficult to see. Juvenile lacks tail streamers, is barred black above and has *black or dull red bill*. **Habitat:** Tropical seas; in NZ region, breeds at Kermadecs. Rare vagrant to northern NZ mainland. **Breeding:** Dec–Aug. **[Sp 85]**

WHITE-TAILED TROPICBIRD *Phaethon lepturus* Rare tropical vagrant

38 cm, (+ up to 40 cm for tail streamers), 300 g. Smaller and more graceful in flight than Red-tailed Tropicbird. Adult white with prominent *diagonal black band on inner wing and solid black patch near the tip of the upperwing*; tail streamers *white; bill yellow to orange.* Juvenile like that of Red-tailed Tropicbird but has black patch on the outer upperwing and pale yellow bill. **Habitat:** Tropical seas. **[Sp 86]**

Frigatebirds are large dark seabirds with very long thin pointed wings, long deeply forked tail and long hooked bill. The sexes differ in the amount of white on their underparts; males are mostly black and have a dark bill, whereas females have a prominent white chest and a pale bill. Immatures are hard to separate, having gingery heads and white chests like females. Usually seen soaring high over tropical seas or pursuing other birds, particularly boobies and terns, forcing them to drop their food, which they catch in midair. They feed entirely on the wing, snatching flying fish and picking fish and squid from the surface of the sea.

LESSER FRIGATEBIRD *Fregata ariel* Rare tropical vagrant

76 cm, 1000 g. Diagnostic *thin white tab extends from the chest onto the armpits and base of the underwing.* Adult male is otherwise *all dark.* Adult female has white of chest and flanks extending to hindneck as *a white collar* contrasting with the *dark hood, chin and throat.* Juvenile has a white chest and gingery head, blotched white when worn. **Habitat:** Tropical seas. **[Sp 105]**

GREATER FRIGATEBIRD *Fregata minor* Rare tropical vagrant

95 cm, 1500 g. Largest frigatebird. Adult male *all dark.* Adult female and juveniles have white of chest and flanks *extending up to chin and throat* and *not* onto underwing. Juveniles have a gingery head, blotched white when worn. **Habitat:** Tropical seas. **[Sp 104]**

RED-TAILED TROPICBIRD

WHITE-TAILED TROPICBIRD

juv

juv

imm

♂

♀

LESSER FRIGATEBIRD

imm

♂

♀

GREATER FRIGATEBIRD

Plate 22

GANNETS and BOOBIES

Large mainly black and white or brown and white seabirds. Streamlined body with long narrow wings and a long tapering tail. Conical bill, bare facial skin; fully webbed feet. Sexes alike. Juveniles and immatures darker than adults, taking several years to attain full adult plumage. Flight steady and direct; short periods of deliberate flapping and long glides. Feed on fish and squid caught by spectacularly diving into the sea, often from a considerable height. Often sit on the surface between feeding bouts. Gannets favour temperate and subtropical seas, whereas boobies favour tropical and subtropical seas. Gannets nest on the ground in large dense colonies; boobies nest on the ground or in trees singly or in loose colonies. Lay 1–4 plain pale eggs.

AUSTRALASIAN GANNET (Takapu) *Morus serrator*   Common native

89 cm, 2.3 kg. *White with buff-yellow head and most flight feathers black* (but not the three innermost secondaries or tertials as in Masked Booby); amount of black in the tail varies with age and moult, adults typically have only 4 central feathers black. Bill pale bluish grey; feet slate grey with blue-yellow lines on legs and toes. Juvenile is grey-brown spotted above, white with brown streaks below, and a dark bill. Adult plumage is attained over 3–5 years, head and underparts whitening first, whereas the rump and tail often remains blotched. **Habitat:** Breeds on many islands and some headlands around the NZ coast. Feeds mostly in coastal waters over the continental shelf. Most juveniles move to the seas off eastern and southern Australia and return when 3–7 years old. **Breeding:** Jul–Jan.   **[Sp 88]**

MASKED BOOBY *Sula dactylatra*   Locally uncommon native

80 cm, 1700 g. Adult resembles adult Australasian Gannet but has *white head, orange-yellow or pink bill, black face mask* with yellow eye. Black trailing edge of upperwing includes tertials and so extends to body; tail all dark. Feet purplish grey. Juvenile has mottled brown upperwings, paler back, heavily streaked (almost brown) head and neck grading to white on the collar and lower neck, and a pale yellowish bill. **Habitat:** Tropical and subtropical seas; in NZ region, breeds at Kermadecs. **Breeding:** Aug–Apr.   **[Sp 90]**

BROWN BOOBY *Sula leucogaster*   Rare tropical vagrant

70 cm, 1200 g. *Dark chocolate brown, sharply cut off at mid-breast from white undersurface of body;* centre of underwing white. Legs yellow or greenish yellow. Male has blue facial skin and yellowish-grey bill; female has yellow facial skin and base of bill. Juvenile like adult, but brown parts paler, white parts mottled grey-brown, and less white on underwing. Bill and facial skin blue-grey; legs flesh-grey. **Habitat:** Tropical seas.   **[Sp 89]**

AUSTRALASIAN GANNET

juv

juv

imm

MASKED BOOBY

juv

juv

BROWN BOOBY

juv

juv

Plate 23 # SHAGS and DARTER

Shags are medium to large aquatic birds. Most are all black, or black above and white below. Bill long, strongly hooked at the tip. Upright posture when perched. Short legs; feet are fully webbed. Many have brightly coloured facial skin when breeding. Sexes alike. In flight, wings short and broad, and neck is extended. Swim with head held uptilted and body low in the water.

BLACK SHAG (Kawau, Great Cormorant) *Phalacrocorax carbo* — Common native

88 cm, 2.2 kg. Largest shag. Black with browner wings and tail, and white patch on cheeks and throat. Facial skin yellow, but early in breeding season it becomes orange-red below eye. Breeding adult also has a white thigh patch, a small black crest on nape and upper neck, and thin white streaks (filoplumes) on the crown and upper neck. Bill grey; eye green; feet black. Immature similar but dull brown above, brown mottled white below, and no throat patch. **Habitat:** Rivers, streams and lakes, also estuaries, harbours and sheltered coastal waters. **Breeding:** Apr–Jan. **[Sp 91]**

PIED SHAG (Karuhiruhi) *Phalacrocorax varius* — Locally common native

81 cm, 2 kg. Large. Glossy black above, face from above eye and all underparts white, except for black thighs. Long grey bill; bare skin buff in front of green eye, pink below bill; eye-ring blue; feet black. Immature similar but brownish above, white underparts streaked and mottled brown. **Habitat:** Coastal, ranging inland only to coastal lagoons and lakes. **Breeding:** All year. **[Sp 92]**

LITTLE BLACK SHAG *Phalacrocorax sulcirostris* — Locally common native

61 cm, 800 g. Small elegant shag. Wholly black with green gloss, *dark-edged feathers give a scalloped effect on back. Long, slender lead-grey bill;* dark facial skin; eye green; feet black. Immature similar but brownish. *Tail short* compared with that of Little Shag. *Gregarious,* often feeding as a co-ordinated pack and flying in V-formation low to the water. **Habitat:** Lakes, estuaries and harbours. Common in North I but rare in South I. **Breeding:** Nov–Apr. **[Sp 93]**

LITTLE SHAG (Kawaupaka) *Phalacrocorax melanoleucos* — Common native

56 cm, 700 g. Smallest shag. Highly variable plumages from all black to pied, but *all have short stubby bills,* yellow in adults, dark in juveniles; eye brown; feet black. Adults have yellow facial skin and small black crest on forehead. *Tail long* compared with that of Little Black Shag. Usually feed solitarily or in small loose groups, but gregarious when roosting and nesting. **Habitat:** Lakes, farm ponds, rivers and streams, also estuaries, harbours and sheltered coastal waters. **Breeding:** Aug–May. **[Sp 94]**

Darters are rather like slim, long-necked shags. When swimming, only their head and neck are visible. They spend long periods perched, mostly in trees, with wings and tail spread.

DARTER *Anhinga melanogaster* — Rare Australian vagrant

90 cm, 1750 g. Large but slim, *very long thin neck, straight dagger-like yellow bill* and very long tail. A white stripe runs from below eye down side of *strongly kinked neck;* prominent *cream streaks on upper wings and long scapular feathers.* Male otherwise all brownish black except for red patch on foreneck. Female and immatures paler with upperparts grey-brown and underparts white or pale buff. In flight, long broad wings and kinked neck; rapid shallow wingbeats interspersed with glides. **Habitat:** Lakes, coastal lagoons and estuaries. **[Sp 103]**

BLACK SHAG

juv

breeding

PIED SHAG

juv

DARTER

♂

♀

LITTLE BLACK SHAG

juv

white-throated phase

pied phase

intermediate phase

LITTLE SHAG

juv

Plate 24   **SHAGS**

SPOTTED SHAG (Parekareka)   *Stictocarbo punctatus*   Locally common endemic

70 cm, 1200 g. Slender *grey* shag with *yellow* feet and long slender brown bill. Breeding adult has small black spots on back and wings; rump, tail and thighs black; underparts grey; *a broad white stripe from above eye down sides of the neck*, and sparse white streaks (filoplumes) on neck and thighs; conspicuous double crest, curled forward; green facial skin. Non-breeding adult lacks crests and has obscure white stripe on neck, yellow facial skin, and paler underparts. Immature is paler and browner, lacks distinct head or neck markings. In flight, looks very slender and pale with darker rump and tail. Flies low to the water, often in strings, with rapid wingbeats. **Habitat:** Estuaries, harbours and coastal waters around mainland NZ. **Breeding:** All year.   **[Sp 101]**

PITT ISLAND SHAG   *Stictocarbo featherstoni*   Locally common endemic

63 cm, 1200 g. Like Spotted Shag but darker, no white neck stripe and facial skin apple green in breeding season. **Habitat:** Coastal waters around Chatham Is only. **Breeding:** Aug–Mar.   **[Sp 102]**

KING SHAG   *Leucocarbo carunculatus*   Rare endemic

76 cm, 2.5 kg. Large black and white shag with *pink* feet. White patches on wings appear as a *white bar on the folded wing*; yellow-orange fleshy swellings (caruncles) above base of bill; other facial skin and throat (gular) pouch reddish in breeding season, otherwise grey-blue; eye-ring blue. **Habitat:** Coastal waters of Marlborough Sounds only. **Breeding:** May–Nov.   **[Sp 95]**

STEWART ISLAND SHAG   *Leucocarbo chalconotus*   Locally common endemic

68 cm, 2.5 kg. Large *pink-footed* shag with pied and bronze phases and some intermediates. Pied phase is like King Shag, but caruncles orange and facial skin purplish; juvenile is brown above and white below, and usually lacks white patches on wings and back. Adult bronze phase is all brownish black with green and blue sheen, orange caruncles and purplish facial skin; juvenile is brown except for some white streaks on breast. Breeding birds develop long black crest on forehead and scattered faint white streaks (filoplumes) on head. **Habitat:** Coastal waters off southeastern South I and Stewart I. **Breeding:** Aug–Mar.   **[Sp 96]**

CAMPBELL ISLAND SHAG   *Leucocarbo campbelli*   Locally common endemic

63 cm, 2 kg. Like King Shag, but caruncles absent and entire head and neck black, apart from a white chin. **Habitat:** Coastal and offshore waters around Campbell I only. **Breeding:** Nov–May.   **[Sp 100]**

AUCKLAND ISLAND SHAG   *Leucocarbo colensoi*   Locally common endemic

63 cm, 2 kg. Like King Shag, but caruncles absent. **Habitat:** Coastal and offshore waters around Auckland Is only. **Breeding:** Nov–May.   **[Sp 99]**

BOUNTY ISLAND SHAG   *Leucocarbo ranfurlyi*   Locally common endemic

71 cm, 2.5 kg. Like King Shag, but caruncles absent. **Habitat:** Coastal and offshore waters around Bounty Is only. **Breeding:** Oct–Mar.   **[Sp 98]**

CHATHAM ISLAND SHAG   *Leucocarbo onslowi*   Locally common endemic

63 cm, 2.25 kg. Like King Shag, but orange caruncles are large and prominent. **Habitat:** Coastal and offshore waters around the Chatham Is only. **Breeding:** Aug–Mar.   **[Sp 97]**

SPOTTED SHAG

imm

breeding

non-breeding

PITT ISLAND SHAG

non-breeding

STEWART ISLAND SHAG

KING SHAG

juv

bronze phase

pied phase

juv pied phase

CHATHAM ISLAND
SHAG

CAMPBELL ISLAND
SHAG

AUCKLAND
ISLAND
SHAG

BOUNTY
ISLAND
SHAG

Plate 25   # HERONS and EGRETS

Medium to large elegant wading birds with long neck and legs, straight dagger-like bill and long unwebbed toes. Flight strong, typically with heavy languid wingbeats on broad wings, neck folded back and head tucked in, and legs trailing. Sexes alike. Immatures of most species are like adults but duller. Many species have ornamental plumes, which may be on the head, back and chest, sometimes distinctively coloured. The colours of bill, facial skin, legs and feet may become brighter or change as birds come into breeding condition. They feed in shallow water or on damp pasture, walking slowly or standing motionless and lunging at prey. Diet is mainly aquatic animals. All may make a harsh grating call in flight; otherwise silent except at breeding colonies. Many species breed and roost communally, others are solitary. Lay 2–5 blue-green eggs on a platform of sticks built in trees or on cliffs.

REEF HERON   *Egretta sacra*   Rare Pacific vagrant

66 cm, 400 g. White phase is stocky with *short legs and long heavy brownish-yellow bill*. Legs yellowish green to grey. In breeding season, strap-like plumes form on nape, chest and back. Feeding stance typically hunched and horizontal. **Habitat:** Coasts. All NZ resident birds are dark (see Plate 26), but a vagrant or colour variation has been seen once in NZ: Canterbury, June 1987.   **[Sp 111]**

INTERMEDIATE EGRET   *Egretta intermedia*   Rare Australian vagrant

64 cm, 400 g. All-white heron, smaller than White Heron, larger than Little Egret, and stockier than both. Fully stretched *neck about same length as body* and thicker than White Heron's. *Black line of gape ends level with eye*. In breeding plumage, extensive filamentous *plumes on back and chest*. Legs and bill reddish; facial skin green. In non-breeding, bill and facial skin yellow; legs black, paler grey above 'knees'. **Habitat:** Freshwater and coastal wetlands, occasionally pasture.   **[Sp 110]**

WHITE HERON (Kotuku)   *Egretta alba*   Uncommon native

92 cm, 900 g. Clearly the largest all-white heron. Long thin S-shaped neck with a distinct kink one-third back from the head; fully stretched *neck is longer than the body*; *black line of gape extends past the eye*. In breeding plumage, elegant filamentous *plumes on back* extend beyond the folded wings and the tail. Bill black; facial skin green; legs black, yellowish above 'knees'. In non-breeding, plumes absent, bill yellow, facial skin greenish yellow and legs black. Usually solitary, standing or walking sedately in shallow water. **Habitat:** Coastal freshwater wetlands and estuaries, occasionally wet pasture. In NZ, breeds only at Okarito, West Coast, but disperses throughout mainland. **Breeding:** Sep–Jan.   **[Sp 108]**

LITTLE EGRET   *Egretta garzetta*   Uncommon Australian migrant

60 cm, 300 g. Small *dainty* all-white heron with *long slender black bill*; facial skin yellow; legs and feet black except for *yellow soles*. *Black line of gape ends level with eye*. In breeding season, plumes on *nape, chest and back*; the 2 nape plumes are strap-like, whereas chest and back plumes are filamentous. *Very active when feeding*, dashing about in pursuit of fish, often with wings raised and with a high-stepping gait. Often solitary but may associate with White Herons. **Habitat:** Coastal lakes and estuaries.   **[Sp 109]**

CATTLE EGRET   *Bubulcus ibis*   Locally common Australian migrant

50 cm, 360 g. *Small stocky and short-necked* (shorter than body) heron with *yellow bill*, grey legs and feet, and a *heavy jowl* of feathers under the bill. In breeding plumage, orange-buff plumes on head, neck and breast. Transitional stages from all white to buff common from September onwards. Non-breeding and immature birds all white but can have a faint buff wash on the crown. **Habitat:** *Usually associate with farm animals, especially cattle*, in damp pasture. May return to the same farms or group of farms for autumn and winter year after year.   **[Sp 112]**

REEF HERON
white phase

INTERMEDIATE EGRET

breeding

non-breeding

WHITE HERON

LITTLE EGRET

breeding

CATTLE EGRET

breeding

Plate 26

HERONS, EGRETS and BITTERNS

WHITE-FACED HERON   *Ardea novaehollandiae*   **Abundant native**

67 cm, 550 g. Slim *bluish-grey heron with white face, chin and upper throat*; bill black, legs greenish yellow. Strap-shaped plumes, more prominent in the breeding season, are long and pale grey on the back and short and pinkish brown on the chest. Juvenile like adult but lacks plumes and the white face is reduced, often white chin only. Flight slow, often high, with steady beats of 2-toned wings. **Habitat:** Occupies a wide variety of habitats from coastal estuaries and lagoons to rivers, lakes and farmland. Nests in solitary pairs high in trees, especially eucalypts and shelterbelt pines on farmland. **Breeding:** Jun–Feb.   **[Sp 106]**

REEF HERON (Matuku moana)   *Egretta sacra*   **Uncommon native**

66 cm, 400 g. Dark phase uniformly *slaty-grey* heron with a long *heavy horn-coloured-to-yellowish bill*; legs relatively short, yellow-green. Early in breeding season, long strap-like plumes form on back and short ones form on nape and foreneck. Juvenile browner and lacks plumes. *Feeding stance hunched and almost horizontal;* flight slow just above the water surface. Usually solitary or in pairs. **Habitat:** Mangrove inlets, rocky shores, wave platforms and sometimes on intertidal mudflats. Commonest in Northland, decreasing southward and uncommon in South, Stewart and Chatham Is. **Breeding:** Sep–Mar.   **[Sp 111]**

Bitterns are specialised for living in swamps; typically short-necked and camouflaged brown with dark and pale streaks, especially on underparts. Sexes alike. When disturbed, they 'freeze', with body and bill pointing skywards, sometimes swaying with raupo or reeds moving in the breeze.

AUSTRALASIAN BITTERN (Matuku)   *Botaurus poiciloptilus*   **Rare native**

71 cm; ♂ 1400 g, ♀ 1000 g. *Large bulky thick-necked bittern, mottled brown and buff.* Secretive, partially nocturnal, generally keeping within dense cover where its plum-age blends with the vegetation. When flushed, rises with broad rounded wings labouring. Flight direct, neck withdrawn, legs trailing and with slow steady wing-beats. Usually solitary. During breeding, distinctive *deep booming calls*, like air being blown over an open bottle. **Habitat:** Mainly freshwater wetlands, especially with dense cover of raupo or reeds. Some movement to coastal wetlands in autumn and winter. **Breeding:** Sep–Feb.   **[Sp 114]**

LITTLE BITTERN   *Ixobrychus minutus*   **Rare Australian vagrant**

30 cm, 85 g. *Very small bittern.* Adult male has *large buff wing patches* contrasting with black flight feathers, back and tail; ginger sides to face and neck. Adult female like male, but black replaced with brown. Juvenile yellowish buff, heavily streaked dark brown. Flight as in Australasian Bittern; adults show *prominent pale patches on dark upperwings.* **Habitat:** Freshwater wetlands. One NZ record: Westport, February 1987.   **[Sp 115]**

WHITE-FACED HERON

juv

REEF HERON

juv

AUSTRALASIAN BITTERN

♂   ♀   juv ♀

LITTLE BITTERN

Plate 27

CRANES, PELICANS and HERONS

Cranes are tall elegant birds with a stout straight bill, longer than the head. The inner secondary flight feathers form plumes that overhang the tail, like a 'bustle'. Sexes alike. They often soar in thermals.

BROLGA   *Grus rubicundus*   **Rare Australian vagrant**

115 cm; ♂ 7 kg, ♀ 5 kg. *Very tall stately grey crane* with *scarlet head and nape*, except for grey crown and ear coverts; eye yellow. Juvenile has pink face and crown. In flight, shallow wingbeats, *neck and legs extended*, grey wings with black primaries. **Habitat:** Swampy margins of lakes and ponds, and damp pasture.
[Sp 166]

Pelicans are large bulky birds with an enormous bill and gular (throat) pouch. Short legs make them ungainly on land, but they swim gracefully. Fly strongly with head tucked in, often in a flock in V formation, or soar high on thermals. They feed mainly on fish scooped from the water, often feeding in a group to surround a shoal of fish. Favour large open waterbodies.

AUSTRALIAN PELICAN   *Pelecanus conspicillatus*   **Rare Australian vagrant**

170 cm, 5 kg. *Enormous white bird with huge pink bill and pouch;* upperwing black with a large white panel; underwing white with black primaries. Juvenile brown where adult black. **Habitat:** Occasionally recorded in freshwater and tidal wetlands in NZ.   **[Sp 87]**

WHITE-NECKED HERON   *Ardea pacifica*   **Rare Australian vagrant**

90 cm, 900 g. Robust *dark grey heron with a white head, neck and upper breast;* variable line of dark spots down the front of the neck. Greenish sheen and maroon plumes on back are prominent in the breeding season. Juvenile lacks plumes and is more heavily spotted and barred brown on neck and breast. In flight, upperparts dark with a striking *white patch at the bend of the wing.* **Habitat:** Margins of swamps, ponds and dams, and damp pasture.   **[Sp 107]**

NANKEEN NIGHT HERON   *Nycticorax caledonicus*   **Rare native**

57 cm, 800 g. *Stocky rounded short-necked heron, rufous brown or heavily streaked and spotted brown.* Thick black bill; short yellow legs. Adult has rufous-brown (nankeen) upperparts, paler underparts, black cap. When breeding, 2 long slender white plumes hang from the nape. Juvenile dark brown, heavily spotted and streaked pale buff. In flight, looks heavy-headed, round-winged and short-tailed, and has shallower and faster wingbeats than other herons. Usually feeds at dusk or night and roosts in trees by day. **Habitat:** Margins of freshwater wetlands or tidal lagoons. Vagrant until it started breeding on Whanganui River in 1990s. **Breeding:** Season unknown in NZ.   **[Sp 113]**

BROLGA

AUSTRALIAN PELICAN

NANKEEN NIGHT HERON

WHITE-NECKED HERON

juv

Plate 28

SPOONBILLS and IBISES

Large heron-like waterbirds with flat spoon-shaped bill (spoonbills) or strongly downcurved bill (ibises). Sexes alike. They fly with neck outstretched, rapid wingbeats alternating with long glides. Roost in trees; breed in colonies with platform nests made from twigs and tidal debris. Disperse widely after breeding. Silent away from colonies. Diet is fish, crustaceans and other aquatic invertebrates.

ROYAL SPOONBILL *Platalea regia* Locally common native

77 cm, 1700 g. *Large brilliantly white bird with long black spoon-shaped bill* and black legs. Adult has black facial skin marked with a yellow patch above each eye and a red spot in the centre of the forehead, and the surface of the bill is wrinkled. In breeding plumage, large white drooping plumes on the rear of the head and a yellowish wash across breast. Juvenile has plain black facial skin, smooth bill and small black tips to wings. Feeds by walking slowly forwards in shallow water, *sweeping partly open bill from side to side.* **Habitat:** Tidal mudflats, occasionally on margins of freshwater lakes. Main breeding colonies at Okarito, Vernon Lagoons (Marlborough), islands just off Otago, and Invercargill Estuary. **Breeding:** Sep–Feb.
[Sp 118]

YELLOW-BILLED SPOONBILL *Platalea flavipes* Rare Australian vagrant

88 cm, 1900 g. Like Royal Spoonbill, but plumage off-white and *bill and legs pale yellow.* Facial skin pale grey, bordered by a black line. In breeding plumage, medium-length stiff white plumes on lower neck, thin black lace-like plumes on wings, and red patches in front of eye. Feeds by sweeping partly open bill from side to side in shallow water. **Habitat:** Mainly inland wetlands and wet pasture.   [Sp 119]

GLOSSY IBIS *Plegadis falcinellus* Uncommon Australian vagrant

60 cm, 500 g. Slender *glossy dark brown ibis with long downcurved bill.* At a distance, stance like a feeding Pukeko. In breeding plumage, head, neck and upperparts deep glossy reddish brown, wings iridescent green; bill and facial skin grey, bordered at the base with a conspicuous white line. Non-breeding and juvenile dull brown with variable white mottling on head and neck. Flies with head and neck outstretched like a shag, but alternates rapid wingbeats with short glides. Feeds mainly by probing in soft mud. **Habitat:** Margins of freshwater lakes and swamps, and damp pasture. Occasional irruptions into NZ.
[Sp 116]

AUSTRALIAN WHITE IBIS *Threskiornis molucca* Rare Australian vagrant

70 cm, 2 kg. Large scruffy *white ibis with long heavy downcurved bill and unfeathered black head.* In breeding plumage, short yellowish plumes on foreneck, and long frilly black tertials droop over tail and folded wing. Non-breeding lacks neck plumes, and tertials shorter and greyer. Juvenile has head and neck fully feathered dark grey and white. In flight, neck outstretched, wings tipped black, and in adults a line of red bare skin shows on the underwing. Walks slowly, probing in mud. **Habitat:** Freshwater or brackish wetlands and wet pasture.
[Sp 117]

breeding

juv

non-breeding

ROYAL SPOONBILL

YELLOW-BILLED SPOONBILL

GLOSSY IBIS

breeding

non-breeding

AUSTRALIAN WHITE IBIS

Plate 29 **WATERFOWL**

Aquatic birds with a small rounded head, short flattened bill, rounded body, short legs, webbed feet and a waddling gait on land. They fly strongly with neck outstretched. Sexes alike in swans and geese, but male ducks are usually more colourful than females. Lay large clutches. Chicks leave the nest within days but are guarded for several months until they can fly.

BLACK SWAN   *Cygnus atratus*   Common Australian introduction

120 cm; ♂ 6 kg, ♀ 5 kg. *Very large black swan.* Bill crimson with white tip and bar near tip. Juvenile is ashy brown with a dull red bill. Takes off laboriously and noisily, running across the surface, wings striking on each downstroke. Flies with long neck extended and slow deep wingbeats, showing *prominent white wing tips.* Flocks fly in long skeins. *Voice a musical bugling.* Feeds mainly on vegetation by dabbling at the surface, upending to reach bottom plants, or grazing on nearby damp pasture. **Habitat:** Lakes, estuaries and parks; sometimes seen at sea or on pasture. **Breeding:** Jul–Feb.   **[Sp 122]**

MUTE SWAN   *Cygnus olor*   Rare European introduction

150 cm; ♂ 12 kg, ♀ 10 kg. *Very large white swan.* Bill orange with a black knob at the base, larger in breeding males. Juvenile grey-brown, paler than juvenile Black Swan; grey bill bordered with black at the base and lacking knob. Not mute but usually silent. Noisy 'swishing' flight with long neck extended. **Habitat:** Lakes, parks and private waterfowl collections. **Breeding:** Sep–Jan.   **[Sp 121]**

CANADA GOOSE   *Branta canadensis*   Common North American introduction

83 cm; ♂ 5.4 kg, ♀ 4.5 kg. *Large brown goose* with pale brown and white barring below; *black neck and head with conspicuous white patch on cheeks and chin.* Loud *honking* call given when alarmed and in flight. Flocks fly in V formation. Grazes on pasture, young crops and aquatic plants. **Habitat:** High-country pasture, freshwater lakes and margins, and coastal lagoons. **Breeding:** Sep–Dec.   **[Sp 123]**

CAPE BARREN GOOSE   *Cereopsis novaehollandiae*   Rare Australian introduction

87 cm, 5 kg. *Large bulky pale grey goose* with dark spots on scapulars and wing coverts. *Bill short and largely covered by a greenish-yellow cere;* legs pink and feet black. In flight, uniformly grey with black tail and wingtips. Grazes on pasture plants. **Habitat:** Parks, occasionally on lakes. Vagrants may occasionally reach NZ.   **[Sp 124]**

FERAL GOOSE   *Anser anser*   Common European introduction

80 cm, 3 kg. The familiar domestic goose of farms and parks, often feral. Males are all white, females white with brown on wings and thighs. Juveniles all grey-brown. Bill, legs and feet orange-pink. Usually graze away from water. **Habitat:** Lakes, estuaries and farmland.   **[Sp 125]**

BLACK SWAN

juv

MUTE SWAN

juv

CANADA GOOSE

CAPE BARREN GOOSE

♂ ♀

FERAL GOOSE

PARADISE SHELDUCK (Putangitangi)   *Tadorna variegata*   Common endemic

63 cm; ♂ 1700 g, ♀ 1400 g. Large goose-like duck with *orange-chestnut undertail* and tertials. Male has *black head with greenish gloss, body dark grey finely barred black*. Female has *brilliant white head, body bright orange-chestnut*, obscured by darker fine barring in eclipse plumage. Juveniles like male, but immature females develop white patches around eyes and at base of bill. In flight, prominent white patches on upperwings. Often call; male a deep 'zonk-zonk . . .', female a shrill 'zeek, zeek . . .' Mostly seen as pairs or in large flocks, especially during the moult in Dec–Mar. **Habitat:** Farmland, lakes, ponds and high-country riverbeds. **Breeding:** Aug–Dec.   [Sp 126]

CHESTNUT-BREASTED SHELDUCK   *Tadorna tadornoides*   Rare native

65 cm; ♂ 1600 g, ♀ 1300 g. Like male Paradise Shelduck, but *undertail black and chest and lower neck orange-chestnut, bordered above by thin white collar*. Male has upper back and breast pale orange-chestnut, thin white collar, and occasionally has a small white patch at base of bill. Female has darker orange-chestnut upper back and breast, very thin white collar and white patches at base of bill and around eye. Juvenile like female but smaller, duller and lacks collar. Often seen with Paradise Shelduck in NZ. **Habitat:** Freshwater and brackish lakes. First recorded in 1973 and have bred at least twice in eastern South I. **Breeding:** Season unknown in NZ.   [Sp 127]

BLUE DUCK (Whio)   *Hymenolaimus malacorhynchos*   Uncommon endemic

53 cm; ♂ 900 g, ♀ 750 g. *Blue-grey duck with a pale pink bill*, tipped with black flaps. Adult has yellow eyes, breast spotted reddish chestnut. Sexes similar. Juvenile has dull grey bill and eyes, and fewer breast spots. Uniformly grey in flight. Male call a whistling 'whio, whio' (fee-o, fee-o); female call a rattling growl; often call together in flight. Remain in territorial pairs all year. Seen standing on rocks or feeding with head and neck underwater. **Habitat:** Fast-flowing mountain streams and rivers, mainly in native forest or tussock grassland, occasionally on lakes. **Breeding:** Jul–Jan.   [Sp 129]

AUSTRALIAN WOOD DUCK   *Chenonetta jubata*   Rare Australian vagrant

48 cm, 800 g. Pale grey duck with chest spotted brown, head dark brown, and short thin bill. Male has dark brown head and neck, with a short black mane on back of head; grey flanks. Female has pale lines above and below eye; flanks broadly barred brown and white. Juvenile like female but duller. In the water, sits higher than other ducks. Spends much time out of water grazing or roosting. Upright stance. Call a rising 'mew' or 'wee-ow'. **Habitat:** Grassland near wetlands.   [Sp 128]

GRASS (Plumed) WHISTLING DUCK   *Dendrocygna eytoni*   Rare Australian vagrant

50 cm, 800 g. Pale brown duck with goose-like profile and *stiff cream plumes curving up from the flanks* to above back. Bill flecked pink and grey. Sexes alike. Juvenile paler with small plumes. In flight, head held below the horizontal, back hunched and legs trailing. When flying, constantly twittering and whistling; the wings also whistle. **Habitat:** Grassland near wetlands.   [Sp 120]

PARADISE SHELDUCK

♀

♂

♀ eclipse

♂

♀

♀ imm

CHESTNUT-BREASTED
SHELDUCK

♂

♀

♀

BLUE DUCK

GRASS WHISTLING DUCK

AUSTRALIAN WOOD DUCK

Plate 31

WATERFOWL

MALLARD *Anas platyrhynchos* **Abundant European introduction**

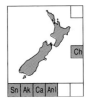

58 cm; ♂ 1300 g, ♀ 1100 g. The familiar duck of parks and farm ponds. *All have orange legs and feet, and a blue speculum bordered with thin black and broader white bands front and back.* Breeding male has dark glossy green head, chestnut breast, pale grey body, black rump and undertail; bill yellow-green. Female is streaked and spotted brown and buff on body and wings; bill brownish grey with orange at base, sides and tip. Eclipse male like female but has greyer head and neck, with remnants of green on crown and nape, and chestnut wash on breast. Juvenile similar to female. Variable plumage because of interbreeding with Grey Duck. Feeds by dabbling on water surface or by upending; also grazes and eats cereals. Rises nearly vertically from water and flies with fast shallow wingbeats. Female call the well-known 'quack, quack'; male call a soft high-pitched 'quek'. **Habitat:** Wetlands, estuaries, rivers, farm ditches, parks and cereal crops. **Breeding:** Jul–Jan. **[Sp 130]**

GREY DUCK (Parera) *Anas superciliosa* **Common native**

55 cm; ♂ 1100 g, ♀ 1000 g. Like female Mallard but *darker with conspicuously striped pale head, grey bill, greenish-brown legs and feet. Green speculum with black borders and thin white band on trailing edge only.* Sexes alike. In flight, looks dark with a very pale head and upper neck. Calls like Mallard. Has interbred extensively with the Mallard to produce paler birds with less distinct facial stripes and greyish bills, yellowish-brown legs and feet, and blue speculum. **Habitat:** Pure birds mainly in remote wetlands, including forest lakes and rivers; uncommon in agricultural and urban habitats dominated by Mallards. **Breeding:** Aug–Jan. **[Sp 131]**

AUSTRALASIAN SHOVELER (Kuruwhengi) *Anas rhynchotis* **Common native**

49 cm; ♂ 650 g, ♀ 600 g. Duck with heavy spatulate bill. Sits low in the water and profile shows no apparent forehead. Breeding male has *blue-grey head with a white crescent in front of golden eye*; breast off-white with extensive dark brown mottling; flanks bright chestnut with prominent *white patch at base of tail.* Bill dark grey; legs orange. Eclipse male has head speckled blue-grey, underparts mottled bronzy chestnut, with paler (sometimes almost white) breast, and lacks white flank patch. Female streaked and spotted brown and buff on body; bill grey with some pale orange at base and sides in some birds. In flight, *upperwing has sky-blue panel on inner forewing, narrow white wingbars and dark green speculum.* Flight swift, wings noticeably narrow and pointed. Whistling wings and jinking flight as it approaches to land. Birds utter a quiet 'cuck-cuck-cuck . . .' Feeds by sieving seeds and small aquatic animals through immersed bill. **Habitat:** Mainly shallow lowland wetlands, and muddy estuaries. **Breeding:** Oct–Feb. **[Sp 135]**

NORTHERN SHOVELER *Anas clypeata* **Rare Arctic vagrant**

50 cm, 650 g. Like Australasian Shoveler, including the same profile and upperwing pattern, but male in breeding plumage has *pure dark green head, and clean white breast extends to shoulders.* Eclipse male can have crescent on face, but head greener and flanks and undertail paler than Australasian Shoveler. Female paler and greyer than Australasian Shoveler, and usually has more orange on sides of bill and more white on outer tail. **Habitat:** Lowland wetlands. **[Sp 136]**

PINK-EARED DUCK *Malacorhynchus membranaceus* **Rare Australian vagrant**

40 cm, 400 g. Small duck with a large square-ended bill, black flaps at the tip. Back and wings grey-brown, distinctly *striped dark brown and white on lower neck, breast and flanks*; white flank patch extends across rump; undertail yellow-brown. *Large dark patch around eye*, contrasting white eye-ring, and small pink patch on ear coverts. In flight, *white rump contrasts with grey-brown upperwing and back, and dark brown white-tipped tail.* Constant chirruping call on the water and in flight. Feeds by filtering with bill submerged up to eyes. **Habitat:** Lakes. One NZ record: Auckland, June 1990. **[Sp 137]**

MALLARD

♂

♂ eclipse

♀

GREY DUCK

♂ eclipse

♂

AUSTRALASIAN SHOVELER

♀

♂ eclipse

♂

NORTHERN SHOVELER

♀

PINK-EARED DUCK

Plate 32

WATERFOWL

GREY TEAL (Tete) *Anas gracilis*   Common native

43 cm; ♂ 525 g, ♀ 425 g. *Delicate light grey-brown duck with pale grey cheeks, chin and foreneck.* Silhouette rounded, including head. Sits high and upright on the water. Bill blue-grey; *eye red.* Sexes alike. Juvenile paler, eye brown. In flight, speculum black with a green sheen, a narrow white bar behind, and a *prominent white triangle* in front; underwing white in the centre. Wingbeats very fast. Feeds by filtering on water surface or dredging bill in soft mud. **Habitat:** Lowland lakes and lagoons, and estuaries. **Breeding:** Jun–Feb.   **[Sp 132]**

CHESTNUT TEAL *Anas castanea*   Rare Australian vagrant

45 cm, 650 g. Like larger and darker-faced Grey Teal. Breeding male has *dark glossy green head and neck, bright chestnut underparts, a large white flank patch and a black undertail.* Female and juvenile like Grey Teal, but *pale buff rather than whitish chin and throat*, and dark crown is less distinct. Eclipse male like a dark female, but traces of colour are usually apparent. Bill blue-grey; *eye red.* In flight, wing pattern like Grey Teal. **Habitat:** Lowland lakes and estuaries.   **[Sp 133]**

BROWN TEAL (Pateke) *Anas aucklandica*   Rare endemic

48 cm; ♂ 600 g, ♀ 500 g. Like Chestnut Teal, but *eye brown with narrow white eye-ring* in all plumages. In flight, *lacks white triangle* in front of speculum. Breeding male has a glossy green head, an *indistinct narrow white collar* and a conspicuous white flank patch. Eclipse male, female and juvenile are warm brown; breast is mottled dark brown. Bill blue-black. Auckland I Teal flightless, with more subdued colouring. Campbell I Teal also flightless and with prominent white eye-ring. Gather to roost in flocks by day, and feed at dusk and at night. **Habitat:** Tidal creeks, lagoons and swamps, and adjacent wet pasture. Subantarctic subspecies feed in peaty creeks and soaks, and on coastal platforms and kelp beds. Brown Teal mostly on Great Barrier I and in Northland. **Breeding:** Jun–Nov; Auckland I Teal: Dec–Feb.   **[Sp 134]**

WHITE-EYED DUCK *Aythya australis*   Rare Australian vagrant

48 cm, 900 g. Diving duck like NZ Scaup, but *chocolate brown with white undertail; forehead slopes gently.* Bill dark grey with whitish band near the end, tipped black. Male has *white eye*; female brown eye. Female and juvenile lighter browner than male, and white patch on bill is smaller. In flight, upperwing has a broad white trailing band *from wingtip to body*; underwing white. Feeds and roosts on water, rarely coming onto land. **Habitat:** Large deep freshwater lakes, occasionally estuaries.   **[Sp 138]**

NEW ZEALAND SCAUP (Papango) *Aythya novaeseelandiae*   Uncommon endemic

40 cm, 650 g. Small blackish diving duck with *rounded toy 'rubber duckie' profile* and a *steep forehead.* Male *glossy black*, maroon on flanks and brown on belly. Bill blue-grey, tipped black; eye *golden-yellow.* Female *blackish brown*, usually with *vertical white band at the base of the bill.* Bill with faint black tip; eye brown. Juvenile like female but lacks white on face and bill dark grey. In flight, upperwing has a broad white trailing band from wingtip, but *not reaching body*; underwing white. Patters along water when taking off and flies low to the surface. Feeds on bottom weeds and invertebrates by diving. **Habitat:** Large deep freshwater lakes, including hydro lakes; also coastal dune lakes. **Breeding:** Oct–Mar.   **[Sp 139]**

GREY TEAL

CHESTNUT TEAL

♀

♂

BROWN TEAL

♀

♂ breeding

Auckland Island Teal

♂

♀

WHITE-EYED DUCK

♂

♀

juv

♂

♀

NEW ZEALAND SCAUP

Plate 33   **RAPTORS**

Diurnal birds of prey with long fingered or pointed wings; long tail; short hooked bill with coloured facial skin at the base of the bill (cere); powerful, largely unfeathered legs with long sharp talons for grasping prey or gripping carrion. Sexes usually alike, but females larger. Juveniles darker than adults.

AUSTRALASIAN HARRIER (Kahu)   *Circus approximans*   Abundant native

♂ 55 cm, 650 g; ♀ 60 cm, 850 g. *Large brown hawk with long fingered wings held in shallow V*, and a long slightly rounded tail. Becomes paler with age. Juvenile very dark brown with a prominent *white patch on back of head*; brown uppertail and brown eye. In adult, head and upperparts dark brown, face paler; *uppertail white*, tail light brown barred dark brown; underparts reddish brown streaked dark brown, underwings barred at tips and on trailing half. Some very old males have frosty-grey upperparts, pale buff underparts and white underwings. Eye yellow in males, very pale yellow in females. Commonly soars and glides in search of prey or carrion; often feeds on road-killed animals. **Habitat:** Farmland, tussockland and swamps, also forest edges. **Breeding:** Sep–Feb.   **[Sp 142]**

NEW ZEALAND FALCON (Karearea)   *Falco novaeseelandiae*   Uncommon endemic

♂ 43 cm, 300 g; ♀ 47 cm, 500 g. *Fast-flying raptor with rapid beats of long pointed wings*; also soars and glides. Adult has head, sides of face and vertical patch (like drooping moustache) below eye dark brownish black, faint rufous eyebrow; nape, back, wings and tail bluish black, faintly barred buff. Base of bill and chin white, throat and sides of neck buff streaked dark brown; breast and belly dark brown narrowly barred white; thigh and undertail rufous. Bill black, greyer at base; cere, legs and feet yellow; eye dark brown. Juvenile distinctly darker brown and less boldly marked. Bush Falcon (North and northwestern South Is) as above; eastern form (eastern South I) larger and paler; southern form (southwestern South, Stewart and Auckland Is) intermediate, more rufous on Auckland I. Often perches high in trees or on a rock, swoops to catch prey. Call a loud rapid 'kek-kek-kek'. **Habitat:** Forests and bush patches, open tussockland of South I. Juveniles wander to cities, orchards, riverbeds and offshore islands. **Breeding:** Sep–Feb.   **[Sp 143]**

BLACK KITE   *Milvus migrans*   Rare Australian vagrant

♂ 50 cm, 550 g; ♀ 55 cm, 600 g. Large *dark-brown* raptor with paler head and shoulder patches. Soars or glides on long fingered wings held flat, and frequently twists its *long forked tail*. Adult has forehead and chin grey merging into brown on the crown, cheeks and throat; rest of body dark brown with some darker streaks. Pale shoulder patch when bird is at rest. Bill black, cere yellow, legs and feet yellow. Juvenile paler, and head, neck and breast heavily streaked buff; upperwing mottled buff; bill black, cere grey, legs and feet yellow. **Habitat:** Open country.   **[Sp 141]**

BLACK FALCON   *Falco subniger*   Rare Australian vagrant

♂ 50 cm, 600 g; ♀ 54 cm, 800 g. Like *large* NZ Falcon but uniformly sooty brown except for pale streaked chin and face, and dark grey glossy wash on underwing and undertail. Juvenile darker with pale feather edges and faint barring under tail and wings. **Habitat:** Open country and scattered forest.   **[Sp 145]**

NANKEEN KESTREL   *Falco cenchroides*   Uncommon Australian vagrant

♂ 32 cm, 160 g; ♀ 34 cm, 180 g. Small long-winged and long-tailed raptor with *habit of hovering*, poised in mid-air facing into the wind with tail fanned. In flight, back and upperwings cinnamon brown with black wingtips; underparts white with buff wash on breast and variable fine dark streaks. Male has *blue-grey head* streaked black, and *tail blue-grey* with black band near tip and narrow white tip. Female and juvenile have *pale rufous head*, finely streaked black; *tail pale rufous* with black band near tip and narrow white tip. **Habitat:** Open country.   **[Sp 144]**

AUSTRALASIAN HARRIER

juv

ad

juv

ad ♀

ad ♂

imm

NEW ZEALAND
FALCON

ad

juv

BLACK KITE

BLACK FALCON

NANKEEN
KESTREL

♂

♂

♀

Plate 34

GAMEBIRDS

All gamebirds are introduced, often with great persistence and cost. Small to large plump birds that feed on the ground. Omnivorous but mainly take plant food, scratching and digging at the ground surface with legs and strong claws, and bill. When disturbed, they crouch, run to cover, or burst from cover with whirring wings and alarm notes, flying fast and low to pitch a short distance away. Sexes usually differ: females and immatures have subdued plumage that blends with the surroundings; males are sometimes brightly coloured, but even strongly patterned males blend with their surroundings. Immatures are usually seen with adults, so identity should not be a problem.

PHEASANT *Phasianus colchicus* Common European introduction

♂ 80 cm, 1400 g; ♀ 60 cm, 1200 g. Long-tailed gamebird. Male colourful, mainly rich orange-reds, glossy dark green head, red facial wattles. Female smaller, pale brown heavily mottled dark brown, lacks facial wattles. Male territorial call a loud, abrupt crow: 'kok-kok', with emphasis on the second syllable. Explodes suddenly from undergrowth when disturbed, with noisy wingbeats and rapid calls, and glides back to cover. **Habitat:** Open scrubland, vegetated sand dunes, riverbanks, and agricultural land with plenty of cover. **Breeding:** Jul–Mar.   [Sp 152]

PEAFOWL *Pavo cristatus* Uncommon Asian introduction

90 cm (+ male's 100 cm tail); ♂ 4.5 kg, ♀ 3.5 kg. Peacock distinctive and well known; peahen smaller, brown mottled black and white, and with a pointed tail. The peacock's loud wailing *trumpet-like cry* – 'kay-yaaw' – draws attention. Roosts in trees. **Habitat:** Parks and private gardens, rough agricultural land with good cover in warm, dry districts.   [Sp 153]

WILD TURKEY *Meleagris gallopavo*
Locally common North American introduction

♂ 120 cm, 8 kg; ♀ 90 cm, 4 kg. Large black bird with blue and red head; familiar farmyard Turkey. Male black with paler barred wings and tail; beard of long feathers hangs from upper chest; head and neck naked and wrinkled, blue and red. Female smaller and browner, and lacks beard and neck wattles. The familiar territorial gobbling is mainly by males. Seldom flies, except to roost in trees. **Habitat:** Farmland, especially where there is good cover.   [Sp 154]

TUFTED GUINEAFOWL *Numida meleagris* Rare African introduction

60 cm, 1500 g. Large rounded gamebird with a small blue-grey bare head, red wattles, and a bony horn protruding from the crown. Body slate grey thickly spotted white. Sexes alike. Roosts in trees. **Habitat:** Semiferal at many farms and rural homesteads; a few are feral in rough agricultural land in Northland, Waikato, Rotorua and Wanganui.   [Sp 155]

PHEASANT

♂

♀

PEAFOWL

♂

♀

WILD TURKEY

♀

♂

TUFTED GUINEAFOWL

Plate 35

GAMEBIRDS

GREY PARTRIDGE *Perdix perdix* Rare European introduction

30 cm. Medium-sized *grey* partridge, mottled brown on back and barred chestnut on flanks. Male has *orange-brown face and throat and dark horseshoe-shaped patch on breast*. Female has paler face and less distinct patch on breast. Bill and legs blue-grey. In flight, *mottled upperparts and rusty tail*. Flight fast direct and low with rapid whirring wingbeats; when flushed, a covey usually keeps together. Voice is sharp 'kirrik', likened to rusty gate hinges. **Habitat:** Open country with dense cover.   **[Sp 150]**

RED-LEGGED PARTRIDGE *Alectoris rufa* Rare European introduction

31 cm. Like Chukor in size, plumage, bright red bill and legs, and voice, but has *black necklace higher on throat, streaked black and white* on lower throat and sides of neck; *crown, nape and hindneck brown*. Flank bars are more chestnut than black. Sexes alike. In flight, shows *plain grey-brown back*. **Habitat:** Open country with dense cover, such as riverbeds flanked by willows and gorse.   **[Sp 148]**

CHUKOR *Alectoris chukar* Locally common Asian introduction

31 cm; ♂ 600 g, ♀ 500 g. Like Red-legged Partridge but has *solid clear-cut black necklace that crosses low on the throat; crown, nape and hindneck grey*. Flank bars are more black than chestnut. Sexes alike. In flight, *upperparts plain grey with rusty wash at base of wings* and rusty outer tail feathers. When flushed, a covey usually scatters. Voice a loud 'chuck-chuck-chuck-per-chuck-per-chuck-chuckar-chuckar-chuckar'. **Habitat:** South I hill country, especially rocky hillsides with tussock and sparse scrub. **Breeding:** Sep–Feb.   **[Sp 149]**

CALIFORNIA QUAIL *Callipepla californica*
Common North American introduction

25 cm, 180 g. Small partridge with *forward-curving topknot crest plume*, smaller in female. Male has a black throat bordered by a white band, blue-grey breast and scaly upperparts. Female duller. Male has a loud *3-syllable call:* 'chi-ca-go' or 'where are you?', with emphasis on the second syllable. **Habitat:** Open country with patches of low scrub, riverbeds flanked by willows and gorse. **Breeding:** Sep–Mar.   **[Sp 146]**

BROWN QUAIL *Synoicus ypsilophorus* Locally common Australian introduction

18 cm, 100 g. *Very small rounded brown quail.* Mottled black and chestnut above; fine wavy bars below. Bill dark, eye reddish, legs yellowish. Sexes alike. Call a plaintive languid 'ker-wee', the second syllable drawn out and with rising inflexion. **Habitat:** Scrub edges in rough farmland; most common in Northland, uncommon further south. **Breeding:** Sep–Feb.   **[Sp 151]**

BOBWHITE QUAIL *Colinus virginianus* Rare North American introduction

23 cm, 180 g. Small quail with *longitudinal pale chestnut stripes on the flanks,* dark grey bill and yellowish-brown legs. Male has *white face, black cap and line through eye* to join black necklace across throat, trailing down onto breast. Female has yellowish-buff face and brown markings. Male call a whistling 'poor-bob-white', with accent on the last note. **Habitat:** Low scrub with grassy clearings; may persist in South Auckland and northern Hawke's Bay.   **[Sp 147]**

GREY
PARTRIDGE

♂

♀

RED-LEGGED
PARTRIDGE

CHUKOR

CALIFORNIA
QUAIL

♂

♀

BROWN QUAIL

BOBWHITE QUAIL

♂

♀

Plate 36

RAILS and CRAKES

Most are secretive birds of wetlands and are rarely seen except when attracted by taped calls. Plumage is usually a pattern of black, white, brown and chestnut. Immatures are duller. Sexes alike. Body is narrow, for slipping through dense vegetation. Long unwebbed toes spread their weight. The short tail flicks as they walk. Bill stout and dagger-like in rails, shorter in crakes. Fly reluctantly when disturbed but are capable of sustained flight, mainly at night.

WEKA   *Gallirallus australis*   **Locally common endemic**

53 cm; ♂ 1000 g, ♀ 700 g. *Flightless. Brown, streaked black*. Sturdy short bill and legs. The 4 subspecies are separated by plumage colour. Rare North I Weka is greyer below and has brown legs; Buff Weka, introduced to Chatham Is, is the palest; Western Weka (Nelson to Fiordland) is noticeably chestnut, except in Fiordland, where a dark form is common; Stewart I Weka is the smallest and also has a dark form, but paler than Western Weka. Sometimes very inquisitive. Walks quietly, flicking leaves aside with bill in search of food. Runs fast, neck outstretched. *Territorial call a loud repeated 'coo-eet', rising in pitch*. **Habitat:** Forests, scrub and open country with good cover. **Breeding:** Aug–Feb.   **[Sp 158]**

BANDED RAIL (Moho-pereru)   *Rallus philippensis*   **Locally common native**

30 cm, 170 g. Strikingly marked but secretive. *Upperparts olive brown and black with white spots, and underparts barred black and white*. A chestnut band crosses chest, and a narrower one passes through eye to hindneck; whitish eye stripe, grey chin and throat. Long stout bill, brown. Juvenile less distinctly marked. Can fly well but, when flushed, flies for a short distance with legs dangling. Call a creaky 'swit', heard mostly at dusk and dawn. **Habitat:** Saltmarshes, mangroves and, less often, freshwater swamps; also some offshore islands. **Breeding:** Sep–Mar.   **[Sp 156]**

AUCKLAND ISLAND RAIL   *Rallus pectoralis*   **Locally common native**

21 cm, 90 g. Secretive subspecies of Lewin's Rail of Australia and New Guinea. Smaller and darker than Banded Rail. Back, wings and uppertail olive brown streaked black. Crown, sides of head and neck rufous to gingery brown. Throat and bill grey. Flanks and undertail finely barred black and white. Long slim bill, reddish. Legs pale brown. **Habitat:** Dense scrub cover, tussock and herbfields on Adams and Disappointment Is of the Auckland Is only. **Breeding:** Oct–Dec.   **[Sp 157]**

SPOTLESS CRAKE (Puweto)   *Porzana tabuensis*   **Locally common native**

20 cm, 45 g. Small dark rail, secretive but responds to taped calls. Head and underparts leaden grey with a bluish sheen, *upperparts plain dark chocolate brown*, undertail black barred white. Bill short, black; eye and eye-ring red; legs reddish. Juvenile lacks sheen, and chin and throat dull white. Varied calls; usually sharp 'pit-pit', a repeated 'book' and a distinctive *rolling 'purrrrrrrr'*, like an alarm clock going off and gradually running down. **Habitat:** Freshwater wetlands with raupo or sedge, especially in the North I; forest on some offshore islands. **Breeding:** Aug–Feb.   **[Sp 159]**

MARSH CRAKE (Koitareke)   *Porzana pusilla*   **Locally common native**

18 cm, 40 g. Tiny slim secretive rail. Like a miniature Banded Rail, but upperparts cinnamon brown *streaked* black and white. Sides of head and underparts blue-grey; flanks, abdomen and undertail are black barred white. Bill, legs and feet greenish; eye red. Juvenile barred brown and buff on underparts, pale buff on cheeks and throat. Readily walks on duckweed and other floating vegetation. Call a harsh 'krek', like a fingernail being drawn along a comb. **Habitat:** Dense beds of reeds and rushes in freshwater and estuarine wetlands. **Breeding:** Oct–Jan.   **[Sp 160]**

Western
dark phase

WEKA

Buff

Western

AUCKLAND ISLAND RAIL

BANDED RAIL

juv

MARSH CRAKE

SPOTLESS CRAKE

juv

Plate 37

SWAMPHENS and COOTS

Birds of marsh and open water. Most are black, brown and purple-blue. Sexes alike. Wings short and broad. The bill extends onto their forehead as a shield, usually with diagnostic colour. Their strong legs and long toes aid walking on floating vegetation. Toes may be lobed (coots) for specialised swimming. They run well, walk with flicking tail, exposing a white undertail, and swim with bobbing head.

TAKAHE (Notornis) *Porphyrio mantelli* **Rare endemic**

63 cm, 3 kg. Like an enormous Pukeko. *Flightless.* Colour ranges from iridescent dark blue head, neck and breast and peacock-blue shoulders to olive-green and blue back and wings. *Bill and shield massive, scarlet,* paler toward the tip; legs and feet red; eye brown. Immature duller; bill and shield dark grey. Mainly vegetarian; *leaving behind chewed and abandoned stems of tussock or other grasses* and 8 cm long *sausage-shaped fibrous droppings.* Male and female duet with a loud Weka-like, but *slow and deep, 'coo-eet';* alarm note a *deep resonant 'oomf'.* **Habitat:** Natural range now tussock grassland and beech forest in mountains west of Lake Te Anau. Introduced to rank grassland on Tiritiri Matangi, Kapiti, Mana and Maus Is. **Breeding:** Oct–Jan.   **[Sp 164]**

PUKEKO (Purple Swamphen) *Porphyrio porphyrio* **Abundant native**

51 cm; ♂ 1050 g, ♀ 850 g. *Deep blue* with black head and upperparts. *Undertail white, flirted with every step.* Bill and shield scarlet; eye red; legs and feet orange-red. Sexes alike. Immature has much brown and buff in the plumage and on bill and legs. Voice a loud unmusical screech. Runs well and swims with tail held high. Clambers about and may perch in scrub and trees. When disturbed in the open, runs to cover or flies, legs dangling, for a short distance. Flies high at night, calling – a loud harsh screech. **Habitat:** Wetlands, estuaries, short damp pasture and parks. Often in extended family groups. **Breeding:** Aug–Mar.   **[Sp 163]**

AUSTRALIAN COOT *Fulica atra* **Locally common native**

38 cm; ♂ 570 g, ♀ 520 g. *Black with white bill and shield. No white under tail.* Eye red; legs dark grey, *feet lobed.* Immature dark brown-grey, shield small and pinkish grey. Mainly aquatic; swims with head jerking back and forth, *dives* with a short forward jump to pluck submerged aquatic plants, patters across the surface as it labours to take off. Sometimes comes ashore to graze on short grass. Often in flocks. Main call a loud harsh 'krark'. **Habitat:** Small freshwater lakes and shallow bays of larger lakes. **Breeding:** Aug–Mar.   **[Sp 165]**

DUSKY MOORHEN *Gallinula tenebrosa* **Rare Australian vagrant**

37 cm, 500 g. Like a Coot but wings olive brown, *shield orange-red, bill red with a yellow tip, and undertail dark with white sides*; legs green with red at 'knee' joint. Immature browner; bill varying from greenish yellow to brown. Wings project high above tail when swimming. Common call a loud explosive 'prurk'. **Habitat:** Weedy shallows or edge of reedbeds of freshwater wetlands, sometimes on nearby pasture.   **[Sp 162]**

BLACK-TAILED NATIVE-HEN *Gallinula ventralis* **Rare Australian vagrant**

35 cm, 400 g. Similar in size and shape to Dusky Moorhen but more *upright stance with tail held cocked.* Olive brown above, slate grey below, with prominent *white pear-shaped spots on the flanks.* Tail and undertail black; tail flicked constantly. *Shield, upper bill and bill tip green, lower bill orange*; eye yellow; legs brick red. **Habitat:** Feeds on dry land near freshwater wetlands.   **[Sp 161]**

TAKAHE

PUKEKO

imm

AUSTRALIAN
COOT

imm

DUSKY MOORHEN

imm

BLACK-TAILED NATIVE-HEN

Plate 38   **WADERS**

A large diverse group of birds of estuaries, coasts, riverbeds and farmland. Most are long-legged and feed in or near shallow water. Bill shape is varied; short and stubby in those (e.g. dotterels) that peck from the surface, but longer in those that feed in shallow water (e.g. stilts), or probe deeply (e.g. godwits). Flight strong and direct. Often form flocks while roosting or flying, but disperse to feed. Many species seen in NZ breed in the Arctic and arrive in September, with remnants of breeding plumage, and depart in March, often in breeding plumage. Most subadults and a few adults spend the southern winter here.

PIED OYSTERCATCHER (Torea)   *Haematopus ostralegus*   **Abundant native**

46 cm, 550 g. Striking black and white wader with long stout red bill and short stubby pink legs. *Sharp border on lower chest between black upperparts and white underparts*, a *white tab* extends upwards in front of folded wing. In flight, *white wingbar, rump and lower back*. Orange eye-ring. Sexes alike. Immature has browner plumage, dusky-red bill and dull legs. Forms large roosting and feeding flocks. Flight call a loud shrill 'kleep'. **Habitat:** Breeds inland on riverbeds and farmland, mainly in South I. Migrates to estuaries for autumn and winter. **Breeding:** Aug–Jan.   **[Sp 168]**

CHATHAM ISLAND OYSTERCATCHER   *Haematopus chathamensis*   **Rare endemic**

48 cm, 600 g. Like pied phase Variable Oystercatcher in having a slightly smudgy border on chest, but *shorter bill and thicker legs and feet*. **Habitat:** Rocky and sandy coasts of Chatham Is. **Breeding:** Oct–Mar.   **[Sp 170]**

VARIABLE OYSTERCATCHER (Torea, Toreapango)   *Haematopus unicolor*
Uncommon endemic

48 cm, 725 g. Variable plumage, from black to pied, with continuous gradient between. Long robust red bill and short stubby pink legs. Pied phase like Pied Oystercatcher but *larger*, bill heavier, and *smudgy* border on chest; most lack tab in front of folded wing. In flight, white wingbar and rump have smudgy edges, and lower back is black or smudgy. Black phase, commonest south of Taranaki and Gisborne, is pure black. Immature has browner plumage, dusky-red bill and dull legs. Flight call a loud shrill 'kleep'. **Habitat:** Breeds on rocky and sandy coasts, rarely on shores of coastal lakes. Some gather on estuaries in autumn and winter. **Breeding:** Sep–Feb.   **[Sp 169]**

SPUR-WINGED PLOVER   *Vanellus miles*   **Abundant native**

38 cm; ♂ 370 g, ♀ 350 g. Conspicuous *noisy* large plover. Black crown, hindneck and shoulders in front of bend of wing; smooth brown back and wings; white rump and tail tipped black. White underparts; wings have dark trailing edge. *Yellow facial patch, wattles and bill*; legs and feet reddish. Spur on bend of wing usually hidden. Juvenile has small wattles, and feathers on upperparts are narrowly edged black and buff. *Flies with slow deliberate beats* of rounded wings. Call a *loud staccato rattle*: 'kerr-kick-ki-ki-ki'. **Habitat:** Farmland, rough grassland, wetland margins and estuaries. **Breeding:** Jun–Dec.   **[Sp 189]**

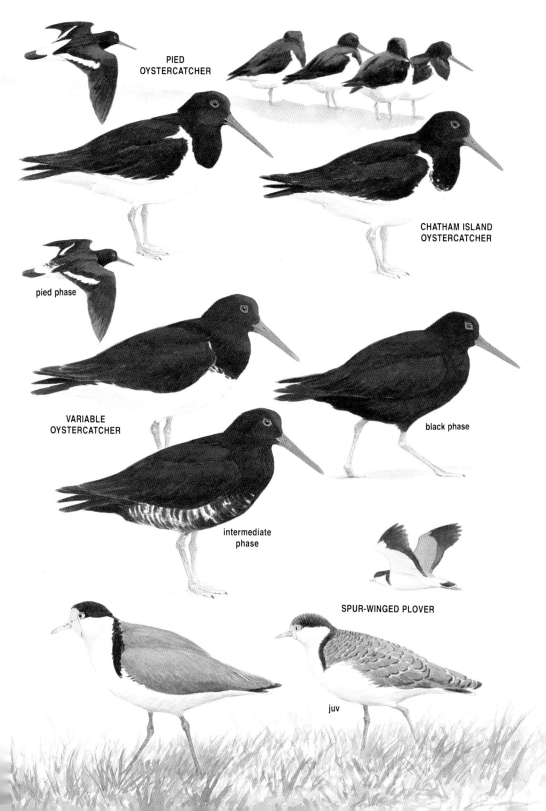

PIED
OYSTERCATCHER

CHATHAM ISLAND
OYSTERCATCHER

pied phase

VARIABLE
OYSTERCATCHER

black phase

intermediate
phase

SPUR-WINGED PLOVER

juv

Plate 39 # WADERS

PIED STILT (Poaka) *Himantopus himantopus* Common native

35 cm, 190 g. Distinctive black and white wader with *extremely long pinkish-red legs* and *long fine black bill*. Variable black on crown, nape, hindneck and collar on the lower neck; black wings and back; grey wash at end of tail. Face, throat and under-parts white. Eye red. Juvenile has grey wash on head and neck, dull pink legs, dark brown back and wings. Distinctive *yapping calls*, often heard at night or when breeding birds are disturbed. Hybridises naturally with Black Stilt; intermediate forms not uncommon. **Habitat:** Breeds on riverbeds, lake margins and damp pasture. Form flocks at estuaries and lakes outside breeding season. Many South I and southern North I birds migrate to northern North I after breeding season. **Breeding:** Jul–Jan.
[Sp 171]

BLACK STILT (Kaki) *Himantopus novaezelandiae* Rare endemic

40 cm, 220 g. Pure adults *entirely black* with a greenish gloss on upper surface.*Very long pinkish-red legs, very long fine black bill*, red eye. Juvenile has white on head, neck and breast, with black patch around eye and grey wash on back of neck. Wings, belly, flanks and undertail black. Full black plumage acquired over the first year, but throughout the bill is longer than in Pied Stilt and the legs slightly shorter. Naturally hybridises with Pied Stilt; adult hybrids are very variable, but longer bill and shorter legs are apparent in darker birds. Unlike juvenile Black Stilt, hybrid adults have some solid black on the breast. **Habitat:** Breeds on riverbeds, lake margins and ponds of Mackenzie Basin, inland South Canterbury. After breeding, most move to river deltas of major lakes in the Mackenzie Basin, but some move to estuaries of eastern South I and western North I. **Breeding:** Sep–Jan.   [Sp 172]

AUSTRALIAN RED-NECKED AVOCET *Recurvirostra novaehollandiae*
Rare Australian vagrant

44 cm, 300 g. Distinctive *black and white wader with chestnut head and neck, and fine upcurved bill* (more steeply in male) and long pale blue-grey legs. White body; black and white pattern on wings and back especially noticeable in flight. Juvenile has paler chestnut head and neck, and brown and white wing markings. *Feeds with scythe-like sweep of the bill.* **Habitat:** Formerly bred on South I riverbeds; now a vagrant to lakes and estuaries.   [Sp 173]

PIED STILT

imm

juv

BLACK STILT

imm

juv

Hybrid Black/Pied Stilts

AUSTRALIAN RED-NECKED
AVOCET

Plate 40   **WADERS**

BANDED DOTTEREL (Tuturiwhatu)   *Charadrius bicinctus*   Abundant endemic

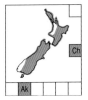

20 cm, 60 g. Medium-sized dotterel with a confusing range of plumages according to age, sex and time of year. Breeding adult has white underparts except for *2 bands, a thin black band on the lower neck and a broad chestnut band on the breast*. Male has bolder and darker bands, and also has a thin black band above white forehead, and a dark line through eye. Non-breeding adults of both sexes are highly variable: black facial markings are lost; breast bands fade and often lost except as yellow to grey-brown tabs at the shoulders; upper band usually shows as a faint incomplete necklace of spots, but some retain a distinct upper band. Juvenile like non-breeding, but *whole head washed yellowish buff*, brown mottling on breast usually forms dark shoulder tabs, and upperparts grey-brown with fawn or off-white edges to the feathers. All have short dark grey bill, black eye, variable yellowish-grey-green legs. Main calls a loud 'pit' and a fast rolling 'che-ree-a-ree'. **Habitat:** Breeds on sandy beaches, shellbanks and riverbeds. After breeding, form flocks at estuaries, lake margins and sometimes short grassland, e.g. airfields. Some, especially those breeding in high-country South I, migrate to Australia. **Breeding:** Jul–Jan.   **[Sp 176]**

NEW ZEALAND DOTTEREL (Tuturiwhatu)   *Charadrius obscurus*
Uncommon endemic

25 cm, 160 g. *Large squat tame dotterel with large head and robust bill.* Breeding adult has upperparts brown, finely streaked dark brown, and whitish feather edges; *under-parts range from pale orange-buff to rich rufous*; darker red in males and in southern subspecies (*obscurus*). Non-breeding adult is nondescript but *distinctly pale*; grey-brown upperparts have broad whitish feather edges; underparts white with obscure pale grey-brown breast band, often restricted to just the shoulders. Juvenile like a pale breeding adult but with buff feather edges and pale orange-buff wash on breast and belly, flecked dark brown on breast and flanks. In flight, white wingbar and white edges to rump and tail. Heavy black bill, tip slightly upturned; proportionately short olive-grey legs. Usual call a penetrating 'chip'. **Habitat:** Beaches, rivermouths and estuaries of northern NZ (*aquilonius*); also breeds on mountain tops of Stewart I (*obscurus*), after breeding moves to estuaries of Stewart I, Southland and Farewell Spit. **Breeding:** Aug–Feb.   **[Sp 175]**

MONGOLIAN DOTTEREL   *Charadrius mongolus*   Rare Asian migrant

20 cm, 60 g. *Medium-sized leggy dotterel with heavy short black bill.* Breeding adult has broad brick-red breast band with *thin black line on upper margin*, red extends onto nape and upper forehead; black facial mask sometimes with thin line down centre of forehead. Non-breeding like non-breeding Banded Dotterel and Large Sand Dotterel, separated only with care. *Forehead and eyebrow clean white*; upperparts *plain grey-brown*, greyer than Banded Dotterel; *conspicuous dark eye patch*; underparts white, with *broad grey shoulder tabs*, sometimes meeting to form a band on lower neck. In flight, distinct wingbar just onto primaries. Sexes alike. Usual call 'chirrip' with rolled 'r'. **Habitat:** Breeds Asia. Only a few reach NZ estuaries each year, most regularly at Manukau, Firth of Thames and Farewell Spit.   **[Sp 181]**

LARGE SAND DOTTEREL   *Charadrius leschenaultii*   Rare Asian migrant

24 cm, 90 g. *Large leggy dotterel with long heavy black bill.* Like Mongolian Dotterel but larger, much longer legs and body held more horizontal, and bill much more robust. Breeding adult has a narrow pale reddish-orange breast band, extending upwards on sides of neck to behind eye; black line through eye to bill and across top of forehead. Non-breeding has white forehead and eyebrow, *plain grey-brown upperparts* and white underparts except for grey-brown shoulder tabs, which may meet to form a thin breast band. Legs *long*, yellowish grey to green. In flight, distinct wingbar well onto primaries. Sexes alike. Usual call is a soft *trill*. **Habitat:** Breeds Central Asia. Only a few reach NZ estuaries each year, mostly at Kaipara, Manukau, Firth of Thames and Farewell Spit.   **[Sp 180]**

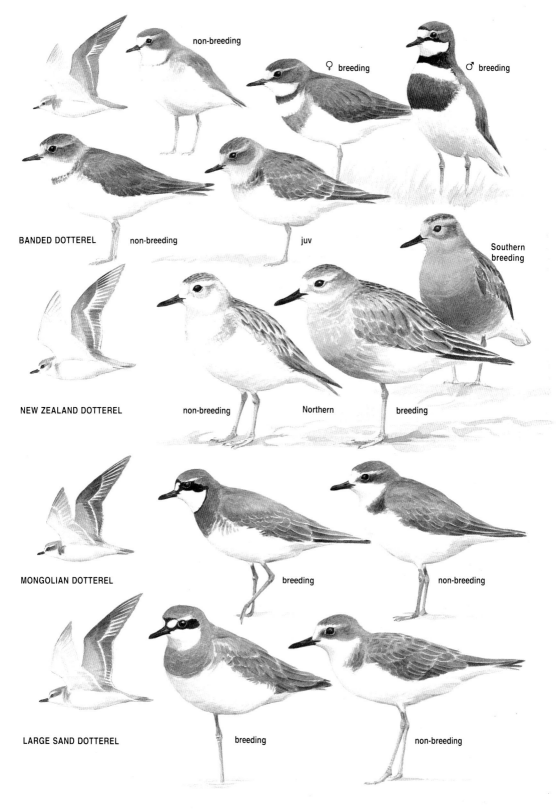

non-breeding

♀ breeding

♂ breeding

BANDED DOTTEREL   non-breeding   juv

Southern
breeding

NEW ZEALAND DOTTEREL   non-breeding   Northern   breeding

MONGOLIAN DOTTEREL   breeding   non-breeding

LARGE SAND DOTTEREL   breeding   non-breeding

Plate 41

WADERS

BLACK-FRONTED DOTTEREL *Charadrius melanops* Locally common native

17 cm, 33 g. Distinctive small dotterel with *slow jerky flight, black wingtips and metallic 'pit' flight call.* Upperparts mottled light brown with chestnut shoulder patch; black forehead, vertical patch onto crown, eyeline and *V-shaped breast band*; white eyebrow, side of neck and underparts. *Bill bright red, tipped black*; legs dull pink. Sexes alike. Juvenile lacks breast band, black forehead and shoulder patch. **Habitat:** Recently colonised from Australia. Breeds on riverbeds (especially near backwaters), gravel pits and bare ground. Form flocks after breeding, especially on lake margins and damp paddocks. **Breeding:** Aug–Mar. [Sp 178]

SHORE PLOVER (Tuturuatu) *Thinornis novaeseelandiae* Rare endemic

20 cm, 60 g. Distinctive *small stocky dotterel* of South East I and the Western Reef in the Chathams, but recently introduced on Motuora I in the Hauraki Gulf and near Mahia in Hawke's Bay, and seen on nearby estuaries. Crown, neck and upperparts greyish brown; white ring around back of head above eyes and across forecrown; black forehead, sides of face and throat in males, dirty brown in females; underparts white. Bill red, tipped black; legs orange. Juvenile has white head and neck with brown-grey cap and eye patch; bill brown with orange base. Usual call a quiet 'kleet', but loud ringing aggressive calls sound like oystercatcher piping calls. **Habitat:** Wave platforms, marsh-turf and estuaries. **Breeding:** Oct–Feb. [Sp 184]

RED-KNEED DOTTEREL *Erythrogonys cinctus* Rare Australian vagrant

18 cm, 50 g. Distinctive dotterel with *broad white trailing edge to chocolate brown wings* and *white tail with dark central stripe.* Black head and breast band boldly contrasts with white chin and sides of neck. Back brown, underparts white with chestnut patch under bend of wing. Bill red, tipped black; long legs, pink above 'knee', grey below. Sexes alike. Juvenile has head grey-brown, breast band absent or smudgy grey-brown. **Habitat:** In Australia, usually feeds in freshwater or brackish wetlands. One NZ record: Manawatu Estuary, March 1976. [Sp 183]

RED-CAPPED DOTTEREL *Charadrius ruficapillus* Rare Australian vagrant

15 cm, 38 g. Small active pale *greyish-brown dotterel with bright white underparts and black legs*, rufous head and nape, black bill and thin white wingbar. Male has white forehead edged black above, black line through eye edging rufous neck. Bill and legs black. Female has much less extensive rufous and lacks black markings. Juvenile duller and mottled above. **Habitat:** Formerly bred on shingle riverbeds of South I; now a rare vagrant. [Sp 177]

RINGED PLOVER *Charadrius hiaticula* Rare Arctic vagrant

19 cm, 60 g. Small plump dotterel with a short stubby bill and a *white ring around neck* separating the brown nape from the back. Breeding adult has black breast band, eye patch, forecrown and line from eye to bill; bill orange, tipped black. Non-breeding has white forehead and pale buff eyebrow to well behind eye. Crown, eye patch, line to bill, back and breast band grey-brown. Bill black with dull orange base; orange legs. **Habitat**: Breeds Arctic. Two NZ records, at Firth of Thames. [Sp 179]

BLACK-FRONTED DOTTEREL

juv

juv

♀

♂ **SHORE PLOVER**

imm **RED-KNEED DOTTEREL**

imm

♀

♂ **RED-CAPPED DOTTEREL**

non-breeding

breeding

RINGED PLOVER

Plate 42

WADERS

PACIFIC GOLDEN PLOVER   *Pluvialis fulva*   Common Arctic migrant

25 cm, 130 g. Medium-sized speckled wader, often in marsh-turf or short grass. Wary; when alert stands tall, looking slim with long neck and large head. Breeding adult has brown upperparts heavily speckled golden yellow and white; black face and underparts (*mottled on flanks*) separated by broad white stripe from bill, above eye and down neck to flanks. Non-breeding has head and upperparts pale brown with golden-buff or cream spots; tail barred brown and buff; pale buff eye stripe; throat and chest buff, speckled brown and yellow, grading into pale buff flanks, belly and undertail. Sexes alike. Juvenile has more heavily speckled upperparts and yellower head and underparts; more dark markings on breast and flanks. In flight, dark brown upperwing with an indistinct pale wingbar, and uniform brownish-grey underwing and armpits. At rest, tip of tertials level with tip of tail, and wings just longer than tail. Large black eye, short black bill. Long dark grey legs give leggy appearance. Flight fast and direct, often in small flocks. *Flight call a musical 'too-weet'.* **Habitat:** Breeds Arctic tundra of Siberia and W Alaska. In NZ, at estuaries with extensive *Zostera* and *Sarcocornia/Samolus* beds (especially Parengarenga, Manawatu, Farewell Spit, Awarua Bay) or freshwater wetlands with marsh-turf on fringes (Kaimaumau, Lakes Wairarapa and Ellesmere); rarely on short grassland in NZ. Very few overwinter.   **[Sp 186]**

AMERICAN GOLDEN PLOVER   *Pluvialis dominica*   Rare Arctic vagrant

26 cm, 165 g. Like Pacific Golden Plover but slightly *larger*, deeper chested with stouter bill and shorter legs (especially tibia). *Tip of tertials falls well short of tip of tail*, and wing usually much longer than tail. Breeding plumage male has *completely black flanks*; non-breeding adults and juveniles are *greyer* than Pacific Golden Plover, golden tones restricted to the back and scapulars. Juvenile has more mottling and barring on underparts, and ear coverts and cap are darker, making white eyebrow more prominent. **Habitat:** Breeds Arctic America. Migrates to inland S America. One confirmed NZ record.   **[Sp 187]**

GREY PLOVER   *Pluvialis squatarola*   Uncommon Arctic migrant

28 cm, 250 g. Much *larger heavier-billed and greyer than Pacific Golden Plover*. Has spangled appearance, and black face, throat and underparts in breeding plumage. Non-breeding is very pale, speckled grey and white head, upperparts and breast; white underparts. In flight, white underwings have diagnostic *black armpits*, thin white wingbar, *white rump*, and barred tail. Sexes alike. Juvenile grey-brown above with white and a few yellow spots. Large black eye, stout black bill and long ash-grey legs. Flight call a 3-note 'hee-oo-ee'. **Habitat:** Breeds high Arctic. In NZ, at estuaries, especially Parengarenga, Firth of Thames and Farewell Spit.   **[Sp 188]**

UPLAND SANDPIPER   *Bartramia longicauda*   Rare American vagrant

28 cm, 140 g. A brown-streaked wader with *large body, long slender neck, long tail, small head*, large black eye and short thin straight bill. Head, throat and upperparts olive-buff, streaked dark brown; flanks white with dark brown chevrons, abdomen white. In flight, rump and tail have dark centre and thin white or creamy margins, dark upperwing with black primaries. *Wings held upright on landing* to show pied barring on underwings. **Habitat:** Breeds N America. Migrates to S America. One NZ record.
[Sp 217]

ORIENTAL DOTTEREL   *Charadrius veredus*   Rare Asian migrant

24 cm, 95 g. Medium-sized plover with a *slim elegant build, long legs and an erect stance*. Breeding adult has broad chestnut breast band with black lower margin. Non-breeding has plain grey-brown upperparts, but some have narrow buff margins to feathers; pale buff eyebrow, face and throat, broad grey-buff breast band contrasts with off-white abdomen. Juvenile like non-breeding but broad pale margins to feathers on upperparts. In flight, no clear wingbar, underwing grey. Fine black bill; proportionately long dull yellow legs. **Habitat:** Breeds N China. In NZ, at estuaries, in areas of dried mud or short pasture, often with Banded Dotterel or Pacific Golden Plover.   **[Sp 182]**

PACIFIC GOLDEN PLOVER

breeding

juv

non-breeding

Pacific

moulting

AMERICAN
GOLDEN PLOVER

juv

GREY PLOVER

breeding

non-breeding

UPLAND SANDPIPER

breeding

ORIENTAL
DOTTEREL

non-breeding

Plate 43 # WADERS

PAINTED SNIPE *Rostratula benghalensis* **Rare Australian vagrant**

25 cm, 120 g. Distinctive large-bodied chestnut, olive and white wader with short greenish legs and long (5 cm) slightly decurved bill. Buff stripe over centre of head from bill to nape; white band sweeps up in front of wings from breast to back; broad olive or buff and black patterned wings. Adult male has brown head with pale buff eye patch; nape, throat and breast streaked greyish brown; wings, back and uppertail spangled buff and grey; belly white. Adult female has maroon-brown head with white eye patch; reddish-brown nape, throat and breast; dark olive-grey wings, back and uppertail; white belly. When flushed, flies with slow wingbeats, legs dangle like in Pukeko, and gives repeated 'kuk' call. **Habitat:** Breeds Africa and Australasia. One NZ record, at Lake Ellesmere, August 1986. Usually in long grass near freshwater wetlands. **[Sp 167]**

JAPANESE SNIPE *Gallinago hardwickii* **Rare Arctic migrant**

24 cm, 160 g. Richly variegated rotund brown wader with *very long (7 cm) straight bill*, short grey legs, heavily streaked head with large eyes set high on the head. *Fast zig-zagging flight when flushed* from thick cover near wetland margins; gives harsh call: 'kok'. Head streaked dark brown and buff; upperparts heavily streaked brown, buff and black; breast buff, speckled dark brown; flanks barred; belly and undertail creamy white. **Habitat:** Breeds Japan and eastern Russia. Migrates to Australasia. Only a few reach NZ, mainly in long grass near freshwater wetlands. **[Sp 193]**

CHATHAM ISLAND SNIPE *Coenocorypha pusilla* **Locally common endemic**

20 cm, 80 g. Like NZ Snipe but smaller, shorter (3 cm) bill, and pale unmarked lower breast and belly. **Habitat:** Forest and thick vegetation on offshore islands in Chathams group, mainly South East and Mangere Is. **Breeding:** Sep–Feb. **[Sp 192]**

NEW ZEALAND SNIPE (Hakawai) *Coenocorypha aucklandica*
Locally common endemic

23 cm, 105 g. Small rotund richly variegated brown wader with *long (5 cm) slightly drooping brown bill* and short yellowish-brown legs. Head marked boldly with buff central stripe over head from forehead to nape, long buff eyebrows and brown line through eye; pale buff cheek patch, streaked darker. Upperparts heavily mottled with black feather centres and brown or buff edges. Throat, neck and breast buff, streaked brown. Female larger than male. Male calls a low 'trerk trerk trerk' and 'queeyoo, queeyoo', but sometimes a *ghostly whistle at night* caused by vibrating tail feathers as air passes through the spread tail during aerial display. Confined to NZ subantarctic islands. **Habitat:** Forest and scrub of The Snares (*heugeli*), Antipodes (*meinertzhagenae*), Jacquemart I (Campbell I), and Ewing and Adams Is in the Auckland Is (*aucklandica*). **Breeding:** Aug–Feb. **[Sp 191]**

PAINTED SNIPE

♂

♀

♀

JAPANESE SNIPE

Japanese
Snipe

NEW ZEALAND SNIPE

CHATHAM ISLAND SNIPE

Plate 44   # WADERS

LESSER KNOT (Huahou) *Calidris canutus*   Abundant Arctic migrant

24 cm, 120 g. A stocky rather nondescript wader with a heavy (3 cm) straight black bill and short dull green legs, but distinctive rusty red head and underparts in breeding plumage. Head and upperparts of non-breeding adult plain grey with paler feather edges, whitish eyebrow; underparts pale grey to off-white, with lightly speckled grey on neck, breast and flanks. Head, neck and breast of breeding adult become *rusty red*, and back black with rust and white speckling; females less richly coloured. Juvenile like non-breeding, but back more scaly with white feather tips and subterminal black lines. In flight, indistinct white wingbar, *pale rump barred white and grey*. Often seen in flocks and with Bar-tailed Godwits. **Habitat:** Breeds Arctic. Second most common migrant visiting NZ estuaries each summer; many overwinter. Favours northern and western estuaries, especially Kaipara, Manukau, Firth of Thames and Farewell Spit; only occasionally on margins of freshwater lakes.   **[Sp 194]**

GREAT KNOT *Calidris tenuirostris*   Rare Arctic migrant

27 cm, 160 g. Like Lesser Knot but larger, with a *heavier longer (4 cm) black bill and white rump*. Head and upperparts of non-breeding adult plain grey with paler feather edges, finely streaked dark grey on crown, neck and breast; indistinct eyebrow; flanks usually marked with *dark arrowhead-shaped spots*. Breeding adult has head and neck heavily streaked black; breast very heavily blotched blackish brown, extending onto flanks as bold arrowhead-shaped spots; rusty-red feathers on base of upperwing only. Juvenile like non-breeding, but back and wing feathers have darker centres with buff fringes; brownish-buff wash on breast. **Habitat:** Breeds Siberia. Migrates to Australasia. Only a few reach NZ, normally with Lesser Knots at northern or western estuaries.   **[Sp 195]**

CURLEW SANDPIPER *Calidris ferruginea*   Uncommon Arctic migrant

19 cm, 60 g. A small slender wader with *long thin downcurved bill*, black legs, *white rump* and white wingbar. Non-breeding adult has *pale* plain grey-brown head and upperparts; white eyebrow; underparts white with pale grey wash and streaks on breast. Breeding adult has distinctive rusty-red head and underparts, with feathers initially edged white; back feathers black, notched grey and rust red. Juvenile like non-breeding, but back feathers darker, edged white, and lightly streaked neck and breast washed buff. **Habitat:** Breeds Arctic Asia. Regular summer visitor to NZ, and some overwinter. Favours tidal flats, brackish pools and margins to coastal lakes, mainly at Firth of Thames, Lake Ellesmere and Awarua Bay.   **[Sp 198]**

DUNLIN *Calidris alpina*   Rare Arctic straggler

18 cm, 50 g. Like Curlew Sandpiper but shorter legs, *a shorter only slightly downcurved bill, and black central stripe through white rump*. Non-breeding adult browner with streaked buff-washed upper breast, and less distinct eyebrow. Breeding adult has rusty red on crown and edges of dark-centred back feathers, breast and flanks streaked black, *belly black*, and undertail white. **Habitat:** Breeds Holarctic. Migrates to northern tropics. A few have reached northern NZ estuaries in summer.   **[Sp 197]**

WHITE-RUMPED SANDPIPER *Calidris fuscicollis*   Rare Arctic vagrant

16 cm, 35 g. Small slender wader with short black legs, short slightly drooping black bill, usually with pale base to lower mandible; *white rump*. Folded wings project well beyond tail to give elongated appearance. Non-breeding adult has drab grey head and upperparts with paler feather edges, neck and breast streaked and washed grey; underparts off-white. Breeding adult has dark streaked head, washed pale rufous on crown and ear coverts; rufous fringes to feathers of back and inner wing; breast heavily streaked brown, often extending onto flanks as chevrons. In flight, narrow white wingbar. **Habitat:** Breeds Arctic N America. Migrates to S America. A few have reached NZ estuaries. **[Sp 202]**

juv

non-breeding

breeding

LESSER KNOT

non-breeding

breeding

GREAT KNOT

breeding

non-breeding

CURLEW SANDPIPER

non-breeding

breeding

non-breeding

DUNLIN

breeding

non-breeding

WHITE-RUMPED SANDPIPER

Plate 45   WADERS

WRYBILL   *Anarhynchus frontalis*   Locally common endemic

20 cm, 60 g. Very pale grey stocky confiding wader with short thick neck and black bill with *tip curved to the right*. Legs grey-green. Breeding adult has white forehead edged above with thin black frontal band in male; crown, nape and upperparts plain ashy grey. Underparts white except *black band across upper breast*, narrower in female. Non-breeding lacks frontal band, and breast band is indistinct or absent. Juvenile has back feathers edged white, and breast band always absent. In flight, small white wingbar and white sides to grey rump. Form dense flocks at roosts, usually apart from most other waders. **Habitat:** Breeds shingle riverbeds of Canterbury and Otago. Migrates to estuaries of North I, especially Firth of Thames, Manukau and Kaipara. Feeds on wet mudflats. **Breeding:** Aug–Jan.   **[Sp 185]**

TURNSTONE   *Arenaria interpres*   Common Arctic migrant

23 cm, 120 g. Very striking stout wader with *variegated white, black, brown and tortoise-shell plumage*, short black bill and *short orange legs*. Horizontal stance and habit of busily fossicking along the tideline, probing under debris and bulldozing or flicking over tide-wrack. Non-breeding has head and upperparts dark brown, mottled black and chestnut; face variegated black, white and brown; upperbreast black, underparts white. In breeding plumage, male more boldly marked with white cap, finely streaked black; female has brown cap, streaked black and white. In flight, striking complex pattern of black, white and chestnut. **Habitat:** Breeds high Arctic. In NZ, favours wave platforms, coastal lagoons and some estuaries, especially Parengarenga, Kaipara, Farewell Spit, Motueka, Lake Grassmere, Kaikoura Peninsula, Awarua Bay and Te Whanga Lagoon (Chathams).   **[Sp 190]**

TEREK SANDPIPER   *Tringa terek*   Uncommon Arctic migrant

23 cm, 70 g. Plain pale grey-brown wader with *long thin upcurved black bill with orange base, short orange-yellow legs*, and dark patch at bend of wing. Moves actively with crouched run and bobs head and tail. Non-breeding has head and upperparts pale brownish grey with faint white eyebrow; throat and breast variably streaked grey; underparts white. Breeding has browner back, finely flecked grey, and black streak at base of upperwing appears as a black line along back. In flight, *broad white trailing edge to upperwing* near body, pale sides to rump and tail. **Habitat:** Breeds Eurasia. A few reach NZ estuaries each summer, often roosting with Wrybills.   **[Sp 224]**

SANDERLING   *Calidris alba*   Rare Arctic migrant

20 cm, 50 g. Very pale wader with *black patch at bend of wing*, short stout black bill and short black legs. *Feeds actively; runs along water edge on sandy beaches*. Non-breeding has head and back pearly grey; sides of face white with grey wash through eye; underparts white. Breeding has head, breast and upper back pale rusty red, speckled black. Juvenile like non-breeding, but back scalloped black and grey, and head and sides of lower neck streaked black. In flight, *prominent white wingbar*, enhanced by dark grey leading edge and tips to wing; black stripe down centre of tail; white sides to rump and grey sides to tail. **Habitat:** Breeds Arctic. A few reach NZ each summer, on sandy beaches and estuaries.   **[Sp 196]**

COMMON SANDPIPER   *Tringa hypoleucos*   Rare Arctic migrant

20 cm, 50 g. Small dark solitary sandpiper with *white tab in front of folded wing*. *Often perches on rocks or logs and bobs head and tips tail. Jerky, flickering flight interspersed with glides on stiffly held wings*. Head and upperparts olive brown except white eye-ring and eyebrow, boldest in front of eye; throat and sides of neck washed brown; underparts white. Tail long, extending well beyond folded wings. Short straight dark brown bill; short greenish-grey legs. In flight, white wingbar and white sides to brown rump and tail. Flight call a distinctive clear 'hee-dee-dee'. **Habitat:** Breeds Eurasia. A few reach NZ, usually in small muddy estuaries.   **[Sp 220]**

WRYBILL

non-breeding

♀ breeding

♂ breeding

TURNSTONE

♂ breeding

non-breeding

♀ breeding

TEREK SANDPIPER

breeding

non-breeding

SANDERLING

breeding

juv

non-breeding

Sanderling

COMMON SANDPIPER

Plate 46 # WADERS

SHARP-TAILED SANDPIPER   *Calidris acuminata*   Uncommon Arctic migrant

22 cm, 60 g. A medium-small richly speckled brown wader with *rufous crown*, finely streaked black, and white eyebrow. Bill (2.5 cm) slightly downcurved, *grey-brown with greenish base. Legs yellowish green.* Non-breeding has upperparts dull brown with pale feather edges; neck and breast mottled grey or buffish with irregular streaks, *fading* to white on lower breast and belly. In breeding plumage, upperparts richly coloured with chestnut and buff edges to feathers; breast heavily streaked and marked with *small boomerang-shaped streaks on lower breast and along flanks.* Juvenile like non-breeding adult but more rufous, especially on crown, neck and *edges of tertials.* In flight, faint white wingbar and white sides to black rump and uppertail. **Habitat:** Breeds Siberia. Migrates to Australasia. In NZ, favours low-growing saltmarsh of estuaries and open marsh-turf flats of coastal lakes, mainly at Kaimaumau, Firth of Thames, Ahuriri and Manawatu Estuaries, Lakes Wairarapa and Ellesmere, and Awarua Bay.   **[Sp 199]**

PECTORAL SANDPIPER   *Calidris melanotos*   Rare Arctic migrant

23 cm, 80 g. Non-breeding like Sharp-tailed Sandpiper, but darker, *crown streaked brown and buff*, neck and breast *heavily streaked dark brown that ends abruptly* and contrasts with white underparts. Bill (2.5 cm) slightly downcurved, *brown with yellowish base; legs yellow.* In breeding plumage, upperparts become darker, with chestnut and buff feather edges; breast heavily streaked in male, blackish brown flecked white in female. Juvenile like non-breeding adult but more rufous on head and back. In flight, faint white wingbar and white sides to black rump and uppertail. **Habitat:** Breeds Arctic N America. Migrates to S America. A few reach NZ each summer, often with Sharp-tailed Sandpipers on open marsh-turf flats of coastal lakes, especially Lakes Wairarapa and Ellesmere, or in low-growing saltmarsh of estuaries.   **[Sp 200]**

RUFF (Reeve)   *Philomachus pugnax*   Rare Arctic vagrant

29 cm, 170 g. Non-breeding like large *upright* Sharp-tailed Sandpiper, but lacks rufous crown and has *small head, short fine bill, long neck and legs.* Head and upperparts scaly grey-brown with grey feather edges, wings darker; throat and sides of face white; breast buff, washed grey brown; belly, undertail and underwings white. Bill (3.5 cm) slightly downcurved, brown with paler base. Legs from orange to green. Breeding plumage (not recorded in NZ) is highly variable, especially in males, which have many colours and large neck ruffs and head tufts; female like non-breeding but dark barring on upperparts and black blotches on breast. Juvenile like non-breeding but upperparts have buff feather edges and neck and breast washed buff. In flight, looks long-winged with narrow white wingbar; *prominent white oval patches on sides of rump.* **Habitat:** Breeds Arctic. Straggles to Australasia. Only a few NZ records, mainly at margins of freshwater or brackish lakes.   **[Sp 208]**

BAIRD'S SANDPIPER   *Calidris bairdii*   Rare Arctic vagrant

18 cm, 40 g. Small buff-brown wader with *straight fine black bill*, short black legs, *broad black centre to white rump and tail*, and *long wings that project well beyond tail*, giving it an elongated look. Complete finely streaked buff breast band. Non-breeding adult has head and upperparts uniformly scaly brown, with buff feather edges. In breeding plumage, crown and breast become strongly streaked dark brown, upperparts dark brown and black with white feather edges, and some rufous on the back. Juvenile has rusty brown upperparts and chest; pale edges to feathers give a scaly effect on the back and wings. In flight, a very narrow short wingbar. **Habitat:** Breeds Arctic N America. Migrates to S America. A few reach NZ estuaries.   **[Sp 201]**

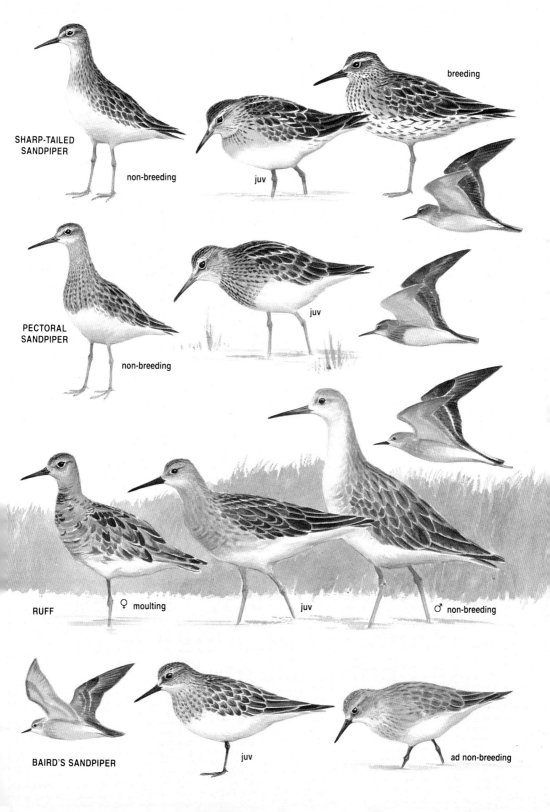

SHARP-TAILED SANDPIPER

non-breeding

juv

breeding

PECTORAL SANDPIPER

non-breeding

juv

RUFF

♀ moulting

juv

♂ non-breeding

BAIRD'S SANDPIPER

juv

ad non-breeding

Plate 47 # WADERS

RED-NECKED STINT   *Calidris ruficollis*   Common Arctic migrant

15 cm, 30 g. Tiny wader with short straight black bill and short black legs. Non-breeding adult has forehead and eyebrow white; crown, neck and upperparts *pale grey* with brownish tinge, paler feather edges and black feather shafts. Breeding adult has crown and back blackish brown with rufous feather edges, *contrasting* with grey-brown pale-edged feathers on wing coverts; *sides of face, neck, chin and throat brick red*; underparts white. Juvenile like non-breeding, but crown and sides of breast washed pale rufous; back feathers dark rufous-edged, contrasting with greyer pale-edged wing coverts. Some show thin white V on back and double white eyebrow. In flight, white wingbar reaches base of primaries; white sides to uppertail contrast with black central stripe down rump and tail. Feeds by pecking with rapid sewing-machine action. **Habitat:** Breeds Siberia and Alaska. Migrates to Australasia. Several hundred reach NZ in summer, and some overwinter. Mainly at estuaries and coastal lakes, especially at Parengarenga, Manukau, Porangahau, Farewell Spit, Lake Ellesmere and Awarua Bay.   **[Sp 203]**

LITTLE STINT   *Calidris minuta*   Rare Arctic vagrant

15 g, 25 g. Tiny wader, like Red-necked Stint but slightly smaller, slightly longer black legs, and slightly longer bill, decurved at the tip; shorter wings give less attenuated rear end. Non-breeding adult has upperpart feathers dark-centred, edged brown, giving a browner appearance. Breeding adult has head, neck and upper breast *orange-rufous*, streaked and mottled darker; *chin and throat white*; back dark brown with creamy-white V-shaped line, broad orange-rufous feather edges and *no contrast between back and wing coverts*. Juvenile has upperpart feathers with *broad orange-rufous fringes, a prominent white V on the back* and a double eyebrow. In flight, white wingbar does not reach primaries; white sides to black stripe down rump and tail. **Habitat:** Breeds Arctic Eurasia. Migrates to Europe, Africa and Asia. Rare vagrants have reached Lake Ellesmere.   **[Sp 204]**

LEAST SANDPIPER   *Calidris minutilla*   Rare Arctic vagrant

15 cm, 25 g. Tiny wader, like Red-necked Stint but browner and with *dull yellow legs*, and more crouched bent-legged feeding posture. Very difficult to identify from slightly larger Long-toed Stint (*C. subminuta*) seen regularly in Australia. Shrill *'kreep-kreep-kreep'* call and thicker all black bill are best field features of Least Sandpiper; also crown paler and more streaked, dark line from bill to eye, and heavily streaked breast. In flight, narrow white wingbar, and white sides to thin black line down rump. **Habitat:** Breeds Arctic N America. Migrates to S America. One record in NZ (Wairoa 1952), but several other yellow-legged stints have been recorded.   **[Sp 205]**

BROAD-BILLED SANDPIPER   *Limicola falcinellus*   Rare Arctic migrant

17 cm, 35 g. Small wader with short *olive-green legs, very long (3 cm) heavy black bill* slightly drooped at tip, and *double eyebrow; a broad white eyebrow joining a thinner, higher stripe in front of each eye*. Non-breeding adult has crown, neck and upperparts pale brown-grey with dark feather shafts and pale edges giving a scaly appearance; grey stripe down centre of head to bill; underparts white, lightly streaked grey on sides of neck and breast. Breeding adult has head, neck and breast streaked black; upperparts very dark, feathers thinly edged buff or rufous, giving a streaked appearance; central stripe on head becomes black. Juvenile has prominent V on mantle, rufous edges to mantle and inner scapulars, buff and white edges to rest of upperparts. In flight, dark grey leading edges to upperwing and narrow white wingbar; white sides to rump contrast with broad dark grey stripe down centre of tail. **Habitat:** Breeds Arctic Eurasia. Migrates to SE Asia. Scarce visitor to NZ estuaries.   **[Sp 207]**

WESTERN SANDPIPER   *Calidris mauri*   Rare Arctic vagrant

17 cm, 30 g. Tiny wader with short black legs, like Red-necked Stint but with distinctly *longer (2.5 cm) slightly drooping black bill*. Non-breeding adult has pale grey upperparts with paler feather edges, white eyebrow, breast finely streaked grey, underparts white. Breeding adult has rufous crown, nape and patch behind eye, prominent white eyebrow; back grey-brown, mottled rufous and black on scapulars; breast and flanks marked with black streaks and chevrons. Juvenile like breeding adult but paler rufous on head; breast washed buff and lightly streaked black at sides. In flight, narrow white wingbar, white sides to black rump. **Habitat:** Breeds Arctic N America and eastern Siberia. Migrates to Central America. A few reach NZ estuaries.   **[Sp 206]**

RED-NECKED STINT breeding non-breeding

juv

LITTLE STINT breeding non-breeding

juv

Little
Stint

LEAST SANDPIPER non-breeding

BROAD-BILLED
SANDPIPER breeding non-breeding

WESTERN
SANDPIPER breeding non-breeding

Plate 48 # WADERS

EASTERN CURLEW *Numenius madagascariensis* Uncommon Arctic migrant

63 cm, 900 g. Largest wader in NZ. Distinctive *very long (19 cm) downcurved bill*. Body streaked greyish brown and buff, paler on underparts, with indistinct white eyebrow and brown rump. Bill dark brown with pink base to lower bill. *Flight call a distinctive carrying 'croo-lee'*. **Habitat:** Breeds northeastern Asia. Migrates to Australasia; c. 30 visit NZ each summer, mainly at Firth of Thames and Farewell Spit.

[Sp 210]

WHIMBREL *Numenius phaeopus* Uncommon Arctic migrant

43 cm, 450 g. Medium-sized curlew with *long (9 cm) downcurved bill*, head marked boldly with white eyebrows and centre stripe over top of dark brown head. Asiatic subspecies (*variegata*) has *off-white rump*. American subspecies (*hudsonicus*) has *speckled brown rump*. Body completely streaked greyish brown and buff. Bill black, legs bluish grey. *Flight call a rippling whistle of about 7 notes: 'ti-ti-ti-ti-ti-ti-ti'*. Often very wary and stands alert near roosting flocks of waders. **Habitat:** Breeds Arctic. 100–200 visit NZ each summer (mainly Asiatic), especially at Parengarenga, Firth of Thames and Farewell Spit. [Sp 211]

BRISTLE-THIGHED CURLEW *Numenius tahitiensis* Rare Arctic straggler

43 cm, 400 g. Medium-sized *buff and brown* curlew with *long (9 cm) downcurved bill and very boldly marked head*. Dark eye stripe, pale buff eyebrow and central stripe over top of dark brown head. Body streaked brown and buff; *rump smooth cinnamon*; tail rusty buff, barred black; belly whitish, and upper legs have a few long loose white feathers. *Flight call a clear 'kee-vee'*, unlike trilling call of other curlews. **Habitat:** Breeds western Alaska. Common migrant to central Pacific. Only a few straggle to NZ, all records from the Kermadecs. [Sp 213]

LITTLE WHIMBREL *Numenius minutus* Rare Arctic migrant

29 cm, 160 g. *Small curlew* with *long (5 cm) downcurved bill* and boldly marked head. Dark eye stripe, buff eyebrow and thin central stripe over top of brown head. Body streaked brown and warm buff, brown rump, and upperwing in flight looks dark and unmottled. Bill dark brown, pink base to lower bill; legs bluish grey. *Flight call a 3-note 'te-te-te'*. **Habitat:** Breeds Siberia. Migrates to Australasia. A rare visitor to NZ, mostly in short pasture or ploughed ground, often with Banded Dotterels or rather similar-looking Golden Plovers. [Sp 212]

EASTERN CURLEW

American

Asiatic

WHIMBREL

BRISTLE-THIGHED
CURLEW

LITTLE WHIMBREL

Plate 49   # WADERS

BAR-TAILED GODWIT (Kuaka) *Limosa lapponica* Abundant Arctic migrant

♂ 39 cm, 300 g; ♀ 41 cm, 350 g. Commonest migrant wader. Long (♂ 8.5 cm, ♀ 10.5 cm) *slightly upturned black bill with a pink base*. Legs and feet black. Non-breeding has head, upperparts and upperwings streaked grey-brown; lower back, *rump and tail barred brown and white*; underparts dirty white, washed grey on breast; underwings extensively flecked grey-brown. Breeding adult, seen from February onwards, has black and buff upperparts; brick-red head, neck, breast and underparts in males; buffy red with fine barring in females. Juvenile like non-breeding but buffer and with more heavily marked upperparts, but unmarked breast. In flight, wingbar indistinct, pale rump and barred tail. Flies fast with twisting and turning, or direct in long lines or chevrons. **Habitat:** Breeds Arctic in Eurasia and Alaska. Eastern race *baueri* migrates to Australasia, especially NZ estuaries, sandy beaches and shores of coastal lakes. Main sites, where 10,000+ spend the southern summer, are Kaipara, Manukau and Farewell Spit.
[Sp 214]

HUDSONIAN GODWIT *Limosa haemastica* Rare Arctic migrant

39 cm, 300 g. In non-breeding plumage like Bar-tailed Godwit, but *smooth* grey upperparts and grey wash on breast. Conspicuous *white rump contrasts with broad black tip to the tail; narrow white wingbar. Black armpits* and extensive black on underwing separate from non-breeding Black-tailed Godwit. Breeding adult male has head and neck finely barred black and white, upperparts dark brown spotted buff, breast and belly chestnut; female paler on breast and belly. **Habitat:** Breeds N America. Migrates to S America. Vagrants reach NZ most summers, usually with Bar-tailed Godwits at estuaries. **[Sp 216]**

BLACK-TAILED GODWIT *Limosa limosa* Rare Arctic migrant

39 cm, 350 g. In non-breeding plumage like Bar-tailed Godwit, but more elegant with *smooth* grey plumage and *long straight bill*. In flight, conspicuous *white wingbars, and white rump contrasts with broad black tip to the tail. White underwings and armpits with thin black margins* separate from non-breeding Hudsonian Godwit. Breeding adult has head, neck and breast brick red; belly barred black and white; upperparts mottled rusty and black. **Habitat:** Breeds temperate Eurasia. Race *melanuroides* migrates to Asia and Australasia. Only a few reach NZ each summer, usually with Bar-tailed Godwits at estuaries or with Pied Stilts on lake margins. **[Sp 215]**

ASIATIC DOWITCHER *Limnodromus semipalmatus* Rare Asian vagrant

34 cm, 180 g. Like a small godwit but with *short legs* and a *long (8 cm), straight stout black bill*. In non-breeding plumage, face clearly marked with white eyebrow and dark line from bill to eye. Upperparts dark grey-brown, streaked paler; back, rump and tail barred brown and off-white; underparts flecked grey on breast and along flanks, belly white and *underwings mainly white*. Feeds with sewing-machine action of rapid probes with bill pointed straight down. **Habitat:** Breeds Central Asia. Migrates to S Asia and Australasia. Rarely reaches NZ estuaries. **[Sp 209]**

juv

BAR-TAILED GODWIT

♂ breeding

♀ non-breeding

HUDSONIAN GODWIT

♂ breeding

non-breeding

BLACK-TAILED GODWIT

juv

♂ breeding

non-breeding

ASIATIC DOWITCHER

non-breeding

Plate 50   **WADERS**

MARSH SANDPIPER   *Tringa stagnatilis*   Uncommon Arctic migrant

22 cm, 70 g. Elegant *pale grey* wader, like small Greenshank but *very long greenish legs* and *needle-like (4 cm) black bill*. Non-breeding has crown and eye stripe streaked grey, eyebrow white, upperparts ash grey, *darker at shoulder*. Underparts white. Breeding adult has head and neck flecked dark grey, upperparts brownish grey heavily barred and spotted dark brown, breast spotted dark brown and black; legs can turn yellowish. In flight, *lacks wingbar, white rump extends as a V well up back*; tail white, lightly barred grey in centre. Wades in shallow water and feeds with *head-down, tail-up, triangular stance*. **Habitat:** Breeds Central Asia. Reaches NZ estuaries and lake margins each summer, often with Pied Stilts.   **[Sp 222]**

GREENSHANK   *Tringa nebularia*   Uncommon Arctic migrant

32 cm, 170 g. Large elegant grey wader with long (5.5 cm) heavy *slightly upturned bill, blue-grey at base*; long green legs. Non-breeding has head and neck finely streaked grey, indistinct white eyebrow, upperparts dark grey, lightly flecked white and black; underparts white. Breeding adult has head, neck and upperbreast heavily flecked blackish brown; irregular dark mottling on upperparts. In flight, *lacks wingbar, white rump extends as a V well up back*; tail white, broadly barred dark grey. Wades in shallow water with *horizontal stance*. Distinctive voice, a loud ringing *'tew-tew-tew'*. **Habitat:** Breeds Eurasia. A few reach NZ each summer, often associated with Pied Stilts in muddy estuarine creeks and on lake margins.   **[Sp 221]**

LESSER YELLOWLEGS   *Tringa flavipes*   Rare Arctic vagrant

24 cm, 75 g. Elegant grey wader, like Marsh Sandpiper but *long slender yellow legs*, and *lower back greyish brown*. Bill (4 cm) fine and straight, slightly longer than head. Non-breeding has upperparts brownish grey, *white eyebrow only in front of eye*; wing feathers pale-edged giving a spotted look; underparts white except upper breast streaked brownish grey. Juvenile like non-breeding, but upperparts browner, strongly spotted white; neck and breast spotted and streaked brown. In flight, lacks wingbar, *square white rump not extending up back*. **Habitat:** Breeds N America. Migrates to S America. Occasionally recorded at NZ estuaries and lake margins.   **[Sp 223]**

WANDERING TATTLER   *Tringa incana*   Uncommon Arctic migrant

27 cm, 120 g. Medium-sized wader with smooth slate-grey back and *short yellow legs*. Like Siberian Tattler but call a clear *rippling trill of 6–10 notes*. Bill grey, *nasal groove extends 70% of length*. Non-breeding has head, upperparts and upperbreast slate grey, *white eyebrow only in front of eye*, underparts white. Breeding adult has all underparts, including flanks and undertail, heavily barred dark grey. In flight, smooth grey upperparts; flies on stiffly held wings. When alert, bobs head and tips tail. **Habitat:** Breeds western N America. Migrates to Central America and Pacific Is. A few regularly reach NZ estuaries and especially rocky shores each summer.   **[Sp 218]**

SIBERIAN (Grey-tailed) TATTLER   *Tringa brevipes*   Uncommon Arctic migrant

25 cm, 100 g. Like Wandering Tattler, but call a sharp high-pitched *'too-weet'*. Usually slightly paler and browner, and *white eyebrow extends behind eye* and as a thin line over the base of the bill. Bill grey, *nasal groove extends 50% of length*. In breeding plumage, underparts heavily barred dark grey, but flanks and undertail remain white. In flight, smooth grey-brown upperparts; flies on stiffly held wings. When alert, bobs head and tips tail. **Habitat:** Breeds Siberia. Migrates to Australasia. A few reach NZ estuaries and sometimes rocky shores each summer.   **[Sp 219]**

Pied Stilt juv

Marsh Sandpiper

MARSH SANDPIPER

breeding

non-breeding

non-breeding

GREENSHANK

breeding

non-breeding

juv

LESSER YELLOWLEGS

WANDERING TATTLER

non-breeding

breeding

non-breeding

breeding

SIBERIAN TATTLER

Plate 51 # WADERS

RED-NECKED PHALAROPE   *Phalaropus lobatus*   Rare Arctic straggler

19 cm; ♂ 30 g, ♀ 35 g. Unusual small slim and graceful wader. *Feeds by swimming jerkily or in circles, pecking from the water surface. Short very fine black bill*; very short dark grey legs with lobed feet; white wingbar; large white patches at sides of rump contrast with black stripe down grey-tipped tail. Non-breeding adult like Grey Phalarope, but bill finer, back feathers have dark centres and broad white edges, giving a *scaly* appearance. Breeding adult unmistakable: mainly grey above, with rufous patch sweeping from behind eye down sides of neck to throat; male duller. Juvenile has grey patch behind and below eye, and grey on crown extends down hindneck to back. **Habitat:** Breeds Arctic. Migrates to pelagic waters off western N America, Arabia, Micronesia and Namibia. A few have straggled to NZ estuaries or coastal lakes. **[Sp 226]**

GREY (Red) PHALAROPE   *Phalaropus fulicarius*   Rare Arctic vagrant

20 cm; ♂ 50 g, ♀ 60 g. Unusual dainty wader. *Feeds by swimming jerkily or in circles, pecking from the water surface. Short thick black bill* (yellow with black tip in breeding adult); short brownish-grey legs with yellow lobes on feet; white wingbar; small white patches at sides to grey tail. Non-breeding adult like non-breeding Red-necked Phalarope but bill stouter, back feathers have very thin white edges giving a *smooth* appearance. Breeding adult unmistakable: neck and underparts mainly brick red, back black and buff, and white patch around back of head behind eye; male duller. Juvenile initially a warm pinkish buff but quickly becomes like non-breeding adult; however, retains buff edges to wing feathers. **Habitat:** Breeds Arctic. Migrates to pelagic areas of tropical Atlantic Ocean, off Namibia and S America. A few have reached NZ estuaries and coastal lakes. **[Sp 225]**

WILSON'S PHALAROPE   *Phalaropus tricolor*   Rare American vagrant

22 cm; ♂ 50 g, ♀ 65 g. Unusual slim and graceful wader. *Feeds by swimming jerkily or in circles pecking at the water surface*, or by wading, or running actively with *waddling gait on dry land with short yellow legs. Long needle-like black bill*, no wingbar, and *white rump* distinguish from other phalaropes. Non-breeding adult resembles small very short-legged Marsh Sandpiper, with very pale grey head and upperparts, darker on wings and back; white eyebrow and underparts. Breeding adult unmistakable: silver-grey and chestnut head, neck and upperparts on female; male duller and lacks grey areas. **Habitat:** Breeds N America. Migrates to wetlands of S America. Rare vagrant to NZ estuaries and lakes. **[Sp 227]**

ORIENTAL PRATINCOLE   *Glareola maldivarum*   Rare Asian migrant

23 cm, 75 g. Distinctive atypical wader with *graceful buoyant tern-like flight while feeding by hawking*, swooping and soaring; sometimes feeds on ground with rapid tip-toeing run. Non-breeding adult has dull olive-brown crown, back and upperwings; throat buff, enclosed by a streaked black necklace; neck and upper breast pale olive-grey-brown, lower breast and belly white. Breeding adult has brighter olive-brown on head and upperparts; throat enclosed by bold black necklace; lower breast becomes buff. Juvenile has flecked appearance from back and upper breast feathers being tipped dark and edged buff. In flight, *underwing chestnut with dark grey trailing edge and tip, deeply forked white tail with olive brown tip.* **Habitat:** Breeds SE Asia. Migrates to Australasia, occasionally reaching NZ estuaries, coastal lakes and over open grassland. **[Sp 174]**

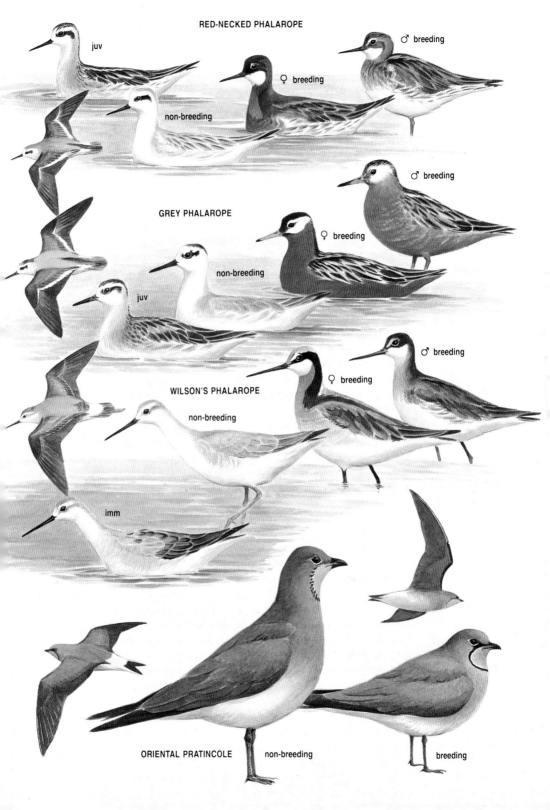

RED-NECKED PHALAROPE

juv

non-breeding

♀ breeding

♂ breeding

GREY PHALAROPE

♂ breeding

♀ breeding

non-breeding

juv

WILSON'S PHALAROPE

♂ breeding

♀ breeding

non-breeding

imm

ORIENTAL PRATINCOLE   non-breeding   breeding

Plate 52 SKUAS

A small group of widespread and highly mobile coastal or marine birds, medium to large. Plumages are highly variable but mainly brown and white, with white flashes in the outer wing. The small skuas are difficult to separate during moult from juvenile to immature, or immature to adult plumages, or between breeding and non-breeding plumages. Sexes alike. Flight is fast and direct, or twisting and turning in pursuit while relentlessly chasing terns and gulls to force them to drop or disgorge food. Strongly territorial when breeding, and aggressively defend their territory from intruders. Usually lay 2 brown eggs in a shallow scrape or cup of vegetation.

ARCTIC SKUA *Stercorarius parasiticus* Common Arctic migrant

43 cm (+ projecting tail feathers), 400 g. Small elegant skua with highly variable plumages: two main phases (about 80% dark in NZ), intermediates and a wide range of juvenile and immature plumages. Difficult to distinguish from larger Pomarine Skua unless in mixed groups 'working' a flock of terns. Bill black; *legs and feet black* in adults, *or grey-blue tipped black* in juveniles. Dark phase breeding adult is blackish brown with slightly paler yellowish nape and ear coverts; pale phase has black cap, white cheeks, yellowish nape and ear coverts; brown back, wings and tail, white underparts with variable dark breast band and dark undertail. Continuous variation between; all adults have *dark underwing with single pale patch at base of primaries*, upperparts uniformly dark except for *3–4 pale shafts at base of primaries*, and *pointed central tail feathers project 10 cm beyond rest of tail.* Non-breeding similar but lacks tail projection; dark phase can have white flecks on rump; pale phase has less distinct cap, underparts and flanks barred and washed brown, *undertail streaked*, pale flecks on rump and uppertail. Juvenile highly variable, but all have barred underwings with *single pale patch* and upperwings as in adults; most have rusty-brown body, mottled and barred darker, and paler streaked neck. Immatures acquire adult plumage over several years; mostly like non-breeding adult, but pale phase more heavily barred and washed brown on underparts and face, and rump and undertail lightly barred; *rump is darker than the neck.* **Habitat:** Breeds Arctic and subarctic. Migrates to southern oceans. Commonest skua seen off NZ coast and in harbours, especially Jan–Apr, when often seen harrying slightly smaller White-fronted Terns or Red-billed Gulls. Sometimes roosts on beaches. [Sp 230]

POMARINE SKUA *Stercorarius pomarinus* Uncommon Arctic migrant

48 cm (+ projecting tail feathers), 600 g. Similar range of plumages and pattern of plumage changes with age as Arctic Skua, but larger, *more heavily built and broader-winged; underwing dark with two pale patches at base of primaries;* upperwing shows 3-4 pale shafts on primaries. Breeding adult has twisted pair of tail feathers with *broad blunt ends* projecting 10 cm beyond rest of tail. Juvenile and immature have *rump paler than the neck.* Flight similar to Arctic Skua but less dashing as twisting and turning after distinctly smaller White-fronted Terns and Red-billed Gulls; direct flight with slower steadier wingbeats. **Habitat:** Breeds Arctic. Winters in tropics and southern oceans, especially off W Africa and eastern Australia. Regularly summer and autumn visitor to NZ coast, especially open coasts, e.g. Manawatu coast, Farewell Spit; rarely in harbours. [Sp 231]

LONG-TAILED SKUA *Stercorarius longicaudus* Rare Arctic migrant

35 cm (+ projecting tail feathers), 300 g. Smallest skua. Like small slender Arctic Skua but more *buoyant tern-like flight; greyer upperparts with darker primaries, which have only 1–2 pale shafts; legs short and blue.* Similar variety of plumages and changes with age as in Arctic Skua. Pale phase usual in NZ, dark phase rare, and intermediates very rare. Breeding adult has greyish-brown upperparts contrasting with dark brown primaries and trailing edge to secondaries; very long and thin central *tail streamers project 20 cm beyond rest of tail.* Non-breeding adult lacks or has short pointed tail projection, and undertail is barred brown and white. Juvenile and immature have short tail projection, heavily barred underwing and undertail, and often a barred rump. **Habitat:** Breeds Arctic and subarctic. Winters in tropical and southern temperate oceans. Mostly straggles to North I, sometimes in moderate numbers. [Sp 232]

ad light phase
non-breeding

ARCTIC SKUA

ad dark phase
moulting

ad dark phase

ad light phase

juv

juv

imm

imm

POMARINE SKUA

ad ♂ breeding

juv

juv

LONG-TAILED SKUA

ad

imm moulting

juv

ad
non-breeding

ad breeding

Plate 53

SKUAS and GULLS

BROWN SKUA (Hakoakoa) *Catharacta skua* Locally common native

63 cm; ♂ 1675 g, ♀ 1950 g. Very large stocky skua, like a large juvenile Black-backed Gull but *chocolate brown* except for some variable bronzy-yellow flecking on hindneck and *conspicuous white flashes on wings*. Wings broad and rounded; large hooked black bill; legs and feet black. Juvenile lacks yellow on hindneck, often more mottled and rusty on upperparts. In flight, slow powerful wingbeats and short glides. On breeding grounds, defends territory with raucous calls and low dives. **Habitat:** Breeds circumpolar subantarctic; in NZ region, on Chathams, Fiordland coast, islands around Stewart I, Solanders, The Snares, Antipodes, Auckland and Campbell Is, especially near seabird colonies. Disperse through southern oceans; occasionally seen on NZ mainland in winter, often at beach-washed offal. **Breeding:** Sep–Feb.

[Sp 228]

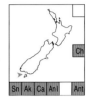

SOUTH POLAR SKUA *Catharacta maccormicki* Locally common native

59 cm; ♂ 1275 g, ♀ 1425 g. Large stocky skua, like Brown Skua but smaller; *shorter stubbier black bill*; more yellow feathering on hindneck. Variable plumages from pale to all dark, but all have *prominent white wing flashes*. Wings broad and rounded; tail short; legs and feet black. Pale phase has head and underparts pale ashy grey-brown with yellowish collar and brown back, wings and tail. Dark phase has body brown; back, wings and tail paler brown; white flecks at base of bill; buff collar. Juvenile lacks collar and has pale feather edges on upperparts, giving a scaly appearance. **Habitat:** Breeds Antarctica, including Ross Sea, usually near seabird colonies. Occasionally beach-wrecked or seen off coast of NZ mainland while on passage to N Pacific, usually Jan–Apr. **Breeding:** Nov–Mar. [Sp 229]

Gulls, terns and noddies are a large cosmopolitan group of mainly coastal birds. Most have short straight bills and short legs. Sexes alike. Usually grey, black or brown above, and white below in adults; juveniles usually have brown barring on back and wings. Bill and legs are often brightly coloured but usually change with age and/or season.

BLACK-BACKED GULL (Karoro) *Larus dominicanus* Abundant native

60 cm; ♂ 1050 g, ♀ 850 g. The only large gull in NZ. Languid shallow wingbeats interspersed with long glides separate it from distant skuas and mollymawks. Juvenile dull brown, pale feather edges give a mottled appearance, especially on head, neck and underparts; bill and eye dark brown; legs pinkish brown. In flight, looks dark brown with a paler rump. 2nd year has head, neck and underparts white, mottled and flecked brown; back and upperwings scruffy brown and black; bill dull yellowish or greenish, darker at tip; legs pinkish brown to greyish green. In flight, rump white, mottled brown, tail usually barred brown and white, wings darker towards tips. 3rd year has head and underparts white; neck lightly flecked brown; back and upperwings brown and black, the extent of black depending on the stage of moult; rump and tail white, with black band across tip. Bill dull yellow, darker at tip; legs yellowish green. Adult has head, neck, underparts, rump and tail white, back and upperwings black with narrow white trailing edge; bill yellow with red spot at tip of lower bill; eye pale yellow; legs greenish yellow. **Habitat:** Breeds circumpolar subantarctic; in NZ region, on coast of mainland, offshore and outlying islands, except only straggles to Kermadecs and The Snares; also breeds far inland on riverbeds, near lakes and alpine tarns. Ranges widely, feeds at rubbish tips, farmland, ploughed fields, beaches, harbours and behind boats, but rarely ventures far out to sea. **Breeding:** Oct–Feb. [Sp 233]

BROWN SKUA

SOUTH POLAR SKUA

dark phase

pale phase

pale phase

Black-backed Gull
juv

ad

juv

3rd year

2nd year

BLACK-BACKED GULL   ad

Plate 54 # GULLS and TERNS

RED-BILLED GULL (Tarapunga) *Larus novaehollandiae* Abundant native

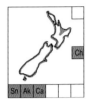

37 cm; ♂ 300 g, ♀ 260 g. Grey and white gull, mainly of the coast. Like Black-billed Gull but *shorter deeper bill* and boldly patterned wingtips. Adult has head, underparts and tail white, sometimes pinkish on breast; back and *wings pearly grey, except wingtips black with small white window*. Short deep bright red bill; legs and feet red; eye white. Juvenile and 1st year have larger dark patch at wingtip and very small, if any, white window. Bill dark with pink near base; legs pale flesh to reddish black; eye brown. **Habitat:** Breeds subantarctic from Africa to Chathams; in NZ region, on coast from Three Kings to Campbell Is; inland colony at Lake Rotorua. Common in coastal waters, beaches and estuaries; only occasionally (but sometimes in large flocks) inland to wet paddocks, playing fields and lakes. **Breeding:** Oct–Feb.   [Sp 234]

BLACK-BILLED GULL *Larus bulleri* Common endemic

37 cm; ♂ 300 g, ♀ 250 g. *Very pale* gull of inland South I and coasts. Like Red-billed Gull but *longer thinner bill* and very pale wingtips. Adult has back and *wings pale silvery grey, wingtips only thinly bordered black*. Long thin black bill; legs and feet black or reddish black; eye white. Juvenile quickly loses small grey patch behind eye; has more extensive black on wingtips; bill pale flesh with dark tip; legs from pinkish to reddish black; eye brown. **Habitat:** Breeds on riverbeds and lake margins of South I, some also in southern North I and at Lake Rotorua; a few coastal colonies in both islands. Feeds inland in wet paddocks, ploughed fields and over lakes; also coastal waters, beaches and estuaries. **Breeding:** Sep–Feb.   [Sp 235]

CASPIAN TERN (Taranui) *Sterna caspia* Uncommon native

51 cm, 700 g. *Very large silver-grey tern with massive red bill* tipped black and yellow; short white, slightly forked tail; underparts white with dark tips to underwing. Adult has black cap when breeding, heavily flecked white in non-breeding plumage; legs black. Juvenile has browner cap; back feathers sparsely edged buff and white; bill orange-red; legs dull orange. Flight direct, with steady shallow beats of broad wings; head and bill pointing downward when hunting. Dives into water. Adult call a loud harsh 'kaaa'; juveniles beg with a persistent high-pitched mewing. **Habitat:** Breeds widely; in NZ, colonies on isolated sandspits and shellbanks of coast and harbours; some pairs on riverbeds or lake shores. Feeds in inshore waters, up rivers and over coastal lakes. Vagrant to Kermadecs and Chathams. **Breeding:** Sep–Jan. [Sp 240]

CRESTED TERN *Sterna bergii* Rare tropical vagrant

47 cm, 350 g. *Large tern with long slender greenish-yellow bill*. Breeding adult has white forehead, black cap and a *straggly crest*; upperparts *slate grey*, paler on rump and tail; underparts white; legs black. Non-breeding adult has crown white or streaked black. Juvenile similar, but cap browner and extends around eye, wings brownish grey and mottled. Looks rakish yet graceful in flight. Plunge-dives. Noisy; call a rasping 'kerrcrik'. **Habitat:** Breeds eastern Asia, S Pacific and Australia. A few reach NZ coasts.
[Sp 248]

GULL-BILLED TERN *Gelochelidon nilotica* Rare subtropical vagrant

43 cm, 230 g. *Robust pale tern with long broad wings, short slightly forked tail, short thick gull-like black bill and long black legs*. Breeding adult has black cap; back and wings very pale grey; neck and underparts white. Non-breeding adult has a *black patch from eye to ear coverts*, and grey flecking on nape. Hawks and skims over water or land, picking up prey in flight; rarely dives into water. **Habitat:** Breeds tropics and subtropics, including Australia. A few reach NZ estuaries and coastal marshes.   [Sp 238]

RED-BILLED GULL

juv

BLACK-BILLED GULL

juv

juv

CASPIAN TERN

juv

non-breeding

breeding

CRESTED TERN   juv

non-breeding

breeding

non-breeding

Crested Tern
juv

breeding

GULL-BILLED TERN

Plate 55

TERNS

WHITE-FRONTED TERN (Tara)   *Sterna striata*   Abundant native

40 cm, 160 g. Commonest tern on NZ coast, often in large flocks. *Long black bill*; short legs, black or reddish black. Breeding adult is very pale pearly grey and white; *black cap separated from bill by white forehead*; neck and underparts white, sometimes pinkish on breast. In flight, *upperwing entirely pale grey* except for black outer web to outer primary; *underwing white to tips*. At rest, deeply forked tail extends well beyond wings. Non-breeding adult similar, but cap recedes to above eyes; at rest, tail level with wings. Juvenile heavily marked brown and white on upperparts; dark mottling on upperwing (carpal bar), prominent at rest, and in flight forms a dark triangle on inner forewing; primaries mid-grey; tail even with or shorter than wings. Immature similar, but mottling on inner forewing shows as black line at shoulder. Feeds by plunge-diving. Call a high-pitched 'siet'. **Habitat:** Breeds coast of NZ mainland, Chatham and Auckland Is; visitor to other subantarctic islands. Favours coastal waters and harbours. Large flocks form over shoaling fish, especially in summer and autumn. Roosts on shellbanks or sandspits. Rarely seen inland. Many, including most juveniles, winter in Australian waters. **Breeding:** Oct–Feb.   **[Sp 241]**

COMMON TERN   *Sterna hirundo*   Rare Arctic migrant

36 cm, 120 g. Like small dark White-fronted Tern, but bill shorter and finer; legs rather long. At rest, deeply forked tail even with or slightly shorter than wings. Breeding adult has black cap *sloping* down to black bill with dull red base; pearl-grey underparts. In flight, *outermost 3–4 dark grey primaries contrast with paler grey inner primaries*, which appear as a *translucent patch* against the light, diffuse trailing edge to tip of underwings; dark outer edge to tail; reddish-black legs. In non-breeding plumage, black cap recedes to level of eye; underparts white; many have prominent carpal bar at rest; bill black; legs reddish black. Immature similar, but primaries darker, and tertials often have brownish tips. Flight more buoyant than White-fronted Tern, wingbeats faster and deeper. Feeds by plunge-diving; frequently hovers. Calls a short 'kik' and a raspy 'kreer'. **Habitat:** Breeds subarctic. Migrates to temperate oceans. Only a few identified in NZ, mainly from North I coasts or coastal lakes.   **[Sp 247]**

ARCTIC TERN   *Sterna paradisaea*   Rare Arctic migrant

34 cm, 110 g. Like small dark White-fronted Tern and similar to Common Tern, but paler, smaller-bodied and longer-winged. Head rounded except *steep forehead*; bill rather short; *legs very short, brilliant red to reddish black*. Breeding adult has black cap down to blood-red bill; underparts darker grey than upperparts; small amount of black on tips of outer 3–4 primaries; *all of outerwing appears translucent* against the light except for a *thin well-defined dark trailing edge to tip of underwing*; thin dark outer edge to tail; at rest, deeply forked tail even with or longer than wings; red legs. In non-breeding plumage, cap recedes to *behind eye*; underparts white; some develop a faint carpal bar; bill black. Immature has thin carpal bar and darker primaries. In flight, looks slim, long-winged and long-tailed. Flight buoyant, with deeper, faster wingbeats than White-fronted Tern. Calls like Common Tern. **Habitat:** Breeds Arctic. Migrates to southern oceans. A few seen each summer at NZ estuaries or coastal lakes.   **[Sp 246]**

ANTARCTIC TERN   *Sterna vittata*   Locally common native

36 cm, 140 g. Medium-sized tern with white rump and forked tail. Breeding adult has black cap down to red bill; white cheeks; even grey body; wings grey with black only on the outer web of the outer primary; legs red. Non-breeding adult similar, but cap recedes to just behind eye; underparts white; bill dull pinkish red. Juvenile initially marked brown and white on back; bill dark brown, legs dull reddish. In flight, thinner-winged and more delicate than White-fronted Tern, and wings lack dark markings. Feeds by dipping and plunge-diving. **Habitat:** Breeds circumpolar subantarctic, including NZ subantarctic south of Stewart I. Stays close to breeding sites and not recorded off mainland. **Breeding:** Sep–Apr.   **[Sp 243]**

WHITE-FRONTED TERN

imm

non-breeding

imm

ad

breeding

juv

imm

ad Common

non-breeding

breeding

COMMON TERN

imm Common

imm

imm Arctic

non-breeding

breeding

ad Arctic

ARCTIC TERN

imm

ad

non-breeding

ANTARCTIC TERN

breeding

juv

Plate 56

TERNS

BLACK-FRONTED TERN (Tarapiroe)   *Sterna albostriata*   Common endemic

29 cm, 80 g. The common inland tern of the South I. Smaller and greyer than White-fronted Tern. *Blue-grey body, wings and short shallow-forked tail contrasts with white rump* in flight; undertail white; *bill and legs orange*. Breeding adult has black cap down to bill; thin white streak across cheeks; *bill and legs bright orange*. Non-breeding adult similar, but cap recedes to arc from eye to eye around back of head, except crown flecked grey; bill and legs dull orange. Immature has crown flecked black; dark patches around eye; chin white; breast very pale grey; bill dusky brown, becoming yellow with age; legs dull orange. Feeds mainly by hawking insects over riverbeds and dropping to pick prey from the surface of lakes, swamps and farmland. **Habitat:** Breeds in small colonies on gravel riverbeds of South I, mainly east of Alps. Migrates to coast to feed at sea, especially in Cook Strait and off eastern coast of North and South Is, as far north as Bay of Plenty. **Breeding:** Oct–Feb.   [Sp 239]

WHITE-WINGED BLACK TERN   *Chlidonias leucopterus*   Uncommon Asian migrant

23 cm, 65 g. Distinctive very small tern with slow buoyant flight. Black and white in breeding plumage; grey and white in non-breeding, but with distinctive *black 'ear-muffs' and club-shaped patch on nape*. Breeding adult has black head, neck, back and underparts: white rump and only barely forked tail; upperwing very pale grey, darker at tips; underwing black at base, white at tips; bill and legs red. Non-breeding adult has white head except crown streaked black, and black club-shaped band extends over top of head from behind eyes and also down nape; grey back; upperwing grey, darker at tips and along trailing edge of secondaries; shows dark carpal bar at rest; rump, tail and underparts white; bill and legs black, some with reddish tinge. Immature similar, but upperwings darker grey, rump very pale grey and tail grey. Hawks insects over water or land; flies persistently back and forth, dropping down to pick insects from water surface; rarely plunges. **Habitat:** Breeds Eurasia. Migrates to tropics and subtropics. A few reach NZ coastal lakes, swamps and estuaries each year.   [Sp 237]

WHISKERED TERN   *Chlidonias hybrida*   Rare Australian vagrant

26 cm, 90 g. Small tern with slow buoyant flight, long legs and gull-like stance; *even grey on rump and slightly forked tail*. Breeding adult has black cap down to red bill; white cheeks; dark grey underparts and sooty belly contrasts with white undertail; red legs. Non-breeding is pale grey above and dull white below with black arc from eye to eye around back of head, solid on ears but flecked on nape; wingtips darker than rest of wings; bill and legs dull red-brown. Immature similar but narrow dark borders to upperwing, and rump slightly paler than rest of upperparts. Feeds by hawking insects, picking prey from the water surface or by taking shallow plunges into water. **Habitat:** Breeds Africa to Australia; nomadic or migratory. A few reach NZ, mainly at coastal lakes or sewage ponds.   [Sp 236]

breeding

non-breeding

imm

juv

BLACK-FRONTED TERN

non-breeding

imm

moulting

breeding

WHITE-WINGED BLACK TERN

imm

breeding

WHISKERED TERN

imm

breeding

imm

Plate 57

TERNS

LITTLE TERN   *Sterna albifrons*   Uncommon Asian migrant

25 cm, 50 g. Very small vocal tern; very like dark Fairy Tern, but *dark primaries contrast with rest of upperwing*. Flight erratic with rapid deep wingbeats, often hovers. Breeding adult has white *sloping forehead* and *sharp recess to just behind eye*; black crown, nape and *line through eye to yellow bill with black tip*; upperparts pale grey, darker on wingtips with outermost 2–3 primaries black; deeply forked white tail; underparts white; legs orange-yellow. In non-breeding plumage (seen in NZ summer), cap recedes to band from eye to eye around back of head and down nape; bill dull yellow, dusky at tip; legs dull yellow. Immature similar, but bill black and *dark leading edge to wing* prominent as dark shoulder (carpal) bar at rest; some retain brown feather tips on upperparts; legs blackish brown. Flight call a sharp chattering 'kik, kik, kik . . .' and a rasping 'kree-ik'. **Habitat:** Breeds widely in Northern Hemisphere and Australia. Most in NZ are in non-breeding plumage in Oct–Mar, probably migrants from E Asia. Single birds and small flocks regularly seen at NZ estuaries or coastal lakes, mainly at North I harbours, especially Firth of Thames.   **[Sp 245]**

FAIRY TERN   *Sterna nereis*   Rare native

25 cm, 70 g. Very small tern, very like pale Little Tern but *upperwing almost uniform pale grey*. Flight erratic with rapid deep wingbeats; often hovers. Breeding adult (Oct–Mar) has white *steep forehead* and *rounded recess to above eye*; black crown, nape and *line to eye; white feathering between eye and pure yellow-orange bill*; upperparts uniform pale grey; deeply forked white tail; underparts white; legs orange-yellow. In non-breeding plumage, cap recedes to above eye and down nape; bill orange-brown, dusky at tip and base; legs dull orange. Immature similar, but bill black with dusky-yellow base, thin *dark leading edge to wing* faintly visible as dark shoulder (carpal) bar at rest; legs brown. Flight call a high-pitched 'zwit'. **Habitat:** Breeds Australia, New Caledonia and NZ. The NZ subspecies, which is endangered, breeds on a few Northland sandspits, and feeds on nearby estuaries, especially Kaipara Harbour in winter. **Breeding:** Nov–Feb.   **[Sp 244]**

GREY TERNLET   *Procelsterna cerulea*   Locally common native

28 cm, 75 g. Distinctive small delicate *blue-grey tern. Wings darker grey, especially at tips, and with a thin white trailing edge.* Prominent eye owing to small black patch in front of eye; long forked tail; bill black; long black legs, feet black with yellow to pink webs. Juvenile has head streaked and upperparts and wings washed brownish. Flight graceful. Feeds by hovering, fluttering and paddling on sea surface like a huge Storm Petrel; sometimes settles on the surface. **Habitat:** Tropical and subtropical Pacific; in NZ region, breeds at Kermadecs, in some years also at Three Kings Is and rock stacks off eastern coast of Northland and in Bay of Plenty. Occasionally seen in northern NZ coastal waters; straggles as far south as Canterbury. **Breeding:** Aug–Feb.   **[Sp 252]**

WHITE TERN   *Gygis alba*   Rare native

31 cm, 110 g. *Delicate pure white tern* with almost translucent wings and short forked tail; prominent eye owing to narrow black ring of feathers around eye; long straight bill, black with bluish base; legs and feet blue-grey with yellowish webs. Juvenile has smudgy brown patch behind eye and across back of head, and rusty brown flecks on back and upperwings. Flight swift and graceful; often circles over breeding areas by day. **Habitat:** Tropical seas; in NZ, breeds at Kermadecs, vagrants occasionally reach NZ mainland. **Breeding:** Oct–Mar.   **[Sp 253]**

breeding

LITTLE TERN

non-breeding

imm

imm

FAIRY TERN

breeding

non-breeding

imm

imm

GREY TERNLET

WHITE TERN

Plate 58

TERNS and NODDIES

SOOTY TERN   *Sterna fuscata*   Locally common native

45 cm, 210 g. Large tropical tern. Adult has white forehead and eyebrow to just above eye; cap, line through eye to bill, nape and *upperparts dark brownish black*; sides of neck and underparts white, washed pale grey towards long deeply forked tail. Bill and legs black. Juvenile dark brown except feathers on back and upperwings edged white or buff, underwings pale grey, and underparts white towards tail. Distinctive harsh 'wideawake' call. **Habitat:** Breeds tropics and subtropics, including Kermadecs. After breeding, ranges widely over deep water and a few reach northern NZ, especially after autumn and winter gales. **Breeding:** Oct–Mar.   **[Sp 242]**

BRIDLED TERN   *Sterna anaethetus*   Rare tropical vagrant

41 cm, 120 g. Like small pale Sooty Tern. Adult has white forehead and eyebrow extending well behind eye; black cap, line through eye to bill, and nape contrasts with dark grey-brown upperparts; sides of neck and underparts white, long deeply forked tail. Bill and legs black. Juvenile similar, but crown streaked white, incomplete black line between eye and bill, and feathers on back and upperwings edged white or buff. **Habitat:** Breeds tropics, including northern Australia. One NZ record: Canterbury, November 1987.   **[Sp 249]**

COMMON NODDY   *Anous stolidus*   Rare native

39 cm, 200 g. Medium-sized dark tropical tern with *very long broad tail* with shallow central notch. Like large White-capped Noddy but *browner*, and in flight, *underwing has pale central panel*. Adult has whitish-grey forehead and cap, merging into brown on sides of face and nape; black line from bill to eye; body, upperwing and tail dark brown; underwing grey-brown, edged dark brown. Thin straight (4.5 cm) black bill; legs and feet black. Juvenile similar but duller, cap less clearly defined, and back and wing feathers edged pale. Flight buoyant. Feeds mainly from sea surface and sometimes settles on the water. **Habitat:** Tropics and subtropics; recently found breeding on Curtis I, Kermadecs. After breeding, disperses to feed in flocks over deep warm waters. Three records from near the NZ mainland. **Breeding:** Sep–Jan.
          [Sp 250]

WHITE-CAPPED (Lesser) NODDY   *Anous tenuirostris*   Locally common native

37 cm, 100 g. Medium-sized dark tropical tern with long broad tail, square or slightly notched. Like small Common Noddy but *blacker, and in flight has completely dark underwings*. Adult has silvery-white forehead, cap to level of eyes, and hindcrown; black line from bill to eye; sooty black neck, body and wings; tail brownish black, underwings black. Fine slightly decurved (4 cm) black bill; legs and feet dark brown. Juvenile similar but less white on hindcrown, sharper separation of pale crown from dark neck, and feathers on back and wings edged pale. Flight buoyant; feeds mainly from sea surface but sometimes dives; occasionally settles on the water. **Habitat:** Breeds tropics and subtropics, including Kermadecs. After breeding, remains close to breeding sites, but vagrants occasionally reach NZ mainland, mostly in autumn after northerly gales. **Breeding:** Aug–Apr.   **[Sp 251]**

SOOTY TERN

juv

juv

BRIDLED TERN

juv

COMMON NODDY

WHITE-CAPPED NODDY

Plate 59

PIGEONS and DOVES

Medium to large landbirds with short bill, small head, rounded wings and short feathered legs. Sexes alike. Calls simple and often repetitive variations of 'coo'. Flight strong, direct and often noisy. Aerial displays of stall dives are part of breeding displays. Can breed at any time of year if food supplies are suitable. Lay 1–2 white eggs on a flimsy platform of sticks. Short incubation and nestling periods; young fed 'crop milk' and, later, other regurgitated food. They often fledge well below adult weight, with short wings and tail, and dull bill and feet. All are herbivorous; the New Zealand Pigeon feeds on fruit and foliage, the three introduced species feed on seeds, especially grain.

NEW ZEALAND PIGEON (Kereru, Kukupa, Parea) *Hemiphaga novaeseelandiae*
Common endemic

51 cm, 650 g (mainland); 55 cm, 800 g (Chathams). Largest pigeon in NZ. Head, throat, upper breast and upperparts metallic green with purplish sheen and bronze reflections, especially around neck (mainland), or with ashy-grey wash (Chathams); sharp line separates upper breast from white lower breast, belly and legs. Eye crimson; bill red with orangish tip; feet crimson. Juvenile similar, but upperparts duller, smudgy upper breast, dull bill and feet, and often the tail is shorter. In flight, strong steady wingbeats, broad rounded wings and long broad tail; *noisy swish of wings* is distinctive. Call a single soft penetrating 'kuu'. **Habitat:** Native forests, especially in lowland areas, scrub, forest patches among farmland, rural and city gardens and parks. **Breeding:** Variable, depending on availability of ripe fruit; usually Oct–Apr. **[Sp 254]**

ROCK (Feral) PIGEON *Columba livia*
Common European introduction

33 cm, 400 g. Highly variable plumages seen in descendants of domestic and racing pigeons. In the wild form, the plumage is mainly blue-grey, with sides of neck glossy green and purple; rump whitish; two prominent black bars across the wings; dark tip to the tail. Bill leaden; feet pinkish. Flight fast and direct, with flicking wingbeats; pointed angled wings, and short tail. **Habitat:** City parks and streets; grain stores, wharfs and railway stations. In rural areas, favours drier arable farmland. Often nests on cliffs and caves in river gorges and on sea coast. **Breeding:** All year, peak Sep–Feb. **[Sp 255]**

BARBARY DOVE *Streptopelia roseogrisea*
Rare African introduction

28 cm, 140 g. *Pale creamy buff*, shading to white on chin, belly and undertail coverts; distinctive *black half-collar* around back of neck. Eye red; bill horn-black; feet crimson. Juvenile similar but lacks black half-collar and has pale bill. Distinctive call: a *persistent 'coo-crooo'*. **Habitat:** Parks, gardens and orchards in South Auckland and near Whangarei, Rotorua, Whakatane and Havelock North. **Breeding:** Oct–Feb. **[Sp 256]**

SPOTTED DOVE *Streptopelia chinensis*
Uncommon Asian introduction

30 cm, 130 g. Head grey, tinged pink; *nape and back of neck black, finely spotted with white*; back, wings and rump mottled brown; tail long, with darker outer feathers, broadly tipped with white. Eye red; bill black; feet pink. Juvenile similar but lacks patterning on nape. Calls mellow, varying from 1 to 4 notes: 'coo', 'croo-croo', 'coo-coo-croo', 'coo-coo-croo-coor'. **Habitat:** Suburban parks, gardens, farmland and orchards of Auckland, South Auckland, and near Te Puke and Opotiki. **Breeding:** Oct–Feb. **[Sp 257]**

Chatham Island

NEW ZEALAND PIGEON

ROCK PIGEON

BARBARY DOVE

SPOTTED DOVE

juv

Plate 60

PARROTS

A large cosmopolitan family of often very colourful birds, but the NZ species are relatively drab, mainly green. All have a short bill with a horn covering (cere) enclosing the nostrils. The upper mandible is strongly curved, fitting neatly over the lower mandible. Their legs are short, and their feet have two toes pointing forward and two back.

SULPHUR-CRESTED COCKATOO   *Cacatua galerita*
Uncommon Australian introduction

50 cm, 900 g. A large *white parrot with a bright yellow crest*; a yellow tinge on underwing and undertail; bill and legs grey-black. Female slightly larger. Flies strongly on broad rounded wings, screeching raucously. Often feeds on the ground. **Habitat:** Forest patches in open country, especially western Waikato and Turakina River. **Breeding:** Aug–Jan.   [Sp 258]

KAKAPO   *Strigops habroptilus*   Rare endemic

63 cm; ♂ 2.5 kg, ♀ 2 kg. Large flightless nocturnal parrot. *Moss green above, greenish yellow below;* feathers mottled with fine brown and yellow bars. Owl-like facial disc. Male has broader head and larger bill. Feeds on ground or by clambering into shrubs. Male call a *loud repetitive booming* for hours, from cleared track-and-bowl system on ridge of prominent hill. **Habitat:** Formerly in forests of three main islands; introduced and now confined to Chalky, Codfish and Pearl Is, unless a few persist in Fiordland. **Breeding:** Usually every 3–5 years, Dec–Jul.   [Sp 260]

KEA   *Nestor notabilis*   Locally common endemic

46 cm; ♂ 1000 g, ♀ 800 g. A large, often bold parrot, olive green with scarlet underwings and rump. Dark-edged feathers make it look sculpted. Bill, cere, eye and legs dark brown; upper mandible longer in the male. Juvenile has pale crown, yellow cere, eye-ring and on bill; yellow fades in a couple of years to bill only. *Call a loud ringing 'keee-aa',* mainly in flight. Delights in aerobatics and playful but sometimes destructive behaviour. **Habitat:** Mainly in alpine zone, but also in forest and descends to lowland river flats. **Breeding:** Jul–Mar.   [Sp 262]

KAKA   *Nestor meridionalis*   Locally common endemic

45 cm; ♂ 525 g, ♀ 475 g. A large sometimes inquisitive *forest parrot* with crimson underwings and rump. North I birds are mainly olive brown with darker feather edges; crown paler and greyer; golden wash on cheeks; dark crimson collar, undertail and lower belly. Bill longer and more arched in the male. Juvenile has yellow base of lower mandible. South and Stewart Is birds (illustrated) brighter, and crown almost white. Noisy; many varied calls from liquid whistling notes to harsh grating calls. **Habitat:** Favours native forest and predator- and possum-free offshore islands, but a few visit gardens and orchards. **Breeding:** Sep–Apr.   [Sp 261]

GALAH   *Cacatua roseicapilla*   Rare Australian introduction

36 cm, 325 g. A noisy *pink and grey parrot* with paler crown and crest. Immature duller than adult, with grey about the face. **Habitat:** Forest patches in open country; recently established in South Auckland, especially near Hunua Ranges, Pukekohe, and Pakihi and Ponui Is. **Breeding:** Season unknown in NZ.   [Sp 259]

SULPHUR-CRESTED COCKATOO

KAKAPO

KEA

KAKA

GALAH

Plate 61 **PARROTS**

CRIMSON ROSELLA *Platycercus elegans* **Rare Australian introduction**

35 cm, 130 g. Distinctive medium-sized parrot with a long tail. Adult *rich crimson with blue cheeks*, wings and tail, mottled black on the back. Immature green but with crimson on forehead, breast and undertail, blue on chin, wings and tail. **Habitat:** Parks and gardens in Wellington. **Breeding:** Sep–Feb. **[Sp 263]**

EASTERN ROSELLA *Platycercus eximius* **Locally common Australian introduction**

32 cm, 110 g. Distinctive long-tailed parrot with a bell-like *'kwink, kwink' flight call.* Head, upper breast and undertail crimson; *cheeks white;* lower breast yellow; back, rump, flanks and belly yellowish green, mottled black on back; leading edge of inner wing black, contrasts with pale blue on the central wing and dark blue on the wingtips; tail dark bluish green, edged pale blue. Female and immature more heavily mottled black on back, and red areas duller and patchy. Loud ringing calls and chattering notes. **Habitat:** Favours lightly wooded country (e.g. scattered totara) but uses forest and urban parks and gardens. **Breeding:** Oct–Jan. **[Sp 264]**

YELLOW-CROWNED PARAKEET (Kakariki) *Cyanoramphus auriceps*
Locally common endemic

♂ 25 cm, 50 g; ♀ 23 cm, 40 g. Long-tailed bright yellow-green parrot of native forest. *Crown golden yellow;* forehead and band from bill *to* eye red, and small patch on sides of rump crimson; violet-blue on wing coverts and some outer flight feathers. Orange-fronted colour phase is plainer green, lacking yellow; forehead and band from bill to eye orange. Flight fast and direct, with rapid wingbeats. *Flight call a rapid high-pitched chatter.* **Habitat:** Native forests; rare orange-fronted phase is seen mostly in North Canterbury. **Breeding:** Oct–Feb. **[Sp 267]**

RED-CROWNED PARAKEET (Kakariki) *Cyanoramphus novaezelandiae*
Locally common native

♂ 28 cm, 80 g; ♀ 25 cm, 70 g. Very like the Yellow-crowned Parakeet but larger and with red crown, forehead and band from bill to *behind* eye; rump patches crimson. Flight direct and rapid, often above the canopy, or side-slipping through the trees. *Flight call a rapid loud chatter,* lower-pitched than Yellow-crowned Parakeet. **Habitat:** Rare in native forests on the main islands but common in forest and scrub on Stewart I and many predator-free offshore and outlying islands. **Breeding:** Oct–Mar. **[Sp 266]**

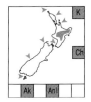

ANTIPODES ISLAND PARAKEET *Cyanoramphus unicolor*
Locally common endemic

♂ 32 cm, ♀ 29 cm; 130 g. Visibly larger and plumper than other NZ parakeets. *Entirely green head* and body, except for blue on wing coverts and some flight feathers; underparts tinged yellow. **Habitat:** Tussock and scrub of Antipodes Is only. **Breeding:** Oct–Mar. **[Sp 265]**

CRIMSON ROSELLA

juv

EASTERN
ROSELLA

♂

♀

orange-fronted
phase

YELLOW-CROWNED
PARAKEET

RED-CROWNED
PARAKEET

ANTIPODES ISLAND
PARAKEET

Plate 62

CUCKOOS

A diverse group ranging in size from the Shining Cuckoo to the Channel-billed Cuckoo. Generally grey or brown, often with conspicuous barring, especially on the underparts; long tail with transverse bars and white notches; short bill and short legs. Sexes alike. Most lay 1 egg in nests of other insectivorous species. Young cuckoos make insistent penetrating begging calls. The adults are vocal when breeding and are more often heard than seen.

SHINING CUCKOO (Pipiwharauroa) *Chrysococcyx lucidus*   Common native

16 cm, 25 g. Short-tailed *metallic bronze-green cuckoo, barred dark green on white face and underparts.* Juvenile duller and less distinctly barred. Song a distinctive *series of high-pitched upward-slurring whistles: 'coo-ee, coo-ee . . .' followed by 1–2 downward-slurring notes: 'tsee-ew';* the latter often given when flying at night. Usual host is Grey Warbler. **Habitat:** Native forest, scrub, parks and gardens from Sep–Apr. Migrates to Solomon Is and Bismark Archipelago for NZ winter. **Breeding:** Oct–Feb.
[Sp 271]

LONG-TAILED CUCKOO (Koekoea) *Eudynamys taitensis* Locally common endemic

40 cm, 125 g. Large *brown cuckoo with very long tail.* Adult has upperparts rich brown, barred black; face and underparts pale buff, boldly streaked brown and black. Juvenile has upperparts dull brown, spotted white; face and underparts buff, lightly streaked. Main call a *loud harsh shriek – 'zzwheesht' –* from a high perch or in flight, any time of day. In flight, tail as long as body. Usual hosts are Whitehead, Brown Creeper and Yellowhead. **Habitat:** Mainly native and exotic forest, Oct–Mar, but almost anywhere on migration. Migrates to Pacific islands. **Breeding:** Nov–Jan.
[Sp 272]

CHANNEL-BILLED CUCKOO *Scythrops novaehollandiae*   Rare Australian vagrant

61 cm. Huge grey cuckoo with a long black and white-tipped tail, and large powerful yellow bill. Red skin round the red eye. **Habitat:** Breeds Australian forests. Winters in Indonesia. Rarely seen in NZ, spring and summer. [Sp 273]

PALLID CUCKOO *Cuculus pallidus*   Rare Australian vagrant

30 cm, 85 g. Medium-sized cuckoo with long wings and tail and falcon-like profile in flight. Adult plain grey, barred only on undertail; a dark grey line passes through the eye; pale eyebrow and patch on the nape. Immature boldly marked brown and buff on head and upperparts; pale buff underparts. Feeds by swooping to ground from a perch. Male song a series of *slowly rising and accelerating melancholy notes: 'too, too . . . too, too'.* **Habitat:** Breeds Australia. Winters northern Australia, New Guinea and Indonesia. A few reach NZ, mainly in lightly forested open country. [Sp 269]

ORIENTAL CUCKOO *Cuculus saturatus*   Rare Asian straggler

33 cm. Like large Pallid Cuckoo but darker grey, and *lower chest, belly and undertail boldly barred black on white.* Rare brown phase rich brown above, paler below and heavily barred black all over. Feeds by swooping to ground from a perch. Usually silent in NZ. **Habitat:** Breeds Asia. Migrates to Indonesia and Australia. A few reach NZ, mainly in lightly forested open country. [Sp 268]

FAN-TAILED CUCKOO *Cacomantis flabelliformis*   Rare Australian vagrant

26 cm. Slim cuckoo with habit of cocking and fanning tail on alighting on a perch. Adult *blue-grey above, mostly rust red below, but with tail notched black on white.* Immature speckled rufous and brown with pale brown belly and undertail coverts, dark bars on chest and undertail. Feeds by swooping to ground from a perch. Call a repeated rapid descending trill. **Habitat:** Breeds Australia and SW Pacific. Vagrants reach NZ, mainly in lightly forested open country. [Sp 270]

SHINING CUCKOO

CHANNEL-BILLED
CUCKOO

juv

LONG-TAILED CUCKOO

FAN-TAILED
CUCKOO

PALLID CUCKOO

ORIENTAL
CUCKOO

juv

brown phase

Plate 63

OWLS and KINGFISHERS

Owls are mainly nocturnal birds of prey. They are chunky, and usually streaked brown and buff and spotted white. Large head and flat-faced with large eyes in a paler facial disc. Bill short and hooked. Powerful feet and talons. Sexes alike; females slightly larger. Plumage is soft, and so flight is silent. Voice ranges from plaintive calls to harsh screeches.

LITTLE OWL *Athene noctua*   Locally common European introduction

23 cm, 180 g. *Small grey-brown owl, heavily streaked and spotted white.* Flatter head and shorter tail than Morepork. Often seen by day perching on posts and farm sheds. Flight undulating. Call a clear high-pitched 'kiew'. **Habitat:** Farmland of South I only, especially near east coast. **Breeding:** Oct–Jan.   [Sp 276]

MOREPORK (Ruru) *Ninox novaeseelandiae*   Common native

29 cm, 175 g. *Dark brown owl,* obscurely spotted and barred buff. Yellow eyes set in dark facial mask. Larger rounder head and longer tail than Little Owl. Nocturnal; roosts by day in thick vegetation, especially in tree ferns. Main call a loud double hoot – '*more-pork*' – also repeated monotonous 'more' and rising vibrating 'cree'. **Habitat:** Forest, scrub, lightly forested open country, parks and gardens. **Breeding:** Sep–Mar.   [Sp 274]

BARN OWL *Tyto alba*   Rare Australian vagrant

34 cm. *Large pale buff and white owl;* looks white when seen at dusk or in headlights. Heart-shaped white facial disc. Call a rasping screech: 'skiirrr'. **Habitat:** Almost worldwide in open country.   [Sp 277]

Kingfishers are small to large birds with a dumpy body, short neck, short legs, large head, and a bill that looks too large and heavy. Sexes alike. Often but not always associated with water. They sit patiently on a branch, powerline or other prominent perch and dart or glide to snatch prey from the ground surface, or to plunge into shallow water. Calls are harsh.

KOOKABURRA *Dacelo novaeguineae*   Rare Australian introduction

45 cm, 350 g. *Very large bird with heavy black and yellow bill;* pale head and underparts, brownish back; tail rufous, barred black. Perches prominently on bare branch or powerline. In flight, clear white wing flashes. Voice a *raucous laughing cackle,* mainly at dawn and dusk. **Habitat:** Lightly forested open country, mainly from Orewa and Kaukapakapa to Whangarei, especially south of Wellsford. **Breeding:** Nov–Mar.
[Sp 280]

KINGFISHER (Kotare) *Halcyon sancta*   Abundant native

24 cm, 65 g. *Small deep green-blue and buff bird;* green grading to blue on the head and upperparts. Pale yellowish-buff to off-white underparts and collar round back of neck. Immature duller with buff feather edges on upperparts and brownish mottling on chest. Often seen *perched on powerlines, or on branches and rocks near water.* Call a *loud penetrating 'kek-kek-kek-kek'.* **Habitat:** Forest, river margins, farmland, lakes, estuaries and rocky coastlines; movement towards the coast in winter. **Breeding:** Oct–Feb.   [Sp 281]

MOREPORK

LITTLE OWL

BARN OWL

KOOKABURRA

KINGFISHER

imm

Plate 64 # SWIFTS, SWALLOWS and MARTINS

Swifts are reminiscent of swallows but designed for aerial feeding and speed, with wide flattened bill and very long thin swept-back wings. Generally black, with white patches and distinctive tail shape. Sexes alike. They fly high, with bursts of rapid wingbeats alternating with long swift glides, dives and banking turns; at dusk and in bad weather, they fly low over water or circle headlands, hilltops and stands of tall trees. Rarely land (clinging to side of tree or building) except when breeding. Voice an excited twittering.

SPINE-TAILED SWIFT   *Hirundapus caudacutus*   Rare tropical straggler

20 cm. Large swift with *short square tail*. All dark except for *white patches on throat and undertail*. In the hand, each tail feather has a short projecting spine. **Habitat:** Breeds E Asia. Migrates to Australia. Most stragglers to NZ seen over open country, mainly Nov–Mar.   **[Sp 278]**

FORK-TAILED SWIFT   *Apus pacificus*   Rare tropical straggler

18 cm. Slightly smaller and slimmer than Spine-tailed Swift, with long *deeply-forked tail*. All dark except for *white rump and pale throat and lightly barred upperbreast*. **Habitat:** Breeds E Asia. Migrates to Australia. Stragglers to NZ seen over open country, mainly Oct–Feb, but some in winter.   **[Sp 279]**

Swallows and martins are small birds with rapid erratic darting and gliding flight in pursuit of flying insects or snatching them from the surface of water or the ground. NZ species mostly blue above, pale below; each species has distinctive combination of pattern of red on head, colour of rump, and shape of tail. Sexes alike. Juveniles duller. Perch and come to ground readily; often seen gathered on powerlines, fences, shed roofs and riverbed shingle. Build distinctive mud nests under bridges, in caves or rock outcrops, trees or around buildings. Lay 3–5 pale pink eggs, speckled brown.

WELCOME SWALLOW   *Hirundo tahitica*   Abundant native

15 cm, 14 g. Adult has head and back blue-black; forehead, throat and chest rufous; underparts dull white; *deeply forked tail* with a row of white spots near the tip. Juvenile duller on upperparts, paler rufous markings, and tail less deeply forked. Often in swirling groups low over open water or crops, or sit on wires like clothes pegs. **Habitat:** Open country, especially near water. Often builds cup-shaped mud nest under bridges and under eaves of houses. **Breeding:** Aug–Mar.   **[Sp 287]**

AUSTRALIAN TREE MARTIN   *Hirundo nigricans*   Rare Australian vagrant

13 cm. Smaller and stockier than Welcome Swallow. Head and back blue-black; forehead of adult rufous, juvenile pale rufous; underparts and *rump dull white; tail short, almost square*. **Habitat:** Vagrants regularly reach NZ in autumn and early winter, mainly in open country in company with Welcome Swallows.
[Sp 288]

FAIRY MARTIN   *Hirundo ariel*   Rare Australian vagrant

12 cm. Much smaller than Welcome Swallow. *Whole head pale chestnut*; back blue-black; *rump bright white*; underparts dull white; *tail short, almost square*. **Habitat:** Rare vagrants reach NZ in Nov–Mar, mainly in open country. Distinctive bottle-shaped nest found in shed near Lake Wairarapa in 1970s.   **[Sp 289]**

SPINE-TAILED SWIFT

FORK-TAILED SWIFT

WELCOME SWALLOW

juv

juv

FAIRY MARTIN

AUSTRALIAN
TREE MARTIN

Plate 65

AUSTRALIAN PASSERINES and DOLLARBIRD

Passerines are the largest group of birds. They are small to medium sized land birds found worldwide, except on Antarctica. All species have four toes, three pointing forward and one back, well-adapted for perching. Most species are song-birds, with complex musical calls, but there are exceptions (e.g. crows). They show great diversity of form, behaviour and breeding biology.

BLACK-FACED CUCKOO-SHRIKE *Coracina novaehollandiae*
Rare Australian vagrant

33 cm. Large pale grey bird with a long tail, and *habit of folding and refolding its wings on alighting* at a perch. Adult has black face and throat. Immature has black patch from bill to ear coverts, and pale faintly barred throat and upper breast. Sexes alike. Flight undulating. Feeds mainly on insects taken in foliage or by swooping to the ground from a perch. Call a short soft croaky 'prurr'. **Habitat:** Lightly forested open country. Vagrants, mostly immatures, seen mainly in autumn, sometimes in spring. **[Sp 291]**

DOLLARBIRD *Eurystomus orientalis*
Rare Australian straggler

29 cm. Stout short-tailed greenish bird with a large brownish head and glossy blue throat. Short broad red bill; red legs. In flight, *prominent pale 'silver dollar' patches on wings*. Immature has brown-grey body, dark bill and brown legs. Sexes alike. Perches high on dead branches, in an upright posture, before swooping out to catch large insects. Call a *loud raspy cackle*. **Habitat:** Lightly forested open country. Breeds Australia. Winters Asia. Most NZ records are of adults in Nov–Dec, and immatures in Mar–May.
[Sp 282]

SATIN FLYCATCHER *Myiagra cyanoleuca*
Rare Australian vagrant

16 cm. Small slim bird with a rather long tail; a small crest gives a *peaked back of head*. Male dark glossy *blue-black*, except lower chest and belly white. Female slate grey with bluish gloss on upperparts; throat and upperbreast reddish buff, *contrasts sharply* with white lower breast and belly. Feeds on insects by darting out from a perch to snatch them in mid-air. On realighting, quivers tail. **Habitat:** Of 3 NZ records, 2 seen in gardens. **[Sp 303]**

WHITE-BROWED WOODSWALLOW *Artamus superciliosus*
Rare Australian vagrant

19 cm. In flight, like a small slim Starling soaring and gliding gracefully. Head, throat and upperparts dark blue-grey; chestnut underparts; a prominent broad white eyebrow in males, less distinct in females. Feeds on insects taken in the air and on the ground; also nectar. **Habitat:** Open country. Two NZ records.
[Sp 325]

MASKED WOODSWALLOW *Artamus personatus*
Rare Australian vagrant

19 cm. In flight, like a small slim Starling soaring and gliding gracefully. Males two-tone grey, darker above; *black face and throat mask*, bordered white. Females duller with less distinct mask. Feeds on insects taken in the air and on the ground; also nectar. **Habitat:** Open country. Only NZ record was a pair that bred in Otago in early 1970s. **[Sp 324]**

WHITE-WINGED TRILLER *Lalage tricolor*
Rare Australian vagrant

18 cm. Breeding male black and white with a grey rump. Female and immature brown with buff feather edges. Non-breeding male like female, but wings black and white. Feeds mainly on insects taken in foliage or by swooping to ground from a perch. Male song, uttered while perched and in flight, is Chaffinch-like in form, a descending 'chiff-chiff-chiff-joey-joey-joey', ending with a Canary-like trill. **Habitat:** One NZ record: in a Dunedin garden, 1969. **[Sp 292]**

BLACK-FACED CUCKOO-SHRIKE

imm

DOLLARBIRD

WHITE-BROWED
WOODSWALLOW

♀

♂

♂

♀

SATIN FLYCATCHER

♀

♂

♀

♂ breeding

MASKED WOODSWALLOW

WHITE-WINGED TRILLER

Plate 66

NATIVE PASSERINES

RIFLEMAN (Titipounamu) *Acanthisitta chloris*   Locally common endemic

8 cm; ♂ 6 g, ♀ 7 g. *NZ's smallest bird. Rounded wings; very short stumpy tail;* bill fine
and slightly upturned. Male bright yellow-green above, green on rump; female
streaked dark and light brown above, brownish yellow on rump. Both whitish below,
conspicuous white eyebrow stripe, and yellowish flanks. Immature like female but
streaked on breast. Feeds by working its way up trees and shrubs, flicking wings
and exploring bark and lichen of trunks, branches and leaves. Call a very high-
pitched sharp repeated 'zipt', beyond the hearing range of some people. **Habitat:**
Native forest and scrub; favours beech and tawa forest. Some in exotic forest, gorse
and willows, especially in South I. **Breeding:** Sep–Feb.   **[Sp 283]**

ROCK WREN *Xenicus gilviventris*   Uncommon endemic

10 cm; ♂ 16 g, ♀ 20 g. Small alpine bird with short tail, rounded wings, long legs and
toes, fine black bill, cream eyebrow. Male dull green above, grey-brown below, flanks
yellow; brighter green and yellow in Fiordland. Female plainer olive brown. *Bobs
vigorously up and down.* Usually hops and runs, flying only short distances. **Habitat:**
Alpine regions of South I only, among rockfalls, screes and subalpine scrub. **Breeding:**
Oct–Feb.   **[Sp 285]**

SILVEREYE (Tauhou) *Zosterops lateralis*   Abundant native

12 cm, 13 g. Small green bird with conspicuous *white eye-ring.* Head and upperparts
olive green with grey back and wash on lower neck and onto breast; underparts
creamy white with pinkish-brown flanks and white undertail. Sexes alike. Juvenile
lacks eye-ring. Usually in small flocks, except when breeding. Readily attracted to
bird tables in cold winters. Flight call from flocks an excited 'cli-cli-cli'; single birds
give a plaintive 'cree'. Song a melodious mix of warbles, trills and slurs. **Habitat:**
Forests, scrub, orchards, parks and gardens. **Breeding:** Sep–Mar.   **[Sp 308]**

GREY WARBLER (Riroriro) *Gerygone igata*   Abundant endemic

10 cm, 6.5 g. Very small grey bird with a darker *tail, conspicuously tipped white,* and a
habit of *hovering* to pick insects and spiders from plants. Adult is grey-brown above,
pale grey on face, throat and breast; off-white belly and undertail, red eye. Sexes
alike. Juvenile similar but yellowish on face and underparts, brown eye. Flits and
hovers among outer foliage and twigs to catch invertebrates. Song a distinctive *long
musical wavering trill.* **Habitat:** Scrub (especially manuka and kanuka), forest, parks
and gardens. Builds a distinctive domed hanging nest, with small side entrance hole.
Breeding: Aug–Jan.   **[Sp 301]**

CHATHAM ISLAND WARBLER *Gerygone albofrontata*   Locally abundant endemic

12 cm; ♂ 10 g, ♀ 8.5 g. Like large Grey Warbler but browner and bill much larger.
Male has olive-brown head and upperparts, darker on wings and tail; prominent
white forehead, eyebrow and underparts; flanks and undertail pale yellow; red eye.
Female lacks white forehead and has duller greyish-white underparts and yellowish
eyebrow, face and throat. Juvenile like female, but upperparts olive grey; underparts
yellower; eye brown. Gleans invertebrates from leaves and crevices in trunks and
branches; rarely hovers. **Habitat:** Forest and scrub. Builds a distinctive domed
hanging nest, with small side entrance hole. **Breeding:** Sep–Jan.   **[Sp 302]**

RIFLEMAN

♂

♀

ROCK WREN

♂

♀

SILVEREYE

juv

GREY WARBLER

♂

CHATHAM ISLAND
WARBLER

Plate 67

INTRODUCED PASSERINES and NEW ZEALAND PIPIT

BLACKBIRD   *Turdus merula*   Abundant European introduction

25 cm, 90 g. Adult male *black with a bright orange bill*. Adult female *dark brown* with paler throat and smudgy mottled breast; bill brown and dull orange. Juvenile *rusty brown*, especially on head; pale streaks on back and wing coverts; brown barring on underparts; bill dark brown. Immature male (Apr–Jan) has brown wings contrasting with black body. *Long tail*. Feeds mainly on the ground; *hops* rather than walks. *Song a loud clear tuneful warble, mellower than Song Thrush and not repetitive.* Alarm call a persistent sharp 'tchink-tchink'. **Habitat:** Forest, scrub, farmland with scattered trees or hedges, orchards, parks and gardens. **Breeding:** Aug–Jan.   **[Sp 295]**

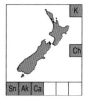

SONG THRUSH   *Turdus philomelos*   Abundant European introduction

23 cm, 70 g. Warm brown above, buff-white below, with *breast boldly spotted dark brown*. Bill yellowish brown with yellow gape; legs pinkish brown. Sexes alike. Juvenile similar but more yellowish buff, spotted and streaked paler above and smaller spots below; bill dark brown with prominent yellow gape. Feeds mostly on the ground, where it hops and runs. Hammers snails open on a regular 'anvil'. Song *a loud string of repeated clear-cut musical phrases*, each separated by a brief pause: 'chitty-choo chitty-choo, oo-eee oo-eee . . .' Song perch usually high and conspicuous. **Habitat:** Forest, scrub, farmland with scattered trees or hedges, orchards, parks and gardens. **Breeding:** Aug–Feb.   **[Sp 296]**

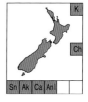

Starling (juvenile — see Plate 73)   **[Sp 319]**

DUNNOCK   *Prunella modularis*   Common European introduction

14 cm, 21 g. *Nondescript, dark and unobtrusive bird*, rather like a female House Sparrow but has *slim body, fine black bill*. Upperparts brown streaked darker; face, collar and breast washed grey; flanks streaked brown; red eye; orange-brown legs. Sexes alike. Juvenile similar but has brown eye. Usually feeds alone on the ground, keeping close to cover; shuffles along in a crouched posture, delicately picking at the surface. Sings from the top of a bush or hedge, a thin hurried warble. Call a high-pitched insistent 'tseep'. **Habitat:** Forest, scrub, farmland with hedges, orchards, parks and gardens. **Breeding:** Aug–Feb.   **[Sp 294]**

SKYLARK   *Alauda arvensis*   Common European introduction

18 cm, 38 g. Dull yellow-buff bird, streaked and spotted brown on upperparts and breast. Adult has a *small crest*, raised when alert. Juvenile yellower and spottier, and lacks crest. In flight, *white outer tail feathers and white trailing edge to broad wings*. Male in territorial flight display (Aug–Jan) soars with whirring wings up to 100 m, and slowly descends, all the time singing a *sustained and vigorous torrent of varied trills and runs*. Call, usually in flight, a liquid 'chirrup'. **Habitat:** Open country, from coast to subalpine. **Breeding:** Sep–Feb.   **[Sp 286]**

NEW ZEALAND PIPIT (Pihoihoi)   *Anthus novaeseelandiae*   Uncommon native

19 cm, 40 g. Like Skylark, including white outer tail feathers, but more slender and has the distinctive habit of frequently *flicking its long tail up and down*. Head and upperparts brown, streaked darker; prominent *white eyebrow*; underparts whitish, streaked brown on breast. Runs and walks jerkily on long legs; often flies a short distance ahead, calling a shrill 'scree' or drawn-out 'zwee'. **Habitat:** Open habitats from coast to alpine tops, but avoids intensively farmed areas; mainly near coast, on shingle riverbeds, gravel roads, and scree slopes. **Breeding:** Aug–Mar. **[Sp 290]**

BLACKBIRD

♂

juv

♀

juv

SONG THRUSH

Starling juv

SKYLARK

DUNNOCK

NEW ZEALAND PIPIT

Plate 68

NATIVE PASSERINES

FERNBIRD (Matata) *Bowdleria punctata*

Locally common endemic

18 cm, 35 g. Warm brown above, paler below, heavily streaked and spotted dark brown; *forehead and crown chestnut*; whitish eyebrow stripe. Distinctive *long frayed tail*. Sexes and juveniles alike. Secretive, often remaining hidden in thick vegetation or moving mouse-like through the rushes, appearing inquisitively in the scrub canopy. Reluctant to fly. Flight weak and whirring, tail drooping. Often detected by sound alone. Common call a short sharp 'tchip', and *metallic double-note 'uu-tick'* often produced by pair in duet. **Habitat:** Freshwater and tidal wetlands, especially reedbeds or pakihi with emergent scrub; also drier sparse scrub and bracken. **Breeding:** Aug–Mar.

[Sp 297]

BROWN CREEPER (Pipipi) *Mohoua novaeseelandiae*

Locally common endemic

13 cm; ♂ 13.5 g, ♀ 11 g. Crown, back, rump and tail reddish brown; ash grey on face and neck; small white stripe behind eye; light buff underparts; dark bar near tip of tail. Sexes and juveniles alike. Usually in small fast-moving *noisy* flocks high in canopy, uttering nasal notes and rapid slurred trills. Male song includes slurs, musical whistles and harsh notes: 'chi-roh-ree-roh-ree-ree', the second note being lower than the first. Females sing a rapid sequence of brief notes, the last being higher and prolonged. **Habitat:** Forest and scrub of South and Stewart Is. **Breeding:** Sep–Feb.

[Sp 300]

WHITEHEAD (Popokatea) *Mohoua albicilla*

Locally common endemic

15 cm; ♂ 18.5 g, ♀ 14.5 g. Male has *white head and underparts*, with contrasting black bill, eye and legs; upperparts pale brown. Female and immature similar, but crown and nape shaded brown. Usually in small fast-moving *noisy* feeding flocks or family groups, high in canopy, uttering harsh chattering calls, trills and slurs. Male song can be clear and Canary-like: 'peek-o, peek-o, peek-o'. **Habitat:** Native and exotic forest, and scrub of North I. **Breeding:** Sep–Jan.

[Sp 298]

YELLOWHEAD (Mohua) *Mohoua ochrocephala*

Rare endemic

15 cm; ♂ 30 g, ♀ 25 g. Male has *bright yellow head and underparts* with contrasting black bill, eye and legs; upperparts yellowish brown. Female and immature similar, but crown and nape shaded brown. Tip of tail often worn to spine-like shafts. Usually in small *noisy* feeding flocks or family groups, high in canopy, uttering loud staccato chattering calls and trills and slurs. Male song clear and Canary-like. **Habitat:** Tall native forest, especially red beech of South I. **Breeding:** Oct–Feb.

[Sp 299]

FANTAIL (Piwakawaka) *Rhipidura fuliginosa*

Abundant native

16 cm (including 8 cm tail), 8 g. Small bird with small head and bill; *long tail, often fanned*. Pied phase has grey head, white eyebrow, brown back; yellow underparts, with white and black bands across chest; black and white tail. Juvenile similar, but browner body, rusty-brown wing coverts, and indistinct chest markings. Island subspecies have variable white in tail, most in Chathams. Black phase, mainly in South I, all sooty black except white spot behind eye. Restless movements; twists and jerks on a perch, tail fanned, flies out to seize flying insects. Erratic flight as it hawks over forest or scrub canopy, into an insect swarm over a clearing, paddock, pond or garden. Call a penetrating 'cheet'; song a harsh rhythmical 'saw-like' 'tweet-a-tweet-a-tweet-a-tweet . . .' **Habitat:** Forest, scrub, farmland with hedges and shelterbelts, river margins, parks and gardens. **Breeding:** Aug–Mar.

[Sp 304]

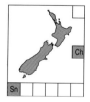

FERNBIRD

BROWN CREEPER

YELLOWHEAD

WHITEHEAD

juv pied

FANTAIL

pied phase

black phase

Plate 69

NATIVE PASSERINES

TOMTIT (Miromiro – North I, Ngiru-ngiru – South I)   *Petroica macrocephala*
Common endemic

13 cm, 11 g. Small forest bird with a large head and short tail. Five subspecies vary slightly in size and colour; the most distinctive is the Snares subspecies, which is wholly black but glossier in the male. Adult male (North I) has black head with small white spot above bill; glossy black upperparts and upper breast; white underparts, sharply divided at breast; white wingbar and sides to tail. South, Chatham and Auckland Is subspecies similar, but have underparts yellowish, brighter or orange on upper breast near dividing line. Juvenile males similar, but have white shaft streaks to black feathers and always have white underparts. Adult females (North and South Is) have brown head and upperparts; grey-brown chin and upper breast fading to white on underparts; wingbar and sides of tail pale buff. Chatham I female similar but darker brown above. Auckland Is female like male but dull black upperparts and upper breast. Feeds in the understorey by perching on branch or trunk, scanning, then flying to ground or tree to catch invertebrates. *Male song a loud jingling burst: 'ti oly oly oly oh'*, varies regionally. Male call a short high-pitched 'swee'; female call a reedy 'seet'. **Habitat:** Scrub, native and exotic forest and scrub. **Breeding:** Sep–Feb.
[Sp 305]

BLACK ROBIN   *Petroica traversi*
Rare endemic

15 cm; ♂ 25 g, ♀ 22 g. Small completely black forest bird with short fine black bill, long thin legs and an upright stance. Feeds mostly on the forest floor or in low branches. Male song a clear simple phrase of 5–7 notes. Call a high-pitched single note. Formerly extremely rare; in 1979 there were just 5 birds, including 1 productive female 'Old Blue' (depicted), but with intensive management the population has recovered to about 150. **Habitat:** Forest and scrub of predator-free islands in Chatham group and Pitt Island. **Breeding:** Oct–Jan.
[Sp 307]

NEW ZEALAND ROBIN (Toutouwai)   *Petroica australis*
Uncommon endemic

18 cm, 35 g. Inquisitive and confiding *dark slaty-grey forest bird with long thin legs and an upright stance.* Male (North I) is dark, almost black, except for white spot above bill, pale greyish-white lower breast and belly; black feathers have pale shaft streaks, and so very faintly streaked upperparts; wings dark brownish black. Female and juvenile (North I) similar, but greyer with variable paler patches on breast and throat. Male (South I) has dark grey upperparts and upper chest, distinctly divided from yellowish-white lower chest and belly; flanks variably greyish; white spot above bill; wings dark brownish black. Female and juvenile (South I) similar, usually greyer on breast with variable whitish patches. Stewart I birds have similar patterns to North I. Perches on a low trunk or branch and flies to *feed on the forest floor;* hops about and sometimes trembles one leg to induce prey to surface. Male song loud clear and sustained string of phrases, usually descending and including 'pwee-pwee-pwee' phrases; varies regionally. Call a soft 'chirp'. **Habitat:** Native and exotic forest, sometimes tall scrub. **Breeding:** Jul–Jan.
[Sp 306]

TOMTIT

North Island

♂

♀

South Island

juv ♂

♂

Snares Island

BLACK ROBIN

♀

North Island

South Island

♂

♂

♀

juv

NEW ZEALAND ROBIN

Plate 70

NATIVE PASSERINES

KOKAKO   *Callaeas cinerea*   Rare endemic

38 cm, 230 g. *Large dark bluish-grey* bird with a *black facial mask*, short strongly arched black bill, long black legs, long tail and rounded wings. North I adult has blue wattles; South I adult has orange wattles. Juvenile has smaller pinkish wattles, smaller facial mask, and dull brown wash in plumage. Leaps around in trees and takes short flights, never sustained for long. More often heard than seen. Calls mostly at dawn; *song is a slow string of very loud rich mournful organ-like notes.* **Habitat:** Tall podocarp hardwood forest in North I, Little Barrier, Tiritiri Matangi and Kapiti Is; formerly beech and mixed forest in South and Stewart Is, probably extinct. **Breeding:** Oct–Mar.
                                                                        [Sp 321]

TUI   *Prosthemadera novaeseelandiae*   Common endemic

30 cm; ♂ 120 g, ♀ 90 g. Dark bird with two *white throat tufts*, or poi. Looks black in dull light, but has *green, bluish-purple and bronze iridescent sheen*, back and flanks dark reddish brown; a lacy collar of filamentous white feathers on neck; white wingbar; slightly decurved black bill and strong black legs. Sexes alike. Juvenile dull slate black with glossy wings and tail, greyish-white throat, lacks tufts. Energetic and acrobatic while feeding in trees on nectar and fruit. In flight, round wings with white shoulder patches; long broad tail; *noisy whirring flight* between short glides. Song has rich fluid melodic notes (often repeated) mixed with coughs, clicks, grunts and wheezes; varies regionally. **Habitat:** Native forest and scrub, farmland with kowhai, gums and flax, parks and gardens. **Breeding:** Sep–Feb.   [Sp 311]

STITCHBIRD (Hihi)   *Notiomystis cincta*   Rare endemic

18 cm; ♂ 40 g, ♀ 30 g. Male has white erectile tufts behind eyes; velvety black head, upper breast and back, bordered golden yellow across breast and folded wings; rest of underparts pale brown. Female greyish brown with white wingbar; lacks ear tufts. Often cocks tail. Call an loud explosive whistle: 'see-si-ip'. **Habitat:** Forest on a few predator-free islands, especially Little Barrier, Tiritiri Matangi and Kapiti Is; recently released at Karori Sanctuary in Wellington. **Breeding:** Sep–Apr.   [Sp 309]

BELLBIRD (Korimako, Makomako)   *Anthornis melanura*   Common endemic

20 cm; ♂ 34 g, ♀ 26 g. Green bird with a short curved bill, slightly forked tail, and noisy whirring fast and direct flight. Adult male olive green, paler on underparts, head tinted with purple gloss; wings and tail dark bluish black, except for yellow patch at bend of folded wing; eye red. Female browner with *narrow white stripe across cheek from bill* and bluish gloss on forehead and crown. Juvenile like female, but with *brown eye and yellowish cheek stripe*. Song varies regionally but always loud clear liquid ringing notes, without grunts and wheezes. Alarm call a rapidly repeated harsh scolding 'yeng, yeng, yeng'. **Habitat:** Native and exotic forest, scrub, farm shelterbelts, parks and gardens. **Breeding:** Sep–Feb.   [Sp 310]

SADDLEBACK (Tieke)   *Philesturnus carunculatus*   Rare endemic

25 cm; ♂ 80 g, ♀ 70 g. Head and body glossy black with *bright chestnut saddle*, rump and tail coverts; *pendulous orange-red wattles at base of black bill*. North I subspecies has thin buff line at upper edge of saddle. North I juvenile has smaller wattles and lacks buff line; South I juvenile (Jackbird) *chocolate brown*, paler below, with reddish-brown tail coverts, and small wattles. Often feeds on the forest floor, and bounds from branch to branch rather than flies. Main call is a *strident ringing 'cheet, te-te-te-te'*; often duet. **Habitat:** Forest and scrub on several offshore islands. **Breeding:** Aug–May.   [Sp 322]

KOKAKO

North Island

juv

South Island

TUI

juv

STITCHBIRD

♂

♀

juv ♂

BELLBIRD

SADDLEBACK

juv South Island

ad North Island

♂

♀

Plate 71

INTRODUCED PASSERINES

HOUSE SPARROW *Passer domesticus* Abundant European introduction

14 cm, 30 g. A gregarious, garrulous and quarrelsome associate of humans. Conical bill. Adult male chestnut brown above, streaked black on back; crown *dark grey*; rump greyish brown; underparts greyish white. Black bib and bill in breeding season, bib smaller and bill greyish pink rest of year. Female and juvenile drab sandy brown above, streaked darker on back; greyish white below; pale buffy eyebrow and sides to neck. Young juvenile often shows fleshy yellow gape. Flight fast and direct, showing small white wingbar. Voice a variety of monotonous unmusical cheeps and chirps. **Habitat:** Towns, arable farmland and farm shelterbelts, orchards; sometimes edges of native forest well away from human habitation. **Breeding:** Sep–Feb.

[Sp 318]

CHAFFINCH *Fringilla coelebs* Abundant European introduction

15 cm; ♂ 22 g, ♀ 21 g. Sparrow-sized finch with *conspicuous white shoulder, wingbar and outer tail feathers*. Adult male has black forehead, blue-grey crown and nape; *rich pinkish-brown face and underparts*, fading to white on belly; reddish-brown back; olive rump. Female and juvenile lack male colours; mainly soft brownish grey, except greenish rump and prominent white wingbars on darker wing. Flight undulating; flight call a soft single 'tsip'. *Male song a series of short loud notes, ending in a flourish: 'chip chip chip tell tell tell cherry-erry-erry tissi cheweeo'*, usually given from a high perch. Usual calls a metallic 'pink' or 'chwink-chwink', and a whistling 'huit'. **Habitat:** Native and exotic forest, scrub, farmland, tussockland, parks and gardens. **Breeding:** Sep–Feb.

[Sp 314]

REDPOLL *Carduelis flammea* Common European introduction

12 cm, 12 g. Small dull brown-streaked finch, but seen closely *forehead crimson and chin black*. Male in breeding season develops a pink to crimson flush on its breast, varying in intensity with individual and region. Juvenile lacks the crimson and black on the head and can look pale-headed. Often seen feeding or flying in large flocks, especially near weed-infested crops. Flight erratic and undulating; *flight call a fast harsh rattling metallic 'chich-chich-chich'*, sometimes followed by a 'bizzzz'. Main call a plaintive, questioning 'tsooeet?'. **Habitat:** Farmland, orchards, tussockland, forest and scrub margins, parks and gardens. **Breeding:** Oct–Feb.

[Sp 317]

GOLDFINCH *Carduelis carduelis* Abundant European introduction

13 cm; ♂ 16 g, ♀ 15 g. Small finch with *striking gold bars on black wings*. Adults have *brilliant red face*, slightly more extensive on the male, especially above and behind the eye; white ear coverts and sides to neck; black crown and half-collar; upperparts and breast soft brown; rest of underparts and rump white; tail black, spotted white near tip. Juvenile pale buff, streaked and spotted darker; wings and tail as in adult. Outside breeding season, usually in flocks, often feeding on seeds of thistles or other weeds. Flight undulating. *Male song a pleasant liquid twittering 'tsitt-witt-witt'*. **Habitat:** Farmland, orchards, parks and gardens. **Breeding:** Oct–Mar.

[Sp 316]

♂ breeding ♂ non-breeding

♀

HOUSE SPARROW

♀ ♂

CHAFFINCH

♀

juv

REDPOLL

♂ breeding

juv

GOLDFINCH

Plate 72

INTRODUCED PASSERINES

GREENFINCH *Carduelis chloris*   **Common European introduction**

15 cm, 28 g. *A robust olive-green finch with a pale heavy bill and prominent yellow on the sides of the tail and the edges of the closed wing.* Males olive green, the brightest have a conspicuous yellow eyebrow and yellowish belly. Females browner, dull olive green, the dullest a washed-out greenish brown. Juvenile and many immatures duller again, mainly brown, streaked darker with yellowish-green wash on rump and upper tail coverts. Flight undulating, looking heavy-bodied and short-tailed, and showing yellow wing flashes. Out of breeding season, often form large flocks in weed-infested crops. In breeding season, male repeatedly calls a *harsh drawn-out 'dzwee'*. Other common calls are a pleasant twittering 'chichichichichit-teu-teu-teu-teu', sometimes just the 'teu' notes; and a sweet rising 'tsooeet'. **Habitat:** Farmland, pine plantations, native bush and scrub fringes, pine and macrocarpa shelterbelts, parks and gardens. **Breeding:** Oct–Mar.   [Sp 315]

YELLOWHAMMER *Emberiza citrinella*   **Common European introduction**

16 cm, 27 g. Sparrow-sized mainly *yellow bird of open country* with reddish-brown upperparts, streaked darker; *rufous rump and white outer tail feathers.* Adult male has *bright yellow head and underparts,* head lightly marked brown on crown and on sides of face; *cinnamon wash across breast,* and pale yellow flanks. Adult female duller and paler yellow, more heavily marked brown on head, and *breast band greyish green.* Juvenile and immature even paler yellow or pale buff, heavily streaked, but still with rufous rump. Hops on ground when feeding, often with crouched posture. Outside breeding season, often form flocks on weed-infested crops and where hay has been scattered. Male song is rendered 'little bit of bread and no cheese'. Call a ringing metallic 'tink', or 'twick'. **Habitat:** Open country from sea level to sub-alpine, especially arable farmland or rough pasture with scattered scrub. **Breeding:** Oct–Mar.   [Sp 312]

CIRL BUNTING *Emberiza cirlus*   **Uncommon European introduction**

16 cm, 25 g. Sparrow-sized bird of open country, similar to Yellowhammer in size and shape and also with white outer tail feathers, but much less yellow and *rump greyish olive.* Adult male distinctive with black throat, head boldly striped black and yellow, crown and nape dark grey, fading to pale grey wash across breast; upperparts brown, streaked darker; cinnamon patches on wings and sides of lower breast, rest of underparts pale yellow streaked darker. Adult female and juvenile nondescript mix of buff, yellow and brown, heavily streaked on crown and finely streaked on breast and flanks. Hops on ground when feeding, often with crouched posture. Outside breeding season, often form small flocks on waste ground. Male song a *monotonous metallic cricket-like rattling buzz.* Calls include a thin 'zit' or 'see', and a soft brief 'tyu'. **Habitat:** Dry pastoral or arable farmland with scattered scrub, and pine and macrocarpa shelterbelts, mainly in Nelson and eastern South I, especially Marlborough and Central Otago. Some move to coastal wasteland and saltmarsh in winter. **Breeding:** Oct–Feb.   [Sp 313]

House Sparrow (female — see Plate 71)   [Sp 318]

GREENFINCH

juv

YELLOWHAMMER

♀

♂

juv

CIRL BUNTING

♀

juv

♂

♀ House Sparrow

Plate 73

INTRODUCED PASSERINES

STARLING   *Sturnus vulgaris*   **Abundant European introduction**

21 cm, 85 g. *Short-tailed dark bird with waddling jerky walk*. Breeding adult glossy black with purple sheen on head and breast; dark green sheen and buff spangling on wings and abdomen; pointed yellow bill, bluish base in male, pinkish in female. Non-breeding head and body spotted buff and white; bill dark. Juvenile smooth grey-brown, throat paler; bill dark. Flight fast and direct, often in large co-ordinated flocks. Distinctly *pointed triangular wings*. Large winter roosts; flocks converge at dusk and disperse at dawn. Feeds on ground by jabbing bill into soil. *Noisy*; call a descending whistle: 'cheeoo'; song, a rambling collection of clicks, rattles, warbles and gargles, interspersed with musical whistles. A good mimic. **Habitat:** Farmland, orchards, parks, gardens, city streets, forest margins and beaches. **Breeding:** Oct–Jan.

[Sp 319]

RED-VENTED BULBUL   *Pycnonotus cafer*   **Rare Asian introduction**

20 cm. Slim dark bird with long *white-tipped tail and red patch on undertail*. Head, upperparts and breast blackish, fading to grey on belly; rump white. Feathers on back of head can be raised into triangular crest. A popular cage-bird because of cheerful attractive call: 'pee pee-plo' or 'be-care-ful'. **Habitat:** Parks and gardens of central Auckland; established in 1950s, then exterminated, but others have been illegally released in 1990s.   [Sp 293]

MYNA   *Acridotheres tristis*   **Locally abundant Asian introduction**

24 cm, 125 g. *Cheeky brown bird with jaunty walk*. Adult *cinnamon brown with glossy black head and neck*, white undertail and underwing; yellow legs, bill and bare patch of skin near eye. Sexes alike. Juvenile has dark brown head, paler bill and facial skin. In flight, prominent *white patches on wings*, and white-tipped tail. Roosts communally all year, largest in winter; flocks converge at dusk and depart at dawn. Feeds mainly on the ground, *often at roadsides*. Voice jangling; song a rapid medley of raucous gurgling, chattering and bell-like notes. **Habitat:** Parks, gardens, orchards and farmland, sometimes on forest margins. **Breeding:** Oct–Mar.   [Sp 320]

AUSTRALIAN MAGPIE   *Gymnorhina tibicen*   **Abundant Australian introduction**

41 cm, 350 g. Large *black and white bird with pale blue black-tipped bill*. White-backed form has *hind neck and back white* in male, *finely barred grey* in female. Black-backed form (mostly in Hawke's Bay), has *black back*; hind neck white in male, finely barred grey in female. Juvenile like female, but underparts brownish grey and bill dark. Hybrids have variable black on back. Flight direct, with pointed wings and rapid shallow wingbeats. Feeds on the ground, sometimes in loose flocks. Song distinctive flute-like carolling, especially at dawn and dusk, rendered 'quardle oodle ardle wardle doodle'. **Habitat:** Open farmland with tall shelterbelts and scattered trees or forest, parks and gardens. **Breeding:** Jul–Dec.   [Sp 326]

ROOK   *Corvus frugilegus*   **Locally common European introduction**

45 cm; ♂ 425 g, ♀ 375 g. A *large glossy black crow with shaggy feathered thighs*. Adult has bare whitish face. Juvenile and immature have faces feathered black. In flight, *long broad 'fingered' wings*, broad roundish tail. *Flight strong and direct, but languid*. Feeds mainly on ground; walks sedately with occasional hops. Feeds, roosts and nests in flocks. Often wary and give *coarse 'caw' or 'kaah' calls* if disturbed or in flight. **Habitat:** Pasture and cultivated paddocks, farm shelterbelts, especially tall gums and pines. **Breeding:** Aug–Dec.   [Sp 328]

juv

RED-VENTED
BULBUL

breeding

STARLING

non-breeding

MYNA

juv

juv
white-backed

♀

ROOK

white-backed

lack-backed

AUSTRALIAN
MAGPIE

♂

imm

Plate 74

SPECIES EXTINCT SINCE 1900

New Zealand, like many other isolated island groups, has a long history of bird extinction. About 32 species died out in the 800 years between the arrival of Polynesians and the arrival of Europeans, most notably all the moa species. In the 200 years since European contact, 9 further species have become extinct, 5 of which have probably died out since 1900. The main factors that contributed to extinction were loss of habitat, introduced mammalian predators and overharvesting.

PIOPIO *Turnagra capensis*   Probably extinct endemic

26 cm. Plump olive-brown Blackbird-sized forest bird. Upperparts olive brown; upper tail coverts and tail rust red, except olive-brown central tail feathers; short robust dark brown bill; legs dark brown. North I subspecies had *white throat*; olive-grey breast and belly, the under tail coverts washed yellow. South I subspecies was *boldly streaked brown and white below*, throat and sides of neck tinged reddish brown, and feathers of forehead, crown and face tipped rust red. Song varied and sustained with 5 distinct bars, each repeated 6–7 times. Common call a short, sharp, whistling cry, quickly repeated. **Habitat:** Native forest and scrub; last confirmed record King Country, 1902, but more recent reports from inland Taranaki, Urewera, western Nelson and Fiordland.   **[Sp 327]**

LAUGHING OWL (Whekau) *Sceloglaux albifacies*   Extinct endemic

38 cm. A large owl with *yellowish-brown plumage heavily streaked brown. Face white around dark reddish-brown eye*, chin greyish; white splashes on scapulars, sometimes also on hindneck and mantle; wings and tail brown with brownish-white bars; bill horn-coloured, black at base; long well-feathered yellowish to reddish-buff legs. Calls, mainly on dark nights, 'a loud cry made up of a series of dismal shrieks frequently repeated', and 'a peculiar barking noise'. **Habitat:** Forests, scrub and open country with rock and limestone outcrops for cover. Last recorded South Canterbury, 1914.   **[Sp 275]**

HUIA *Heteralocha acutirostris*   Extinct endemic

♂ 45 cm, ♀ 48 cm. Glossy black with bluish iridescence, last 3 cm of long tail white; rounded orange wattles at base of ivory-white bill with greyish base: *male had stout straight 60 mm bill, female had slender curved 105 mm bill*; legs bluish grey. Immature had duller plumage, white tip of tail tinged reddish buff, wattles small and pale. Call a soft clear whistle; also a whistling note of higher pitch. **Habitat:** Native forest of southern North I since 1840. Last accepted record 1907.   **[Sp 323]**

BUSH WREN *Xenicus longipes*   Probably extinct endemic

9 cm, 16 g. Larger and darker than Rifleman but easily missed in the gloom of the forest. *Head dark olive brown with clear white eyebrow-stripe*; upperparts dark yellowish green, dark green tail; chin greyish white, *ash-grey underparts* except yellow flanks; long feet and toes. Female and Stewart I subspecies browner. Like the Rock Wren, *bobs on alighting on the ground*. **Habitat:** Forest and scrub. Last records: Urewera, 1955; Nelson Lakes NP, 1968; Kaimohu I (off Stewart I), 1972.   **[Sp 284]**

AUCKLAND ISLAND MERGANSER *Mergus australis*   Extinct endemic

58 cm. Distinctive slim shag-like bird. *Dark red-brown head* with long feathers on back of head forming a wispy crest; upperparts dark greyish brown; underparts grey with white mottling. *Long slender orange-yellow bill*, browner above and serrated along cutting edges; legs orange. In flight, white wing-patch and underwing white mottled grey. Sexes alike. **Habitat:** Restricted to coastal waters and streams of Auckland Is since European settlement. Last recorded 1902.   **[Sp 140]**

PIOPIO

North Island

South Island

LAUGHING OWL

HUIA

♂

♀

BUSH WREN

♀

♂

AUCKLAND ISLAND
MERGANSER

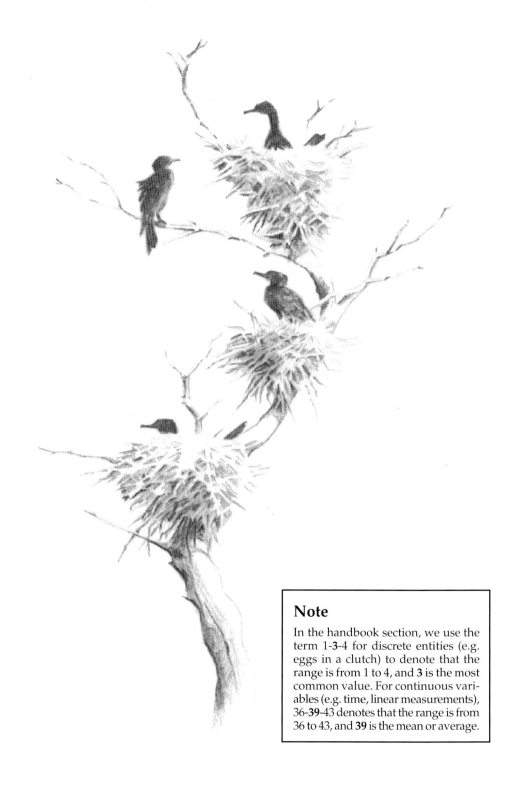

Note

In the handbook section, we use the term 1-**3**-4 for discrete entities (e.g. eggs in a clutch) to denote that the range is from 1 to 4, and **3** is the most common value. For continuous variables (e.g. time, linear measurements), 36-**39**-43 denotes that the range is from 36 to 43, and **39** is the mean or average.

KIWI

3 species: family endemic to New Zealand.

Kiwi are flightless birds standing up to 45 cm high. They are evidently an early offshoot from the evolutionary line of the primitive flightless ratites (moa, emu, cassowary, ostrich and rhea). Kiwi are more closely related to emus than moa. They are one of the oldest members of the New Zealand avifauna as their ancestors are believed to have been in New Zealand when it broke away from Gondwanaland about 65 million years ago.

Kiwi are usually nocturnal, but on Stewart Island some forage by day. They have small eyes but apparently good night vision. Large ears enable good hearing. Kiwi have a very well-developed sense of smell; the nostrils are uniquely placed near the tip of the long, sensitive bill. They can be heard breathing through the nostrils as they explore the ground for food, producing a snuffling sound like that of a hedgehog.

Long, tactile facial bristles surround the base of the bill. The feathers have a simple structure with a single rachis and unlinked barbs, and they hang loose like hair. The wings are minute and largely unfeathered, but they have a soft claw at the tip. They have no tail, and thus look distinctively rounded or pear-shaped. The legs are short and powerful; the three forward-pointing toes and small hind toe have long sharp claws, used for fighting and digging. Other unusual physical features of kiwi are that females have a pair of functional ovaries rather than just one, and that the body temperature and metabolic rate are lower than in most other birds.

Kiwi live from sea level to alpine tussock-land and herbfields at about 1500 m asl. They are mostly in native forest but are also found in scrubland, rough farmland, swamps and pine forests, especially where native vege-tation remains in the gullies. Diet is mainly invertebrates, particularly insect larvae, worms and spiders, taken from the soil by plunging their bill deep into the earth, often right up to the 'hilt'. Kiwi also eat fallen fruits.

Females are larger and heavier than males. In proportion to the size of the female, the egg is very large at about 15–20% of body weight. It is also very rich in nutrients and energy. She lays 1–2 white or greenish eggs in a burrow, in a hollow log or under dense vegetation, the eggs laid 2–4 weeks apart. The very long incu-bation of 65–85 days is by the male only in the Little Spotted Kiwi and the Brown Kiwi in the North Island, by the male and female in the Great Spotted Kiwi and the Brown Kiwi in the South Island, and by the pair and helpers in the Brown Kiwi on Stewart Island. Brood patches develop on incubating birds. Each chick hatches fully feathered and first leaves the nest about a week later. It feeds unaccompanied, and returns less and less often to the nest. The young usually stay in the territory for several months, but they disperse as the next breeding season approaches, except on Stewart Island, where family groups remain together.

Although seldom seen, kiwi indicate their presence by their penetrating calls. Call rates are highest in the two hours after dusk and before dawn. Males and females often duet, with the male call being a drawn-out, ascending, shrill whistle note, repeated 15–25 times, whereas the female call is a hoarse, guttural note, repeated 10–20 times.

The range and number of all kiwi species has been reduced since humans arrived in New Zealand, but especially over the last hundred years. Forest clearance has reduced available habitat, and populations have become fragmented and isolated, but the main impact now is from introduced predators: possums damage eggs, and mustelids and feral cats kill young chicks, and adults are especially at risk from dogs, ferrets and poorly set possum traps. Kiwi are sometimes killed on roads at night. Injured kiwi have been kept in captivity, and much has been learned of their habits. Brown Kiwi and, recently, Little Spotted Kiwi have been bred in captivity, and Brown Kiwi are on display at captive breeding facilities in New Zealand and overseas.

Reading: www.kiwirecovery.org.nz. *DoC Threatened Species Rec Plan Ser* No. 2. Fuller, E. (ed) 1990. *Kiwis*. Auckland: SeTo Publishing. Peat, N. 1999. *Kiwi: NZ's Remarkable Bird*. Auckland: Godwit. Reid, B. & Williams, G.R. 1975. In *Biogeography and Ecology in New Zealand*. The Hague: Junk.

1. BROWN KIWI *Apteryx australis* Plate 1

Other names: Rowi (Okarito), Tokoeka (Fiordland and Stewart Island)
Size: 40 cm; male 2.2 kg, female 2.8 kg
Geographical variation: Results of recent genetic studies show that the Brown Kiwi should be split into three quite distinct, but similar looking species: 'Brown Kiwi' *Apteryx mantelli* in the North Island, 'Rowi' *Apteryx rowi* near Okarito, and 'Tokoeka' *Apteryx australis* with distinct varieties near Haast, in northern Fiordland, in southern Fiordland and on Stewart Island.

Distribution: Subfossil and Maori midden remains indicate that Brown Kiwi were widespread throughout mainland New Zealand in pre-European times. Since 1900, their range has contracted markedly and many populations have become fragmented and isolated, while others have become locally extinct. Still locally common north of Whangarei and well established on Little Barrier, Kawau and Ponui Islands in the Hauraki Gulf. Sparsely distributed, but sometimes locally common, in the Coromandel Peninsula, the Bay of Plenty, from Gisborne to the northern Ruahine Range, and from Tongariro through the Whanganui/Taranaki hinterland and on Mt Taranaki. A small population (c. 50 birds) on the higher parts of Kapiti Island seems to be partly from Fiordland stock introduced in the early 1900s. The South Island has three separate and sparse populations: in lowland forests between Okarito and the Waiho River (West Coast), in the mountains just south of Haast, and in Fiordland from the Hollyford Valley to Preservation Inlet. Brown Kiwi remain common on Stewart Island.

Population: North Island, widespread and locally common; Okarito 200 in 2004; Haast 200–300; Fiordland, widespread; Stewart Island widespread and common; captivity c. 120 in 2005.

Conservation: Protected threatened endemic. The fragmentation and decline of populations has been alarming and continues even though forest clearance has almost ceased. Since the 1970s, the disappearance of Brown Kiwi from apparently suitable habitat has been noted in Northland, King Country, Kaimanawa Range, Hawke's Bay and parts of eastern Fiordland. Many populations are not self-sustaining because adult mortality (from ferrets, dogs, pigs, possum traps and natural causes) exceeds breeding productivity, which is low because possums, mustelids and cats eat eggs or young chicks.

In the 1990s, much effort has been directed at identifying the main threats to kiwi and trying to manage key mainland populations in the wild by controlling predators. The small number of Brown Kiwi in captivity at nocturnal houses in New Zealand and overseas has provided opportunities for research and education, and is managed in a way to maintain genetically pure lines from different parts of the country. Although breeding success is variable, the captive population is close to self-sustaining.

Breeding: Most eggs are laid in June–December, in a burrow, hollow log or sometimes under dense vegetation. North Island birds lay 1–**2**–3 clutches of 1–2 white eggs (124 x 80 mm; 440 g). The eggs are laid 3–4 weeks apart, and the male incubates for 75–90 days. Other species lay 1–2 clutches of 1 pale green egg (133 x 84 mm; 530 g), which male and female incubate for 65–75 days. On Stewart Island, juveniles remain with their parents and share with incubation. Incubating birds develop a brood patch.

The chick hatches fully feathered and remains in the nest about a week before venturing out unaccompanied. The chick returns to the nest by day for several weeks. Brown Kiwi chicks in the North Island become independent at 2–5 weeks old and disperse from the natal territory, but elsewhere juveniles remain in their parental territory for up to 5 years. Growth continues up to 5 years. First breeding is at 1–8 years old. Most pairs are monogamous and persist through the year and between years. The oldest bird recorded in the wild is over 30 years old, but some probably live at least 60 years.

Behaviour: Most vocal in winter and spring. The male call (higher-pitched and clearer) is often answered immediately by its mate; sometimes they call simultaneously. The male and female of a pair usually feed separately at night, but spend about 20% of days together. During courtship, a pair often remains together for hours, with the birds making loud grunts and snuffling sounds. **Feeding:** Diet is mostly invertebrates but includes some fallen fruits and occasional leaves. Main prey are earthworms, larvae of beetles, cicadas and moths, spiders, orthopterans (weta and crickets) and centipedes, with the proportions varying from place to place and with season. Most are taken from the soil, rotting logs or the surface. When feeding, the bird walks slowly along, tapping the ground and sniffing loudly; it often plunges its bill deep into the earth, right up to the 'hilt'. Sometimes the bird digs a small crater up to 15 cm deep and 10 cm wide when it is struggling to extract a large earthworm.

In the hand: Sexes of adults are distinguished by bill length: males 81–**100**–120 mm, females 111–**130**–157 mm with much regional variation, but little overlap within populations. Females are heavier (2090–**2750**–4010 g for non-gravid birds) than males (1720–**2250**–3060 g). The bill of some birds continues to grow for at least the first 5 years.

Reading: Baker, A.J. *et al.* 1995. *Proc. Natl. Acad. Sci. USA* 92: 8254–8258. Burbidge, M.L. *et al.* 2003, *Cons. Genetics* 4: 167–177. Colbourne, R. & Kleinpaste, R. 1984. *Notornis* 31: 191–201. McLennan, J.A. 1988. *NZ J Ecol* 11: 89–97. McLennan, J.A. & Potter, M.A. 1992. *NZ J Ecol.* 16: 91–97. McLennan, J.A. *et al.* 1987. *NZ J Ecol* 10: 97–107. McLennan, J.A. *et al.* 1996. *NZ J Ecol* 20: 27–35. Potter, M.A. 1990. *NZ J Ecol* 14: 17–24. Taborsky, B. & Taborsky, M. 1992. *Ibis* 134: 1–10. Tennyson, A.J.D. *et al.* 2003. *Rec. Auck Mus.* 40: 55–64.

2. LITTLE SPOTTED KIWI *Apteryx owenii* Plate 1

Other name: Kiwi-pukupuku
Size: 30 cm; male 1150 g, female 1325 g
Distribution: Subfossil and Maori midden remains indicate that Little Spotted Kiwi were widespread throughout mainland New Zealand in pre-European times. A single specimen collected in the Tararua Ranges in 1875 is the only recent record in the North Island. Many specimens were collected in the South Island. They were still common in Westland at the start of the twentieth century, but they have declined dramatically and now only a few scattered birds may persist in forests between Fiordland and northwestern Nelson. A few survived on D'Urville Island, Marlborough Sounds, until the 1980s, when the final two were shifted to nearby predator-free Long Island, where they have bred with birds brought from Kapiti Island. The main population is on Kapiti Island; their origin is not clear, but they were probably introduced in the 1920s from the South Island. Small populations have been established recently on Hen Island, Tiritiri Matangi Island, Red Mercury Island, and Long Island (Marlborough Sounds).

Population: 1400 in 2005: Kapiti Island c. 1200, Hen Island 100, Tiritiri Matangi Island 60, Red Mercury Island 40, Long Island 30, captivity 3.
Conservation: Protected endangered endemic. The main population, on Kapiti Island, is apparently stable, has many juveniles and may have benefited from the eradication of possums in the 1980s. The population seems near carrying capacity, because gaps created by transfers to other islands are filled quickly. Fire or the introduction of predators is a risk for the species, and so a programme is under way to establish populations on other islands also free from mustelids and cats. In 1983, 12 birds were transferred to Red Mercury Island, and by 2001 there were at least 50 birds. In 1988–89, 38 birds were transferred to Hen Island, and by 1995 there were at least 50 birds. Two birds from D'Urville Island and three from Kapiti Island were introduced to Long Island between 1981 and 1987, and by 2003 there were at least 30 birds on the island. In 1993, five pairs were transferred from Kapiti to Tiritiri Matangi Island, and a further six birds were added in 1995; by 2002 the

population stood at 50 birds. In 2000–01, 40 Kapiti Island birds were transferred to Karori Sanctuary, Wellington, and they have bred well.

Breeding: Most eggs are laid in September–January. They lay **1**–2 white eggs (110 x 70 mm; 300 g) in a burrow, in a hollow log or under dense vegetation. In two-egg clutches (rare), the eggs are laid 2–3 weeks apart. Incubation is by the male only and takes 65–75 days. The chick hatches fully feathered and remains in the nest 4–5 days before venturing out unaccompanied. It returns to the nest for several weeks but may stay away for the odd day. Chicks seem to stay close to their natal territory for at least 6–9 months before dispersing to find a vacant territory. Growth continues for at least 30 months, but sometimes they form pairs before fully grown. Pairs are monogamous and persist all year and between years. The oldest bird recorded in the wild was at least 22 years old in 2002, but life expectancy on Kapiti Island is c. 45 years.

Behaviour: Most vocal in spring and summer. The male call (higher pitched and clearer) is often answered immediately by its mate. The male and female of a pair usually feed separately at night but spend about 25% of days together. During courtship, pairs often remain together for hours and make loud grunts and snuffling sounds.

Feeding: Diet is mostly small invertebrates but includes some fallen fruits and occasional leaves. Main prey are earthworms, larvae of beetles, cicadas, flies and moths, spiders and adult beetles, with the proportions varying from place to place and with season. Most are taken from the upper layer of the soil, leaf litter or rotting logs. When feeding, the bird walks slowly along, tapping the ground and sniffing loudly; it sometimes plunges its bill into the earth, but rarely right up to the 'hilt'.

In the hand: The adult male develops a brood patch in summer. Sexes can be distinguished by size, with no overlap in adult bill measurements: males 62–**68**–73 mm, females 75–**84**–94 mm. Adult females are heavier (1010–**1350**–1920 g for non-gravid birds) than adult males (880–**1125**–1450 g). Birds in good condition under 1000 g are considered juveniles, but males in poor condition (e.g. after incubation) can be as light as 880 g. The bill of juveniles continues growing for at least the first 30 months. Adult females have greyer backs and smaller, paler legs and toenails than the otherwise similar juvenile Great Spotted Kiwi.

Reading: Colbourne, R. *et al.* 1990. *NZ J Zool.* 17: 533–542. Colbourne, R. 1992. *J Roy Soc NZ* 22: 321–328. Colbourne, R.M. & Robertson, H.A. 1997. *Notornis* 44: 253–258. Jolly, J.N. 1989. *J Roy Soc NZ* 19: 433–448. Jolly, J.N. 1990. In *Kiwis*. Auckland: SeTo Publishing. Robertson, H.A. *et al.* 1993. *Notornis* 40: 253–262.

3. GREAT SPOTTED KIWI *Apteryx haastii* Plate 1

Other names: Roroa, Roa
Size: 45 cm; male 2.4 kg, female 3.3 kg
Distribution: Subfossil and Maori midden remains indicate that Great Spotted Kiwi have always been restricted to the South Island. In the 1800s, they were recorded throughout Westland, western Canterbury and north-western Nelson, but in the 1900s their range in Westland has contracted from the south to about the Taipo River, near Hokitika. Great Spotted Kiwi remain locally common in three recently isolated populations: from north-western Nelson (e.g. Heaphy Track) to north of the Buller River near Westport, in the Paparoa Ranges, and in the Southern Alps from the Hurunui River to Arthur's Pass. Ten

birds released at Lake Rotoiti in 2004–05.
Population: 20,000 birds. Northwestern Nelson to Buller River, widespread and locally common; Paparoa Range, widespread and common in some areas; Hurunui River to Arthur's Pass, widespread and locally common in higher forests.
Conservation: Protected threatened endemic. The fragmentation and decline of populations this century has been slower than for the Brown Kiwi, and apparently stable populations remain in remote wet country in northwestern Nelson and northern Westland. However, since 1900, the disappearance of local populations from apparently suitable habitat has been noted in parts of the Grey

Valley and northern Westland. Some populations are likely to be not self-sustaining because adult mortality (from dogs, pigs, possum traps and natural causes) exceeds breeding productivity, which is low because possums, mustelids and possibly cats eat eggs or young chicks.

One concern for Great Spotted Kiwi is that none are established on a predator-free island (19 birds transferred from Nelson to Little Barrier Island in 1915 failed to establish). Since the 1980s, effort has been directed at studying the ecology of Great Spotted Kiwi, identifying their distribution and monitoring the three main populations.

Breeding: Most eggs are laid in July–December. They lay **1** white egg (124 x 77 mm; 435 g) in a hole among roots of a tree, in a hollow log, in a burrow or sometimes under a fallen log or in dense vegetation. The male incubates during the day and for about half the night, but the female incubates for half the night while the male feeds. The incubation period is c. 70 days. Little is known of chick development, but like other kiwi the Great Spotted hatches fully feathered and remains in the nest for a week before venturing out; it reaches adult size at c. 4 years. Pairs are monogamous and persist all year and between years.

Behaviour: Call rate is fairly even throughout the night, with a peak just before dawn, and they are most vocal in summer. The male call (higher-pitched and clearer) is often answered immediately by its mate. The male and female of a pair usually feed separately at night, but spend about 40% of days together. Great

Spotted Kiwi are much warier of humans than are other kiwi, and often slip away from their daytime shelters well before they are seen.

Feeding: Diet is mostly invertebrates and fallen fruits, along with occasional leaves. Main prey are earthworms, beetles, spiders, centipedes and fruit, but weta, freshwater crayfish and *Powelliphanta* snails have also been recorded. Most food is taken from the soil, leaf litter or rotting logs. When feeding, the bird walks slowly along, tapping the ground and sniffing loudly; it sometimes plunges its bill deep into the earth, right up to the 'hilt'. Sometimes the bird digs a distinctive small crater up to 15 cm deep and 10 cm wide when it is struggling to extract a large earthworm.

In the hand: Sexes are distinguished by size, with little overlap in adult bill measurements: males 83–**97**–104 mm, females 103–**120**–135 mm. Females are significantly heavier (2850–**3300**–4300 g) than males (1750–**2400**–3000 g). Great Spotted Kiwi are considered to be juvenile if the product of body weight (kg) and bill length (cm) is less than 16.0 for males and 27.6 for females, but young females pass through a stage when they cannot be distinguished from adult males. Juvenile Great Spotted Kiwi can look like adult Little Spotted Kiwi, but have a browner back and legs, and have brown (not ivory or pale pink) claws.

Reading: McLennan, J.A. 1990. In *Kiwis*. Auckland: SeTo Publishing. McLennan J.A. & McCann, A.J. 1991. *DSIR Land Resources Contract Report* 91/48, Department of Conservation. McLennan J.A. & McCann, A.J. 1991. *NZ J Ecol* 15: 163–166. McLennan, J.A. & Potter, M.A. 1993. *Notornis* 40: 294–297. McLennan J.A. *et al.* 1996. *NZ J Ecol*. 20: 27–35.

GREBES   Podicipedidae

20 species; 4 in New Zealand region, including 1 endemic.

An ancient group of diving birds, quite unrelated to the family Anatidae (swans, geese, ducks), grebes may have diverged early

on from the lineage that gave rise to the penguins, petrels, pelicans and storks.

Grebes are aquatic specialists, usually living on clear, shallow freshwater lakes and ponds, particularly those with mud, clay or sand on the bottom and emergent or floating vegetation. Their lobed toes (not webbed) propel and steer them underwater. Their tails are a vestigial tuft only, not a rudder. Their large feet are set well back, making them efficient swimmers but clumsy on land, which they avoid. Their small narrow wings are not used in swimming but are used for flight, mainly at night. In winter, many gather on large lakes or (seldom in New Zealand) in estuaries and harbours.

Sexes are alike, but males are larger than females on average and have longer bills. Fish-eating grebes have long, pointed bills, whereas invertebrate-eaters have short, stubby bills. Most, especially fish-eaters, swallow their own feathers, especially breast and flank feathers, which may help in the forming of pellets.

The nest is a mass of sodden waterweed and sticks, attached to submerged or emergent vegetation. The eggs, laid at intervals of about two days, are white but soon become stained brown. They are covered with vegetation when the bird leaves the nest. Young chicks often ride on their parents' backs. The chicks of almost all grebes have stripes on the head and neck, remnants of which remain for several months after they have become independent juveniles. After breeding, most grebes moult all their flight feathers at once and so are flightless for several weeks; presumably true of New Zealand grebes also.

4. AUSTRALASIAN CRESTED GREBE   *Podiceps cristatus*   Plate 2

Other names: Puteketeke, Kamana, Southern Crested Grebe, Great Crested Grebe
Size: 50 cm, 1100 g
Geographical variation: Three subspecies: *cristatus* breeds in the Palaearctic, *infuscatus* in Africa, and *australis* in Australasia.
Distribution: Throughout Europe, Africa and parts of Asia to Australia and New Zealand. In New Zealand, Crested Grebes breed in the South Island only, on lowland lakes west of the Southern Alps and on subalpine and alpine lakes within and east of the main ranges, with the greatest density in inland Canterbury.

In some winters, some move to coastal lakes and estuaries; e.g. 64 gathered for the winter of 1995 on Lake Forsyth, near Lake Ellesmere. A few, perhaps vagrants from Australia, have been seen in the North Island at Lake Rotorua (1975–76 and two in 1979). Subfossil and midden records in the North Island suggest that they formerly had a wider distribution.
Population: c. 350 birds in 2004: c. 10 in Marlborough, c. 20 on the West Coast, c. 200 in Canterbury, c. 100 in Otago and c. 20 in Fiordland.
Conservation: Protected threatened native. Since 1900, Crested Grebes have disappeared from Lakes Rotoiti and Rotoroa in Nelson, except as occasional visitors. Moderately common on inland lakes of Marlborough, such as McRae and Guyon, and up to 15 were seen in 1985–86 on Lake Rotorua, near Kaikoura. They have declined severely on the West Coast, in Fiordland and western Southland; e.g. they are absent from traditional strongholds such as Lakes Gunn and Fergus and have become very rare on Paringa, Brunner, Ianthe, Te Anau, Manapouri and Monowai. They remain stable in inland Canterbury and have occupied several artificial hydro lakes, but their low numbers and concentration on four groups of lakes (Pearson, Coleridge, Ashburton and Alexandrina) leave them vulnerable to human interference and habitat changes.
Breeding: Prefer large clear lakes of glacial origin, provided there is some aquatic vegetation for building and anchoring the nest. Both sexes build the nest, which is attached to submerged branches, often under willows in water over a metre deep. They lay 1–**3**–7 eggs (57 x 36 mm) in September–February, mostly December–January. Both sexes incubate for 23–**26**–31 days, starting when the first egg is laid. The chicks stay near the nest until all have hatched. Both adults feed the chicks and often carry them on their backs.
Behaviour: Usually breed as territorial pairs but come together in loose flocks in winter.

They are silent except when breeding.
Feeding: Diet is mainly fish and aquatic invertebrates. They feed underwater and can tolerate rough water and poor underwater visibility. Larger fish are brought to the surface for swallowing. They also swallow feathers, removed mostly from their breast and flanks while preening, and feed chicks small fish mixed with these wetted and pulverised feathers.

Reading: O'Donnell, C.F.J. 1981. *Notornis* 28: 212–213. O'Donnell, C.F.J. 1982. *Notornis* 29: 151–156. Sagar, P.M. 1981. *Notornis* 28: 301–310. Sagar, P.M. & O'Donnell, C.F.J. 1982. *Notornis* 29: 143–149.

5. NEW ZEALAND DABCHICK   *Poliocephalus rufopectus*   Plate 2

Other name: Weweia
Size: 29 cm, 250 g
Distribution: Well distributed in the North Island, on coastal lakes from North Cape to Pukekohe and from southern Taranaki to Paraparaumu; on the lakes and dams of the Volcanic Plateau, especially Rotoiti and southern Taupo; and in the east, on the lakes and dams of Gisborne, Hawke's Bay and the Wairarapa. In autumn, many birds gather on favoured lakes, especially the southern end of Taupo, on Rotoiti, Okareka (Rotorua district), Hatuma (Waipukurau), Horo-whenua (Levin), and sewage oxidation ponds, especially those of Masterton, Waikanae and Marton. They do not flock on estuaries or coastal bays, as small grebes do elsewhere. Wintering birds appear in some localities where few breed, e.g. Lakes Hatuma and Horowhenua. Vagrants reach Marlborough.
Population: c. 1700 (c. 100 Northland, c. 500 Volcanic Plateau, c. 400 Hawke's Bay, c. 150 Wairarapa, c. 400 Manawatu). Extinct in the South Island.
Conservation: Protected threatened endemic. Formerly sparingly distributed on lowland lakes of the South Island but declined rapidly in the nineteenth century, of unknown causes. The last certain breeding record was on Lake Fergus, upper Eglinton Valley (1941). The only recent records are three single birds in Marlborough (June 1987, October 2001 and December 2001). The widespread construction of farm dams and ponds, which Dabchicks may use for breeding, and sewage oxidation ponds, which they often winter on, has been to their advantage recently.

Breeding: An extended breeding season, with laying in June–March, mostly September–December. They lay **2**–3 eggs (43 x 29 mm, 18 g) in a depression in a pile of decomposing plant material, which is usually floating and anchored to a willow branch or emergent vegetation, or in shallow water resting on the bottom. The eggs are white but soon become stained brown. Both sexes incubate for 22–23 days, starting when the first egg is laid. Whenever an adult leaves the nest without being flushed, it covers the eggs. Newly hatched chicks swim and dive freely, and travel on an adult's back, where they are fed. They may need 10 weeks to become fully independent.

Behaviour: In pairs in the breeding season but congregate to form large loose flocks in autumn and winter. They seem unaffected by duck shooting, being small and not rising from the water when disturbed. They fly from one water body to another only at night; by day they dive, swim or skitter across the surface if disturbed. In mild alarm, a Dabchick floats stern-on with the rear-end fluffed out, presenting a white eye-like pattern to the human intruder or another Dabchick approaching its territory. Dabchicks are silent.

Feeding: Diet is mainly aquatic insects (especially water-boatmen) and their larvae, and small molluscs taken underwater. Larger food, such as fish and freshwater crayfish are sometimes taken. Unlike many grebes, the Dabchick does not eat feathers, presumably because of its invertebrate diet.

In the hand: Males are larger than females, but most measurements overlap. Birds with a bill longer than 22.5 mm are considered males, those with shorter bills are considered females.

Reading: Buddle, G.A. 1939. *Emu* 39: 77–84. Heather, B.D. 1988. *Notornis* 35: 185–191. Lusk, C.H. & Lusk, J.R. 1981. *Notornis* 28: 203–208.

6. HOARY-HEADED GREBE *Poliocephalus poliocephalus* Plate 2

Size: 28 cm, 250 g

Distribution: Australia, mostly south of 20°S, and in Tasmania. First New Zealand records were in 1975, at The Snares and at Lake Horowhenua. A pair bred near Te Anau in 1975–76, and later two pairs bred until 1978. In the late 1970s, there were many widely scattered sightings, mostly of single birds that did not stay long, from Northland to Southland. Records after 1980 are few and mainly in the South Island, but to date they have failed to become established.

Breeding: Similar to New Zealand Dabchick. In Australia, they lay 4–5 eggs (40 x 28 mm, 16 g), mostly in October–January, and chicks are recorded November–February.

Feeding: Their diet of aquatic invertebrates taken underwater is similar to that of the New Zealand Dabchick.

Reading: Storer, R.W. 1987. *Emu* 87: 150–157.

7. AUSTRALASIAN LITTLE GREBE
Tachybaptus novaehollandiae Plate 2

Other name: Australasian Grebe
Size: 25 cm, 220 g
Geographical variation: Six subspecies confined to Australasia; the nominate subspecies *novaehollandiae* is in Australia, southern New Guinea and New Zealand.
Distribution: Widely distributed through Australasia from Java to New Caledonia and New Zealand. They are mainly found in southern Australia, including Tasmania. The first New Zealand records were near Arrowtown (1968–69) and Dargaville (1972). In the North Island, Little Grebes have become established on sheltered reed-fringed small lakes, dune lakes and farm ponds from Cape Reinga to Lake Kereta, South Kaipara Head. They form small flocks of up to 20 birds in autumn, especially on the Aupouri Peninsula. A pair bred at Lake Rotoehu, Rotorua, in 2002. In the South Island, pairs or family parties were

seen until the mid-1980s on widely scattered lakes from Marlborough to Southland, but despite a promising start, breeding pairs have persisted only in coastal South Canterbury, and more recently at Farewell Spit.

Population: Over 100 birds in 2005, mainly in Northland and South Canterbury.

Conservation: Protected self-introduced native, maintaining a tenuous hold in New Zealand. Sometimes seen on the same lakes as Dab-chicks, but it is not known if they compete.

Breeding: In New Zealand, young have been recorded in January–April. The nest is a floating pile of decomposing plant material, anchored to reeds, water lillies or willows. In Australia, they lay 2–4–5 eggs (36 x 25 mm), which both sexes incubate for c. 23 days.

Behaviour: Very wary and secretive when nesting. At the first hint of danger, they sink silently beneath the surface, leaving only the periscope of the head above the water. Usually silent but utter loud trills when courting.

Feeding: Diet in Australia is mostly small fish, snails and aquatic insects, which they catch mainly by diving, but they also swim on the surface with head and neck immersed and turned from side to side, or snatch from the surface or from plants. They swallow feathers deliberately.

Reading: Chance, G.R. 1969. *Notornis* 16: 3–4. Marchant, S. *et al.* 1989. *Aust Birds* 23: 2–6. Miller, P. 1973. *Notornis* 20: 272–275.

ALBATROSSES   Diomedeidae

14 species, 11 with breeding restricted to the Southern Hemisphere and 3 in the North Pacific.* In the New Zealand region, 10 species have been recorded including 2 endemic species and 5 other breeding species.

Albatrosses and mollymawks (the common name in New Zealand for smaller albatrosses) are a clearly defined group of very large seabirds belonging to the tube-nosed petrel order (Procellariiformes). Although they are among the largest of all flying birds, alba-trosses are noted for their perfection of soaring flight behind boats and among the tempes-tuous seas of the southern oceans. In strong winds, they wheel effortlessly on very long, narrow and stiffly held wings for hours, but in almost calm conditions they have a flapping flight and more usually rest on the surface until the wind picks up. Their webbed feet are used for swimming and as rudders in flight, especially when coming in to land.

Albatrosses have long bills with a strongly hooked tip and small, raised tubular nostrils on either side near the base. The shape and colour of the bill plates can be useful in identifying beach-wrecked specimens, but at sea the head colour and pattern of black on the wings is also important to note.

They nest in loose colonies, mainly on uninhabited and often inaccessible islands of the southern oceans. At their breeding grounds they have an elaborate series of displays accompanied by neighs, groans, baahs, wails, croaks, cackles, and bill-snapping and clappering. All species lay 1 white egg, usually in a shallow depression on top of a pedestal ('chimney pot') made of vegetation and mud. Incubation takes 66–83 days. Nestlings are downy and take many months to reach flying age. With this long breeding cycle, some species can nest only every second year if they have bred successfully.

Albatrosses feed mainly on various squids, fish and offal, on or close to the surface. Some species are readily attracted to boats and follow them for hours, occasionally alighting to pick up scraps cast overboard or food disturbed in the wake. Some are especially attracted to fishing boats, and in recent years several species have suffered high mortality from being drowned in trawl nets or after

---

*The Black-footed Albatross *Diomedea nigripes* of the North Pacific has been recorded once in the Southern Hemisphere, at Dusky Sound, Fiordland, in 1884.

taking baited fish-hooks on tuna long-lines. Research is under way to develop new methods to reduce seabird by-catch problems.
Reading: Harrison, P. 1987. *Seabirds of the World: a photographic guide.* London: Christopher Helm. Harrison, P. 1988. *Seabirds: an identification guide.*

London: Christopher Helm. Murphy, R.C. 1936. *Oceanic Birds of South America.* New York: MacMillan. Serventy, D.L. *et al.* 1971. *The Handbook of Australian Sea-birds.* Sydney: Reed. Warham, J. 1990. *The Petrels: their ecology and breeding systems.* London: Academic Press.

8. WANDERING ALBATROSS *Diomedea exulans* Plate 3

Other names: Toroa, Wanderer, Snowy Albatross
Size: 115 cm, 6.5 kg
Geographical variation: Recent taxonomic research suggests that the four subspecies should be reclassified as full species, two of which breed in the New Zealand region: *antipodensis* on the Antipodes and Campbell Islands, and *gibsoni* on the Auckland Islands. The Snowy Albatross *chionoptera* regularly visits New Zealand waters, whereas *dabbenena* of Tristan da Cuhna and Gough Island in the South Atlantic is not definitely known from New Zealand.
Distribution: Circumpolar, breeding on islands between 37 and 55°S in the South Atlantic and South Indian Oceans, Macquarie Island and, in the New Zealand region, at the Antipodes, Auckland and Campbell Islands. They wander widely in southern oceans between the pack ice off Antarctica and the subtropics. Birds breeding in the New Zealand subantarctic remain in the Tasman Sea and South Pacific Ocean, but *chionoptera* regularly reach New Zealand waters, judging by records of banded birds found dead on the coast. Wandering Albatrosses are seen in all months, but mainly in winter, off the coast, especially around Stewart Island and in Cook Strait.
Population: c. 15,000 breeding pairs in New Zealand out of a world population of about 30,000 pairs, estimated on the basis that c. 60% of the breeding birds are at their colony each year. *antipodensis*: the Antipodes c. 5500 pairs or 33,000 birds in 1995–6; Campbell Island <10 pairs; *gibsoni*: Auckland Islands c. 6000 pairs or 40,000 birds, mostly on Adams Island, but 200–300 pairs nest on Disappointment Island and a few are still on the main Auckland Island.
Conservation: Protected threatened native. Wandering Albatrosses are attracted to feed on offal behind fishing boats and are often

hooked on tuna long-lines (14% of seabird deaths recorded in 1988–97). Females are apparently more likely to be accidentally killed than males. Deaths of breeding adults are particularly worrying in such a long-lived species. Repetition in 1997 of a 1973 transect count on one ridge on Adams Island indicated a 63% decline in the intervening 24 years; however, as Wandering Albatrosses are biennial breeders, the numbers vary from year to year, depending on breeding success the previous year. Similar declines have been noted at other colonies in the southern ocean. Banding studies are under way on Adams Island and at the Antipodes, and accurate censuses are now under way in most years in major colonies to determine population trends in the New Zealand races of Wandering Albatross.
Breeding: Detailed studies have not been carried out in New Zealand. At the Auckland Islands, eggs are laid from mid-January to February, but on the Antipodes and at Campbell Island they do not usually start laying until late January. They lay 1 white egg (126 x 78 mm, 425 g) in a shallow depression on top of a 20–50 cm tall mound of grass and soil. The mound is built on flat ground close to a ridge, where adults can easily catch enough wind for takeoff. Incubation is by both sexes in alternating shifts of 6–10 days during the incubation period of 75–83 days. Chicks are initially covered in very pale grey down and are brooded by both adults for the first month, but are then left unguarded except during feeding visits and occasional longer visits until the chick fledges at c. 9 months old in late December–March and is immediately independent of its parents.

If breeding is successful, adults miss a year before breeding again; but if they fail early in the breeding cycle, most pairs breed in successive years. Pair bonds are life-long, but if a bird loses its mate it can re-pair with another bird. Pairs return to the same nest location year after year, and young return to their natal colony at 3–14 years old, but usually do not start breeding until 7–16 years old. The oldest New Zealand bird recorded was over 24 years old, but some probably live to over 40 years.

Behaviour: Gregarious at breeding colonies and form flocks around fishing boats, but usually wander the oceans alone or in small groups. At sea, they are generally silent except for a hoarse croak, made when they are fighting for scraps.

Feeding: Diet is mainly squid, with occasional fish, octopuses and crustacea, mostly caught at night on the surface or by plunging down a metre or two. During the day, food is scavenged from around whales and dolphins, and recently from behind boats, which has made them vulnerable to accidental capture on baited fish-hooks.

In the hand: The various subspecies are difficult to identify because of the wide variety of immature plumages and the incomplete knowledge of the rate of aquisition of a mature adult plumage. Adult females of *antipodensis* retain dark brown plumage similar to the immature plumage of other subspecies, males often have a prominent dark patch on their crown and an oily smudge across the breast, and both male and female have very little white on their upperwings. Overall, *gibsoni* is paler than *antipodensis* at all ages, and usually shows prominent white patches on the inner upperwing. As the common name Snowy Albatross suggests, adults of the subspecies *chionoptera* are very pale on their head, back and inner upperwings; they also have longer bills than New Zealand birds (males 160–180 mm cf. 145–160 mm; females 155–170 mm cf. 135–150 mm).

Reading: Bailey, A.M. & Sorensen, J.H. 1950. *Subantarctic Campbell Island.* Denver: Denver Mus Nat Hist. Croxall, J.P. *et al.* 1990. *J Anim Ecol* 59: 775–796. Murray, T.E. *et al.* 1993. *Bird Cons Int* 3: 181–210. Robertson, C.J.R. & Warham, J. 1992. *Bull BOC.* 112: 74–81. Robertson, C.J.R. & Warham, J. 1994. *Bull BOC.* 114: 132–134. Walker, K. *et al.* 1991. *DoC Sci & Res Int Rep* No. 109. Weimerskirch, H. *et al.* 1987. *Oikos* 49: 315–322.

9. ROYAL ALBATROSS *Diomedea epomophora* Plate 3

Other name: Toroa
Size: 115 cm, 9 kg
Geographical variation: Recent taxonomic research suggests that the two subspecies should be reclassified as full species: the large Southern Royal Albatross *epomophora* breeding on the Auckland Islands and Campbell Island, and the smaller Northern Royal Albatross *sanfordi* breeding at the Chathams and at Taiaroa Head, Otago. The two forms have interbred at Taiaroa Head.
Distribution: Breed only in New Zealand; on outlying southern islands and on the mainland at Taiaroa Head, at the southern side of the entrance to Otago Harbour near Dunedin. Ranges through New Zealand coastal waters and the Tasman Sea all year but are most commonly seen in winter, especially in Cook Strait, off East Cape and in Foveaux Strait. Most non-breeders, juveniles and young birds migrate eastwards to seas off South America and the Falkland Islands, returning by the South Indian Ocean and below Australia. Occasional stragglers

have been recorded in the subtropical Pacific near Tonga, off Rarotonga and in the Tuamotu Archipelago of French Polynesia.
Population: c. 15,000 pairs. *epomophora*: Campbell Island 8400 pairs, Enderby, Adams and Auckland Islands 70 pairs; *sanfordi*: Sisters Islands, northern Chathams, c. 2500 pairs, Motuhara (Forty Fours Islands), eastern Chathams, c. 4000 pairs, Taiaroa Head 25 pairs.
Conservation: Protected uncommon endemic. Numbers on the subantarctic islands were much reduced by sealers, whalers, farmers and introduced animals, but since the islands have been protected, and sheep, pigs and cattle have been reduced on Campbell Island and removed from Enderby in the Auckland Islands, numbers have increased.

On the Chathams, the northern subspecies was traditionally harvested by Moriori and then Maori until they were legally protected in 1921. Although some illegal harvest continued, the numbers in the Chathams have apparently remained moderately stable since the first detailed counts were made in 1972–75. However, a deterioration of nesting habitat related to soil loss in severe storms and a drier climate has led to a decline in breeding success in recent years because many eggs break in the rudimentary nests built in poor rocky habitats.

A small colony of Northern Royal Albatrosses has become established on Taiaroa Head. Birds prospected the colony as early as the 1890s, but it was not until 1938 that they bred successfully. The colony has grown steadily, mainly from returning chicks but also with some continued immigration from the Chathams, so that by 1999 there were about 25 pairs.

Royal Albatrosses seem moderately stable with few reports of birds being killed on tuna long-lines. Series of carefully timed aerial photographs of some colonies, together with banding recoveries, are being used to monitor long-term population trends.

Breeding: About a month after returning to their colony, Northern Royal Albatrosses lay between 27 October and 6 December, whereas the southern subspecies lays between 24 November and 25 December. They lay 1 white egg (126 x 78 mm, 421 g) in a shallow depression on top of a 10–30 cm tall mound of tussock, thin woody branches, fern and moss. The nest is built on sheltered flat ground, often a long way from a ridge or cliff where adults can catch strong winds or an updraught for takeoff. Incubation is by both sexes in alternating shifts of 2–12 days during the incubation period of 77–81 days.

Chicks are initially covered in white down and are brooded by both parents for the first 5–6 weeks, but are then left unguarded except during feeding visits and occasional longer visits until the chick fledges at c. 8 months old from mid-August to December. It is immediately independent of its parents. If breeding is successful, the adults miss a year before breeding again; but if they fail early in the breeding cycle, most pairs breed in successive years. Pair bonds are life-long, but if a bird loses its mate it can re-pair with another bird. Pairs return to the same nest site year after year, and young return to their natal colony at 3–8 years old, but usually do not start breeding until 6–10 years old. The oldest wild bird recorded in New Zealand is a Northern Royal Albatross, 'Grandma', which reached a banded age of 51.5 years and a probable actual age of over 61 years.

Behaviour: Gregarious at breeding colonies, and small flocks form around fishing boats, but at sea they are usually solitary. Generally silent at sea but noisy when displaying at their nest.

Feeding: Diet of adults is mainly squid, with some fish, crustacea and salps. Food is caught on the surface, and only rarely do birds plunge down a metre or two. They do not seem to regularly take baited long-line hooks.

In the hand: Males are larger than females, with only a slight overlap within subspecies, but female *epomophora* overlap extensively with male *sanfordi*. The southern subspecies *epomophora* is the largest of all albatrosses and is distinctly larger than *sanfordi* in all measurements, e.g. wing 680–705 mm cf. 635–670 mm in males, 650–680 mm cf. 615–635 mm in females; bill 180–190 mm cf. 165–175 mm in males, 165–180 mm cf. 155–165 mm in females.

Reading: Bailey, A.M. & Sorensen, J.H. 1950. *Subantarctic Campbell Island*. Denver: Denver Mus Nat Hist. Richdale, L.E. 1950. *Biol. Monographs* 3. Dunedin: Published privately. Richdale, L.E. 1952. *Biol. Monographs* 4. Dunedin: Published privately. Robertson, C.J.R. 1991. *DoC Sci & Res Ser* No. 35. Robertson, C.J.R. 1993. *Emu* 93: 269–276. Robertson, C.J.R. & Kinsky, F.C. 1972. *Notornis* 19: 289–301.

10.   BLACK-BROWED MOLLYMAWK   *Diomedea melanophrys*   Plate 5

Size: 90 cm, 3 kg

Geographical variation: Recent taxonomic research suggests that the two subspecies should be reclassified as full species: the widespread Subantarctic Black-browed Mollymawk *melanophrys*, and the slightly smaller endemic New Zealand Black-browed Mollymawk *impavida* which breeds only on the Campbell Islands.

Distribution: Circumpolar, breeding on subantarctic islands between 46 and 56°S.

Subantarctic Black-browed Mollymawks breed on islands in the South Atlantic and South Indian Oceans, on Macquarie Island and, in the New Zealand region, at Bollons Island (Antipodes), the Western Chain (The Snares) and at Campbell Island. Non-breeders, juveniles and young birds of this subspecies wander extensively through the southern oceans between about 30°S and the Antarctic coast, and further north off the western coasts of South America and Africa; a few stragglers even cross the equator.

New Zealand Black-browed Mollymawks breed on the northern coast of Campbell Island and on Jeanette Marie, and range widely in New Zealand waters and through the Tasman Sea to eastern Australia. Many immatures move northwards to the Coral Sea and the South Pacific Ocean to about New Caledonia and Fiji, and stragglers have been recorded further east in the subtropical Pacific near Tonga, Samoa, the Cook Islands and in French Polynesia.

Population: The most plentiful of all albatrosses, with a world population of c. 700,000 breeding pairs, mainly breeding on islands off southern Chile and at the Falkland Islands, but c. 24,000 are in the New Zealand region. *melanophrys*: Bollons Island (Antipodes) 120 pairs, Western Chain (The Snares) a few pairs, Campbell Island c. 20 pairs; *impavida*: Campbell Island 23,000 pairs.

Conservation: Protected native. The New Zealand Black-browed Mollymawk is a threatened endemic subspecies; on Campbell Island the population increased until about 1970, declined rapidly until the early 1980s, but has since increased slowly.

Most of the decline in the 1970s was attributed to changes in food supplies as sea temperatures changed and to birds being killed accidentally in fishing operations. Black-browed Mollymawks are attracted to feed on offal behind fishing boats and may be caught on baited hooks of tuna long-lines (the commonest species accidentally caught), or drowned in trawl nets. Males and females appear equally likely to be caught accidentally on long-lines, but juveniles seem especially vulnerable.

Breeding: On Campbell Island, birds return in August and most eggs are laid over a short period between mid-September and early October. Pairs are stable from year to year and return to the same nest site each year. They lay **1** white egg (102 x 66 mm, 230 g), with pinkish speckling at the broader end, in a shallow cup on top of a small pedestal of soil and vegetation. The adults share incubation for c. 70 days, and then share duties guarding the downy chick until it is 15–**23**–34 days old. The chick fledges at 122–**130**–141 days old in mid-April.

Chicks are independent once they fledge and apparently disperse quickly from the colony: one was found dead on Foxton Beach 7 days after it had been banded on Campbell Island. Young return to land from 5 years old, but do not start breeding until 6–**10**–13 years old. Adult survival is about 94.5%, with the oldest banded bird being over 26 years old.

Behaviour: Nest in large close-knit colonies, sometimes intermingling with Grey-headed Mollymawks. At sea, they form large flocks to feed on offal from fishing boats and elsewhere are often found in large mixed flocks of seabirds. At their breeding ground, they have an elaborate series of displays accompanied by baas, wails, croaks, cackles, groans and bill-snapping.

Feeding: Diet has not been studied in New Zealand, but elsewhere in the southern oceans it is mainly fish (often scavenged from fishing boats), squid, krill and carrion. Prey is mainly seized on the surface, and only rarely do birds plunge or dive for food. Their affinity for feeding on scraps from fishing boats has made Black-browed Mollymawks vulnerable to accidental capture.

In the hand: The pale honey-coloured eye of adult birds of the New Zealand subspecies is distinctive in live or freshly dead birds, but they also have a more extensive black eyebrow and are on average smaller than the Subantarctic subspecies (bill 106–**112**–118 mm cf. 114–**117**–122 mm; wing 490–**520**–540 mm cf. 510–**535**–560 mm). Males are slightly larger than females in all measurements.

Reading: Bailey A.M. & Sorensen, J.H. 1950. *Subantarctic Campbell Island.* Denver: Denver Mus Nat Hist. Moore, P.J. & Moffat, R.D. 1990. *DoC Sci & Res Int Rep* No. 59. Waugh, S. *et al.* 1999. *Ibis* 141: 216–225. Warham, J. & Fitzsimons, C.H. 1987. *NZ J Zool* 14: 65–79. Weimerskirch, H. *et al.* 1986. *Ibis* 128: 195–213.

11. SHY MOLLYMAWK   *Diomedea cauta*   Plate 4

Size: 90 cm, 4 kg

Geographical variation: Recent taxonomic research suggests that the four subspecies should be reclassified as full species, three of which breed in the New Zealand region and the fourth (*cauta*) breeds around Tasmania and occasionally visits New Zealand waters. New Zealand White-capped Mollymawks *steadi* breed on Disappointment, Auckland and Adams Islands, Auckland Islands; and a few breed on Bollons Island, Antipodes, and the Forty-Fours, Chathams; Salvin's Mollymawks *salvini* breed at the Bounty Islands and the Western Chain of The Snares; and Chatham Island Mollymawks *eremita* breed at Pyramid Rock, Chathams.

Distribution: Breed widely in the New Zealand subantarctic and on islands off southwestern Tasmania and in Bass Strait, but elsewhere only a few pairs (*salvini*) breed at the Crozet Islands in the South Indian Ocean. At sea, they range widely in the southern oceans, with most records from subantarctic and subtropical waters of the South Pacific north to about 25°S, off South America and off South Africa.

Birds of all local subspecies are seen in New Zealand coastal waters and are the species of mollymawk most often beach-wrecked, mainly from early winter to late spring. Shy Mollymawks are very abundant over continental shelf waters around southern and central New Zealand during most of the year, except that Chatham Island Mollymawks are rarely seen off the mainland coast and most migrate to seas off Chile and Peru.

Population: All but c. 5000 pairs of the world population of 150,000 pairs breed in the New Zealand subantarctic. *steadi*: Auckland Islands – Disappointment Island c. 75,000 pairs, 3000 pairs on Auckland Island, 100 pairs on Adams Island, 20 pairs on Bollons Island and a single pair on the Forty-Fours in 1991 and 1996. *salvini*: Bounty Islands c. 31,000 pairs in 1997, Western Chain of The Snares 1200 pairs; and *eremita*: Pyramid Rock, Chathams 5300 pairs.

Conservation: Protected native. The Chatham Island Mollymawk is a threatened endemic subspecies and has been caught on long-lines

set for tuna, ling and swordfish. Feral pigs have almost wiped out all accessible breeding colonies on main Auckland Island. In the 1980s many White-capped Mollymawks were killed accidentally by fishing operations, most being drowned after having collided with and become entangled in squid trawling gear, but changes to fishing gear seem to have largely alleviated the problem. Many White-capped Mollymawks (15% of all seabirds in 1988–97) are killed on tuna long-lines in New Zealand and Australian waters.

Breeding: On the Auckland Islands, eggs are laid from early November, whereas the other subspecies lay from late August to early October. They lay **1** white egg (103 x 67 mm, 238 g), with reddish-brown flecking at the broader end, in a shallow cup on top of a pedestal of dried mud, feathers, guano and vegetation. The adults share incubation for c. 70 days and then share duties guarding the downy chick for c. 3 weeks. Chicks of *steadi* on the Auckland Islands fledge in August, whereas chicks of the other subspecies fledge in April, aged c. 4.5 months old. The oldest Shy Mollymawk recorded is an Australian bird aged over 16 years.

Behaviour: Breed in large densely packed colonies with nests averaging 1.2 m apart on the Bounty Islands, where they intermingle with Erect-crested Penguins. At sea, Shy Mollymawks sometimes form huge flocks of 2000–3000 birds around fishing boats and are often in large mixed flocks of seabirds.

Feeding: Diet is mainly squid, fish, krill, salps, and offal from fishing boats, mostly seized on the surface. Their affinity for feeding on scraps near fishing boats makes Shy Mollymawks vulnerable to accidental capture or entanglement.

In the hand: Males are larger than females for all measurements, but the ranges overlap extensively. The bill of *eremita* (120 mm) is much shorter than in *salvini* (128 mm), *cauta* (130 mm) or *steadi* (135 mm). The wing of *steadi* (595 mm) is longer than in the similar-looking *cauta* (560 mm).

Reading: Bartle, J.A. 1991. *Bird Cons Int* 1: 351–359. Robertson, C.J.R. & van Tets, G.F. 1982. *Notornis* 29: 311–336.

12. GREY-HEADED MOLLYMAWK *Diomedea chrysostoma* Plate 5

Size: 80 cm, 3.25 kg

Distribution: Circumpolar, breeding on subantarctic islands between 46 and 56°S, with the biggest colonies being on Diego Ramirez Islands near Cape Horn, and on South Georgia. In New Zealand, Grey-headed Mollymawks breed only at Campbell Island, although about 50 pairs nest nearby on Macquarie Island. At sea, they range widely in the southern oceans, generally over deep oceanic waters between 40°S and the Antarctic coast. They are occasionally seen in New Zealand coastal waters and are one of most frequent mollymawk species to be beach-wrecked, especially in July–October when juveniles are moving north into the Tasman Sea.

Population: The annual number of breeding pairs in the world is estimated at c. 92,000 pairs of which c. 7500 pairs nest each year on Campbell Island. The actual breeding population is higher because breeding is biennial for successful pairs.

Conservation: Protected native. Numbers on most subantarctic islands are stable or declining; indications are that Campbell Island birds have declined by about 80% since the 1940s and is currently declining by about 3% per annum due to low recruitment and poor breeding success. Although few Grey-headed Mollymawks are accidentally caught in New Zealand waters because the species feeds in deep water, many are killed on tuna long-lines in Australian waters and elsewhere in the Southern Ocean. The decline on Campbell Island at the same time as New Zealand Black-browed Mollymawks could be associated with changes in food supplies as a result of oceanic warming, which has apparently caused the dramatic decline of Rockhopper Penguins there.

Breeding: Grey-headed Mollymawks, like the large albatrosses, are biennial breeders; if they raise a chick successfully, they will not attempt to breed the following year; but if they fail

(especially in the early part of the nesting cycle), they will breed the following year. On Campbell Island, birds return in late August and most eggs are laid over a short period between 26 September and 9 October. They lay **1** white egg (107 x 67 mm), with brownish-red speckling at the broader end, in a shallow cup on top of a small pedestal of soil and vegetation. The adults share incubation for c. 72 days and then share duties guarding the downy chick until it is 15–**27**–39 days old. The chick fledges at 143–**152**–157 days old in early to mid-May. Chicks are independent once they fledge. Young return to land at 5 years old, but do not start breeding until 10–**13**–17 years old. Adult survival is about 95.3%, with the oldest banded bird being over 28 years old.

Behaviour: Nest in large colonies, intermingling with New Zealand Black-browed Mollymawks on Campbell Island. At sea, Grey-headed Mollymawks feed alone but may form flocks with other seabirds. They seldom follow ships and, except near the Falkland Islands, tend not to congregate around fishing boats as most other mollymawks do. Generally much quieter and more docile than other albatrosses.

Feeding: Diet has not been studied in New Zealand, but elsewhere in the southern oceans it is mainly squid and fish (rarely scavenged from fishing boats) and sometimes krill and carrion such as small seabirds. Prey is mainly seized on the surface, but occasionally birds plunge or dive for food.

In the hand: Males are slightly larger than females in all measurements, but there is considerable overlap.

Reading: Bailey A.M. & Sorensen, J.H. 1950. *Subantarctic Campbell Island.* Denver: Denver Mus Nat Hist. Moore, P.J. & Moffat, R.D. 1990. *DoC Sci & Res Int Rep* No. 59. Waugh, S. *et al.* 1999. *Ibis* 141: 216–225. Weimerskirch, H. *et al.* 1986. *Ibis* 128: 195–213.

13. YELLOW-NOSED MOLLYMAWK
Diomedea chlororhynchos Plate 4

Size: 75 cm, 2.5 kg

Geographical variation: Two subspecies: *chlororhynchos* in the South Atlantic, and *carteri* in the South Indian Ocean. Most Yellow-nosed Albatrosses seen in New Zealand waters are *carteri*, but the nominate subspecies has been recorded three times.

Distribution: Breed on islands in the Atlantic and Indian Oceans between 37 and 47°S and range through the South Atlantic and South Indian Oceans and east to southern Australia and New Zealand. Both adults and juveniles have recently become regular winter visitors to warm coastal waters off eastern Northland, the Hauraki Gulf and the Bay of Plenty, where they often loosely associate with Australasian Gannets. They are occasionally reported off the South Island, especially at Tasman Bay and Kaikoura. South Atlantic birds prospected on Middle Sister Island, Chathams in 1975, 1976 and 1996. Indian Ocean birds bred on The Pyramid, Chathams, 1998–2000.

Feeding: Diet has not been studied in New Zealand, but elsewhere it is mainly fish and squid, with some fish scavenged from fishing boats. Prey is mainly seized on the surface, but birds occasionally plunge or dive for food.

In the hand: The nominate subspecies has a prominent black triangle around and in front of the eye, and the culminicorn broadens behind the nares and is rounded, not pointed, at the base.

Reading: Latham, P.C. 1980. *Notornis* 27: 393–394. Robertson, C.J.R. 1975. *Notornis* 22: 342–344.

14. BULLER'S MOLLYMAWK *Diomedea bulleri* Plate 5

Size: 80 cm, 3 kg

Geographical variation: Recent taxonomic research suggests that the two subspecies should be reclassified as full species: the Southern Buller's Mollymawk *bulleri* breeding on The Snares and on the Solander Islands, and the Northern Buller's Mollymawk *platei* breeding at the Chatham Islands and on Rosemary Rocks, Three Kings Islands.

Distribution: Breed only in New Zealand, near or north of the Subtropical Convergence. The largest colony is on Motuhara Island (Forty Fours), to the east of the Chathams. They are regularly seen in coastal waters and over the continental shelf around southern New Zealand and the Tasman Sea, and they are quite often beach-wrecked in winter, especially on the Southland, Otago and Wellington coasts. Buller's Mollymawks are uncommon in northern New Zealand waters. After breeding they disperse across the South Pacific Ocean, north of the Antarctic Convergence, to the west coast of South America; a few stray into the South Atlantic and South Indian Oceans.

Population: Total population is c. 30,000 breeding pairs: Rosemary Rock, Three Kings Islands, 20 pairs; Sisters Islands, Chathams, 2100 pairs; Forty Fours, Chathams, 16,000 pairs; Solander Islands 4900 pairs; The Snares 8700 pairs.

Conservation: Protected endemic. Numbers of Buller's Mollymawks breeding on The Snares increased 78% between 1969 and 1992, but declined on the Solanders between 1985 and 1996, and the nesting density has apparently declined on the Forty Fours since the 1970s. Many Southern Buller's Mollymawks (8% of all seabirds caught in 1988–97) are caught on tuna long-lines and some are caught in trawl nets, but the many deaths caused by flying into netsonde cables behind squid boats have ceased since these cables were phased out after 1992. On balance, they may have derived some benefit from the increased fishery in southern New Zealand waters; however, further close monitoring of all breeding populations is needed.

Breeding: Northern Buller's Mollymawks return to the Chathams in late September and eggs are laid between 26 October and 23 November, whereas Southern Buller's Mollymawks return to The Snares in mid-December and eggs are laid over a long season, from late December to mid-February. They lay **1** white egg (104 x 65 mm, 246 g), with brownish-red speckling at the broader end, in a shallow cup on top of a small pedestal of soil, rock chips and vegetation. The adults share incubation in stints of 2–4 days in the northern subspecies, but of 10–14 days in the southern form. Incubation lasts 68–72 days and the parents share duties guarding the downy chick until it is c. 21 days old. The chicks fledge at c. 5–6 months old, in June at the Chathams but August–October at The Snares.

Birds apparently mate for life and retain the same nest site from year to year – one pair banded in 1948 was still using the same nest 23 years later, and the female was last seen there in 1993, aged at least 50 years old. **Behaviour:** Nest in large colonies, generally keeping apart from other species. At sea, they are usually solitary but are sometimes seen in small groups and occasionally in large mixed flocks around fishing boats.

Feeding: Diet during the breeding season is mostly squid, with some fish, krill, octopuses, tunicates and carrion such as small seabirds. Prey is mainly seized on the surface, and only rarely do birds plunge or dive for food.

In the hand: Males are slightly larger than females. Although there is much overlap, most can be sexed from a combination of tarsus width and minimum bill depth. The nominate *bulleri* has a narrower bill (male 26.3–30.2 mm, female 25.5–28.1 mm) than *platei* (male 30.7–34.5 mm, female 28.7–32.4 mm).

Reading: Richdale, L.E. & Warham, J. 1973. *Ibis* 115: 257–263. Robertson, C.J.R. 1991. *DoC Sci & Res Ser* No. 35. Robertson, C.J.R. 1994. *DoC CAS Notes* No. 70. Sagar, P.M. *et al.* 1998. *Notornis* 45: 271–278. Sagar, P.M. *et al.* 1994. *Notornis* 41: 85–92. Sagar, P.M. & Warham, J. 1993. *Notornis* 40: 303–304. Warham, J. & Fitzsimons, C.H. 1987. *NZ J Zool* 14: 65–79. West, J.A. & Imber, M.J. 1986. *NZ J Zool* 13: 169–174.

15. LIGHT-MANTLED SOOTY ALBATROSS
Phoebetria palpebrata   Plate 6

Size: 80 cm, 2.75 kg
Distribution: Circumpolar, breeding on subantarctic islands between 46 and 56°S, including the Antipodes, Auckland and Campbell Islands. The biggest colonies are on South Georgia, the Kerguelen and Auckland Islands. At sea, they range widely in the southern oceans, generally over deep oceanic waters between 40°S and the Antarctic coast, but are occasionally seen in New Zealand coastal waters and are most frequently beach-wrecked in July–October, especially on the Auckland west coast.
Population: World population is estimated at 21,500 breeding pairs, of which c. 250 are on the Antipodes, c. 2000 on the Auckland Islands and >1600 pairs on Campbell Island.
Conservation: Protected native. The size and trends of breeding populations in the New Zealand subantarctic are poorly known, but moderate numbers of birds (6% of seabirds identified in 1988–97) have been caught recently on tuna long-lines in New Zealand waters.

Breeding: Biennial breeders; if they raise a chick successfully, they will not attempt to breed the following year; but if they fail (especially in the early part of the nesting cycle), they will breed the following year. On Campbell Island, birds return in early October to the same nesting site on a coastal cliff ledge or a small terrace on a steep slope of an inland peak, but they build a new nest each time. Most eggs are laid over a short period between 24 October and 7 November. They lay **1** white egg (102 x 65 mm, 233 g), with brownish-red speckling at the broader end, in a shallow cup on top of a small pedestal of soil and vegetation. The adults share incubation for c. 67 days in shifts of 12–17 days initially and then shorter shifts as hatching approaches. The parents take 2–4-day shifts brooding the downy chick until it is c. 19 days old. The chick fledges at c. 141 days old in late May to early June. Chicks are independent once they fledge. Young return to their natal colony for several years before starting to breed at an average of 12 years old. Annual survivorship is high and life expectancy is over 30 years.

Behaviour: Nest solitarily or rarely in groups of three or four pairs. At sea, they feed alone or sometimes in small flocks and sometimes gather to feed on scraps tossed from fishing boats. At their breeding ground they have an elaborate series of courtship displays accompanied by a distinctive clear two-syllable 'pee-oo', baas and bill-snapping.

Feeding: Diet has not been studied in New Zealand, but elsewhere in the southern oceans it is mainly squid and krill, also fish and carrion such as small seabirds. Prey is mainly seized on the surface, but birds occasionally plunge for food from just above the surface.

Reading: Bailey A.M. & Sorensen, J.H. 1950. *Subantarctic Campbell Island.* Denver: Denver Mus Nat Hist. Jouventin, P. & Weimerskirch, H. 1990. *Proc 19th Int Orn Congr.* Sorensen, J.H. 1950. *DSIR Cape Exped Series Bull* No. 8. Weimerskirch, H. *et al.* 1987. *J Anim Ecol* 56: 1043–1056. Weimerskirch, H. *et al.* 1986. *Ibis* 128: 195–213.

16. SOOTY ALBATROSS   *Phoebetria fusca*   Plate 6

Size: 80 cm, 2.5 kg

Distribution: Circumpolar, breeding on subantarctic islands between 36 and 49°S in the South Atlantic and South Indian Oceans. The biggest colonies are on Gough Island and Tristan da Cunha. They disperse eastwards along the Subtropical Convergence to deep waters south of Australia and up the eastern seaboard towards the Great Barrier Reef. Three records in New Zealand waters: Auckland Islands (February 1991); Pukaki Rise, southeast of Otago (November 1993); and Antipodes (November 1995).

Feeding: Diet is mainly squid, but fish, krill and carrion such as small seabirds are also taken. Most prey is seized while swimming, but birds occasionally plunge from just above the surface. Sooty Albatrosses often follow boats and feed on scraps cast overboard.

Reading: Weimerskirch, H. *et al.* 1987. *J Anim Ecol* 56: 1043-1056. Weimerskirch, H. *et al.* 1986. *Ibis* 128: 195-213.

SHEARWATERS, FULMARS, PRIONS and PETRELS   Procellariidae

The Procellariidae is the largest and most diverse family of seabirds, with about 72 species. In the New Zealand region, 49 species have been recorded, including 11 endemic species and 23 other breeding species.

The Procellariidae includes a wide variety of seabirds from the giant petrels to the diving petrels. All have distinctive external nostrils encased in a tube on the top or sides of the bill. They have 11 primaries. The 11th (outermost) is minute, but the 10th is at least as long as the 9th, giving the wing a pointed tip. All seabirds have webbed feet with three forward-pointing toes of about the same length.

Most species nest in burrows or crevices, normally clumped into colonies. Birds return to their colony months before egg-laying to claim their nest sites (usually the same site is used year after year) and to court. After copulation, females leave the colony for one to six weeks on a 'pre-laying exodus' to form the egg. Males also leave but often make occasional visits to the nest site.

All species lay one white egg, which is very large relative to the female's size. The few instances of two eggs in a nest are from two females using the same site. A long incubation period is typically split up into several incubation stints lasting from several days to several weeks between changeovers. Occasionally the changeovers do not coincide and the egg is left unattended for several days; however, eggs have hatched successfully after being chilled for six days. Incubation stints shorten as incubation proceeds, and when the egg hatches the downy chick is brooded and guarded for only a few days in hole-nesting species, but for several weeks in surface-nesting species, until it is able to maintain body temperature.

Throughout its development, the chick is fed large meals at irregular intervals. It gains weight rapidly, becoming much heavier than its parents, but this declines towards adult weight before it fledges. Chicks normally spend some time on the surface exercising their wings before they eventually leave the colony. Once they have flown, they are completely independent of their parents. Young birds usually return to their home colony at 2–7 years old, and spend several years visiting the colony, especially when breeders are incubating or feeding chicks, before attempting to breed. The Procellariidae are typically long-lived, with several species known to live over 25 years.

Most species now breed only on offshore and outlying islands because mainland colonies have been ravaged by introduced mammalian predators. They generally return to their colonies at night, and once on land they are clumsy and unable to take flight rapidly; their only defence is by biting or by spitting stomach oil. The nestling is particularly vulnerable to predators because it is often left unattended for long periods while the parents feed at sea and it emerges from the nest at night to exercise its wings in the week or two before it can fly.

The Procellariidae feed on a wide variety of sea life, ranging from some of the prions, which sieve zooplankton on comb-like lamellae along the edge of their bills, to the giant petrels, which scavenge on dead marine mammals and occasionally kill small seabirds. Most species feed within a few metres of the sea surface, but some shearwaters dive to at least 20 m. These seabirds have well-developed nasal glands for extracting salt from their blood and exuding it out of the prominent nostrils.

The shearwaters (*Calonectris, Puffinus*) include about 15 medium to large species with long slender bills and flat nasal tubes. They are usually brown to black above and white or brown below. Some have large sternums and dive well for fish and squid, using their wings for propulsion, while others have small sternums and feed on, or close to, the surface.

The four species of diving petrel (*Pelecanoides*) are small, stocky black and white seabirds with short wings adapted for propulsion under water. They have a fast, direct, whirring flight and readily dive for small krill and copepods.

The four species of *Procellaria* are large stocky seabirds with large, heavily hooked pale bills with dark markings and prominent nostrils. They feed mainly at night on bioluminescent squid but also now take offal discarded from fishing boats.

The three species of *Pseudobulweria* are medium-sized seabirds with exceptionally large feet and a notch on the cutting edge of the upper bill caused by the latericorns having blunt ends.

The fulmarine petrels (*Lugensa, Pagodroma, Daption, Thalassoica, Fulmarus* and *Macronectes*) are a diverse group of 8 species, all of which have robust bills with prominent joined nasal tubes, rising from the base.

The six species of prion (*Pachyptila*) are small seabirds pale blue above and white below with a prominent M-shaped mark across the upperwings and a dark-tipped tail. Comb-like lamellae on the inside of the bill are used to filter zooplankton.

The single *Halobaena* species looks like the prions but has a white-tipped tail and the upper bill has small tooth-like serrations at the base.

The gadfly petrels (*Pterodroma*) consist of 29 species of highly agile seabirds with long wings and short, laterally compressed black bills with a strongly hooked nail. They feed mainly on squid and small fish.

Reading: Harrison, P. 1987. *Seabirds of the World: a photographic guide.* London: Christopher Helm. Harrison, P. 1988. *Seabirds: an identification guide.* London: Christopher Helm. Imber, M.J. 1985. *Ibis* 127: 197–229. Murphy, R.C. 1936. *Oceanic Birds of South America.* New York: MacMillan. Serventy, D.L. *et al.* 1971. *The Handbook of Australian Seabirds.* Sydney: Reed. Warham, J. 1990. *The Petrels: their ecology and breeding systems.* London: Academic Press.

17. CORY'S SHEARWATER *Calonectris diomedea* Plate 7

Other name: North Atlantic Shearwater
Size: 46 cm, 900 g
Geographical variation: Three subspecies: *diomedea* breeds in the Mediterranean, *borealis* breeds in the subtropical eastern North Atlantic, and *edwardsii* breeds on the Cape Verde Islands of the tropical North Atlantic. Only *borealis* is known from the New Zealand region.
Distribution: Breed widely in the Mediterranean Sea and between 15 and 40°N in the eastern North Atlantic Ocean. They migrate to spend November–May in temperate and tropical waters of the South Atlantic, but many disperse into the temperate and cooler waters of the southwestern Indian Ocean. One New Zealand record: Foxton Beach (January 1934).

Feeding: Diet is mainly fish and squid, mostly seized on the surface or during shallow plunges. Cory's Shearwaters associate with cetaceans and follow boats to feed on scraps tossed overboard.

In the hand: Males are larger than females, e.g. bill depth 21.0–**22.6**–24.1 mm cf. 19.3–**20.4**–21.6 mm and bill length 54.4–**58.8**–61.7 mm cf. 52.0–**55.7**–59.9 mm.

Reading: Oliver, W.R.B. 1934. *Emu* 34: 23–24. Robertson, H.A. & James, P.C. 1988. *Bull BOC* 108: 79–87. Zino, P.A. 1971. *Ibis* 113: 212–217.

18. PINK-FOOTED SHEARWATER *Puffinus creatopus* Plate 7

Size: 48 cm, 900 g
Distribution: Breed on the Juan Fernandez Islands on Mas-a-Tierra and Santa Clara, and on Mocha Island, Chile. They migrate north to the eastern North Pacific, usually in continental-shelf waters from Mexico to British Columbia, but as far north as Alaska. Stragglers reach Hawai'i, and vagrants reach the Line Islands, eastern Australia and New Zealand. Five New Zealand records: outer Canterbury Bight (June 1979) and off Kaikoura (January 1994, December 1998, February 1999 and January 2003).

Feeding: Diet is mainly fish and squid seized on the surface or during shallow plunge-dives. Pink-footed Shearwaters follow boats and feed on scraps tossed overboard.

Reading: Tunnicliffe, G.A. 1982. *Notornis* 29: 85–91. Tunnicliffe, G.A. 1984. *Notornis* 31: 130.

19. FLESH-FOOTED SHEARWATER *Puffinus carneipes* Plate 8

Other name: Toanui
Size: 44 cm, 600 g
Distribution: Breed on subtropical islands at St Paul Island (Indian Ocean), around the southern coast of Western Australia, off Eyre Peninsula (South Australia), at Lord Howe Island and in northern New Zealand. The main colonies in the New Zealand region are off the eastern coast of the North Island from Northland to East Cape, especially at Coppermine, Whatupuke and Lady Alice Islands in the Hen and Chickens group, Green and Middle Islands of the Mercury group, and Karewa Island in the western Bay of Plenty. Smaller colonies are at Kauwahaia Island (Bethells Beach), Ohinau Island, East Island, Saddleback Island (off New Plymouth) and the Titi Islands in Cook Strait.

During the breeding season, they range over continental-shelf waters of the North Island and Cook Strait, but non-breeders also move south to the eastern Cook Strait and to the Subtropical Convergence from Foveaux Strait east to the Chathams. New Zealand birds migrate north in March to late May to winter in the North Pacific Ocean, mainly off the eastern coast of Korea and off Japan, but some winter off the western coast of North America. They return to New Zealand waters in late September.
Population: 25–50,000 pairs in New Zealand. Often seen in inshore waters off eastern New

Zealand in summer. The largest New Zealand colony is of 20,000+ birds on Coppermine Island.

Conservation: Protected native. Subfossil and midden records from the North Island and Chatham Island indicate a wider breeding distribution in the past, and this has probably been reduced by predators and 'mutton-birding'. Current breeding colonies are largely protected, and only a few chicks are illegally harvested. Flesh-footed Shearwaters are attracted to feed on offal behind fishing boats and are sometimes drowned after being hooked on baited fishing lines or becoming entangled in nets. Little data are available to determine population trends, and banding studies and monitoring of key breeding colonies are needed.

Breeding: No detailed studies in New Zealand. Birds return to their colonies in late September to early October, and eggs are laid over about three weeks from 21 November to 12 December. They lay **1** white egg (69 x 46 mm, 75 g) in a burrow c. 1 m long. Both sexes incubate for c. 53 days. The chick is initially covered in pale grey down and is guarded by either parent for 2–3 days and fed about every second night for 12 days, then increasingly infrequently until the chick fledges in late April or early May, at c. 92 days old. It is immediately independent of its parents. The oldest bird recorded was an Australian one over 30 years old.

Behaviour: Breed on some islands in large dense colonies, on others interspersed with Grey-faced Petrels, Sooty Shearwaters and Little Shearwaters. Early in the season, they sometimes take over a burrow occupied by a Grey-faced Petrel chick (winter bred) that is about to leave, and at some northern colonies they share burrows with tuatara. Grey-faced Petrels in turn often oust Flesh-footed Shearwater chicks when they return to their colonies in April.

At sea, Flesh-footed Shearwaters are usually solitary, but they form feeding flocks and rafts off their colonies. They are generally silent at sea except when they are fighting for scraps. At their colonies, they are noisy on moonless nights, especially just after dusk and before dawn. The main call, given on the ground and sometimes in the air, is a series of high-pitched moans somewhat resembling the sound of cats fighting.

Feeding: Diet is mainly squid and fish. Much food is probably caught at night on the surface or by pursuit-plunging, but during the day food is scavenged from around whales and dolphins, and recently from behind boats, which makes them vulnerable to accidental capture on baited fish-hooks and in seine nets.

Reading: Brown, R.G.B. *et al.* 1978. *Condor* 80: 123–125. Falla, R.A. 1934. *Rec Auck Inst Mus* 1: 245–260. Warham, J. 1958. *Auk* 75: 1–14.

20. WEDGE-TAILED SHEARWATER   *Puffinus pacificus* Plates 7 and 8

Size: 46 cm, 450 g

Geographical variation: Two subspecies: *pacificus* breeds only in the southwest Pacific, at the Kermadecs, Norfolk, Fiji and Tonga; *chlororhynchus* breeds widely in the South Indian Ocean, around Australia and across the subtropical and tropical Pacific, including Lord Howe Island and New Caledonia.

Distribution: Breed on islands of the tropical and subtropical Indian and Pacific Oceans and range widely in adjacent seas. Some populations are migratory; band returns show that birds from southeastern Australia migrate to the western North Pacific. In the New Zealand region, Wedge-tailed Shearwaters breed only at the Kermadec Islands and apparently migrate to the southeastern part of the North Pacific. Recorded at sea to the northeast of New Zealand in autumn, and a few stragglers of both subspecies have been recorded beach-wrecked on the North Island coast, mainly November–April.

Population: A very common and widely distributed shearwater. In New Zealand, they breed only at the Kermadec Islands, where a few still breed on Raoul Island on headlands and along the tops of coastal cliffs, but they are very common on the smaller offshore islands without cats and rats such as the Meyer Islets (e.g. c. 10,000 pairs on North

Meyer) and Dayrell Island. The largest colonies are in the southern Kermadecs, where c. 40,000 pairs nest on Macauley Island and 2500 pairs nest on Curtis Island.

Conservation: Protected native. Virtually extinct on Raoul Island, where 'immense numbers' were recorded in 1908, but its status was only 'abundant' in 1944, because of predation by feral cats and Norway rats. Numbers breeding on predator-free islands elsewhere in the group have probably remained stable, except for an increase on Macauley Island since the removal of goats.

Breeding: No detailed studies in New Zealand through the whole season. In the Kermadecs, timing of breeding varies a week or two from year to year. Birds return to their colonies in October and clean out their burrows in November. The colony is virtually abandoned during the first half of December while birds are on their pre-laying exodus, but they return and lay in mid- to late December, mostly c. 18 December. They lay **1** white egg (67 x 43 mm) in a burrow up to 2.5 m long, but sometimes they lay on the surface under an overhanging rock, in a small cave or under vegetation. Both sexes incubate for c. 54 days.

Chicks hatch in early February and are initially covered in pale grey down. They are left unattended within days after hatching and fledge from late May to early June,

at c. 90 days old, at which time they are immediately independent of their parents. Some yearlings attend colonies, but they do not start breeding until at least 4 years old. The oldest bird recorded was an Australian one aged over 19 years.

Behaviour: Breed in large dense colonies on some islands, sometimes interspersed with other petrels and shearwaters, especially Black-winged Petrels at the Kermadecs. At sea, Wedge-tailed Shearwaters are usually solitary but sometimes form small feeding flocks or large rafts off colonies. They are generally silent at sea and over their colonies, but occasional wails are given by circling birds. Wedge-tailed Shearwaters are very noisy on land at the colony. They often come ashore in the late afternoon, with numbers increasing towards dusk, and the noise builds to a peak in the first couple of hours of darkness. The main call given on the ground is a soft wailing moan: 'ka-whoooo-ahh'.

Feeding: Diet is mainly fish, but squid, krill and jellyfish are also taken. Feeding birds sometimes look for prey by gliding along with head and neck just under the water. Prey is seized near the surface or sometimes by pursuit-plunging. They scavenge around whales and dolphins, and from behind boats.

Reading: Crockett, D.E. 1975. *Notornis* 22: 1–9. Jenkins, J.A.F. 1979. *Notornis* 26: 331–348. Merton, D.V. 1970. *Notornis* 17: 147–199.

21. BULLER'S SHEARWATER   *Puffinus bulleri*   Plate 7

Other name: New Zealand Shearwater (North America)
Size: 46 cm, 425 g
Distribution: Breed only on the Poor Knights Islands off the eastern coast of Northland. Between early September and mid-May, birds disperse widely throughout New Zealand seas, mainly over North Island continental-shelf waters, particularly off Northland, in the Hauraki Gulf and the Bay of Plenty, and off East Cape; but they reach Foveaux Strait, seas off Fiordland and the Chatham Islands. From December, some birds move across the Tasman Sea to coastal waters off eastern Australia.

During April to late May, Buller's Shearwaters depart on migration to the northern and eastern North Pacific, from Japan across to the western coast of North America. The migration route is not known exactly, but most seem to reach the subarctic waters of the northwestern Pacific in June, then many drift northwards to the Gulf of Alaska and eastwards to be off the North American coast by August, and then they head directly back in early September. Some non-breeders remain all year in the North Pacific, with many seen off the west coast of North America in September–October, and some move south to spend the summer in the Humboldt

Current, off Peru and Chile.
Population: c. 2.5 million birds, breeding only at the Poor Knights Islands.
Conservation: Protected endemic. Numbers breeding on the Poor Knights Islands have increased greatly since the removal of feral pigs from Aorangi Island in 1936. On Aorangi Island, the population was estimated at 100 pairs in 1938, but c. 200,000 pairs were breeding by 1981, the increase probably coming from a mix of recruitment and immigration from nearby Tawhiti Rahi Island. The Poor Knights Islands are protected as a Nature Reserve and are predator-free.
Breeding: Birds return to their colonies in mid-September and court and clean out their burrows during October. They are then virtually absent from the colony for c. 30 days from late October on their pre-laying exodus, but return and most eggs are laid during just a few days from 26 to 30 November. They lay **1** white egg (65 x 43 mm, 67 g) in a burrow 0.5–**1**–3 m long, but occasionally in caves, cavities and old stone-walls. Both sexes incubate in stints of 4–7 days for c. 51 days. The chick is initially covered in smoky blue-grey down and is left unattended within days after hatching between 17 and 26 January. Most chicks fledge in the second half of May, at c. 90 days old.

Behaviour: Breed in large dense colonies, interspersed with Fairy Prions. They have apparently ousted Fluttering Shearwaters and Grey-faced Petrels from Aorangi Island since the 1930s as their numbers have increased. At sea, Buller's Shearwaters are usually found alone or in small flocks, but they migrate across a broad front in ones and twos and in groups of up to 12 birds. Feeding aggregations or resting rafts of 50–600 birds are often seen off the east coast of New Zealand in summer, and occasionally flocks of 5000–10,000 birds are seen off the eastern coast of Northland and off North America. They are generally silent at sea but noisy in the air and on the ground at their colonies, especially when they return in the first couple of hours of darkness.
Feeding: Diet is small (9–17 mm) krill, small fish, salps and jellyfish, taken while sitting on the surface. Birds searching for food glide along with head and neck just under the water. Buller's Shearwaters rarely plunge into the sea or dive underwater. They have recently started to scavenge scraps from around fishing boats.

Reading: Harper, P.C. 1983. *Notornis* 30: 299–318. Jenkins, J.A.F. 1974. *Notornis* 21: 109–120. Jenkins, J.A.F. 1988. *Notornis* 35: 203–215. Wahl, T.R. 1985. *Notornis* 32: 109–117.

22.   SOOTY SHEARWATER   *Puffinus griseus*   Plate 8

Other names: Titi, Muttonbird
Size: 44 cm, 800 g
Distribution: Circumpolar, breeding in the subantarctic and temperate zones on islands off the coast of Chile and around Cape Horn; on Kidney Island, Falklands; on Tristan da Cunha; on islands off Tasmania and New South Wales; Macquarie Island; and in New Zealand on many islands and some headlands on the mainland, from the Three Kings Islands to Campbell Island and the Chatham Islands. The main colonies in the New Zealand region are on islands off Stewart Island (especially Codfish and Big South Cape), The Snares, Auckland, Campbell and Chatham Islands. Subfossil and midden evidence and historical records suggest that Sooty Shearwaters formerly bred in large colonies on the mainland, but only small colonies persist on Banks Peninsula, on Cape Wanbrow (Oamaru), on the Otago coast and on isolated headlands along the west coast of the South Island.

Between September and mid-May, breeding and pre-breeding birds disperse widely throughout New Zealand seas, mainly over continental-shelf and deeper waters off southern New Zealand, and some may move south to the pack ice. Most adults depart on migration to the North Pacific between late March and early May, moving along the east coast of the South and North Islands. Fledglings leave their colonies from mid-April to late May and follow a similar route.

The migration path is directly north over a broad front to subarctic waters between Japan and the west coast of North America, which they reach in April–May. Some then drift northwards to reach the Gulf of Alaska in June. Breeding birds return directly south muttonbirds is not certain, but because the huge colonies on The Snares, Auckland Islands and the Chathams are protected, the overall population is secure.

Breeding: Birds return to their colonies in September and court and clean out their

in August and arrive back in New Zealand waters in September, but non-breeders return a month or two later. Sooty Shearwaters are often found dead on the New Zealand coast during the northward migration of fledglings in May, and again in November–December when pre-breeders return to New Zealand waters.

Population: 20 million+ birds; the largest colony is at The Snares, where c. 2.75 million pairs breed.

Conservation: Protected native, except that a large traditional take of muttonbirds (the fattest chicks) is permitted on some islands in Foveaux Strait and around Stewart Island. Sooty Shearwaters have undoubtedly declined since 1840, with the demise of many mainland and some island colonies being due to the spread of introduced predators and the conversion of forest for farming, over-harvesting of muttonbirds, and drift-netting in the North Pacific. The impact of the annual legal take by Maori of an estimated 250,000

burrows through October. After a pre-laying exodus of c. 3 weeks in early November, most eggs are laid in late November and early December. They lay **1** white egg (77 x 48 mm, 93 g) in a burrow 0.5–3 m long, or occasionally in a crevice, under bushes or huts. Both sexes incubate. Eggs hatch from mid-January after c. 53 days. Chicks are initially covered in smoky blue-grey down and are left unattended within days of hatching. Chicks reach their maximum weight, of 1000–1800 g, at c. 7 weeks old, but then lose weight to fledge at c. 750 g at 86–**97**–106 days old in late April to mid-May. Young return to their natal colony at 3–4 years old but do not start breeding for several years. The oldest bird recorded in New Zealand lived over 25 years.

Behaviour: Breed in large dense colonies, interspersed with other seabirds. At sea, Sooty Shearwaters are gregarious, with large flocks of up to 500,000 birds recorded feeding, on migration or in the seas near breeding colonies. They are generally silent at sea but noisy in the air and on the ground at their colonies when they return in the two hours after dusk, and are even noisier as they depart just before dawn. The main call is a series of hoarse moans: 'oo-oo-ah', getting louder and faster each time.

Feeding: Diet is small fish, squid, krill and other small crustaceans, taken mainly by plunging and then swimming metres under the surface.

Reading: Ainley, D.G. & Boekelheide, R.J. 1983. Studies in Avian Biol 8: 2–23. Richdale, L.E. 1963. Proc Zool Soc (Lond) 141: 1–117. Spear, L.B. & Ainley, D.G. 1999. *Condor* 101: 205–218. Warham, J. & Wilson, G.J. 1982. Notornis 29: 23–30. Warham, J. et al. 1982. Notornis 29: 269–292.

23. SHORT-TAILED SHEARWATER *Puffinus tenuirostris* Plate 8

Other name: Tasmanian Muttonbird
Size: 42 cm, 550 g
Distribution: Breed only on islands off southern Australia from Western Australia to northern New South Wales, especially in Bass Strait and around Tasmania. Subfossil and midden records from the North, South and Chatham Islands suggest they may have once bred in the New Zealand region. From September to April, adults range through waters south of Australia to the edge of the pack ice and across the Tasman Sea to continental-shelf waters of the Hauraki Gulf and Bay of Plenty. They are occasionally beach-wrecked on the New Zealand coast in October–March.

Adults go directly to the northern North Pacific and the Bering Sea in March–April, but fledglings leave between late April and mid-May, and some drift across the Tasman and are wrecked on the west coast of New Zealand in May–June. Adults return past Fiji and Samoa to their colonies in Australia in late September, but subadults return a month or two later. Many pass through New Zealand waters as far south as Foveaux Strait, and in some years (e.g. 1968 and 1986) many are beach-wrecked in October–December.

Population: c. 23 million birds. The main colonies are on islands in Bass Strait and around Tasmania, with vast colonies (1 million+ pairs) on Babel Island and Trefoil Island. Each year an estimated 500,000 chicks are harvested, and a similar number of birds, mainly subadult, were accidentally caught in gill nets in the North Pacific in the 1980s; however, the population is apparently stable or even expanding.

Behaviour: At sea, they are seen in large flocks of up to 500,000 birds while on migration.

Feeding: Diet is mainly krill, amphipods, and small fish and squid. Although similar to that of the Sooty Shearwater, this diet probably has more plankton. They catch most food beneath the surface after plunging in or diving from the surface.

Reading: Bradley, J.S. *et al.* 1991. *Ibis* 133 Suppl 1: 55–61. Holmes, G. 1977. *Notornis* 24: 286–287. Serventy, D.L. 1967. *Proc 14th Int Orn Congr* 165–190. Skira, I.J. 1986. *Aust Wildl Res* 13: 481–488. Wooller, R.D. *et al.* 1990. *J Anim Ecol* 59: 161–170.

24. CHRISTMAS ISLAND SHEARWATER
Puffinus nativitatis Plate 8

Size: 38 cm, 350 g
Distribution: Breed on tropical and sub-tropical islands throughout the central Pacific Ocean from the Leeward Islands of Hawai'i to Easter Island, including Christmas Island (Kiribati). Their distribution at sea is poorly known, but most are seen in tropical waters of the central and eastern Pacific. Two New Zealand records: a bird wrecked at Dargaville Beach (February 1976) after a tropical cyclone, and a bird found alive on Curtis Island in the southern Kermadecs (November 1989).

Reading: Crockett, D.E. 1977. *Notornis* 24: 285–286. Taylor, G.A. & Tennyson, A.J.D. 1994. *Notornis* 41: 287–291.

25. MANX SHEARWATER *Puffinus puffinus* Plate 9

Size: 36 cm, 450 g
Distribution: Breed on islands in the temperate and subarctic North Atlantic. They migrate to the South Atlantic, mainly to seas off Brazil and Argentina, but sometimes to waters of southern Africa. A few wander to Australasia; a British-banded yearling was found dead in South Australia in November 1961, and two immature birds have since been beach-wrecked in New Zealand: Pukerua Bay (June 1972) and Waikanae Beach (January 1985).

In the hand: As the Manx Shearwater is very difficult to distinguish at sea from the Fluttering Shearwater, most acceptable records are likely to be from beach-wrecked specimens. It can be separated from Fluttering and Hutton's Shearwaters on measurements and undertail and underwing colours. Bill length is 31–**34.5**–38 mm and wing length is 225–**237**–245 mm, the side feathers of the undertail coverts have black outer vanes (as in Hutton's Shearwater), the longest axillaries reach near the trailing edge of the wing and are white with a broad black subterminal band (immatures) or a moderate black band (adults) and white tip, and apart from the dark leading edge (especially at the elbow) the underwing is mainly white.

Reading: Brooke, M.deL. 1990. *The Manx Shearwater*. London: T. & A.D. Poyser. Kinsky, F.C. & Fowler, J.A. 1973. *Notornis* 20: 14–20. Tennyson, A.J.D. 1986. *Notornis* 33: 59–61.

26. FLUTTERING SHEARWATER *Puffinus gavia* Plate 9

Other name: Pakaha
Size: 33 cm, 300 g
Distribution: Breed only in New Zealand, on many islands and islets along the northeastern coast of the North Island from the Three Kings Islands to islands near Gisborne, and on islands in the Marlborough Sounds. In spring and summer, they are in inshore waters close to their breeding colonies, but in autumn and winter, they range over continental-shelf waters, inshore waters and harbours, as far south as Foveaux Strait. In autumn, many fledglings migrate to the southeastern seaboard of Australia, from South Australia to Queensland, and stragglers have been recorded from New Caledonia and Vanuatu. Most return in July–August, when often found beach-wrecked. Subfossil and midden remains from North, South and Chatham Islands suggest a wider breeding distribution in the past.
Population: A very common shearwater in the Hauraki Gulf, in the Bay of Plenty and in Cook Strait. The total is 100,000+ breeding pairs, with the largest colonies being on the Three Kings Islands, Channel Island, the Aldermens and the Trio Islands.
Conservation: Protected endemic. Chicks were harvested by Maori until legal protection in 1953. Numbers of Fluttering Shearwaters have declined with the spread of predators such as cats and rats to headlands on the mainland and to offshore islands. The colonies on Little Barrier, Cuvier and Motuhora (Whale) Islands were destroyed by cats and rats, and within the Mercury Group, Fluttering Shearwaters are common only on islands free of Pacific rats. Efforts to eradicate mammalian predators from offshore islands will undoubtedly benefit small seabirds such as the Fluttering Shearwater.
Breeding: Some birds visit their colonies throughout the year. Most return to their colonies on forest- or scrub-covered islands in August to court and clean out their burrows. Eggs are laid from early September to mid-October. They lay 1 white egg (57 x 40 mm) in a burrow 0.5–1 m long, or occasionally in a crevice or among rock-falls. Eggs hatch in November and chicks fledge in late January and early February.
Behaviour: Breed in dense or scattered colonies, often interspersed with other seabirds, especially Diving Petrels, Little Shearwaters, Grey-faced Petrels, and Fairy Prions in Cook Strait. At sea, Fluttering Shearwaters are sometimes found in flocks of up to 20,000 birds while feeding, roosting or on passage. When feeding they occasionally give a soft chattering cackle, but when they are circling their breeding colonies they are

very noisy with rapid, staccato two-syllable calls, with much variation on the main call: 'ka-how ka-how ka-how ka-how, kehek kehek kehek kehek - errr'.

Feeding: Diet is mostly small fish and krill, taken mainly by plunging from a few metres above the surface or paddling slowly forwards searching with their head submerged, then diving with their partly opened wings used for propulsion.

In the hand: Fluttering Shearwaters can be separated from Hutton's and Manx Shearwaters on measurements and on undertail and underwing colours. Bill length is 28–**33.5**–37 mm and wing length is 190–**210**–225, the side feathers of the undertail coverts are normally white, the longest axillaries do not reach the trailing edge of the wing and are light buff-grey, squarish-ended and white-tipped, and apart from the dark leading edge the underwing is mainly white.

Reading: Edgar, A.E. 1962. *Notornis* 10: 1–15. Powlesland, R.G. & Pickard, C.R. 1992. *Notornis* 39: 27–46.

27. HUTTON'S SHEARWATER *Puffinus huttoni* Plate 9

Size: 36 cm, 350 g

Distribution: Breed only in New Zealand, 1200–1800 m asl in the Seaward Kaikoura Range of the northeastern South Island. Formerly they also bred in the Inland Kaikoura Range. As subfossil and midden material is not readily distinguishable from that of Fluttering Shearwaters, it is not possible to tell if they used to have an even wider breeding distribution. During spring and summer, they range over continental-shelf and deeper waters mainly east of the South Island from Cook Strait to Otago, especially north of Banks Peninsula.

In autumn, Hutton's Shearwaters migrate to coastal and continental-shelf waters of Australia as far north as Torres Strait and around the southern and western coasts to off northwestern Western Australia. It is not yet clear whether they circumnavigate the continent or follow the same route outwards and back. Adults return to New Zealand in August, followed by subadults in October–November, but younger pre-breeders apparently remain in Australian waters all year. The pattern of recovery of beach-wrecked birds reflects this migration pattern; very few specimens are found between April and August, but numbers increase to peak in October–November, when the subadults return.

Population: c. 100,000 breeding pairs, nesting in one large and one small, scattered colony in the Seaward Kaikoura Range.

Conservation: Protected endemic. Although the species was first described in 1912, its breeding grounds were not found until 1965. Reports from high-country runholders indicated that Hutton's Shearwaters formerly bred in the Inland Kaikoura Range, where Maori formerly collected the young as muttonbirds. Recent studies have shown that stoat predation on adults and young is sometimes very intense and some subcolonies have declined seriously. Some parts of the colonies are in steep, unstable sites, and erosion (perhaps induced by the heavy browsing of deer, chamois, goats, hares and possums) has obliterated some of them. Stoats are now trapped at the accessible main subcolonies, but many nesting sites are too remote to be protected. Control of browsing mammals has led to better vegetation cover at the colonies.

Breeding: Birds return to their colonies on soil-covered slopes high in the mountains from late August to mid-September. In some years the colonies are still snow-covered and birds wait up to a month before they can clean out their burrows. Eggs are usually laid between 25 October and 18 November, but later in some subcolonies where snow persists longer. The whole population may breed later in years when snow persists long into the spring. They lay **1** white egg (60 x 41 mm) in a burrow 0.6–**1.2**–2.5 m long, but usually running parallel with and just below the surface. Eggs hatch in late December–January and most chicks fledge during March–early April. Young return to the colony from 3 years old but probably do not start breeding until 4–6 years old.

193

Behaviour: Breed in large, patchily dense colonies. At sea, Hutton's Shearwaters are difficult to distinguish from Fluttering Shearwaters, with which they may mix. Large flocks of 20,000 birds, presumed to be primarily of this species, have been seen feeding and roosting off the Marlborough coast. Off Australia, they have been seen in small flocks, sometimes intermingling with other shearwaters. When circling above their breeding colonies they are noisy, uttering a rapid staccato cackle, more wheezy than that of the Fluttering Shearwater. There is much variation on the main call: 'ko-uw ko-uw ko-uw ko-uw, kee kee kee kee - aaah'.

Feeding: Diet is mostly small fish and krill, taken mainly by plunging from a few metres above the surface or by paddling slowly forwards searching with their head sub-merged, then diving with their partly opened wings used for propulsion.

In the hand: Hutton's Shearwaters can be separated from Fluttering and Manx Shearwaters on measurements and on undertail and under-wing colours. Bill length is 32–**36**–39 mm and wing length is 210–**225**–235 mm, the side feathers of the undertail coverts have dark brown edges in most birds, the longest axillaries reach near the trailing edge of the wing and are dark brown, rounded at the tip, and only rarely or slightly tipped with buff or white, and the underwing is smudged with brown, especially near the base of the wing.

Reading: Halse, S.A. 1981. *Emu* 81: 42–44. Halse, S.A, & Halse, N.J. 1988. *West Aust Nat* 17: 97–106. Harrow, G. 1965. *Notornis* 12: 59–65. Harrow, G. 1976. *Notornis* 23: 269–288. Kinsky, F.C. & Fowler, J.A. 1973. *Notornis* 20: 14–20. Powlesland, R.G. & Pickard, C.R. 1992. *Notornis* 39: 27–46. Tarburton, M.K. 1981. *Notornis* 28: 9–10.

28. LITTLE SHEARWATER *Puffinus assimilis* Plate 9

Other name: Allied Shearwater
Size: 30 cm, 200 g
Geographical variation: Seven subspecies, three of which breed in the New Zealand region: the Kermadec Little Shearwater *kermadecensis*, the North Island Little Shearwater *haurakiensis* and the Subantarctic Little Shearwater *elegans*. The Norfolk Island Little Shearwater *assimilis* occasionally visits New Zealand waters.

Distribution: Little Shearwaters have a highly disjunct breeding distribution; on islands in the North and South Atlantic Oceans, in the Indian Ocean at St Paul Island and on islands off the coast of Western Australia, on Lord Howe, Norfolk and Kermadec Islands, around northern and subantarctic New Zealand including the Chathams, and at Rapa Island in the central South Pacific Ocean. All subspecies are quite sedentary, except for the Subantarctic Little Shearwater, which ranges widely in subantarctic waters.

Kermadec Little Shearwaters breed on the Herald Group, on Macauley Island and have an especially large colony on Curtis Island; young birds are sometimes beach-wrecked on western and northern North Island beaches in November–December.

North Island Little Shearwaters breed on islands around the northern North Island, with main colonies on the Poor Knights, Chickens, Mokohinau, Mercury and Aldermen Islands, and smaller colonies on the Cavalli Islands and Ohena Island; they are commonly seen in the outer Hauraki Gulf and the Bay of Plenty.

Subantarctic Little Shearwaters breed on the Star Keys and probably Little Mangere in the Chathams, and on islands around Antipodes Island (especially Bollon's Island); this race has been seen off the Auckland and Bounty Islands and is occasionally wrecked on South Island and southern North Island beaches.

Norfolk Island Little Shearwaters, which breed at Lord Howe and Norfolk Islands, stray to the west coast of the North Island.

Population: The Kermadec race has 100,000+ breeding pairs, with most on Curtis Island, and several hundred on Macauley and the Meyer Islands. The North Island race has c. 10,000 pairs, with moderate numbers on the Poor Knights, Hen and Chickens (especially Lady Alice Island), Mokohinau group (especially Lizard Island), Mercury Group (e.g. c. 1000 pairs on Red Mercury Island) and the

Aldermens (4000+ pairs). The Subantarctic race has only c. 150 pairs on the Star Keys and Little Mangere in the Chathams, but 100,000+ pairs on Bollons, Archway and Inner Windward Islands of the Antipodes.

Conservation: Protected native. Being the smallest shearwater, Little Shearwaters are easily preyed on by introduced mammals and do well only on islands without mammalian predators, although they survive in reduced numbers in the presence of Pacific rats. They have become extinct on Raoul Island since cats and Norway rats became established.

Breeding: Mostly winter or spring breeders, but birds return to their colonies irregularly all year. Laying is from mid-June to late July in the Kermadecs, from early July to mid-August around the northern North Island, and in September in the subantarctic. They lay **1** white egg (54 x 37 mm) in a burrow 0.3–2 m long. Eggs hatch after 52–58 days. Chicks fledge at 70–75 days old, in mid-October to late November on the Kermadecs, November–December around the northern North Island, and January–February on the subantarctic islands.

Behaviour: Breed in colonies ranging from small, loose aggregations mingling with Grey-faced Petrels and Pycroft's Petrels on such islands as Red Mercury Island, to large, dense colonies on Curtis Island (Kermadecs) and Bollons Island (Antipodes). At sea, Little Shearwaters are usually solitary or in small flocks, and seldom associate with other seabirds. They are noisy over and at their breeding colonies, particularly just after dusk and before dawn, with their main call being a rapidly repeated 'kakakakakakak-urrr'.

Feeding: Diet is mostly small fish, krill, squid and octopuses, taken mainly by diving from the surface or by plunging from a few metres above the surface.

In the hand: This is the only shearwater with bright blue feet. The subspecies are impossible to determine at sea, and even in the hand plumage differences are slight and measurements overlap extensively. *kermadecensis*: bill 24–**25.3**–27 mm, wing 180–**189**–195 mm; *haurakiensis*: bill 23–**26.1**–29 mm, wing 181–**192**–201 mm, greater upperwing coverts have white tips; *elegans*: bill 23–**24.5**–26 mm, wing 170–**187**–197 mm, many lower back feathers and upperwing coverts have distinctive narrow white tips; *assimilis*: bill 22–**23.3**–24.3, wing 173–**182**–189 mm.

Reading: Fleming, C.A. & Serventy, D.L. 1943. *Emu* 43: 113–125. Imber, M.J. 1983. *Notornis* 30: 283–298. Powlesland, R.G. & Pickard, C.R. 1992. *Notornis* 39: 27–46. Warham, J. & Bell, B.D. 1979. *Notornis* 26: 121–169.

29. COMMON DIVING PETREL *Pelecanoides urinatrix* Plate 9

Other name: Kuaka
Size: 20 cm, 130 g
Geographical variation: Four subspecies, two of which breed in the New Zealand region: Richdale's Diving Petrel *urinatrix*, and the Subantarctic Diving Petrel *exsul*.
Distribution: Circumpolar, breeding on islands between 34 and 55°S and staying mainly in adjacent seas. Richdale's Diving Petrels breed on islands off Tasmania and in Bass Strait; and on many islands from the Three Kings to the Bay of Plenty, off Taranaki, in the Marlborough Sounds, on islands in Foveaux Strait and around Stewart Island, on the Solander Islands, The Snares and small islands in the Chathams. Subantarctic Diving Petrels are circumpolar, breeding mainly in the subantarctic zone, including the Antipodes and Auckland Islands and on islets off Campbell Island.

Both subspecies are quite sedentary, remaining mainly in seas near the breeding colonies, which they visit occasionally during the non-breeding season. Common Diving Petrels are quite often wrecked on beaches close to breeding colonies with peaks of recoveries in winter and again in early summer, when young have just left the nest.
Population: 1 million+ pairs. Large colonies are on scattered islands off Northland and in the Bay of Plenty, on Sugarloaf Island near New Plymouth, Brothers and Trios Islands in Cook Strait, on South East Island in the Chathams, on Little Solander Island, at The Snares, and on the Antipodes.
Conservation: Protected native. Common

Diving Petrels are vulnerable to predation by introduced mammals and survive best on islands without mammalian predators. They have become extinct or rare on islands with rats or cats, or where grazing mammals accidentally destroy burrows. Recent efforts to eradicate rats from offshore islands will probably benefit Common Diving Petrels.

Breeding: The breeding season is a couple of months earlier in northern New Zealand than in Foveaux Strait. On Green Island in the Mercury group, Common Diving Petrels return to their colonies from March onwards, with a peak of activity around the end of May to prepare their burrows.

Eggs are laid in August in northern New Zealand, but from late September to early October in Foveaux Strait. They lay **1** white egg (38 x 30 mm) in a burrow 0.25–1.5 m long. Eggs hatch after c. 53 days. Chicks are brooded for 10–15 days and fledge at 45–**52**–59 days old in late November–December in northern New Zealand, and in January–February in Foveaux Strait. Some young birds return to their natal colony as yearlings but do not start breeding until 2–3 years old.

Behaviour: Breed in colonies, and at sea they are seen in small groups. They are noisy at their breeding colonies with a variety of calls given in the air, on the ground and from their burrows. The main calls are a harsh 'kuaka-did-a-did' and 'kuaka' given by females only; 'kooo-ah', given by males only.

Feeding: Diet is mostly small krill and copepods, taken mainly by diving into the sea from a metre or two above the surface, then swimming underwater using their wings for propulsion.

In the hand: The two species of diving petrel can be reliably separated only in the hand. The Common Diving Petrel has dusky-brown inner webs on its three outer primaries, not white or very pale grey as in the South Georgian; the septal process is near the base of the nostril rather than near the centre; and the underwing coverts vary from heavily smudged brown-grey to pale grey, but never white as in the South Georgian, which usually also has a black line on the rear of the tarsus. Richdale's Diving Petrel is larger than the Subantarctic subspecies, but measurements overlap. *urinatrix*: bill 15–**16.7**–18.5 mm, wing 113–**127**–137 mm; *exsul*: bill **16.1** mm, wing **119** mm.

Reading: Payne, M.R. & Prince, P.A. 1979. *NZ J Zool* 6: 299–318. Powlesland, R.G. *et al.* 1992. *Notornis* 39: 101–111. Richdale, L.E. 1943. *Emu* 43: 24–48; 97–107. Richdale, L.E. 1965. *Trans Zool Soc (Lond)* 31: 1–86. Thoresen, A.C. 1969. *Notornis* 16: 241–260.

30.   SOUTH GEORGIAN DIVING PETREL
Pelecanoides georgicus   Plate 9

Size: 18 cm, 120 g
Distribution: Circumpolar, breeding in the subantarctic zone. The only colony in New Zealand is on Codfish Island (Whenua Hou), although as recently as 1943 they bred on Dundas and Enderby in the Auckland Islands, and subfossil remains indicate huge colonies were at Mason Bay, Stewart Island and probably on Chatham Island. They are thought to be sedentary, but judging by stomach contents of Codfish Island birds, they apparently feed well offshore near the edge of the continental shelf.
Population: A common species, with millions of pairs nesting on South Georgia, the Kerguelen, Prince Edward, Crozet and Heard Islands. Codfish Island has 60–70 pairs.
Conservation: Protected native. The colony

on Codfish Island, identified in 1978, was previously assumed to be of Common Diving Petrels. The former colonies in sand dunes on Dundas and Enderby Islands were probably destroyed by trampling of cattle and Hooker's sea lions, and by the interference of rabbits. Weka, a potential predator of fledglings on Codfish Island, were eradicated by 1986. The breeding habitat on Codfish Island is limited to a small area of sand dunes, and people are now prevented from walking over these dunes, and the population is increasing steadily.
Breeding: On Codfish Island, birds spend September–October cleaning out their deep burrows in unstable and sparsely vegetated sand dunes, 1–5 m above the high-tide line. Eggs are laid in early November, a month

earlier than at other, more southern breeding colonies. No other New Zealand information on breeding. Elsewhere, they lay 1 white egg (39 x 32 mm), incubation is for 44–47–52 days, and chicks fledge at 43–50–60 days old.

Behaviour: On Codfish Island, they breed in a loose colony scattered along about 1 km of sand dunes, separate from other seabirds. Adults call in the air over the colony but return directly to their burrows, spending little time on the surface.

Feeding: Diet of the Codfish Island birds is small krill, fish and squid, taken mainly by diving into the sea from a metre or two above the surface, then swimming underwater using their wings for propulsion.

In the hand: The two species of diving petrel can be reliably separated only in the hand – see Common Diving Petrel.

Reading: Imber, M.J. & Nilsson, R.J. 1980. *Notornis* 27: 325–330. Jouventin, P. *et al*. 1985. *Notornis* 32: 157–220. Payne, M.R. & Prince, P.A. 1979. *NZ J Zool* 6: 299–318. Weimerskirch, H. *et al*. 1989. *Emu* 89: 15–29. West, J. & Imber, M.J. 1989. *Notornis* 36: 157–158. Worthy, T.H. 1998. *Notornis* 45: 229–246.

31. GREY PETREL *Procellaria cinerea* Plates 7 and 10

Other name: Pediunker
Size: 48 cm, 1000 g
Distribution: Circumpolar, breeding on many subantarctic islands, including the Antipodes (Antipodes and Bollons) and Campbell Islands. They range widely over deep water between 25 and 60°S and follow the Humboldt Current to the seas off Peru. Birds from the New Zealand colonies feed mainly in deep water to the east of New Zealand. In summer and autumn, immature Grey Petrels move north off the eastern coast of the North Island, but adults are rarely found north of 45°S. During the breeding season, adult females move further north than adult males, with a winter and spring concentration of adult females in nutrient-rich waters off East Cape and the Gisborne coast. Because Grey Petrels are more common in seas to the east of New Zealand than in the Tasman Sea, the few that are beach-wrecked are mainly on the east coast in summer, when young have just fledged.

Population: Uncommon, with main colonies (100,000+ birds) on Gough Island in the South Atlantic, and in the New Zealand region where there are 10,000–50,000 pairs, mainly on the Antipodes. The colonies on islands off Campbell Island are small, and fewer than 100 pairs remain in the remnant colonies on main Campbell Island.

Conservation: Protected native. At the Campbell Island colonies, almost all chicks are killed by cats and Norway rats. Of greatest concern, however, is that Grey Petrels are attracted to feed on offal discarded from fishing boats, and because breeding females feed in important fishery areas, they are especially susceptible to being drowned after being accidentally hooked on tuna or ling long-lines. They made up 27% of seabirds reported killed in New Zealand waters in 1988–97. The impact on their breeding populations has not been assessed.

Breeding: No detailed study has been made in New Zealand. The timing of breeding seems similar to that on Tristan da Cuhna, with laying in April–June and chicks fledging October–December. They lay 1 white egg (81 x 56 mm) in a burrow 1–3 m long. Eggs hatch after 52–61 days and chicks fledge after 110–120 days.

Behaviour: Breed in loose colonies inter-mingled with White-headed Petrels on Antipodes Island. At sea, they are often seen alone, but occasionally they form large mixed flocks around fishing boats or feeding whales. They are silent while flying but noisy on land, with two main calls given on the ground and in their burrows: a drawn-out moan and, more commonly, a few wheezy moans followed by loud, far-carrying, staccato bleats.

Feeding: Diet is mostly squid, fish and offal, mainly taken on the surface or by diving from about 3 m.

Reading: Bartle, J.A. 1990. *Notornis* 37: 146–150. Imber, M.J. 1983. *Notornis* 30: 283–298. Jouventin, P. *et al*. 1985. *Notornis* 32: 157–220. Murray T.E. *et al*. 1993. *Bird Cons Int* 3: 181–210. Warham, J. 1988. *Notornis* 35: 169–183. Warham, J. & Bell, B.D. 1979. *Notornis* 26: 121–169.

32. BLACK PETREL *Procellaria parkinsoni* Plate 10

Other names: Taiko, Parkinson's Petrel
Size: 46 cm, 700 g
Distribution: Breed only in New Zealand, on Little Barrier and Great Barrier Islands. They formerly bred widely on mountain ranges in the North Island and the north-western South Island. During the summer breeding season, they range mainly through subtropical waters between 30 and 42°S around northeastern New Zealand and across the Tasman Sea to the southeastern coast of Australia. A few birds are wrecked on North Island beaches in November–April. Recently fledged chicks are sometimes found beach-wrecked on the east coast of the North Island in May.

Black Petrels migrate in March–July to the eastern tropical Pacific Ocean from west of the Galapagos Islands to southern Mexico (15°N) and northern Peru (5°S), and return in October–December. A few younger non-breeders may stay there all year.
Population: c. 10,000 birds, including non-breeders. Little Barrier c. 100 pairs, Great Barrier 2500+ pairs.
Conservation: Protected threatened endemic. Although Maori and early Europeans harvested chicks from mainland colonies, introduced predators probably caused their demise. The colony on Little Barrier Island was severely reduced until cats were eradicated in 1980. Since then the number of chicks raised has improved and the colony is slowly increasing. On Great Barrier Island, where breeding was not discovered until 1964, cat predation at the colony is slight and productivity is high, probably because, unlike Little Barrier, there are few nesting Cook's Petrels to sustain high numbers of cats near the colony.

Black Petrels associate with fishing boats and are sometimes accidentally caught on long-lines or in nets. Between 1986 and 1990, 249 fledglings were transferred from Great Barrier to Little Barrier Island in the hope of boosting the small Little Barrier colony; however, only a few were recaptured there, but some have returned to Great Barrier.
Breeding: Black Petrels are summer breeders.

They return to their mainly high, ridgetop colonies between mid-October and December to court and clean out burrows. Males make frequent visits to the burrow and often stay there during the day, whereas females make only occasional visits. The pre-laying exodus of each pair lasts c. 23–24 days.

Eggs are laid in November–January, mostly between 20 November and 25 December. They lay **1** white egg (69 x 51 mm, 99 g) in a burrow 1–3 m long. The female incubates for the first 0–4 days, then the male takes a long shift of 4–17 days, and then alternating shifts get shorter towards hatching. Eggs hatch in January–February after c. 57 days. The chick is rarely left unattended during the first 2–3 days but is then fed every 2–3 nights until close to fledging, when feeding becomes infrequent. Chicks emerge from their burrows about 10 nights before they finally fledge from mid-April to early July at 96–**107**–122 days old. Young birds have been recorded breeding at 6 years old. The oldest bird recorded lived at least 17 years.
Behaviour: Breed in loose colonies inter-mingled with Cook's Petrels. At sea, they are often seen alone but sometimes form flocks of up to 300 birds around feeding cetaceans, or fishing boats. At the colony, they are usually silent in the air but sometimes give a low moan followed by a series of clacks. On the ground they have loud, far-carrying calls, the main one being a rapid series of staccato clacks. Quieter clacks and moans are given from the burrow.
Feeding: While breeding, Black Petrels feed mainly on squid, supplemented by fish, crustaceans and other marine invertebrates. Judging from the diet composition and the importance of bioluminescent forms, much food is probably taken at night; however, observations in the eastern tropical Pacific show that much squid is scavenged from around feeding melon-headed whales and false killer whales by day. Some prey is taken by sitting on the surface with head immersed and then taking a shallow dive, but they are capable of diving down at least 10 m.

Reading: Imber, M.J. 1976. *NZ J Mar Fresh Res* 10: 119–130. Imber, M.J. 1987. *Notornis* 34: 19–39. Pitman, R.L. & Ballance, L.T. 1992. *Condor* 94: 825–835. Powlesland, R.G. 1989. *Notornis* 36: 299–310. Warham, J. 1988. *Notornis* 35: 169–183.

33. WESTLAND PETREL *Procellaria westlandica* Plate 10

Other name: Westland Black Petrel
Size: 48 cm, 1100 g
Distribution: Breed only in New Zealand, in the densely forested coastal foothills of the Paparoa Range, Westland. Most nest below 200 m asl between the Punakaiki River and Lawsons Creek. During the winter breeding season, they range mainly over continental-shelf waters between Cape Egmont and Fiordland and through Cook Strait to between East Cape and Banks Peninsula, and into pelagic waters of the Tasman Sea and Pacific about and just north of the subtropical convergence. A few adults and recently fledged chicks are beach-wrecked around Cook Strait in November–January. In late summer, Westland Petrels disperse more widely, mainly to the east of New Zealand beyond the Chathams, and also regularly to both coasts of South America, where two banded subadults have been found. In summer, a few visit coastal waters of southeastern Australia.
Population: c. 20,000 birds, including c. 2000 breeding pairs.
Conservation: Protected threatened endemic. Maori and early European settlers used to harvest chicks from colonies. Commercial trawling for hoki within 200 km of the colony since the 1960s has made much extra food (fish scraps) available, and the population has more than trebled from the 3000–6000 birds in 1958; however, the population stabilised in the 1980s, and may now be declining because a few birds, mainly adult females, have been killed accidentally on tuna long-lines. The sites where Westland Petrels breed is legally protected, and feral cats are killed around the colonies.
Breeding: Westland Petrels are winter breeders. They return to their colonies on the steep sides of forested valleys from mid-February to mid-March to court and clean out burrows. Males make frequent visits to the burrow and often stay there during the day, whereas females make only occasional visits. Although there is no clear pre-laying exodus, with females making occasional visits in the weeks before laying, one female with a forming egg was caught over 400 km southwest of the colony.

Eggs are laid over 3 weeks from 12 May, with a peak c. 23 May. They lay 1 white egg (81 x 56 mm) in a burrow 1–2 m long. Eggs hatch in late July after c. 64 days incubation. The chick is rarely left unattended during the first 2 weeks and is fed by each parent about every third night, but less frequently close to fledging. Chicks fledge from 5 November to 26 December at c. 125 days old. Young birds have been recorded back at the colonies at 5 years old, but minimum age recorded for first breeding is 12 years old. The oldest bird recorded lived at least 22 years.
Behaviour: Breed in colonies. At sea, they are often seen alone but join large mixed flocks feeding on scraps from fishing boats. At the colony, they are normally silent in the air, apart from occasional 'quack' calls, but on the ground they are noisy and produce a wide range of sounds. The two main calls are a succession of duck-like quacks, often given in duets, and males give a barrage of pulse-like notes, reminiscent of the call of a Kookaburra.
Feeding: Nowadays, Westland Petrels take mostly fish offal during the breeding season, but their natural diet is mainly squid, fish and planktonic crustacea, taken on the surface or from shallow dives.

Reading: Baker, A.J. & Coleman, J.D. 1977. *Notornis* 24: 211–231. Bartle, A.J. 1990. *Notornis* 37: 146–150. Freeman, A.N.D. 1998. *Emu* 98: 36–43. Freeman, A.N.D. & Wilson, K-J. 1997. *DoC CAS Notes* No. 160. Imber, M.J. 1976. *NZ J Mar Fresh Res* 10: 119–130. Murray, T.E. *et al.* 1993. *Bird Cons Int* 3: 181–210. Powlesland, R.G. 1989. *Notornis* 36: 299–310. Warham, J. 1988. *Notornis* 35: 169–183.

34. WHITE-CHINNED PETREL *Procellaria aequinoctialis* Plate 10

Other name: Shoemaker
Size: 55 cm, 1250 g
Geographical variation: Two subspecies; only *aequinoctialis* is known from the New Zealand region.
Distribution: Circumpolar, breeding on many subantarctic islands, including Antipodes Island, the Auckland Islands (Auckland, Adams, Ewing, Disappointment) and the Campbell Islands (Dent, Jacquemart and other offshore islets). They range widely over deep water between 30 and 65°S, but to 10°S off the western coasts of South America and Africa. Birds from the New Zealand colonies feed mainly to the south and east of New Zealand; adults feed over continental-shelf waters up to the latitude of Cook Strait during their summer breeding season and North Cape in winter. Immatures are occasionally seen off the coast in all seasons, and are most often beach-wrecked in November–February. Few recently fledged chicks are beach-wrecked, so they may disperse mainly to the south and east.
Population: Abundant, with 1 million+ pairs on each of South Georgia and Kerguelen Islands and large colonies at the Crozet and Prince Edward groups. In New Zealand, 100,000+ pairs on the Antipodes, 100,000+ pairs on Disappointment Island and 10,000 pairs on Monowai Island, off Campbell Island.
Conservation: Protected native. The colony on main Campbell Island has gone because adults were killed by cats, and eggs and chicks were eaten by Norway rats. Trends in New Zealand populations are not known, but they are the second most common petrel caught on tuna long-lines in New Zealand waters, and are also caught frequently on the high seas and off Australia and South America. They are sometimes drowned in trawl nets.

Breeding: Summer breeders; eggs are laid from late November to December. They lay 1 white egg (82 x 55 mm, 135 g) in a burrow 1–2 m long. The burrow is sometimes quite wet, but the nest itself remains dry because it is on a raised pedestal. Eggs hatch from late January to February after 57–**59**–62 days. Chick are brooded initially but left unguarded from about the fifth day, and then fed at intervals of 1–6 days. Chicks fledge in April–May after 87–**97**–106 days.
Behaviour: Breed in scattered colonies intermingled with Grey Petrels on Antipodes Island, although some colonies are dense warrens of burrows. At sea, they are usually alone but occasionally form small groups at food and sometimes follow ships. They return to their colonies in the late afternoon and circle in loose flocks. Some land in daylight, but most visits are at dusk or after dark. At the colony, they are silent in the air but very noisy on land, with two main calls given on the ground and in their burrows: a succession of clacks or rattles (apparently the origin of the sealers' name 'shoemaker') and a harsh groan or squeal.
Feeding: The diet of three birds from the Auckland and Campbell Islands included squid, salps, crustacea and fish. Most prey is taken on the surface, by diving from the surface or by diving from just above the water.

Reading: Hall, A.J. 1987. *J Zool* (Lond) 212: 605–617. Imber, M.J. 1976. *NZ J Mar Fresh Res* 10: 119–130. Imber, M.J. 1983. *Notornis* 30: 283–298. Jouventin, P. *et al.* 1985. *Notornis* 32: 157–220. Powlesland, R.G. 1989. *Notornis* 36: 299–310. Warham, J. 1988. *Notornis* 35: 169–183. Warham, J. & Bell, B.D. 1979. *Notornis* 26: 121–169.

35. TAHITI PETREL *Pseudobulweria rostrata* Plate 16

Size: 38 cm, 400 g
Geographical variation: Three subspecies: *becki* of the Solomon Islands, *trouessarti* of New

Caledonia and Fiji, and *rostrata* of French Polynesia.
Distribution: Breed on mountainous tropical

and subtropical islands of the South Pacific Ocean, in New Caledonia and on Tahiti, Moorea and in the Marquesas Islands. They may still breed in the Solomons and possibly on Taveuni and Gau Islands of Fiji. They range over deep water of the tropical Pacific and into the western Tasman Sea and the eastern Indian Ocean, off northwestern Australia. One New Zealand specimen from Dargaville Beach (June 1988), but several were also seen east of Northland and in the Bay of Plenty in the winter of 1988.

In the hand: Tahiti Petrels (and other *Pseudobulweria*) have disproportionately large feet, and a notch in the cutting edge of the upper mandible like that found in *Procellaria*. The notch is caused because the latericorn has a blunt end, rather than ending in a point as in *Pterodroma*. The Tahiti Petrel is larger than the other two *Pseudobulweria* species.

Reading: Imber, M.J. 1985. *Ibis* 127: 197–229.
Plant, A.R. et al. 1989. *Notornis* 36: 149–150.
Powlesland, R.G. & Pickard, C.R. 1992. *Notornis* 39: 27–46.

36. KERGUELEN PETREL *Lugensa brevirostris* Plate 15

Size: 33 cm, 350 g
Distribution: Breed on subantarctic islands of the Atlantic and Indian Oceans, including large colonies at Marion Island, Crozet Islands and Kerguelen Island. They range widely in the southern ocean between 35°S and the edge of the pack ice. Fewer than 40 Kerguelen Petrels were recorded in New Zealand before 1973, but they have since become much more regular winter–spring visitors, with 1800+ birds beach-wrecked in the next 20 years, including 600 in 1984. Most are wrecked on the west coast of the North Island in July–November, at a time when adults are nesting (eggs are laid 2–**13**–25 October) 8000 km away, and so must be subadults.

Reading: Imber, M.J. 1984. *Notornis* 31: 89–91.
Jouventin, P. *et al.* 1985. *Notornis* 32: 157–220.

37. SNOW PETREL *Pagodroma nivea* Plate 11

Size: 35 cm, 325 g
Geographical variation: Two subspecies: the Greater Snow Petrel *nivea* breeds on the Balleny Islands in the Ross Dependency and hybridises with the other subspecies at some other colonies, and the Lesser Snow Petrel *minor* breeds widely in Antarctica, including the Ross Dependency.
Distribution: Circumpolar, breeding on ice-free areas of Antarctica and on small islands around the coast, and on southern subantarctic islands in the Atlantic Ocean. Most remain within or close to the edge of the pack ice, and they are rarely recorded north of 55°S. No confirmed records from around the New Zealand mainland.
Population: Abundant, with many colonies, but no data are available on the size of colonies in the Ross Dependency.
Conservation: Protected native.
Breeding: Snow Petrels arrive at their colonies in October and take a pre-laying exodus of 2–3 weeks in late November. Laying is highly synchronous, in the last few days of November and the first week of December. They lay **1** white egg (55 x 40 mm) in a scrape on a ledge, in a crevice or under a rockfall. Eggs hatch in early January after c. 44 days, and the chick is brooded at first but left unguarded from about the fifth day. Chicks fledge in late February and early March at c. 48 days old.
Behaviour: Breed in scattered colonies, but they are probably forced together by limited sites that are relatively free from snow and ice. At sea, they are usually alone but form small groups at food. They do not normally follow ships. Usually silent at sea, but at their colony they have an aerial display accompanied by a chirring call, and they are very noisy on land with a rapid burst of guttural notes.
Feeding: Diet is mainly squid, fish and krill, mostly obtained from the sea surface, either from the air or while resting on the surface.

In the hand: Snow Petrels show great size variation. Wing length ranges from 240 to 320 mm, with 280 mm being used to separate the two subspecies. At some colonies (e.g. Balleny Islands), all are long-winged, at some all are short-winged, whereas at other colonies (e.g. Cape Hallett) there is a mix of forms, and so two races may be hybridising. Overlapping this racial variation, males are heavier and have longer bills than females.

Reading: Brown, D.A. 1966. *ANARE Sci Rep Ser B* 89: 1–63. Cowan, A.N. 1981. *Notornis* 28: 169–188. Croxall, J.P. 1982. *Notornis* 29: 171–180. Falla, R.A. 1937. *Rep BANZARE Ser B.* Harper, P.C. 1987. *Notornis* 34: 169–192. Jouventin, P. & Voit, C.R. 1985. *Ibis* 127: 430–441. Maher, W.J. 1962. *Condor* 64: 488–499.

38. CAPE PIGEON *Daption capense* Plate 11

Other name: Pintado Petrel
Size: 40 cm, 450 g
Geographical variation: Two subspecies: Southern Cape Pigeon *capense* breeds around the Antarctic continent and on many subantarctic islands in the Atlantic and Indian Oceans, whereas the smaller Snares Cape Pigeon *australe* breeds only on subantarctic islands of New Zealand.

Distribution: Circumpolar, breeding on ice-free areas of Antarctica and on small islands around the coast, and on many subantarctic islands. In the New Zealand region, *capense* breeds at the Balleny Islands and at Scott Island in the Antarctic, and *australe* breeds at The Snares, Bounty, Antipodes, Auckland (Beacon Rock) and Campbell Islands. Recently *australe* have extended their range to the Chathams (Forty Fours and probably The Pyramid).

In winter and early spring, many *capense* move north and east and mingle with *australe* in temperate seas as far north as about 25°S in the southwestern Pacific. In winter and spring, Cape Pigeons often follow fishing boats around the mainland coast, but especially to the east of the South Island. They are mainly beach-wrecked in July–November.

Population: Abundant, with many colonies, but no data are available on the size of colonies of *capense* in the Ross Dependency. c. 8500 pairs, with 7500 pairs on The Snares, and <50 pairs at each of the Auckland, Campbell, Bounty and Chatham Islands.

Conservation: Protected native. Cape Pigeons are opportunist feeders, deriving much food as offal from fishing boats, and so have probably benefited from fishing. In the 1960s, when whales were caught in Cook Strait, huge flocks of Cape Pigeons congregated at the entrance to Tory Channel to feed on scraps from the whaling station there. Occasionally Cape Pigeons are accidentally killed on tuna long-lines and in nets, but band recoveries show that adult mortality is low and so such deaths are probably insignificant.

Breeding: The race *australe* at The Snares and the Bounty Islands breeds 2–3 weeks earlier than *capense* on the Antarctic coast. Some birds are at the colonies on The Snares all year, but eggs are laid only from 4–**11**–20 November. They lay **1** white egg (61 x 43 mm, 60g) in a slight scrape on a rocky ledge, in a crevice or cave, or under a rockfall. Eggs hatch in late December to early January after c. 45 days. The chick is brooded for the first 8–10 days, but left unguarded from 8–15 days old. Chicks fledge in mid-February at c. 52 days old. Young return to their natal colony from 16 months old, but do not start breeding until 3–**6**–10+ years old. The oldest bird recorded in New Zealand lived at least 28 years.

Behaviour: Breed in loose colonies and form large flocks at schools of krill and around fishing boats, and formerly around whaling stations and sewer outfalls. They are noisy and aggressive in feeding flocks. At their colonies, they make a range of churring calls.

Feeding: Diet is mainly krill, amphipods, squid, fish and offal, mainly taken on the surface with rapid pigeon-like pecking or by diving from just above the surface. Sometimes they catch crustaceans by filtering water through their bill or by picking them from the surface while still flying.

In the hand: The race *australe* is smaller than *capense*, but measurements overlap extensively.

Males are larger than females; most males of *australe* on The Snares have a head and bill of 77+ mm, and a mid-toe and claw of 60+ mm, whereas females are smaller.

Reading: Beck, J.R. 1969. *Br Ant Surv Bull* 21: 33–44. Harper, P.C. 1987. *Notornis* 34: 169–192. Pinder, R. 1966. *Br Ant Surv Bull* 8: 19–47. Sagar, P.M. 1979. *Notornis* 26: 23–36. Sagar, P.M. 1986. *Notornis* 33: 259–263.

39. ANTARCTIC PETREL *Thalassoica antarctica* Plate 11

Size: 45 cm, 650 g
Distribution: Circumpolar, breeding on ice-free areas of Antarctica and on small islands around the coast, including the Theron, Rockefeller and Shackleton Mountains, and possibly the Balleny and Scott Islands in the Ross Dependency. Most remain within or close to the edge of the pack ice and seldom venture north of 50°S.

No confirmed records from the New Zealand mainland until 1973, when three were beach-wrecked. In August–September 1978, during an influx into New Zealand waters, 73 were wrecked, mainly on beaches on the west coast of the North Island and Southland, and many were seen from Fiordland to Stewart Island. Since then, moderate numbers were recorded in 1987 (9) and 1991 (18), indicating a possible change in their wintering distribution.
Population: c. 3.9 million pairs in the Ross Dependency.
Conservation: Protected native. The greater frequency in New Zealand waters since the mid-1970s may indicate population growth

or a change in feeding patterns related to the decline in whaling, which used to provide good feeding opportunities.
Breeding: Antarctic Petrels arrive at their colonies in early October. Laying is highly synchronous, in the last third of November and the first few days of December. They lay 1 white egg (70 x 49 mm, 90 g) in a shallow scrape on a cliff ledge or in a crevice. Eggs hatch in early January after c. 46 days and chicks fledge in late February at c. 45 days old.
Behaviour: Breed in dense colonies, but they are probably forced together into sites relatively free of snow and ice. At sea, they are usually seen in flocks, with up to 5000 birds recorded feeding around whaling ships. Usually silent at sea, but at their colony they have a variety of churring, clucking and cackling calls.
Feeding: Diet is mainly krill, squid and small fish picked from the sea surface.

Reading: Ainley, D.G. *et al.* 1984. *AOU Orn Monogr* 32: 1–97. Barlow, M. 1979. *Notornis* 26: 313. Falla, R.A. 1937. *Rep BANZARE* Ser B. Orton, M.N. 1968. *Emu* 67: 225–229.

40. ANTARCTIC FULMAR *Fulmarus glacialoides* Plate 11

Other name: Silver-grey Fulmar
Size: 50 cm, 800 g
Distribution: Circumpolar, breeding on ice-free areas of Antarctica and on small islands around the coast, including the Balleny Islands in the Ross Dependency. They also breed on southern subantarctic islands of the Atlantic Ocean. Most remain close to the edge of the pack ice in summer, but they disperse through the southern oceans to about 35°S and further north in the Humboldt Current off South America.

Fewer than 10 Antarctic Fulmars were recorded from New Zealand beaches before

1970, but they have since become much more regular winter–spring visitors to New Zealand waters. Over 2000 birds were beach-wrecked in the 25 years following 1970, including major wrecks in 1975 (639), 1978 (458) and 1985 (366). Most are beach-wrecked in September–November on the west coast of the North Island and in Southland. Because adults are starting to return to their Antarctic colonies in early October, most birds wrecked are presumably subadults.
Population: Common; colonies are scattered around the Antarctic coast and 1 million+ pairs breed on the South Sandwich Islands.

No estimate of the size of the Balleny Islands population is available.

Conservation: Protected native. The greater frequency in New Zealand waters since the mid-1970s may indicate population growth or a change in feeding patterns related to the decline in whaling, which used to provide good feeding opportunities.

Breeding: Antarctic Fulmars arrive at their ice-free colonies in early October. Laying is highly synchronous, in early December. They lay 1 white egg (76 x 51 mm, 103 g) in a shallow scrape on a steep shingle scree, on a cliff ledge, or in a crevice. Eggs hatch in mid-January after c. 45 days and chicks fledge in early March at c. 52 days old.

Behaviour: Breed in colonies. At sea, they are often seen alone, but when feeding they often join large mixed flocks at schools of krill or around whaling ships or fishing boats. When feeding in flocks, they are often noisy and aggressive, but otherwise they are usually silent at sea. At their colony, they give loud cackling calls, sometimes as a duet.

Feeding: Diet is mainly krill, squid and small fish picked from the sea surface.

Reading: Ainley, D.G. *et al.* 1984. *AOU Orn Monogr* 32: 1–97. Falla, R.A. 1937. *Rep BANZARE Ser B.* Mougin, J.-L. 1967. *Oiseau* 37: 57–103. Mougin, J.-L. 1967. *Com Natn Fr Rech Ant* 36: 1–195. Orton, M.N. 1968. *Emu* 67: 225–229. Powlesland, R.G. 1986. *Notornis* 33: 171–184.

41. SOUTHERN GIANT PETREL *Macronectes giganteus* Plate 6

Other name: Nelly
Size: 90 cm, 4.5 kg
Distribution: Circumpolar, breeding on ice-free areas of Antarctica, on small islands around the coast, on many subantarctic islands and on islands off the Chilean coast. In the New Zealand region, one pair has nested at Cape Crozier, Ross Dependency. The nearest stronghold is Australia's Macquarie Island, where c. 4000 pairs breed. Most remain near Antarctica and in the subantarctic zone during the summer and autumn. Some adults and many subadults disperse eastwards and northwards to about 30°S in winter and spring, and some follow the Humboldt Current to 10°S off South America.

Although the two species are difficult to distinguish at sea, Southern Giant Petrels are probably more common than Northern Giant Petrels in New Zealand waters in winter and spring. Of 77 banded Southern Giant Petrels recovered in New Zealand, most were fledglings that left South Atlantic colonies in April–May and were recovered June–September.

Population: Moderately common, with main colonies (5000+ pairs) on South Orkney, South Shetland and South Georgia Islands in the South Atlantic Ocean.

Behaviour: At sea, they are often seen alone, but they join large mixed flocks when feeding around fishing boats, and formerly they used to gather around whaling ships, sewer and abattoir outfalls. When feeding in flocks they are often noisy and aggressive, but otherwise they are usually silent at sea.

Feeding: Voracious scavengers and predators, feeding on dead penguins and marine mammals, and offal. Giant petrels often kill penguins and other small seabirds, and are even known to have drowned and eaten small albatrosses. The diet also includes crustaceans, squid and fish taken from the sea surface.

In the hand: Separated from Northern Giant Petrel *M. halli* by having a green, not brownish, tip to the bill. Males are larger than females, and most adults can be sexed on bill length: males >97 mm, females <95 mm.

Reading: Hunter, S. 1984. *J Zool* (Lond) 203: 441–460. Johnstone, G.W. 1974. *Emu* 74: 209–218. Powlesland, R.G. 1986. *Notornis* 33: 171–184. Warham, J. 1962. *Auk* 79: 139–160.

42. NORTHERN GIANT PETREL   *Macronectes halli*   Plate 6

Other name: Nelly
Size: 90 cm, 4.5 kg
Distribution: Circumpolar, breeding on many subantarctic islands, including The Sisters and Motuhara (Forty Fours Islands) of the Chathams, on an island in Port Pegasus in southern Stewart Island, and on the Antipodes, Auckland and Campbell Islands. They range widely in the subantarctic zone during the summer and autumn. Some adults and many subadults disperse eastwards and northwards to about 35°S in winter and spring, and some follow the Humboldt Current to about 20°S off South America.

Although the two species are difficult to distinguish at sea, Northern Giant Petrels are probably more commonly beach-wrecked than Southern Giant Petrels in New Zealand waters in summer and autumn, but they are outnumbered by the southern species in winter and spring. Birds banded on Campbell Island have been recovered mainly around New Zealand and in the Tasman Sea, but also on the coast of Argentina. Up to the 1970s, when sewage and abattoir waste were dumped into Wellington Harbour and a whaling station operated just inside the entrance to Tory Channel in the Marlborough Sounds, hundreds of giant petrels (probably mainly of this species) were seen in the Cook Strait area, especially in October–March. Now that these sources of offal have gone, only the odd bird is now seen following fishing boats and the Cook Strait ferries.
Population: Uncommon, with main colonies (1500+ pairs) on South Georgia in the South Atlantic Ocean and Kerguelen Island in the Indian Ocean. New Zealand colonies total c. 2500 pairs, including c. 2000 pairs in the Chathams (mainly on the Forty Fours), 230 pairs on the Antipodes, 230 pairs on Campbell Island and 50+ pairs in the Auckland Islands.
Conservation: Protected native. The size and trends of New Zealand populations are not well known, but appear to be moderately stable even though some offal sources have decreased, and some birds are caught on tuna long-lines.
Breeding: In the New Zealand region, Northern Giant Petrels lay from mid-August to early September. They lay 1 white egg (102 x 66 mm) in a cup-shaped nest built of tussock and other vegetation. Eggs hatch in October–November after c. 60 days. Chicks are brooded for the first 2–3 weeks and then guarded for another fortnight. They fledge in February at c. 112 days old.
Behaviour: Nest in colonies. At sea, they are often seen alone, but they join large mixed flocks when feeding around fishing boats, and they used to gather around whaling ships, sewer outfalls and abattoir outfalls. When feeding in flocks they are often noisy and aggressive, but otherwise they are usually silent at sea.
Feeding: Males tend to be voracious predators and scavengers, killing penguins and feeding on dead birds and marine mammals, whereas females tend to feed more on crustaceans, squid and fish taken from the sea surface.

In the hand: Separated from the dark phase of the Southern Giant Petrel *M. giganteus* by having a brownish, not green, tip to the bill. Males are larger than females, and most adults can be sexed on bill length: males >97 mm, females <95 mm.

Reading: Bailey, A.M. & Sorensen, J.H. 1950. *Subantarctic Campbell Island.* Denver: Denver Mus Nat Hist. Hunter, S. 1984. *J Zool* (Lond) 203: 441–460. McIlwaine, C.P. 1964. *Emu* 64: 33–38. Powlesland, R.G. 1986. *Notornis* 33: 171–184. Robertson, H.A. 1992. *Notornis* 39: 263–289.

43. FAIRY PRION   *Pachyptila turtur*   Plate 12

Other name: Titi Wainui
Size: 25 cm, 125 g
Distribution: Circumpolar, breeding on many subantarctic islands, in Bass Strait and on many islands around the New Zealand mainland and at the Chathams, The Snares, Antipodes Islands and possibly on islets off Campbell Island. The main colonies around

the mainland are at the Poor Knights, in Cook Strait (Stephens, Trios and Brothers Islands), Motunau Island, Foveaux Strait islands and the muttonbird islands off Stewart Island. Some small colonies exist on islands off the Otago coast and also on ledges on nearby sea cliffs on the mainland.

In summer, they range through temperate waters around the mainland coast, in the Tasman Sea and east into the South Pacific. In winter, many are in Foveaux Strait, in the Cook Strait and Taranaki Bight area, and east of Northland, but some disperse further north into subtropical waters as far as the Coral Sea and the Kermadecs. Elsewhere, some reach waters off South America and South Africa. Birds banded on Stephens Island have been recovered mainly around New Zealand and eastern Australia. Fairy Prions are the most common bird beach-wrecked in New Zealand, with peaks of recoveries in February, when fledglings disperse to sea, and July–November, when many subadults are wrecked on west coast beaches after severe storms or persistent westerly winds.

Population: Abundant; 1 million+ pairs in New Zealand, but little data are available on numbers nesting at each colony.

Conservation: Protected native. Chicks used to be harvested by Maori but are now protected. Introduced predators (cats, rats and mustelids) have exterminated many colonies on offshore islands, but the existing colonies seem secure as long as they remain free of predators. At Stephens Island, tuatara are responsible for the loss of over 25% of eggs and chicks, but this probably has little effect. Occasional large wrecks (e.g. in the mid-1970s and mid-1980s) of mainly subadults are also natural events.

Breeding: Adults start returning to their breeding colonies from late March, but do not start cleaning out burrows until late July. Laying varies from mid-October at the Poor Knights, 19 October to 10 November at Stephens Island, to early November at Whero Island and at the Chathams. They lay **1** white egg (44 x 32 mm, 23 g) in a burrow 0.6–2 m long, or in a shallow crevice. Incubation shifts are of 1–**2**–5 days on the Poor Knights, but the other partner often returns each night; whereas on Whero Island, incubation spells are of 6–7 days. Eggs hatch 21 November to 4 December on the Poor Knights, 3–12 December on Stephens Island, and 18 December to 19 January on Whero Island. The incubation period is 44–**47**–54 days.

Chicks are brooded continuously for the first 1–**2**–5 days and then left unguarded. Chicks fledge from the Poor Knights in January, from Stephens Island from mid-January to early February, and from Whero Island from early February to early March. The fledging period is **45** days on the Poor Knights but 43–**50**–56 days on Whero Island. Pairs usually occupy the same nest site each year, and divorces are uncommon. Annual adult survivorship is estimated at 84%, giving a mean life expectancy of 5.9 years, but the oldest bird recorded lived over 22 years.

Behaviour: Nest in colonies. At sea, they are often seen in flocks as they feed, roost or stream back to their colonies at dusk. They are silent at sea but very vocal at their colonies, both in the air and on the ground. Males give a harsh, repeated three-note call: 'poor, pop, per', and a very rapid rattling call, whereas females give a harsh two-note call: 'errr, errr'.

Feeding: Diet is mainly krill, supplemented by other planktonic crustacea and invertebrates, and small fish. Most prey is taken from the sea surface.

In the hand: Fairy Prions have a much wider (35–45 mm) black band at the tip of the tail than other prions (except Fulmar Prions), the wing is 170–**179**–189 mm, and the bill is 20–25 mm long and 10–12 mm wide (but note that bills of beach-wrecked birds, especially juveniles, shrink as they dry out).

Reading: Harper, P.C. 1976. *NZ J Zool* 3: 351–371. Harper, P.C. 1980. *Notornis* 27: 235–286. Harper, P.C. 1987. *Notornis* 34: 169–192. Powlesland, R.G. 1989. *Notornis* 36: 125–140. Richdale, L.E. 1965. *Trans Zool Soc* (Lond) 31: 87–155. Walls, G.Y. 1978. *NZ J Ecol* 1: 91–98.

44. FULMAR PRION   *Pachyptila crassirostris*   Plate 12

Size: 26 cm, 140 g
Geographical variation: Three subspecies: *crassirostris* breeds at the Bounty Islands and The Snares, *pyramidalis* breeds at the Chathams, and *flemingi* breeds at the Auckland Islands and Heard Island (South Indian Ocean).
Distribution: Breed at the Chathams (Motuhara [Forty Fours] and The Pyramid), Bounty Islands, The Snares (Western Chain), Auckland (Rose, Ewing and Ocean) and Heard Islands. They are apparently quite sedentary, but some are storm-drifted to mainland New Zealand coasts in winter and spring.
Population: Uncommon; probably fewer than 40,000 pairs, of which c. 30,000 nest on the Bounty Islands, 1000–5000 on the Chathams, 1000 on the Auckland Islands and 400–600 on the Western Chain of The Snares.
Conservation: Protected native. No information is available about historical changes in numbers or breeding distribution.
Breeding: No detailed studies. As eggs hatch on The Snares in mid-December, they are probably laid in late October. They lay **1** white egg (46 x 33 mm) in a shallow scrape, sometimes lined with feathers, under rockfalls, in caves or in crevices. Chicks have fledged from The Snares by 11 February.

Behaviour: Nest in colonies. The birds nesting on the Bounty Islands and The Snares are unusual among prions in visiting their nests in daylight and in courting and calling by day and not at night. On the Bounty Islands, flocks of about 100 prions mob any gulls or skuas venturing over the islands in daylight. They are very vocal at their colonies, both in the air and on the ground, with males apparently giving a clear four-note call and females responding with a slurred three-note call.
Feeding: Diet is mainly crustaceans and juvenile barnacles picked from the sea surface.

In the hand: Fulmar Prions are quite similar to Fairy Prions, but Fulmar Prions have a slightly narrower tail band and generally longer wing (175–**188**–203 mm, but this varies considerably from colony to colony), and the bill is flattened and the hook is smaller. The race *pyramidalis* is the largest, with long wings (182–**193**–203 mm) and wide bill (12–13 mm), *crassirostris* is intermediate (175–**183**–193 mm and 10–12 mm respectively), and *flemingi* is the smallest (174–**179**–187 mm and 9.5–11 mm respectively).

Reading: Harper, P.C. 1980. *Notornis* 27: 235–286. Harper, P.C. 1987. *Notornis* 34: 169–192. Miskelly, C.M. 1984. *Notornis* 31: 209–223. Robertson, C.J.R. & van Tets, G.F. 1982. *Notornis* 29: 311–336. Sagar, P.M. 1977. *Notornis* 24: 178–183.

45. THIN-BILLED PRION   *Pachyptila belcheri*   Plate 12

Other names: Narrow-billed Prion, Slender-billed Prion
Size: 26 cm, 145 g
Distribution: Breed on Isla Noir (off the Pacific coast of Chile), Falkland Islands, East Island in the Crozet Islands and on Kerguelen Island. In autumn, birds from the Patagonian region disperse westwards into the South Pacific but are not known to reach New Zealand; however, birds from the large colonies on Kerguelen Island in the South Indian Ocean disperse eastwards and many, mainly young birds, reach New Zealand waters in winter. About 50 are beach-wrecked on west coast beaches each year in July–August, but they are occasionally wrecked in large numbers in June–August (e.g. 1300

in 1974, and 1400 in 1986).
Feeding: Diet is mainly small amphipods, fish, squid and krill. Food is obtained at night by picking from the sea surface while resting on the surface, by dipping from in flight or while pattering along the surface.

In the hand: Thin-billed Prions are one of the three smaller prions: wing 165–**180**–190 mm; bill 23–**25**–27 mm, but with a moderately long culminicorn (8–10 mm) compared with Fairy Prion (4–6 mm). They have paler wingtips than other prions, and, unlike others, the undertail lacks a black terminal band.

Reading: Harper, P.C. 1972. *Notornis* 19: 140–175. Harper, P.C. 1980. *Notornis* 27: 235–286. Harper, P.C. 1987. *Notornis* 34: 169–192.

46. ANTARCTIC PRION   *Pachyptila desolata*   Plate 12

Size: 26 cm, 150 g
Geographical variation: Two subspecies: *desolata* breeds at the Kerguelen and Crozet Islands in the central South Indian Ocean, and *banksi* breeds in the South Atlantic Ocean, on Heard Island, on Macquarie Island and in the New Zealand region.

Distribution: Circumpolar, breeding on many subantarctic and antarctic islands, including the Auckland Islands, Scott Island in the Ross Dependency, and possibly on islets off Campbell Island. Vagrants reach the Chathams, and one may have been prospecting on Houruakopara Island. Most remain close to their breeding colonies during summer, but they disperse widely through southern oceans to about 35°S in winter, and some straggle into subtropical waters to reach the Kermadec Islands and Vanuatu. A few *desolata* reach the west coast of New Zealand, but *banksi* regularly appears in small numbers in New Zealand waters in winter. About 50 Antarctic Prions are found beach-wrecked on west coast beaches each year in May–October, but they are occasionally wrecked in large numbers in June–August (e.g. 3200 in 1974, and 1000 in 1986).

Population: Abundant, with huge numbers breeding on South Georgia (22 million pairs) and Kerguelen Island (2–3 million pairs). In the New Zealand region, between 100,000 and 1 million pairs breed on the Auckland Islands, and fewer than 200 pairs breed on Scott Island.

Conservation: Protected native. Introduced cats and pigs have exterminated many colonies on Auckland Island, but they remain common on offshore islands. Occasional large wrecks of mainly subadults probably have little effect on the species.

Breeding: Not studied in New Zealand, but probably like other colonies, where adults return in October and lay in December. They lay 1 white egg (47 x 35 mm, 33 g) in a burrow or rock crevice. Eggs hatch in late January to early February after c. 45 days and young fledge from mid-March to early April at c. 50 days old.

Behaviour: At sea, they are often seen in flocks as they feed, roost or stream back to their colonies at dusk. They are silent at sea but very vocal at their colonies, both in the air and on the ground.

Feeding: Diet is mainly crustaceans and other planktonic invertebrates, but some small fish and squid are eaten. Most are taken while the bird is swimming, by sieving minute prey on to the comb-like lamellae inside the upper bill.

In the hand: Antarctic Prions have a wider bill (11–15.5 mm) than Fairy Prions (9–12.5 mm). They are similar to Salvin's Prions, except that the bill is usually narrower (cf. 13.5–17.5 mm) and when the closed bill is viewed from the side the lamellae are not visible at the base.

Reading: Harper, P.C. 1972. *Notornis* 19: 140–175. Harper, P.C. 1980. *Notornis* 27: 235–286. Harper, P.C. 1987. *Notornis* 34: 169–192. Powlesland, R.G. 1989. *Notornis* 36: 125–140. Tickell, W.L.N. 1962. *Falkland Is Dep Surv Sci Rep* 33: 1–55.

47. SALVIN'S PRION   *Pachyptila salvini*   Plate 12

Other name: Lesser Broad-billed Prion
Size: 27 cm, 170 g
Geographical variation: Two subspecies: *salvini* breeds on islands in the eastern and central subantarctic South Indian Ocean and regularly reaches New Zealand waters, whereas the rare *macgillivrayi* breeds on St Paul and Amsterdam Islands in the temperate South Indian Ocean and has not been recorded in New Zealand.

Distribution: Breed only in the South Indian Ocean, on Marion, Prince Edward, Crozet, St Paul and Amsterdam Islands. They remain close to their breeding colonies during summer, but in winter they disperse eastwards between 35 and 55°S as far as New Zealand. About 50–100, mainly juveniles, are found beach-wrecked on west coast beaches each winter, but subadults are occasionally wrecked in large numbers in June–August (e.g. 1300 in 1970, and 5200 in 1974).

Feeding: Diet is mainly crustaceans and other planktonic invertebrates, but some small fish and squid are eaten. Most are taken while the bird is swimming, by sieving minute prey on to the comb-like lamellae inside the upper bill.

In the hand: Salvin's Prions have a much a wider bill (13.5–17.5 mm) than Fairy Prions (9–12.5 mm). They are similar to Antarctic Prions, except that the bill is usually wider (cf. 11–15.5 mm) and when the closed bill is viewed from the side the lamellae are clearly visible at the base.

Reading: Harper, P.C. 1980. *Notornis* 27: 235–286. Powlesland, R.G. 1989. *Notornis* 36: 125–140.

48. BROAD-BILLED PRION   *Pachyptila vittata*   Plate 12

Other names: Parara, Whalebird
Size: 28 cm, 200 g
Distribution: Broad-billed Prions have a disjunct distribution, with breeding populations on Tristan da Cunha, Nightingale, Inaccessible and Gough Islands in the South Atlantic Ocean, and on many islands about southern New Zealand: in Fiordland, Solander Islands, Foveaux Strait and on islands and stacks around Stewart Island, The Snares and most islands in the Chathams group. New Zealand birds range through temperate waters close to the Subtropical Convergence between 35 and 50°S in the Tasman Sea and Bass Strait, and in the central South Pacific. About 50–100 are wrecked on Southland and North Island west coast beaches each year in June–January, but wrecks are large in some winters (e.g. 1400 in 1961, and 1200 in 1984).
Population: Abundant, with large colonies on the Chathams (especially South East Island, c. 330,000 pairs) and on Foveaux Strait islands.
Conservation: Protected native. Chicks used to be harvested by Maori but are now protected. Introduced predators (cats, rats and Weka) have exterminated many colonies, but the species remains safe on predator-free islands. Occasional large wrecks of mainly subadults are unlikely to affect the species.
Breeding: Adults return to their colonies from February onwards to prepare burrows and to court. Laying is in late August to mid-September at all New Zealand colonies. They lay **1** white egg (50 x 36 mm) in a burrow, rock crevice or cave. Eggs hatch in mid-October to early November after c. 45 days and young fledge in mid-December to mid-January at c. 55 days old.
Behaviour: Nest in huge colonies, often interspersed with other burrowing petrels. At sea, they are often seen in flocks as they feed, roost or stream back to their colonies at dusk. They are silent at sea but very vocal at their colonies, with persistent harsh calls given both in the air and on the ground; similar to those of Fairy Prions, but louder, faster and with more notes.
Feeding: Diet is mainly copepods, other crustaceans and other planktonic invertebrates, but some small fish and squid are eaten. Most are taken from the sea surface while the bird is scurrying forwards rapidly with beak held partly open under the sea surface and moving its head from side to side, or by shallow plunging from the surface. Minute prey are sieved on to the well-developed comb-like lamellae inside the upper bill.

In the hand: Broad-billed Prions are the largest prion (wing 195–225 mm) and have a large head and grotesquely wide bill (19–24 mm), which does not overlap in size with that of any other prion.

Reading: Harper, P.C. 1980. *Notornis* 27: 235–286. Harper, P.C. 1987. *Notornis* 34: 169–192. Imber, M.J. 1981. In *Proc Symp Birds Sea Shore*. Cape Town: African Seabird Group. Powlesland, R.G. 1989. *Notornis* 36: 125–140. Richdale, L.E. 1944. *Emu* 43: 191–217. Richdale, L.E. 1965. *Trans Zool Soc* (Lond) 31: 87–155.

49. BLUE PETREL *Halobaena caerulea* Plates 11 and 12

Size: 29 cm, 200 g

Distribution: Circumpolar, breeding on many subantarctic islands but not in the New Zealand region. The closest colony is 500–600 pairs on stacks off Macquarie Island. They are sedentary during the summer breeding season, but then range widely through the southern oceans between the pack ice and about 40°S. Blue Petrels are regular winter–spring visitors to New Zealand waters and have become more common since about 1980. Each year, 10–100 are usually beach-wrecked on west coast beaches in July–November; however, subadults are occasionally wrecked in large numbers in August–October (e.g. 343 in 1981, 881 in 1984, 527 in 1985, and 372 in 1991).

Feeding: Diet is mainly crustaceans, small fish and squid, taken from the sea surface by dipping in flight or while the bird is swimming. Blue Petrels occasionally follow ships or attend feeding whales.

Reading: Jouventin, P. *et al.* 1985. *Notornis* 32: 157–220. Prince, P.A. 1980. *J Zool* (Lond) 190: 59–76. Reed, S. 1981. *Notornis* 28: 239–240.

50. STEJNEGER'S PETREL *Pterodroma longirostris* Plate 13

Size: 28 cm, 150 g

Distribution: Breed only on Mas-a-Feura Island (Isla Alejandro Selkirk) in the Juan Fernandez archipelago off Chile. About 130,000 pairs breed there, but they are in decline owing to predation by cats. They migrate to the subtropical North Pacific Ocean between Hawai'i and Japan, where they stay from June to November. Vagrants reach temperate seas around the North Island in November– February, with 11 records up to 1995.

In the hand: Stejneger's Petrels have similar plumage to Cook's and Pycroft's Petrels, but they have a white forehead contrasting with the black cap, and their wing (200–220 mm) is shorter than that of Cook's Petrel (220–245 mm). Gould's Petrel has much more extensive black on the nape and sides to the neck.

Reading: Brooke, M.deL. 1987. *Condor* 89: 581–586. Powlesland, R.G. 1985. *Notornis* 32: 23–41.

51. PYCROFT'S PETREL *Pterodroma pycrofti* Plate 13

Size: 28 cm, 160 g

Distribution: Breed only in New Zealand, on islands off the northeastern coast of the North Island. They nest on Stephenson, Poor Knights (Aorangi), Hen and Chickens (Hen, Lady Alice, Whatupuke, Coppermine and Mauitaha) and Mercury (Red Mercury, Korapuki, Double and Stanley) Islands. Subfossil remains from Norfolk and Lord Howe Islands indicates that they formerly had a wider breeding distribution. Judging from the distribution of Pycroft's Petrels found beach-wrecked, they spend the summer in temperate or subtropical waters off the northern North Island, mainly to the east. They migrate to the North Pacific Ocean in the non-breeding season (May–September).

Population: c. 5000 pairs, and a total population of c. 20,000 birds. The largest colonies are on Red Mercury Island (3000–5000 pairs), Chickens Islands (500 pairs) and Double Island (100 pairs).

Conservation: Protected threatened endemic. They breed only on predator-free islands or those with only the Pacific rat present. However, it seems that Pacific rats are responsible for most breeding failures, so recent programmes to eradicate them from some of the Mercury group and some of the Chickens should improve breeding success, but conflict with Little Shearwaters for nesting sites may increase if they also increase in numbers.

Breeding: Adults return to their colonies in October to prepare burrows and to court. Egg-laying is from c. 15 November to c. 20

December. They lay **1** white egg (49 x 35 mm, 32 g) in a burrow 30–130 cm long. Eggs hatch in late January after c. 47 days and young fledge from mid-March to mid-April at c. 80 days old.

Behaviour: Nest in small, localised colonies, interspersed with other burrowing petrels. They are very vocal at their colonies, with a rapid, high-pitched 'kek-kek-kek . . .' aerial call and a variety of calls given on the ground.

Feeding: Diet is not known, except that remains of small squid have been found in stomachs.

In the hand: Pycroft's Petrels are very similar to, though smaller than, Cook's Petrels and were not separated until 1933. They have shorter wings (207–229 mm) than Cook's Petrels (223–245 mm) and shorter bills (22.5–26 mm cf. 24.5–30 mm), but longer tails (88–103 mm cf. 82–95 mm).

Reading: Bartle, J.A. 1968. *Notornis* 15: 70–99. Dunnet, G.M. 1985. *Notornis* 32: 5–21. Powlesland, R.G. 1987. *Notornis* 34: 237–252.

52. GOULD'S PETREL *Pterodroma leucoptera* Plate 13

Size: 29 cm, 175 g

Geographical variation: Two subspecies: *leucoptera* breeds off New South Wales and has not been recorded in New Zealand; *caledonica* breeds on New Caledonia and straggles to New Zealand. The Collared Petrel (*P. brevipes*) of Vanuatu, Fiji, the Cook Islands and possibly the Solomon Islands and French Polynesia is sometimes treated as a subspecies of Gould's Petrel.

Distribution: Breed only on Cabbage Tree Island, New South Wales, and along the central mountain range of New Caledonia. They migrate to the eastern tropical Pacific, especially to the southwest of the Galapagos Islands in July–October. During the breeding season, non-breeders are regularly seen in the Tasman Sea as far south as Foveaux Strait, and 27 have been beach-wrecked to 1997, mainly on the west coast of the North Island,

in December–May.

In the hand: Gould's Petrels have a distinctive black cap, nape and sides to the neck and have slightly shorter wings (213–238 mm) than Cook's Petrel's (220–245 mm) and shorter bills (23–27.5 mm cf. 24.5–30 mm). The most reliable feature to separate *caledonica* from *leucoptera* is that the inner web of the outermost tail feather of *caledonica* is white, or mainly white, with a variable amount of grey flecking near the tip, whereas in the nominate *leucoptera* the outer feather is grey to brownish grey, apart from the basal inner half being off-white. Also, *caledonica* is larger than *leucoptera* (wing: 219–**229**–235 mm cf. 213–**225**–238 mm; bill 23.5–**25.4**–27.5 mm cf. 23–**24.6**–26.5 mm) and has more of a contrast in colour between the grey of its back and uppertail coverts and the dark grey of the rest of the upperparts.

Reading: Imber, M.J. & Jenkins, J.A.F. 1981. *Notornis* 28: 149–160. Powlesland, R.G. 1985. *Notornis* 32: 23–41.

53. COOK'S PETREL *Pterodroma cookii* Plate 13

Other name: Titi
Size: 29 cm, 200 g
Distribution: Breed only in New Zealand, on Little Barrier, Great Barrier and Codfish Islands. Subfossil and midden evidence suggests that they formerly bred on the mainland of both North and South Islands. During the summer breeding season, they range mainly east of New Zealand, especially off the North Island between East Cape and Cook Strait, and east of Foveaux Strait.

Cook's Petrels migrate to the eastern

Pacific Ocean, mainly between 34°S and 30°N and straggle further north into the Gulf of Alaska. They leave New Zealand waters in April and return about August, although a few remain through the winter. They are the commonest small gadfly petrel beach-wrecked on the New Zealand coast. About 25 are found each year, mainly on Auckland and Bay of Plenty beaches with peaks in December and March–April, when chicks have just fledged.

Population: c. 50,000 pairs on Little Barrier

Island, <5 pairs on Great Barrier Island and 100 pairs on Codfish Island (Whenua Hou). **Conservation:** Protected endemic. Chicks used to be collected by Maori, and adults were killed when attracted to fires lit on flight paths to colonies, but they are now protected. About 20,000 pairs of Cook's Petrels bred on Codfish Island in the early 1900s, but predation by Weka reduced them to 100 pairs by 1980; however, they are showing signs of recovery since Weka were removed from the island in 1985. Likewise, the numbers on Little Barrier Island have increased after the eradication of cats there in 1980 and further gains are expected after the eradication of kiore in 2004. Pacific rats are at all breeding sites and still cause serious losses of eggs and chicks.

Breeding: Adults return to their colonies in August to prepare burrows and to court. Laying is from 23 October to 3 December on Little Barrier Island, but about a month later on Codfish Island. They lay **1** white egg (53 x 39 mm, 43 g) in a deep burrow 1–5 m long. Eggs hatch on Little Barrier from mid-December to mid-January after c. 47 days, and young fledge from mid-March to mid-April at c. 88 days old. Chicks fledge from Codfish Island from mid-April to early May.

Behaviour: Nest in large colonies, often interspersed with Black Petrels in the north. They are very vocal over their colonies, with a rapid three-note 'kek-kek-kek' and other aerial calls, and they make high-speed dives above the colony with vibrating feathers making a whistling sound. On the ground, they give a loud purring call. Cook's Petrels often call over land as they are heading for their breeding colonies, and are heard over Northland, Auckland and Stewart Island at night.

Feeding: Diet is mainly squid, crustaceans and small fish. Judging from the composition of the diet, most prey is probably taken at night.

In the hand: Cook's Petrels are similar to about 10 other small gadfly petrels, but they have a very pale underwing with only a small black line extending from the bend of the wing towards the body. Their wing (223–245 mm) and bill (24.5–30 mm) are longer than most similar species (Pycroft's, Stejneger's and Gould's Petrels), and they have a white wedge-shaped patch covering about 60% of the inner web of the primaries, which is not as large on other species, with the exception of some Pycroft's Petrels.

Reading: Powlesland, R.G. 1987. *Notornis* 34: 237–252. West, J.A. 1990. *DoC Sci & Res Int Rep* No. 85.

54. BLACK-WINGED PETREL   *Pterodroma nigripennis*   Plates 13 and 14

Size: 30 cm, 175 g

Distribution: Breed in the southwestern Pacific, at Lord Howe Island, Philip Island off Norfolk Island, islets off New Caledonia, in the New Zealand region, Tonga, the Cook Islands, on islets off Rapa Island and on Bass Rock in French Polynesia. In New Zealand, they breed at the Kermadecs, Three Kings, East and Portland Islands and in the Chathams (South East, Mangere and possibly Star Keys). Black-winged Petrels, expanding their breeding range, have been seen prospecting for nest sites on islands off Australia and on some headlands and islands around the northern North Island.

During the summer breeding season, they range through the subtropical southwestern Pacific and temperate waters of the Tasman Sea, as far south as Foveaux Strait. In May,

they migrate to the subtropical North Pacific Ocean, mainly between 0 and 30°N, from Japan to Mexico. They return to New Zealand waters in late October. About 130 were beach-wrecked on the New Zealand coast from 1960 to 1990, with most found on the west coast of the North Island in December–April.

Population: Common and increasing breeding range, including the recent establishment of breeding pairs on East and Portland Islands off the Gisborne coast and on Mangere Island in the Chathams. Although now rare on Raoul Island, other islands in the Kermadec group have large colonies, with 2–3 million pairs on Macauley Island.

Conservation: Protected native. Huge colonies on Norfolk and Raoul Islands were exterminated by cats and rats, but those on predator-free islands are flourishing and

Black-winged Petrels are expanding their range, even though this leads to many prospecting birds being killed on the ground at some mainland headlands.

Breeding: Adults return to their colonies in mid-October to early December to prepare burrows and to court. Laying is from late December to mid-January in the Kermadecs and about a fortnight later on East Island and in the Chathams, where eggs are laid in mid-January. They lay 1 white egg (52 x 37 mm, 37 g) in a burrow 0.5–1 m long. Chicks hatch in late February to early March at the Chathams, and fledge April–May at the Kermadecs.

Behaviour: Very vocal over their colonies, with a low 'ahh-oo' followed by a rapid 'wi-wi-wi-wi' call. On the ground, the main calls are a rapid, hysterical 'haa-ha-haa-ha . . .', and a low 'orrrrrr . . .' lasting up to 3–4 seconds.

Feeding: Diet is squid, small fish and crustaceans taken on the surface at night.

In the hand: Black-winged Petrels have an unmistakable underwing pattern with a broad black band along the leading edge of the outer upperwing, angling diagonally across the wing towards the body from the elbow but stopping before the axillaries. The bill is more robust than in the otherwise similar Pycroft's Petrel (bill length x depth x width: 23–26 x 10.5–12 x 9–12 mm cf. 22.5–26 x 9.5–10.5 x 7.5–9.5)

Reading: Jenkins, J.A.F. & Cheshire, N.G. 1982. *Notornis* 29: 293–310. Powlesland, R.G. 1985. *Notornis* 32: 23–41. Tanaka, Y. *et al.* 1985. *J Yamashina Inst Orn* 17: 23–31. Tennyson, A.J.D. 1991. *Notornis* 38: 111–116.

55. CHATHAM PETREL *Pterodroma axillaris* Plate 14

Size: 30 cm, 200 g

Distribution: Breed only in New Zealand, on South East Island in the Chathams, but subfossils show that they used to breed more widely in the Chatham group. They are assumed to feed mainly near to or east of the Chathams because they have not been beach-wrecked on the New Zealand mainland. They are assumed also to migrate to the North Pacific Ocean in June–November as the closely related Black-winged Petrel does.

Population: 250 pairs, and a total population of c. 1000 birds in 2004.

Conservation: Protected endangered endemic. Colonies on Chatham, Pitt and Mangere Island were exterminated in pre-European times, but Chatham Petrels were rediscovered on South East Island in 1973 after over 30 years with no records. As Broad-billed Prions compete for nest sites and kill chicks and even adults, they have been culled in and around known burrows, and natural burrows have been replaced with prion-proof artificial nest chambers, to reduce nest competition. Breeding success has improved from 10–30% to over 50% per year.

Breeding: Adults return to South East Island in late November and early December to prepare burrows and to court. Laying is from 20 December to late February. They lay 1 white egg (52 x 39 mm, 47 g) in a deep burrow 0.5–2 m long. Eggs hatch in February to early April and chicks fledge in May to early July. Some birds return to their natal colony at 2 years old. Mean life expectancy of adults is c. 20 years.

Behaviour: Nest solitarily, interspersed with nesting Broad-billed Prions, Common Diving Petrels and storm petrels. They are very vocal over their colonies, with a rapid 'chee-chee-chee . . .' call, sometimes answered by a 'coooo' or 'wikooo'. Also reported is a rapid 'wek-wek-wek . . .' and a purring ground call.

Feeding: Diet includes squid and small fish.

In the hand: Chatham Petrels are similar to Black-winged Petrels, but they have black axillaries (base of the underwing), and their wings are shorter (212–228 mm cf. 215–235 mm).

Reading: Fleming, C.A. 1939. *Emu* 38: 380–413. Imber, M.J. 1985. *Ibis* 127: 197–229. West, J.A. 1994. *Notornis* 41(S): 19–26.

56. MOTTLED PETREL *Pterodroma inexpectata* Plate 14

Other name: Korure
Size: 34 cm, 325 g
Distribution: Breed only on islands in southern New Zealand; in Fiordland (Shag and Front Islands and an island in Lake Hauroko), Solander Islands, islands around Stewart Island, including Codfish and Big South Cape, and The Snares. Subfossil, midden and historical records indicate a former breeding distribution through the North, South and Chatham Islands. During the breeding season, Mottled Petrels range through subantarctic waters to the pack ice, but some, mainly non-breeders, are found up to about 35°S, and cross the Tasman Sea to southeastern Australia. In March–June they migrate to subarctic waters of the North Pacific Ocean and the Bering Sea, where they stay until September. They return directly to New Zealand, arriving back from mid-October to November. A few non-breeders follow the American coast south to reach cool waters of the Humboldt Current and the seas off Cape Horn. About 30 Mottled Petrels are beach-wrecked in New Zealand each summer, mostly on Southland beaches (notably Mason Bay, Stewart Island).
Population: Common. The largest colony is on Codfish Island (Whenua Hou) with 300,000–400,000 pairs. Other major colonies of 10,000+ pairs are on Main Island (The Snares) and Big South Cape Island.
Conservation: Protected endemic. Maori used to harvest chicks in the inland North Island, but colonies on the mainland have gone as a result of forest clearance, fires and predators. Weka kill many birds on islands around Stewart Island, and so breeding success has improved on Codfish Island since Weka

were removed in 1985.
Breeding: Adults return to their colonies in late October and early November to prepare burrows and to court. Eggs are laid from early December to early January, mostly 15–23 December. They lay 1 white egg (61 x 44 mm, 61 g) in a burrow or crevice. Both sexes share incubation in stints of 2–**13**–22 days. Eggs hatch in early February after 48–**50**–53 days. The chick is brooded for the first couple of days and fed about every second day during the first 3 weeks of life. Chicks leave in May and early June at 90–105 days old.
Behaviour: Nest in colonies and sometimes share their cavity with Fairy Prions. At sea, they are usually alone or in small flocks. They arrive at their breeding colonies about 50 minutes after sunset, much later than Sooty Shearwaters. They are very vocal over their colonies, with rapid 'ti-ti-ti . . .' or 'kek-kek-kek . . .' calls and rarer 'oooi' and 'gorr' calls. On the ground, a wide range of calls is given, including the main flight call and the resonant 'gorr', followed by a short staccato 'wik'.
Feeding: Diet is mainly lantern fish, with some crustaceans and squid. Most prey is taken while sitting on the sea surface or by dipping or plunging from the air.
In the hand: Mottled Petrels are distinctive, with their grey belly patch and prominent black band running diagonally across the underwing from the bend in the wing towards the body. The wing length (245–275 mm) is greater than that of most petrels with a similar underwing pattern. Juveniles are paler than adults and have white mottling on most tail feathers, whereas only the outer tail feathers of adults are mottled.
Reading: Harper, P.C. 1987. *Notornis* 34: 169–192. Imber, M.J. 1991. *Acta Int Orn Cong* 20: 1402–1412. Warham, J. *et al.* 1977. *Auk* 94: 1–17.

57. WHITE-NAPED PETREL *Pterodroma cervicalis* Plate 14

Other names: White-necked Petrel, Sunday Island Petrel
Size: 43 cm, 450 g
Geographical variation: Birds collected near Vanuatu are smaller than those from the Kermadecs and may represent an undescribed subspecies.

Distribution: Since the extinction of White-naped Petrels from Raoul Island in the northern Kermadecs in the early 1900s, the only known breeding site was on Macauley Island in the southern Kermadecs, until a few were found recently on Philip Island off Norfolk Island. They may also nest on islands in Vanuatu. During the summer breeding season, they range within the southwestern Pacific, especially to the north and northeast of New Zealand south to the seas off East Cape and westwards into the northern Tasman Sea as far as eastern Australia. Some straggle to northern New Zealand (Mamaku Range, April 1968; off Muriwai Beach, February 1972; Gisborne, 1977; Hokianga Harbour, June 1982; and Karikari Bay, January 1986). In May–July, they migrate to the North Pacific Ocean, mainly to the southeast of Japan. They start returning in September, but some stay until November.

Population: Macauley Island, c. 50,000 pairs in 1988.

Conservation: Protected native. Many used to breed on Raoul (Sunday) Island, but by 1908 only about 500 pairs were breeding and were being ravaged by cats. As a result, they became extinct on Raoul Island before 1970. The Macauley Island population may be expanding now that the habitat has improved with removal of goats from the island, but the species remains vulnerable because it is largely confined to one island.

Breeding: Little information is available. Adults return to their colonies in late September and eggs are laid in December–

January. They lay **1** white egg (66 x 47 mm) in a burrow. Eggs hatch in late February and chicks depart May–June.

Behaviour: At sea, White-naped Petrels are usually alone or in small flocks at food. They are noisy over their colonies, with a harsh 'ka-ka-ka' call. They respond well to warwhoops. On the ground, the main call is 'kukooowik-ka-ha', with variations on the number and pitch of the concluding notes.

Feeding: Diet is mainly squid, taken while sitting on the surface of the sea or by dipping from the air.

In the hand: The white collar is diagnostic, but this may not show up clearly in beach-wrecked specimens. White-naped Petrels can be separated from slightly larger Juan Fernandez Petrels (*P. externa*) by having a brownish-black cap, the outermost primary dusky, with little or no white on the inner web (rather than having a clear white wedge on the inner web), and the underwing has a broad black leading edge beyond the bend of the wing. In *P. externa* the leading edge of the outer underwing is only flecked grey or black. The wing is 299–**310**–323 mm cf. 302–**316**–336 mm, and the bill is 34.5–**36.2**–39 mm cf. 34.5–**37.3**–41 mm in Juan Fernandez Petrels.

Reading: Dowding, J. E. 1987. *Notornis* 34: 325–326. Falla, R.A. 1976. *Notornis* 23: 320–322.

58. JUAN FERNANDEZ PETREL *Pterodroma externa* Plate 14

Size: 43 cm, 500 g

Distribution: Breed only on Mas-a-Fuera (Isla Alejandro Selkirk), Juan Fernandez Islands, in the eastern South Pacific Ocean. They migrate to the tropical North Pacific Ocean mainly between the equator, Hawai'i and Mexico. Vagrants reach the southwestern Pacific, including Australia and New Zealand. One was blown inland near Hamilton in October 1971, and at least two birds have been recorded prospecting nest sites at South East Island and Mangere Island in the Chathams in 1984–92. Seen in a burrow at South East Island, and over Chatham Island in 1997.

In the hand: Apart from the lack of a white collar (except when in moult), they are similar to the slightly smaller White-naped Petrel. They have only flecks of grey or black on the leading edge of the outer underwing, a large white wedge on the inner shaft of the outermost primary, and a brownish-grey cap. The wing is 302–**316**–336 mm cf. 299–**310**–323 mm, and the bill is 34.5–**37.3**–41 mm cf. 34.5–**36.3**–39 mm in White-naped Petrels. The similar Barau's Petrel (*P. baraui*) of the South Indian Ocean, which has been recorded as far east as Victoria, Australia, is smaller (wing 280–300 mm, bill 30–33 mm).

Reading: Falla, R.A. 1976. *Notornis* 23: 320–322. Imber, M.J. *et al.* 1991. *Notornis* 38: 60–62.

59. PHOENIX PETREL   *Pterodroma alba*   Plate 16

Size: 35 cm, 275 g

Distribution: Breed in the tropical and subtropical central Pacific Ocean on the Phoenix, Line, Marquesas, Oeno, Henderson and Ducie Islands. They possibly breed at Tonga, and probably bred on Raoul Island, where four were seen ashore in March 1913. They range widely in the central Pacific Ocean, but the only recent possible record from New Zealand was of a bird flying over Curtis Island, southern Kermadecs, in May 1982.

In the hand: Similar to Tahiti Petrels (*Pseudobulweria rostrata*), but they have a small white patch on the chin and a thin white patch along and just behind the leading edge of the base of the underwing, and Tahiti Petrels have a larger bill (33–39 mm) and a different bill structure from *Pterodroma* petrels. Size separates them clearly from the similar Chatham Island Taiko (*P. magentae*): wing 265–**276**–290 mm cf. 284–**302**–316, and bill 25.5–**27.9**–29.5 mm cf. 30.5–**33.0**–35 mm. The similar pale and intermediate phases of the Herald Petrel (*P. heraldica*), breeding in the central Pacific and seen in the Tasman Sea, have white patches at the base of the primaries (as have Kermadec Petrels *P. neglecta*), and the white patch on the inner underwing of Herald Petrels sometimes goes right to the leading edge of the wing.

Reading: Sorensen, J.H. 1964. *Notornis* 11: 69–81.

60. KERMADEC PETREL   *Pterodroma neglecta*   Plates 15 and 16

Size: 38 cm, 500 g

Geographical variation: Two subspecies: *neglecta* breeds widely across the western and central South Pacific, and *juana* breeds on the Juan Fernandez Islands and San Ambrosia Island in the eastern Pacific.

Distribution: Breed widely across the subtropical Pacific at Balls Pyramid (Lord Howe Island), Kermadec Islands, French Polynesia, Pitcairn group, Juan Fernandez Islands, San Ambrosia Island, in the South Atlantic at Ilha da Trinidade, Brazil, and in the Indian Ocean at Round Island, Mauritius. They range mainly in the subtropical Pacific, but a few stragglers reach New Zealand: six beach-wrecked on the west coast of Northland to 2004; singles off the Chathams (1975), at Cuvier Island (1976–81), Hawke's Bay (1995) and Kaikoura (1999). Some migrate to the tropical North Pacific between the Philippines, Japan and Mexico.

Population: Good numbers in the eastern part of the range, but only 5000-10,000 pairs on the Kermadecs, mainly on North and South Meyer Islets (6000 pairs), <50 pairs on Macauley Island.

Conservation: Protected native. In 1908, c. 500,000 Kermadec Petrels were nesting on Raoul Island, but these were ravaged by Norway rats (eggs) and cats (adults), together with the harvesting of birds by settlers early in the 1900s. They had virtually gone from Raoul Island by 1970 and are now just visitors from nearby breeding colonies.

Breeding: Kermadec Petrels can breed at any time of the year. Eggs or chicks are recorded in almost all months. Most adults return to their colonies in August, and most eggs are laid October–March, but young close to fledging have been recorded in November. Most eggs are laid on the Meyer Islets in January, a couple of months after the peak used to be on Raoul Island. They lay 1 white egg (64 x 47 mm) in a shallow scrape on the surface, usually under thick vegetation. Eggs hatch after 50–52 days, and chicks depart at 110–130 days old.

Behaviour: At sea, Kermadec Petrels usually feed alone. They are noisy over their colonies and on the ground, with a distinctive loud 'yuk-ker-a-ooo-wuk' call, the explosive final note being given 0–3 or more times.

Feeding: Diet is squid and crustaceans, taken while sitting on the surface of the sea or dipping from the air.

In the hand: Kermadec Petrels have a wide range of plumages, but all have a skua-like white patch on the underwing at the base of the primaries.

Equally variable Herald Petrels (*P. heraldica*), which breed in the central Pacific and have been seen in the Tasman Sea, also have white patches at the base of the primaries but lack the white shafts to the primaries on the upperwing, and have a smaller bill (25–**26.8**–28.5) than Kermadec Petrels (28–**30.4**–33 mm).

Reading: Merton, D.V. 1970. *Notornis* 17: 147–199.

61. PROVIDENCE PETREL *Pterodroma solandri* Plate 15

Other name: Bird of Providence
Size: 40 cm, 500 g
Distribution: c. 100,000 Providence Petrels breed on Lord Howe Island and, more recently, on Philip Island (Norfolk Islands) in the subtropical Tasman Sea. During the winter breeding season, they range mainly through the western Tasman Sea near the edge of the Australian continental shelf from Queensland to Tasmania. Surprisingly few have been recorded in New Zealand, with only three records: beach-wrecked birds at Muriwai (1921) and Dargaville (1984), and one seen off Whangaroa Harbour (2004). Providence Petrels migrate to the North Pacific Ocean in November–February, but some stay behind off eastern Tasmania until late December.

In the hand: Very similar to Grey-faced Petrels (*P. macroptera*), but Providence Petrels have a mottled face, a white patch on the underwing at the base of the primaries and are slightly smaller (wing 285–**304**–325 mm cf. 295–**318**–330 mm, and bill 32.5–**34.5**–38.5 mm cf. 33–**37**–40.5). Dark-phased Kermadec Petrels (*P. neglecta*) have a similar wing patch, but they have white primary shafts visible on the upperwing and a much shorter wing (270–**289**–305 mm) and bill (28–**30.5**–33 mm). Dark-phased Herald Petrels (*P. heraldica*) have even shorter wings (270–**278**–290 mm) and bill (25–**27**–29 mm).

Reading: Miller, P. 1986. *Notornis* 33: 76.

62. GREY-FACED PETREL *Pterodroma macroptera* Plate 15

Other names: Oi, Great-winged Petrel, Northern Muttonbird
Size: 41 cm, 550 g
Geographical variation: Two subspecies: *macroptera* breeds on subtropical and subantarctic islands in the Atlantic and Indian Oceans and off southwestern Australia; *gouldi* breeds around the northern North Island of New Zealand.
Distribution: Breed on Gough and Tristan da Cunha in the South Atlantic Ocean, Prince Edward, Crozet and Kerguelen Islands in the South Indian Ocean, on islands off southwestern Australia and around northern New Zealand. Colonies are scattered on mainland headlands and clifftops, and on offshore islands from the Three Kings to near New Plymouth on the west coast and to near Gisborne on the east coast. The main colonies are on the Three Kings, Mokohinau and Mercury groups, and on the Alderman, Whale (Moutohora) and White Islands, but small mainland colonies at Mt Maunganui and near New Plymouth are well known.

Grey-faced Petrels are moderately sedentary. New Zealand birds range between 30 and 48°S in the Tasman Sea and the South Pacific to about 130°W. They turn up off eastern Australia in February–March after breeding and remain common there until May. Grey-faced Petrels are commonly beach-wrecked on Northland and Bay of Plenty beaches, especially in January and February when young have just fledged.
Population: c. 250,000 breeding pairs. The largest colony, with c. 95,000 pairs is on Whale Island (Moutohora).
Conservation: Protected native. Chicks are still legally harvested by Maori from colonies on privately owned islands, but this take has declined recently and so they may now be increasing. Many island populations have benefited from the recent eradication of rats, cats and rabbits. Mainland colonies are declining from predation by rats, cats, dogs, mustelids and humans, and some island populations have been ravaged by introduced predators or interference to breeding birds

by rabbits. The species remains secure, with many colonies protected on island reserves free of large mammalian predators, and continuing programmes to eradicate rabbits and rats from islands will improve breeding performance.

Breeding: Winter breeders. Adults return to New Zealand colonies in March to clean out their burrows and to court. They have a long pre-laying exodus of c. 60 days in females and c. 50 days in males. Laying is 21 June to 29 July, mostly 28 June to 9 July. Females return first from their exodus and lay **1** white egg (67 x 48 mm, 86 g) in a burrow 0.5–2 m long. Incubation is by the female for the first 0–**4**–14 days, but then in three long shifts of 8–**16**–23 days, two by the male.

Eggs hatch from mid-August to mid-September after 51–**55**–58 days, or after **54** days of incubation excluding periods of 0–**1.4**–5 days when the egg is left unattended during change-overs. The chick is continuously guarded for the first 1–**1.7**–3 days and then fed about every 4 nights. Chicks depart from about 7 December to late January,

with a peak at the end of December at 108–**118**–128 days old. Most chicks return to their natal colony and start breeding from 7 years old. The oldest Grey-faced Petrel recorded lived over 26 years.

Behaviour: At sea, they are usually seen alone or in small feeding or roosting flocks. They are noisy over their colonies and on the ground, the main flight call being 'o-hi', which gives rise to the Maori name.

Feeding: Diet is mainly squid, with some fish and crustaceans. Most prey is taken at night while sitting on the surface of the sea or dipping from the air.

In the hand: Grey-faced Petrels are all dark apart from the face and lack the prominent white patch at the base of the primaries found on similar species (Providence Petrel, and dark-phased Kermadec and Herald Petrels). Wing (295–**318**–330 mm) and bill (33–**37**–40.5 mm) measurements help to separate beach-wrecked specimens from similar species.

Reading: Harrison, M. 1992. *DoC Sci & Res Ser* No. 48. Imber, M.J. 1973. *J Anim Ecol* 42: 645–662. Imber, M.J. 1976. *Ibis* 118: 51–64. Johnstone, R.M. & Davis, L.S. 1990. *Ibis* 132: 14–19.

63.   CHATHAM ISLAND TAIKO   *Pterodroma magentae*   Plate 16

Other names: Magenta Petrel
Size: 38 cm, 475 g
Distribution: Breed only in dense forest near the Tuku-a-Tamatea River in the southwest of Chatham Island. Subfossil and midden evidence suggests that they formerly bred in huge numbers on the Chatham Islands. Little is known of their distribution at sea; the only confirmed record of Chatham Island Taiko away from the Chathams was the first specimen, collected in winter 1867 in the central South Pacific near 40°S. Radio-tracking during the breeding season shows that they probably feed in subantarctic seas to the south of the Chathams.
Population: One of the rarest birds in the world; c. 100 birds and only about six nesting burrows are known, all on Chatham Island.
Conservation: Protected critically endangered endemic. Chicks were harvested in huge

numbers by Moriori and Maori up to the start of the 1900s. Former colonies were ravaged by pigs, cats, rats and Weka, and possums compete for burrows. Taiko were thought extinct until Ornithological Society parties led by David Crockett attracted two birds to bright lights in the Tuku Valley, Chatham Island, in January 1973, and finally caught and banded two birds on 1 January 1978. Photographs and measurements confirmed that the Magenta Petrel and the Chatham Island Taiko were the same species.

Up to December 1999, 92 Taiko have been banded in the southwest part of Chatham Island, and six active nesting burrows have been found, mainly by following radio-tagged birds. The Department of Conservation is trapping cats, possums, rats and Weka near the known burrows, and monitoring breeding attempts each year.
Breeding: Adults return in late September

to clean out their burrows and to court. Females have a long pre-laying exodus of 40–55 days and males are away for 25–45 days. Females return to lay at the end of November. **1** white egg (65 x 47 mm) is laid in a burrow up to 3 m long. Eggs hatch in mid- to late January after c. 55 days, and chicks depart 25 April to 10 May at c. 105 days old.

Behaviour: Generally silent over their nesting area. The calls from their burrows, or rarely while being handled, are 'or-wik', 'si si si' and 'orrrr'. They sometimes emerge from their burrows in response to war-whooping.

Feeding: Apart from the regurgitated remains of squid, the diet and feeding methods are not known.

In the hand: Chatham Island Taiko resemble Phoenix Petrels (*P. alba*), but Taiko are larger (wing 284–**302**–316 mm cf. 265–**267**–290 mm, and bill 30.5–**33.0**–35 mm cf. 25.5–**27.9**–29.5 mm). Tahiti Petrels (*Pseudobulweria rostrata*) are similar, but have a different bill structure to *Pterodroma* petrels, and their bill is larger (33–**35.7**–39 mm) but wings are shorter (283–**294**–309 mm).

Reading: Crockett, D.E. 1994. *Notornis* 41(S): 49–60. Imber, M.J. *et al*. 1994. *Notornis* 41 (S): 61–68. Imber, M.J. *et al*. 1994. *Notornis* 41 (S): 69–96. Taylor, G.A. 1991. *DoC Threatened Spec Occ Publ No. 2.*

64. WHITE-HEADED PETREL *Pterodroma lessonii* Plate 15

Size: 43 cm, 600 g

Distribution: Breed on Crozet and Kerguelen Islands in the South Indian Ocean, on Macquarie Island and in the New Zealand subantarctic on the Antipodes and Auckland Islands. They range widely in the southern oceans between the pack ice and 45°S but move northwards to about 30°S in the winter. They are regularly beach-wrecked on the west coast of the North Island in winter and spring, especially around October.

Population: A common subantarctic petrel, with large colonies on Kerguelen, Macquarie, Antipodes (100,000+ pairs on the main island but few on its offshore islands) and the Auckland Islands (all but the main island) including 100,000+ pairs on Disappointment Island.

Conservation: Protected native. Cats have caused massive declines of the colonies on Macquarie Island and Auckland Island. Brown Skuas kill many White-headed Petrels on the Antipodes and Auckland Islands, but the populations are probably stable.

Breeding: No detailed studies in New Zealand, but timing seems similar to that on Macquarie Island. Adults return to their scattered colonies in late August to clean out their burrows and to court. Laying is from mid-November to late December. They lay **1** white egg (69 x 49 mm) in a burrow up to 2 m long. Eggs hatch in late January and February after c. 60 days, and chicks depart in May at c. 102 days old.

Behaviour: At sea, White-headed Petrels usually feed alone or in small groups and do not follow ships. They are very vocal at their colonies from about one hour after dark, with a variety of calls, including a characteristic harsh, chattering 'ti-ti-ti' flight call.

Feeding: Feed on squid, lantern fish, mysid crustacea and other planktonic invertebrates.

Reading: Brothers, N.P. 1984. *Aust Wildl Res* 11: 113–131. Warham, J. 1967. *Emu* 67: 1–22. Warham, J. & Bell, B.D. 1979. *Notornis* 26: 121–169.

65. SOFT-PLUMAGED PETREL *Pterodroma mollis* Plate 16

Size: 34 cm, 300 g

Geographical variation: Two closely related species (*P. feae* and *P. madeira* in the North Atlantic) are sometimes treated as part of this species.

Distribution: Subtropical and subantarctic islands of the South Atlantic and South Indian Oceans, and in the New Zealand subantarctic, on Antipodes Island. They range mainly between 25 and 60°S in the Atlantic and Indian Oceans but are rare in the South Pacific Ocean; however, now regularly seen on subantarctic cruises near the Antipodes. They have straggled to the mainland of New Zealand only recently, with 12 records since 1971, mainly on the east coast and around Cook Strait in May–June, when fledglings have just left their colony on the Antipodes, or in November–December. Three records from on or near the Chatham Islands (1980, 1987, 1997).

Population: Several thousand pairs breed on Antipodes Island, where the population is growing rapidly, and very large numbers breed at Gough Island and on Indian Ocean islands.

Conservation: Protected native. Soft-plumaged Petrels were first discovered in the New Zealand region in February 1969, when they were seen flying over Antipodes Island. In 1978, burrows were located and the colony

appeared to be expanding, and by 1994 there were several thousand pairs breeding.

Breeding: Not studied in New Zealand. Elsewhere, adults return to their colonies in August–September to clean out their burrows and to court. Laying is generally in December, and apparently some time after 5 December on the Antipodes. They lay 1 white egg (60 x 43 mm, 54 g) in a burrow 1–1.5 m long, under dense tussock and fern. Eggs hatch in January–February after c. 50 days, and most chicks depart in May at c. 90 days old.

Behaviour: Call over their nesting area with strange, mournful, low-pitched, fluting cries like a lamb bleating; this call is also uttered on the ground and in burrows.

Feeding: Diet is mainly squid, with some small fish and crustacea.

In the hand: Soft-plumaged Petrels have pale and dark phases, but all recorded from the New Zealand region have been of the pale phase. White-headed Petrels and Chatham Island Taiko are the most similar species, but Soft-plumaged Petrels are much smaller (wing 235–**255**–275 mm, bill 25.5–**28.4**–32 mm). The rare dark phase is similar to the Kerguelen Petrel but lacks the silvery outer underwing.

Reading: Harper, P.C. 1973. *Notornis* 20: 193–201. Imber, M.J. 1983. *Notornis* 30: 283–298. Jouventin, P. *et al.* 1985. *Notornis* 32: 157–220. Warham, J. & Bell, B.D. 1979. *Notornis* 26: 121–169.

STORM PETRELS Oceanitidae

The Oceanitidae are very small seabirds, ranging from Antarctic waters to the tropics. There are 21 species, of which 5 breed in the New Zealand region, and 1 is a vagrant.

The storm petrels are small, delicate birds with a weak black bill. They have prominent nostrils encased in a single, often upturned tube at the base of the bill. They have 11 primaries, but the 11th (outermost) is minute. The 10th primary is shorter than the 9th, giving the wing a rounded tip. The legs and

webbed toes are long and are used to skip or patter along the sea surface as the birds look for zooplankton.

The biology of storm petrels and the threats to them are like those of the Procellariidae (see page **184**). The main differences are that females are larger than males, they lay the heaviest egg relative to female weight of any birds (typically in the range of 25–29% of female weight for the smaller species), and the egg is regularly unattended for one or more days at a time during incubation, which makes the total incubation period highly variable.

Reading: Harrison, P. 1987. *Seabirds of the World: a photographic guide*. London: Christopher Helm. Harrison, P. 1988. *Seabirds: an identification guide*. London: Christopher Helm. Lockley, R.M. 1983.

Flight of the Storm Petrel. Newton Abbot: David & Charles. Murphy, R.C. 1936. *Oceanic Birds of South America*. New York: MacMillan. Serventy, D.L. *et al*. 1971. *The Handbook of Australian Seabirds*. Sydney: Reed. Warham, J. 1990. *The Petrels: their ecology and breeding systems*. London: Academic Press.

66. LEACH'S STORM PETREL *Oceanodroma leucorhoa* Plate 17

Size: 20 cm, 45 g
Geographical variation: Four subspecies: *leucorhoa* breeds widely in the North Atlantic and North Pacific, and straggles to New Zealand; three others (*beali, chapmani* and *socorroensis*) breed on the Pacific coast of North America.
Distribution: Breed on small islands in the North Atlantic and North Pacific, mainly between 42 and 68°N, except along the Pacific coast of North America down to northern Mexico. They migrate south to tropical and subtropical waters after breeding, and stay from September to March, with some non-breeders remaining all year. A few have straggled to New Zealand: Muriwai Beach (August 1922); Matamata (April 1978); Dargaville Beach (August 1978); Rabbit Island,

Chathams (two prospecting in November 1980) and 90 Mile Beach (October 1998).
Behaviour: At Rabbit Island, two birds gave soft chuckles – 'kuk-ku-huk' – in flight and on the ground, and a prolonged loud churring with a rising pitch, interspersed with 'ik' notes, was given by a bird in a burrow.

In the hand: Leach's Storm Petrels are similar to Wilson's Storm Petrel, the only other black storm petrel with a white rump known from the region, but have a larger bill: 13.5–**16.0**–17.5 mm cf. 11–**12.5**–13.5 mm. The white rump patch of Leach's Storm Petrel is divided or partially divided by a dark central line of feathers, whereas Wilson's Storm Petrel has a pure white rump.

Reading: Imber, M.J. & Lovegrove, T.G. 1982. *Notornis* 29: 101–108.

67. WILSON'S STORM PETREL *Oceanites oceanicus* Plate 17

Size: 18 cm, 35 g
Geographical variation: Two subspecies: *oceanicus* breeds on subantarctic islands in the South Atlantic and South Indian Ocean; *exasperatus* breeds on coasts and islands off Antarctica and is an uncommon passage migrant through New Zealand waters.
Distribution: Circumpolar, breeding at many sites on the coast of Antarctica and on many islands in antarctic and southern subantarctic waters to 46°S. In the Ross Dependency, they breed at many sites along the coast of the Ross Sea and on Balleny and Scott Islands. After breeding, they migrate to the Northern Hemisphere and are beach-wrecked or seen passing through New Zealand waters, heading north in March–May and returning south in November–December. The main migration routes appear to avoid New

Zealand waters; they are regularly seen in Perserverance Harbour, Campbell Island. In most years, the main southward migration route passes to the east of New Zealand, judging by records at sea near the Chathams, on the Chatham Rise, near the Bounty Islands, and at Campbell Island.
Population: One of the most abundant species of bird in the world; c. 125,000 pairs breed in the Ross Dependency.
Conservation: Protected native. Numbers are huge despite skua predation and reductions in some subantarctic colonies after the introduction of cats and rats.
Breeding: Not studied in Ross Dependency, but elsewhere in Antarctica, adults return to their colonies in November to early December to claim nest sites and to court. Laying is in December–January. They lay **1** white egg (33

221

x 24 mm, 10 g) in a crevice in a cliff or scree slope. Eggs hatch in January–February after c. 45 days, and chicks depart March–April at c. 50 days old. Young breed at 3 years old, and average life expectancy is at least 10 years.
Behaviour: Breed in large dense colonies and often feed in flocks, but migrate singly.

In the hand: Wilson's Storm Petrels are like Leach's

Storm Petrels, the only other black storm petrel with a white rump known from the region, but have a smaller bill: 11–**12.5**–13.5 mm cf. 13.5–**16.0**–17.5 mm. The white rump patch of Wilson's Storm Petrel is not divided or partially divided by a dark central line of feathers as in Leach's Storm Petrel.

Reading: Falla, R.A. 1933. *Rep BANZARE* B 2: 1–288. Lacan, F. 1971. *Oiseau* 41: 65–89. Pryor, M.E. 1968. *Ant Res Ser* (Wash) 12: 57–82.

68. GREY-BACKED STORM PETREL *Oceanites nereis* Plate 17

Size: 18 cm, 35 g

Distribution: Circumpolar, breeding on many subantarctic islands in the Atlantic and Indian Oceans, and in the New Zealand region. They breed at the Chathams on many small islands and stacks, with main colonies on South East and Mangere Islands; also on the Antipodes and Auckland Islands, and on islets off Campbell Island. Breeding birds return to their colonies almost all year round, but some New Zealand birds move north to about 30°S and westwards into the southern Tasman Sea, and they are regular visitors to coastal waters off southeastern Australia. Grey-backed Storm Petrels are occasionally beach-wrecked in June–December, especially around Cook Strait. Several times they have been recorded well inland in the southern South Island, and so may breed somewhere in Fiordland.

Population: Moderate numbers. Possibly 10,000–12,000 pairs breed in the Chathams; smaller colonies are on the Antipodes and Auckland Islands.

Conservation: Protected native. Little is known of the numbers of this species, but because they nest above the ground they are vulnerable to mammalian predators, and so most are now on islands free of ground predators and grazing mammals.

Breeding: Adults return to their colonies at almost any time of year. Numbers build up in August and eggs are laid from mid-September to December. They lay **1** white egg (31 x 23 mm, 8.5 g) in a shallow cup of leaf fibres above ground in a 'rat hole' at the base of flax, ferns, herbs or tussock clumps, or under iceplants. The incubation period is 39–45 days; because the egg is often left unattended for a day or more, the period is quite variable. The chick is brooded for only a few hours and then guarded for up to 4 days. It is fed every 1–**1.6**–3 days and reaches adult weight by 17 days old, but it does not fledge until c. 50 days old.

Behaviour: Breed in loose colonies and feed alone or in small flocks. Silent in the air. A monotonous cricket-like chirping is given on the ground.

Feeding: Studies at the Chathams have found that Grey-backed Storm Petrels specialise in feeding on the free-swimming stage of immature barnacles, supplemented with other zooplankton.

In the hand: Grey-backed Storm Petrels are the smallest storm petrel in the New Zealand region (wing 117–**131**–139 mm). Females average longer in the wing and tail than males, but measurements overlap. The outermost primary is rounded in adults but pointed in juveniles.

Reading: Imber, M.J. 1981. In *Proc Symp Birds Sea Shore*. Cape Town: African Seabird Group. Imber, M.J. 1983. *Notornis* 30: 283–298. Plant, A. R. 1989. *Notornis* 36: 141–147. Warham J. & Bell, B.D. 1979. *Notornis* 26: 121–169.

Storm petrels seen off the Mercury Islands (January 2003) and more recent sightings of flocks of up to 20 birds in the Hauraki Gulf may be the New Zealand Storm Petrel (*Oceanites maorianus*), a species presumed extinct because only three birds had ever been recorded; two collected off East Cape in February 1827, and one possibly collected off Banks Peninsula later in the 19th century. The birds seen recently all had a white belly and undertail coverts streaked black on the flanks and undertail coverts, an indistinct breast band with black brown 'bleeding' projections onto the white belly, and feet projecting beyond the tail.

69. WHITE-FACED STORM PETREL   *Pelagodroma marina*   Plate 17

Other names: Takahikare-moana, Frigate Petrel
Size: 20 cm, 45 g
Geographical variation: Six subspecies, of which three have been recorded in New Zealand: *dulciae*, breeding around southern Australia; *maoriana*, breeding around the mainland of New Zealand and at the Chathams and Auckland Islands; and *albiclunis*, breeding in the Kermadecs.

Distribution: There are widespread colonies of White-faced Storm Petrels in subantarctic to subtropical parts of the Atlantic, Indian and southwestern Pacific Oceans. In New Zealand, *maoriana* breed on many islands of northern New Zealand from the Three Kings Islands to Motumahunga (off New Plymouth) in the west and to Motunau (Bay of Plenty) in the east. They also breed on Sentinel Rock (Cook Strait), Motunau (Canterbury), several islands around Stewart Island, and at the Chatham (especially South East Island) and Auckland Islands. The breeding ground of the rare *albiclunis* has not yet been discovered but may be on or near Macauley Island, southern Kermadecs, where a bird was caught in 1988; there have been about 30 records of this subspecies at sea near the Kermadecs.

After breeding, most New Zealand birds migrate to warmer tropical waters of the eastern Pacific in May–August: a bird banded on South East Island in February was recovered 1000 km west of Peru three months later. About 30 White-faced Storm Petrels are beach-wrecked each year, mostly on Northland and Bay of Plenty beaches in spring and summer. One of the few beach-wrecked in winter has been identified as the Australian subspecies *dulciae*, and part of the population of this subspecies may migrate to the seas north of New Zealand in winter.

Population: The New Zealand subspecies *maoriana* is common and breeding on many islands. The largest colony is on South East Island with c. 850,000 breeding pairs. The Kermadec Storm Petrel *albiclunis* is very rare (<100 pairs).

Conservation: Protected native. Despite declines caused by the introduction of cats, rats and Weka to many islands, the populations are secure on islands without mammalian predators.

Breeding: Adults return to their colonies in September to early October, and eggs are laid from late October to mid-December. They lay 1 white egg (36 x 26 mm) in a burrow up to 1 m long. Incubation spells are of 1–4–9 days, but the egg is often left unattended between shifts and can hatch even after being left for 92 hours. The incubation period is c. 50 days, but the period depends on the nest attentiveness of the adults. The chick is continuously guarded for 2–3 days and fed nightly during the 52–57–67-day fledging period. Chicks fledge from mid-February to mid-March. A few remain to mid-April.

Behaviour: Breed in dense colonies. At sea, they feed alone or in large flocks. They are silent in the air but give a mournful twitter and a cackling call from burrows and on the surface.

Feeding: Studies at the Chathams have found that White-faced Storm Petrels feed on a wide variety of krill, amphipods and other planktonic crustaceans, and small fish. They take most prey from the surface while flying or pattering along, occasionally while resting on the surface.

In the hand: White-faced Storm Petrels are a distinctive large storm petrel (wing 145–157–175 mm). Females are slightly larger than males, but measurements overlap greatly. The outermost primary is rounded in adults but pointed in juveniles. Subspecies *maoriana* has a deeply forked tail (5–10.5–15 mm), whereas both *dulciae* (2–5.0–8.5 mm) and *albiclunis* (1.5–3.6–6 mm) have only a slightly forked tail. Subspecies *albiclunis* has a white rump, compared with a pale grey rump in both *dulciae* and *maoriana*.

Reading: Imber, M.J. 1981. In *Proc Symp Birds Sea Shore*. Cape Town: African Seabird Group. Imber, M.J. 1984. *Emu* 84: 32–35. Richdale, L.E. 1943. *Trans Proc Roy Soc NZ* 73: 97–115, 217–232, 335–350. West, J.A. & Nilsson, R.J. 1994. *Notornis* 41(S): 27–37.

70. BLACK-BELLIED STORM PETREL *Fregetta tropica* Plate 17

Size: 20 cm, 55 g

Distribution: Breed widely on subantarctic islands in the Atlantic (South Shetland, South Orkney and South Georgia Islands) and Indian Oceans (Prince Edward, Crozet and Kerguelen Islands), and in New Zealand at the Antipodes and Auckland Islands. Recorded from the Chathams in subfossil deposits and seen there in January 1979 and on Campbell Island in 1963. After summer breeding, New Zealand birds migrate to warmer subtropical waters of the Coral Sea and the southwestern Pacific Ocean. They are occasionally seen east of New Zealand and at the Chathams on passage during May–June as they head north and October–November as they return. Only seven birds have been beach-wrecked up to 1997, mainly in Southland or on beaches near Cook Strait.

Population: c. 50,000–100,000 pairs in New Zealand, mainly in the Auckland Islands, but 1000+ pairs recently found on the Antipodes. Elsewhere, large colonies are found on Elephant Island (South Shetland) and Prince Edward Islands.

Conservation: Protected native. Little is known of the trends of New Zealand populations.

Breeding: Little is known in New Zealand. At Signy Island (South Orkney), adults return to their colonies in November and lay in late December and January, which is consistent with the discovery of two freshly laid eggs on the Auckland Islands on 1 February. They lay 1 white egg (37 x 27 mm, 15 g) in a burrow up to 0.5 m long in stream banks and peat hummocks. The incubation period is 35–45 days, and chicks fledge at 65–70 days old from mid-April to late May.

Behaviour: Breed in small scattered colonies. At sea, they feed alone or in small flocks. Silent in the air, but on the ground they give a piercingly shrill whistle, which is often hard to pinpoint.

Feeding: Little known but probably feed on krill, amphipods and other planktonic crustaceans, and small fish and squid. They take most prey from the surface while flying or pattering along. Sometimes feed around whales and trawlers.

In the hand: The few Black-bellied Storm Petrels lacking a central black stripe down the belly are almost identical to some White-bellied Storm Petrels; however, the feet of the former extend well (c. 10 mm) beyond the tail, and they have white (not black) bases to their throat feathers.

Reading: Beck, J.R. & Brown, D.W. 1971. *Ibis* 113: 73–90. Imber, M.J. 1973. *Notornis* 30: 283–298. Turner, D. 1980. *Notornis* 27: 94–95. Warham, J. & Bell, B.D. 1979. *Notornis* 26: 121–169.

71. WHITE-BELLIED STORM PETREL *Fregetta grallaria* Plate 17

Size: 20 cm, 50 g

Geographical variation: Four subspecies: the nominate *grallaria*, which breeds in the Kermadecs and at Roach Island, Lord Howe group, is the only form known from New Zealand.

Distribution: Breed widely on subtropical or temperate islands in the South Atlantic (Tristan da Cuhna Group), South Indian (St Paul Island) and South Pacific Oceans (Lord Howe, Kermadec, Rapa and Juan Fernandez Islands). In the Kermadecs, they breed in the southern group on Macauley and Curtis Islands, and possibly also on Haszard and Cheeseman Islands. Throughout their range, White-bellied Storm Petrels migrate northwards into the tropics after the summer-autumn breeding season; however, birds have been caught on Macauley Island in September and on Curtis Island in October–November, and so some birds remain close to their breeding colonies. They are rare vagrants to waters off the New Zealand mainland at any time of year, with only eight records (three beach-wrecked) as far south as off Farewell Spit.

Population: Nothing is known about the size of New Zealand colonies, but the Roach Island colony is of 1000+ pairs.

Conservation: Protected native. Little is

known of the status of New Zealand populations.

Breeding: Apparently breed in late summer and autumn as on Lord Howe Island; a freshly hatched chick seen on Curtis Island on 21 May 1982 is the only confirmed breeding record in New Zealand. From the age of the chick, it is likely that eggs are laid in March–April. They lay 1 white egg in a crevice, short burrow or small caves. No information on incubation or fledging periods.

Behaviour: Silent in the air, but on the ground they give a soft twittering call and a high-pitched whistle – 'pee-pee-pee . . .' – repeated 20 or more times.

Feeding: Diet is planktonic crustaceans and small squid, taken from the surface while flying or pattering on the water.

In the hand: White-bellied Storm Petrels can be distinguished from the few Black-bellied Storm Petrels that lack a central black stripe down the belly by having the feet extending to about the tip of the tail (but not c. 10 mm beyond) and by having dark bases (not white) to their throat feathers.

Reading: Lovegrove, T.G. 1978. *Notornis* 25: 291–298.

PENGUINS   Spheniscidae

16 species confined to the Southern Hemisphere: 13 in the New Zealand region, including 4 endemic and 5 other breeding species.

Penguins are a clearly defined group of flightless, stocky seabirds standing up to a metre high. They are a primitive group dating back to the late Eocene, about 45 million years ago; fossils of three species have been found in the South Island from this era.

Penguins are covered with a waterproof coat of dense, short and flattened feathers; the wings are modified into flippers, and the tail is short and stiff. They have a large head and a powerful, short, stout bill. Their legs are short and stout, with webs linking the three forward-pointing toes. On land, they walk upright with an ungainly waddling gait, and hop over obstacles, using their flippers to maintain balance. On ice, they sometimes toboggan. In the water, they can swim rapidly, being propelled by their flippers only. Some species porpoise when travelling fast.

Penguins dive to catch food. The extreme example is the Emperor Penguin, which has been recorded diving to 450 m and staying submerged for 11 minutes. They feed on fish, crustaceans (especially krill), squid and a wide range of other marine invertebrates.

Penguins visit land to breed and moult, and some inshore species return to land on most nights to roost. They have ritualised displays, and most give a variety of brays, trumpets and growls. Colonial breeders often engage in fights with neighbouring birds.

They usually lay a clutch of 1–2 whitish eggs each year; a few failed pairs attempt to re-lay. Nests vary from burrows for Little Blue Penguins and some Fiordland Crested Penguins to simple scrapes for most species. The King and Emperor Penguins build no nest and incubate the egg between the top of their feet and their body.

Penguins vary from solitary to colonial, some colonies being of millions of pairs. Eggs are small in relation to their body size, and have a long incubation period of 33–65 days depending on the species. Usually both sexes incubate, except that in the Emperor Penguin only the male incubates. Chicks hatch covered in thick down and are fed irregularly by both parents. In colonial species, chicks group together in crèches from about three weeks old until they have their natal moult into full feathers and leave the colony at 2–6 months old.

During the moult of 2–5 weeks in summer or autumn, birds look ragged and 'sick', as almost all the feathers are replaced simultaneously. During this time, the bird fasts and is unable to swim without getting waterlogged. If you find birds moulting, leave them alone, and do not return them to sea; contact the Department of Conservation if a moulting penguin is in danger from dogs or other predators. Many records of unusual species visiting the New Zealand region are of wandering birds forced to come ashore in autumn to moult.

Reading: Davis, L.S. & Darby, J.T. (eds). 1990. *Penguin Biology*. San Diego: Academic Press.

Harrison, P. 1987. *Seabirds of the World: a photographic guide*. London: Christopher Helm. Harrison, P. 1988. *Seabirds: an identification guide*. London: Christopher Helm. Murphy, R.C. 1936. *Oceanic Birds of South America*. New York: MacMillan. Serventy, D.L. *et al*. 1971. *The Handbook of Australian Sea-birds*. Sydney: Reed. Stonehouse, B. (ed.). 1975. *The Biology of Penguins*. London: MacMillan.

72. EMPEROR PENGUIN *Aptenodytes forsteri* Plate 18

Size: 115 cm, 30 kg

Distribution: Circumpolar, breeding on the coast, islands and sea-ice of the Antarctic continent. In the Ross Sea sector of Antarctica, there are at least six colonies: Cape Roget, Coulman Island, Cape Washington, Franklin Island, Beaufort Island and Cape Crozier. They seldom venture north of the Antarctic Circle, but a single bird came ashore at Oreti Beach, Southland (April 1967).

Population: 50,000 pairs in the Ross Sea sector in 1983, which is c. 30% of the estimated total breeding population in Antarctica. Main colonies were at Coulman Island (21,708 pairs) and Cape Washington (19,364 pairs).

Conservation: Protected common native. Significant declines have been noted at several colonies in the Ross Sea sector in recent years, perhaps as a result of human disturbance or changing food supplies. Cape Roget has dropped from 17,000 pairs in the 1950s to 3777 pairs in 1983, and the Cape Crozier colony dropped from 256 pairs in 1974 to 78 pairs in 1983.

Breeding: Laying is from late April to June; the mean laying date is about a month later at southern colonies. They lay **1** white egg (123 x 82 mm, 442 g), which the male then incubates on the top of his feet for 62–**64**–67 days. The male also broods the chick for c. 10 days and feeds it an oesophageal secretion before the female returns and broods and feeds the chick on demand for the next 3–4 weeks. Meanwhile, the male goes to sea to recover from his three-month fast, during which he has lost about 40% of his body weight. The male and female then alternate their attendance of the chick until it joins a crèche at c. 8 weeks old, and then both parents depart for sea and return about every 10 days.

In December–January, the chicks depart independently of their parents at c. 150 days old, when they average <50% of the normal adult weight. At some colonies, the chicks have to travel over 50 km to reach the sea, and mortality on this journey is high. First breeding is at 3–**5**–9 years old. Birds are monogamous, but most change partners each year. At Point Geologie, to the west of Ross Sea, annual adult survivorship was 95.1%, so life expectancy was 19.9 years.

Behaviour: Breed in colonies and feed in groups outside the breeding season. When preparing to breed, the pair vigorously defends the space around them, but once incubating, the males often huddle together to keep warm.

Feeding: Diet is mainly fish (60–250 mm long) and squid (up to 280 mm long), but krill and a wide range of other marine invertebrates are taken. They feed by diving to great depths (up to 450 m below the surface) to capture large fish (and possibly large squid) living on or near the ocean floor, or feed on immature squid, fish and krill in shallow water near icebergs and floes. About 30% of dives are beyond 100 m deep. Most dives last 2–8 minutes and are at speeds of 10–15 km/hr.

Reading: Budd, G.M. 1962. *Proc Zool Soc* (Lond) 139; 365–388. Henderson, L.E. 1968. *Notornis* 15: 34–35. Kooyman, G.L. *et al*. 1990. *Polar Rec* 26: 103–108. Kooyman, G.L. & Ponganis, P.J. 1990. In *Penguin Biology*. San Diego: Academic Press. Mougin, J-L. 1966. *L'Oiseau* 36: 167–226. Robertson, G. *et al*. 1994. *Ibis* 136: 19–31. Stirling, I. & Greenwood, D.J. 1970. *Notornis* 17: 277–279. Stonehouse, B. 1953. *Sci Rep Falkland Is Dep Surv* 6: 1–33. Wilson, G.J. & Taylor, R.H. 1984. *NZ Ant Rec* 6: 1–7.

73. KING PENGUIN *Aptenodytes patagonicus* Plate 18

Size: 90 cm, 13 kg

Distribution: Circumpolar, breeding on many islands in the subantarctic zone, including 70,000+ pairs nesting on Macquarie Island, but none breed in the New Zealand region. A few midden remains from the Chatham Islands indicates that King Penguins may have visited or bred there in the past. Vagrants are seen regularly at Campbell Island, and birds occasionally turn up in summer and autumn to moult at the Auckland, The Snares and Antipodes Islands (three records). Stragglers occasionally reach the mainland: at Stewart

Island and Moeraki (both before 1930), Timaru (1991) and Punakaiki (2005). It is likely that a bird in Auckland Harbour sometime before 1930 was released from a ship.

Feeding: Diet is mainly fish and squid, with some krill and other marine invertebrates. They can dive to great depths (up to 240 m below the surface) to capture fish and squid living on or near the ocean floor.

Reading: Scarlett, R.J. 1976. *Notornis* 23: 355. Stonehouse, B. 1960. *Sci Rep Falkland Is Dep Surv* 23: 1–81. Warham, J. & Bell, B.D. *Notornis* 26: 121–169.

74. YELLOW-EYED PENGUIN *Megadyptes antipodes* Plate 19

Other name: Hoiho

Size: 65 cm; male 5.5 kg, female 5.25 kg

Distribution: New Zealand only; breeding on the coast and some offshore islands of the southeastern South Island from Banks Peninsula to Bluff, Foveaux Strait islands, Stewart Island and its outliers (particularly Codfish), Auckland Islands and Campbell Island. Most birds are sedentary and feed within 25 km of their colony while breeding, and return regularly throughout the non-breeding season to the vicinity of their breeding site. Stragglers (mainly juveniles) reach The Snares, Fiordland, the Chathams, the northern Canterbury and the Marlborough coasts, the southern North Island, and even as far north as the Bay of Plenty (1980). In some years (e.g. 1972 and 1977) moderate numbers are beachwrecked in the southern North Island. Subfossil and midden remains from the South Island and subfossil remains from Chatham Island indicate a wider distribution in the past.

Population: c. 6000: c. 2000 breeding pairs and c. 2000 non-breeders. Estimated numbers of breeding pairs: South Island 600–650, Stewart Island/Foveaux Strait 220–400, Auckland Islands 520–570, and Campbell Island 490–600 pairs.

Conservation: Protected endangered endemic. The number of birds and their breeding success seem to fluctuate widely,

but in recent years major declines have been noted at a number of sites. The population in the Catlins may have declined 75% since the 1940s, and between 1985 and 1987 the number of pairs breeding on the South Island declined by 50%, because a shortage of food in two successive breeding seasons led to adults not attempting to breed and also increased adult mortality owing to starvation during the annual moult. Yellow-eyed Penguins are occasionally drowned in fishing nets.

On the Otago Peninsula, 30–40% of breeding adults and most chicks died during the 1989–90 breeding season, possibly as a result of an unidentified biotoxin, but the populations have recovered. On Campbell Island, the population declined rapidly between 1988 and 1992, attributed in part to an increase in disturbance from sea lions.

Intensive research on the ecology of Yellow-eyed Penguins is under way, focusing on the diet, feeding behaviour and breeding biology of the Otago coast population. Habitat management around breeding sites aims to exclude stock (which trample nests) and restore coastal scrub and forest. Because mammalian predators (especially ferrets and stoats) cause serious losses in some years, intensive predator control operates on parts of the Otago coast. Population changes on the mainland and the subantarctic islands are being monitored regularly.

Breeding: Most birds return to the same area each year, but fewer than 30% of birds use the same nest site in successive years. Laying in Otago is in September–October, mostly the second half of September; the season is about a fortnight later on Campbell Island. They lay 1–**2** pale bluish-green eggs (77 x 57 mm, 138 g) in a substantial open bowl, generally hard against a bank, flax bush or tussock, which provides shelter from direct sunlight and obscures the view to other breeding pairs. Incubation starts after the second egg is laid 3–5 days after the first. Both sexes incubate in spells of c. 2 days. Most eggs hatch within a day of each other, after 39–**43**–51 days.

Chicks are brooded for the first 25 days, by which time they have developed a thick layer of secondary down. They start making short forays away from the nest site, and after 40–50 days they are attended only at night. Chicks sometimes form small crèches at sites where numbers are high. They fledge after 97–**106**–118 days in February–March and are immediately able to swim and be independent of their parents. First breeding is at 2–3 years in females, 3–4 years in males. Birds are monogamous and retain their partners from year to year. The oldest tagged Yellow-eyed Penguin lived over 20 years.

Behaviour: Breeding distribution is clumped because of a shortage of suitable nesting sites rather than a need to form colonies. Small groups form outside the breeding season, or to avoid sea lions, but apparently birds feed alone.

Feeding: Yellow-eyed Penguins eat mainly small to medium-sized fish (up to 32 cm long), but squid, octopuses and some krill are also taken. One-year-old birds eat more squid and less fish than adults. They dive to 160 m below the surface to capture fish (and possibly squid) living on or near the ocean floor.

In the hand: Males are larger than females, but measurements overlap; over 85% of birds can be sexed correctly from a combination of skull length (from the back of the skull to bill tip) 135–**143**–150 mm cf. 130–**137**–149 mm, and foot length (from the back of the heel to the tip of the pad of the middle toe) 126–**131**–136 mm cf. 121–**125**–131 mm.

Reading: Darby, J.T. & Seddon, P.J. 1990. In *Penguin Biology*. San Diego: Academic Press. Moore, P.J. 1992. *Notornis* 39: 1–15. Moore, P.J. *et al.* 1995. *DoC Sci & Res Ser* No. 83. Ratz, H. & Murphy, B. 1999. *Pacific Cons. Biol.* 5: 16–27. Richdale, L.E. 1951. *Sexual Behavior in Penguins*. Lawrence: Univ Kansas Press. Richdale, L.E. 1957. *A Population Study of Penguins*. Oxford: OUP. Van Heezik, Y. 1990. *NZ J Zool* 17: 201–212. Van Heezik, Y.M. & Davis, L. 1990. *Ibis* 132: 354–365.

75. GENTOO PENGUIN *Pygoscelis papua* Plate 18

Size: 75 cm, 5.5 kg

Geographical variation: Two subspecies: the larger *papua* breeds mainly on the subantarctic islands, and the smaller *ellsworthii* breeds in the South Atlantic Ocean and on the Antarctic Peninsula. All that have reached New Zealand shores are presumed to have been *papua*.

Distribution: Circumpolar, breeding on the Antarctic Peninsula and many islands in the subantarctic zone, including 4700 breeding pairs on Macquarie Island. They feed inshore, and so remain close to their breeding ground. A few vagrants, usually immatures, have been recorded ashore on beaches in the New Zealand region: Campbell Island (several records), Dunedin (September 1970), Bluff (November 1970), Catlins (October 1974),

Banks Peninsula (February 1976, December 1993), Antipodes Island (Novembers 1978 and 1995) and The Snares (Decembers 1985 and 2002).

Feeding: Diet at Macquarie Island in June–November is mainly oceanic fish (up to 18 cm long) and squid. Elsewhere, Gentoo Penguins have been recording eating mostly krill. They usually feed close to the surface but have been recorded diving to over 160 m.

Reading: Croxall, J. P. & Prince, P.A. 1980. *Ibis* 122: 245–253. Darby, J.T. & Wright, A.W. 1973. *Notornis* 20: 28–30. Hindell, M.A. 1989. *Emu* 89: 71–78. Reilly, P.N. & Kerle, J.A. 1981. *Notornis* 28: 189–201. Robertson, G. 1986. *Aust Wildl Res* 13: 583–587.

76. ADÉLIE PENGUIN *Pygoscelis adeliae* Plate 19

Size: 70 cm; 5 kg

Distribution: Circumpolar, breeding in large colonies on ice-free coasts and islands of Antarctica and on South Shetland, South Orkney, South Sandwich and Bouvet Islands. In the Ross Sea sector of Antarctica there are 34 colonies, with the largest (>50,000 pairs) being at Cape Adare, Possession Island, Cape Hallett, Cape Cotter, Franklin Island, Cape Bird and Cape Crozier. Movements are poorly known, but few are recorded north of 60°S. Two have been recorded from the New Zealand mainland: one dead on the Marlborough coast (December 1962) and one alive at Kaikoura (December 1992).

Population: c. 1,082,000 pairs in the Ross Sea sector, which is over 40% of the total world breeding population of c. 2.6 million pairs. The largest colony in the world is at Cape Adare with 282,000 pairs.

Conservation: Protected abundant native. The number of birds seems to be stable, but individual colonies seem to decline after human disturbance. Counts of Adélie Penguins are being used to monitor changes to the Antarctic environment by counting birds in aerial photographs of the main colonies in the Ross Sea sector.

Breeding: Laying is during November and early December, mostly about the middle of November, c. 1–2 weeks after the birds return to the colony. They lay 1–2–3 pale green eggs (69 x 55 mm, 120 g) 2–3–4 days apart. If the first egg is lost shortly after laying, a third egg is often laid, bringing the clutch back to two, but this egg is much smaller than usual (66 x 51 mm, 101 g). The nest is a scrape surrounded by rounded stones. Colonies are on flat or gently sloping surfaces free of snow, up to 100 km from open water when birds first arrive, but the sea-ice quickly breaks up, letting birds reach open water easily. Incubation starts with the first egg but may be only partial until the second egg is laid. The female usually returns to sea while the male takes the first spell of about a fortnight; thereafter, incubation is shared roughly evenly, with the length of incubation spells positively related to the distance to open water. The eggs hatch 1–2 days apart, after 30–33–38 days.

Chicks are guarded by their parents for the first 17–22–32 days, during which time they develop a thick layer of secondary down, and then start to shed this as feathers appear. The parents swap duties every couple of days and feed their chicks soon after they arrive back. The chicks join crèches, but their parents are still able to pick them out in the crowd of chicks. Chicks fledge after 41–51–56 days in late January and February, at c. 56% of adult weight. They are independent of their parents after they leave the colony. First breeding is at 3–4–6+ years in females, 4–7–8+ years in males. Birds are monogamous and usually retain their partners from year to year; most divorces are in pairs that were poorly synchronised arriving back at the colony. The oldest Adélie Penguin recorded lived at least 16 years.

Behaviour: Gregarious, with some colonies of 250,000+ pairs. At sea, they are often seen in small groups roosting on ice floes or feeding in open water.

Feeding: During the breeding season, they eat mainly krill, especially *Euphausia superba* and *E. crystallorophias*, but they also take a few fish, squid and a variety of marine invertebrates. They feed close to the surface or at moderate depths (10–100 m) but are capable of diving to 175 m.

Reading: Ainley, D.G & DeMaster, D.P. 1980. *Ecology* 61: 522–530. Cossee, R.O. & Mills, J.A. 1993. *Notornis* 40: 308–309. Davis, L.S. *et al.* 1988. *Notornis* 35: 15–23. Lishman, G.S. 1985. *Ibis* 127: 84–99. Reid, B.E. 1965. *NZ J Sci* 8: 503–514. Spurr, E.B. 1975. *Ibis* 117: 324–338. Taylor, R.H. 1962. *Ibis* 104: 176–204. Taylor, R.H. *et al.* 1990. *NZ J Ecol* 14: 25–29. Van Heezik, Y. 1988. *Notornis* 35: 23–26.

77.   CHINSTRAP PENGUIN   *Pygoscelis antarctica*   Plate 19

Size: 75 cm, 5.5 kg

Distribution: Circumpolar, breeding mainly on the Antarctic Peninsula and islands in the subantarctic zone of the Atlantic Ocean, especially at the South Sandwich Islands (c. 5 million pairs). A very small breeding colony has recently been found on an islet off Sabrina Island, Balleny Islands, in the Ross Sea sector of Antarctica. Chinstrap Penguins feed inshore during the breeding season and near the northern limit of pack ice during winter, and so are rarely recorded north of 60°S. Vagrants have been recorded at Antipodes Island (1978), Invercargill (1980), Campbell Island (1984), Warrington, Otago (1992) and Kaikoura (2002).

Population: c. 10 pairs breed at the Balleny Islands; this is a minute fraction of the total world breeding population of c. 6.5 million pairs.

Conservation: Protected native. Formerly they were almost entirely confined to the South American quadrant of Antarctica, but they have increased and spread eastward into the Ross Sea sector of Antarctica.

Breeding: No studies in the New Zealand region, but elsewhere laying is in late November and December, about a fortnight after birds return to their colony. They lay 1–2–3 creamy white eggs (67 x 52 mm, 113 g) 3–4 days apart. The nest is a shallow cup on a slightly raised platform of small stones on an ice-free slope, often in mixed colonies with Adélie and/or Gentoo Penguins. Incubation starts after the first egg but may be only partial until the second egg is laid. The male departs to sea once the second egg is laid, and the female takes the first incubation spell of c. 6 days. The male then incubates for 10 days. Shifts then alternate and shorten as incubation proceeds. The incubation period is 31–**35**–39 days; first eggs hatch about a day before the second egg.

Chicks are guarded for the first 3–4–5 weeks, during which time they are fed regularly. They then join small crèches until they fledge in late February to early March at 48–**53**–59 days old and at about 67% of adult weight. They are independent once they have left the colony. First breeding is at 3 years in both sexes.

Behaviour: Gregarious, breeding in large colonies and feeding in loose groups out of the breeding season. Compared with other penguins, they are bold and aggressive towards humans and other animals at their colony.

Feeding: Diet at Signy Island in the breeding season is mostly krill, especially *Euphausia superba*, with just a few fish and amphipods. They feed close to the surface but have been recorded diving to depths of 70 m.

Reading: Conroy, J.W.H. *et al.* 1975. In *The Biology of Penguins*. London: MacMillan. Lishman, G.S. 1985. *Ibis* 127: 84–99. Spurr, E.B. 1985. *Notornis* 32: 1–4.

78.   BLUE PENGUIN   *Eudyptula minor*   Plate 19

Other names: Korora, Little Blue Penguin, Fairy Penguin (Australia)

Size: 40 cm, 1100 g

Geographical variation: Up to six subspecies have been recognised on the basis of back colour, flipper pattern and measurements, but recent genetic analysis showed only two clear forms; the Otago birds being closer to Australian birds than all the others combined. The superficially distinct White-flippered Penguin *albosignata* of Banks Peninsula and Motunau Island was not genetically distinct.

Distribution: Breed on the coasts of southern Australia, Tasmania and New Zealand. In the New Zealand region, Blue Penguins breed on the coasts and offshore islands of North, South, Stewart and the Chatham Islands. They are generally sedentary and are often seen in shallow inshore waters and harbours close to their breeding grounds. Some birds, especially juveniles, wander several hundred kilometres from their breeding or natal site; e.g. birds from Motunau Island have been recovered in Otago and Hawke's Bay, and vagrants occasionally reach The Snares. Subfossil and midden remains indicate that Blue Penguins were widespread and common on the coasts of New Zealand in pre-European times.

Population: Widespread and locally common; the main breeding is on islands off eastern Northland, in the Hauraki Gulf, Great Barrier Island, around Cook Strait, on Motunau Island, around southern Otago and Foveaux Strait, and on the Chatham Islands.

Conservation: Protected native. Locally common on uninhabited islands and on remote parts of the mainland coast away from disturbance by humans, dogs, cats and mustelids, but a few persist in coastal urban areas such as around Wellington Harbour and Oamaru. Populations undergo severe crashes, and many dead birds are washed ashore in some years (e.g. eastern Northland in autumn 1974), probably as a result of food shortage or biotoxins.

Breeding: Laying is in July–December, with peaks in August and November. They lay 1–**2** white eggs (56 x 43 mm, 54 g), 3–5 days apart. The nest is in a burrow, natural cavity or rock pile, or sometimes under driftwood. Some Blue Penguins nest in loose colonies near the shore, but others nest hundreds of metres from any other pair and can be over 500 m inland and above 200 m asl on some islands; some birds are even seen occasionally at 550 m near the summit of Kapiti Island. Incubation starts after the first egg is laid but may be only partial until the second is laid. Both sexes incubate with short shifts of 1–2

days, until the eggs hatch after 33–**36**–43 days.

Chicks are brooded for the first 10 days, guarded continuously for a further 1–3 weeks, guarded only at night for a further 3–4 weeks, and then in the final stages they are visited only briefly at night. Chicks fledge at 48–**54**–63 days old and at about 90% of adult weight. They are independent once they have left the nest. First breeding is at 2–3 years in both sexes. The oldest bird recorded in New Zealand lived over 19 years.

Behaviour: Blue Penguins are very vocal when they come ashore at night. They have a wide range of calls, from mewing notes, not unlike those of a cat, to loud screams, trumpeting and deep-toned growls. A complete body moult usually takes place at the breeding site for 10–18 days in December–March.

Feeding: Birds breeding on Codfish Island in October take mainly arrow squid and small (10–35 mm) fish, and a few octopuses. They feed mostly within 5 m of the surface but have been recorded diving to depths of 69 m.

In the hand: Males have longer and deeper bills than females, but because of the wide geographical variation in the size of Blue Penguins, sexing of birds from bill measurements is reliable only at particular breeding sites.

Reading: Banks, J.C. *et al.* 2002. *Notornis* 49: 29–38. Crockett, D.E. & Kearns, M.P. 1975. *Notornis* 22: 69–72. Dann, P. 1994. *Notornis* 41: 157–166. Gales, R. 1988. *Notornis* 35: 71–75. Kinsky, F.C. 1960. *Rec Dom Mus* 3: 145–218. Kinsky, F.C. & Falla, R.A. 1976. *Rec Nat Mus* 1: 105–126. Montague, T. 1985. *Emu* 85: 264–267. Van Heezik, Y. 1990. *NZ J Zool* 17: 543–548.

79. ROCKHOPPER PENGUIN *Eudyptes chrysocome* Plate 20

Size: 55 cm, 2.8 kg

Geographical variation: Three subspecies, all recorded in the New Zealand region: the Eastern Rockhopper *filholi* breeds at Macquarie Island and in the New Zealand subantarctic, whereas the Western Rockhopper *chrysocome* and Moseley's Rockhopper *moseleyi* are vagrants.

Distribution: Circumpolar, breeding on many subantarctic islands. In the New Zealand region, Eastern Rockhoppers breed on the

Antipodes, Auckland and Campbell Islands. In late summer, up to 20 moult at The Snares, and some reach the Otago and Canterbury coasts and the Chathams. Western Rockhoppers have been seen at The Snares (1985–87, 1993), and Moseley's Rockhoppers have been seen at South East Island (August 1968 to November 1970), Wellington (January 1984), possibly at Gisborne (December 1976), Pitt Island (November 1998) and Star Keys (January 2004).

Population: The Eastern Rockhopper has c. 60,000 pairs in the New Zealand region: c. 3000 pairs on the Antipodes, 51,500 pairs on Campbell Island and 2700–3600 pairs on the Auckland Islands. The main breeding site for this subspecies is Macquarie Island (200,000 pairs).

Conservation: Protected native. Locally common on subantarctic islands, but they have declined 94% at Campbell Island from c. 800,000 pairs in 1942 to just over 50,000 pairs in 1985, perhaps because of rising sea temperatures affecting the penguins' food supply. A similar decline has been noted recently at the Antipodes, and a lesser decline at the Auckland Islands.

Breeding: Laying is in October–November, slightly earlier at the Antipodes than at Campbell Island or the Auckland Islands. They lay 2 white eggs, the first (64 x 48 mm, 80 g) being much smaller than the second (71 x 54 mm, 112 g), which is laid 4–5 days later. The nest is a lined scrape in a large colony on terraces, scree slopes and sometimes among tussock or in caves from near the coast to several hundred metres inland. Incubation starts before the second egg is laid, but the second egg usually hatches first. The first egg is often lost from the nest during squabbles or taken by Brown Skuas, and only rarely are two chicks reared. Both sexes incubate; the female takes the first long shift of 10–19 days, followed by the male for 7–13 days. The incubation shifts shorten until the eggs hatch after 33–34 days.

Chicks are brooded initially and guarded almost continuously by the male (which fasts for 5 weeks), and occasionally by the female during daily feeding visits, until they are about 3 weeks old. Thereafter, they form small crèches and are fed only by their own parents. Chicks depart in February and early March at about 9–10 weeks old, and they are independent once they have left the colony.

Behaviour: Gregarious, breeding in colonies of over 10,000 pairs on Campbell Island, and they are seen in groups at sea. Moult usually takes place at the breeding grounds over 3–4 weeks during April, about a month after their chicks have fledged.

Feeding: At Campbell Island, the diet in the breeding season is mainly fish with some small crustaceans, squid, octopus and other marine invertebrates. Elsewhere, krill forms most of the diet. Rockhopper Penguins feed by pursuit-diving to depths of up to 100 m.

In the hand: Adult males have longer, deeper and wider bills than females, with little overlap at any single breeding site. At Campbell Island, males had a product (in mm) of these three bill measurements of over 8700, whereas females were under 7800; on the Antipodes the corresponding figures were 10,200 and 9400. Races are distinguished by underflipper pattern and the colour of skin at the base of the bill: in *filholi* it is pink, whereas in *chrysocome* and *moseleyi* it is black. Race *moseleyi* is larger, with much longer flippers (175–190 mm) than the other two races (160–175 mm).

Reading: Cooper, W. 1992. *Notornis* 39: 66–67. Cunningham, D.M. & Moors, P.J. 1994. *Emu* 94: 27–36. Tennyson, A.J.D. & Miskelly, C.M. 1989. *Notornis* 36: 183–189. Warham, J. 1963. *Auk* 80: 229–256; Warham, J. 1972. *Auk* 89: 86–105. Warham, J. 1975. In *The Biology of Penguins*. London: MacMillan.

80. MACARONI PENGUIN *Eudyptes chrysolophus* Plate 20

Other name: Royal Penguin
Size: 70 cm, 4.5 kg
Geographical variation: Two subspecies: the Macaroni Penguin *chrysolophus* breeds on islands off Chile, in the South Atlantic and South Indian Oceans, and the Royal Penguin *schlegeli* breeds on Macquarie Island. Both have been recorded as vagrants to the New Zealand region.
Distribution: Circumpolar, breeding on many subantarctic islands. Macaroni Penguins have been recorded from Cape Hallett and the Balleny Islands in the Ross Sea sector of Antarctica, at Campbell Island and The Snares. Royal Penguins are more regular vagrants, with records from Hawke's Bay, Wellington, Otago (three), The Snares (two), Auckland and Campbell Islands (regular visitors in summer and autumn).
Feeding: At Macquarie Island, the diet during

the breeding season is mainly krill, especially during incubation and moulting, but it is more varied, with more fish and squid, during chick-feeding.

In the hand: Adult males have longer and deeper bills than females, with little overlap at any single breeding site. Royal Penguins have larger bills than Macaroni Penguins and normally have white or pale grey cheeks, chin and throat, but rarely black. Macaroni Penguins have jet-black cheeks, chin and throat, but rarely some are white, so positive identification to race is difficult.

Reading: Hindell, M.A. 1988. *Emu* 88: 219–226. Warham, J. 1971. *Notornis* 18: 91–115.

81. FIORDLAND CRESTED PENGUIN
Eudyptes pachyrhynchus   **Plate 20**

Other names: Tawaki, Pokotiwha
Size: 60 cm, 4 kg
Distribution: Fiordland Crested Penguins breed only in New Zealand. They breed in small colonies on headlands, on islets, around entrances to fiords and sometimes in sandy bays, southwards from near Bruce Bay in Westland and the Open Bay Islands, to Fiordland, Solander Island, Green Islets (Foveaux Strait), Codfish Island and on and around western and southern Stewart Island. During breeding, adults stay in continental shelf waters close to their nesting colonies. They return to their colonies to moult before dispersing in autumn. Immatures often moult away from the breeding grounds and are occasionally recorded beach-wrecked or moulting around the coast of the North and South Islands in summer and early autumn. A pair attempted to breed on Banks Peninsula in 1945, and a pair bred in Palliser Bay in 1953. Yearlings and occasional older birds are common on The Snares in summer but do not breed there. Vagrants reach Chatham, Auckland, Campbell and Macquarie Islands and southern Australia from New South Wales to Western Australia. Subfossil and midden remains from North and South Islands indicate a wider distribution in the past.
Population: c. 2500–3000 pairs; main populations are on Taumaka Island (Open Bay Islands) 150 pairs, between Paringa River and Murphy Beach 180 pairs, Breaksea Island and adjacent islets 215 pairs, Solander Islands 115 pairs, Codfish Island 140 pairs.
Conservation: Protected endangered endemic. Until recently the numbers of birds have not been assessed because most breed on the remote coastline of South Westland

and on islands in Fiordland. An estimate of 5000–10,000 pairs in 1984 seems to have been optimistic, although there is some evidence that the breeding population on Solander Island has declined markedly since the 1950s, as have the Dusky Sound birds since Richard Henry noted 'thousands' at the turn of the century. At mainland colonies, breeding and moulting birds are threatened by dogs, mustelids and human disturbance. Weka take many eggs and chicks at some island and mainland colonies, even after the chicks are old enough to join crèches.
Breeding: Laying is in July–August. They lay **2** white eggs, the first (67 x 51 mm, 99 g) is smaller than the second (71 x 54 mm, 117 g), which is laid 3–**4**–6 days later. The nest is a shallow lined scrape in a deep cavity under tree roots, among rockfalls, in crevices or caves, or under dense coastal bush or scrub; usually in a small colony of 10 or fewer pairs. Incubation starts when the second egg is laid, and it usually hatches first, after 30–**32**–35 days. Both sexes incubate; for the first week each takes short incubation spells, but then does long spells of 10–14 days. The first egg is sometimes displaced from the nest, but many pairs hatch both eggs. The chick from the smaller egg usually starves, and it is very rare that both chicks are reared successfully.

Chicks are brooded initially and guarded almost continuously by the male (who fasts), and occasionally by the female during feeding visits, until they are c. 3 weeks old. Thereafter, chicks form small crèches and are fed by both parents. Chicks depart in November and early December at c. 10–11 weeks old, and are independent once they have left the colony. First breeding is probably at 5–6 years old.

Behaviour: Moderately gregarious, breeding in small loose colonies of 10 or fewer pairs, and they are sometimes seen in small groups at sea. Adults moult at their breeding site over 20–30 days in January–March, about three months after their chicks have fledged.

Feeding: During the crèching phase in South Westland and Fiordland, adults mainly eat juvenile squid, octopus, krill and a wide variety of small fish; whereas birds feeding chicks on Codfish Island in October mainly eat small (25–35 mm) fish, with a few squid and octopuses.

In the hand: Adult males have longer, deeper and wider bills than females, with little overlap in bill depth or in the product of length, width and depth within particular populations.

Reading: Murie, J.O. *et al.* 1991. *Notornis* 38: 233–238. St. Clair, C.C. 1992. *Behav Ecol Sociobiol* 31: 409–416. St. Clair, C.C. & St. Clair, R. 1992. *Notornis* 44: 37–47. McLean, I.G. *et al.* 1993. *Notornis* 39: 60–63. McLean, I.G. *et al.* 1997. *Notornis* 40: 85–94. Van Heezik, Y.M. 1989. *Notornis* 36: 151–156. Van Heezik, Y.M. 1990. *NZ J Zool* 17: 543–548. Warham, J. 1972. *Auk* 89: 86–105. Warham, J. 1974. *Ibis* 116: 1–27. Warham, J. 1975. In *The Biology of Penguins*. London: MacMillan.

82. SNARES CRESTED PENGUIN *Eudyptes robustus* Plate 20

Size: 60 cm, 3 kg

Distribution: Breed only on The Snares. Most are on Main and Broughton Islands, but a few nest on Toru and Rima islets of the Western Chain. While breeding, adults stay in continental shelf waters close to their nesting colonies, and they return to their colonies to moult before dispersing in winter. Some immatures moult away from the breeding grounds and are occasionally recorded beach-wrecked or moulting around the coast of Stewart Island and the South Island in summer and early autumn. Vagrants have been recorded in Hawke's Bay, on the Wellington coast, at the Chatham, Antipodes, Campbell and Macquarie Islands, southern Australia and Tasmania.

Population: c. 23,000 pairs: Main Island 19,000 pairs, Broughton Island 3500 pairs, Toru 300 pairs, Rima 200 pairs.

Conservation: Protected locally common endemic, little influenced by humans or introduced predators.

Breeding: Laying is in September–October on Main and Broughton Islands, but c. 3–6 weeks later on the Western Chain. They lay 2 white eggs, the first (68 x 52 mm, 100 g) smaller than the second (73 x 56 mm, 130 g), which is laid 4–5 days later. The nest is a shallow lined cup often raised slightly. They breed in small dense colonies of 50–200 pairs, mostly in clearings under *Olearia* or *Brachyglottis* forest, but sometimes among boulders

or in the open. Incubation starts when the second egg is laid, and it usually hatches first, after 31–33–37 days. Both sexes incubate. For the first few days the pair take short incubation spells, but then the male leaves the female to incubate for a fortnight and then returns to incubate until the chicks hatch. The first egg is sometimes displaced from the nest and is often more accessible to Brown Skuas while being incubated. Many pairs hatch both eggs, but the chick from the smaller egg often starves and it is extremely rare that both chicks are reared successfully.

Chicks are brooded initially and guarded almost continuously by the male (which fasts) and are fed by the female during daily visits until c. 3 weeks old. Thereafter, chicks form small crèches (6–12 birds) and are fed only by their parents. Chicks leave in January–February at c. 10–11 weeks old, and are independent after they have left the colony. First breeding is probably from 4 years old. The oldest banded bird recorded lived over 20 years.

Behaviour: Gregarious, breeding in small to large, dense colonies of 5 to 2000 pairs, and they are sometimes seen in small groups at sea. Adults moult at their breeding site for 24–30 days in March–May, c. 3 months after their chicks have fledged.

Feeding: While breeding, they eat mainly krill, small fish and squid, obtained at depths down to 20–80 m.

In the hand: Adult males have longer, deeper and wider bills than females, with a product (in mm) of over 17,800 being a male, and under 13,320 being a female.

Reading: Miskelly, C.M. 1984. *Notornis* 31: 209–223. Warham, J. 1972. *Auk* 89: 86–105. Warham, J. 1974. *J Roy Soc NZ* 4: 63–108. Warham, J. 1975. In *The Biology of Penguins*. London: MacMillan.

83. ERECT-CRESTED PENGUIN *Eudyptes sclateri* Plate 20

Size: 60 cm, 4.5 kg
Distribution: Endemic to New Zealand, breeding in large numbers on the Antipodes and Bounty Islands, and a few breed on Disappointment Island in the Auckland Islands. While breeding, adults stay in continental shelf waters close to their nesting colonies, and they return to their colonies to moult before dispersing in winter. Some immatures moult away from the breeding grounds and are occasionally recorded beach-wrecked or moulting on the east coast of the North and South Islands and at Stewart Island and The Snares. Vagrants have been recorded on the coast of the North Island, at the Chathams, Macquarie Island, on the coast of southern Australia between Victoria and Western Australia, and once even at the Falkland Islands. Formerly bred on Campbell Island.
Population: c. 81,000 pairs. Bounty Islands 28,000 pairs, Antipodes 53,000 pairs, with fewer than 10 pairs elsewhere.
Conservation: Protected endemic with rapidly declining populations, perhaps affected by rising sea temperatures altering their food supply.
Breeding: Little information is available. Laying is in October–November, 2–3 weeks later on Bounty Island than on the Antipodes.

They lay **2** white eggs, the first (77 x 48 mm, 98 g) much smaller than the second (89 x 57 mm, 149 g). The nest is a shallow lined cup, often raised slightly. They nest in huge dense colonies of thousands of pairs among Shy Mollymawks or near Rockhopper Penguins, mostly among boulder-strewn slopes and terraces. Both sexes incubate. The incubation period is c. 36 days. About 10–11 weeks after hatching, the chicks depart in late January to February.
Behaviour: Gregarious, not only breeding in dense colonies of several thousand pairs but also forming small groups at sea. Adults moult at their breeding site for 26–30 days in March–April, c. 6 weeks after their chicks have fledged.
Feeding: While breeding, they eat krill and squid, and may also take small fish.

In the hand: Adult males have longer, deeper and wider bills than females, with a product (in mm) of over 16,000 being a male, and under 14,000 being a female.

Reading: Richdale, L.E. 1941. *Emu* 41: 25–53. Richdale, L.E. 1950. *Emu* 49: 153–166. Robertson, C.J.R. & van Tets, G.F. 1982 *Notornis* 29: 311–336. Warham, J. 1972. *Ardea* 60: 145–184. Warham, J. 1975. In *The Biology of Penguins*. London: MacMillan. Warham, J. & Bell, B.D. 1979. *Notornis* 26: 121–169.

84. MAGELLANIC PENGUIN *Spheniscus magellanicus* Plate 18

Size: 70 cm, 3.5 kg
Distribution: Breed on the Juan Fernandez Islands in the Pacific, along the coast of southern Chile south to the islands near Cape Horn, along the Patagonian coast of Argentina, and in the Falkland Islands. There have been two records of Magellanic Penguins on the New Zealand mainland: Waimarama, Hawke's Bay (March 1972), and in Otago

Harbour (March 1990). Both birds were moulting, but as they readily took fish from the hand they may have had an assisted passage by ship.

Reading: Boswall, J. & MacIver, D. 1975. In *The Biology of Penguins*. London: MacMillan. Darby, J.T. 1991. *Notornis* 38: 36. Robertson, C.J.R. *et al.* 1972. *Notornis* 19: 111–113.

TROPICBIRDS   Phaethontidae

3 species; 2 in the New Zealand region, including 1 species breeding at the Kermadec Islands.

Sailors called tropicbirds 'bos'n birds' because the projecting middle tail feathers resembled the marlin spike of the boatswain and their call is like his whistle. These white seabirds are confined to tropical and subtropical seas, often far from land. They are usually solitary or in pairs, flying strongly well above the surface, approaching ships with a steady flight and briefly escorting them. Tropicbirds feed on fish and squid, taken mostly by plunge-diving. They breed on the ground, solitarily or in loose colonies, the density depending on available nest sites rather than social need.

85. RED-TAILED TROPICBIRD   *Phaethon rubricauda*   Plate 21

Other name: Amokura
Size: 46 cm, plus up to 40 cm for tail streamers; 800 g
Geographical variation: A single species but with a gradual increase in size and of the pink suffusion on the white plumage from the northern Pacific to the Kermadecs.
Distribution: Breeds on many islands of the tropical Indian and Pacific Oceans, including Lord Howe, Norfolk and the Kermadec Islands. They remain at sea when not breeding, although a few are seen near the Kermadecs in winter. In summer, and usually after tropical cyclones, a few birds are seen around northern New Zealand, mainly off Northland or in the Hauraki Gulf, or beach-wrecked on the coasts of Northland and occasionally as far south as the Waikato, Taranaki and Wanganui coasts. They have twice been recorded inland at Lake Taupo. The only South Island record is of a bird at Akaroa in the 1950s.
Population: c. 120 birds breed at the Kermadec Islands.
Conservation: Protected native. No information available on population trends.
Breeding: Laying is in December–April, mostly December–January. They lay **1** fawn egg, spotted and blotched reddish brown (67 x 47 mm, 80 g) in a scrape on the ground, often in inaccessible positions in cavities and fissures of rugged cliffs. Both sexes incubate in shifts of 2–7 days for 42–46 days. The young stay at the nest for c. 3 months, leaving in April–May, but there are records of large chicks at Macauley Island in August.
Behaviour: When not breeding, Red-tailed Tropicbirds are usually seen as singles, pairs at the most. They are silent at sea but noisy, especially in aerial display in pairs, at breeding islands. In display, they have a special hover that makes them seem to fly in reverse. Their short legs cannot support them, and they shuffle along, their breast touching the ground.
Feeding: Fish and squid are caught by plunge-diving from both high and low altitudes.

In the hand: Much larger than White-tailed Tropicbird (wing 330–360 mm cf. 260–280 mm), and adult plumage is very different. Juvenile upperparts barring is similar, but the bill tends to be all blackish or blackish with red base, whereas the bill of juvenile White-tailed Tropicbirds tends to be yellowish with a blackish tip.

Reading: Merton, D.V. 1970. *Notornis* 17: 147–199. Powlesland, R.G. *et al*. 1992. *Notornis* 39: 101–111. Tarburton, M.K. 1984. *Notornis* 31: 92–94. Tarburton, M.K. 1989. *Notornis* 36: 39–49.

86. WHITE-TAILED TROPICBIRD   *Phaethon lepturus*   Plate 21

Size: 38 cm, plus up to 40 cm for tail streamers; 300 g
Distribution: Breed on islands in the tropical Atlantic, Indian and western Pacific Oceans, and remain at sea when not breeding. The nearest breeding sites to New Zealand are

New Caledonia, Tonga, Niue and Rarotonga. Regularly seen in subtropical waters between New Zealand and Fiji. Rare vagrants to waters off the New Zealand mainland are possibly birds blown south by tropical cyclones. There have been nine records, mainly of beach-wrecked birds on Northland coasts but as far south as the Whakatane and Taranaki coasts. At least five were immatures.

Behaviour: Similar to Red-tailed Tropicbirds but tend to accompany ships more often.

PELICANS   Pelecanidae

7 species; 1 vagrant reaches New Zealand.

Pelicans are very large freshwater or marine birds with four webbed toes and a very long bill with a massive fleshy pouch for catching fish. Small flocks surround a shoal of fish and then feed synchronously by dipping their heads into the centre of the shoal. Unlike some marine pelicans, the Australasian species rarely dives for food. Pelicans have a laboured take-off, but their flight is easy and graceful as they soar on thermals and glide effortlessly, reminiscent of a jumbo jet, as they come in to land. They often fly in flocks in a V formation, roost in flocks and breed in colonies.

87.   AUSTRALIAN PELICAN   *Pelecanus conspicillatus*   Plate 27

Size: 170 cm, 5 kg

Distribution: Breed only in Australia, mainly in the north and east. Usually found on inland and coastal lakes rather than in harbours or estuaries, and often breed near inland lakes, although some colonies are on islands in Bass Strait. They disperse widely from their breeding colonies and are regular visitors to New Guinea, the Bismarck Archipelago and Solomon Islands. Rare vagrant to New Zealand with four records: Whanganui River (1890), Kaipara Harbour (August 1976), Southland (November 1977), three or four birds in South Canterbury (December 1977–June 1978). When the 1977 birds came, there was a simultaneous influx into New Guinea and some reached as far as Palau.

Behaviour: Australian Pelicans are gregarious, breeding in colonies, roosting in flocks on sand or mud banks, feeding in parties to surround shoals of fish and then plunging their heads simultaneously below the water to catch their prey.

Reading: Vestjens, W.J.M. 1977. *Aust Wildl Res* 4: 37–58.

GANNETS and BOOBIES   Sulidae

9 species: 2 breed in the New Zealand region and 1 is a visitor to New Zealand waters.

Gannets and boobies are marine birds, mainly feeding close to shore rather than in open oceans. All plunge-dive – gannets for fish, boobies for flying fish. Whereas gannets are typical of temperate seas, boobies are typical of tropical and subtropical seas. Breeding adults tend to stay permanently around their colony and in local seas, whereas non-breeders and young disperse widely.

Their bill is sturdy and cone-shaped, with its cutting edges serrated for seizing fish. The forehead is flattened, and much of the face is covered with bare skin. Three webbed toes, sometimes with all or some skin brightly coloured. The sexes are alike, but juveniles take two to four years to gain fully adult plumage. They breed in colonies, and gan-

netries are particularly dense, mostly on islands and typically on the ground.

Reading: Nelson, J.B. 1978. *The Sulidae: Gannets and Boobies*. Oxford: OUP.

88. AUSTRALASIAN GANNET *Morus serrator* Plate 22

Other name: Takapu
Size: 89 cm, 2.3 kg
Geographical variation: Three species: *bassana* of the North Atlantic, *capensis* of southern Africa, and *serrator* of New Zealand and Australia. In recent years, *capensis*, which has a gular (throat) stripe 3–4 times as long as in *serrator* (from the base of the bill to the foreneck as opposed to from the base of the bill to the chin), has been recorded in increasing numbers in Australia and has interbred with *serrator*.
Distribution: Breed in New Zealand, Philip Island (Norfolk group) and Australia. In New Zealand, they breed in 28 colonies, from the Three Kings Islands south to Little Solander Island. In 1980–81, 99% were in gannetries on islands off the northern half of the North Island. The largest colonies are Gannet Island, west of Kawhia, with 8000+ pairs in 1980– 81, and White Island. Three of the smallest are in the South Island – an islet in Waimaru Bay (Marlborough Sounds), The Nuggets (Otago coast) and Little Solander Island (Foveaux Strait). There are three mainland colonies; the Muriwai (West Auckland) and Cape Kidnappers colonies are on plateaus on coastal headlands, whereas the other colony has recently established on shellbanks near the tip of Farewell Spit. It grew from c. 75 breeding pairs in 1983 to c. 600 pairs in 1987.

Adults and a few juveniles range widely in New Zealand seas during the winter, mostly north of Cook Strait, but vagrants reach the Chatham and Auckland Islands, and Campbell Island (1968). Almost all juveniles and some adults disperse to coastal waters of Australia, as far west as the Indian Ocean and as far north as Rockhampton, Queensland. Most young New Zealand gannets stay in Australian waters until they are 3–7 years old, but a few return at the age

of 1–2 years. Of the 100–300 gannets beach-wrecked annually, most are found on North-land coasts in November–February, during chick-rearing and with the departure of juveniles across the Tasman.
Population: National counts were 21,100 breeding pairs in 1946–47, 37,800 pairs in 1969–70, and 46,000 (of 53,000 pairs in the subspecies) in 1980–81. The annual increase over the 34 years was 2.3%. Excluded from the counts are the large number of immature birds in Australian waters.
Conservation: Protected native. Numbers are increasing rapidly, and mainland colonies have benefited from strict control of access by sightseers because breeding birds are easily disturbed.
Breeding: The breeding season varies from year to year and between gannetries, depend-ing on latitude. Hauraki Gulf males return in mid-June, eggs are laid between late July and mid-October, and chicks leave the nest from late December. At Cape Kidnappers, they return in late July, eggs are laid in late September to December, and chicks leave the nest from early February.

The nest is a depression in a mound mostly of seaweed and guano. Nests are spaced out according to the striking distance of neigh-bouring sitting birds. They lay 1 pale blue-green chalky-covered egg (77 x 47 mm), which both sexes incubate under the webs of their feet for c. 44 days. The young leave the nest at 93–115 days old. Most cross the Tasman Sea soon after leaving the gannetries, arriving from January onwards. They first breed when at least 5 years old. The oldest banded bird in New Zealand lived over 30 years.
Behaviour: Usually solitary away from the colony, but loose flocks form over shoals of fish, and sometimes the birds commute in small flocks. Except when feeding in flocks, they are usually quiet away from the gannetry.

Feeding: Diet is mainly small fish such as pilchards, anchovy and jack mackerel from shallow water, and saury from deep water. Small squid are also taken. They are almost entirely marine, feeding primarily over continental shelf and inshore waters, but also enter harbours and estuaries.

They dive straight down from up to 30 m high. Just before hitting the water, they fully stretch their wings backwards, entering the water at tremendous speed. Inflatable air sacs beneath the skin on the lower neck and breast cushion the shock of entry. In shallow water, such as surf, they dive at a narrow angle. Most prey is swallowed at the surface.

Reading: Fleming, C.A. & Wodzicki, K.A. 1952. *Notornis* 5: 39–78. Hawkins, J.M. 1988. *Notornis* 35: 249–260. Robertson, D.A. 1992. *NZ J Ecol* 16: 77–81. Wingham, E.J. 1985. *Emu* 85: 231–239. Wodzicki, K.A. *et al.* 1984. *Notornis* 31: 232–261.

89. BROWN BOOBY *Sula leucogaster* Plate 22

Size: 70 cm, 1200 g
Geographical variation: Four subspecies; the only one recorded in New Zealand is *plotus* of eastern Africa, islands of the Indian Ocean, Indonesia, Micronesia, northern Australia, New Guinea and much of the Pacific Ocean.
Distribution: Breed in tropical seas. The nearest breeding sites to New Zealand are on many of the islands and cays off the Queensland coast. Occasionally seen off the Kermadec Islands, and a few reach the New Zealand mainland in most summers. They are seen mostly as singles in Northland and in the Bay of Plenty, but have been recorded as far south as Canterbury.
Feeding: They feed by vertical plunging, but from a lower height than Australasian Gannets. Flying fish are the main prey in the tropics, but they take other fish and some squid.

90. MASKED BOOBY *Sula dactylatra* Plate 22

Other name: Blue-faced Booby
Size: 80 cm, 1700 g
Geographical variation: Four subspecies; the only one recorded from New Zealand is *personata* of Australia and the western and central Pacific Ocean, including Lord Howe, Norfolk and the Kermadec Islands. Sometimes the birds breeding in the Tasman Sea and at the Kermadecs (which have dark brown eyes, not yellow, and longer wings) are separated as a distinct subspecies, *fullagari*.
Distribution: Breed in tropical and subtropical seas in the Pacific, Indian and Atlantic Oceans, and in the Caribbean Sea. In the New Zealand region, they breed on the Kermadec Islands (Meyer, Dayrell, South Chanter, Macauley, and Curtis Islands). They are a rare vagrant to the northern North Island, with only five records: Gannet Island (1883), west of North Cape (1964), Firth of Thames (two between October 1977 and March 1978), Hamilton (July 1983), Dargaville (May 1988).

Population: Kermadec Islands, 100+ pairs, mainly on Curtis Island (70 pairs in 1989).
Conservation: Protected native. The numbers of Masked Boobies breeding at the Kermadecs has increased in recent decades, partially owing to an influx of birds from colonies at Norfolk Island.
Breeding: At the Kermadecs, they breed almost all year, with the peak of laying in late August to November. They lay 1–2 dull white eggs (66 x 46 mm, 75 g) on the ground, often in a site exposed to the wind. Both sexes incubate under the webs of their feet for c. 44 days, starting after the laying of the second egg. Hatching is not synchronous and, although both sexes brood chicks at first and feed them, usually only one is raised. It leaves the nest at c. 120 days old. The young may breed as early as 2 years old. Birds banded in Australia have lived over 18 years.
Behaviour: Masked Boobies fly high and fast, soaring and circling. Like Brown Boobies, they often perch on buoys and posts marking

channels. They are silent at sea but noisy at breeding colonies.

Feeding: Mostly flying fish; also other fish and some squid, taken by plunging from high above, usually in deep oceanic water far from land.

SHAGS   Phalacrocoracidae

33 species worldwide in freshwater and marine habitats; 12 species breed in the New Zealand region, including 8 endemic species.

In New Zealand, all members of the Phalacrocoracidae are called shags, whereas elsewhere the term 'cormorant' is used for members of the genus *Phalacrocorax*. Foot colour varies between the three genera in New Zealand: black in the mainly freshwater *Phalacrocorax*, pink in the marine *Leucocarbo*, and yellow in the marine *Stictocarbo*.

Shags are medium to large, long-necked aquatic birds with a stiff, wedge-shaped tail, and moderately short, rounded wings, which black-footed shags hold out to dry when perched. They feed by diving from the water surface to catch fish and crustacea with their long hooked bill. They use their webbed feet to swim underwater. The outermost toe is longest, and a web connects the inner toe with the long hind toe. In the breeding season, bare skin on the face becomes brightly coloured and contrasts with the eye and bill.

Shags sometimes feed in flocks, but they typically roost in flocks and breed in colonies on cliffs or rocky islets, or in trees overhanging water, sometimes together with other shags. They have an elaborate series of ritualised courtship displays at or near the nest, a bulky platform made of sticks or seaweed. Their eggs have a chalky encrustation on the surface. Both sexes share incubation. The chicks are naked at hatching but soon develop down. Both parents regurgitate food for the chicks. If a predator approaches, chicks in tree nests overhanging water will jump well before they can fly, but they are adept at climbing back up to the nest.

91. BLACK SHAG *Phalacrocorax carbo*   Plate 23

Other names: Kawau, Black Cormorant, Great Cormorant
Size: 88 cm, 2.2 kg
Geographical variation: At least three subspecies: *novaehollandiae* breeds throughout Australia, New Guinea and New Zealand.
Distribution: Breed widely from eastern North America (Newfoundland to Maine), Greenland, Iceland, across Europe and Asia, Africa and Australasia. In New Zealand, they breed throughout the main islands and on the Chatham Islands; vagrant to Macauley Island (Kermadecs), The Snares and Campbell Island. They are found in sheltered coastal waters, estuaries, harbours, rivers, streams, dams and lakes up to the subalpine zone. It seems that some young disperse widely – a nestling banded at Lake Wairarapa was recovered at Lord Howe Island, and one banded in New South Wales was recovered near Westport. There is much local movement between feeding and roosting or nesting areas, but no evidence for regular long-distance migration in New Zealand.
Population: Widespread and moderately common (5000–10,000 pairs). Most nest in small colonies of 5–20 pairs, but colonies of over 50 pairs have been recorded in the Waikato, in the Lake Wairarapa wetlands, and at several sites on Chatham Island.
Conservation: Partially protected native. For many years, Black Shags were persecuted by fishermen who saw them as competitors for commercial fish species and for young trout. Black Shags were given partial protection in 1986 after studies had shown that they ate

many young eels and so were probably of some benefit to game-fishers. They are often caught in fishing nets and occasionally on hooked lines.

Breeding: Nesting colonies are commonly in willows, pines, pohutukawa or beech trees overhanging water, or on cliff ledges in river gorges. Some are on coastal cliffs or in low scrub on offshore stacks, and occasionally they nest on old maimai, on the ground (e.g. Wairau Lagoons, Farewell Spit) or in trees well away from water (e.g. in karaka trees in Gollans Valley, near Wellington). The nest is usually a large platform built of sticks, twigs, and flax, raupo and cabbage tree leaves, up to 10 m above the water or ground.

The breeding season is quite variable from colony to colony, and breeding may be delayed at some sites by disturbance from duckshooters. Most eggs are laid in June–October, but birds at Gollans Valley regularly lay in late April. They lay 2–**3**–5 bluish-green eggs (61 x 38 mm) 2 days apart. Incubation lasts 27–31 days. Chicks are able to scramble from the nest at c. 4 weeks old, but fledge at c. 7 weeks old. They are fed by their parents for 7–10 weeks after fledging. Some young breed at 2 years old, but most start at 3 years old. A Black Shag banded in Europe lived nearly 20 years.

Behaviour: Generally feed alone, but sometimes they form flocks of 100+ birds where food is abundant. They often roost in small groups on logs, on rocks and in trees. They are generally silent away from their colonies, but at the nest they make a variety of croaks, grunts and wheezy whistles.

Feeding: Diet is mainly small and medium-sized fish (<35 cm long), including mullet, wrasse, red cod, spotties, smelt, eels, bullies, galaxids, trout and perch; the proportion of species varies greatly according to habitat. Freshwater crayfish, large invertebrates and molluscs are also taken. Black Shags feed in lakes, pools in rivers, estuaries and tidal inlets, and stay close inshore, mainly in water less than 3 m deep, but have been caught in crayfish pots set 12 m deep. Their dives usually last c. 20 seconds, with c. 6 seconds rest between dives, but dives of up to 58 seconds have been recorded.

Reading: Dickinson, P. 1951. *Aust J Mar Fresh Res* 2: 245–251. Falla, R.A. & Stokell, G. 1945. *Trans Roy Soc NZ* 74: 320–331. Sim, D. & Powlesland, R.G. 1995. *Notornis* 42: 23–26. Stonehouse, B. 1967. *Ibis* 109: 600–605.

92. PIED SHAG   *Phalacrocorax varius*   Plate 23

Other names: Karuhiruhi, Pied Cormorant
Size: 81 cm, 2 kg
Geographical variation: Two subspecies: *varius* breeds in New Zealand, and *hypoleucos* breeds in Australia.
Distribution: Breeds in coastal mainland Australia. In New Zealand, Pied Shags have a patchy breeding distribution, mainly in warmer areas on sheltered coasts, harbours and offshore islands. The main breeding areas are around the Kaipara and Hokianga Harbours, on the east coast of the North Island from Doubtless Bay to Gisborne, in the South Island from Tasman Bay through the Marlborough Sounds and south to Banks Peninsula, in Fiordland and around the east coast of Stewart Island. Colonies are on freshwater lakes at Pupuke (Auckland), Elterwater (Marlborough) and Rotorua (Kaikoura). Pied Shags are generally sedentary and, unlike their Australian counterpart, rarely venture inland. A few birds, mainly juveniles, disperse well away from breeding areas and can turn up in coastal sites almost anywhere.

Population: Widespread and moderately common (5000–10,000 pairs), especially in the Bay of Islands, inner Hauraki Gulf, Coromandel Peninsula and Marlborough. Most nest in small colonies of 5–30 pairs, but over 50 pairs have been recorded in Whangarei Harbour, in Panmure Basin (Auckland) and near Nelson.

Conservation: Protected native. Pied Shags are sometimes illegally persecuted by fishermen who regard them as competitors for fish, and some birds are caught accidentally in fishing nets. Shags are now known to have a minimal impact on fish stocks, and few are now shot. This may have contributed to an apparent increase in numbers of Pied Shags. **Breeding:** Nest in colonies, sometimes together with other shags, especially Black and Little Shags. Colonies are commonly in pines, pohutukawa or rata growing on cliffs and overhanging the sea, but occasionally they nest in pohutukawa, willows or silver poplars, or on navigation lights and artificial structures over estuaries or lakes. The nest is usually a large platform 0.5 m across, built of sticks and seaweed, up to 10 m above the water.

Most colonies are active all year round, but laying peaks in July–October and January–March. They lay 2–**3**–**4**–5 pale bluish-green eggs (59 x 38 mm, 47 g) 2 days apart. Incubation lasts 25–**29**–33 days, but this varies within a clutch so that first eggs take c. 31 days to hatch and fourth eggs take c. 27 days. The chicks hatch over the space of a few days. Chicks first leave the nest at c. 4 weeks old,

but fledge at 47–**53**–60 days old. They are fed by their parents for up to 11 weeks after fledging. In Australia, a banded Pied Shag lived over 20 years.

Behaviour: Mostly feed alone but sometimes form flocks of 20+ birds where food is abundant. They often roost in small groups on logs, on rocks and in trees. Generally silent away from their colonies, but at the nest they are noisy, making a variety of harsh croaks, squeals and wheezy whistles.

Feeding: Diet is mainly fish 6–15 cm long. Flounder, mullet, perch, smelt and eels are usually taken in water less than 10 m deep. Dives usually last 20–30 seconds, depending on water depth. The longest dive recorded was of 225 seconds in 20 m deep water. Rest time between dives is 5–10 seconds.

Reading: Lalas, C. 1979. *Notornis* 26: 94–95. Millener, P.R. 1972. MSc thesis, Univ Auckland. Stonehouse, B. 1967. *Ibis* 109: 600–605. Taylor, M.J. 1987. *Notornis* 34: 41–50.

93.   LITTLE BLACK SHAG   *Phalacrocorax sulcirostris*   Plate 23

Other name: Little Black Cormorant
Size: 61 cm, 800 g
Distribution: Breed in Australasia east of Borneo and Java, in New Caledonia and the North Island of New Zealand, with a few large colonies in the Auckland, Waikato, Rotorua Lakes, Lake Taupo, Hawke's Bay and Lake Wairarapa wetlands. They disperse widely in autumn after breeding, with an influx of birds into coastal areas around Northland and Auckland and into Wellington Harbour. A few regularly winter in the South Island, as far south as Southland. Fledglings banded at Lake Rotorua have been recovered in the Hauraki Gulf and from Wellington.
Population: Widespread and moderately common (1000–5000 pairs), especially in the North Island. A rare visitor to the South Island. Colonies of 300+ pairs have been recorded at Lakes Whangape (Waikato), Rotorua and Taupo, but these normally last only a few years before the birds shift elsewhere. The number of Little Black Shags seems to be increasing, with a marked increase in numbers seen in winter in the southern North Island

and in the South Island since about 1980.
Conservation: Protected native. Little Black Shags are sometimes illegally persecuted by fishermen who regard them as competitors for fish, and some birds are caught accidentally in fishing nets. Shags are now known to have a minimal impact on fish stocks, and few are now shot; this may have contributed to the recent increase in numbers of Little Black Shags.
Breeding: Nest in large colonies, sometimes together with other shags, especially Little Shags. Colonies are commonly in willows overhanging fresh water, but sometimes nests are constructed on the ground on small islands. The nest is usually a platform of sticks about 30 cm in diameter. Laying is mostly in November–December, but some autumn nesting has been recorded. They lay 2–**4**–5 pale bluish-green eggs (48 x 32 mm) 2 days apart. No information is available on incubation or fledging periods. In New Zealand, the oldest Little Black Shag lived at least 9 years.
Behaviour: Feed in flocks of 10–150 birds and

work as a group to herd a shoal of fish. They often roost in large groups on logs, on piers, on rocks and in trees. They are silent away from their colonies, but at the nest they are noisy, making a variety of harsh croaks and whistles.

Feeding: Diet is mainly small fish and freshwater crayfish. The main inland prey are smelt, bullies and goldfish, and smelt and whitebait are probably the main marine species taken, judging by the flocking behaviour of birds in estuaries and sheltered harbours. Most fish are taken close to the surface, and dive times are generally 5–10 seconds. Rest times between dives last only 2–3 seconds.

Reading: Potts, K.J. 1977. *Wildlife – A Review* 8: 34–38.

94. LITTLE SHAG *Phalacrocorax melanoleucos* Plate 23

Other names: Kawaupaka, Little Pied Cormorant

Size: 56 cm, 700 g

Geographical variation: Three subspecies: *melanoleucos* breeds in Palau, Indonesia, New Guinea, Australia, New Caledonia and Solomon Islands (except Renell Island, where *brevicauda* is endemic) and was briefly established on Campbell Island; and *brevirostris* breeds in the rest of New Zealand. The New Zealand birds have a wide range of plumage forms, from pied (like those elsewhere in Australasia) to the common 'white-throated' form, smudgy adults and an almost completely black juvenile form. Paler phases are more common in the north. Pied birds make up 60% of the population in the Far North, 32% in Auckland, 15% in the rest of the North Island, but just 8% in the South Island.

Distribution: Breed in Australasia east of Java and the Moluccas, in New Caledonia and New Zealand. Colonies are scattered throughout the North, South and Stewart Islands, and nearby offshore islands. Little Shags are found in sheltered coastal waters, estuaries, harbours, rivers, dams and lakes up to the subalpine zone. There is much local movement between feeding and roosting or nesting areas. After breeding, they disperse widely from their colonies and large flocks congregate around good food sources (e.g. sewer outfalls) or good roosting sites (e.g. 300+ birds roosting at Freemans Pond at the base of Farewell Spit, and 300+ about Wellington Harbour, places where few are found in summer). Stragglers have been recorded from The Snares and Auckland Island, and a small colony (probably of Australian origin) became established on Campbell Island in 1967.

Population: Widespread and common (5000–10,000 pairs), especially in the northern North Island. Colonies of 200+ pairs have been recorded at Lakes Rotomahana, Rotorua and Taupo. The number of Little Shags seem to be increasing, with a marked increase in numbers in Wellington Harbour between the mid-1970s and late 1990s.

Conservation: Protected native. Little Shags are sometimes illegally shot by fishermen who regard them as competitors for fish, and some birds are caught accidentally in fishing nets. Shags are now known to have a minimal impact on fish stocks, and few are now shot; this may have contributed to the increase in numbers of Little Shags.

Breeding: Nest in large colonies, sometimes together with other shags, especially Pied Shags. Colonies are commonly in willows or silver poplars overhanging fresh water or estuaries, but sometimes they nest on maimai or on ledges in river gorges or on sea cliffs. The nest is usually a platform of sticks and leaves, about 30 cm in diameter. The breeding season is very long; nest-building starts in late July, and laying is August–February, with a peak in September–November. They lay 2–4–5 pale blue-green eggs (48 x 31 mm, 25 g) 2 days apart. Incubation lasts c. 4 weeks, and chicks fledge 6 weeks later.

Behaviour: Normally feed alone or in small groups of up to 10 birds, but often roost in flocks of up to 50 birds on logs, on piers, on rocks and in trees. They are silent away from their colonies and make little noise at their colonies, except while displaying, and a loud, repeated 'coo' is given when an aerial predator approaches the colony.

Feeding: Diet varies greatly with habitat but is mainly small fish (<13 cm long) and freshwater crayfish, with the occasional frog and tadpole. The main inland prey are smelt, bullies and goldfish, whereas the main marine species taken are bullies, flounder, sole and smelt. Little Shags generally feed close inshore in water less than 3 m deep; their dives last c. 15 seconds and up to 37 seconds in deep water. Rests between dives last c. 6 seconds.

Reading: Dickinson, P. 1951. *Aust J Mar Fresh Res* 2: 245–251. Dowding, J.E. & Taylor, M.J. 1987. *Notornis* 34: 51–57. Lalas, C. 1983. PhD thesis, Univ Otago. Matthews, C.W. & Fordham, R.A. 1986. *Emu* 86: 118–121. Millener, P.R. 1972. MSc thesis, Univ Auckland. Potts, K.J. *Wildlife – A Review* 8: 34–38. Stonehouse, B. 1967. *Ibis* 109: 600–605. Taylor, M.J. 1987. *Notornis* 34: 41–50.

95. KING SHAG *Leucocarbo carunculatus* Plate 24

Size: 76 cm, 2.5 kg

Distribution: New Zealand only. Breed on very small islands in the outer Marlborough Sounds – Duffers Reef, North Trio Islands, White Rocks, Sentinel Rock and possibly Stewart Island (southeast of D'Urville Island). They are sedentary and remain within the Marlborough Sounds, especially favouring 20–40 m deep water in the outer parts of Pelorus and Queen Charlotte Sounds.

Population: In 1992, the population was 524 birds, with 166 nests recorded. Duffers Reef 69 nests, Trios 50 nests on two islets, White Rocks 30 nests, Sentinel Rock 17 nests, and possibly a few pairs on Stewart Island.

Conservation: Protected threatened endemic. King Shags are sometimes illegally shot by fishermen, and a few birds are caught accidentally in fishing nets. Shags are now known to have a minimal impact on fish stocks, and few are now shot. King Shags are very wary, and some nests fail if boats approach colonies too closely.

Breeding: Nest in colonies on small exposed islands, sometimes only a few metres above high-water mark. The nest is usually a level platform about 0.5 m in diameter, made of twigs, branchlets and kelp, and cemented with guano. The breeding season is very long: nest-building activity picks up in March and reaches a peak in May. Laying is mostly in May–June. They lay 1–2–3 pale blue eggs (65 x 41 mm). There is no information on incubation or fledging periods.

Behaviour: Sometimes roost in flocks on rocks or on mussel-farm buoys, but feed solitarily. Birds from the Duffers Reef colony fly low and directly to their feeding grounds on average 8 km away. They spend much time early in the season collecting nest material or circling the colony. They are silent away from their colonies and make little noise at their colonies, except while displaying.

Feeding: Diet is mainly seafloor-dwelling fish such as flounder, sand-eels, blue cod and red cod, but sole and other flatfish are likely prey. Crayfish and crabs are occasionally taken. Preferred feeding sites are in 20–40 m deep water with a flat bottom. Average dive times are c. 45 seconds, with a maximum of 90+ seconds recorded.

Reading: Nelson, A. 1971. *Notornis* 18: 30–37. Schukard, R. 1994. *Notornis* 41: 93–108.

96. STEWART ISLAND SHAG *Leucocarbo chalconotus* Plate 24

Other name: Bronze Shag (dark phase)

Size: 68 cm, 2.5 kg

Geographical variation: The two main colour forms, pied and bronze, interbreed freely. Birds breeding in Otago are much larger and have more developed papillae above the bill than those in Foveaux Strait. The bronze phase predominates in the north, while the pied phase predominates in the south; a few birds have intermediate plumage.

Distribution: New Zealand only. Breed from Maukiekie Island (North Otago) to Foveaux Strait and around Stewart Island. About 15 colonies of 10–500 pairs are occupied each year. Numbers fluctuate widely at particular colonies, and some colonies are abandoned only to be reoccupied several years later. Colonies are on small islands and on sea cliffs on the mainland. After breeding, some birds disperse northwards to about the Waitaki River and west to Te Waewae Bay. A vagrant has reached The Snares.

Population: Moderately common around the southeastern South Island and Foveaux Strait. The total population is 1600–1800 pairs.

Conservation: Protected rare endemic. Stewart Island Shags are sometimes illegally shot by fishermen, and a few birds are caught accidentally in fishing nets. Numbers of birds at particular colonies fluctuate from year to year, making long-term population trends hard to assess.

Breeding: Nest in colonies on islands and on sea cliffs, sometimes only a few metres above high-water mark. The nest is usually a level platform about 0.5 m in diameter, made of twigs and seaweed and cemented with guano. The breeding season is long and variable, but laying is mostly in September–November. They lay 1–2–3 pale blue eggs (66 x 42 mm). There is no information on incubation or fledging periods.

Behaviour: Sometimes roost on headlands and islands in huge flocks of 1000+ birds, particularly in April–May. They are silent away from their colonies, and only the male calls at the nest.

Feeding: Diet in Otago is mainly bullies and seafloor-dwelling fish such as flounders and sole. Marine invertebrates such as crabs, shrimps, octopuses and polychaete worms are occasionally taken. Most food is taken in water less than 30 m deep, but they feed up to 15 km from land. Average dive times are 50–70 seconds, but the maximum recorded is close to 3 minutes. Rests between dives last 20–40 seconds.

Reading: Lalas, C. 1983. PhD thesis, Univ Otago. Sansom, M.L. 1956. *Notornis* 7: 16–20. Watt, J.P.C. 1975. *Notornis* 22: 265–272.

97. CHATHAM ISLAND SHAG *Leucocarbo onslowi* Plate 24

Size: 63 cm, 2.25 kg

Distribution: Breed only on Chatham Island (including Motuhinahina Island in Te Whanga Lagoon), Star Keys, and Rabbit Island off Pitt Island. They feed through coastal waters of the Chatham group and rarely in brackish water in Te Whanga Lagoon.

Population: Moderately common (842 pairs at 10 colonies in 1997, but only 271 pairs at 13 colonies in 2003). The largest colony is on the Star Keys.

Conservation: Protected rare endemic. Some are illegally shot by fishermen, and several accessible mainland colonies (e.g. Cape Fournier) have been abandoned because of human disturbance and associated gull predation. Colonies are sometimes disturbed by fur seals.

Breeding: Nest in colonies on islands and exposed rocky headlands, usually well above high-water mark. The nest is a level platform about 0.5 m in diameter, made of twigs, iceplants and seaweed. Laying is mostly in August–December, but there is some variation both between and within colonies. They lay 1–2–3–4 pale blue eggs (61 x 44 mm). There is no information on incubation or fledging periods.

Behaviour: Sometimes roost in flocks of 100+ birds but generally feed alone.

Feeding: Diet is mainly small (<25 cm long) fish, especially flatfish, opalfish and bullies, and the occasional squid, cuttlefish and octopus. Most are taken from deep offshore waters, but birds occasionally feeding close inshore or in rockpools.

Reading: Fleming, C.A. 1939. *Emu* 38: 380–413. Imber, M.J. 1994. *Notornis* 41(S): 97–108. Lalas, C. 1983. PhD thesis, Univ Otago.

98. BOUNTY ISLAND SHAG *Leucocarbo ranfurlyi* Plate 24

Size: 71 cm, 2.5 kg
Distribution: Breed only on the Bounty Islands; commonly feed within the group, but also venture into the open ocean. One seen at The Snares (April–May 1997).
Population: 569 pairs in November 1978; the largest colony was on Lion Island (165 pairs); however, only 120 nests found in 1997/98.
Conservation: Protected rare endemic. The population may be declining rapidly.
Breeding: Nest mainly in colonies on narrow cliff-side ledges, but a few nests are on rocky ridges. The nest is a flattened bowl 35 cm in diameter, made of seaweed, feathers, stones and mud. Laying is in October–November. They lay 2–3 eggs (64 x 41 mm). There is no information on incubation or fledging periods.
Behaviour: Sometimes feed in flocks of up to 300 birds. They are generally silent, but the male only makes calls during displays.
Feeding: Diet includes small fish and squid, snails, isopods and sea urchins.

Reading: Robertson, C.J.R. & van Tets, G.F. 1982. *Notornis* 29: 311–336.

99. AUCKLAND ISLAND SHAG *Leucocarbo colensoi* Plate 24

Size: 63 cm, 2 kg
Distribution: Breed only on the Auckland Islands and have not been recorded elsewhere. Commonly seen around the sheltered harbours and inlets of the southern and eastern side of the islands.
Population: Probably c. 1000 pairs, including c. 500 on Enderby Island, and c. 300 on Ewing Island.
Conservation: Protected rare endemic. The population is limited to one island group, but no known threat exists.
Breeding: Nest in colonies on cliff-side ledges, usually under an overhang or under trees to afford protection from skuas. The nest is a flattened bowl made of twigs, tussock, seaweed, peat and guano. Laying is in November–February. They lay 3 pale blue eggs (62 x 39 mm) at intervals of 2–4 days. The incubation period is about 28 days. The fledging period is not known.
Behaviour: Sometimes feed and roost in flocks. During courtship displays, the male utters barks and ticking sounds, and females give a soft purr.
Feeding: No detailed studies, but their diet includes small fish and marine invertebrates.

100. CAMPBELL ISLAND SHAG *Leucocarbo campbelli* Plate 24

Size: 63 cm, 2 kg
Distribution: Breed only on the Campbell Islands and have not been recorded elsewhere. Commonly seen around the sheltered harbours and inlets of the east coast, especially in winter.
Population: In 1975, c. 2000 nests and an estimated population of 8000 birds.
Conservation: Protected rare endemic. The population is limited to one island group, but no known threat exists.
Breeding: Nest in inaccessible colonies of up to 150 nests on cliff-side ledges, islets and in caves. The nest is a flattened bowl, made of twigs and tussock. Laying is in November–February. They lay 2 pale blue eggs (64 x 39 mm). There is no information on incubation or fledging periods. A banded bird lived at least 13 years.
Behaviour: In winter 1960, a flock of 2000 birds was recorded in Perseverence Harbour, but usually they hunt in co-ordinated packs of 30–100 birds. These flocks spread out as they start to feed but maintain synchronous diving, so that all birds are submerged at once. During courtship, males utter barks and females apparently remain silent.
Feeding: No detailed studies, but their diet includes small shoaling fish and marine invertebrates.

Reading: Bailey, A.M. & Sorensen, J.H. 1962. *Subantarctic Campbell Island.* Denver: Denver Mus Nat Hist.

101. SPOTTED SHAG *Stictocarbo punctatus* Plate 24

Other names: Parekareka, Blue Shag (southern subspecies)
Size: 70 cm, 1200 g
Geographical variation: Two subspecies: the Spotted Shag *punctatus* breeds in the North Island and the northern and eastern South Island, and the Blue Shag *steadi* breeds around the southwestern South Island and Stewart Island.
Distribution: Breed only in New Zealand. In the North Island, Spotted Shags breed in the inner Hauraki Gulf, on the west coast of Auckland and the Waikato, on Kapiti Island and on Somes Island in Wellington Harbour. In the South Island, they nest in the Marlborough Sounds, down the Kaikoura coast to Banks Peninsula, and from North Otago to the Catlins. Blue Shags nest in a few scattered colonies in Westland (e.g. Perpendicular Point at Punakaiki, and the Open Bay Islands) and on islands in Foveaux Strait and around Stewart Island. There is much local movement between feeding and nesting areas.

Spotted Shags favour the marine environment off rocky shores and rarely venture into enclosed estuaries, freshwater habitats or sandy sea coasts. After breeding, most form large winter flocks and often fly in long lines between their feeding and roosting sites. Most birds remain within 200 km of their breeding grounds, but some long-distance movement occurs, such as the annual appearance of a mixed-age flock of 20–50 birds in Hawke's Bay over 300 km from the nearest known breeding site. Odd birds (especially juveniles) can appear almost anywhere, including several records from Lake Taupo, and a juvenile banded on Somes Island in July was caught five months later on the Coromandel Peninsula, 500 km away.
Population: Widespread and locally common (10,000–50,000 pairs), Spotted Shags are probably increasing, with marked increases recorded on Banks Peninsula and in Wellington Harbour in the past 30 years.
Conservation: Protected endemic. Spotted Shags are sometimes illegally shot by fishermen, and some birds are caught accidentally in fishing nets. Shags are now known to have a minimal impact on fish stocks, and few are now shot. Spotted Shags often breed at sites where nests are difficult to count and often change sites, and so population trends are hard to assess.
Breeding: Nest in colonies of 10–700 pairs, normally apart from other shags. The colonies are usually on coastal cliff ledges or rocky islets. The nest is a platform about 0.6 m in diameter, made of seaweed, grass and iceplants. The breeding season is variable from year to year and in different parts of the country; in the Hauraki Gulf, peaks of laying are in March, August and December; on Somes Island, the two peaks are in June and November; but at Banks Peninsula and Otago Harbour, the only peak is in September–November. Laying of Blue Shags at Punakaiki is quite variable, March–April in some years but August–October in others.

They lay 1–**3**–4 pale blue eggs (58 x 36 mm, 42 g) at 2-day intervals. The incubation period is 28–**31**–35 days. Chicks are guarded continuously until c. 30 days old and are fed about four times a day by both parents. Chicks leave the nest and fledge at 57–**62**–71 days old. The oldest Spotted Shag recorded was over 10 years old.
Behaviour: Form large flocks of up to 2000 birds when feeding, or roosting on headlands or sandspits out of the breeding season. They are silent away from their colonies. Displaying males are noisy, but females remain silent.
Feeding: Diet is mainly small fish less than 15 cm long, and marine invertebrates. The main fish taken are ahuru, red cod, gudgeon, bullies and sprats; arrow squid are also taken frequently. Spotted Shags mainly feed in deep water up to 15 km from the shore, but they sometimes feed in harbours. Their average dive time is c. 30 seconds, with a rest of 10–15 seconds between dives. The longest dive recorded lasted 70 seconds.

Reading: Doherty, J.L. & Bräger, S. 1997. *Notornis* 44: 49–54. Fenwick, G.D. & Browne, W.M.M. 1975. *J Roy Soc NZ* 5: 31–45. Lalas, C. 1983. PhD thesis, Univ Otago. Kinsky, F.C. 1970. *Notornis* 17: 102–104. Stonehouse, B. 1967. *Ibis* 109: 600–605. Turbott, E.G. 1956. *Rec Auck Inst Mus* 4: 343–363.

102. PITT ISLAND SHAG *Stictocarbo featherstoni*   Plate 24

Size: 63 cm, 1200 g

Distribution: Breed on Chatham and Pitt Islands and most of the smaller islands in the group. Not recorded elsewhere.

Population: Widespread and moderately common (729 breeding pairs in 1997, but only 547 pairs in 2003).

Conservation: Protected endemic. Pitt Island Shags are sometimes illegally shot by fishermen. As colonies are small and widely scattered, and vary in numbers from year to year, population trends are hard to assess.

Breeding: Nest in small colonies of 5–20 pairs, normally apart from Chatham Island Shags. The colonies are usually on coastal cliff ledges or rocky islets. The nest is a platform c. 30 cm in diameter, made of seaweed, grass and iceplants. The breeding season is extended. The peak of laying is in August–September, but laying continues as late as December. They lay 1–**3**–4 pale blue eggs (58 x 35 mm) probably at 2-day intervals. Incubation and fledging periods are unknown.

Behaviour: Breed in much smaller colonies than Chatham Island Shags or the closely related Spotted Shag. They usually feed alone. Silent away from their colonies; displaying males are noisy, but females remain silent.

Feeding: Diet is mainly small fish, especially bullies, and marine invertebrates such as snails and polychaete worms. They mostly feed in coastal waters up to 20 m deep, but occasionally feed in the brackish water of Te Whanga Lagoon. Their average dive time is c. 30 seconds, with a 15-second rest between dives. The longest dive recorded lasted 68 seconds.

Reading: Fleming, C.A. 1939. *Emu* 38: 380–413. Imber, M.J. 1994. *Notornis* 41(S): 97–108. Lalas, C. 1983. PhD thesis, Univ Otago.

DARTERS   Anhingidae

2 species; 1 vagrant reaches New Zealand.

Between them, the two species of darter have a near worldwide distribution (not Europe or high latitudes) in freshwater habitats. These large birds resemble shags but are slimmer and have a long, thin, unhooked bill and a very long snaky neck. They have long stiff tails and long rounded wings, which are held out to dry when the birds perch after swimming.

103. DARTER *Anhinga melanogaster*   Plate 23

Size: 90 cm, 1750 g

Geographical variation: Three subspecies: *melanogaster* in Asia from India to Indonesia and the Philippines; *rufa* in Africa, Madagascar and the Middle East; and *novaehollandiae* in Australia and New Guinea.

Distribution: Breed widely, from Africa through Asia to Australia. In Australia, most breeding colonies are in the Murray–Darling Basin and along the eastern seaboard, but after breeding they disperse widely. The only confirmed New Zealand records are a fresh skin of an adult female found nailed to the wall of a shed near Hokitika (January 1874), Kaitaia (December 1992) and Wellington Harbour (December 2003). There have been several unconfirmed sightings of Darters in Northland in the 1990s. Given their dispersive nature in Australia, and their use of columns of rising hot air to glide and soar from one place to another, they are expected to reach New Zealand again.

Feeding: Feed in lakes, ponds and slow-moving streams by sinking slowly underwater and then swimming with webbed feet to dart their neck out and stab fish on their needle-like bill. On surfacing, the bird tosses the fish into the air and catches it head first. Sometimes they eat insects caught above the water. Dives last c. 30 seconds, with only a 5-second pause between dives.

Reading: van Tets, G.F. & Scarlett, R.J. 1972. *Notornis* 19: 85–86.

FRIGATEBIRDS   Fregatidae

5 species, of which 2 reach New Zealand.

Sailors called frigatebirds 'man-o'-war birds' because of their piratical habits. They inhabit tropical seas, often hundreds of kilometres from land, soaring high on thermals. They feed entirely on the wing, taking flying fish and squid by surface dipping and, to a lesser extent, pursuing other seabirds, particularly boobies, and forcing them to disgorge their food. Most breed on remote islands, nesting in colonies in trees or on bushes, or, if necessary, on the ground. The nest is made of loosely woven sticks. They lay a single white egg.

104. GREATER FRIGATEBIRD   *Fregata minor*   Plate 21

Other name: Great Frigatebird
Size: 95 cm; 1500 g
Distribution: Breed on islands in the Indian and Pacific Oceans, and a few nest in the southwestern Atlantic Ocean. The nearest breeding places to New Zealand are New Caledonia, Fiji and probably Tonga. At least 12 New Zealand records since 1861, between the Kermadec Islands and Westport, mostly on the east coast of the North Island or inland at lakes.

Reading: Jenkins, J.A.F. 1980. *Notornis* 27: 205–234.

105. LESSER FRIGATEBIRD   *Fregata ariel*   Plate 21

Other name: Least Frigatebird
Size: 76 cm, 1000 g
Geographical variation: Three subspecies: *ariel*, of the central Indian Ocean, Australia and the southwestern Pacific, is the form recorded from New Zealand waters.
Distribution: Breed on islands of the tropical Indian, Pacific and southwestern Atlantic Oceans. They are more often recorded in New Zealand than Greater Frigatebirds because the nearest breeding sites are on islands off Queensland, New Caledonia, Fiji, Tonga and Samoa. About 12 specimens have been collected beach-wrecked in New Zealand since 1907, mostly in the north, but including Cook Strait and the Chatham Islands; also about 12 sightings, mostly at the Kermadecs and in Northland, but as far south as Otago and at Chatham Island. Lesser Frigatebirds probably get swept south by tropical storms, as happened in 1971 when several were seen off the Northland coast.

HERONS, EGRETS and BITTERNS   Ardeidae

About 65 species; 10 in the New Zealand region, including 5 breeding species. An endemic species, the New Zealand Little Bittern *Ixobrychus novaezelandiae*, became extinct in the late 1800s.

This family occurs worldwide, mainly in the tropics. Their broad-winged flight is ponderous but strong, though the smaller species are faster. Apart from the bitterns and night herons, they are active by day. They have a slender body and long neck and legs; night herons have a stouter body and a shorter neck. All have a straight, dagger-like bill and a short tail. The bill, on a long, often kinked neck, is ideal for seizing or skewering fish.

Patches of powder down are on the breast and rump in bitterns, and the thighs also in egrets. The middle of the three forward-pointing toes has serrations along the side like the teeth of a comb and is thought to remove fish-slime and mud during grooming and preening. All species give a low-pitched croak when alarmed but feed silently.

Egrets and herons are very similar: for example, all have bare facial skin, often distinctively coloured. Egrets are white; herons are usually grey: the distinction is useful but not absolute. Egrets are gregarious and breed in colonies, often mixed with other egrets and with ibises; true herons are solitary. Both typically have plumes when breeding. Their nests are untidy platforms of sticks and twigs. Incubation starts with the first or second egg, and so chicks are of different ages and sizes. Adults feed the young with regurgitated food, not offering whole food. The young start breeding at one or two years old, sometimes still in immature plumage.

Herons, egrets and bitterns feed mainly on fish; also frogs and insects. Larger species may take small mammals and birds as chance offers.

Reading: Hancock, J. & Elliott, H. 1978. *The Herons of the World*. London: London Editions. Hancock, J. & Kushlan, J. 1984. *The Herons Handbook*. London: Croom Helm.

106.   WHITE-FACED HERON   *Ardea novaehollandiae*   Plate 26

Other names: Blue Heron, Blue Crane
Size: 67 cm, 550 g
Geographical variation: Two subspecies: *nana* in New Caledonia and the Loyalty Islands, and *novaehollandiae* throughout the rest of Australasia.
Distribution: Breed in southern Indonesia, New Guinea, Australia, Lord Howe and Norfolk Islands and New Zealand. Occasionally reported in New Zealand from 1865 to the 1930s, they became established and are now the most common heron, having benefited from the widespread conversion of forest to farmland. They are open-country generalists, being found in swamp margins, lake shores, farm dams and creeks, riverbeds, town parks; also mudflats, estuaries, rocky shores, and sandy beaches inside harbours and estuaries.

Breeding was initially confirmed in 1941 at Shag River, Otago, but they became widespread on the New Zealand mainland in the 1940s and increased explosively in the late 1950s and early 1960s. They colonised the Chatham Islands by the early 1970s, and vagrants have been recorded from the Kermadecs, The Snares, Auckland and Campbell Islands.

Population: Widespread and common, especially in lowland districts with rough pasture and nearby lakes and estuaries.
Conservation: Protected self-introduced native. White-faced Herons spread and increased rapidly between the 1940s and 1970s, but numbers have probably since declined.
Breeding: Breed solitarily or in loose groups, usually high up in belts of macrocarpas, pines or eucalypts, not necessarily near water. The nest is an untidy bundle of sticks and twigs, not easy to see, in a fork or well out on a branch. At the Chathams especially, they nest on cliff ledges and under rocks just above

high-water mark, in sites usually used by Reef Herons. Laying starts in June in the north, later further south, with the peak about October.

They lay 3–**4**–5 pale blue-green eggs (45 x 33 mm), which both sexes incubate for c. 26 days. Usually only 2 young are raised, fed by both adults. Unlike other herons, the young stay at or near the nest until they are able to fly.

Behaviour: Mainly solitary, but they form loose flocks in winter on damp and flooded pasture, often with Cattle Egrets and Black-backed Gulls. When not breeding, they may roost together. They are often seen perched on a fencepost or the lip of a trough. In flight, a harsh 'graaw' is quite common.

Feeding: Diet is fish, frogs and tadpoles, aquatic and pasture insects, spiders, earthworms and mice. They stalk through the shallows of wetlands, darting a dagger-like bill forwards by straightening out their long neck or pausing to rake one foot rapidly back and forth.

Reading: Hemmings, A.D. & Chappell, R.G. 1988. *Notornis* 35: 245–247. Lo, P.L. 1984. *Notornis* 31: 95. Lo, P.L. 1991. *Notornis* 38: 63–71. Lo, P.L. & Fordham, R.A. *Notornis* 33: 233–245. Lowe, K.W. 1983. *Corella* 7: 101–108. Moore, P.J. 1984. *Notornis* 285–299.

107. WHITE-NECKED HERON *Ardea pacifica* Plate 27

Other name: Pacific Heron
Size: 90 cm, 900 g
Distribution: Breed only in mainland Australia. Six records in New Zealand: Methven (April–July 1952); Houhora (October 1981), Waipu (January 1984), Hokitika (June–July

2002), Oamaru (January–March 2003) and Toko, Taranaki (June 2003).

Behaviour: Favour margins of freshwater swamps and dams and damp pasture inland. Similar to White-faced Herons in feeding and flight behaviour.

108. WHITE HERON *Egretta alba* Plate 25

Other names: Kotuku, Great Egret, Great White Heron
Size: 92 cm, of which length of body is under half; 900 g
Geographical variation: Of the four or more subspecies, the range of the largest, *modesta*, is India, China and Japan to Australia and New Zealand.
Distribution: Breed worldwide in tropical and temperate regions. In New Zealand, they breed only near Okarito, Westland. After breeding, they disperse widely, especially northwards; therefore they can appear at any shallow freshwater lake, swamp, damp pasture, estuary or mangrove creek at some time. Some have reached the Chatham, Auckland and Campbell Islands as strays blown off course during this dispersal. From time to time, their winter number is augmented by irruptions from Australia, such as a small one in 1952 and a large irruption in winter 1957, when 200+ birds were

recorded, mainly in Northland, Waikato, Bay of Plenty, Canterbury and Otago.

Population: 150–200 birds, half of which are non-breeders.

Conservation: Protected rare native. The White Heron colony at Okarito is in a reserve, and public access is controlled to minimise disturbance to breeding birds but allow viewing from observation hides.

Breeding: The Okarito colony has been known since pre-European times. It is in a kahikatea swamp through which the sluggish Waitangiroto River crawls. Some of the nests are in the crowns of tree ferns; others are in kowhai or kamahi. Royal Spoonbills prefer the adjacent taller kahikatea. Both sexes share nest-building. Laying is in September–October. They lay 3–**4**–5 pale bluish-green eggs (52 x 36 mm). Both sexes incubate for c. 25 days and care for the young. The fledging period is c. 42 days, and the young leave the colony at c. 64 days old. The oldest banded

White Heron was a bird in the United States that lived over 22 years.

Behaviour: White Herons make a harsh grating call in flight; otherwise silent, except at the breeding colony.

Feeding: Diet is mainly small fish and eels, frogs, shrimps and aquatic insects, which they swallow whole, and occasionally small mammals such as mice and small birds such as Silvereyes. They feed by quietly walking or standing motionless, lunging with their dagger-like bill and a kinked neck at prey whenever it comes within range.

Reading: Andrew, I.G. 1963. *Notornis* 10: 311–315.

109. LITTLE EGRET *Egretta garzetta* Plate 25

Size: 60 cm, 300 g

Geographical variation: Two subspecies: *garzetta* breeding in Africa and Eurasia, and *nigripes* breeding in Australasia.

Distribution: Breed from Africa and southern Europe, east to India, Southeast Asia, China, Japan, Indonesia and Australia, including Tasmania. They are scarce annual migrants to New Zealand from Australia, usually arriving in autumn and departing in early spring. They sometimes oversummer. Little Egrets have been recorded at many localities, mainly coastal, throughout the North and South Islands. Most are in singles, but occasionally groups of up to five are recorded. Two vagrants reached Raoul Island, Kermadecs (1974).

Behaviour: Little Egrets are quite unlike White Herons or Intermediate Egrets in their feeding methods; they are very active, chasing after fish and other animal food with a high-stepping gait, wings upraised. They prefer estuaries and other tidal wetlands to freshwater habitats.

110. INTERMEDIATE EGRET *Egretta intermedia* Plate 25

Other name: Plumed Egret

Size: 64 cm, 400 g

Geographical variation: Three subspecies: *brachyrhyncha* of Africa, *intermedia* of southern Asia, Japan and the Philippines, and *plumifera* of Australia and southern New Guinea.

Distribution: Africa, south of the Sahara, southern and eastern Asia and Australasia. In Australia, they breed only on the mainland, in the north and east from Broome to Victoria, and mostly in the Murray–Darling Basin. Ten New Zealand records: Manawatu Estuary (early 1970s), lower Waikato, near Lakes Whangape and Ohinewai (1979, 1981, 1985, 1993), Kaikohe (1986), Avon–Heathcote Estuary (1986), Lake Ellesmere (3 in 1998), Motueka (2004) and Lawrence (2004).

Behaviour: Similar to White Herons in their feeding methods but prefer freshwater habitats, seldom visiting estuaries or other saline coastal places. They sometimes feed in pasture, often in the presence of Cattle Egrets.

111. REEF HERON *Egretta sacra* Plates 25 and 26

Other names: Matuku moana, Eastern Reef Egret

Size: 66 cm, 400 g

Geographical variation: Two subspecies, *albolineata* of New Caledonia and the Loyalty Islands, and *sacra* elsewhere. Reef Herons are usually dimorphic, with a dark phase (the only one seen breeding in New Zealand) and a white phase (common in the Pacific islands but recorded only once in New Zealand). Occasionally there is also a third, mottled phase, which is intermediate.

Distribution: Eastern Asia, from Bangladesh to southern Korea and Japan, to Australia and New Zealand, and eastward through the tropical Pacific to the Marquesas, Tuamotu and Austral Islands. Reef Herons are widespread in the North, South and Stewart Islands and adjacent small islands, mainly along rocky shores or in mangrove-filled estuaries and tidal streams, not on long, sandy beaches. They are seldom inland, although occasionally seen at Lake Taupo. Scarce on Stewart Island and a rare vagrant to the Kermadec, Chatham and Auckland Islands. The white phase has been seen in New Zealand once: Avon–Heathcote Estuary (June 1987).

Population: Moderate numbers on the coasts of Northland, Coromandel Peninsula and the Marlborough Sounds.

Conservation: Protected native. In New Zealand, Reef Herons are less widespread than they used to be, probably not because of competition with White-faced Herons but largely owing to increased human disturbance on the coast.

Breeding: Solitary nesters in caves, in crevices between or behind rocks, on rock shelves under an overhang, in cliff-side vegetation under clumps of flax or *Astelia*, or among the roots of pohutukawa. Nests are the usual platform of sticks and twigs, made up of seaweed or such trees and shrubs as are washed up by the tide. Laying is mainly in September–December, with a peak in October. They lay 2–**3**–4 pale blue-green eggs (46 x 35 mm), and both sexes incubate for 25–28 days. The young fledge at 5–6 weeks old. The oldest Reef Heron in Australia lived at least 14 years.

Behaviour: Usually solitary but roost in small flocks, especially in Northland mangroves at high tide. Their daily movements are influenced by the tides; they feed mainly on falling and low tides.

Feeding: Diet is mainly small fish, including eels and flounder; also crabs and molluscs. They feed largely by crouching, body and head horizontal, neck retracted, jabbing at prey, sometimes flicking their wings. Sometimes they stalk with the body above the horizontal, the neck curved but not retracted, and the head above the level of the body.

Reading: Edgar, A.T. 1978. *Notornis* 25: 25–58.

112. CATTLE EGRET *Bubulcus ibis* Plate 25

Size: 50 cm; males 390 g, females 340 g

Geographical variation: Two subspecies: *ibis* of Africa spread in the twentieth century to South and then North America. The larger *coromandus* of southern and eastern Asia, including Japan and southern Korea and China, spread south to Indonesia, Australia and New Zealand.

Distribution: Breed widely in the Americas, Africa, Asia and Australasia. In Australia, they are common and widespread but breed especially in Queensland and New South Wales. First records in New Zealand were in 1963, possibly 1956, and from then they have been recorded annually as steadily increasing winter visitors until they reached a peak in 1986 of well over 3000 birds. They arrive mainly in April–May, making a landfall somewhere on western coasts, stay for a while to feed, and then move to a few favoured farms or open habitats in the North, South, Stewart and Chatham Islands. Vagrants have been recorded from the Kermadecs, The Snares, Auckland and Campbell Islands. Most return to Australia in October–November, but some, mostly juveniles, remain throughout the summer. They have not bred in New Zealand.

The largest wintering flocks are at Rangiriri (Waikato), and Whirokino (Manawatu). Main wintering sites in the North Island are Unahi (Far North), Ruawai (Northland), Parakai (Auckland), Aka Aka and Piako (South Auckland), Rangiriri and Lake Ngaroto (Waikato), Awaiti (Bay of Plenty), Lake Hatuma (Hawke's Bay), Featherston (Wairarapa), Whirokino and Lake Horowhenua (Manawatu). In the South Island: Takaka (Nelson), Grovetown (Marlborough), Karamea, Westport and Kokatahi (West Coast), Ellesmere (Canterbury), West Taieri and Stirling (Otago), and Wyndham and Thornbury (Southland).

Population: National counts in late August rose from 293 in 1977 to a peak in 1986 of 3000+, fell to 2000+ in 1987, and to 1000+ in

1988. By the mid-1990s, numbers had dropped to fewer than 1000 birds each year.

Behaviour: Cattle Egrets are gregarious. In Australia, they nest colonially in trees in or beside swamps and lakes or on islands in settled or industrial areas, often with other egret species and with ibises. In New Zealand, they feed in small parties or in flocks of up to several hundred birds, and they roost in tall trees, mostly macrocarpa, or on or near the ground in swamp or lakeside vegetation. They are shy and wary, and seldom allow close approach.

Feeding: In New Zealand, they associate with cattle and with other domestic stock, especially sheep. They walk slowly forward, neck outstretched, peering at the ground, with backward and forward movement of the head. Mostly they search independently, but sometimes they seem co-ordinated: those at the back of a flock fly to the front and the flock rolls forward along a drain or across a paddock. Their diet is mainly earthworms, grass grubs, larvae of moths and flies, and in the north, crickets. Young birds that oversummer also feed on flies, grasshoppers and a few mice. They may sway their necks from side to side before lunging at flies on grass. Occasionally they perch on resting cattle or sheep, but do not seem to use them as vantage points to scan for prey or to feed on ticks and other parasites of large animals, as they do in tropical countries.

Reading: Bridgman, H.A. & Maddock, M. 1994. *Notornis* 41: 189–204. Jackson, W.R. & Olsen, M. 1988. *Notornis* 35: 83–85. Heather, B.D. 1991. *Notornis* 38: 165–169. Maddock, M. 1993. *Corella* 17: 93–99. McKilligan, N.G. 1985. *Ibis* 127: 530–536.

113. NANKEEN NIGHT HERON *Nycticorax caledonicus* Plate 27

Other name: Rufous Night Heron
Size: 57 cm, 800 g
Geographical variation: Five extant subspecies: *hilli* of eastern Indonesia, New Guinea and Australia is presumably the form recorded in New Zealand.

Distribution: Breed in the Philippines, Micronesia, Indonesia, New Guinea, Bismarck Archipelago, Solomon Islands, New Caledonia, Australia, and recently in New

Zealand. In Australia, they are a vagrant to Tasmania but common in the north, east and southwest, and are especially common along the coastal rivers of southeastern Australia and the inland rivers of the Murray-Darling Basin.

Unsuccessfully liberated in New Zealand in 1852 (a bird shot near Wellington in 1856 may have been one of these). They may have bred near Blenheim, where an adult and two immatures were seen in 1958 and an adult was again seen in 1959. Birds breeding at Wellington Zoo were released in 1982, all with leg bands; after a year most had dispersed, and three of these birds were reported later: Pakawau (1983), Lower Hutt (1984), and Warkworth, Northland (1984).

Nankeen Night Herons were occasional vagrants from Australia, with records of unbanded birds from Wellington (1972), southern Wairarapa (1977), Owaka, Otago (1980), near Whangamomona, inland Taranaki (1983), and upper Taieri River, Otago (1988), but, have bred on the Whanganui River between Pipiriki and Jerusalem since at least 1995. In 1994, nine birds (six immatures and three adults) were seen in willows along this stretch of river.

Population: Less than 50 birds in 2005.

Conservation: Protected apparently self-introduced native.

Breeding: In Australia, Nankeen Night Herons breed in the dense cover of trees, e.g. mangroves and eucalypts, often high above water level in saline or fresh wetlands, both adults building the usual platform of sticks. They lay 2–**3**–5 pale green to blue eggs (52 x 37 mm), which both sexes incubate for 21–22 days. Hatching is not synchronous. The young leave the nest 6–7 weeks after hatching. The oldest banded bird of the North American subspecies lived over 21 years.

Behaviour: Gregarious all year but feed solitarily. In Australia, they roost by day in groups in leafy trees, e.g. willow, often low to the ground and within convenient flying distance of water.

Feeding: In Australia, diet is mostly fish; also frogs, freshwater crayfish and insects, taken as opportunity arises. They usually stand and wait, upright or crouched, or walk slowly, in the manner of most herons. They feed mainly at night or in the evening but may feed by day, especially when breeding. They fly out from their roost at dusk with slow, heavy wingbeats to their feeding sites.

Reading: Marsh, N. 1995. *Notornis* 42: 282–283. Marsh, N. & Lovei, G.L. 1997. *Notornis* 44: 152–155.

114. AUSTRALASIAN BITTERN *Botaurus poiciloptilus* Plate 26

Other name: Matuku
Size: 71 cm; males 1400 g, females 1000 g
Distribution: Breed in southern Australia (including Tasmania), New Zealand, New Caledonia and the Loyalty Islands. In New Zealand, they are widely distributed in the North, South and Stewart Islands, but are found mostly in Northland, Waikato, Bay of Plenty, Manawatu, southern Wairarapa and on the West Coast. Resident on Great Barrier and possibly Mayor Islands. They are in tall, dense beds of raupo and reeds in freshwater wetlands, wet habitats with a mixture of water purslane and willow weed, and damp pasture infested with large clumps of rush or introduced tall fescue.
Population: Estimate in 1980: 580–725 birds.
Conservation: Protected rare native. Bitterns

have declined through drainage and 'reclamation' of wetlands, and cattle grazing in swamps which damages breeding cover. They are possibly more common than estimated because they are cryptic and can live in small swamps not included in national estimates.
Breeding: Nest in dense stands of raupo and reeds surrounding lakes and in swamps. Nests are built by the female, who breaks down all reeds within reach until a platform is made 250–300 mm above water level. Laying is in September–November. The female alone incubates the clutch of 3–**4**–5 olive-brown eggs (51 x 37 mm) for c. 25 days, and then feeds the young. The chicks fledge at c. 7 weeks old.
Behaviour: Usually solitary and stealthy. If

disturbed, they may stand tall, neck fully stretched up, head and bill pointing skywards, or drop slowly down into the vegetation by retracting their head and crouching down, their plumage looking very reed-like. This cryptic 'freeze' posture is a surveillance posture; their eyes can look all around from this pose. On windy days they may also sway to match the movement of the vegetation.

When startled and put to flight, Australasian Bitterns may make their version of the usual heron croak. Calling from within the reedbeds, males advertise their territories by booming – making sounds rather like a muffled foghorn or that produced by blowing across an open bottle.

Feeding: Diet is fish (especially eels), frogs, freshwater crayfish and aquatic insects, caught mostly on or near edges of ponds or waterways. They feed alone, sometimes from traditional feeding platforms made by flattening clumps of reeds. Holding their head and neck parallel to the surface, they sway the head from side to side or keep still for up to 10 minutes; they then lunge and swallow the prey whole or, if too big, by shaking and battering it first. They feed mostly at night, and so are seen mainly at dawn and dusk.

Reading: Whiteside, A.J. 1989. *Notornis* 36: 89–95.

115. LITTLE BITTERN   *Ixobrychus minutus*   Plate 26

Size: 30 cm, 85 g
Geographical variation: Of the four subspecies, *dubius* of Australia and southern New Guinea is the form recorded from New Zealand. The little-known New Zealand Little Bittern *Ixobrychus novaezelandiae*, which is presumed extinct, was much larger (53 cm).
Distribution: Breed widely in Europe, Africa, Asia, southern New Guinea and Australia. One New Zealand record: a juvenile that walked past a Westport supermarket in February 1987 and was caught, examined and released.

Behaviour: Usually more secretive than the much larger Australasian Bittern, and males do not boom, advertising instead with a hoarse, monotonous croaking. In Australia, they skulk in thick reedbeds, flooded shrubland and other dense vegetation in swamps, marshes, the edges of freshwater wetlands.

Reading: O'Donnell, C.F.J. & Dilks, P. 1988. *Notornis* 35: 153–157.

IBISES and SPOONBILLS   Threskiornithidae

30 species; 1 breeds in New Zealand and 3 are vagrants from Australia.

The bills of this group are highly distinctive: long and down-curved in ibises, long and spatulate in spoonbills. All are gregarious; breeding, roosting, and feeding in flocks. They feed mostly in shallow freshwater lakes, brackish coastal lagoons and estuaries, but the ibises that visit New Zealand feed also in dry habitats in Australia , e.g. pasture and public parks. The mid-toe is specialised as a comb-claw in ibises; not in spoonbills. Most develop ornamental plumes when breeding. They disperse widely after breeding and are silent away from the breeding colonies.

116. GLOSSY IBIS   *Plegadis falcinellus*   Plate 28

Size: 60 cm, 500 g
Distribution: Breed widely in eastern North America, Europe, parts of Africa, central Asia, India, Malaysia, Indonesia, New Guinea and Australia. They are frequent vagrants to New Zealand, sometimes irrupting in small flocks,

as in 1953, 1968, 1975 and 1988. One record from Chatham Island (December 1984). In New Zealand, they frequent damp pasture and rough pasture and rushes on the muddy margins of freshwater lakes.

Behaviour: Gregarious all year. They are easily overlooked, resembling the hunched posture of a feeding Pukeko, and in flight they can be confused with a shag. They are usually extremely wary.

Feeding: Peck and probe rapidly for food in soft ground, taking food in the tip of the curved bill. In Australia, they take all sorts of aquatic invertebrates and pasture insects. In New Zealand, they have been known to take fish, small eels, frogs and tadpoles from swamps and insects and earthworms from pasture.

Reading: Lowe, K.W. 1983. *Emu* 83: 31–34.
Sansom, O. *et al*. 1954. *Notornis* 6: 18–19.

117.   AUSTRALIAN WHITE IBIS   *Threskiornis molucca*   Plate 28

Size: 70 cm, 2 kg
Geographical variation: Of the three sub-species, *strictipennis* of Australia, southern New Guinea and part of the Solomon Islands reaches New Zealand.
Distribution: Breed in Australasia from the Moluccas to New Guinea, Solomon Islands and Australia. They were first recorded near Nelson, in 1925. There were minor irruptions in 1957 and 1975–76. Ten or more juveniles arrived in 1957 at scattered localities from Northland to Southland, and were seen at various places during the following five years. A similar influx in 1975–76 was at first in Northland and the Bay of Plenty, but later elsewhere in the North Island. Most remained through 1976 but had gone by 1980. The only record since has been of one bird near Westport (January 1986).

Behaviour: Very like the Glossy Ibis in habitat and habits.

118.   ROYAL SPOONBILL   *Platalea regia*   Plate 28

Other name: Kotuku-ngutupapa
Size: 77 cm, 1700 g
Distribution: Breed in northern, eastern and southeastern Australia and New Zealand. A vagrant to Indonesia, New Guinea and some Pacific islands.

After a century of vagrant records, Royal Spoonbills have successfully colonised New Zealand. They were first reported at Castlepoint in 1861 but did not start breeding until 1949, next to the White Heron colony near Okarito. They now breed also at the Vernon Lagoons, Marlborough (since 1978); on Maukiekie Island, North Otago (since 1984); on Green Island, near Dunedin (since 1988); on Omaui Island, at the entrance to Invercargill Estuary (since 1993); in Parengarenga Harbour (since 1993); on Kapiti Island (since 1994) and Pig Island, Riverton (since 1998).

They disperse in autumn, mainly to traditional wintering sites at Parengarenga, Rangaunu and Whangarei Harbours (North-land), Mangere oxidation ponds (Auckland), Kaituna Cut/Maketu (Bay of Plenty), Ahuriri Estuary (Hawke's Bay), Foxton Estuary (Manawatu), Farewell Spit, Motueka and Waimea Estuaries (Nelson), Avon–Heathcote Estuary and Lake Ellesmere (Canterbury). Individually colour-banded birds move widely; juveniles from the Vernon Lagoon colony have been reported from Parengarenga Harbour to Invercargill Estuary.

Population: From a total of 52 birds in August 1977, Royal Spoonbills have increased rapidly, perhaps at first supplemented by Australian birds but mainly through successful breeding at several new colonies. Winter censuses gave national totals of 242 birds in 1991, 377 in 1992, 502 in 1993, 560 in 1994, 610 in 1995, 659 in 1996 and 956 in 2000.

Breeding: At Okarito, they nest in tall kahikatea, whereas the more recently established colonies are on the ground near Black-backed Gull colonies or on top of low-growing taupata and boxthorn scrub near shag colonies. Laying is in September–December. They lay 2–3–4 dull white eggs with brown blotches (66 x 43 mm). Both sexes incubate for 20–25 days. The age that chicks first leave the nest and fledging period are not known. **Behaviour:** Gregarious; feeding, roosting and flying in small flocks. They fly in lines or chevrons but spread out to feed. Silent away from their breeding colony.

Feeding: Diet is mainly small invertebrates, fish and frogs, taken at night as much as by day, because they rely on touch rather than sight to detect food. They feed mostly in tidal mudflats or around the margins of shallow lakes, by walking along and sweeping their bill, slightly open, in smooth, sideways arcs, by which the water movement pulls small prey from the bottom or from the water column.

Reading: Lowe, K.W. 1982. *Emu* 82: 163–168. Stidolph, R.H.D. 1948. *Notornis* 2: 195–196.

119. YELLOW-BILLED SPOONBILL *Platalea flavipes* Plate 28

Size: 88 cm, 1900 g
Distribution: Breed only in Australia. Two New Zealand records: Rangaunu Harbour and Kaitaia area (1976–78) and Te Whiti, Wairarapa (December 1981).

Behaviour: In Australia, they prefer feeding in shallow dams and pools of fresh or brackish waters rather than tidal mudflats. They also feed on damp or flooded pasture.

Reading: Billing, A.E. 1977. *Notornis* 24: 192.

WATERFOWL   Anatidae

Swans, geese and ducks are found world-wide in freshwater and marine habitats. There are about 160 species, of which 14 (4 endemic, 4 native and 6 introduced) breed or have bred in the wild in the New Zealand region since 1920. A further endemic species (*Mergus australis*) became extinct in the early years of the 1900s, and another 6 species are vagrants to the region.

All species have webbed feet for swimming in freshwater rivers and lakes, or in coastal waters. Their bill is modified for filter-feeding; water and food is sucked in at the tip of the bill and expelled through fine comb-like lamellae at the sides, which catch minute seeds and invertebrates. Although most feed in this way, some species mainly graze on aquatic or terrestrial vegetation and pick seeds (e.g. peas or wheat) off the ground, and the mergansers have serrated bills for catching fish.

In New Zealand, most introduced and some native species of waterfowl are legally harvested during a strictly controlled shooting season. Each year, Fish and Game Councils determine the length and timing of the season and the allowable bag for each species, and monitor the licensing of hunters and annual hunting statistics. A voluntary organisation, Ducks Unlimited, works to create and protect wetland habitats suitable for waterfowl and is also involved in captive breeding programmes for some threatened and rare species.

Reading Frith, H.J. 1982. *Waterfowl in Australia*. Sydney: Angus & Robertson. Madge, S. & Burn, H. 1988. *Wildfowl: An Identification Guide to the Ducks, Geese and Swans of the World*. London: Christopher Helm. Johnsgard, P.A. 1978. *Ducks, Geese and Swans of the World*. Lincoln: Univ Nebraska Press. Williams, M. 1981. *The Duckshooter's Bag*. Wellington: Wetland Press.

120.   GRASS WHISTLING DUCK   *Dendrocygna eytoni*   Plate 30

Other name: Plumed Whistling Duck
Size: 50 cm, 800 g
Distribution: Breed in eastern and tropical Australia. They have recently expanded their breeding range south of 30°S into the Murray-Darling Basin. Partly nomadic, following rains and floods in wet years to colonise temporary wetlands and then returning to permanent water, mainly along the eastern seaboard. Vagrant to other parts of Australia, including Tasmania, and to New Guinea and New Zealand. Five records from New Zealand: Thames (May 1871), up to 14 (three shot) near Balclutha (June 1871), three at Ashburton (1894–96), a flock of 12 near Karamea (January 1975), and a flock of 9–11 in the lower Waikato River area (April–May 1982). Despite flocks of birds appearing in New Zealand, they are not known to have bred.

Feeding: In Australia, they feed mainly on land near lagoon edges, in paddocks and on open plains. Their diet is almost entirely vegetation, especially grasses, grass seed-heads, legumes, herbs and sedges.

Reading: Ellis. B.A. 1975. *Notornis* 22: 244.

121.   MUTE SWAN   *Cygnus olor*   Plate 29

Size: 150 cm; males 12 kg, females 10 kg
Distribution: Natural range is northern Eurasia from Great Britain to eastern Russia. They were introduced to New Zealand from Great Britain from 1866 onwards as ornamental birds, and maintain a tenuous hold in the wild on wetlands in Hawke's Bay, North Canterbury and Lake Ellesmere. Some live in a semi-feral state in many town parks, such as Virginia Lake, Wanganui, and stragglers or escapees from ornamental collections occasionally turn up in other wetlands.
Population: c. 100 in the wild in the 1990s, c. 20 in Hawke's Bay, the rest in Canterbury.
Conservation: Protected introduced species. Mute Swans once numbered several hundred birds in the wild, but the April 1968 *Wahine* storm destroyed much feeding habitat at their stronghold, Lake Ellesmere, and the population crashed. Ducks Unlimited have a captive breeding programme aimed at eventually releasing birds into the wild.
Breeding: Birds establish their territories in August and start building their nest in September. They usually nest solitarily, but at Harts Creek, Lake Ellesmere, they formerly nested in a colony, although each nest was screened by raupo from neighbouring nests. The nest is usually floating in shallow water or beside a slow-flowing stream or lake. It is a huge mound of grass and leaves of raupo, flax and rushes, topped with a shallow bowl lined with a little down.

Laying is from late September to December. They lay 4–7–11 white eggs (120 x 70 mm, 350 g) at 2-day intervals. The female alone incubates for c. 35 days. The eggs hatch within a day of one another, and both parents lead the cygnets to water within a further day and maintain guard through their development. The cygnets are initially covered in light grey down but slowly develop brownish-white juvenile plumage and fledge at 120–150 days old. In Britain, most females start breeding at 3 years old and most males begin at 4 years old. Once paired, they remain together for life. The oldest banded bird in Britain lived over 24 years.
Behaviour: Non-breeding and moulting Mute Swans form small flocks, but breeding adults usually remain as pairs and become very territorial when breeding; the cob (male) aggressively defends his pen (female) and nest from intruding birds and people by hissing at them and striking out with his wings, and they have been known to fight other cobs to the death. Despite their name, Mute Swans are quite vocal, with a variety of quiet honks, snorts and hisses.
Feeding: Diet is mainly leaves of submerged aquatic plants, which they reach by up-ending, willow leaves plucked from overhanging trees, or grass and clover grazed near the edge of the water. These are supplemented

by some aquatic invertebrates and even the odd fish, tadpole or frog.

Reading: Birkhead, M. & Perrins, C. 1986. *The Mute Swan*. London: Croom Helm.

122. BLACK SWAN *Cygnus atratus* Plate 29

Size: 120 cm; males 6 kg, females 5 kg

Distribution: Native to southwestern and eastern Australia and to Tasmania. Although about 100 birds were introduced to New Zealand between 1864 and 1868, it is likely that some also arrived naturally in 1867, because the Black Swan population grew and spread very rapidly. By 1880, they were well established in the wild, and are now widespread and abundant throughout the main islands and on Chatham Island. Greatest numbers are on large lowland or coastal lakes and lagoons and on some estuaries, especially Kaipara Harbour, the lower Waikato valley, Hawke's Bay, Lake Wairarapa, Farewell Spit, Lake Ellesmere, coastal Otago and Southland, and Te Whanga Lagoon (Chatham Island). Good numbers are also found on some inland lakes such as those in the Rotorua district, Lake Taupo and Ashburton Lakes.

Banding and neck-collar studies have shown that Black Swans in New Zealand are moderately sedentary and largely divided into 10 regional populations, each with a major nesting area and one or more coastal feeding and moulting areas. However, at Farewell Spit, the major moulting site in the country, about 10,000 birds from all around the mainland intermingle, although most come from the Wairarapa and Marlborough.

Population: In the early 1960s, well over 100,000 Black Swans were in New Zealand, with 70,000 on Lake Ellesmere alone; however, the April 1968 *Wahine* storm destroyed much feeding habitat at Lake Ellesmere and the population there crashed to fewer than 10,000 birds by 1978. In 1981, the national population was estimated to be 63,000 birds: 60,000 on the mainland and 3000 on Chatham Island.

Conservation: Partially protected introduced species. About 5000 birds are legally shot each year during the duck-shooting season; the number taken is strictly controlled with daily bag limits and seasons set independently for each region, depending on the population trends. Before numbers fell at Lake Ellesmere in the late 1960s, special culls of birds, commercial egg-collecting or egg-pricking were sometimes necessary to keep their numbers in check because they create a nuisance grazing and fouling pastures adjacent to some lakes.

Breeding: Black Swans have a long breeding season, which varies according to local conditions and whether the pairs are solitary or in colonies. Solitary pairs breeding in small wetlands and large deep lakes usually nest in July–October, whereas colonial birds breeding near large shallow wetlands breed only when the lake level starts to drop, at any time from September to January. The nest is usually on land within 100 m of a lake. It is a huge mound of grass and leaves of raupo, flax and rushes, topped with a shallow bowl lined with a little down.

The clutch is of 3–6–14 pale green eggs (104 x 67 mm, 250 g), but clutches of over 10 eggs are probably laid by more than one female. The first three eggs are laid c. 30 hours apart; thereafter daily. Both birds share incubation in spells of 3–4 hours through the day, but the female generally incubates at night. The incubation period is 32–36–43 days. The eggs hatch during less than 48 hours, and both parents lead the cygnets to water within a further day.

Solitary pairs usually guard their brood on territory throughout their development, but sometimes shift to a large body of open water for safety; however, cygnets from colonies form large crèches of up to 40 birds, guarded by some of the adults. The cygnets are initially covered in light grey down, but they slowly develop the grey-brown juvenile plumage and fledge at 95–140 days old. Young birds start breeding when 2–4 years old. The oldest banded bird in New Zealand lived at least 29 years.

Behaviour: Non-breeding and moulting Black Swans form loose flocks of up to several thousand birds. In solitary pairs, the male aggressively defends a large feeding territory around the nest. At a few sites, colonies of up to 5000 nests have been recorded, and only the nest site is defended. The Black Swan is quite vocal, with a musical and far-reaching bugle call given both in flight and on the water, especially at night.

Feeding: Diet is mainly leaves of submerged aquatic plants such as *Ruppia*, *Egeria* and *Zostera*, which they reach by up-ending, but they also graze on lakeside pasture grasses and clover.

Reading: Miers, K.H. & Williams, M. 1969. *Wildfowl* 20: 23–32. Williams, M. 1977. *Aust Wildl Res* 4; 289–299. Williams, M. 1979. *NZ J Ecol* 2: 34–41.

123. CANADA GOOSE *Branta canadensis* Plate 29

Size: 83 cm; males 5.4 kg, females 4.5 kg.

Geographical variation: 12 subspecies; the form in New Zealand is the Giant Canada Goose *maxima* from northern and central states of the USA (North Dakota to Arkansas), although other subspecies (*tavernii* and *canadensis*) from other parts of North America may have mixed with it.

Distribution: Natural range is North America and northeastern Asia (Kamchatka Peninsula and Japan). They were first introduced to New Zealand from North America in 1876, but only with 50 birds introduced in 1905 and other liberations up to 1920 did the present population become established. They are abundant in the wild in the eastern South Island from Marlborough to North Otago (especially at Lake Ellesmere) and common in drier tussock country of eastern Fiordland. Early attempts to introduce Canada Geese to the North Island failed, but they have become well established in the wild since the 1970s in the Waikato, Taupo-Ohakune area, northern Hawke's Bay, coastal Manawatu, and especially near Lake Wairarapa.

In the South Island, most birds breed near high-country lakes and rivers, but many adults and juveniles from inland Marlborough to the Mackenzie Basin migrate to Lake Ellesmere and other coastal lakes and estuaries in November–February for the autumn moult, and then stay through the winter to early September. Recently, more birds have remained on high-country lakes all year, moulting on inland lakes and feeding on pastures nearby, and some breed on coastal lakes such as Ellesmere and nearby Forsyth. In the North Island, most birds are resident on coastal lakes such as Whakaki Lagoons (near Wairoa) and Lake Wairarapa. Vagrants have been recorded from the Kermadec, Chatham and Auckland Islands.

Population: The post-shooting season population is c. 50,000 birds: 10,000 in the North Island and 40,000 in the South Island, including 10,000–15,000 overwintering on Lake Ellesmere.

Conservation: Partially protected introduced species. Up to 30,000 birds are legally shot during the normal May–July shooting season and in special seasons in late summer. Others are legally shot when they damage arable crops such as peas and grain and when they eat grass and foul pastures. Sometimes special culls of moulting birds or egg-pricking have been necessary to keep numbers under control in some districts.

Breeding: Birds return to their breeding sites in early September, and the gander aggressively defends a territory of about a hectare while the female builds the nest in a site with good visibility. Laying is from mid-September to late October, but replacement clutches are laid into November. They lay 2–**4–5**–10 white eggs (88 x 58 mm, 200 g), daily in a shallow bowl in a pile of grass and rushes gathered from within reach of the nest. The bowl is lined with feathers. Incubation, by the female only, takes c. 28 days and the eggs hatch synchronously.

The goslings, which are initially covered in yellow and brown down, are led from the nest within a day of hatching and are guarded by both parents or join crèches of up to 50 goslings during the 80 days to fledging. Family groups remain together until the next breeding season, when the young are driven away. They usually start breeding at 3 years old. Most pairs remain together from year to year and return to the same nesting area each year unless nesting is disrupted. About 30% of adult Canada Geese die each year (20% shot and 10% of natural causes), giving a life expectancy of 2.8 years, but the oldest banded bird lived over 30 years.

Behaviour: When not breeding, they form flocks of up to 2000 birds and are usually very wary. Flocks are often noisy, with a constant chorus of honking as birds maintain contact, especially when they are flying. The main flight call is a musical double honk 'ah-honk'.

Feeding: Mainly graze on land on plants such as grass, clover, lucerne and brassicas. They also eat wetland and aquatic plants, especially rushes and *Potamogeton*. Sometimes feed on stubble or standing crops of peas or grain, and flocks can cause considerable damage.

Reading: Imber, M.J. 1971. *Notornis* 18: 253–261.

124. CAPE BARREN GOOSE *Cereopsis novaehollandiae* Plate 29

Size: 87 cm, 5 kg

Distribution: Natural range is southern Australia, where they are rare but increasing with improvement of habitat on their main breeding islands. They breed mainly in grassland or wetlands on islands in Bass Strait, in the Spencer Gulf of South Australia and in the Recherche Archipelago off Western Australia, and many birds migrate to the mainland of Australia after their winter breeding season. They were first liberated at Lake Hawea in 1914, and a few persisted in open grassland and tussockland in the district until about 1946. Birds recorded from Fiordland in 1947, 1967 and 1990, Ahuriri River (1966), South Auckland (1986) and Takaka (1998) are considered vagrants from Australia, but most other sightings are probably of birds released from captivity. A few have become established in the wild near Waikanae and in South Canterbury.

Behaviour: Generally feed on land, and only rarely swim. They are usually silent on the ground, but both sexes give a low-pitched grunt in flight, and the male also gives a high-pitched trumpet call.

Feeding: Mainly graze grasses, legumes, weeds and herbs in the open, often well away from standing water.

Reading: Williams, G.R. 1968. *Notornis* 15: 66–69.

125. FERAL GOOSE *Anser anser* Plate 29

Other names: Greylag Goose, Domestic Goose

Size: 80 cm, 3 kg

Distribution: Natural range of the wild ancestor of this bird is the wetlands and farmland of Eurasia, from Iceland to China. Greylag Geese have been domesticated for centuries and were brought to New Zealand with the early European settlers. In many parts of the country, they have become truly feral, and numerous others live in a semi-feral state at city parks and on farms.

Population: No information available. Flocks of 50+ birds have been recorded at many sites, including most large lakes and in pastoral farmland.

Breeding: Not studied in New Zealand. In Europe, their usual clutch is of 4–6 creamy-white eggs (85 x 58 mm). They often nest in dense colonies, with nests a few metres apart in reedbeds or in thick grass under willows.

Behaviour: In New Zealand, Feral Geese are usually seen in flocks at lakes, at estuaries or on pastoral farmland. They make loud honks both on the ground and in flight.

Feeding: Graze on grass, clover and weeds, usually away from water.

126. PARADISE SHELDUCK *Tadorna variegata* Plate 30

Other names: Putangitangi, Pari
Size: 63 cm; males 1700 g, females 1400 g
Distribution: Breed only in New Zealand and are widely distributed in hill-country pasture, arable land, tussock grassland and wetlands throughout the mainland and on offshore islands with lakes or farmland such as Great Barrier, Kapiti and Stewart Islands. Although they appear in subfossil and midden deposits in the Chathams, the only recent record is of one bird in January 1984. A male visited Raoul Island in October 1995, and five visited Lord Howe Island for over a month from March 1950. In the North Island, the main concentrations are in Northland, in hill country of Gisborne–Hawke's Bay and Wanganui–Rangitikei, on the Manawatu dune lakes and in the Wairarapa. In the South Island, most are along the eastern foothills of the Southern Alps and on the Southland plains.

Adult Paradise Shelduck are generally sedentary, but movements are complex and depend in part on the habitats being used; those breeding in tussock grasslands tend to be more mobile than those breeding in hill-country farmland. All birds vacate their territories and flock sites for the annual moult. Large flocks of 1000+ birds gather in December–February at traditional moulting sites on farm ponds, lakes, tarns and river-beds. Individuals stay for 6–8 weeks and the big flocks break up in March–April. Juvenile females tend to return to breed in their natal area, but juvenile males disperse widely and often settle over 100 km away from their natal area.

Population: In 1981, the pre-shooting season population was estimated at c. 120,000 birds; 70,000 in the North Island and 50,000 in the South Island.

Conservation: Partially protected endemic. During the summer moult, they were important food for Maori and many were killed at traditional moulting sites. Paradise Shelducks were uncommon in the 1800s and largely restricted to the eastern and southern South Island. The conversion of native forest to exotic pasture, the construction of farm ponds, the introduction of strict controls on their harvest in 1868 and liberations of Southland birds into the central North Island between 1916 and 1921 more than outweighed the effects of introduced predators and drainage of natural wetlands. They have increased greatly through the 1900s, despite periods of localised decline caused by overharvesting. Regional bag limits and seasons are now closely linked to productivity and movements of birds in each part of the country.

Breeding: Birds re-establish their territories in March–April; it is often centred on a rush-covered soak, small farm pond or part of a larger lake or riverbed with an open view. The male aggressively defends the territory and maintains a lookout for predators while the female incubates. The nest is in a hollow log, under fallen logs, in a hayshed, or in a hole in the ground, but in forest patches some birds nest up to 25 m above the ground in a tree-hole.

Laying is mostly in August–September, but a few clutches are laid into November. The clutch is of 5–**9**–15 white eggs (67 x 49 mm, 85 g), laid daily, but clutches of 10+ eggs are probably laid by more than one female. Clutches are only rarely replaced, but two pairs can use the same area of water, giving the false impression that Paradise Shelducks are double-brooded. The female incubates for 30–35 days, during which she leaves the nest 2–3 times a day for about an hour at a time. The eggs hatch about the same time, but late-hatching eggs are often abandoned when the female leads the brood of ducklings to open water, which can be over a kilometre away.

The ducklings have a striking pattern of brown and white down, but when they fledge at c. 8 weeks old they resemble adult males, except females have white patches around the eyes and base of the bill. These patches expand to the whole head after another couple of months and the body colour gradually lightens.

Most Paradise Shelducks start breeding when 2 years old, but females often delay until they are 3 years old. Pairs remain together from year to year and return to the same nesting area each year. If one bird dies, the mate occupies the same territory and re-mates again. About 35% of breeding adults die each year, giving a life expectancy of 2.3 years; however, some birds live much longer, with the oldest banded bird living at least 23 years.

Behaviour: Paradise Shelducks are usually in pairs, but non-breeders flock during the breeding season, when they start their moult, and large flocks of 1000+ breeders and fledglings form for a couple of months during the summer moult. Pairs are alert, and from a high point on the ground or while circling overhead they duet their loud alarm calls: the male's deep 'zonk-zonk . . .' and the female's shrill, penetrating 'zeek, zeek . . .' Both sexes give a piercing flock call when flying to join a flock or when flying birds are approaching.

Feeding: Graze on grass and clover, and also feed on grass and weed seeds and stubble or standing crops of peas or grain. Aquatic vegetation is obtained from the surface or by up-ending. Flocks can sometimes cause considerable damage to young pasture and hay and grain crops, especially near major moulting sites.

Reading: Barker, R.J. 1990. *Notornis* 37: 173–181.
Williams, M.J. 1972. *Wildfowl* 23: 94–102.
Williams, M.J. 1979. *Notornis* 26: 213–272.
Williams, M.J. 1979. *Notornis* 26: 369–390.

127 CHESTNUT-BREASTED SHELDUCK
Tadorna tadornoides   **Plate 30**

Other names: Australian Shelduck, Mountain Duck
Size: 65 cm; males 1600 g, females 1300 g
Distribution: Breed in southwestern and southeastern Australia and in Tasmania. They are mainly sedentary, although birds move several hundred kilometres between breeding territories and traditional moulting sites, including crossing Bass Strait. In drought years, some are forced to seek more distant moulting sites; vagrants reach northern states and Norfolk Island.

First recorded in New Zealand at Hokitika in January 1973, but small invasions occurred in 1982–83 and 1984–85, with many records of singles and some flocks of up to 22 birds throughout the North and South Islands, on The Snares and on Auckland and Campbell Islands. The number seen gradually declined, except around Lakes Elterwater and Grass-mere in coastal Marlborough, where a few have been seen regularly in late summer and autumn during the 1990s. Further individuals or small flocks have appeared from time to time, e.g. a pair at Raoul Island (March 1994), three on Pitt Island (December 1997), and three in the Manawatu (April 1998).
Population: In 1983, at least 56 birds were in New Zealand, but 10 years later there were probably fewer than 20 birds, mostly in Marlborough.

Conservation: Protected self-introduced native. They maintain only a tenuous hold, and breeding has been confirmed only twice: a pair with half-grown young at Lake Tekapo in January 1985, and a pair with three flying young at Lake Grassmere in March 1991. They are probably mistaken for Paradise Shelduck during the shooting season.

Breeding: Not studied in New Zealand. In Australia, laying is mostly in July–October, extending later in wet seasons. The nest is usually in a hole in a living or dead tree, in a hole in the ground, or under dense bushes. The clutch is 4–**9**–19 white eggs (69 x 49 mm, 88 g), laid daily, but those of 10+ eggs are probably laid by more than one female. The female incubates for 30–33 days and the ducklings are led from the nest to open water, which can be over a kilometre away. The ducklings have a striking pattern of brown and white down, but when the chicks fledge at c. 70 days old, they look like the adult but are smaller, duller and have white flecking on the face, lack the white collar and have a light brown chest and upper back.

Behaviour: In New Zealand, Chestnut-breasted Shelducks have been seen mainly in small flocks at lakes likely to be used as moulting sites, seldom at places where they are likely to breed. The male's alarm call, a loud, deep honk, is answered by the female's higher-pitched call.

Feeding: Graze on grass, clover and weeds, and also feed on grass and weed seeds, and on aquatic vegetation, which they obtain from on the surface or by up-ending.

Reading: Heather, B.D. 1987. *Notornis* 34: 71–77.

128.   AUSTRALIAN WOOD DUCK   *Chenonetta jubata*   Plate 30

Other names: Maned Duck, Maned Goose
Size: 48 cm, 800 g
Distribution: Breed widely in Australia and Tasmania. They are highly nomadic, following rains and floods in wet years to colonise temporary wetlands, and then returning to permanent water in southwestern Australia and along the eastern seaboard. Vagrant to New Zealand, with six records of lone birds: Central Otago (1910), Southland (1944), Marlborough (1980), The Snares (1983, 1985–86) and Southland (2002).

Feeding: In Australia, they prefer grassland with scattered trees near water, where they graze on grass, clover and other green foliage. They sometimes graze in shallow water on lagoon fringes, on grain stubble, and in city parks.

129.   BLUE DUCK   *Hymenolaimus malacorhynchos*   Plate 30

Other name: Whio
Size: 53 cm; males 900 g, females 750 g
Distribution: New Zealand only. They are mainly restricted to fast-flowing and turbulent rivers and streams in forested hill country or mountains, but are occasionally seen on mountain tarns or on sheltered harbours of Fiordland. In the North Island, they are found on rivers of the Volcanic Plateau and from the Raukumara Range to the northern Ruahine Range. A few may persist in the Tararua Range. They have been recently reintroduced to Egmont National Park. In the South Island, they are widespread on rivers of northwestern Nelson, the Paparoa Range and Fiordland, and in the headwaters of rivers in the Southern Alps, particularly on the western side. A few birds persist in Peel Forest at the headwaters of the Rangitata River, and in the Catlins.

Colour-banding studies have shown that breeding birds remain on their territories for life, whereas juveniles disperse up or down their natal river and attempt to settle and establish territories close to their natal territory, but will occasionally shift between catchments, even including 1000 m ascents to cross mountain passes. The ability of Blue Ducks to home over long distances was shown by a pair that flew over 100 km from Mt Taranaki back to their territory near Ohakune within a few days.

Population: c. 2000–4000 birds: up to 1000 in the North Island, mainly in and around Tongariro National Park, and up to 3000 in the South Island, widely scattered.

Conservation: Protected threatened endemic. The range and numbers of Blue Ducks have declined since European settlement, especially in the North Island. Clearance of lowland forest and some upland forest, grazing of riverside vegetation, and introduced predators have contributed to the decline. Introduced trout may compete for aquatic invertebrates, and the water flow of some rivers has been altered by hydroelectric dams. Blue Ducks are being bred in captivity for release into suitable habitats such as Egmont National Park.

Breeding: Breeding adults remain on their territory all year. The nest is a simple bowl of twigs, grass and down in a hollow log, small cavity or under dense vegetation near a steep stream bank. Laying is in July–December, mostly August–October. Many late nests are replacement clutches. They lay 4–6–9 creamy white eggs (65 x 45 mm, 72 g) at 48-hour intervals. The female incubates for 30–35 days while the male stands guard nearby.

The young are initially covered in pale creamy-white and olive-grey down. They are quickly led to the stream by the female, and can swim and dive well in fast-flowing water. They are guarded by both parents during their 10-week fledging period. Chicks disperse from the territory soon after fledging. Breeding in their first year of life has been recorded, but most do not manage to establish a territory and obtain a partner until their second year. The oldest Blue Duck recorded in the wild lived over 13 years.

Behaviour: Usually seen in pairs, occupying the same short stretch of river year after year. Records from the 1800s suggested that non-territorial birds sometimes flocked, but with declining numbers this is now not seen. They are usually seen in the early morning and late afternoon fossicking among rapids and small pools in the lee of large boulders, and are rarely observed in flight. When they do fly, they fly low and direct by day, but at night they can sometimes be heard flying 50+ m above the ground. Their flight call, and the male territorial call, is a shrill, somewhat hoarse whistle: 'whio' or 'whio-whio'; the female has a rattling growl: 'cr-ack'.

Feeding: Blue Ducks dabble, dive and up-end in the rapidly flowing white water of mountain streams and rivers. Diet is almost entirely aquatic invertebrates; mostly caddis-fly larvae, but also mayfly, stonefly and chironomid larvae obtained from the downstream sides of stones and boulders. They occasionally catch emerging adult insects on the surface and also take some algae and fruit.

Reading: Harding, M.A. 1994. *Notornis* 41: 293–295. Kear, J. & Steel, T.H. 1971. *Notornis* 18: 187–198. Williams, M.J. 1980. *Notornis* 26: 306–307. Williams, M. 1991. *Wildfowl* 42: 63–86.

130. MALLARD *Anas platyrhynchos* Plate 31

Size: 58 cm; males 1300 g, females 1100 g
Geographical variation: Mallards in New Zealand were derived from both European and North American stock (*platyrhynchos*). In New Zealand, they interbreed with Grey Ducks (*A. superciliosa*), and hybrids are common.

Distribution: Natural range is across the temperate Northern Hemisphere in Europe, Asia and North America. Birds of British game-farm stock were first introduced to New Zealand from Australia in 1867. Acclimatisation Societies made many liberations up to about 1918, particularly in the southern South Island, but Mallards were not particularly successful until they were intensively bred and liberated in the 1930s and 1940s, and North American birds were introduced. Liberations continued up to 1960, when Mallards had become the most numerous and widespread waterfowl on the New Zealand mainland, using a wide variety of wetlands from town parks and small farm ponds to rivers and estuaries. They have colonised many offshore islands and the Chatham, Antipodes, The Snares, Auckland and Campbell Islands. Banding studies show that Mallards disperse widely throughout New Zealand, and one bird banded in Otago was shot in South Australia 16 months later.

Population: In 1981, there were c. 5 million. The Mallard population grew until about 1985, but have declined since to c. 3 million.

Conservation: Partially protected introduced species; legally harvested in the duck-shooting season, with the take controlled by daily bag limits for licensed hunters, and legally shot under licence when they damage farm crops.

Breeding: Pair formation begins in the autumn flocks, and by July pairs have formed and feeding territories established. The nest is a bowl of grass with down added as incubation proceeds, usually under dense vegetation or sometimes simply in tall grass or in a hollow tree or fork; not far from water. First clutches are laid between late July and October, with renesting up to the end of December. They lay 10–**13**–16 pale greenish or creamy eggs (58 x 43 mm, 60 g). Eggs are laid daily, usually about dawn. The male guards the female during laying but then leaves her to incubate alone for 26–28 days. The female leads the ducklings to water soon after they hatch. Broods of up to 35 ducklings following a single female have been reported, but these may have been from a nest in which more than one female laid or when two or more broods had coalesced.

The young are initially covered in dark brown down with yellow facial markings and underparts, but they quickly develop feathers and fledge at 55–60 days old. The young disperse widely. About half die before they start breeding at 1 year old. Adults live on average 2.5 years, but some birds live much longer, the oldest recorded in the wild in New Zealand being over 26 years old.

Behaviour: Males commence moult in November, females start about a month later, and in December–January large flocks of moulting birds congregate on freshwater lakes. They stay well away from the shore during the day but feed on the adjacent shore at night during the 3 weeks they are flightless. At this time, flocks of 1000+ birds have been seen at Lakes Wairarapa, Ellesmere and Tuakitoto. The flocks break up in late summer, but during the duck-shooting season Mallards regroup on protected wetlands such as town lakes and reserves. In autumn and winter, Mallards have an elaborate set of courtship displays and males often gather around and harass lone females. Males have a soft, high-pitched 'quek'; females are more vocal with their characteristic loud, repeated 'quack quack quack'.

Feeding: Diet is mainly aquatic vegetation, which they get by up-ending or dabbling in shallow water, taking seeds from the water surface or growing plants. They often graze grass and clover. Ducklings and females forming eggs take many aquatic invertebrates such as small snails, insect larvae and water beetles. Mallards also feed on grain, peas and beans in stubble after the crop has been harvested, and flocks sometimes feed in standing crops, causing considerable damage by knocking down and trampling plants.

Reading: Balham, R.W. 1952. *Emu* 52: 163–191. Gillespie, G.D. 1985. *J Appl Ecol* 22: 347–356. Gillespie, G.D. 1985. *Auk* 102: 459–469.

131. GREY DUCK   *Anas superciliosa*   Plate 31

Other names: Parera, Pacific Black Duck
Size: 55 cm; males 1100 g, females 1000 g
Geographical variation: Three subspecies are recognised, but banding studies show that there is some exchange between populations, especially between Australia and New Zealand; *rogersi* breeds in Indonesia, New Guinea and Australia, *pelewensis* on islands of the southwest Pacific, and *superciliosa* in New Zealand. Grey Ducks interbreed extensively with Mallards in New Zealand, and many birds have a hybrid origin.

Distribution: Breed in Australasia from Sumatra through Indonesia to New Guinea and Australia, on many islands in the southwestern Pacific, east to French Polynesia and north to the Caroline Islands, and in the New Zealand region. They are in wetlands throughout New Zealand, including many offshore and outlying islands such as the Kermadec, Chatham, Antipodes, The Snares, Auckland and Campbell Islands. On the mainland, they are most common in Northland, Westland, parts of the Waikato and the eastern Bay of Plenty–Gisborne area.

Grey Ducks prefer small lakes, slow-flowing rivers and tidal water surrounded by forest rather than farmland. They have not adapted to the agricultural landscape and are rare on town lakes. Banding studies show that they disperse widely throughout New Zealand; a bird banded in Marlborough was shot in Australia, and a New South Wales bird was shot in Otago. In recent decades, with a marked decline in numbers, they seem to have become more sedentary.

Population: In 1970, there were c. 1.5 million Grey Ducks, but by 1981 they had declined to c. 1.2 million, and the decline has accelerated so that by the 1990s there were fewer than 500,000.

Conservation: Partially protected native; legally harvested in the duck-shooting season, with the take controlled by daily bag limits for licensed hunters. The decline in this species is attributed to a loss of wild habitats, and competition and hybridisation with the Mallard.

Breeding: Pair formation starts in autumn flocks. By late July, most birds are paired and the males start to defend territories. The nest is a bowl of grass with a lining of down added as incubation proceeds. It is generally away from water (cf. Mallard) and usually under dense vegetation or quite often in a tree hole, fork or clump of *Astelia,* up to 10 m above the ground. The first clutch is usually laid between late August and November, but pairs continue to renest to the end of December. They lay 5–**10**–13 pale greenish or creamy eggs (58 x 41 mm, 60 g) about dawn each day. The male guards the female during laying and for about the first week of incubation, but then leaves her to incubate alone for 26–28 days. The female leads the ducklings to water soon after they hatch. Broods of up to 17 ducklings have been reported, but these were probably from a nest in which more than one female laid.

The young are initially covered in dark brown down with yellow facial markings and underparts, but they quickly develop feathers and fledge at c. 60 days old and disperse widely. About 65% die before they start breeding at 1 year old. Adults live on average just 21 months, but some birds live much longer than this, with the oldest recorded in the wild in New Zealand being at least 20 years old.

Behaviour: Grey Ducks are often seen in small flocks outside of the breeding season, but do not remain in family groups once the young have fledged. Males have a soft, high-pitched 'quek', and females the more characteristic loud 'quack quack quack', as in Mallards.

Feeding: Diet is mainly seeds sieved from the water through comb-like lamellae at the sides of the bill, and aquatic vegetation which they get by up-ending or dabbling in shallow water. They sometimes graze grasses along wetland margins. Ducklings and females forming eggs especially take many aquatic or marine invertebrates such as small snails, insect larvae, water beetles and crustacea.

Reading: Balham, R.W. 1952. *Emu* 52: 163–191. Gillespie, G.D. 1985. *Auk* 102: 459–469. Williams, M.J. 1969. *Notornis* 16: 23–32.

132. GREY TEAL *Anas gracilis* Plate 32

Other name: Tete
Size: 43 cm; males 525 g, females 425 g
Distribution: Breed only in Australia and New Zealand, and are vagrants to Indonesia, New Guinea, the Solomons and New Caledonia. In New Zealand, they were rare and local until about the 1950s, but several natural irruptions from Australia (notably in 1957 when a drought followed a year with excellent inland breeding) and the provision of nest boxes has led to a dramatic increase in numbers and range of the species. They are now common in shallow coastal lakes and lagoons with good margins of swamp and willows, in South Auckland and northern Waikato, Hawke's Bay, Manawatu, Wairarapa and the eastern South Island from Marlborough to Southland. They are also in moderate numbers on the Rotorua lakes and along the eastern foothills of the Southern Alps. After breeding, they often gather at estuaries to feed on exposed mudflats. They have been recorded on some offshore islands but not from outliers, except Chatham Island (1951). Banding studies show that, although some Grey Teal are sedentary, many are highly mobile and disperse widely in New Zealand. A bird banded in southern Australia was shot in the Waikato in 1957.
Population: In the early 1970s, there were estimated to be fewer than 20,000 birds, but by 2005 the population had risen to well over 50,000.
Conservation: Protected native. Each year, even though a moderate number are shot accidentally during the duck-shooting season, the population has grown strongly.
Breeding: Pairs remain together all year, but most join large flocks for the late summer moult and then remain in flocks until July.

In Australia, breeding is closely linked to rainfall, but in New Zealand it is more seasonal although still related to water levels. Laying is mostly in June–September, but replacement clutches can be laid through to January. The nest is a bowl of grass with a lining of down added as incubation proceeds. It is generally close to water and usually in a tree hole, nest box or among dense vegetation, e.g. *Carex secta*.

They lay 5–**7**–9 creamy eggs (50 x 36 mm), laid about dawn each day. The male guards the female during laying and incubation. The female incubates for 25–31 days. The pair leads the ducklings to water soon after they hatch. They are initially covered in dark grey-brown down with off-white facial markings and underparts, but quickly develop feathers and fledge at c. 55 days old and then disperse widely. About 68% die before they start breeding at 1 year old. Adults live on average about 3 years, but some birds live much longer; the oldest recorded in the wild in New Zealand being over 9 years old, but a bird in Australia lived at least 21 years.
Behaviour: Normally seen in small flocks of 10–50 birds, but flocks of 1000+ are recorded in autumn at Lake Wairarapa and Bromley Sewage Ponds (Christchurch). Birds in flocks chatter almost constantly. Males give a loud, short whistle, and females a rapid 'cuck-cuck-cuck' call.
Feeding: Diet is mainly seeds of aquatic plants and invertebrates such as water beetles and larvae of midges, caddisflies and mosquitoes, obtained by dabbling in shallow water or by dredging exposed lakeside or estuarine mudflats and filtering out the food.

Reading: Mills, J.A. 1976. *NZ J Zool* 3: 261–267.

133. CHESTNUT TEAL *Anas castanea* Plate 32

Size: 45 cm, 650 g
Distribution: Breed only in Australia, mainly in the southwest and southeast, and particularly in coastal wetlands of Victoria and Tasmania. Most breed on small freshwater

lakes but move to large lakes and estuaries after breeding, and they are among the few ducks that regularly use very saline habitats. Vagrant to northern Australia, New Guinea, Lord Howe Island and New Zealand. One possible Chestnut Teal was seen at the Waikanae Estuary on 31 January 1991, and an immature bird subsequently wintered at the Manawatu Estuary; in winter 1992, up to three birds (two immature males and an immature female) were seen at the Manawatu Estuary. As a few adults or immatures have appeared there in most subsequent years during the annual influx of Grey Teal during the duck-shooting season, Chestnut Teal may be breeding somewhere in the Manawatu

wetlands. Singles at Kowai River, Canterbury (1993) and Balclutha (2003).

Feeding: In Australia, their preferred habitats are coastal wetlands, including estuaries and brackish lagoons. They eat seeds and invertebrates by dabbling in shallow water or by dredging in mud on exposed mudflats or at the front edge of the rising tide.

Reading: Moore, J. & Moore, M. 1992. *Notornis* 39: 289–292.

134. BROWN TEAL   *Anas aucklandica*   Plate 32

Other name: Pateke
Size: 48 cm; male 600 g, female 500 g
Geographical variation: Three subspecies are currently recognised: the Brown Teal *chlorotis* breeds on the New Zealand mainland and some offshore islands, the Auckland Island Teal *aucklandica* breeds in the Auckland Islands, and the Campbell Island Teal *nesiotis* breeds on Dent Island in the Campbell Islands. Recent taxonomic work suggests that the teal breeding on the subantarctic islands result from separate invasions from Australia and should be regarded as full species. The subspecies *chlorotis* is more closely related to the Chestnut Teal of Australia, which suggests that it is a relatively recent colonist.
Distribution: Breed only in New Zealand. They were originally widely distributed in lowland swamps and swamp forest from Northland to Stewart Island, but have declined dramatically. Their stronghold is now Great Barrier Island; their natural range in the North Island is restricted to the eastern coast of Northland from the Bay of Islands to Tutukaka, Coromandel Peninsula and a few on Little Barrier and Great Mercury Islands. In the South Island, they persist only in Fiordland. They have not been seen on Stewart Island since the 1970s. A small population is established on Kapiti Island, derived from a release of captive-bred birds in 1968, and a few birds are still seen in the Manawatu–Horowhenua lowlands from a release of over 300 captive-bred birds in the 1970s and early 1980s. Recent releases on Tiritiri Matangi Island and at Moehau have

been successful.

The Auckland Island Teal has gone from the main Auckland Island, but remains on Enderby, Rose, Ewing, Dundas, Adams and Disappointment Islands. The Campbell Island Teal was found in 1855, but rarely seen until a small population was found on Dent Island in 1975. They have been re-introduced to Campbell Island, via Codfish Island, following eradication of rats there in 2001.
Population: Brown Teal: c.1000 birds in 2004; 550+ on Great Barrier Island, 200+ in Northland, 200 in captivity and 100 scattered widely through the rest of the country. Auckland Island Teal: 2000+ birds. Campbell Island Teal: 50–100 birds.
Conservation: Protected threatened endemic. All three subspecies have declined in numbers and range over the last century. The decline of Brown Teal was probably caused by predation by introduced cats, dogs and mustelids, the drainage of prime lowland swamp habitats and the harvest of birds until they were protected in 1921. Conservation efforts for Brown Teal are aimed at securing suitable coastal habitat in Northland and on Great Barrier Island, and controlling predators. Ducks Unlimited has had great success in breeding Brown Teal in captivity, but releases on the mainland have failed because of predation. Both Auckland Island Teal and Campbell Island Teal have been bred in captivity.
Breeding: Campbell Island Teal have not been seen breeding in the wild. Most Brown Teal lay in June–October, but clutches can be laid

at almost any time of year, whereas Auckland Island Teal do not lay until December–January. Brown Teal lay 3–5–8 cream eggs (60 x 43 mm, 61 g) at about 1.5-day intervals, but Auckland Island Teal lay only 3–4–5 cream eggs (64 x 45 mm, 75 g) at intervals of 2–3 days. The nest is a bowl of grass under dense vegetation such as *Carex*, fern or tussock. The male guards the territory while the female incubates for c. 30 days, and contributes to raising the brood. In captivity, the fledging period is 50–55 days. The oldest Brown Teal in the wild lived over 6 years.

Behaviour: Brown Teal are strongly territorial during the breeding season but form flocks at traditional sites in summer. These flocks break up in winter, but juvenile and unpaired birds continue to use the roosting sites through the breeding season. In contrast, Auckland Island Teal pairs remain on territory all year, but juveniles and unpaired adults form small flocks in protected bays. The males of all forms give soft, high-pitched wheezy whistles and popping calls; females give low quacks and growls.

Feeding: Diet is mainly aquatic or marine invertebrates taken by dabbling from just below the water surface or in mud in shallow water of estuaries, freshwater wetlands, and peaty or muddy pools or trickles on land. Auckland Island Teal often feed among kelp in sheltered bays, and they probe amongst rotting seaweed along the shore.

Reading: Hayes, F.N. & Williams, M.J. 1982. *Wildfowl* 33: 73–80. Weller, M.J. 1974. *Notornis* 21; 25–35. Weller, M.J. 1975. *Auk* 92: 280–297. Williams, M. *et al.* 1991. *Acta XX Cong Int Orn* 876–884. Williams, M. 1995. *Notornis* 42: 219–262.

135. AUSTRALASIAN SHOVELER *Anas rhynchotis* Plate 31

Other names: Kuruwhengi, New Zealand Shoveler, Spoonbill

Size: 49 cm; males 650 g, females 600 g

Geographical variation: Two subspecies: the nominate *rhynchotis* breeds in Australia, and the New Zealand Shoveler *variegata* breeds in New Zealand.

Distribution: Breed in southern Australia, especially in the Murray-Darling Basin, but they disperse northwards in wet years. They are in wetlands throughout both main islands of New Zealand, and straggle to Stewart Island and the Auckland Islands. They became extinct on the Chatham Islands in 1925. Shovelers prefer fertile shallow wetlands and some sewage ponds of the lower Waikato, Hawke's Bay, Manawatu, Wairarapa, Canterbury and Otago, especially those lakes fringed with raupo. Moderate numbers are found on the Rotorua lakes and Lake Taupo. They are uncommon on flowing rivers and high-country lakes of the South Island.

Banding studies have shown that Shovelers are highly mobile within New Zealand, and movements between Southland and the Waikato are not uncommon. A juvenile banded in coastal Manawatu was caught 800 km away in Otago the following May, but by August it had returned to its natal lake to breed.

Population: c. 150,000 birds in the 1980s.

Conservation: Partially protected native; c. 30,000 are legally harvested each year in the duck-shooting season, with the take controlled by daily bag limits for licensed hunters. Numbers of Shovelers appear stable. Construction of farm dams and sewage ponds, and increased fertility of many lowland lakes with farm run-off, may be compensating for the loss of natural wetlands.

Breeding: In July and August, Shovelers are in courtship flocks, but by September pairs disperse to establish a territory. The nest is a bowl of grass, lined with down. It is usually in thick rank pasture, tussock or carex away from water. Laying is mainly in October–November, but a few late or replacement clutches are laid until January. They lay 9–11–13 pale bluish-white eggs (52 x 38 mm) about dawn each day. The male guards the female during laying and for about the first fortnight of incubation, but then leaves her to complete the incubation of c. 25 days. The female leads the ducklings from the nest soon after they hatch. Normally the brood is kept in dense vegetation by day but feeds in open water at night.

The young are initially covered in dark brown down with yellow facial markings and underparts, and the bill quickly develops its distinctive spoon shape. Sometimes crèches of up to 100 well-grown ducklings have been recorded. Chicks fledge at 50–60 days old and disperse widely. About 65% die before they start breeding at 1 year old. Adults survive on average just 21 months, but some birds live much longer, with the oldest recorded in the wild in New Zealand being over 11 years old.

Behaviour: Usually seen in flocks, sometimes of 1000+ birds on large fertile lakes. They tend to shy away from city ponds. Shovelers are often silent by day, but at night they make a soft but far-carrying 'cuck-cuck-cuck . . .' call.

Feeding: Diet is mainly minute aquatic plants such as *Lemna*, seeds, and zooplankton sieved from the water by dabbling in shallow water or in mud. The food is filtered out on very fine comb-like lamellae at the sides of the bill. Large invertebrates such as water beetles and freshwater snails are also eaten.

Reading: Sibson, R.B. 1967. *Notornis* 14: 22–26.

136. NORTHERN SHOVELER *Anas clypeata* Plate 31

Size: 50 cm, 650 g

Distribution: Breed in the cool-temperate Northern Hemisphere from Iceland and England across northern Europe and Asia, and into western North America. They migrate to southern Europe, the Rift Valley of Africa, southern Asia and central America, and are vagrants to Micronesia and occasionally to Australasia. Seven confirmed records in New Zealand, all of males in breeding plumage (when most easily distinguished from Australasian Shovelers): Waikato (May 1968), Horowhenua (May 1969,

August 1971), Wanganui (August 1989), Southland (May 1991), Bay of Plenty (May 1993) and Gisborne (June 1995).

Feeding: In their natural range, Northern Shovelers prefer shallow, reed-fringed, high-fertility freshwater or brackish lakes, sewage ponds and flooded paddocks. They feed on minute invertebrates, seeds and plant material obtained by dabbling in shallow water or mud.

Reading: Kinsky, F.C. & Jones, E.B. 1972. *Notornis* 19: 105–110.

137. PINK-EARED DUCK *Malacorhynchus membranaceus* Plate 31

Size: 40 cm, 400 g

Distribution: Breed only in Australia, mainly in the south and especially in the Murray-Darling Basin of inland New South Wales and Victoria. They disperse widely within Australia in response to inland rains and droughts, but are not common on the eastern seaboard and are only a rare visitor to Tasmania. One New Zealand record: an immature bird at Mangere Sewage Ponds (June 1990).

Feeding: In Australia, Pink-eared Ducks are mainly on shallow stagnant lakes and on sewage ponds. They feed on invertebrates (especially chironomid larvae) and seeds obtained by sieving food onto comb-like lamellae inside the bill. The distinctive bill flaps are apparently used to feel invertebrates touching the bill.

Reading: Eller, G.J. 1991. *Notornis* 38: 109–110.

138. WHITE-EYED DUCK   *Aythya australis*   Plate 32

Other names: Karakahia, Hardhead
Size: 48 cm, 900 g
Distribution: Breed only in Australia, mainly in the south and especially in the deeper swamps of the Murray–Darling catchments, along the Great Dividing Range and in coastal Victoria. They disperse widely within Australia in response to inland rains and droughts, and vagrants reach Indonesia, New Guinea, Vanuatu, New Caledonia, Norfolk Island and New Zealand. The Maori had a name for the White-eyed Duck, and the many records in New Zealand in the late 1800s suggests that they may have bred here until about 1895.

Since then, there have been only six records: Rotorua (1934), Hawke's Bay (one bird shot out of a flock of eight in 1973), Auckland (1980), Otago (1990), West Coast (two in 1994) and New Plymouth (2001).
Feeding: In Australia, White-eyed Ducks prefer large deep lakes with abundant aquatic vegetation, similar to those lakes used by Scaup in New Zealand. They dive to feed on aquatic plants and invertebrates, especially freshwater mussels and snails, although they occasionally up-end or dabble in shallow water or mud.

139. NEW ZEALAND SCAUP   *Aythya novaeseelandiae*   Plate 32

Other names: Papango, Black Teal
Size: 40 cm; 650 g
Distribution: New Zealand only. They are widespread but have a patchy distribution. Most are on dune lakes of Northland, hydroelectric lakes in the upper Waikato, and on lakes in the Rotorua district, Taupo, Hawke's Bay, West Coast, North Canterbury and on the high-country lakes and tarns of the Southern Alps. Elsewhere they are rare, and are not recorded from offshore or outlying islands. Scaup prefer large deep lakes and are rarely found on shallow coastal lakes, lagoons, estuaries or rivers. Little information is available about movements of Scaup within New Zealand, but they are presumed to be mainly sedentary.
Population: c. 20,000 birds in the 1990s.
Conservation: Protected endemic. Midden evidence suggests that Scaup were formerly more widespread, including being on the

Chathams. Numbers and range have declined since European settlement through modification of habitat, shooting and the introduction of predators. However, they have recovered some ground since they were partially protected in 1921 and fully protected in 1934. In the North Island, hydroelectric dams have provided valuable new habitat. Ducks Unlimited has carried out a captive breeding programme and established new populations (e.g. in dune lakes from southern Taranaki to Waikanae).
Breeding: By September, most paired birds have left the winter flocks and the males become territorial. The nest is a bowl of grass and rushes, lined with down, in dense cover close to water. Sometimes Scaup form loose colonies where suitable breeding habitat is scarce. Laying is mostly from late October to December, but a few late or replacement clutches are laid until February. The clutch is

of 2–**7**–**8**–15 creamy-white eggs (64 x 45 mm, 71 g), but clutches of 12+ eggs are probably laid by more than one female. Only the female incubates, for c. 30 days. The female broods the ducklings on the nest for up to 24 hours before leading them to water; they are immediately capable of diving to feed. They are initially covered in pale brown down but with white underparts, and the bill is reddish brown. The female guards the brood during their c. 75-day fledging period. Occasionally, rafts of up to 50 birds are formed by several females and their similarly aged broods. Age at first breeding and survivorship is not known, as few New Zealand Scaup have been banded.

Behaviour: Usually seen in flocks in autumn and winter, sometimes 200+ birds at traditional moulting and wintering sites such as Lakes Rotorua, Taupo and Tutira, Bromley Sewage Ponds (Christchurch), and the Ashburton lakes. They are often silent, but males have a 3–4-note high-pitched whistle, and females 'quack'.

Feeding: They dive to at least 3 m, probably much deeper, to feed on aquatic plants and invertebrates such as freshwater snails, although they occasionally up-end or dabble in shallow water or mud. Most dives last 15–20 seconds, but some last over a minute.

Reading: Soper, M.E. 1976. *New Zealand Birds.* Christchurch: Whitcoulls. Stokes, S.J. 1991. MSc thesis, Univ Canterbury.

140. AUCKLAND ISLAND MERGANSER *Mergus australis* Plate 74

Size: 58 cm, 900 g

Distribution: Auckland Island Mergansers are extinct. Subfossil bones have been found in natural sites and Maori middens widely on the North, South, Stewart and Chatham Islands, showing that Maori hunters and their accompanying dogs probably brought about their extinction on the mainland and at the Chathams. The only historical records are from Auckland and Adams Islands of the Auckland group. European attempts at settlement, together with introduced mammals, led to their decline on the Auckland Islands, but probably the final cause of their extinction was the shooting of about 30 birds for museum specimens. The last pair were shot in 1902. Extensive searches since 1942 have failed to find any birds.

Breeding: The nest, eggs and clutch size of Auckland Island Mergansers were not described. One brood of four ducklings (which lacked the patterned down of northern mergansers) was recorded in summer.

Behaviour: Although their wings were reduced, they could fly. They lived on the fiord-like inlets of the eastern and southern coasts of the Auckland Islands, especially on the extensive coast of Carnley Harbour, and also at the head of estuaries and pools of streams.

Feeding: Little is known. They apparently fed on fish; also on crustaceans, shellfish and marine worms. As with all mergansers, they used the backward-facing serrations on both mandibles to seize and hold their prey.

Reading: Kear, J. & Scarlett, R.J. 1970. *Wildfowl* 21: 78–86. Williams, G.R. & Weller, M.W. 1974. *Notornis* 21: 247–249.

RAPTORS Accipitridae and Falconidae

The raptors, or diurnal birds of prey, are found worldwide from inshore marine habitats to the mountain tops. There are about 217 species of eagle, kite, hawk and harrier (Accipitridae), of which only 1 breeds in New Zealand and 1 is a vagrant, although there are occasional rumours of large eagles, presumably vagrants from Australia. There are 61 species of falcon and kestrel (Falconidae); again only 1 species breeds in New Zealand, but 2 are vagrants. Subfossil bones of a large, long-legged, short-winged eagle

Harpagornis moorei and of a sea eagle *Icthyophaga australis* show that New Zealand used to have a greater variety of raptors.

New Zealand raptors are medium-to-large, mainly brown birds. Raptors have long wings and tail; long, unfeathered powerful feet with very sharp talons; a small, broad, hooked bill with a waxy cere at the base of the upper bill; and large eyes.

Reading: Brown, L.H. *Birds of Prey*. London: Hamlyn. Cade, T.J. 1982. *The Falcons of the World*. London: Collins. Newton, I. 1976. *Population Ecology of Raptors*. Berkhamsted: Poyser.

141. BLACK KITE *Milvus migrans*   Plate 33

Other name: Fork-tailed Kite
Size: Males 50 cm, 550 g; females 55 cm, 600 g
Distribution: Breed widely in Africa and from southern Europe across Asia and Australasia to the eastern states of Australia. In Australia, most breed in inland parts of South Australia, New South Wales and Queensland, but they have frequent irregular irruptions to other states and to coastal areas in response to droughts and local abundance of food.

Vagrant to New Zealand, with five records: Marlborough (1992–94; 2000), Mackenzie Basin (1994), South Auckland (2000–03) and Wairarapa (2002).
Feeding: In Australia, Black Kites scavenge road-killed animals, other dead animals, offal and garbage, but also catch live prey such as young rabbits, birds, reptiles, frogs and large insects. They hunt by soaring, high-quartering and low, hedge-top quartering.

142. AUSTRALASIAN HARRIER *Circus approximans*   Plate 33

Other names: Kahu, Hawk, Swamp Harrier
Size: 55 cm; males 650 g, females 850 g
Distribution: Breed widely in southeastern New Guinea, Australia and the southern Pacific, including Vanuatu, New Caledonia, Fiji, Tonga, Wallis Island, French Polynesia (introduced), and in New Zealand. Vagrants have been recorded from Samoa and the Cook Islands. Harriers are widespread and common throughout open country on the New Zealand mainland, offshore islands and the Chathams. They visit the Kermadec Islands each winter and wander to The Snares, Auckland and Campbell Islands.

In New Zealand, Harriers are common in wetlands, farmland, high-country tussock-land, scrubland, along forest margins and riverbeds and around the coast. The only habitats they rarely use are large dense stands of native or exotic forest, and urban areas. Banding studies show much movement both north and south across Cook Strait, especially of young birds wandering in autumn and early winter. Adults also disperse from their

breeding home range in February–March and sometimes use a regular wintering area up to 100 km away each year.
Population: Widespread and very common, especially compared with the number of raptors seen in other parts of the world.
Conservation: Protected native. Harriers undoubtedly benefited from the conversion

of forest to farmland since European settlement and the introduction of small mammals (especially rabbits) and birds, which form the main part of their diet. For many years they were persecuted by some farmers for attacking young lambs and cast sheep, and sportsmen shot many because Harriers sometimes attack young gamebirds. During the 1930s and 1940s, bounties were paid by Acclimatisation Societies for hundreds of thousands of birds, but Harriers remained abundant. Since the 1950s, numbers have declined as rabbit control has removed a key part of their diet, but they remain common. They were protected in 1985.

Breeding: Males establish their territories in May–June, but females do not return until June–August. In June, some pairs start courtship soaring, and on warm calm days from late July to October pairs are often seen doing their spectacular 'sky dance' or courtship diving, a series of U-shaped dives accompanied by loud calls. In September–October, females start building the nest. It is a low platform of bracken, manuka, raupo and flax stalks, topped with rushes, cabbage-tree leaves and grass. It is sited on the ground in swamps, in wet patches covered in rushes, in bracken fern or rank grass in young pine plantations or on road verges, or in grain crops. Rarely, nests are built on a platform in a tree.

In September–December, they lay 2–**3**–**5**–7 off-white eggs (52 x 39 mm) at 48–72-hour intervals. Only the female incubates for 31–34 days, but the male feeds the female throughout. The eggs hatch over several days and some eggs are abandoned once a few chicks have hatched. Only the female feeds the chicks, but the male gathers food for the female and the chicks, and passes it to the female by dropping it as both birds fly close to the nest. When the chicks are older, both adults hunt, and when the female is away the male occasionally drops food at the nest but does not stay to feed them.

The chicks fledge at 43-46 days old, in December–February. They remain with their parents for a week after leaving the nest, but gradually venture further and finally disperse about 7 weeks after fledging. Yearling females

have been recorded breeding, but males probably do not start breeding until 2–3 years old. Pairs return to the same territory year after year, but occasionally a male will mate with two females. The oldest Harrier recorded in New Zealand lived over 18 years.

Behaviour: Strongly territorial in the breeding season but otherwise usually solitary. However, in winter they often have large (100+ birds) communal roosts in a secluded swamp, and they sometimes form loose flocks when dispersing long distance or when feeding at abundant sources such as at rabbit carcases after a poisoning operation. Harriers are silent outside the breeding season, except for an occasional whistle. During display flights, especially dives, they are very vocal, the male giving a repeated high-pitched 'kee-a', and the female a 'kee-o' response.

Feeding: Diet is varied, with both carrion and live prey eaten. The main carrion are sheep (especially in winter and spring), possums and hedgehogs (from roads), and waterfowl and other gamebirds (during the shooting season). Live prey is mainly small mammals (especially rabbits, hares, hedgehogs, rats and mice), small birds (introduced species and ducks and eggs), frogs, fish, lizards and large invertebrates such as grasshoppers and crickets (in summer and autumn).

Harriers hunt by day and usually search for prey by low slow-quartering followed by a dive attack or by briefly hovering and then dropping vertically. Harriers sometimes soar high, especially when searching for carrion, and they sometimes stoop like a falcon to flush small birds from a crop. Young birds often hunt insects on the ground with a series of pounces and snatches with the feet. Prey is caught by the sharp talons, not with the bill, which has a very weak bite, but the hooked tip is used to lever skin and flesh from the carcase.

In the hand: First-winter Harriers have brown eyes, dark brown plumage with an obvious white nape patch, and do not moult their flight feathers. In females, the eye colour changes to mid-brown in the second winter and yellow in later years; whereas in males yellow specks have appeared at 9 months of age and by the second year they have golden-yellow eyes, which in later years turn sulphur-yellow. As birds get older, their plumage gets paler, and so very old birds can appear almost grey. Females are larger than males, with little overlap in leg and bill measurements: the hind-claw length of females is 21.5–**24.5**–31 mm cf. 18–**21**–26.5 mm in males, and bill length (including cere) is 33–**36.5**–40.5 mm in females and 30–**33**–37 mm in males. Females are also heavier in all seasons, usually weighing over 800 g, whereas males rarely exceed 750 g, even with a full crop.

Reading: Baker-Gabb, D.J. 1979. *Notornis* 26: 325–329. Baker-Gabb, D.J. 1981. *Notornis* 28: 103–119. Baker-Gabb, D.J. 1981. *Notornis* 28: 241–254. Pierce, R.J. & Maloney, R.F. 1989. *Notornis* 36: 1–12. Robertson, H.A. 1980, *NZ J Zool* 7: 579–583.

143.   NEW ZEALAND FALCON   *Falco novaeseelandiae*   Plate 33

Other names: Karearea, Bush Hawk, Sparrow Hawk
Size: 45 cm; males 300 g, females 500 g
Geographical variation: Treated as one highly variable species, with three forms that differ in size, colour and habitats: the 'Bush Falcon' of forests of the North Island and the northwestern South Island, the 'Eastern Falcon' of the open country of the eastern South Island, and the 'Southern Falcon' of coastal Fiordland, Stewart Island and the Auckland Islands. The forms intergrade and show clinal variation with habitat rather than latitude.
Distribution: New Zealand only. They breed in native and exotic forest in the North Island, mainly south of a line from northern Taranaki to Whakatane (Bay of Plenty), although a few pairs breed in the Coromandel Range. In the South Island, they breed in dry tussockland and rough farmland in hills along the eastern side of the Southern Alps from Marlborough to Southland, and in forests of northwestern Nelson, the Southern Alps, West Coast and Fiordland. Rare on Stewart Island and its outliers. Well established on the Auckland Islands. Known from the Chathams from an egg collected before 1888 and from subfossil bones. Adults are quite sedentary, but juveniles wander widely in autumn and winter and account for most sighting of falcons on offshore islands, in farmland and orchards, and in towns and cities.
Population: Widespread but rare; in the 1970s there were c. 4000 pairs: 3150 pairs of Eastern Falcons, 650 pairs of Bush Falcons and 200 pairs of Southern Falcons.
Conservation: Protected threatened endemic. Falcons may have never been common in New Zealand, but the clearance of much lowland native forest has reduced their range, and selective logging of large podocarps has removed their preferred nesting sites. These changes are partly offset by the good hunting opportunities along forest edges created by roading or partial forest clearance and by the introduction of mammals (especially rabbits and hares) and of small birds (especially finches and Skylarks).

Although Falcons have been protected since 1970, they are sometimes shot by pigeon fanciers and poultry farmers when a young bird discovers an easy source of food. Falcons are likely to be illegally caught for falconry, an activity that is strictly controlled in New Zealand. Trained Falcons bred in captivity under permit have been used in experiments to scare birds from airfields and vineyards.
Breeding: Most established pairs remain on territory all year. In late winter and early spring, pairs are often seen together doing aerial displays, including food passes and aerobatics. The nest is a simple scrape on a sheltered cliff ledge, on a slip face, under a rock overhang or a fallen log, or high in a tree in a clump of *Astelia*. Laying is in September–December. They lay 2–**3**–4 eggs (49 x 37 mm, 47 g), which are buff to rich reddish brown with chocolate blotches. Incubation is shared in shifts of 1–4 hours and takes c. 30 days.

The chicks are mainly brooded by the female for the first 10–14 days and are fed by the female only. However, the male gathers most of the food for the female and the chicks and passes the food to the female by dropping it as both birds fly close to the nest. When the chicks are c. 2 weeks old, the female starts hunting too. Male chicks fledge at c. 32 days, but females stay until c. 35 days old. They retain some natal down until about 6 weeks old. Their parents continue to feed them with aerial food passes (drops or talon-to-talon transfers) and at perches for over a month, but chicks start hunting when about 7 weeks old and most are independent 2 months after fledging. They soon disperse widely. Although some attempt breeding at 1 year old, most do not start until they are 2 years old. **Behaviour:** Falcons are fiercely territorial in the breeding season and make repeated dive attacks on people near the nest; this is often the first sign that a pair has established a territory in an area. This attack is accompanied by a characteristic 'kek-kek-kek-' call, which is also the main call heard from both sexes outside the breeding season.

Feeding: Falcons are fierce and fearless predators of live prey, especially small birds (finches, Skylarks, Blackbirds and Song Thrushes), small mammals (young rabbits and hares) and large insects (grasshoppers and beetles). They take some large birds, including New Zealand and Feral Pigeons, Magpies and even White-faced Herons and Black-backed Gulls. They usually wait on a perch until they see the quarry and then directly attack, or sometimes head off in another direction to gain height before turning to dive from behind. Some attacks are mounted by the Falcon flying swiftly around a tree or a corner of forest or a building to startle a feeding flock, and then selecting and attacking one bird. They catch prey by the sharp talons, not the bill, but kill large prey by biting the back of the neck. Rarely feed on carrion.

In the hand: Juveniles are like adults, except the upperparts of juveniles are uniformly coloured rather than having pale feather-tips, and they lack barring on the flanks. Females are much larger than males, and wing measurements of adults do not overlap, despite marked differences in size between the various forms: females 268–308 mm cf. males 226–267 mm. Bush Falcons are smallest, e.g. wing averages 273 mm in females and 236 mm in males cf. 281 mm and 248 mm respectively for Southern Falcons and 297 mm and 255 mm in Eastern Falcons.

Reading: Fox, N.C. 1978. *Notornis* 25: 203–212. Fox, N.C. 1978. *Notornis* 25: 317–331. Fox, N.C. 1988. *Notornis* 35: 270–272. Lawrence, S.B. & Gay, C.G. 1991. *Notornis* 38: 173–182.

144. NANKEEN KESTREL *Falco cenchroides* Plate 33

Other name: Australian Kestrel
Size: Males 32 cm, 160 g; females 34 cm, 180 g
Geographical variation: Two subspecies; *cenchroides* in Australia and Lord Howe and Norfolk Island and a vagrant to New Zealand, *baru* in New Guinea.
Distribution: Widespread and common on mainland Australia but scarce in Tasmania. They are mainly sedentary, but occasionally inland droughts force them to move northwards or towards the coast. They colonised Lord Howe Island in the 1940s and Norfolk Island in 1969. Frequent vagrants appear anywhere in New Zealand, especially in the autumn and early winter. The numerous records since 1889 include small irruptions in 1969 and 1990 when birds were seen widely in both North and South Islands. There is no firm evidence that they have bred in New Zealand, despite conditions being suitable for them judging from repeated sightings of two birds near Te Mata Peak, Hawke's Bay, for over five years from the late 1980s.
Feeding: Kestrels have an unmistakable hunting method of hovering, poised in mid-air with head facing into the wind and tail depressed according to the strength of the wind. They drop by stages before plunging to the ground to seize prey in their talons. Small birds are sometimes taken on the wing. Kestrels are typically in open country, sometimes riding the updraughts around hilltops or sand dunes as they search short grass for mice, small birds, lizards and large insects.

Reading: Edgar, A.T. & Grant, P. 1969. *Notornis* 16: 288–298. Powell, W.J. 1978. *Notornis* 25: 94–95.

145. BLACK FALCON *Falco subniger* Plate 33

Size: Males 50 cm, 600 g; females 54 cm, 800 g
Distribution: A rare species endemic to Australia. They breed inland and occasionally near the coast of southern Australia, but droughts occasionally force birds into coastal areas and cause small eruptions east of the Great Dividing Range. Following an eruption in 1982–83, a probable juvenile male reached Gisborne (November 1983).

Feeding: Black Falcons often glide on slightly drooped wings but can accelerate to very swift flight when chasing small birds, their main prey. Small food items are eaten on the wing or at a perch, rarely on the ground.

Reading: Blackburn, A. 1984. *Notornis* 31: 6.

GAMEBIRDS Phasianidae

213 species worldwide. The only native member of this family, the endemic New Zealand Quail *Coturnix novaezelandiae*, became extinct about 1875.

Some 20 species of gamebirds have been introduced to New Zealand, but about half have failed to establish. All were introduced for domestic or hunting purposes, often with great persistence and at great cost. Some are still supplemented yearly by captive-reared stock raised by Fish and Game Councils (the former acclimatisation societies), paid for from hunters' licence fees.

Most species favour farmland, swamp margins and open ground with plenty of coarse grass or scrub for cover. They feed on the ground and are omnivorous – grain, other seeds, berries, roots, together with whatever invertebrates are revealed as they scratch and dig at the ground surface with stout legs and strong claws and bill. Most roost in trees.

The sexes often differ; females and immatures have subdued plumage that blends with the surroundings, males are often brightly coloured in the larger species or strongly patterned but cryptic in the smaller ones. Many species are polygamous, the male having a harem of females in the breeding period. Their nest is a shallow hollow scraped in the ground with little or no lining. Clutches are large, but, although most eggs hatch, few chicks reach independence. The chicks leave the nest soon after hatching and feed themselves, attended by the adults. Most young can fly within two or three weeks of hatching.

Reading: Delacour, J. 1977. *The Pheasants of the World*. Hindhead, UK: Spur Publications.
Johnsgard, P.A. 1988. *The Quails, Partridges and Francolins of the World*. Oxford: OUP.

146. CALIFORNIA QUAIL *Callipepla californica* Plate 35

Size: 25 cm, 180 g
Geographical variation: Of the seven subspecies in western North America, New Zealand birds seem most like *brunnescens*, perhaps hybridised with *californicus*.
Distribution: Natural range is western North America from southern British Columbia to Baja California, and within this range *brunnescens* is found in southwestern Oregon and California. They were introduced to both main islands of New Zealand in the 1860s and 1870s, with later releases of New Zealand-bred stock. Now widely distributed in both main islands, but rare on the West Coast; a few are on the Chatham Islands.

California Quail are found mainly in areas with a mix of open country and low scrub, particularly tussock grassland or rough pasture associated with manuka scrub and, in the South Island, with such dry-country plants as wild Irishman, gorse, broom and briar. They also frequent vegetated riverbeds and riverbed margins.

Population: Common in certain less intensively developed districts of both main islands.

Breeding: Coveys break up in late winter and pairing begins in late August. Eggs are laid from late September to February, with a peak in early November in Otago but in early December in the central North Island. The nest is commonly in long grass near thick cover of blackberry, gorse or bracken. The female lays 8–**13**–22 creamy-white eggs (31 x 24 mm), spotted dark and yellowish brown. Eggs are laid daily. The female incubates for 22–**23** days. The young first breed when about 1 year old. The oldest California Quail recorded in New Zealand lived over 11 years.

Behaviour: In autumn and winter, family groups combine to form large roosting coveys. By day they break into smaller coveys that disperse to their preferred feeding grounds nearby.

Feeding: In their first weeks, chicks eat mainly small insects, but they soon adopt the adult diet of fallen seeds of a wide variety of plants, supplemented with leaves of clover and grasses and a few small insects. In late winter and spring, however, vegetation becomes the dominant food. They feed mostly in the early morning and in the last couple of hours before dusk.

Reading: Gurr, L. 1951. *Notornis* 4: 144–145. Leopold, A.S. 1977. *The California Quail.* Berkeley: Univ California Press. Williams, G.R. 1952. *J Wildl Management* 16: 460–483. Williams, G.R. 1967. *Proc NZ Ecol Soc* 14: 88–99.

147. BOBWHITE QUAIL *Colinus virginianus* Plate 35

Other name: Virginian Quail
Size: 23 cm, 180 g
Distribution: Natural range is eastern North America, Mexico, Central America and Cuba. Introductions of 1000+ birds to New Zealand from 1898 to 1902 were mostly unsuccessful. They did not thrive, and few pockets, if any, survive. They were most recently recorded in South Auckland and near Wairoa in the 1950s, and at Lake Waikaremoana in the early 1970s.

Breeding: Little is known in New Zealand. The nest is a shallow hollow hidden in thick vegetation. The female lays 7–28 white eggs and the incubation period is c. 23 days.

Reading: Gurr, L. 1953. *Notornis* 5: 164. Westerskov, K. 1957. *Notornis* 7: 95–98.

148. RED-LEGGED PARTRIDGE *Alectoris rufa* Plate 35

Size: 31 cm
Distribution: Natural range is western Europe, Corsica and the Canary Islands. Despite failed introductions into New Zealand in the late 1800s, a programme to establish them has been in progress since 1984, using eggs imported from Britain from 1980 onwards. Birds have been released between the Kaipara Harbour and Taumarunui, in the Bay of Plenty, Gisborne, Hawke's Bay, in the Upper Moutere Valley near Nelson, and in Marlborough and Canterbury. It seems that most releases have been unsuccessful, but in some districts is too early to know whether they will become permanently established.

149. CHUKOR *Alectoris chukar* Plate 35

Other name: Chukar
Size: 31 cm, males 600 g, females 500 g
Geographical variation: The many subspecies described may be only clinal. Two forms were introduced to New Zealand in the 1920s and 1930s, mostly *chukar* of India, but once (into Marlborough) *koroviakovi* of Iran. Although the resulting birds are presumably

hybrids, they look like *chukar*.
Distribution: Natural range is from south-eastern Europe and Turkey east through central Asia, including the Himalayas, to Mongolia and China. They are well established on the dry, rocky country east of the Southern Alps from Marlborough (Nelson Lakes National Park, Wairau River, Seaward Kaikoura Range) to Central Otago (especially between Lakes Coleridge and Wakatipu). North Island liberations, as recently as 1987, have been largely unsuccessful, although a few persist near Tauranga and in Hawke's Bay.
Breeding: Eggs are laid in September–January. The nest is a scrape on the rocky ground under a sheltering tussock. The female lays 8–**13**–

18 cream eggs (43 x 31 mm), flecked reddish brown. Eggs are laid daily. The female incubates for c. 24 days. The oldest Chukor recorded in New Zealand lived over 12 years.
Behaviour: After breeding, the family group remains together as a covey of 5–10 birds, but in winter these groups coalesce to form large coveys of 50–150 birds.
Feeding: Diet is mainly seeds, shoots and leaves of grasses and other ground plants such as thistles, clovers and briars; also some insects, found by scratching at and gleaning from the ground.

Reading: Marples, B.J. & Gurr, L. 1953. *Emu* 53: 283–291. Williams, G.R. 1951. *Notornis* 4: 151–157.

150. GREY PARTRIDGE   *Perdix perdix*   Plate 35

Size: 30 cm, 500 g
Distribution: Natural range is Britain and Europe from southern Sweden to France, Italy, Macedonia and eastern Russia. They were widely liberated in New Zealand without success from the 1860s to 1909. More recently (1959–70), a further 28,000 birds, from Danish stock, were liberated in both North and South Islands. Again, this was apparently also with limited success, although a few birds persisted in Southland until recently.

Breeding: The nest is a shallow scrape on the ground in thick short cover, such as on fallow land and hay crops. The female lays 10–**16**–20 olive-brown eggs and alone incubates for c. 24 days. The oldest Grey Partridge recorded in New Zealand lived over 10 years.

Reading: Westerskov, K.E. 1990. pp 47-62 in *Proc Perdix V: Grey Partridge and Ring-necked Pheasant Workshop*.

151. BROWN QUAIL   *Synoicus ypsilophorus*   Plate 35

Size: 18 cm, 100 g
Geographical variation: About 10 subspecies have been described, two of which, *australis* from mainland Australia and *ypsilophorus* from Tasmania, were introduced to New Zealand.
Distribution: Natural range is southern Indonesia, New Guinea, and Australia, including Tasmania. They were introduced widely in the North and South Islands in the 1860s and 1870s, but now survive only in the North Island. They are common in Northland and many of its offshore islands, and also on some of the developed islands in the Bay of Plenty. Moderately common in the Waikato

and the Bay of Plenty, but scarce south of a line from Kawhia to Lake Taupo to northern Hawke's Bay. They are mainly seen along the dusty edges of country roads, on rough swamp margins and along the edges of salt marshes, as well as in the usual scrub and open rough grassland well supplied with cover.
Population: Common only in Northland and on some Northland and Bay of Plenty offshore islands.
Breeding: Eggs are laid in September–January. The nest is a slight depression lined with grass and leaves, under thick vegetation such as roadside verges and bracken. The female lays

7–12 white eggs (28 x 23 mm), freckled all over with brown. The female alone incubates for c. 21 days.

Behaviour: Brown Quail form small coveys of 5–10 birds when not breeding.

Feeding: Diet is mainly fallen seeds from a wide variety of grasses, weeds and shrubs, but supplemented with vegetation, flowers and insects.

152. PHEASANT *Phasianus colchicus* Plate 34

Other names: Common Pheasant, Ring-necked Pheasant

Size: Males 80 cm, 1400 g; females 60 cm, 1200 g

Geographical variation: New Zealand stock is derived from several subspecies, although most birds resemble the Ring-necked Pheasant from China, *torquatus*, especially in having a broad white neck-ring.

Distribution: Natural range is from Turkey east through central Asia to China. They have been repeatedly introduced to New Zealand from 1842 onwards, and local birds are still reinforced by releases of New Zealand-bred stock. In the North Island, they are most common in the northern and western districts; scattered elsewhere. In the South Island, they are sparse with small numbers in Nelson, Canterbury and Otago.

Population: c. 250,000. Up to 50,000 cocks are shot each year and numbers are reinforced in many districts by captive-reared birds.

Breeding: The New Zealand season is extended, and nests with eggs have been found from late July to late March; most eggs, however, are laid in October–December. The nest is a hollow scantily lined with vegetation and usually in thick cover such as hayfields, under blackberry or bracken, roadside verges, rough pasture, and crops. The female lays 7–**9**–15 olive-brown eggs (46 x 36 mm) and incubates for 23–24 days. The oldest wild Pheasant recorded in New Zealand lived over 15 years.

Feeding: In their first weeks, chicks eat mainly small insects but gradually adopt the adult diet of green-leaf material, seeds, grain, berries and larger insects.

Reading: Barker, R.J. 1991. *Notornis* 38: 125–130.

153. PEAFOWL *Pavo cristatus* Plate 34

Other name: Indian Peafowl

Size: 90 cm plus male's 1 m tail; males 4.5 kg, females 3.5 kg

Distribution: Natural range is India and Sri Lanka. They are now very widely distributed as ornamental species for parks and private gardens. They were brought to New Zealand in the 1840s and have become truly feral in rough, mainly hill-country, farmland in many warmer and drier North Island localities and in northwestern Nelson and the West Coast. When feral, they become shy and wary.

Breeding: Peahens lay 4–6 pale cream to warm buff eggs (69 x 51 mm) and incubate for 28 days.

154. WILD TURKEY *Meliagris gallopavo* Plate 34

Size: Males 120 cm, 8 kg; females 90 cm, 4 kg

Distribution: Natural range is North America, from northeastern and central USA to Mexico. They were first introduced to New Zealand about 1890 and have become common on farms as domestic birds. Some have become truly feral on rough farmland in many North Island and a few South Island localities, as well as on Moturoa Island in the Bay of Plenty.

Feeding: Diet is mainly leaves of clover, grasses and weeds, supplemented with a few large insects.

Reading: Schemnitz, S.D. 1992. *Notornis* 39: 126–129.

155.   TUFTED GUINEAFOWL   *Numida meleagris*   Plate 34

Other name: Helmeted Guineafowl
Size: 60 cm, 1.5 kg
Distribution: Natural range is Africa south of the Sahara Desert. They have been widely introduced to farms and aviaries, and have become feral in rough farmland in parts of Northland, Waikato, Rotorua and Wanganui.
Behaviour: Noisy and gregarious, but wary.

RAILS, GALLINULES and COOTS   Rallidae

About 140 species, of which 8 breed in New Zealand. Midden evidence shows that 8 other endemic species became extinct between the arrival of Maori, and European settlement, and the Chatham Island Rail *Rallus modestus* became extinct in about 1900. Two other species are vagrants to New Zealand, and a Corncrake *Crex crex* was reputedly killed near Nelson in 1865, but this record has not been officially accepted.

The rails are mainly aquatic birds, all capable of swimming well. In New Zealand, they range in size from the small Marsh Crake to the large flightless Takahe. Apart from the Pukeko and Weka, rails and crakes are secretive birds, usually skulking in freshwater swamps, and estuarine mangroves and reedbeds. On some mammal-free islands, however, they live on the forest floor. Rails have slim bodies that help them move through dense vegetation, moderately long powerful legs with long unwebbed toes that help them walk in wetlands, a short tail, which is flicked up and down as they walk or swim, and short broad wings. Apart from the flightless Weka and Takahe, rails have low, laboured flight by day, but at night they fly higher and show good ability to colonise isolated islands. Island forms tend to become flightless.

The two species of gallinule breeding in New Zealand, the Takahe and the Pukeko, are believed to represent two invasions from Australia of the cosmopolitan Purple Swamphen *Porphyrio porphyrio*; the Takahe arrived several million years ago, and the Pukeko much more recently. Typical of ancient New Zealand birds, the Takahe has become larger and flightless.

The gallinules and coots have a bony frontal shield extending from the bill to cover the forehead. The legs of coots are quite short, and the toes have lobes of skin that help them swim.

Most species nest solitarily, but Pukeko form groups and several females can lay in the same nest. The cup-shaped nest is generally well concealed in dense swamp vegetation or among *Carex* clumps; however, coots construct an exposed floating platform attached to raupo or rushes. The downy young are capable of walking, running and swimming within days of hatching.

Reading: Ripley, S.D. 1977. *Rails of the World*. Toronto: M.F. Feheley.

156.   BANDED RAIL   *Rallus philippensis*   Plate 36

Other names: Moho-pereru, Buff-banded Rail
Size: 30 cm, 170 g
Geographical variation: Up to 15 subspecies are recognised. The subspecies *assimilis* is the form breeding on the New Zealand mainland, and *dieffenbachii* was endemic to the Chathams but only one specimen was collected in 1840 before it was exterminated in the mid-1800s.
Distribution: Breed in the South Pacific from Indonesia and the Philippines through Melanesia, Australia and New Zealand to as far east as Niue in western Polynesia. In New Zealand, Banded Rails were formerly common throughout the main islands but had

declined by the 1930s owing to habitat loss and the introduction of mammalian predators.

They are now found mainly in mangrove forests, saltmarshes and rush-covered (not raupo-covered) freshwater wetlands in Northland (including the Three Kings, Poor Knights and Great Barrier Islands), around Auckland, the Waikato, Coromandel Peninsula and Bay of Plenty. They are rarely recorded south of a line from northern Taranaki to Opotiki, except for breeding reported from Mahia. Some are probably overlooked in inland swamps such as those around Lake Wairarapa, where, after 60 years without sightings, one was killed by a cat in 1992. In the South Island, they are now largely confined to unmodified saltmarshes of the northern coast in Whanganui Inlet, Golden Bay, Tasman Bay and at the head of the Pelorus and Queen Charlotte Sounds in the Marlborough Sounds. Banded Rails are occasionally recorded from Stewart Island and are still in moderate numbers on some of the Weka-free islands off the coast and on Little Solander Island.

Population: Locally common near the coast of the northern North Island. The northern South Island population was c. 100 breeding pairs in the early 1980s.

Conservation: Protected native, decreasing through habitat modification with reclamation of estuaries and mangrove swamps, and disturbance and predation by introduced mammals, especially mustelids.

Breeding: Pairs remain on their territories all year. Most eggs are laid in September–December, but clutches have been recorded as late as March, and dependent chicks have been seen in April. They probably lay several clutches each season, comprising 3-**5-6** buff or pale pinkish eggs (40 x 29 mm, 16 g), marked with dark reddish-brown and purplish-grey spots and blotches. The cup-shaped nest is well hidden in thick grass or rushes. The pair incubates for 19–25 days. The chicks, which are initially covered in black down but change to dark brown by a week old, are led from the nest within 24 hours and are accompanied by both parents throughout the c. 60 days to fledging.

Behaviour: Pairs remain together on territory year after year but often only emerge into the open at dawn and dusk or in heavy rain. Sometimes a family party emerges to forage in a secluded creek or ditch, especially on a falling tide, when there are young chicks to be fed. The best way to see Banded Rails is to play tapes of their calls, especially their high-pitched 'quee-quee-' or creaky 'swit-swit-' calls often heard at dusk.

Feeding: Diet is mainly snails (*Potamopyrgus estuarinus*, *Ophicardelus costellaris* and *Amphibola crenata*), crabs, spiders, beetles and worms. They also take seeds, fruits and succulent leaves. Most feeding is in the morning and evening and straight after high tide when crabs are most active and the tide has dislodged snails.

Reading: Elliott, G.P. 1987. *NZ J Ecol* 10: 109–115. Elliott, G.P. 1989. *Notornis* 36: 117–123. Schodde, R. & de Naurois, R. 1982. *Notornis* 29: 131–141.

157. AUCKLAND ISLAND RAIL *Rallus pectoralis* Plate 36

Other name: Lewin's Rail (Australia)
Size: 21 cm, 90 g
Geographical variation: The Auckland Island Rail (*muelleri*) is a subspecies of the Lewin's Rail, a variable species split into about ten subspecies ranging from the Philippines, through eastern Indonesia, New Guinea and Australia to the Auckland Islands.
Distribution: Known only on Adams and Disappointment Islands in the Auckland Islands. On Adams Island, they are wide-spread in habitats with a dense canopy about a metre above ground but with open runways beneath. They are found throughout the tussock and herbfields on Disappointment Island.
Population: Locally common on Adams Island, with an estimated population of c. 1500 birds. Common on Disappointment Island, with several hundred birds.
Conservation: Protected threatened native. Auckland Island Rails were first collected in

the late 1800s but were not seen again until one was caught on Adams Island in 1966 and taken to Mt Bruce Wildlife Reserve. In 1989, they were found to be moderately common on Adams Island, once their habitat preferences were known. Another healthy population was discovered on Disappointment Island in 1993. With two populations, the subspecies is probably safe as long as rats are not accidentally introduced to these islands.

Breeding: Little is known. Two nests were found in November 1989, and at the same time young chicks were heard squeaking. Eggs are therefore laid in October–November. The only clutch recorded was of **2** cream eggs (35.1 x 26.5 mm, 12 g; 32.8 x 24.2 mm, 8.5 g), marked with brown, red-brown and pale grey spots and blotches concentrated at the blunt end. The cup-shaped nests were well hidden among tussock and sedge. Incubation and fledging periods are unknown. An immature bird caught in the wild lived 9 years in captivity at Mt Bruce.

Behaviour: Little known, as birds are shy and cryptic, and live under dense vegetation. In summer, they are active from just before sunrise to just after sunset, and although they do not call at night, they may remain active. The usual distinctive call is a loud, descending 'crek', repeated about 10 times at one-second intervals. The second call is a loud, sharp, whistle-like note, repeated about 50 times in about 12 seconds. They also make a variety of grunts and clicks, and chicks squeak. They respond to their taped calls.

Feeding: Unknown, but presumably the diet is invertebrates such as snails, worms and insects.

Reading: Elliott, G.P. *et al.* 1991. *Notornis* 38: 199–209. Falla, R.A. 1967. *Notornis* 14: 107–113.

158. WEKA *Gallirallus australis* Plate 36

Other name: Woodhen
Size: 53 cm; males 1000 g, females 700 g
Geographical variation: Four subspecies: the North Island Weka *greyi* breeds in the North Island, the Western Weka *australis* breeds in the northern and western South Island, the Buff Weka *hectori* was introduced to the Chatham Islands before it died out from the eastern South Island, and the Stewart Island Weka *scotti* is largely confined to the islands around Stewart Island.

Distribution: Formerly bred throughout the mainland of New Zealand, but in the 1920s and 1930s disappeared from most of the North Island, where they are now confined mainly to the Opotiki district, although they have been successfully introduced to the Bay of Islands, Kawau, Rakitu and Mokoia Islands.

In the South Island, Western Weka remain locally common in the Marlborough Sounds, Golden Bay and northwestern Nelson, northern Westland south to about Hokitika, and on some Fiordland islands; uncommon in Tasman Bay, from Hokitika to Fiordland and inland Southland. They have been introduced to D'Urville and smaller islands in the Marlborough Sounds, and to Kapiti Island.

Buff Weka became extinct in the eastern South Island by the late 1920s, but they had been introduced to the Chathams, where they thrived and have become very common throughout Chatham and Pitt Islands. They have been introduced to Banks Peninsula and Stevensons Island in Lake Wanaka.

Stewart Island Weka are scarce on Stewart Island but have been introduced to many of the nearby islands and to Macquarie Island, where they have since been eradicated. The origin of Weka introduced to several islands (e.g. Solander and Open Bay) has not been established.

Conservation: Protected threatened endemic, except on the Chatham Islands, where a legal harvest is permitted. Maori and early European settlers used Weka for food, oil and feathers, and carried them to many offshore islands. Weka declined dramatically between 1900 and 1940, and became extinct in most of the North Island and disappeared from the eastern South Island. The causes of the rapid decline are not clear, but habitat changes during the conversion of forest and scrubland to farmland, the use of poison baits and the introduction of mammalian predators such as cats, dogs and mustelids may have contributed.

With the exception of a reintroduction to the Bay of Islands, the many attempts to reintroduce Weka back into their former range on the mainland have been unsuccessful, despite some birds persisting and even breeding for a few years. Populations undergo major fluctuations and some become locally extinct for several years before reinvasion and becoming common again. These declines are often attributed to disease, but there is no supporting evidence and it seems more likely that they are due to widespread breeding failure and adult mortality during periods when food is scarce.

The North Island Weka is regarded as threatened because of its very restricted and declining distribution, and because of its failure to re-establish in apparently suitable habitat elsewhere. The Royal Forest and Bird Protection Society and Otorohanga Kiwi House have a successful captive breeding programme aimed at release into suitable North Island habitats. The other subspecies are more secure but remain at risk until the causes of the rapid declines are better understood.

Breeding: Pairs remain on territory or in fixed home ranges all year. The breeding season is highly variable and depends on local weather patterns, food availability and population size. Weka can breed all year if conditions are suitable, and can raise up to four broods in a year. The nest is a bowl of grasses, sedges, rushes and cabbage-tree leaves, lined with finer grasses, feathers, moss or wool. It is on the ground at the hollow base of a tree, in a short burrow, under or inside fallen logs, or in a dry site under tussock, sedges or fern. They lay mostly in August–January, 1–**2**–**3**–6 creamy white or pinkish eggs (58 x 41 mm) about 2–3 days apart.

Both sexes incubate, the female for most of the day, the male from late afternoon to early morning. They incubate for 26–28 days from after the last egg is laid; the chicks hatch over several days and leave the nest at 2–3 days old when still covered in dark brown down. Both adults brood the chicks during cold weather in the first week and feed the chicks until they are nearly fully grown at 6–10 weeks old. The young disperse at 3–4 months old and can breed at 5 months old. The oldest Weka recorded in the wild lived over 15 years.

Behaviour: Adult Weka stay on their territory or home range all year, but juveniles disperse from their natal area. Although Weka are flightless, they can swim across a kilometre or more of river, lake or sea. Weka are usually shy and retiring, and are seen only fleetingly as they run from one patch of cover to another, but some birds, especially those on islands or living around tramping huts, become very bold and readily take food from the hand.

Weka are more often heard than seen. Their main call is a shrill, far-carrying, double-note 'coo-eet', normally heard at dusk and in the early evening. Often when one Weka starts calling, others respond and the hills come alive with calls. Other calls include soft, deep, resonant booming and high-pitched peeping from young begging for food.

Feeding: Diet is mainly invertebrates and fruit, but they take seeds, small vertebrates and carrion. The main invertebrates are worms, beetles, orthopteran larvae, snails, amphipods and isopods found in leaf litter, in long grass or along the tideline. They feed by flicking the litter aside with their bill (surprisingly, not with their feet). They can sometimes become serious pests by feeding on newly sown crops, and come into conflict with conservation programmes by killing invertebrates, reptiles and seabirds, and eating eggs of seabirds and other ground-nesting birds.

Reading: Beauchamp, A.J. 1987. *Notornis* 34: 317–325. Beauchamp, A.J. 1988. *Notornis* 35: 282–284. Beauchamp, A.J. *et al.* 1993. *Notornis* 40: 309–312. Carroll, A.L.K. 1963. *Notornis* 10: 281–300. Coleman, J.D. *et al.* 1983. *Notornis* 30: 93–107.

159. SPOTLESS CRAKE *Porzana tabuensis* Plate 36

Other names: Puweto, Putoto, Sooty Rail
Size: 20 cm, 45 g
Geographical variation: The subspecies *plumbea* of Australia and New Zealand is doubtfully distinct from the nominate *tabuensis* of the Philippines, Moluccas, New Guinea, Micronesia, Melanesia and south-western Polynesia.
Distribution: Widely distributed in Australasia and the South Pacific from the Philippines and Micronesia east to the Marquesas Islands of French Polynesia. Within New Zealand, they are in raupo- and sedge-dominated swamps throughout the North Island, but are sparsely distributed in raupo swamps and reedbeds in the South Island and on Stewart Island. They are seldom in flax-dominated wetlands. Spotless Crakes are common on some offshore islands such as the Three Kings, Motukawanui, Poor Knights, Tiritiri Matangi and Great Barrier Islands. They are also on small islands in the Kermadecs, and on Chatham Island.

Spotless Crakes are secretive and rarely seen; many records are of cat-killed birds being brought to houses, or by duck-shooters who have seen crakes lurking near their maimai. They are apparently quite mobile, probably flying at night, judging by occasional records of birds found in towns, far from their usual habitats, and their widespread distribution around New Zealand and in the Pacific. In the Waikato, a bird released 25 km from its banding site had returned within 6 weeks.
Population: Locally common on mammal-free offshore islands such as the Meyer Islets in the Kermadecs, the Poor Knights Islands, and in many raupo and sedge swamps in the northern North Island and in the Manawatu/Horowhenua dune lakes.
Conservation: Protected native. The drainage of many lowland wetlands and introduced mammalian predators have undoubtedly had a major impact on Spotless Crakes, but because of their very secretive nature, they are probably more common than the number of records suggest.

Breeding: Pairs remain on territory all year. They lay from late August to January, mostly September–October, 2–**3**–**4**–5 pinkish cream eggs (30 x 22 mm, 9 g) in a bulky, cup-shaped nest loosely woven out of grass and sedge. In swamps, the nest site is usually raised 30–50 cm above the water level beside the pedestal of a *Carex*, and often under a canopy of dead *Carex* tillers and an overstorey of tall raupo, willow, manuka or cabbage trees to protect the nest from the elements. On islands, they nest on the ground, under dense cover. Clutch size and egg size increases through the season. Both sexes incubate for 20–22 days. The chicks, which are initially covered with black down, leave the nest within 2 days and are looked after by both parents during the 4–5 months until they reach adult size.
Behaviour: Little is known, as the birds are shy and cryptic, and live in dense vegetation. Spotless Crakes are more often heard than seen, and usually they are found by playing their taped calls in suitable habitat. They have a wide variety of calls; those usually heard from swamps are sharp 'pit-pit' calls, a single or repeated 'book' and a distinctive rolling 'purrrrrrrr' call like an alarm clock going off and gradually running down. Most unsolicited calls are heard at dawn and dusk, when the birds are probably most active.
Feeding: Diet is a mixture of invertebrates such as worms, spiders, beetles, snails and insect larvae, and seeds of aquatic plants or fallen fruits. In swamps, they rarely come into the open but sometimes feed on muddy margins or in channels through raupo; however, on predator-free islands they readily feed in leaf litter on the forest floor by day.

In the hand: From a small sample (n = 12), it appears that male Spotless Crakes have longer bills than females (18–21 mm [8] cf. 16–17.5 mm [4]).

Reading: Hadden, D. 1970. *Notornis* 17: 200–213. Kaufmann, G. 1987. *Notornis* 34: 207–216. Kaufmann, G. & Lavers, R. 1987. *Notornis* 34: 193–205. O'Donnell, C.F.J. 1994. *Notornis* 41: 211–213. Onley, D. 1982. *Notornis* 29: 9–21.

160. MARSH CRAKE *Porzana pusilla* Plate 36

Other names: Koitareke, Ballion's Crake
Size: 18 cm, 40 g
Geographical variation: Five subspecies; three in Africa, Europe and Asia to Irian Jaya, *palustris* in Papua New Guinea, Australia and Tasmania, and *affinis* in New Zealand.
Distribution: Breed throughout the Old World from Africa and Europe across Asia to Australasia. In New Zealand, they are scattered sparsely in raupo swamps of the North, South and Stewart Islands, but are also in saltmarsh habitats and high-altitude wetlands of the South Island. They were in the Chatham Islands in the early 1900s, but none has been seen recently.

Marsh Crakes are secretive and rarely seen, many records are of cat-killed birds being brought to houses, or from duck-shooters who have seen crakes lurking near their maimai. They are apparently quite mobile, probably flying at night, judging from occasional records of birds found at lighthouses or in towns, far from their usual habitats.
Population: Locally common in some salt-marsh habitats, such as on the southern side of Farewell Spit, and generally more common than Spotless Crakes in the South Island.
Conservation: Protected native. The drainage of many lowland wetlands and introduced mammalian predators have undoubtedly had a major impact on Marsh Crakes, but because of their very secretive nature, they are probably more common than the number of records suggest.

Breeding: Little information is available from New Zealand, as few nests have been found. Pairs apparently remain on territory all year. They lay in October–December, 5–6–7 olive-brown eggs (28 x 20 mm) in a shallow dished platform made of short lengths of rushes or sedge. The nest is usually 30–40 cm above the water beside the pedestal of a *Carex* and with a hood of dead *Carex* tillers to protect the nest from the elements. Unlike the Spotless Crake, nests are generally not in dense raupo stands. Both sexes incubate for 16–20 days. The chicks are initially covered with black down and have yellow bills.
Behaviour: Little is known, as Marsh Crakes are extremely shy and cryptic, and live in dense vegetation. By day, they are more silent than Spotless Crakes and seldom respond to taped calls; however, they occasionally respond aggressively to taped calls of Spotless Crakes. At dusk and at night, they have a variety of calls, that most often heard being a harsh trill 'krek', like the sound of a fingernail being drawn along a comb.
Feeding: Diet is a mixture of invertebrates and seeds of aquatic plants. In swamps, they rarely come into the open, but sometimes feed on muddy margins of swamps or in tidal runnels in saltmarshes.

Reading: Barlow, M. & Sutton, R.R. 1975. *Notornis* 22: 178–180. Elliott, G. 1989. *Notornis* 36: 117–123. Kaufmann, G. 1987. *Notornis* 34: 207–216. Kaufmann, G. & Lavers, R. 1987. *Notornis* 34: 193–205.

161. BLACK-TAILED NATIVE-HEN *Gallinula ventralis* Plate 37

Size: 35 cm, 400 g
Distribution: Breed only in Australia. They are widespread and highly nomadic, moving inland to breed following heavy rain and dispersing back towards the coast in drier spells. They are vagrants to New Zealand, with at least five records: Colac Bay, South-land (June 1923); Tukituki River, Hawke's Bay (May 1957 to mid-1958); Karamea (August–November 1984), lower Waikato (May 1986) and Lake Hood, Ashburton (August 2002).

Reading: Brathwaite, D.H. 1963. *Notornis* 10: 228–233.

162.   DUSKY MOORHEN   *Gallinula tenebrosa*   Plate 37

Size: 37 cm, 500 g
Distribution: Breed in southern Western Australia, in the eastern states of Australia (excluding Tasmania) and in New Guinea. They are moderately nomadic, with some heading inland to breed following heavy rains. A single vagrant has been recorded in New Zealand, at Lake Hayes, near Arrowtown (August–October 1968).
Reading: Barlow, M.L. 1969. *Notornis* 16: 81–84.

163.   PUKEKO   *Porphyrio porphyrio*   Plate 37

Other names: Purple Gallinule, Purple Swamphen
Size: 51 cm; males 1050 g, females 850 g
Geographical variation: About 15 subspecies have been described. The form *melanotus* breeds in northern and eastern Australia, Tasmania and New Zealand, including the Kermadec and Chatham Islands.
Distribution: The range of the Pukeko, or Purple Gallinule/Swamphen as it is known overseas, includes southern Europe, Africa, India, Southeast Asia, New Guinea, Melanesia, western Polynesia, Australia and New Zealand. It is found throughout the North, South and Stewart Islands and many of their offshore islands, including Great Barrier, Great Mercury, Waiheke and Kapiti Islands, and on the Chatham Islands. A few are in the Denham Bay swamp and the Blue Lake on Raoul Island, Kermadecs. A vagrant to the Three Kings Islands and to Campbell Island. Because few are known from subfossil material or middens on the New Zealand mainland, it seems likely that the Pukeko became established within the past 1000 years and became abundant only several hundred years ago as forest was cleared.
Population: Abundant in most districts throughout their range, especially favouring rough damp pasture near wetlands.
Conservation: Partially protected native; legally harvested during the duck-shooting season but not a highly prized gamebird. In some areas, Pukeko are regarded as a pest for their grazing and damage to grain and vegetable crops. They have adapted well to the changes humans have made to swamps and forests, and so have prospered particularly on farmland.
Breeding: Eggs are usually laid in August–February, with the peak in October–November, but a few may breed in any month. Pukeko build their nests on a tussock or rush clump usually standing in water, the grass or rushes being beaten down into a platform; usually several nests are made at once. Territories are often occupied by groups rather than pairs. Groups can consist of two laying females and at least two males, and all share the incubation. Groups can contain non-breeding 'helpers', offspring from previous broods that help in feeding and caring for the chicks. Each adult female lays 4–**5**–6 buff eggs (50 x 35 mm) with blotches of brown distributed evenly or in a ring at the larger end, but as several females can lay in the same nest, clutches of 10–15 eggs are not uncommon. The incubation period is 23–**25**–27 days. Young Pukeko may breed at the end of their first year but often not until their second year. Life expectancy depends on the harshness of the climate; it averages 3–4 years in Otago but 5–6 years near Auckland. The oldest Pukeko recorded in New Zealand lived over 9 years.
Behaviour: In places with plenty of cover, Pukeko prefer to run (if on land) or swim to cover, but in more open places they readily take flight for short distances. When they do fly, their take-off is laboured: running across the surface with rapid wingbeats, taking to the air with feet dangling and head and neck stretched out. Sometimes they land in the top of raupo, scrub or willows, and clumsily perch and clamber about there. They often call loudly, with a harsh screech.
Feeding: Diet is a wide variety of swamp and pasture vegetation; also animals, mainly small insects and spiders, but also frogs, small birds and eggs. From late summer to mid-winter, they form flocks to graze on pasture,

especially clovers, usually near a swamp, pond, ditch or clump of rushes, to which they return if disturbed. Larger food, e.g. raupo *Typha* or other seed-head stem, may be held by one foot like a parrot and stripped or macerated by the powerful bill.

In the hand: Birds may be sexed by the measurements front of nostril to tip of bill and depth of bill, males being larger.

Reading: Carroll, A.L.K. 1966. *Notornis* 13: 133–141. Carroll, A.L.K. 1969. *Notornis* 16: 101–120. Craig, J.L. 1980. *Anim Behav* 28: 593–603. Craig, J.L. *et al.* 1980. *Notornis* 27: 287–291. Fordham, R.A. 1983. *NZ J Ecol* 6: 133–142. Jamieson, I.G. 1994. *NZ Geographic* 21: 54–70. Jamieson, I.G. & Craig, J.L. 1993. *Natural History* 102: 50–57.

164.   TAKAHE   *Porphyrio mantelli*   Plate 37

Other names: Notornis, Moho
Size: 63 cm; 3 kg
Geographical variation: The subspecies *hochstetteri* was originally throughout the South Island, while the larger, extinct *mantelli* was in the North Island.
Distribution: Takahe are widespread as subfossils and in middens, but there were only four confirmed sightings during the nineteenth century, all in or near Fiordland. They were thought extinct until 1948, when G.B. Orbell found them again in the Murchison, Kepler and Stuart Mountains, west of Lake Te Anau, Fiordland. Their natural range is now confined to the Murchisons. There are successful small groups established on four islands, Tiritiri Matangi (Hauraki Gulf), Kapiti and Mana (western Wellington) and Maud (Marlborough Sounds); introduced captive-bred stock in the Stuart Mountains; and a few captive breeding birds at the National Wildlife Centre (Mt Bruce), Te Anau Wildlife Centre and Burwood Bush (near Te Anau).
Population: At their rediscovery in 1948, the total was c. 250, at most 300, birds. They declined in the 1960s and 1970s, and since 1982 total numbers in the wild have fluctuated between 110 and 225 birds. In 2004, there were c. 150 Takahe in Fiordland, c. 75 on offshore islands and c. 30 in captivity.
Conservation: Protected endangered endemic. The aims of current management efforts are to raise breeding success and so restore the population in the Murchisons and expand numbers elsewhere in Fiordland to about the 500 that the area is thought able to support, and to consolidate the four island

populations. Breeding is closely monitored, and eggs that are infertile and 'extra' eggs beyond one per clutch are removed so that every Takahe has one fertile egg to incubate, and the 'surplus' goes to the Burwood Rearing Unit to be raised for release into the wild. A special effort is made to prevent Takahe from being imprinted on people, and so chicks are fed by puppets. The main competitor, red deer, and the main predator, the stoat (and possibly the Weka), are being controlled to improve the quality of the mainland habitat.
Breeding: Laying is in October–December. They lay 1–**2**–3 pale buff eggs (74 x 49 mm, 97 g) with irregular, widely spaced brown blotches. Both sexes incubate for 29–**30**–31 days. Eggs hatch c. 48 hours apart, and the chicks soon leave the nest and are attended by both adults. Young are capable of breeding at the end of their first year but usually begin in their second year. They may stay with their parents for 1–2 years and share the chick-rearing role. They are potentially very long-lived (14–20 years).
Behaviour: Takahe are fiercely territorial in the breeding season, and some males will attack human intruders. Following breeding, the family party usually stays together close to the nesting territory, and sometimes yearlings will help their parents with incubation and care of young. The main contact call by day or night is a loud, Weka-like 'coo-eet', and the alarm note is a very deep, resonant 'oomf'. Pairs often duet.
Feeding: The main foods of the naturally distributed high-altitude birds are snow tussocks (*Chionochloa* spp.) and, in winter in

the beech-forested valleys, the rhizomes of the fern *Hypolepis millefolium*. On islands, they take mainly introduced grasses. They dig up fern rhizomes and pull out snow-tussock leaf bases with their bill. Holding them in their feet, they macerate the bases, digesting only the plant juices, not the fibres, which remain as typical green, sausage-shaped droppings of largely unaltered fibres.

Reading: Crouchley, D. 1994. *Takahe Recovery Plan*. Wellington: DoC. Mills, J.A. & Lavers, R.B. 1974. *Notornis* 21: 312–317. Mills, J.A. *et al.* 1984. *NZ J Ecol* 7: 57–70. Mills, J.A. *et al.* 1991. *Ornis Scand* 22: 111–128.

165. AUSTRALIAN COOT *Fulica atra* Plate 37

Other name: Eurasian Coot
Size: 38 cm; males 570 g, females 520 g
Geographical variation: Four subspecies; the form *australis* breeds throughout Australasia, including New Zealand.
Distribution: Ranges from Europe and parts of northern Africa across Asia to Japan, south to New Guinea, Australia and New Zealand. Coots were recorded in New Zealand as vagrants on eight occasions between 1875 and 1953, all in the South Island. One was recorded at Lake Tutira, Hawke's Bay, in 1954, but then Coots invaded from Australia in 1957, when nine were shot in Southland, one was shot near Blenheim, one was shot on Lake Wairarapa and another was seen on Lake Pupuke, Auckland. The first breeding record in the South Island was at Lake Hayes, near Arrowtown, in 1958, and in the North Island at Lake Okareka, near Rotorua, in 1962. Coots spread to all districts in the 1960s and 1970s and are now widespread and common on certain lakes.

Coots favour shallow, sheltered bays fringed with extensive raupo beds and willows, especially in Auckland, on Hamilton Lake, on the Volcanic Plateau lakes, on Lake Tutira, Virginia Lake (Wanganui), Centennial Lagoon (Palmerston North), Lake Elterwater (Marlborough), St Annes Lagoon (near Cheviot), Lake Heron and the Ashburton lakes (Canterbury). They are still largely absent from Wellington, Nelson, the West Coast and Southland.
Population: c. 2000 birds in 1995.
Conservation: Protected self-introduced native. Coots are now widespread and firmly established in New Zealand, and slowly increasing as they colonise new lakes.
Breeding: Eggs are laid in August–February,

and often two broods are raised. The nest is an untidy, floating platform of twigs, rushes and waterweed anchored in emergent vegetation on the margins of inland waters. Rushes are often bent over to form the nest itself or a cover above it. Both sexes collect material. They lay 4–8 creamy white eggs (50 x 34 mm), uniformly marked with dark spots. Both sexes incubate for 22–26 days and care for the young. The age of first breeding of the smaller Eurasian Coot is at 1–2 years old, and the oldest known banded bird in Europe lived over 18 years.
Behaviour: Coots form large flocks in the non-breeding season, but in spring and summer, while territorial breeding birds are occupied in or near reedbeds, non-breeders form small flocks in more open water. Although highly mobile, they are presumed to move at night, because they are not seen to fly by day; rather, they skitter across the surface, rather like New Zealand Dabchicks, feet trailing and with rapid, shallow wingbeats, to splash down breast first. Their usual call is a series of loud, harsh notes uttered singly, sometimes rendered 'krark'.
Feeding: Diet is mainly vegetarian but includes some aquatic invertebrates. They reach most of the plants in submerged weedbeds by diving; they jump upwards and forwards, disappearing bill first. Their lobed feet alone propel them under water. They bring plants to the surface, jerkily swallowing what is in the bill. Dives last 2–15 seconds, depending on the water depth. They sometimes graze grass of mown lawns at some city lakes.

Reading: Bakker, B.J. & Fordham, R.A. 1993. *Notornis* 40: 131–136. Granville, I. 1973. BSc (Hons) thesis, Univ Canterbury. Macdonald, R. 1968. *Notornis* 15: 234–237.

CRANES   Gruidae

About 15 species worldwide, except in South America and much of the Pacific. One species is a rare vagrant to New Zealand.

Cranes are very large, long-legged and long-necked birds with a large head and a long straight bill. The Australian species are often associated with water but also frequent dry floodplains and open grassland. They fly strongly with neck extended and legs trailing.

Reading: Johnsgard, P.A. 1983. *Cranes of the World*. Bloomington: Indiana Univ Press.

166. BROLGA   *Grus rubicundus*   Plate 27

Size: Males 125 cm, 7 kg; females 100 cm, 5 kg
Distribution: Breed in southern New Guinea and northern, eastern and southeastern Australia, and are especially common in Queensland. Two vagrants have been recorded in New Zealand: Clevedon (March–May 1947), and Punakaiki, West Coast (January 1968).
Behaviour: Cranes, Brolgas included, are noted for their graceful dances (year-round) and their high flying, often out of sight but with audible trumpeting. They fly with their neck stretched out, unlike herons but like spoonbills and ibises.

Reading: McKenzie, H.R. & Cunningham, J.M. 1952. *Notornis* 4: 198. Westerskov, K.E. 1968. *Notornis* 15: 248–253.

PAINTED SNIPE   Rostratulidae

2 species; 1 is a rare vagrant to New Zealand.

In the field, their long bill, squat body and large eyes makes these birds look like the true snipes of the Scolopacidae. In fact, they are more closely allied with rails (Rallidae) and jacanas (Jacanidae). Sex roles are reversed, females being brighter and bigger, and they visit males purely for courtship and mating. The rest of nesting duties are the responsibility of the male. They are polyandrous, i.e. a female mates with more than one male.

167. PAINTED SNIPE   *Rostratula benghalensis*   Plate 43

Size: 25 cm, 120 g
Geographical variation: Two subspecies: *benghalensis* breeds in central and southern Africa, southern Asia, southern Japan, China, the Philippines and western Indonesia; and *australis* breeds in Australia.
Distribution: Eastern Australia from Queensland to Victoria. They are nomadic and head to inland swamps and lakes to breed following heavy rains. When the interior dries out, they return to coastal lakes and swamps. A single vagrant has reached New Zealand: a male at Lake Ellesmere (August 1986).
Behaviour: Little is known about Painted Snipe, as they feed mainly in thick vegetation at dusk and at night, and they freeze rather than fly when disturbed. When they do fly, they fly low, directly and only briefly, unlike the steep, towering flight of true snipe. Like rails, they jerk the rear of their body up and down.

OYSTERCATCHERS

Haematopodidae

7 species worldwide; 3 breed in New Zealand, including 2 endemic species.

Oystercatchers are all black, or black and white, shorebirds with a very long, straight, reddish-orange bill, a squat body and short, thick, pinkish-red legs. They have loud, shrill calls and elaborate 'piping' displays, in which several birds gather and move around with neck stretched, bill pointed downwards and body hunched with wings touching the ground, accompanied by loud, insistent calling.

Oystercatchers are gregarious, feeding in loose flocks but generally roosting and flying in tight flocks. They are mainly coastal, although Pied Oystercatchers are unusual in that they breed well inland on gravel river-beds and on farmland. In winter, all species sometimes roost or feed inland on short grass or beside shallow lakes. Their nest is a simple scrape, partially lined with small twigs. Both sexes share incubation and feed the precocial young.

Reading: Baker, A.J. 1973. *Notornis* 20: 128–144.

168. PIED OYSTERCATCHER *Haematopus ostralegus* Plate 38

Other names: Torea, South Island Pied Oystercatcher, SIPO
Size: 46 cm, 550 g
Geographical variation: The New Zealand subspecies of the widely distributed Pied Oystercatcher is *finschi*; some authors treat it as a separate species.
Distribution: Almost worldwide, mainly near the coasts of the Americas, Europe, Africa, Asia and Australasia. In New Zealand, they breed inland in the South Island, mainly east of the Southern Alps, on braided riverbeds, farmland, fringes of lakes and in subalpine bogs. Since 1980, a few pairs have bred on the Ngaruroro River, Hawke's Bay, and since 1988 a few have bred near Lake Onoke, Wairarapa. After breeding, some shift to estuaries of the South Island, but in late December to early March most migrate directly to estuaries and sandy beaches of the North Island and the northern South Island, although many also remain through the winter at estuaries of the South and Stewart Islands. Stragglers have reached Australia, Vanuatu and the Kermadec, Chatham and Campbell Islands.

The largest wintering populations (10,000+ birds) are at Kaipara and Manukau Harbours, the Firth of Thames, and the coast between Nelson and Farewell Spit. 1000+ birds are regularly at Whangarei and Kawhia Harbours, the Avon–Heathcote Estuary, near Dunedin and at Southland harbours. Birds start returning to their South Island breeding grounds from early June, but most breeding birds return in late July to early August. In spring and summer, about 15,000 (18% of the total population), mainly subadult birds, stay at the main wintering sites, especially in the Manukau–Firth of Thames area (7000) and the Nelson region (3000).
Population: c. 85,000 birds: North Island 60,000 (Kaipara Harbour 14,000, Manukau Harbour 26,000 and Firth of Thames 12,000); South Island 25,000 (mainly Nelson to Farewell Spit 16,000); Stewart Island 300.
Conservation: Protected abundant native. From the mid-1800s, the population was in serious decline from hunting; however, with conversion of tussockland to pasture, and their protection in 1940, they have increased rapidly. This is especially obvious at the northern North Island wintering sites of Manukau Harbour and the Firth of Thames, where numbers have increased from fewer than 1000 in the 1940s to 17,000 in 1972 and to 38,000 in the 1990s. At southern wintering sites, they have also increased, but not to the same extent. The total population has increased by about 75% from the 49,000 birds estimated in 1970–71.
Breeding: Pairs usually reclaim the same territory year after year, even though the birds generally overwinter at different sites. The

293

nest is a shallow scrape; on riverbeds it is usually on a slightly raised area of sand, often near a piece of driftwood or a prominent stone, but on farmland it is often placed randomly, although away from fences or trees. Eggs are laid in August–December, mostly September–November; earlier in lowlands. They lay 1–**2**–3 brownish-stone eggs (56 x 39 mm; 44 g), blotched dark brown. Eggs are laid 2 days apart, mainly in the afternoon. Both sexes incubate for 25–**28**–30 days, starting when the penultimate egg is laid. The downy chicks remain in the nest 1–2 days and then stay in the parents' territory until they first fly at c. 5 weeks old. Young return to their natal area at 3–4 years old but generally do not start breeding until 4–5 years old. The oldest bird recorded in New Zealand lived over 27 years.

Behaviour: Much behaviour is highly ritual-ised, and many displays are common to other oystercatchers. The most conspicuous breed-ing display is 'social piping'. Birds mob aerial predators and lead ground predators away from nest or chicks with conspicuous walking, false brooding and feigning wing injury.

Feeding: Diet is mainly molluscs (especially bivalves), estuarine worms, earthworms and insect larvae (especially grassgrub), but other small invertebrates and small fish are taken. They feed in estuaries, on sandy shores, in pasture, on ploughed paddocks and riverbeds by surface picking and deep probing. They open bivalves by stabbing between the shells and twisting the bill to part the shells, but some birds hammer through the shell.

In the hand: Females are larger than males, especially for bill length, but measurements over-lap slightly: males **81** mm, females **91** mm. First-year birds are distinguished by their dull brown-black upperparts, brownish-orange bill, grey legs and brown eyes, and they retain juvenile primaries through their first year. Second- and third-year birds still have a brownish tinge to their back but develop the pink legs and orange-red eyes of adults.

Reading: Baker, A.J. 1973. *Notornis* 20: 128–144. Baker, A.J. 1974. *Notornis* 21: 219–233. Baker, A.J. 1974. *NZ J Mar Fresh Res* 8: 211–219. Baker, A.J. 1975. *J Zool* (Lond) 175: 357–390. Baker, A.J. 1975. *Notornis* 22: 189–194. Sagar, P.M. *et al.* 2000. *Notornis* 47: 71–81. Sibson, R.B. 1966. *Notornis* 13: 94–97. Twydle, M. & Twydle, W. 1983. *Notornis* 30: 197–198. Veitch, C.R. 1978. *Notornis* 25: 1–24.

169.   VARIABLE OYSTERCATCHER   *Haematopus unicolor*   Plate 38

Other names: Torea, Toreapango (black phase), Black Oystercatcher
Size: 48 cm, 725 g
Geographical variation: The distribution of the three colour phases (black, pied and intermediate) varies with latitude: in the northern North Island, 43% are black, 22% are pied and 35% are intermediates; in central New Zealand (39–44°S), 85% are black and 7% pied; and in the southern South Island and Stewart Island, 94% are black and 5% pied.

Distribution: New Zealand only. They are on coasts of the main islands and offshore islands but not the outlying islands. Breeding and wintering distributions are similar, but there is some local movement to estuaries outside the breeding season. In the North Island, they are most abundant along the northeastern coast from North Cape to Mahia Peninsula, and near Wellington, but scarce on the west coast between Manawatu and Auckland. In the South Island, they are common around Tasman and Golden Bays, Marlborough Sounds and Fiordland, but scarce on the east coast between Cloudy Bay and Dunedin. Common on the beaches of Stewart Island and its offshore islands.

Population: c. 4000 birds: North Island 2700 (Northland 1100, Coromandel–Bay of Plenty 800, Gisborne 250, Wellington 150); South Island 1150 (Fiordland 450, Nelson 250); Stewart Island 150.

Conservation: Protected rare endemic. In the early 1900s, they were in serious decline from hunting; however, since they were protected in 1940 they have increased dramatically. This is especially so in the northern North Island, where many nests on sandspits are now also protected from predators and human disturbance. The total population has approximately doubled from c. 2000 birds in the early 1970s.

Breeding: Pairs remain stable from year to year; some occupy their territory all year, but others join small winter flocks or join flocks of Pied Oystercatchers. The nest is a shallow scrape, usually on a sandy beach just above spring-tide level, but also on shingle beaches,

rock platforms and rarely on lake shores up to 30 km inland (e.g. Lake Wairarapa). Eggs are laid in September–February, mostly November–December; earlier in southern New Zealand. They lay 1–**2**–**3**–5 stone to pale olive eggs (59 x 41 mm; 49 g), spotted dark brown. They are laid 2 days apart, mainly in the afternoon. Both sexes incubate, but the female does most during daylight, for 25–**28**–33 days, starting when the last egg is laid. The downy chicks remain in the nest 1–2 days and then stay in their parents' territory and are solely fed by them for the first 3 weeks. They first fly at 6–7 weeks old, but stay close to their natal territory for at least 2–3 months before dispersing to join winter flocks. They start breeding from 3 years old. The oldest bird recorded lived over 27 years.

Behaviour: Much behaviour is highly ritualised, and many displays are common to other oystercatchers. The most conspicuous breeding display is 'social piping'. Birds mob aerial predators and lead ground predators away from nest or chicks with conspicuous walking, false brooding and feigning wing injury.

Feeding: Diet is mainly molluscs (especially bivalves), worms and crabs, also other small invertebrates and occasionally small fish. They take these mainly from rocky or sandy shores and estuaries, occasionally lake shores and grassland, by surface picking and deep probing. They open bivalves by stabbing between the shells and twisting the bill to part the shells, but some birds hammer through the shell.

In the hand: Females are larger than males, especially for bill length, but measurements overlap: males **82** mm, females **91** mm. First-year birds are distinguished by their dull brown-black upperparts, brownish bill, grey legs and brown eyes, and they retain juvenile primaries through their first year. Second- and third-year birds still have a brownish tinge to their back but develop the pink legs and orange-red eyes of adults.

Reading: Baker, A.J. 1973. *Notornis* 20: 128–144; 330–345. Baker, A.J. 1974. *Notornis* 21: 219–233. Baker, A.J. 1974. *NZ J Mar Fresh Res* 8 211–219. Baker, A.J. 1975. *J Zool* (Lond) 175: 357–390.

170. CHATHAM ISLAND OYSTERCATCHER

Haematopus chathamensis   Plate 38

Size: 48 cm, 600 g

Distribution: Confined to the Chatham Islands. Most are widely scattered on the coast of Chatham and Pitt Islands, and on wave platforms of South East and Mangere Islands and the Star Keys. Breeding and wintering distributions are similar, but some local movement of juveniles between islands has been noted, and some pairs breeding on South East Island regularly feed 2 km away on Pitt Island.

Population: c. 300 birds in 2004. Of 84 known or likely breeding pairs, 64 were on Chatham Island, 13 on Pitt Island, 4 on South East Island and 3 on Mangere Island.

Conservation: Protected endangered endemic. In the 1930s, the Chatham Island Oystercatcher was widely distributed but scarce. Numbers have increased spectacularly since 1970, when the population was estimated at c. 50 birds. The main increase has been in the northern part of Chatham Island, where nests have been protected from predators and storm surges since the early 1990s. The population on South East Island has, however, declined from 13 pairs in 1978 to 8 pairs in 1989 and to just 4 pairs in 2004.

Breeding: Most pairs occupy their territory all year, but juveniles and subadults form small flocks or settle alone on a vacant section of coast. The nest is a shallow scrape, usually on a sandy beach just above spring-tide level, or among rocks above the shoreline. On offshore islands, nests are usually well away from centres of Brown Skua territories and are often under the cover of small bushes or rock overhangs. Eggs are laid in October–February, mostly November–December. They lay 1–2–3 olive-grey eggs (57 x 40 mm; 46 g), spotted dark brown. They are laid 2 days apart. Both sexes incubate, but the female does most during daylight, for about 25 days.

The downy chicks remain in the nest 1–2 days and are then led away by their parents; they continue to be brooded at least during the first week. They first fly at c. 7 weeks old but stay close to their natal territory for several months before dispersing. They start breeding from 3 years old, but most start when 5–6. Mean life expectancy is 7.7 years; the oldest bird lived over 19 years.

Behaviour: Much behaviour is highly ritualised, and many displays are common to other oystercatchers. The most conspicuous breeding display is 'social piping'. Birds mob aerial predators, including Brown Skuas, and lead ground predators away from nest or chicks with conspicuous walking, false brooding and feigning wing injury.

Feeding: Diet is mainly molluscs and marine worms, supplemented with other small invertebrates. They take these mainly from rocky shores (especially from small pools on wave platforms and from algal mats) or sandy shores by surface picking and deep probing. They open bivalves by stabbing between the shells and twisting the bill to part the shells, but some birds hammer through the shell. Limpets and chitons are struck vertical blows, prised off rocks and eaten whole.

In the hand: Females are larger than males, especially for bill length, but measurements overlap slightly: males **68** mm, females **77** mm. First-year birds are distinguished by their dull brown-black upperparts, pinkish-brown bill, grey legs and brown eyes, and they retain juvenile primaries through their first year. Second- and third-year birds still have a brownish tinge to their back but develop the pink legs and orange-red eyes of adults.

Reading: Baker, A.J. 1973. *Notornis* 20: 128–144. Baker, A.J. 1974. *Notornis* 21: 219–233. Baker, A.J. 1974. *NZ J Mar Fresh Res* 8: 211–219. Baker, A.J. 1975. *J Zool* (Lond) 175: 357–390. Schmechel, F. & O'Connor, S. 1999. *Notornis* 46: 155–165.

STILTS and AVOCETS Recurvirostridae

Of 7 species, 2 breed in New Zealand and a third may have bred in the nineteenth century.

These are medium-sized waders with long, slender bills, necks and especially legs, which suit their wading up to the belly to feed in shallow fresh, salt or brackish water. Stilts have a fine, almost straight bill. Avocets have a fine, upturned bill, more sharply turned in females, with complex lamellae which they use to sift out tiny food particles. Sexes are alike, but males have longer legs. Most species have a pattern of black above and white below. Webbing between the front three toes is much reduced in stilts. Although having long legs, which trail behind the short, square tail in flight, they are slim and graceful. Adult plumage is gained in their first or second year; they first breed at 2–3 years.

171. PIED STILT *Himantopus himantopus* Plate 39

Other names: Poaka, Black-winged/White-headed Stilt
Size: 35 cm, 190 g
Geographical variation: Of the five sub-species, *leucocephalus* extends from the Philippines, Indonesia and the Bismarck Archipelago to Australia and New Zealand.
Distribution: Pied Stilts, more generally known as Black-winged Stilts overseas, breed right around the world in tropical and warm temperate regions. They breed prolifically throughout New Zealand but are rare on Stewart and Chatham Islands and absent from Fiordland and the subantarctic islands. They may have colonised New Zealand as recently as the early 1800s. They expanded rapidly from about the 1870s to the early 1900s, and continued to increase at least until the 1940s.

The migration routes taken by the various regional populations of Pied Stilts have been studied by the Ornithological Society of New Zealand by a national programme of colour-banding adults and juveniles. Birds on riverbeds in the southern North Island and the South Island move in December–February to coastal places and some, especially those from inland Southland, Central Otago, Mackenzie Basin and Mid-Canterbury, move to northern North Island harbours. Coastal breeders in both main islands and birds breeding in the north are usually sedentary. Pied Stilts can be heard calling as they fly high overhead on migration.
Population: c. 30,000 birds in 1984–93. Maximum autumn–winter counts are: Parenga-renga 1500, Rangaunu 3000, Kaipara 3000+, Firth of Thames 5000, Tauranga 1500, Whakaki Lagoon 1000, Lake Poukawa 1500, Lake Wairarapa 1500, Lake Ellesmere 3000, Lake Wainono 1000. Favoured also, but accommodating hundreds not thousands, are Houhora, Whangarei, Kawhia/Aotea, Maketu, Ahuriri, Lake Hatuma and Manawatu Estuary in the North Island, and Nelson Haven, Lake Grassmere, Avon–Heathcote Estuary, Green Island Lagoon and Southland lagoons and estuaries in the South Island. Smaller flocks are at many places around the New Zealand coast. They are least common where the habitat is unsuitable, e.g. in Taranaki and the West Coast.
Conservation: Protected common native. Pied Stilts are probably a relatively recent colonist of New Zealand and have thrived with the conversion of lowland swamp forest into seasonally wet farmland. In South Canterbury, Pied Stilts have hybridised with the endemic Black Stilt when its numbers have dwindled to such a level that Black Stilts have difficulty finding a mate of their own species.
Breeding: Pied Stilts return to their breeding grounds in June–July in lowland places and August–October in inland places. They breed in loose colonies of up to 100 pairs, but typically 3–20 pairs, on mounds surrounded by or near water in wetlands in open country, both coastal and inland. Mainly in flooded pasture, muddy pasture resulting from chewed-down, trampled turnips and chou-moellier, margins of swamps, edges of ponds

297

and estuaries and other permanent wetlands, and gravel riverbeds. Both sexes build the nest. In lowland places, the peak of laying is in August–October; October–November inland. They lay 2–4–5 greenish eggs (44 x 32 mm) with blackish-brown blotches and streaks. Starting with the last egg, both sexes incubate for about 25 days. The fledging period is 30–37 days. Pied Stilts usually start breeding at 2 years old, occasionally at 1 year old. The oldest banded bird of the European subspecies lived over 12 years.

Behaviour: Gregarious at all seasons; adults breed together in loose colonies, feed together and, in autumn and winter, roost together in often large compact flocks. Their yapping is persistent and noisy when feeding and flying, including at night; juveniles utter a higher-pitched chipping, sometimes hoarse, until their first winter.

Feeding: Diet is mainly aquatic and terrestrial invertebrates. If the habitat is tidal, they feed at low tide, day or night. At inland ponds and swamps, they take mainly insects; on inland riverbeds mainly larvae of mayflies, caddisflies, stoneflies and midges, plus adult waterboatmen and molluscs. Common methods of feeding are plunging, in which birds peck underwater; snatching, in which birds capture flying insects; probing, in which birds insert their bill into mud or wet soil; and scything, in which birds sweep the bill from side to side in soft mud, like avocets, particularly when wind or darkness makes prey less visible.

Reading: Pierce, R.J. 1984. *Notornis* 31: 7–18. Pierce, R.J. 1984. *Notornis* 31: 106–130. Pierce, R.J. 1985. *NZ J Zool* 12: 467–472. Pierce, R.J. 1986. *Auk* 103: 273–280.

172. BLACK STILT *Himantopus novaezelandiae* Plate 39

Other name: Kaki
Size: 40 cm, 220 g
Distribution: New Zealand only. In the nineteenth century, Black Stilts bred on the braided shingle riverbeds and associated wetlands of the lower North Island and the whole South Island (except Fiordland) on both sides of the Southern Alps. In the 1930s and 1940s, they were still common in lowland South Canterbury, Central Otago and the Mackenzie Basin. They have declined drastically, and since about 1960 breeding has been confined to the Mackenzie Basin. They now breed only in the upper Waitaki system from the Godley and Macaulay Rivers in the north to the Cass, Tasman, Tekapo, Ohau, Hopkins, Dobson and Ahuriri Rivers in the centre and south. After nesting, most move to ponds or lakes before wintering on the nearby river deltas around major lakes, but a few migrate north to Kawhia and Kaipara Harbours. Birds paired with Pied Stilts or with strongly Pied hybrids sometimes follow their mates to northern North Island estuaries, leaving in January and returning in July at the earliest.
Population: c. 160 birds in 2004: 72 adults in the wild and 47 others held in captivity at Twizel.

Conservation: Protected endangered endemic. The decline of Black Stilts has been from predation by introduced mammals, loss of habitat, and hybridisation with Pied Stilts. The main predators, feral cats and ferrets, may be short of their main food, the rabbit, when Black Stilts start nesting in August. They breed alone on the banks of small streams and side braids of major rivers, but also on islands or swamps. Unlike Pied Stilts, they do not have the mutual protection of nesting in colonies, they have lost some of their distraction displays, and their fledging period is a long c. 40 days, cf. the Pied Stilt's 30–37 days. Habitat was lost to hydroelectric development, to the drainage of swamps and to the spread on riverbeds of introduced plants such as willows and lupins.

As Black Stilts declined, they became so widely separated that often not enough Black Stilts were on a river, and as Pied Stilts became abundant they interbred, resulting in hybrids. Management aims to control predation, partly by trapping round each Black Stilt nest, partly by maintaining predator-free exclosures;

incubating eggs and hand-rearing about 30 chicks each year and passing them to Black Stilt adults in the wild so that they stay in the Mackenzie Basin for the winter and mate with other Black Stilts; and restoring habitat by removing exotic plants from waterways.

Breeding: Nest as solitary pairs in braided shingle rivers and nearby wetlands such as sidestreams, swamps, tarns and ponds. They arrive on territory in July or August and select a nest site on stable shingle, usually on islands or the banks of a river. Both sexes build the nest. Eggs are laid in September–December. They lay 3–**4**–5 eggs (45 x 32 mm), greenish with dark brown or black blotches and streaks. Incubation starts after the third or fourth egg is laid. Both sexes incubate for 24–**25**–27 days. The fledging period is 30–**40**–55 days. They can breed at 2 years old, but most breed first when 3 years old. The oldest bird known in

the wild lived over 19 years.

Behaviour: Less gregarious than Pied Stilts. They make a loud, monotonous yapping, like that of Pied Stilts but higher-pitched.

Feeding: Insectivorous, taking mostly aquatic invertebrates, especially mayflies. Other foods of some importance are several kinds of caddisfly, molluscs, fish, midges and waterboatmen. They catch their prey by pecking at them in the water column, probing beneath shingle or rocks or, in mud, scything sideways by feel only, in the manner of avocets. Favourite feeding places are the riffles of braided rivers.

Reading: Pierce, R. 1986. *Black Stilt*. Wellington: John McIndoe & NZ Wildlife Service. Reed, C.E.M. 1986. Unpubl MSc thesis, Massey Univ. Reed, C.E.M. *et al*. 1993. *Black Stilt Recovery Plan*. Wellington: DoC.

173. AUSTRALIAN RED-NECKED AVOCET
Recurvirostra novaehollandiae   Plate 39

Size: 44 cm, 300 g

Distribution: Breed only in Australia, mainly in southern parts. Between 1859 and 1892, avocets were reported widely from Whangarei to Invercargill, and they attempted breeding at several estuarine localities in Canterbury. Only two recent records, both of single birds: Lake Ellesmere (1912), and Westport (1968–70).

Behaviour: Gregarious. They feed in flocks at shallow wetlands of fresh, brackish or preferably saline water. In Australia, they are often inland at saltlakes, especially when evaporation has raised the salinity, but they move to coastal wetlands in summer–autumn. They utter loud barking and wheezing whistles.

Reading: Kaigler, C.G. 1968. *Notornis* 15: 123.

PRATINCOLES and COURSERS Glareolidae

Of the 15 species, 1 reaches New Zealand as a rare vagrant. Recent research suggests that this family is closely related to the gulls, terns and skuas, rather than the waders, as currently placed.

Pratincoles are graceful and highly aerial

birds, similar to terns. They have very long, narrow wings, a forked tail and a wide gape with which they catch flying insects on the wing. They also feed on the ground like other waders; in spite of their short legs, they can run fast. Their bill is short and strongly arched. The sexes are alike.

174. ORIENTAL PRATINCOLE *Glareola maldivarum* Plate 51

Size: 23 cm, 75 g
Distribution: Breed in southern Asia from Pakistan and India to Mongolia, China, Taiwan and the northern Philippines. They are partially sedentary in winter, but many migrate to winter in northern Australia, often in thousands, much smaller numbers reaching southern and eastern Australia. A few occasionally wander to New Zealand. Eight records: Westport (1898), a flock of at least five at Appleby, Nelson (1959), Stewart Island (1963), Raoul Island, Kermadecs (1976), two sightings in South Canterbury (1977), Kaipara Harbour (1985), Ruapuke Island, Foveaux Strait (1988), Farewell Spit (1994), New Plymouth (1999) and Lake Ellesmere (2002).
Behaviour: Oriental Pratincoles fly like over-large swallows, usually near water.

Reading: Falla, R.A. 1959. *Notornis* 8: 126–127. Pierce, R.J. 1978. *Notornis* 25: 290.

PLOVERS, DOTTERELS and LAPWINGS
Charadriidae

About 65 species, most of which are migratory. There are about 29 plovers and dotterels, of which 5 (formerly 6) breed in New Zealand and 8 visit as migrants from the Northern Hemisphere; 26 lapwings, 1 of which breeds in New Zealand. Some authorities place the Red-kneed Dotterel with the lapwings rather than the plovers.

In New Zealand, the terms plover and dotterel mean the same thing; there is no clear distinction. All are plumpish with a thick, short neck, short tail, small, rounded head with a high forehead and bill shorter than the head, pointed and slightly swollen at the tip. The plumage is a blend of black, white, brown and grey, sometimes more colourful in breeding plumage. They often have a bold pattern in flight. They have a characteristic 'walk and stop' way of feeding.

Lapwings tend to be inland on pasture and around coastal wetlands. They have wattles on the face and spurs on the bend of the wing, and are noisy on the ground and in flight, by night as well as by day.

175. NEW ZEALAND DOTTEREL *Charadrius obscurus* Plate 40

Other names: Tuturiwhatu, Red-breasted Dotterel,
Size: 25 cm; 160 g (*obscurus*), 145 g (*aquilonius*)
Geographical variation: Two subspecies have recently been described: the larger and more boldly coloured Southern New Zealand Dotterel *obscurus* breeds on Stewart Island, and the smaller Northern New Zealand Dotterel *aquilonius* breeds on the coast of the northern North Island.
Distribution: New Zealand only. Two discrete populations: North and Stewart Islands. In the North Island, New Zealand Dotterels breed on beaches, and especially near stream mouths, of Northland, Auckland, South Auckland, the Waikato and the Bay of Plenty, and have recently colonised the Gisborne and northern Hawke's Bay coast. They breed from North Cape to Taharoa South Beach (south of Kawhia Harbour) in the west and to Mahia Peninsula in the east. They also breed on some offshore islands, including the Cavalli, Hauraki Gulf (Great Barrier, Waiheke, Motu-ihe, Browns, Ponui, Beehive), Great Mercury and Whale Islands, Rurima Rocks and Portland Island. A scarce visitor south to the coasts of Taranaki, Manawatu, western Wellington, and Hawke's Bay.

Some northern birds are sedentary and stay in their breeding places; others move a short distance to a flocking site at an estuary. The first arrivals are in mid-January; most arrive by late February. Most leave the flock site and return to their breeding places by the end of April.

On Stewart Island, they breed above the bushline, but some descend to tidal estuaries, mudflats and beaches to feed. In January–March, they move down to Paterson Inlet, and others cross Foveaux Strait to winter in coastal Southland, particularly near Cow Island in Awarua Bay. A few birds have been recorded in coastal parts of Nelson (Farewell Spit and Motueka Sandspit), the West Coast, Marlborough and Canterbury. Southern birds usually arrive back at their breeding grounds in September.

New Zealand Dotterels were apparently breeding till the mid-1800s throughout the South Island, particularly in the Southern Alps and their foothills and on the braided riverbeds of Canterbury, moving to the coast in winter. They were probably exterminated partly by introduced predators and partly by being shot for food.

Population: c. 1400 birds. *aquilonius* c. 1350 birds; holding their own or increasing with nest protection, but in some places where human disturbance is high their habitat is diminishing. *obscurus*: c. 65 birds in 1994; rapidly reduced by cat predation, especially on males, which incubate at night, and so probably only about 15 breeding pairs remain.

Conservation: Protected threatened endemic. The dune areas and beaches preferred by northern birds are often changed by housing, pine plantations and plantings of marram grass to stabilise foredunes and sandspits. Human disturbance by people, their vehicles, dogs and stock may crush eggs and chicks, or leave eggs, chicks and adults open to predation, particularly by stoats, feral cats and Black-backed Gulls. Recent efforts to protect northern birds at selected breeding sites have greatly improved breeding success and may have led to their recent expansion of range.

With the southern birds, the aim is to control feral cats in the breeding areas and former breeding areas of Stewart Island, and to find ways of breeding birds in captivity and releasing them in the wild to boost numbers.

Breeding: Northern New Zealand Dotterels breed on sandspits, at stream mouths, on beaches, shellbanks, sandbanks and among low dunes from August to February. The nest is a scrape in the sand with little or no lining, often near an obvious marker such as a piece of driftwood, seaweed or a clump of vegetation. They also use harbour dredgings, oil-refinery grounds and areas beside airport runways.

Southern New Zealand Dotterels breed inland on open, subalpine mountain tops, usually where vegetation is sparse or very low and often in rocky places. The nest is a depression among cushion plants lined with dried vegetation. Until recently, a few pairs also bred in the sand dunes at Mason Bay, Stewart Island.

Northern New Zealand Dotterels lay 2–3 pale olive to buff-brown eggs (44 x 31 mm), heavily marked with dark brown or black blotches; Southern New Zealand Dotterels lay 2–3 eggs (46 x 33 mm). The few clutches of 5 and 6 are probably laid by two females. Both sexes incubate for 28–32 days, females mostly by day, males mostly at night. The fledging period is 6–7 weeks. Juveniles of both subspecies are likely to wander, usually until c. 18 months old. Most young first breed in their second year, occasionally in their third year. The oldest bird lived over 31 years, but one individual, 'Wimble', may have lived at least 42 years if worn band numbers were read correctly.

Behaviour: Tame and approachable; often heard before being seen. The common call, often accompanied by head-bobbing, is a penetrating 'chrp', 'trrt' or 'prrp'. It is associated with alertness and mild alarm in the presence of a human or other intruder.

Feeding: A wide variety of feeding habitats and foods, according to what is available. Commonest habitats are tidal estuaries, stream mouths and sandy beaches. They use a version of the 'walk or run-stop-peck' method typical of plovers. Diet is mainly aquatic and terrestrial invertebrates but includes some small fish. Crabs are commonly taken, the larger ones bashed and eaten in pieces. Foot-paddling is recorded, as is sand-scratching, which is a means of flushing sandhoppers.

On the subalpine breeding grounds of Stewart Island, some birds fly down to tidal flats in Paterson Inlet to feed, but they also feed on wet herbfields and in seepages, eating a variety of invertebrates, including insects, spiders and earthworms.

Reading: Barlow, M. 1993. *Notornis* 40: 15–25. Dowding, J. 1993. *New Zealand Dotterel Recovery Plan*. Wellington: DoC. Dowding, J.E. 1994. *Notornis* 41: 221–233. Dowding, J.E. & Chamberlin, S.P. 1991. *Notornis* 38: 89–102. Dowding, J.E. & Murphy, E.C. 1993. *Notornis* 40: 1–13. Edgar, A.T. 1969. *Notornis* 16: 85–100.

176. BANDED DOTTEREL *Charadrius bicinctus* Plate 40

Other names: Tuturiwhatu, Double-banded Plover (Australia)
Size: 20 cm, 60 g; Auckland Island birds larger
Geographical variation: Two subspecies: *bicinctus*, the common breeding bird of the North, South and Chatham Islands and partial migrant to Australia; and *exilis*, confined to the Auckland Islands.
Distribution: Breed only in New Zealand. They are found throughout the North and South Islands, and on several offshore islands (including Great Mercury and Ruapuke), Stewart Island, the Chatham and Auckland Islands. A high proportion of the population migrates to southeastern Australia in winter, a few regularly visit Lord Howe and Norfolk Islands, and some straggle to Vanuatu, New Caledonia and the Kermadecs.

Some Banded Dotterels breed around the sandy coasts, especially near stream or rivermouths of both main islands, but their breeding concentrations are on the shingle riverbeds of Hawke's Bay, Manawatu and the Wairarapa in the southern North Island, and especially on the braided riverbeds of Marlborough, Canterbury, Otago and Southland in the South Island. The main stronghold is Canterbury, where 5000 pairs breed on riverbeds and river terraces, and the coastal lakes, lagoons and beaches, and another 5000 pairs breed on rivers in the Mackenzie Basin.

The migration routes taken by the various regional populations of Banded Dotterel have been studied in a co-operative programme of colour-banding in New Zealand and Australia. After breeding, most birds from the inland and high-altitude southern South Island migrate to Australia in March, whereas those breeding in the Canterbury lowlands and in the northern South Island mostly migrate to northern New Zealand in February. For example, winter band recoveries in Australia are: Southland 74%, Central Otago 95%, Mackenzie Basin 65%, Canterbury 27%, Westland 15%, Marlborough–Nelson 3%, North Island 1%. Westland birds move mainly to Farewell Spit. Birds breeding at coastal sites are mainly sedentary, from the Southland coast to North Island beaches. Birds breeding inland in the North Island generally winter on nearby coasts or move to Auckland or the Bay of Plenty in January–February. Movements of birds breeding in the Chatham and Auckland Islands are not known.
Population: c. 50,000, mainly in the South Island. Probably 30,000 reach Australia each winter. On the Auckland Islands, there were at least 730 *exilis* in November 1989.
Conservation: Protected endemic. Widespread and moderately common. They suffer from predation by introduced mammals and loss of some habitat to hydroelectric development and irrigation schemes, but seem to be holding their own.
Breeding: Banded Dotterels start returning to North Island breeding sites in July, but those in inland Canterbury arrive in August–September. Nest sites are in consolidated sand, shingle, shell and dirt, with or without prostrate vegetation. Males prepare a series of scrapes, one of which is chosen as the nest. Eggs are laid in July–November in lowland areas, September–December in the Rangipo Desert of the central North Island and in the Mackenzie Basin, but start as late as Novem-

ber on the mountain ranges of Central Otago. They lay 2–**3**–4 eggs (34 x 25 mm, 12 g), pale grey through blue-green to olive and brown, with black spots, streaks and blotches. Both sexes incubate for 25–27 days, starting usually after the second or third egg; the female incubates for most daylight hours, the male may incubate mainly at night. Hatching is synchronised. The chicks soon leave the nest and feed independently. The fledging period is 5–6 weeks. Most birds breed in their first year. The oldest banded bird lived over 10 years.

Behaviour: Gregarious at winter roosts but often form loose flocks, and are even territorial, while feeding. They breed solitarily with well-defended territories. Their usual calls are a fast, rolling 'che-ree-a-ree', accented on the second syllable, in defence of the breeding or winter feeding territory, and a loud, high-pitched, far-carrying 'pit' or 'chip',

given in flight or on the ground.

Feeding: Diet includes a variety of terrestrial and aquatic invertebrates, supplemented by occasional berries of prostrate plants. On pasture and tilled ground, they mostly take earthworms and beetles. On riverbeds, marsh-turf habitats of lakeshores and estuarine mudflats, they take worms, the larvae of chironomids, mayflies and caddisflies, and emerging adult insects. Like all plovers, they feed visually by using 'run-stop-look-step-peck' on dry sand and 'run-stop-peck' on wet sand and saltmarsh; they also foot-tremble in damp habitats.

Reading: Bomford, M. 1988. *Notornis* 35: 9–14. Pierce, R.J. 1980. *Notornis* 27: 309–324. Pierce, R.J. 1989. *Notornis* 36: 13–23. Pierce, R.J. 1999. *Notornis* 46: 101–122. Robertson, H.A. & Dennison, M.D. 1979. *Notornis* 26: 73–88. Walker, K. *et al.* 1991. *Notornis* 38: 257–265.

177. RED-CAPPED DOTTEREL *Charadrius ruficapillus* Plate 41

Other name: Red-capped Plover
Size: 15 cm, 38 g
Distribution: Breed only in Australia, mainly in the southeast and in Tasmania. They have apparently failed in a recent attempt to colonise New Zealand; the first record was an adult male collected near Waikanae in 1878, the next was a female mated to a Banded Dotterel in 1947–50 on the Ashley River, Canterbury, raising hybrid young. In the 1960s and 1970s, several pairs of Red-capped Dotterels bred on the Ashley, Leader and Waipara Rivers of northern Canterbury, and

raised chicks. Between 1955 and 1975, there were several records of birds at the Ashley and Waipara River mouths, Lake Tuakitoto, Manukau Harbour and the Firth of Thames. The last sighting was in 1981 at Lake Ellesmere. Birds were not found in an intensive search of former breeding grounds in 1986–87.

Behaviour: Gregarious and often join flocks of Banded Dotterels in New Zealand. General behaviour and feeding methods are similar to those of the Banded Dotterel.

Reading: Hughey, K.F.D. 1989. *Notornis* 36: 24–26.

178. BLACK-FRONTED DOTTEREL *Charadrius melanops* Plate 41

Other name: Black-fronted Plover (Australia)
Size: 17 cm, 33 g
Distribution: Breed throughout Australia and, since the late 1950s, in New Zealand. They first colonised Hawke's Bay, then spread to Manawatu, Wairarapa and across Cook Strait to Marlborough and South Canterbury in the late 1960s. Now they breed on the shingle riverbeds of the eastern and southern North Island, south of Wairoa and Wanganui,

and are found sparsely in the northeastern South Island and in increasing numbers on the shingle beds of smaller rivers in Canterbury, Otago and Southland. Elsewhere they are seen only as rare non-breeding vagrants, except that a small number regularly visit estuaries in the eastern Bay of Plenty, and a pair bred at Mangere Sewage Ponds in 2002.

When not breeding, most birds stay on

the rivers, but in autumn some move to dried lake beds (e.g. Pukepuke and Omanuka Lagoons), and when river levels rise they gather on nearby muddy places and wetlands such as Whakaki Lagoon, Ahuriri Estuary, Lakes Poukawa, Hatuma and Wairarapa, and Te Whiti sewage ponds near Masterton, Feilding sewage plant, Longburn abattoir sludge ponds (now in disuse). A regular few are in winter on the Bay of Plenty coast, their origin unknown. Some non-breeding flocking in the South Island has begun at Lakes Elterwater and Ellesmere, and at Spider, Wainono and Washdyke Lagoons.

Population: c. 1700 in New Zealand. North Island c. 1400 (Hawke's Bay 800, Wairarapa 300, Manawatu 300); South Island c. 300 (Marlborough 50, Canterbury 150, Otago 50, Southland 50).

Conservation: Protected uncommon self-introduced native. Black-fronted Dotterels have recently established as a breeding species in New Zealand, and do not seem to compete significantly with any native species.

Breeding: Eggs are laid c. 2–3 days apart in August–February, early in Hawke's Bay, where riverbeds are wider, and late in Wairarapa, where floods are common in early summer. The nest is a shallow depression on the ground, usually lined with fine pebbles or wood chips, dry grass and leaves, often on the shingle ridge nearest to the feeding area. They lay 2–3 khaki eggs (29 x 21 mm), with the grey or cream background obscured by a mass of brown spots, flecks and fine wavy lines. Both sexes incubate for 22–26 days.

Behaviour: Some birds remain on territory all year in solitary pairs, but in winter others form loose groups of up to 100 birds. The contact call is a sharp 'pit', more high-pitched and metallic than that of Banded Dotterels and given more often in flight. The threat call is a vigorous rippling 'ree-ree-ree-ree-ree'. The main territorial call is a languid churring 'rrrr-reep' given by the male while circling above its territory in butterfly flight. In the presence of a human intruder, they crouch back-on in the shingle, becoming almost invisible. When more alarmed, they spread and depress their tail, rocking from side to side. They run among stones rather than over them, as other riverbed waders do.

Feeding: Diet is mainly molluscs, crustaceans, insects and earthworms, taken by the 'walk or run-stop-peck' typical of plovers. They also foot-tremble, followed by pecking to take prey disturbed by tapping (on hard surfaces) or leg-shaking (over soft soil or mud).

Reading: Child, P. & Child, M. 1984. *Notornis* 31: 31–39. Heather, B.D. 1977. *Notornis* 24: 1–8. Tarburton, M.K. 1989. *Notornis* 36: 249–259.

179. RINGED PLOVER   *Charadrius hiaticula*   Plate 41

Size: 19 cm, 60 g

Distribution: Breed in northeastern Canada, Greenland, Iceland, northern Europe and northern Asia east to the Bering Sea. They winter mainly in Africa, but a few winter on the coasts of Japan, Korea and China, and vagrants reach Indonesia, New Guinea, Australia and New Zealand. The two New Zealand records of single birds are both at the Firth of Thames (December 1970–May 1971 and November 1983–October 1985).

Reading: Brown, J.A. *et al.* 1971. *Notornis* 18: 262–266.

180. LARGE SAND DOTTEREL   *Charadrius leschenaultii*   Plate 40

Other names: Large Sand Plover, Greater Sand Plover

Size: 24 cm, 90 g

Geographical variation: Of the three subspecies, *leschenaultii* breeds in eastern central Asia and migrates to Australasia.

Distribution: Breed across central Asia from Turkey to northwestern China, and winter in Africa, southern Asia and Australasia. The subspecies *leschenaultii* breeds in southern

Siberia, Mongolia and northwestern China, and migrates to Australasia, especially to the coasts of northern Australia and down the eastern seaboard to Victoria and Tasmania. In New Zealand, they are recorded almost annually as a rare visitor, mostly in September–April. Favoured sites are the Kaipara and Manukau Harbours, the Firth of Thames and Farewell Spit, but they have been recorded on estuaries from Parengarenga Harbour to coastal Southland. The most seen together is 9 in the Firth of Thames in 1983.

Population: Normally, fewer than 10 visit New Zealand each summer, whereas about 75,000 visit Australia.

Behaviour: Gregarious, feeding and roosting with other species, especially with Banded Dotterels on mudflats and estuaries. They feed in the 'run-and-stop' manner typical of plovers. The call is a soft trill similar to that of the Mongolian Dotterel.

Reading: Sibson, R.B. 1953. *Notornis* 5: 179–181.

181. MONGOLIAN DOTTEREL   *Charadrius mongolus*   Plate 40

Other names: Mongolian Plover, Lesser Sand Plover

Size: 20 cm, 60 g

Geographical variation: Birds of both *mongolus* and *atrifrons* groups of subspecies reach New Zealand, but most are of the latter group, which includes the two easternmost subspecies *mongolus* and *stegmanni* that breed in eastern and northeastern Siberia, and winter through the Western Pacific from Japan to Australasia.

Distribution: Breed in two widely separated groups: in central Asia and in far-eastern Asia. They winter on coasts of eastern and southern Africa, southern Asia and in Australasia, east to Fiji. In Australia, they are common on northern coasts and down the eastern seaboard to Victoria, Tasmania and South Australia. In New Zealand, they are a scarce but regular visitor, mostly in late September to mid-April or even early May. Most records are in the Manukau Harbour, the Firth of Thames and Farewell Spit, but they have been recorded at estuaries from Parengarenga Harbour to Oreti Estuary, Invercargill. The most seen together is four at Karaka, Manukau Harbour, in 1981. Several birds have overwintered, and an individual stayed at Porangahau Estuary from March 1986 to January 1988 without going into breeding plumage.

Population: Normally, fewer than 5 birds visit New Zealand each summer, whereas c. 20,000 visit Australia.

Behaviour: Gregarious; in New Zealand they feed and roost with Banded Dotterels on mudflats and estuaries. They feed in the 'run-and-stop' manner typical of plovers, pausing often to crouch and lunge at prey seen moving. Their voice is similar to that of the Banded Dotterel but distinctive to the experienced observer, with a rolled 'r' component not present in a Banded Dotterel's voice.

Reading: Heather, B.D. & Robertson, H.A. 1981. *Notornis* 28: 82–83. Sibson, R.B. 1975. *Notornis* 22: 347–349.

182. ORIENTAL DOTTEREL   *Charadrius veredus*   Plate 42

Other name: Oriental Plover

Size: 24 cm, 95 g

Distribution: Breed in Mongolia and Manchuria, and migrate to winter mostly in Indonesia and Australia. About 40,000 birds visit the coasts and open grassy plains, airfields and sports fields of northern Australia, but they are stragglers to southern states, and a rare straggler to Lord Howe Island and New Zealand. Eleven New Zealand records, mainly of single birds: Raoul Island, Kermadecs (1908); a flock of ten at the Firth of Thames (1954–55), Parengarenga Harbour (1955, 1968–69); Manukau Harbour (1975, three in 1994), Lake Wainono (1977), Greymouth airfield (1982), Invercargill Estuary

(1988), Lake Ellesmere (1989) and Te Whanga Lagoon, Chathams (2000).

Behaviour: Gregarious, feeding in loose flocks. They take mainly insects by the usual plover 'run-and-stop' method. Their call is a whistled 'chip' in flight, but a sharp, rippling trill when chasing one another on the ground.

183.   RED-KNEED DOTTEREL   *Erythrogonys cinctus*   Plate 41

Size: 18 cm, 50 g

Distribution: Breed only in Australia, mainly on inland freshwater lakes and swamps. They head inland to breed following heavy rains, but when the interior dries out they move towards estuaries and brackish coastal lagoons. One seen in New Zealand: Mana-watu River estuary (March 1976).

Behaviour: Usually solitary and seen gleaning and probing for invertebrates on the edge of freshwater wetland margins or brackish coastal ponds. They swim readily.

Reading: Robertson, H.A. & Dennison, M.D. 1977. *Notornis* 24: 193–194.

184.   SHORE PLOVER   *Thinornis novaeseelandiae*   Plate 41

Other name: Tuturuatu

Size: 20 cm, 60 g

Distribution: South East Island and Western Reef in the Chathams and rarely wandering to other islands of the group. They live on the coastal rocky wave platforms and on the 'Clears', an open, exposed area of saltmeadow at the southern end of the island.

Shore Plovers were recorded in the South Island at Queen Charlotte Sound (Marl-borough Sounds) and Dusky Sound (Fiord-land) in 1773, and were probably distributed widely round the South Island coast until exterminated soon after the arrival of Norway rats and feral cats. The last reliable mainland record was at Waikawa River, Otago, about 1871. At that time they were still on Mangere and Pitt Islands in the Chathams, but they disappeared soon after the introduction of cats to those islands.

Shore Plover reared in captivity have been released on Motuora Island (Hauraki Gulf) and near Mahia (Hawke's Bay) since 1994, and some of these birds have been seen on the mainland coast, as far away as the Manawatu Estuary.

Population: c. 250 in 2004; c. 130 on South East Island, 15 on Mangere Island and c. 100 in captivity or released.

Conservation: Protected endangered endemic. Very vulnerable to predators such as cats, and naturally survive on two small predator-free islands, despite hundreds being collected for museum specimens between 1890 and 1910. Faced by the constant risk of introduced predators reaching South East Island, the loss of marsh-turf habitat since the removal of sheep in 1961, and the risk of fire, disease or the encroachment of breeding fur seals onto key feeding and breeding areas, the aim is to establish several self-sustaining populations on islands and in captivity.

Since 1994, over 150 captive-bred birds have been released on Motuora Island and near Mahia but only the latter is self-sustaining. In February 1999, a new population of c. 20 birds was discovered on the rarely visited Western Reef off the north-western tip of Chatham Island, but is has since died out.

Breeding: Eggs are laid from mid-October to January. Nests are hidden under thick vegetation, occasionally under boulders near the shore or under large rocks inland. They lay 2–3 pale buff eggs (37 x 26 mm, 13 g), blotched or spotted darker brown. Both sexes, but mostly females, incubate for about 28 days, usually starting when the last egg is laid. The fledging period is 36–55 days. Some young breed at 2 years, but most start when 3 years old. A bird banded as an adult lived to over 20 years old.

Behaviour: Strongly territorial in the breeding season, but in winter they may roost and feed in flocks of up to 35 birds. They are noisy, making loud, ringing calls, especially in aggression with neighbours. The normal call of both sexes is a quiet 'kleet' or 'pip', higher-pitched in females.

Feeding: Diet includes crustaceans (copepods, ostracods, amphipods, isopods), spiders, molluscs (gastropods, bivalves), insects and their larvae. They glean and peck among the tide-wrack and on wet rock platforms covered in algae and barnacles. They may take rapid, short steps – 'step-peck-peck-peck-step' – or foot-tremble on algae-covered rock platforms.

Reading: Davis, A. 1994. *Notornis* 41 (S): 171–194. Davis, A. 1994. *Notornis* 41 (S): 195–208. Dowding, J.E. & Kennedy, E.S. 1993. *Notornis* 40: 213–222. Fleming, C.A. 1939. *Emu* 39: 1–15.

185. WRYBILL *Anarhynchus frontalis* Plate 45

Other names: Ngutuparore, Wrybilled Plover
Size: 20 cm, 55 g
Distribution: New Zealand only. Wrybills breed in Canterbury and parts of inland Otago on the braided rivers that flow east from the Southern Alps or their foothills, from the Waiau and Hurunui Rivers in the north to the Makarora and Matukituki Rivers in the south. The main breeding rivers are the Rakaia, Rangitata, Waimakariri and the upper Waitaki.

After breeding, most birds fly north to the large tidal harbours of Northland, Auckland and South Auckland, i.e. Kaipara, Manukau and, above all, the Firth of Thames. Flocks of 100+ birds reach Parengarenga, Houhora, Whangarei and Waitemata Harbours. Smaller flocks regularly winter at other Northland estuaries, Tauranga Harbour, Muriwai Lagoon, Porangahau Estuary and Manawatu Estuary. A few Wrybills remain in the South Island in winter, mainly on the Waimea Estuary and at Farewell Spit. A vagrant has reached the Chathams.

Fledglings and failed breeders start leaving in late November, often staging at Lake Ellesmere. The main northward movement of birds is in the last couple of weeks of December and early January. The last adults and late fledglings leave in early February. Their return from northern mudflats starts in early August, the peak being in mid-August, often staging in flocks at Lakes Ellesmere and Wainono. Some 5–10% of winter visitors stay in the north through the summer.

Population: 4100–4200 birds in 2001.
Conservation: Protected rare endemic. The breeding of Wrybills has apparently been confined to eastern South Island rivers in historic times. In the late 1800s and early 1900s, many were collected for museum specimens, especially because of their unique sideways-bent bill. They were legally protected in 1940. Numbers have declined over recent decades, in some cases probably as a result of predation, hydroelectric developments and water extraction for irrigation, and because of the invasion of shingle riverbeds by exotic weeds such as willows, gorse and lupins.

Breeding: Eggs are laid from late August to January; many adults lay two clutches. The usual nesting sites are on islands of bare shingle, with the stones slightly larger than the eggs, or a shingle bank near water at a high point without vegetation. The blue-grey adults, eggs and chicks blend well with the blue-grey of the greywacke shingle. A few nest on the shores of adjacent lakes, e.g. Lake Tekapo. Males scrape a hollow in the shingle by bulldozing with their breast.

They lay **2** pale grey eggs (35 x 26 mm, 11 g), tinged blue or green, and covered with minute dark-brown spots and lines. Both sexes incubate for c. 30 days. Hatching is synchronous, and the chicks are led away to a riffle, backwater or other suitable feeding place. The fledging period is 36–37 days. About 50% of first year birds return to the breeding grounds, but few breed until they are 2 years old. The oldest bird recorded lived over 16 years.

Behaviour: Gregarious when not breeding; they roost quietly together, almost all on one leg, which they keep to, preferring to hop rather than lower the second leg when disturbed. They swirl as one in the air, especially before southward migration, when a flock has been likened to smoke or to a flung scarf. Their usual call is not prominent, on the ground or in flight.

Feeding: The last third of the long bill turns to the bird's right at an angle of 15–22°, and the upper mandible is slightly broader than the lower and overlaps it on the outside of the curve; inside the curve the two halves do not meet, and so the lower mandible collects invertebrates from under stones. Feeding is by pecking directly or by tilting the head to the left followed by clockwise movements of the bill under stones in shallow riffles. Diet is mainly aquatic or near-aquatic

mayflies, caddisflies, bugs, beetles, flies and stoneflies. When rivers are in flood, they are forced on to stream banks and the water's edge, where their diet is more general: beetles, flies, mayflies and spiders.

On tidal mudflats in the north, they prefer silty mud with a surface film of water. They catch small crustaceans by scything the wet mud, the bill dabbing slightly from left to right.

Reading: Davies, S. 1997. *Notornis* 44: 1–14. Hughey, K.E.D. 1985. *Notornis* 32: 42–50. Hughey, K.D. 1997. *Notornis* 44: 185–193. Pierce, R.J. 1979. *Notornis* 26: 1–21. Rawlings, M. 1993. *Forest & Bird* 24: 10–15. Stead, E.F. 1932. *The Life Histories of New Zealand Birds*. London: Search.

186. PACIFIC GOLDEN PLOVER *Pluvialis fulva* Plate 42

Other names: Asiatic/Eastern/Least Golden Plover

Size: 25 cm, 130 g

Distribution: Breed on the arctic and subarctic tundra of Siberia and western Alaska. They migrate south on a broad front, mainly to the coasts of India, Pakistan, Sri Lanka, Southeast Asia, southern China, Japan, Malaysia, the Philippines, Australasia and most Pacific islands. In New Zealand, they are the fourth most common Arctic migrant wader. They are seldom seen far from the coast. Favoured places are Parengarenga and Rangaunu Harbours, Lake Ohia (Far North), Whangarei, Kaipara and Manukau Harbours, the Firth of Thames, Bay of Plenty estuaries, Muriwai Lagoon (Gisborne), Wairoa and Ahuriri Estuaries, Manawatu Estuary, Lake Wairarapa, Farewell Spit, Lake Ellesmere, the Southland coastal lagoons and estuaries, and Te Whanga Lagoon, Chatham Island. They are recorded regularly at the Kermadecs and at many other mainland localities, and stragglers have reached the Auckland Islands.

The earliest birds arrive in September, but most arrive from October to early November.

Almost all depart northwards in late March to early April.

Population: 300–1200 birds visit New Zealand each summer, but very few overwinter, the highest winter total being only 6 birds.

Behaviour: Pacific Golden Plovers usually stay separate from other waders at high-tide roosts and sometimes roost away from the water's edge, often in a ploughed paddock or on short pasture. Flocks are usually small, 10–50. In New Zealand, unlike in the Pacific Islands, they are notably alert and wary. They are usually silent on the ground. In flight, which is fast, they give a clear, melodious, two-syllable 'tlu-ee'.

Feeding: They feed on grassland, saltmarsh and the upper levels of tidal flats on a wide range of animal food. On grassland, they eat insects and their larvae, including beetles, crickets, grasshoppers, caterpillars, flies, ants and earwigs; also spiders, earthworms and plant seeds. On tidal flats, they take mainly small crustaceans such as crabs, molluscs and marine worms.

Reading: Robertson, H.A. & Dennison, M.D. 1979. *Notornis* 26: 73–88.

187. AMERICAN GOLDEN PLOVER *Pluvialis dominica* Plate 42

Size: 26 cm, 165 g
Distribution: Breed on the arctic and subarctic tundra from northern and central Alaska east to Baffin Island (Canada). They migrate to winter in the interior of South America from Bolivia and southern Brazil to central Argen-

tina. One New Zealand record accepted: Karikari Peninsula (January 1991); but two other likely records: two birds ·on Farewell Spit (1981) and one at Pollen Island, Auckland (1989). All were birds in non-breeding plumage and with Pacific Golden Plovers.

188. GREY PLOVER *Pluvialis squatarola* Plate 42

Other name: Black-bellied Plover
Size: 29 cm, 250 g
Distribution: Breed throughout the arctic tundra and are almost circumpolar, except for Greenland, Iceland and Scandinavia. They migrate to the coasts of North and South America, Africa, southern Asia and Australasia. In New Zealand, they are a rare but annual visitor between mid-August and mid-April, but a few birds have overwintered. Since they were first recorded in the 1940s, there have been over 70 sightings, from Parengarenga Harbour to the Southland coast, and from the Kermadecs and the Chatham Islands. Most records are from Northland, the Firth of Thames and at Farewell Spit. The

largest group seen together was 12 at Farewell Spit in 1994.
Population: Usually fewer than 5 visit New Zealand each summer, the maximum being c. 15 in 1994; whereas c. 12,000 visit Australia.
Behaviour: In New Zealand, they usually roost on the coast on sandbanks or shellbanks rather than in ploughed fields or on short pasture, as Pacific Golden Plover do. Their call in flight is a loud, far-carrying, three-syllable, slurred whistle: 'tlee-oo-ee', the second syllable lower in pitch.
Feeding: Grey Plovers are birds of tidal estuaries, feeding in wet, muddy conditions, close to and often wading in the tideline.

189. SPUR-WINGED PLOVER *Vanellus miles* Plate 38

Other names: Masked Lapwing, Masked Plover
Size: 38 cm; males 370 g, females 350 g
Geographical variation: Two subspecies: *miles* in northern Australia and New Guinea and *novaehollandiae* from mid-Queensland to southeastern Australia, Tasmania and New Zealand. The subspecies overlap extensively and hybridise in Queensland and in the interior of the continent.
Distribution: New Guinea, Australia, Lord Howe Island and New Zealand. A vagrant to the Moluccas, Christmas Island (Indian Ocean), Norfolk Island and the Cook Islands. Vagrants were recorded at Kai-iwi (1886) and at Hokitika (1892). A pair bred for the first time in New Zealand at Invercargill Airport about 1932. By 1951, there were c. 100, and by 1971 c. 1250 breeding birds within a 16

km radius of the original breeding site. During the 1950s, they expanded to inland Southland and appeared near Lake Wanaka, Central Otago, but remained rare outside Southland to the mid-1960s. From the late 1960s to the 1980s, they spread to Stewart Island and to the rest of the South Island. The first breeding records in the North Island were in the early 1970s near Gisborne, Dannevirke and Paraparaumu. Now abundant in coastal Manawatu and southern Wairarapa, and becoming more common throughout the North Island, including Northland. They have become well established on the Chatham Islands since breeding was first recorded there in 1981, and have apparently established at Raoul Island, Kermadecs, since 1993. Recorded from the Auckland (1995), Antipodes (1995) and Bounty Islands (1998).

ground (e.g. chewed-down turnips or chou-moellier, or consolidated riverbed shingle). The nest is a scrape in the ground, unlined or scantily lined with whatever material is nearby.

They lay 1–4 khaki eggs (49 x 35 mm, 31 g) with brownish-black spots and blotches. Both sexes incubate for 30–31 days after the last egg is laid. The chicks soon leave the nest and follow the adults, but find their own food. The fledging period is 7–8 weeks. Young are capable of breeding at the end of their first year, but most pair for life in their first year and breed in their second year. The oldest bird recorded in New Zealand lived over 16 years.

Behaviour: Often gregarious when not breeding; flocks of up to 600, presumably juveniles and non-breeders, have been recorded at Lake Wairarapa in October–December. Spur-winged Plovers are extremely noisy; their main call is a loud, penetrating and staccato 'rattle', often at night, on the ground and in the air. Among their various displays is the conspicuous piping party; in a loose circle on raised ground, six or seven birds face one another in an upright stance with legs straight, breast pushed out and wings held slightly open, exposing the spurs; they call harshly at one another, alternating with silence; some birds stiffly advance and retreat.

When alarmed, they are wary and alert with an upright stance, although an incubating bird usually creeps unobtrusively away from the intruder. They are aggressive in defence of their nest and chicks, screaming and dive-bombing to divert intruders, and attacking Australasian Harriers and Australian Magpies as they fly over.

Feeding: Diet on short-grassed pasture and ploughed paddocks is mainly earthworms and insects and their larvae, but also seeds and leaves; in tidal and other coastal habitats, crustaceans and molluscs are taken. They feed with a slow, stalking walk, shoulders hunched and head forward, with a sudden dip to catch prey.

Population: Abundant in Southland, coastal Otago and Canterbury, Manawatu and southern Wairarapa; common or becoming so elsewhere.

Conservation: Protected common self-introduced native. Spur-winged Plovers are a recent arrival in New Zealand and are clearly suited to the arable and pasture habitats. They are probably beneficial to farmers, as they eat a wide range of invertebrates, including pests such as grass grubs and porina larvae.

Breeding: Laying is from June to late November, with the peak in August. Several clutches are laid each year. The preferred site is rough, open pasture without farm animals, or a flat, wet area with some surface irregularity and a wide outlook. They also breed on bare

Reading: Barlow, M. 1972. *Notornis* 19: 201–211. Barlow, M. 1983. *The Year of the Spur-winged Plover*. Invercargill: Craig Printing. Barlow, M.L. et al. 1972. *Notornis* 19: 212–249.

190. TURNSTONE *Arenaria interpres* Plate 45

Other name: Ruddy Turnstone
Size: 23 cm, 120 g
Geographical variation: Two subspecies: the nominate *interpres*, which breeds throughout the Arctic and migrates to tropical and temperate coasts of both hemispheres; and *morinella*, which breeds in subarctic North America and migrates to South America and the Pacific Islands. Both visit New Zealand.
Distribution: Breed along the northern coasts and islands of Greenland, Scandinavia, Siberia, Alaska and the islands of northern Canada. Almost worldwide in autumn and winter on the coasts of the Americas, Africa, Madagascar, southern and southeastern Asia, the islands of the Pacific, and Australasia. In New Zealand, they concentrate in certain favoured localities: Parengarenga, Rangaunu, Kaipara, Manukau and Tauranga Harbours and the Firth of Thames in the North Island; Farewell Spit, Motueka Estuary, Lake Grassmere, Kaikoura Peninsula and the coastal lagoons and estuaries of Southland in the South Island; Chatham Island and the Auckland Islands. Small numbers are likely to turn up at any coastal lagoon or estuary, especially when they are migrating southwards in late September to October, or northwards in March–April. A straggler to the Kermadec, Antipodes and Campbell Islands. A bird banded near Auckland by the New Zealand Wader Study Group was recaptured in Queensland on southward migration and then recaptured a month later back at its original capture site.
Population: Turnstones are the third most numerous of the arctic waders to visit New Zealand: 4000–7000 birds, evenly divided between the North and South Islands, and

including c. 400 on Chatham Island and 100 on the Auckland Islands. Over 3000 have been recorded gathering at Parengarenga Harbour in March of some years, before their northward migration. Between 100 and 1500 (3–45% of the previous summer visitors) overwinter, perhaps mainly yearlings, and so reflecting the highly variable breeding success in the previous northern summer.
Behaviour: Gregarious, in small flocks of the same species or with Banded Dotterels, sometimes visiting rough farmland near the sea. Flocks in flight or when disturbed utter a twittering 'kititit'.
Feeding: Turnstones feed actively by deftly flicking over shells, seaweed and pieces of wood with their longish, wedge-shaped bill in search of such food items as sandhoppers. They tend to avoid smooth, sandy beaches and open mudflats, preferring to feed on shelly or stony foreshores, among rockpools or on exposed rocky reefs. Their actions depend on what is available; at Farewell Spit, some feed on the Ocean Beach, bustling between waves to dab at wet sand and fossick through stranded debris. Most feed on the Bay Flats; on the falling tide flicking aside or pushing into eel-grass strands, looking for animals hidden underneath, on the rising tide probing for crabs in their burrows in the small runnels among the plants. On rocky coasts, they feed differently; in Victoria, they take mostly small gastropod molluscs and some barnacles.

Reading: Houston, P. & Barter, M. 1990. *Stilt* 17: 17–23. Robertson, H.A. & Dennison, M.D. 1979. *Notornis* 26: 73–88.

SNIPE, SANDPIPERS, GODWITS and CURLEWS Scolopacidae

About 79 species, of which 2 breed in New Zealand (non-migratory snipe) and 32 reach New Zealand as migrants for the northern winter.

Apart from stints (known as peeps in North America), these waders have a slender bill that is as long as or longer than the head. In curlews and godwits, the bill is sensitive and flexible at the tip, and the mandibles open during probing in soft mud or shallow water. All have long, pointed wings, rapid flight, a long neck, long legs and, for birds, a short tail. Their eyes are smaller than those of plovers and dotterels, as suits their more tactile, less visual, feeding. Gregarious when not breeding.

Their food has not been studied in detail in New Zealand. They take a variety of mudflat-burrowing crabs, small amphipod and ostracod crustaceans, polychaete worms and small gastropod and bivalve molluscs. Their diet includes insect larvae and pupae of craneflies (Tipulidae), midges (Chironomidae), beetles and flies; they may also take spiders and earthworms. They swallow grass, sedge and rush seeds, but whether by accident or design is not known for certain. The various species probe to different depths according to the length of their bill. Most of the rapid, vigorous, sewing-machine probing of medium and smaller waders is exploratory, as often is the slower, more careful probing of godwits, curlews or whimbrels.

The waders that migrate to New Zealand mostly breed in the arctic or subarctic tundra of the Northern Hemisphere and are strongly migratory. Those that breed furthest north tend to migrate furthest into the Southern Hemisphere, from the largest curlews to the smallest stints. The routes taken by the various species of wader are being elucidated by an extensive co-operative programme of banding and leg-flagging throughout the East Asian flyway. The New Zealand Wader Study Group have caught over 4000 Arctic migrants in the Auckland area, and some of these have been marked, to enable resightings, with white plastic leg flags.

The first Arctic migrants arrive in September-October, but others trickle into the country through November. Most leave in March–April, but a variable proportion of the summer population stays behind to spend the southern winter in New Zealand; most are probably yearlings, as few adopt breeding plumage, and so the number left behind provides an indication of the success of the previous northern breeding season.

New Zealand is at the southern limit of many species, and some of the distances travelled are huge; it is possible that some of the migrants fly between New Zealand and China, Japan or the Aleutian Chain in a single flight, although most stop at least once to refuel. In order to undertake such a long journey, waders feed voraciously in the weeks before departure and often arrive late to their roosts. They lay down extensive fat deposits, their weight can increase to 50–75% above their normal non-breeding weight. On arrival, they are often exhausted and quite approachable, but quickly regain their condition. The adult Arctic migrants moult all their flight feathers during the southern summer, and so can be distinguished from juveniles, which do not moult or lose only a few feathers until the southern autumn.

The sexes are alike, but females are often noticeably larger than males. The non-breeding plumage, as is mostly seen in New Zealand, is dull, the upperparts mottled or a uniform brown and grey, the underparts paler, sometimes with streaks and spots. Before leaving and while breeding, they are brighter, many species becoming much more rufous above and rufous or black below. The age of first breeding is 1–2–3 years, and many birds live to at least 15 years old.

191. NEW ZEALAND SNIPE *Coenocorypha aucklandica* Plate 43

Other names: Hakawai, Hokioi
Size: 23 cm, 105 g
Geographical variation: Five subspecies; two of which are extinct: the Stewart Island Snipe *iredalei* died out on Jacky Lee Island when Weka were introduced and on Big South Cape Island when ship rats got ashore in 1964, and the Little Barrier Snipe *barrierensis* is known only from one caught on Little Barrier Island in 1870. The remaining three subspecies are *huegeli* on The Snares, *meinertzhagenae* on the Antipodes Islands and *aucklandica* on the Auckland Islands. The subspecific status of snipe on the Campbell Islands has not yet been determined.
Distribution: New Zealand only. New Zealand Snipe are now confined to subantarctic islands that mammalian predators have not reached. Snares Island Snipe are on the three largest islands in The Snares, Antipodes Island Snipe are on all islands in the Antipodes group, and Auckland Island Snipe are on all islands in the group except the main island, which has cats and pigs. In November 1997, a small population of snipe was discovered living on Jacquemart Island, off Campbell Island, but snipe had been recorded on Campbell Island in the 1800s.
Population: Common on predator-free islands in the subantarctic, but no estimates of numbers are available
Conservation: Protected locally common endemic. Snipe were present on the New Zealand mainland before European settlement, but probably died out with the arrival of the Pacific rat with the Maori, about 1000 years ago. Snipe nest on the ground, are confiding and rarely fly, and so are extremely vulnerable to ground-hunting predators such as cats, rats and Weka, all of which have been implicated in the recent extinction of snipe on small islands. The only introduced mammal that snipe have survived alongside is the house mouse on Antipodes Island. An attempt to save the Stewart Island Snipe by transferring them to a predator-free island in 1964 failed when the two birds caught died before release.

Breeding: Laying is in August–January, the season varying between island groups. The nest is on or near the ground, among dense vegetation such as tussock, sedge or fern. It is a simple depression in leaf litter, or a bowl of grass or sedge leaves. They lay 2 pale brown eggs (42 x 32 mm, 23 g) with dark spots and blotches. The eggs are laid 3 days apart. Incubation is shared equally by the sexes for c. 22 days. The chicks leave the nest on the day of hatching, and each is cared for independently by one of the adults. The chicks are fed entirely by their parents initially and remain with them for about 9 weeks. Snipe can breed at 1 year old, but most can not obtain a territory until 2–3 years old.
Behaviour: New Zealand Snipe prefer areas of dense groundcover, only venturing into more open areas at night. They are capable of flight but rarely do so unless disturbed at close range or when displaying. Although cryptically patterned and shunning open areas, snipe are confiding and allow close approach. Their presence is often revealed by the male territorial calls: 'trerk trerk trerk' and 'queeyoo queeyoo', particularly at dawn and dusk. The extinct Stewart Island Snipe was apparently the source of the Maori legend of the hakawai or hokioi, a frightening creature that called only at night. This nocturnal aerial display, a call followed by the sound of vibrating tail feathers, is also given by the Chatham Island and Auckland Island Snipe and perhaps the Antipodes Island subspecies, but not by the subspecies on The Snares.
Feeding: Diet comprises a wide variety of invertebrates, including earthworms, amphipods, insects and their larvae. They favour damper areas of tussock, scrub or forest, where they get all their food by probing in the peaty soil and around the bases of plants.

Reading: Miskelly, C.M. 1987. *Notornis* 34: 95–116. Miskelly, C.M. 1990. *Ibis* 132: 366–379. Miskelly, C.M. 1990. *Emu* 90: 28–32.

192. CHATHAM ISLAND SNIPE *Coenocorypha pusilla* Plate 43

Size: 20 cm, 80 g

Distribution: Chatham Islands only. Formerly on Chatham, Pitt and Mangere Islands, but since cats eradicated them from Mangere Island in the 1890s they have been confined to South East Island. More recently found on Star Keys, and reintroduced to Mangere Island, from which they have colonised Little Mangere Island and now a vagrant to Pitt Island.

Population: Common on South East Island, increasing elsewhere.

Conservation: Protected locally common endemic. Although capable of strong flight, Chatham Island Snipe rarely fly during the day, and their confiding nature makes them easy prey to ground-hunting predators. Successfully reintroduced to Mangere Island from South East Island in 1970 and 1972 when cats were no longer present. Attempts at rearing young in captivity have had little success.

Breeding: Eggs are laid in September–January.

The nest is on or near the ground, among dense vegetation such as tussock, sedge or fern. It is a simple depression in leaf litter, or a bowl of grass or sedge leaves. They lay 2–3 pinkish-brown eggs (39 x 28 mm, 16 g) with spots and blotches of dark brown and grey around the widest part. Chicks leave the nest on the day of hatching and the brood is split between the adults. The chicks are fed entirely by their parents initially but become independent at about 6 weeks.

Behaviour: Chatham Island Snipe remain under forest or among dense cover during the day but will feed in open areas at night. They fly during the day only if disturbed at close range, but do so readily at night when they display aerially.

Feeding: Diet includes earthworms, amphipods, insects and their larvae. They obtain all their food by probing in soil and at the bases of plants.

Reading: Miskelly C.M. 1990. *Ibis* 132: 366–379. Miskelly, C.M. 1990. *Emu* 90: 28–32.

193. JAPANESE SNIPE *Gallinago hardwickii* Plate 43

Other name: Latham's Snipe (Australia)

Size: 24 cm, 160 g

Distribution: Breed in Japan, especially in the north, on the southern Sakhalin Peninsula and the southern Kurile Islands, and on the mainland coast of eastern Siberia. They migrate to winter in New Guinea and Australia, mainly in the eastern and south-eastern states. They have been recorded in New Zealand about 15 times, from Auckland to The Snares, usually at freshwater wetlands surrounded with rank rushes, sedges and reeds. Apart from two early specimens (Auckland 1898 and Wanganui 1914) and

recent records from Manawatu Estuary (1999–2000) and Lake Ellesmere (2002), the rest are sight records where the identity of Japanese Snipe is assumed in preference to the other similar, but less likely, snipes. Seen as singles, except for two at Cooper's Lagoon (1973) and Colac Bay (1984–86) and three at Lake Wairarapa (1993).

Behaviour: Solitary or in small groups. When approached, they generally crouch in thick vegetation, blending with their surroundings, but if disturbed they rise suddenly, zig-zag up steeply and pitch suddenly or circle fairly high, calling a harsh 'krek' repeatedly, before landing.

194. LESSER KNOT *Calidris canutus* Plate 44

Other names: Huahou, Red Knot

Size: 24 cm, 120 g

Geographical variation: Four or five subspecies: *rogersi*, which breeds on the Chukut-

ski Peninsula of eastern Siberia is the form that migrates to Australasia, including New Zealand.

Distribution: Breed in widely separated parts

of the high Arctic and winter in temperate and tropical estuaries of both hemispheres. In New Zealand, they are unevenly distributed around the coast, with large concentrations (10,000+ birds) regularly at the Kaipara and Manukau Harbours and at Farewell Spit. Flocks of 1000–10,000 birds are often recorded from Parengarenga, Houhora, Rangaunu and Whangarei and Waitemata Harbours, and the Firth of Thames. Smaller flocks of 250–1000 birds regularly spend the summer at Mangawhai Estuary, Tauranga Harbour, Manawatu Estuary, Golden and Tasman Bays, in Southland coastal lagoons and estuaries, at Paterson Inlet, Stewart Island, and at Te Whanga Lagoon, Chatham Island. Smaller groups, often mostly transients in September–October and March–April, are at other estuaries and coastal lagoons. A surprisingly rare bird on the Aotea, Kawhia and Ohiwa Harbours, Ahuriri Estuary, Avon–Heathcote Estuary and the Otago coast. A straggler to the Kermadec, Auckland and Campbell Islands. Usually 7–15% of summer visitors remain to overwinter, mainly in the Manukau Harbour.

The New Zealand Wader Study Group has shown from banding recoveries and leg-flag sightings that adult Lesser Knots reach New Zealand in September–October from their breeding grounds in far-eastern Siberia after four to five flights down through eastern Asia and Australia or Irian Jaya. Many juveniles stop in Australia before moving on to New Zealand in their second year. The return from New Zealand to eastern Siberia, starting in March–April, is apparently mainly through staging areas in the Gulf of Carpentaria and New Guinea, and then on the coast of China or Korea.

Population: Lesser Knots are the second most numerous Arctic wader to reach New Zealand: between 45,000 and 70,000 each summer. About 4000–8000 birds overwinter.

Behaviour: Gregarious; flying, roosting and feeding in packed masses. In flight, a flock will twist and turn like swirling smoke clouds. In New Zealand, Lesser Knots are usually silent, but feeding flocks and roosting flocks disturbed by the rising tide may keep up a subdued, not unmusical chatter. Birds in flight may utter a throaty 'knut, knut', and before migration they give a clear 'weet, weet' call.

Feeding: Diet is mainly small (5–15 mm) thin-shelled bivalves *Myodora*, *Tellina* and *Nucula*, with other thicker-shelled molluscs (e.g. the cockle *Chione*) and gastropods, which are swallowed whole. They feed close to the tideline on intertidal mudflats and sandflats, often with Bar-tailed Godwits. A tactile rather than visual feeder, feeding as a flock with remarkable co-ordination, they rapidly drill soft mud or wet sand, with a sewing-machine action, head held low and bill nearly vertical.

Reading: Barter, M. *et al.* 1988. *Stilt* 12: 29–32. Piersma, T. 1991. *Stilt* 19: 30–36. Riegen, A.C. 1999. *Notornis* 46: 123–142.

195. GREAT KNOT *Calidris tenuirostris* Plate 44

Size: 27 cm, 160 g

Distribution: Breed in northeastern Siberia and migrate to southern Asia, the Philippines and Australasia, especially to the northern and northwestern coasts of Australia, where 200,000+ spend the southern summer. A rare migrant to New Zealand, with some 25 records up to 2004, from Northland to Mason Bay, Stewart Island. Mostly singletons except at Manawatu Estuary (three in 1967, four in 2003), Firth of Thames (two in 1970) and Wanganui Estuary (three in 1992).

Behaviour: Gregarious. In New Zealand, they are usually found roosting or feeding with Lesser Knots, and may be overlooked amongst huge flocks of these at some sites.

Reading: Andrew, I.G. 1968. *Notornis* 15: 207–210.

196. SANDERLING   *Calidris alba*   Plate 45

Size: 20 cm, 50 g
Distribution: Breed in the high Arctic in
Greenland, Spitzbergen and parts of Siberia,
including the Taimyr Peninsula and the delta
of the Lena River, and on northern islands
of Canada. They winter widely on coasts in
tropical and temperate regions of both
hemispheres. A rare but probably annual
visitor to New Zealand. They have been
recorded from Northland to Southland and
from Chatham Island. Usually singles, but
sometimes in small flocks, e.g. five at Parengarenga Harbour (1950), five (1967) and four
(1988) at Kaituna Cut/Maketu, six at Farewell
Spit (1983); five (1966) and four (1971) at
Waituna Lagoon, Southland and four at
Tapora, Kaipara Harbour (1999).
Behaviour: Sanderlings always seem in a
hurry as they feed busily close to the tideline;
on the sandy ocean beaches that they prefer,
they rush in and out of the waveline, following
each backwash and jabbing and probing
rapidly. They also peck and probe on estuarine
and mudflat pools, but prefer the sandier
parts. They hold their body horizontal and
move their legs so fast that they have been
likened to clockwork toys.

197. DUNLIN   *Calidris alpina*   Plate 44

Size: 18 cm, 50 g
Distribution: Breed from eastern Greenland,
across northern Europe and Siberia to Alaska
and northern Canada. The eastern subspecies
sakhalina is the one most likely to reach
Australia and New Zealand. Dunlins winter
mainly north of the tropics, from Europe east
to southern China, Korea and Japan. The few
records in Australia and New Zealand are
of rare vagrants, including sight records of
single birds at Kaipara Harbour (1974),
Manukau Harbour (1969 and 1979) and at
the Firth of Thames (1977).
Behaviour: In general behaviour, including
feeding, very much like the like Curlew
Sandpiper. In flight, they give a high, flat
'trrree'.

Reading: Brown, B. 1975. *Notornis* 22: 241–243.
Brown, B. 1979. *Notornis* 26: 202–203.

198. CURLEW SANDPIPER   *Calidris ferruginea*   Plate 44

Size: 19 cm, 60 g
Distribution: Breed in high arctic central
Siberia between the Yenesei and Kolyma
Rivers. A few have bred in Alaska, well to
the east of their normal range. They winter
in Africa, southern Asia and Australasia, and
are a regular migrant to New Zealand in small
numbers. Flocks of 10–50 (exceptionally 100+)
are recorded each summer at Parengarenga
and Manukau Harbours, the Firth of Thames,
Lake Ellesmere and Awarua Bay. Smaller
numbers are recorded at many other estuaries
and coastal lagoons from Northland to
Southland. Recorded from the Kermadec,
Chatham and Auckland Islands. A few
overwinter.
Population: Curlew Sandpipers are the
seventh most numerous Arctic wader to visit
New Zealand, with c. 50–150 birds each
summer; c. 20–50 usually overwinter.
Behaviour: They roost and feed mainly with
Wrybills, when they are present, or with
Banded Dotterels or Lesser Knots. Their call
is a clear, soft, liquid 'chirrup'.
Feeding: Curlew Sandpipers feed in wet mud
or in shallow water, often belly-deep, probing
deeply and often submerging the head to
do so.

199. SHARP-TAILED SANDPIPER *Calidris acuminata* Plate 46

Size: 22 cm, 60 g
Distribution: Breed in northeastern Siberia, in a limited range from the Lena to the Kolyma Rivers. Most birds migrate to New Guinea and Australia, particularly in eastern South Australia, Victoria and southern New South Wales, but some reach New Zealand, Vanuatu, New Caledonia and Fiji. In New Zealand, they are a regular migrant in small numbers. Small flocks of 10–30 birds are often recorded on Parengarenga and Manukau Harbours, the Firth of Thames, Lakes Wairarapa and Ellesmere, and on the Southland coastal lagoons and estuaries. Smaller numbers are found at other estuaries or coastal lagoons from Northland to Southland in October–March. A transient at the Kermadec Islands; a straggler to The Snares and the Chathams. Few overwinter.

Population: Sharp-tailed Sandpipers are the eighth most numerous Arctic wader to reach New Zealand: 50–200 each summer, but usually fewer than 10 overwinter.
Behaviour: Gregarious, often feeding and roosting quietly in small flocks at pools in beds of *Sarcocornia*, or roosting on shellbanks or sandbanks with Wrybills, Lesser Knots, Curlew Sandpipers and Red-necked Stints. They are usually silent in New Zealand, but birds, when flushed, may utter a soft, metallic 'pleep-pleep'.
Feeding: Sharp-tailed Sandpipers forage on the shallow edges of lagoons, both fresh and brackish, preferring low-growing saltmarsh vegetation to open mudflats, although in New Zealand they may also visit higher parts of the shore away from the tideline.

200. PECTORAL SANDPIPER *Calidris melanotos* Plate 46

Size: 23 cm, 80 g
Distribution: Breed across northern Siberia from the Taimyr Peninsula to the Bering Sea, enclosing the known breeding range of the Sharp-tailed Sandpiper, and in northern Alaska and Canada. Most migrate through the United States and Mexico to winter in southern South America, but a few apparently migrate due south to Australia and New Zealand, with occasional records in southeastern Asia, Micronesia, New Guinea, Kiribati and Vanuatu. In New Zealand, they favour eastern estuaries and coastal lagoons, especially Lakes Wairarapa, Ellesmere and Wainono, but have been recorded at many sites from Northland to Southland.

Population: Fewer than 20 Pectoral Sandpipers come to New Zealand every year, mainly in November–April. The largest flock recorded was 11 at Lake Ellesmere in February 1993.
Behaviour: Gregarious, usually in small flocks or with but feeding apart from Sharp-tailed Sandpipers. They are usually silent in New Zealand but, when disturbed into flight, they call a clear, husky 'prrrt, prrrt'.
Feeding: Like Sharp-tailed Sandpipers, they prefer the edges of wet grassy areas and shallow pools with scattered low vegetation, but are even more likely to avoid the open tideline.

201. BAIRD'S SANDPIPER *Calidris bairdii* Plate 46

Size: 18 cm, 40 g
Distribution: Breed from the Chukotski Peninsula of eastern Siberia, across arctic Alaska and Canada to Greenland, and winter in central and southern South America. Rare vagrants to Australia and New Zealand,

including five records of single birds in the North Island: Manukau Harbour (1970, 1976), Firth of Thames (1970, 1972) and Manawatu Estuary (1976).
Reading: McKenzie, H.R. *et al.* 1971. *Notornis* 18: 58–60.

202. WHITE-RUMPED SANDPIPER   *Calidris fuscicollis*   Plate 44

Size: 16 cm, 35 g
Distribution: Breed in far-northern Alaska and Canada, and winter in southern South America. Rare vagrants to eastern and southeastern Australia and New Zealand, including two at Manukau Harbour (December 1969) and one at Parengarenga Harbour (March 1971).

Behaviour: If flushed, they often utter a distinctive, high-pitched 'jeet', like a mouse's squeak.

Reading: Edgar, A.T. 1971. *Notornis* 18: 116–117.
McKenzie, H.R. 1970. *Notornis* 17: 236–237.

203. RED-NECKED STINT   *Calidris ruficollis*   Plate 47

Size: 15 cm, 30 g
Distribution: Breed in northern Siberia from the Taimyr Peninsula to the Bering Sea, and in northwestern Alaska. They migrate to the coasts of Malaysia, the Philippines, and Australasia, especially to southeastern Australia. In New Zealand, they are widespread in small flocks, which seldom exceed 40 birds. Favoured sites are Parengarenga and Manukau Harbours, the Firth of Thames, Porangahau Estuary, Farewell Spit, Lakes Grassmere, Ellesmere and Wainono, and Awarua Bay, but they use many coastal lagoons and estuaries from Northland to Southland. Stragglers have been recorded at Chatham Island and the Auckland Islands.
Population: The fifth most numerous Arctic wader to reach New Zealand, but only some 100–250 visit each summer, whereas 200,000+

visit Australia. In winter, 5–50 remain, mainly at Lake Ellesmere.
Behaviour: Gregarious; feeding in small single-species flocks, or with Banded Dotterels and Wrybills, and usually roosting with Wrybills, if present. Quiet in New Zealand; in flight, they sometimes utter a thin, high-pitched call.
Feeding: Red-necked Stints feed mainly on tidal mudflats, sandflats and coastal lagoons with a thin film of moisture. They feed eagerly, with legs flexed and bodies low to the mud, running about with mouse-like rushes, their bills busily probing up and down like sewing machines. They also snatch and jab at the surface.

Reading: Thomas, D.G. & Dartnall, A.J. 1971. *Emu* 71: 20–26.

204. LITTLE STINT   *Calidris minuta*   Plate 47

Size: 15 cm, 25 g
Distribution: Breed in the Arctic from Scandinavia east to Siberia, and migrate mainly to southern Europe, Africa and southern Asia. They are rare vagrants to Australasia, including several possible New Zealand records at Kaipara Harbour, the Firth

of Thames and Lake Ellesmere, and an accepted record of a bird at Lake Ellesmere (1992–93).
Behaviour: Like Red-necked Stints in habits and habitat; the New Zealand bird was consorting with them.

205. LEAST SANDPIPER   *Calidris minutilla*   Plate 47

Size: 15 cm, 25 g
Distribution: Breed in subarctic North America from Alaska through northern

Canada to Labrador, Nova Scotia and Maine. They migrate to southern United States, the Caribbean, Central America and northern

South America. A rare vagrant to Australasia, including a sight record of a yellow-legged stint at Wairoa Estuary (1952) that fits this species, and two other probable sight records (certainly of yellow-legged stints) at Ahuriri Estuary (1953) and the Firth of Thames (1972).

Reading: Stidolph, R.H.D. 1953. *Notornis* 5: 115.

206. WESTERN SANDPIPER *Calidris mauri* Plate 47

Size: 17 cm, 30 g
Distribution: Breed from the Chukotski Peninsula of eastern Siberia to northern Alaska, and winter in coastal California, Mexico, Central America and northern South America. Rare vagrants to Australasia, including five New Zealand records: Farewell Spit (1964), Rangaunu Harbour (1970), Firth of Thames (1970–71, 1984) and Parengarenga Harbour (1979).

Reading: Blackburn, A. & Bell, B.D. 1965. *Notornis* 12: 109–110.

207. BROAD-BILLED SANDPIPER *Limicola falcinellus* Plate 47

Size: 17 cm, 35 g
Geographical variation: Two subspecies: *falcinellus* breeds in northern Europe and Asia and migrates to East Africa and southern Asia; *sibiricus* breeds in eastern Siberia and migrates mainly to southeastern Asia and northwestern Australia.
Distribution: Breed in widely scattered parts of the Arctic from Scandinavia to eastern Siberia, and winter in Africa, southern Asia and in Australasia. A few reach New Zealand. They were first recorded at the Firth of Thames, January–March 1960, and since then singles, or at most two birds, have been recorded occasionally between Northland and Canterbury. Most sightings have been on the Firth of Thames.
Behaviour: Often solitary, but also with Wrybills or Red-necked Stints at high-tide roosts,
Feeding: In New Zealand, they feed on soft intertidal mudflats with the bill held vertically, probing vigorously up and down, sometimes inserting the full length of the bill and submerging the head; occasionally peck at the surface.

Reading: Sibson, R.B. & McKenzie, H.R. 1960. *Notornis* 8: 233–235.

208. RUFF *Philomachus pugnax* Plate 46

Other name: Reeve (female)
Size: 29 cm, 170 g
Distribution: Breed from northern Europe east to eastern Siberia, and winter mostly in southern Europe, Africa and India. A scarce vagrant to many parts of Australasia, including about 12 sight records in New Zealand: Manukau Harbour, (possible in 1964); Colac Bay, Southland (1984–85); Lake Ellesmere (two in 1984–85; 1991–92, 1999); Lake Poukawa, Hawke's Bay (1985), Lake Wainono (1987, 2002), Miranda (2001), Ahuriri Estuary (2001), Taranaki (2002) and Rakaia Rivermouth (2003).
Behaviour: Gregarious and usually silent when not breeding. They favour muddy edges of shallow freshwater lagoons, probing and pecking to feed. Well known for their lek breeding, in which males congregate to display their spectacularly variable ruffs and ear tufts of breeding plumage. Females visit the lek solely to copulate.

209. ASIATIC DOWITCHER   *Limnodromus semipalmatus*   Plate 49

Size: 34 cm, 180 g

Distribution: Asiatic Dowitchers are very rare and their distribution is not well known. They breed patchily from central Asia to Manchuria, and in winter they are thinly distributed from coastal Arabia, across southern Asia (especially in Sumatra) to northern Australia, where several hundred may spend the southern summer. Four records in New Zealand: Avon–Heathcote Estuary (August–September 1985), Firth of Thames (February–May 1987), Maketu (November 1998) and Ohiwa Harbour (December 2002).

Reading: Fennell, J. *et al.* 1985. *Notornis* 32: 322–323. Paige, J.P. 1965. *Ibis* 107: 95–97.

210. EASTERN CURLEW   *Numenius madagascariensis*   Plate 48

Other name: Far-eastern Curlew

Size: 63 cm, 900 g

Distribution: Breed in northeastern Asia, including the Kamchatka Peninsula and eastern Manchuria, and migrate to coasts of Australasia, especially to northern and eastern Australia. In New Zealand, Eastern Curlews are an annual migrant in small numbers. Favoured places for small flocks of 5–20 birds are Manukau Harbour, the Firth of Thames, Farewell Spit and the Southland coast. Smaller flocks have been recorded frequently at Parengarenga, Kaipara and Kawhia Harbours, Kaituna/Maketu in the Bay of Plenty, and the Manawatu, Ashley and Avon–Heathcote Estuaries. Recorded at the Kermadec and Chatham Islands. A few non-breeders stay in New Zealand over the southern winter.

Population: In the 1980s and 1990s, 20–50 birds visited New Zealand each year, whereas c. 6000 visit Australia. Numbers have declined in southeastern Australia and New Zealand since the 1960s, when probably c. 100 birds visited each summer; e.g. at Farewell Spit, 20–30 were usual in the 1960s, while only 5–10 visit now.

Behaviour: Gregarious and wary when roosting on sand dunes and shellbanks and among mangroves. Their call, given mostly in flight, is a loud, haunting 'croo-lee, croo-lee'.

Feeding: Diet is mainly crustaceans, especially ghost shrimps and crabs, and marine polychaete worms, caught by probing down their burrows deep into the mud, by probing sideways into shallow burrows or by picking at the surface. They feed mainly in muddy, tidal estuaries and harbours.

Reading: Close, D. & Newman, O.M.G. 1984. *Emu* 84: 38–40. Robertson, H.A. & Dennison, M.D. 1979. *Notornis* 26: 73–88.

211. WHIMBREL   *Numenius phaeopus*   Plate 48

Size: 43 cm, 450 g

Geographical variation: Three subspecies: the nominate *phaeopus* breeds in far-northern Europe and western Siberia; the Asiatic Whimbrel *variegata* breeds in eastern Siberia and is the common form in Australasia; and the American Whimbrel *hudsonicus* breeds in northern North America and regularly reaches New Zealand in small numbers.

Distribution: Breed widely in the lower Arctic and migrate to many estuaries and coasts in tropical regions and in the temperate Southern Hemisphere. Asiatic Whimbrels are a regular summer visitor to New Zealand. The most favoured places for small flocks of 10–60 birds are Parengarenga, Rangaunu, Whangarei, Kaipara and Manukau Harbours, the Firth of Thames and Farewell Spit. Smaller groups, usually ones and twos, may appear at any estuary or coastal lagoon in New Zealand. Recorded at the Kermadec and Chatham Islands.

American Whimbrels are also regular summer visitors; groups of up to five birds join flocks of Asiatic Whimbrels at mainly the same favoured estuaries. Recorded at Chatham Island.

Population: Whimbrels are about the sixth most numerous Arctic wader to visit New Zealand, c.100–200 each year. Approximately 95% are Asiatic and 5% American. A few birds of both subspecies overwinter.

Behaviour: Gregarious, usually seen feeding in small groups of up to five birds, but they form small flocks at roost. Often they warily stay in water at the edge of a flock of Bar-tailed Godwit roosting on the tideline. They take off before the godwits take any notice of a distant intruder. Their tittering call – 'ti-ti-ti-ti-ti-ti-ti' – is readily heard from a passing flock of godwits.

Feeding: Diet is mainly crabs and marine worms, picked from the surface or taken by shallow probing.

212. LITTLE WHIMBREL *Numenius minutus* Plate 48

Other name: Little Curlew
Size: 29 cm, 160 g
Distribution: Breed on the dry, open steppes of central and northeastern Siberia, and mainly winter in New Guinea and Australia, especially inland in the north and northwest. In New Zealand, they are a rare annual migrant. Usually singles, occasionally twos or threes, feed in short grassland or ploughed paddocks near estuaries and coastal lakes from Parengarenga to Lake Wainono.

Behaviour: In New Zealand, they are usually alone or at roost with Pacific Golden Plovers, New Zealand Dotterels or Pied Stilts. The usual flight call is a soft chattering 'te-te-te', changed to a harsh 'tchoo-tchoo-tchoo' when flushed or alarmed.

Feeding: Diet is mainly large insects, picked from the surface in grassland or on the drier parts of mudflats.

Reading: Heather, B.D. & MacKenzie, N.B. 1973. *Notornis* 20: 167. McGill, A.R. 1960. *Emu* 60: 89–94.

213. BRISTLE-THIGHED CURLEW *Numenius tahitiensis* Plate 48

Size: 43 cm, 400 g
Distribution: Breed in remote mountains of western Alaska, and winter on oceanic islands and atolls of the central and South Pacific, from Fiji to French Polynesia. Records at Papua New Guinea, Solomons, New Caledonia and the Kermadec Islands (Macauley 1966, North Meyer 1972, Raoul 1972) are at the southwestern limit of their range.

Feeding: Diet includes invertebrates, molluscs and hermit crabs. In French Polynesia and in Rarotonga, they feed in saltpans, in channels and pools in the outer coral reef, and along the line of beach wrack. Unusually for curlews, they are known for stealing the eggs of seabirds.

Reading: Gill, R.E. & Redmond, R.L. 1992. *Notornis* 39: 17–26.

214. BAR-TAILED GODWIT *Limosa lapponica* Plate 49

Other name: Kuaka
Size: male 39 cm, bill 85 mm, 300 g; female 41 cm, bill 105 mm, 350 g
Geographical variation: Two subspecies are currently recognised, but this is under review: *lapponica* breeds from Scandinavia east to central Siberia, and migrates to Europe, Africa and southern Asia; *baueri* breeds from the Lena River across eastern Siberia into northern Alaska, at least as far east as Point Barrow, and migrates to southeastern Asia and Australasia. Recent studies in Australia have shown that Bar-tailed Godwits in north-western Australia have longer bills and shorter wings than those in southeastern Australia and New Zealand, and as neither

321

group seems to fit the published measurements of *baueri*, further subspecies may be raised.

Distribution: Breed from northern Scandinavia across northern Siberia to Alaska. They migrate mainly to estuaries and coasts of tropical and temperate regions from Europe and Africa to Australasia and southwestern Pacific islands, such as Vanuatu, New Caledonia and particularly Fiji. In New Zealand, they are found on estuaries and sandy coasts throughout, but especially on inlets and estuaries with broad intertidal mudflats; south to Stewart Island and east to Chatham Island. Over 10,000 birds visit the Kaipara and Manukau Harbours and Farewell Spit each southern summer, and flocks of 1000–10,000 birds visit other harbours in Northland, the Firth of Thames, Bay of Plenty estuaries, Tasman Bay, Avon–Heathcote Estuary, and Southland estuaries and coastal lagoons. They are a regular visitor to the Kermadecs, and a few straggle to subantartic islands.

The New Zealand Wader Study Group has shown from banding recoveries and leg-flag sightings that some adult Bar-tailed Godwit reach New Zealand in late September or early October by flying non-stop the 11,000 km across the Pacific from their breeding grounds in western Alaska, but others, and perhaps most juveniles, travel the 3500 km longer route through eastern Asia and Australia, arriving here in October–December. At least some of the juveniles stay in Australia until moving here in their second year. Bar-tailed Godwits leave mainly in March or early April and head for the Yellow Sea and Japan, with some stopping briefly in northern Australia or Irian Jaya. They reach their breeding grounds in western Alaska in May and early June, after another refuelling stop on the Kamchatka Pensinsula of eastern Russia.

Population: Bar-tailed Godwits are the most common Arctic wader to visit New Zealand: between 85,000 and 110,000 are present each summer, of which c. 70% are in the North Island and 30% in the South Island. Each year, 8000–18,000 birds remain for the southern winter; presumably mainly youngsters, as few are in breeding plumage in winter.

Behaviour: Gregarious; they feed in loose flocks on mudflats and fly and roost in large tight flocks, often in company with Lesser Knots. Just before landing, a flock may split apart, its members side-slipping erratically; on landing they run together with an excited chattering. Their call in a flying flock is a clear, excited 'kew-kew', and a soft 'kit-kit-kit-kit' is heard from passing flocks. Roosting flocks, if uneasy, may keep up a steady conversational chatter.

Feeding: Diet is mainly polychaete worms and molluscs. They feed on tidal flats, most moving with the tideline, but birds slowly scatter as the tide falls. They make trial probes at intervals as they walk across mud or wet sand and probe, for the full length of the bill if necessary and sometimes with head under water, often walking round the bill to reach down better to where their prey is hiding. They also dig out crabs from sandy burrows or in eelgrass beds.

Reading: Barter, M. 1989. *Stilt* 14: 43–48. Riegen, A.C. 1999. *Notornis* 46: 123–142.

215.   BLACK-TAILED GODWIT   *Limosa limosa*   Plate 49

Size: 39 cm, 350 g
Geographical variation: Three subspecies: *islandica* breeds in Iceland; *limosa* breeds in northern Europe and western Asia; and *melanuroides* breeds in eastern Asia.
Distribution: Breed in the subarctic from Iceland across Asia to the Bering Sea. The Asiatic Black-tailed Godwit *melanuroides* breeds in northern Asia from Mongolia and the upper Yenesei River eastwards to the Bering Sea. They winter in a wide arc from eastern India to Australasia, especially in Arnhem Land and the Gulf of Carpentaria

in northern Australia. Since they were first recognised in New Zealand in 1952, they have been seen annually in many estuaries between Parengarenga and the Southland coast, and have strayed to the Chatham Islands (2000) and the Auckland Islands (1963 and 1976). Occasionally they are in small flocks, with a maximum group of 11, at Lake Ellesmere in 1985. A few sometimes overwinter.
Behaviour: Very like that of Bar-tailed Godwits, which the usual singles or small groups normally associate with in New Zealand.

216.   HUDSONIAN GODWIT   *Limosa haemastica*   Plate 49

Size: 39 cm, 300 g
Distribution: Breed in two disjunct regions of northern North America, one in north-western Canada and Alaska, the other along the southern side of Hudson Bay. Most migrate to South America, but some reach the southwestern Pacific, including New

Zealand. A few are recorded on estuaries and coastal lagoons every year from Parengarenga to the Southland coast. A few sometimes overwinter.
Behaviour: Very like that of Bar-tailed Godwits, which the usual singles or twos normally associate with in New Zealand.

217.   UPLAND SANDPIPER   *Bartramia longicauda*   Plate 42

Other name: Bartram's Sandpiper
Size: 28 cm, 140 g
Distribution: Breed in North America, mainly on grasslands east of the Rockies. They migrate to South America, from southern Brazil to southern Argentina and Chile. A rare vagrant to Australasia, including a sight record of a single bird at Karaka, Manukau Harbour (1967).

Behaviour: They feed mainly inland in grassland, away from water. They readily perch on fenceposts, being in the habit of holding their wings upward briefly when landing, revealing the black barring on the white underwing and flanks. Their rolling trill is rather like that of curlews.
Reading: McKenzie, H.R. 1968. *Notornis* 15: 216–218.

218.   WANDERING TATTLER   *Tringa incana*   Plate 50

Size: 27 cm, 120 g
Distribution: Breed in far-eastern Siberia, coastal Alaska, the Yukon and northwestern British Columbia. Most winter on the coast

of America from California to Peru and on islands of the central and eastern Pacific Ocean as far south as French Polynesia, Cook Islands, Tonga and Fiji. A few wander to the coasts of New Zealand and eastern Australia. In New Zealand, they are rare but possibly annual visitors; sight records from the Kermadecs, on the mainland from Northland to Canterbury, mainly in the east except for Farewell Spit, and from the Chatham and Auckland Islands.

Behaviour: Usually wary and solitary. They bob their head and teeter up and down with their tail. Wandering Tattlers prefer rocky shores to tidal mudflats and beaches. Their usual flight call is a clear, sweet whistle or rippling trill of 6–10 notes, with the accent on the second note, the following notes diminishing a little in volume and given more rapidly than the first two or three.

219. SIBERIAN TATTLER *Tringa brevipes* Plate 50

Other name: Grey-tailed Tattler
Size: 25 cm, 100 g
Distribution: Breed patchily across northern Asia from the upper Yenesei River and Lake Baikal to the mountains of eastern and far-eastern Siberia and the Kamchatka Peninsula. They migrate to winter in southeastern Asia, the Philippines, Australasia and islands in the southwestern Pacific as far east as Fiji. They are a scarce annual visitor to the New Zealand mainland; numerous sight records of ones or twos, especially from the north and at Farewell Spit, but recorded from Northland to Southland and Stewart Island. Stragglers have reached The Snares and the Auckland Islands. A few birds may overwinter.

Behaviour: Usually wary and solitary. They bob their head and teeter up and down with their tail. Siberian Tattlers prefer tidal mudflats but also frequent rocky coasts. Their usual flight call is a sharp, high-pitched two syllables: 'tloo-weet'.

220. COMMON SANDPIPER *Tringa hypoleucos* Plate 45

Size: 20 cm, 50 g
Distribution: Breed across Europe and Asia from Spain and Britain to the Kamchatka Peninsula and Japan. They winter on the coasts of Africa, Madagascar, southern and southeastern Asia, the Philippines, and Australasia, especially in New Guinea. They are an uncommon visitor to New Zealand, with less than 20 sight records since they were first recorded in 1964. Only four sightings have been in the South Island: Lake Wainono (1980), Whanganui Inlet (1981–83), Waipara Estuary (1992) and Farewell Spit (1992).

Behaviour: Usually solitary and often in places not frequented by other waders; the bird in Whanganui Inlet was by itself for three years, feeding on the same stretch of muddy tidal creek apart from other species. Common Sandpipers bob their heads, teeter up and down with their tail and fly on flickering downcurved wings.

221. GREENSHANK *Tringa nebularia* Plate 50

Other name: Common Greenshank
Size: 32 cm, 170 g
Distribution: Breed from Scotland and Scandinavia, across Asia to the Kamchatka Peninsula. They winter widely in Africa, Arabia, India, China, Malaysia, the Philippines and Australasia. A few reach New Zealand annually and have been recorded from Parengarenga Harbour to Southland coastal lagoons and estuaries. Mostly seen as singles or in small parties of up to four. Rare stragglers have reached the Chathams and The Snares. A few may overwinter, and one bird remained in the Bay of Plenty for nine years and assumed breeding plumage in the New Zealand summer.

Behaviour: Gregarious; in New Zealand they are usually seen in the company of Pied Stilts on shallow brackish or freshwater lagoons and muddy tidal creeks rather than on tidal mudflats, which, however, they occasionally use. Their flight call is a loud, ringing 'tchew-tchew-tchew', but they sometimes utter a quiet 'tchew' during feeding.

Feeding: Greenshanks prod and probe at the margins of pools and lagoons, walking briskly, sometimes up to their belly in water, and often running after small fish.

222. MARSH SANDPIPER *Tringa stagnatilis* Plate 50

Size: 22 cm, 70 g

Distribution: Breed from eastern Europe across central Asia to Mongolia, and winter in Africa, southern Asia and Australasia. In New Zealand, since they were first recognised in 1959, there have been about 50 records at coastal lagoons, lakes and estuaries from Parengarenga to Southland, mostly since 1980. Usually singles, but up to four seen together at Kaituna, Bay of Plenty (1969–70), Lake Ellesmere (1981–82), Kaipara Harbour (1989, 1994) and Mangere Ponds (1993), and six at Miranda (1998). A few overwinter.

Behaviour: Very like that of Greenshanks but more graceful in all their activities. They, too, prefer the company of Pied Stilts, and also prefer freshwater lakes and pools, both inland and coastal, to tidal mudflats or even the upper reaches of estuaries.

Reading: Battley, P. 1991. *Stilt* 19: 28–29.

223. LESSER YELLOWLEGS *Tringa flavipes* Plate 50

Size: 24 cm, 75 g

Distribution: Breed in Alaska and Canada east to Hudson Bay, migrating to Central and South America. A rare vagrant to Australasia, including over a dozen records in New Zealand since 1964, from Manukau Harbour to Lake Wainono and Chatham Island. Most sightings have been in coastal marshes and pools, including four widely spaced records from Ahuriri Estuary. Two sightings have been inland on the muddy edges of freshwater lakes.

Behaviour: In New Zealand, very like that of Greenshanks and Marsh Sandpipers, and often in the company of Pied Stilts. Their flight call is a double 'wheep-wheep'.

Feeding: Lesser Yellowlegs walk gracefully and snatch invertebrates from the surface. Often wading up to their bellies and holding the bill and neck stretched forward, they jab at the water surface.

224. TEREK SANDPIPER *Tringa terek* Plate 45

Size: 23 cm, 70 g

Distribution: Breed from the Baltic coast of Finland, across Siberia to the Kolyma River. They migrate to the coasts of Africa, Madagascar, Arabia, southern and southeastern Asia, the Philippines and Australasia; especially common in many parts of northern and eastern Australia. Terek Sandpipers are a scarce but annual visitor to New Zealand, especially to estuaries of Northland and Auckland, Manawatu Estuary and Farewell Spit, and south to the Southland lagoons. The largest flock recorded was eight at Kaipara Harbour in 1986. A few overwinter.

Behaviour: Terek Sandpipers often remain alert and active at high-tide roosts, which they usually share with Wrybills. They bob their heads and teeter up and down with their tail. Their call is a musical trill: 'weeta-weeta-weet'.

Feeding: The restlessly active feeding of these birds draws attention as they keep abruptly changing direction to dash after animals they have seen, which they get by pecking eagerly at the surface. They also probe deeply into soft mud. They favour places where shallow water covers mud such as tidal creeks, both within and apart from mangroves, coastal lagoons and estuarine mudflats.

PHALAROPES   Phalaropodidae

3 species, all of which are rare visitors to New Zealand.

A small anomalous family of medium to small waders with reversed breeding roles, in which the females are larger and brighter than the males and confine their breeding activities to courtship, mating and laying eggs. Gregarious when not breeding. All are expert swimmers, even in shallow water, with dense plumage on the breast and belly that traps air and makes them float high and buoyantly. Two of the three have a circumpolar breeding range and spend the autumn and winter at sea; they have the salt gland highly developed. The third species, the Wilson's Phalarope,

prefers freshwater wetlands and has normal salt glands.

All phalaropes are slim, having a small head on a slender neck and a sharp, straight bill. Their legs are laterally compressed, and their toes are lobed like those of grebes and coots. They spin, or pirouette, while swimming, stirring plankton or other invertebrates up from below – a technique used more on terrestrial lagoons rather than at sea. They also dab the bill into the water and wade in algal mats and, darting this way and that, feed on flies gathered there. New Zealand records are mainly at coastal lagoons, lakes and estuaries.

225. GREY PHALAROPE *Phalaropus fulicarius*   Plate 51

Other name: Red Phalarope
Size: 20 cm; males 50 g, females 60 g
Distribution: Breed through the high Arctic in Greenland, Iceland, Spitzbergen and extreme northern parts of Asia, Alaska and Canada. They migrate to three zones of plankton-rich oceanic upwelling: off Senegal and Sierra Leone, off Namibia and western South Africa, and off the western coast of South America. Vagrants, presumably from the group that winters off South America,

have been recorded seven times in New Zealand, mainly in the east and all in June or July, when they should have been breeding: Lake Wainono (1883, 1987), Lake Ellesmere (1925), Hastings (1934), Kaituna Cut (1977), Manukau Harbour (1992) and Inchclutha, South Otago (1993). All but the second Wainono bird were in breeding plumage or almost so.

Reading: Brown, B. & Latham, P.C.M. 1978. *Notornis* 25: 198–202.

226. RED-NECKED PHALAROPE *Phalaropus lobatus*   Plate 51

Other name: Northern Phalarope
Size: 19 cm; male 30 g, female 35 g
Distribution: Breed on arctic tundra in Greenland, Iceland, Scandinavia and the northern parts of Asia, Alaska and Canada. They migrate to three main zones of oceanic upwelling: off western North America, off Arabia, and between the Philippines and New Guinea, although some winter off Namibia. They are an annual migrant in small numbers

to most Australian states, particularly in the northwest and southeast. Seven New Zealand records: Lake Ellesmere (1929, December 2000, October 2002), Wanganui Estuary (April 1935), Washdyke Lagoon (March 1961), Manukau Harbour (June 1985), Miranda (December 1996), Farewell Spit (November 2000, October 2002) and Lake Grassmere (November 2002).

Reading: Crockett, D.E. 1961. *Notornis* 9: 266. Jenkins, J.A.F. *et al*. 1986. *Notornis* 33: 191–192.

227. WILSON'S PHALAROPE   *Phalaropus tricolor*   Plate 51

Size: 22 cm; male 50 g, female 65 g
Distribution: Breed on the prairie marshes of central North America and migrate to wetlands in southern South America, particularly Argentina. Unlike the other two phalaropes, they do not go to sea but prefer wetlands of the interior. They are a rare vagrant to Australasia, including a single bird at the Manawatu Estuary (September 1983) and two birds at Lake Ellesmere (November 1983–April 1984).

Behaviour: Wilson's Phalaropes swim as actively as the other species, including spinning, but tend to feed like other waders, by walking and running in shallow water or on dry land, often with the neck extended.

Reading: Moore, J.L. & Moore, M. 1984. *Notornis* 31: 330–333. Sagar, P.M. & Harrison, K.C. 1984. *Notornis* 31: 333–334.

SKUAS   Stercorariidae

8 species: 2 breed in the New Zealand region, 2 are regular transients in spring and autumn as they pass between their Arctic breeding grounds and Southern Ocean seas, and 1 is a straggler from non-breeding areas in the central Pacific.

Skuas are strong-flying pelagic birds allied to the gulls. They have hooked beaks with a distinctive sheath covering the base of the upper bill. Most species have light- and dark-plumage phases, with some intermediate forms; all have conspicuous white flashes in the outer wing. The three small species have highly developed central tail feathers that extend well beyond the remainder of the tail, but these are rarely seen in birds in New Zealand waters.

Skuas are piratic, pursuing terns, gulls, shags and shearwaters, and forcing them to drop or disgorge their food. These spectacular aerobatic chases are most often seen in autumn when large flocks of White-fronted Terns usually have Arctic and/or Pomarine Skuas in attendance.

During breeding, the large native skuas feed mainly on shoaling fish, petrels and their eggs and chicks, or penguin eggs and chicks. They also take carrion from beaches or coastal farmland. They are also renown for their fierce territorial defence, diving noisily at people or other large intruders venturing into their breeding area. They strike at people with their legs as they pass close overhead.

Reading: Furness, R.W. 1987. *The Skuas*. Calton: Poyser. Harrison, P. 1983. *Seabirds: An Identification Guide*. Beckenham: Croom Helm. Serventy, D.L. *et al.* 1971. *The Handbook of Australian Seabirds*. Sydney: A.H. & A.W. Reed. Young, E.C. 1994. *Skua and Penguin: Predator and Prey*. Cambridge: Cambridge Univ Press.

228. BROWN SKUA   *Catharacta skua*   Plate 53

Other names: Hakoakoa, Southern Great/Southern/Subantarctic Skua
Size: 63 cm, males 1675 g, females 1950 g
Geographical variation: Many experts treat the subspecies *lonnbergi* of New Zealand and elsewhere in the subantarctic as a distinct species, *Catharacta lonnbergi*.
Distribution: The subspecies *lonnbergi* is circumpolar, breeding in the subantarctic and antarctic zones. In New Zealand, they breed on the Chatham, Solander, Stewart and outliers, The Snares, Antipodes, Auckland and Campbell Islands, and also on the Balleny Islands of the Ross Dependency. A few pairs also nest in southern Fiordland. In the summer, they remain close to their breeding

colonies, but transients appear at the Bounty Islands, and vagrants reach the Ross Sea. Although most northern breeding birds remain on their territory all year, most birds leave the southern colonies and disperse northward in autumn, especially to southern Australia and the western Tasman Sea. In winter, they are occasionally seen along the coast of the North and South Islands, and seldom inland, usually feeding on dead sheep and lambs.

Population: Widespread in the subantarctic, with many small populations. New Zealand probably has fewer than 2000 birds, with the main populations being on the Chathams (c. 260 birds), The Snares (c. 170 birds), Antipodes, Auckland (especially Enderby) and Campbell Islands.

Conservation: Partially protected native. In the Chathams, some Brown Skuas are shot by fishermen and farmers, but elsewhere few are harmed.

Breeding: Most breeding birds at The Snares and the Chathams defend their territory all year, although in winter their defence is less aggressive; at the more southern colonies, birds rarely overwinter. In the northern colonies, about 15% of territories are defended by trios (always two unrelated males and a female), but groups of up to seven birds have been recorded, whereas south of The Snares most Brown Skuas breed in simple pairs. Numbers at the colonies build up from September with members of each territorial group arriving back independently.

Laying is from mid-September to December, with a clear latitudinal gradient from the Chathams, where birds start laying in mid-September, to Campbell Island, where laying starts in early November. The nest is usually a bowl of dry grass, moss and lichen. They lay 1–2–3 brown eggs (74 x 52 mm) with dark brown blotches. Eggs are laid about 2 days apart. The adults share incubation for c. 30 days and feed the chicks during the c. 60-day fledging period. They continue to feed the chicks for at least 70 days after fledging. On the Chathams, young birds return to the colony at 4–5 years old, but do not start breeding until 5–8–14 years old. Many birds live to 20–30 years old.

Behaviour: Non-breeding birds normally form 'clubs' and then fill gaps as territorial members disappear. Brown Skuas normally maintain the same breeding territory and partner(s) year after year. Territorial displays include a conspicuous 'heraldic' display in which a bird, normally on the ground but sometimes while airborne, holds its wings stiffly upwards to display the white wing patches and extends its neck and head and utters a long call: 'charr-charr-charr'. They defend their territory very aggressively against other skuas and, with a screeching call, repeatedly and fearlessly dive at people or other intruders, striking out with their feet as they pass overhead. Usually solitary at sea away from the breeding grounds.

Feeding: While breeding, the diet is mainly penguin eggs and chicks, or petrels. The latter are caught at night on the ground or are sometimes forced to the ground and then killed. Brown Skuas carry seabirds to a 'midden', where they leave the wings, head and legs in a pile, or they regurgitate pellets containing the remains of small seabirds, especially storm petrels. They also feed on fish, eggs of other birds, dead marine mammals or seal placenta, and scavenge dead sheep and cattle in the Chathams. Goose barnacles and Broad-billed Prions form the main part of their winter diet in the Chathams. Away from their colonies, their winter diet is presumed to be mainly pelagic fish, although the few seen on the New Zealand mainland coast are often feeding on carrion, or occasionally harassing other birds such as gulls and shags.

Reading: Hemmings, A.D. 1989. *J Zool* (Lond) 218: 393–405. Hemmings, A.D. 1990. *Emu* 90: 108–113. Hemmings, A.D. 1994. *J Roy Soc NZ* 24: 245–260. Moors, P.J. 1980. *Notornis* 27: 133–146. Young, E.C. 1978. *NZ J Zool* 5: 401–416. Young, E.C. 1994. *Notornis* 41(S): 143–163. Young, E.C. 1998. *Condor* 100: 335–342. Young, E.C. *et al.* 1988. *NZ J Ecol* 11: 113–117.

229. SOUTH POLAR SKUA   *Catharacta maccormicki*   Plate 53

Other names: Antarctic Skua, MacCormick's Skua

Size: 59 cm; males 1275 g, females 1425 g

Distribution: Breed on the shores and offshore islands of Antarctica, mainly near penguin and petrel colonies. They winter at sea, some ranging into the North Pacific, North Indian and North Atlantic Oceans. In New Zealand, they breed at over 50 sites around the Ross Dependency; the main colonies (>300 pairs) are at Cape Crozier, Possession Island, Cape Bird, Sven Foyn Island and at Cape Adare. They presumably migrate well offshore, as they are rarely seen near the New Zealand coast and only a few have been beach-wrecked, mainly along the west coast of the North Island. A bird banded at Cape Hallett in 1964 was recovered in Japan in 1966.

Population: Moderately common around Antarctica; in 1981–83 c. 15,000 birds were at 55+ sites in the Ross Dependency, with Cape Crozier (c. 1000 pairs) having the largest population.

Conservation: Protected native. About 80% of breeding South Polar Skuas are associated with penguin colonies, and, in the long term, numbers may change in line with the penguin population. Numbers showed a minor decline in the northern Ross Sea area between the 1950s and early 1980s, but an increase, especially in non-breeders, in the southern McMurdo Sound, where birds had access to the refuse dump associated with McMurdo Station.

Breeding: Birds arrive at their Ross Sea colonies in mid- to late October, slightly earlier at more northern colonies. Usually a pair occupies the same territory year after year; however, a pair will occasionally shift their territory several kilometres between years. They rarely change mates, except when one bird dies. A single communally breeding trio has been reported from Ross Island. Laying is from mid-November to late December, but the season varies slightly from colony to colony and year to year, depending on weather and food availability.

They lay **2** tan eggs (71 x 50 mm) speckled brown, c. 3–5 days apart, in a simple scrape. Both birds share incubation evenly in spells of 90–180 minutes, and the female is regularly fed by the male during this time; however, where pairs have access to penguin eggs or chicks, both sexes forage. Incubation starts when the first egg is laid, and the eggs hatch 1–**2**–5 days apart, after 24–**29**–35 days. In the Ross Dependency, the second chick is virtually always evicted from the nest by the older one and dies, but at some sites two chicks are usually reared. The fledging period is 49–59 days. The chick continues to be fed by its parents for several weeks after fledging. Young normally return to their natal colony at 1–**3**–5 years old. A few females breed at 4 years old, and males at 5, but most females start breeding when 6–7 years old, and most males start when 8–9. South Polar Skuas are very long-lived; the annual survivorship of birds aged over 10 at Cape Crozier is 96%, giving a life expectancy of over 35 years. As a further indication of the good survival at Cape Crozier, 42 of 224 chicks banded in 1961 were still alive 22 years later.

Behaviour: Non-breeding birds normally form 'clubs' near the colony before the breeding season, and they start courting and forming pairs. Territorial displays are similar to those of the Brown Skua, with a conspicuous 'heraldic' display, in which a bird holds its wings stiffly upwards to show off the white wing patches and calls 'charr-charr-charr'. They defend their territory very aggressively against other skuas and, with a screeching call, repeatedly dive at people or other intruders. Little is known of the social behaviour of South Polar Skuas away from the breeding grounds, but they appear to be solitary at sea.

Feeding: While breeding, the incubating or brooding female is mainly fed by the male, who disgorges food a short distance from the nest. Diet is mainly a shoaling fish, the Antarctic Silverfish *Pleuragramma antarcticum*, but if a territory includes a penguin rookery or petrel colony, a major part of the owners' diet during part of the season will be eggs and chicks and spilt krill. Some skuas specialise at attacking breeding penguins to gain eggs and chicks, and a pair sometimes works as a team to displace an incubating or brooding penguin from its nest. They also feed on dead birds and seals, and some feed at rubbish dumps associated with research bases. In the New Zealand sector of Antarctica, refuse disposal has improved markedly and this source of food is substantially reduced. In the non-breeding season, they feed on shoaling fish, and in the seas off Japan they constantly harass feeding shearwaters and get much food by piracy.

In the hand: Females are 10% heavier than males but measurements overlap, e.g. bill 47–**51**–53.5 cf. 48–**49.5**–51.5 mm and wing 400–**415**–430 cf. 390–**410**–420 mm.

Reading: Ainley, D.G. *et al.* 1985. *Condor* 87: 427–428. Ainley, D.G. *et al.* 1986. *Notornis* 33: 155–163. Ainley, D.G. *et al.* 1990. *J Anim Ecol* 59: 1–20. Hemmings, A.D. 1994. *J Roy Soc NZ* 24: 245–260. Pietz, P. 1987. *Auk* 104: 617–627. Reid, B.E. 1966. *Notornis* 13: 71–89. Spellerberg, I.F. 1970. *Notornis* 17: 280–285. Spellerberg, I.F. 1971. *Ibis* 113: 357–363. Wang, Z. & Norman, F.I. 1993. *Notornis* 40: 189–203. Young, E.C. 1963. *Ibis* 105: 203–233. Young, E.C. 1963. *Ibis* 105: 301–318. Young, E.C. 1994. *Skua and Penguin: Predator and Prey.* Cambridge: Cambridge Univ Press.

230.   ARCTIC SKUA   *Stercorarius parasiticus*   Plate 52

Size: 43 cm excluding central tail feathers; 400 g

Distribution: Breed on the arctic and subarctic tundra of North America, Greenland, Iceland, Scandinavia and Russia. They migrate south in September and pass through the tropics to winter at sea in the Southern Hemisphere. A common visitor to New Zealand waters in November–May, and are easily the most numerous skua seen off the coasts of the

mainland and the Chatham Islands. A few immatures remain over the winter. They are often seen in coastal waters and in large sheltered harbours and sounds, but are seldom seen over land, except that they sometimes join roosting flocks of terns or gulls.

Behaviour: Arctic Skuas are conspicuous as they aerobatically chase White-fronted Terns or small gulls and harry them until they are forced to drop their fish or to regurgitate. Between chases, they usually fly low and purposefully between feeding flocks of terns or settle on the water with a characteristic posture of high head and high tail. They usually feed solitarily, but sometimes small flocks of four or five birds work a flock of terns. Gatherings of up to 50 birds have been reported off the northern North Island.

In the hand: Non-breeding Arctic Skua and Long-tailed Skua can be hard to separate even in the hand; see under 'Long-tailed Skua'.

Reading: O'Donald, P. 1983. *The Arctic Skua: A Study of the Ecology and Evolution of a Seabird.* Cambridge: Cambridge Univ Press.

231. POMARINE SKUA *Stercorarius pomarinus* Plate 52

Size: 48 cm, excluding central tail feathers; 600 g

Distribution: Breed in the arctic and subarctic of North America, Greenland, Iceland, Scandinavia and Russia. They migrate south in September and pass through the tropics to winter at sea in the Southern Hemisphere. A common visitor to eastern and southeastern coasts of Australia, but an uncommon though regular visitor to New Zealand waters from Northland to Foveaux Strait and east to the Chathams in December–April. They are mainly pelagic but occasionally join Arctic Skuas inshore to harass White-fronted Terns, and sometimes also chase Red-billed, Black-billed and Black-backed Gulls. On the New Zealand coast, they tend to be seen off sandy ocean beaches such as Farewell Spit and the Manawatu coast, rather than in sheltered waters, and quite often fly over land near the sea.

Behaviour: Pomarine Skuas are conspicuous as they rather clumsily chase White-fronted Terns or gulls and harry them until they are forced to drop their fish or to regurgitate. Between chases, they usually fly low and purposefully between feeding flocks of terns or settle on the water with a characteristic posture of high head and high tail. They often feed solitarily but sometimes join small flocks of Arctic Skuas working a flock of terns and gulls. An exceptional gathering of 38 birds was reported in the Tasman Sea, 100 km off the Waikato coast.

232. LONG-TAILED SKUA *Stercorarius longicaudus* Plate 52

Size: 35 cm, excluding central tail feathers; 300 g

Distribution: Breed in the arctic and subarctic of North America, Greenland, Scandinavia and Russia. They migrate south in September and pass through the tropics to winter at sea in the Southern Hemisphere. In the South Pacific, most winter in central and eastern waters, but a few visit the southwestern Pacific. The first accepted record in New Zealand was a beach-wrecked bird at Muriwai (January 1964). Since then there have been three small 'wrecks': in summer 1981/82, two were found dead on Northland and Auckland beaches, an immature was seen alive at Lake Taupo and two immatures were seen near Picton; in January–February 1983, at least 16 birds, perhaps 50+, were seen or beach-wrecked between Northland and Wellington; and in November–December 1988, two birds were wrecked on Horowhenua and Northland beaches.

Behaviour: Little is known of the wintering behaviour of Long-tailed Skuas, but generally they are more pelagic than Arctic Skuas and are usually solitary; however, 'El Niño' weather patterns may occasionally force birds west from their usual wintering range to New Zealand. None of the birds seen in New Zealand were harrying terns, as is usual with Arctic Skuas.

In the hand: Non-breeding Long-tailed Skuas and Arctic Skuas can be hard to separate even in the hand; however, about 50% of Long-tailed Skuas have diagnostic blue tarsi, the rest have grey tarsi

like Arctic Skuas. Long-tailed Skuas recorded in New Zealand generally have shorter wings (272–295–315 mm cf. 298–**315**–325 mm), bill (26.5–**28**–31 mm cf. 29–**31**–33 mm), tarsi (37.5–**42**–45.5 mm cf. 41.5–**43**–48 mm) and mid-toe and claw (34.5–**38**–41.5 mm cf. 41–**43.5**–45 mm) than Arctic Skuas in Australasia. A combination of these measures should reliably separate most birds.

Reading: Melville, D.S. 1985. *Notornis* 32: 51–73.

GULLS, TERNS and NODDIES   Laridae

About 88 species (47 gulls, 37 terns and 4 noddies) worldwide: 3 gulls, 6 terns and 4 noddies breed in the New Zealand region, and 8 terns visit regularly or as rare vagrants.

Gulls are coastal or inland birds in New Zealand. Adults have white bodies and grey or black backs, and broad wings with black and white patterning at the tips. Juvenile plumage has a distinctive buff barring on the back and wings. Gulls have a strong bill with a distinctive shape, deepest about a third of the way back from the tip. They walk well on quite long legs. Gregarious; breeding in colonies and feeding and roosting in large numbers. The ground nest is a shallow cup in a low, well-formed mound of vegetation. Chicks are fed by regurgitation. Gulls feed on a wide variety of foods, including human refuse, fish, shellfish, crustaceans and other invertebrates (including earthworms and grubs exposed by ploughing) and eggs of other birds.

Terns and noddies are mostly pelagic or coastal, except some are inland on rivers or over coastal lakes. Noddies breed only in the tropics or subtropics, and sailors may have named them for their absurd-seeming nodding courtship displays. Terns are usually

white below and shades of black or grey above, while noddies are more uniformly white, grey or brown. Juvenile plumage has buff barring, especially on the back and wings. Terns and noddies are more aerial than gulls and are more delicate; their wings are narrower and more pointed and their tail is often forked, sometimes deeply. They have straight, slender, tapering bills. They shuffle or waddle along on short legs. Gregarious; breeding in colonies and feeding and roosting in tight flocks. The nest is a simple scrape or depression in sand, shingle, shell or rock, but some noddies build a small platform nest in a tree or shrub, and White Terns simply lay their egg in a depression on a tree branch. Whole small fish, caught mainly by plunge-diving or by picking from the surface of water and held crosswise in the bill, are usually brought in courtship display and to the chicks, but some tropical terns and noddies feed by regurgitation. Chicks go on begging for months after they can fly.

Reading: Grant, P.J. 1981. *Gulls: An Identification Guide*. Calton: Poyser. Harrison, P. 1983. *Seabirds: An Identification Guide*. Beckenham: Croom Helm. Serventy, D.L. *et al.* 1971. *The Handbook of Australian Sea-birds*. Sydney: A.H. & A.W. Reed.

233.   BLACK-BACKED GULL   *Larus dominicanus*   Plate 53

Other names: Karoro, Kelp Gull (Australia), Dominican Gull, Southern Black-backed Gull
Size: 60 cm; males 1050 g, females 850 g

Geographical variation: Two subspecies: *vetula* breeds in South Africa, and *dominicanus* which breeds widely in the subantarctic and temperate Southern Hemisphere, including New Zealand.

Distribution: Breed on coasts and offshore islands of South America, South Africa, Australia and New Zealand, on many sub-antarctic islands and on the coast of Antarctica. In New Zealand, they breed in colonies or in pairs along the mainland coasts, on most offshore islands and on the Chatham, Bounty, The Snares, Antipodes, Auckland and Campbell Islands, but are strangely absent from the Three Kings. They straggle to the Ross Dependency and the Kermadec Islands, and as far as Norfolk Island and Niue. They also breed on riverbeds, lake shores and subalpine tarns high in the mountains of the North and South Islands.

Black-backed Gulls use estuaries, harbours and open coastlines, rivers, lakes, wet pasture, lambing paddocks and freshly ploughed farmland, rubbish tips and city parks. They are mainly sedentary, but flocks commute 30 km or more each day between roosting sites near the coast and inland feeding sites. At sea, they are mainly restricted to coastal waters; however, they readily follow ships out into pelagic waters.

Population: Widespread and locally common.

Conservation: Unprotected native. Black-backed Gulls have benefited from human settlement in New Zealand, especially with the creation of readily available food supplies from meatworks, fish processors, fishing boats, rubbish tips and sewer outfalls. With offal and sewage discharges into the sea being greatly reduced, and with improved waste management limiting refuse available, numbers are now declining in some areas.

Breeding: Most Black-backed Gulls nest in large colonies of up to several thousand pairs on coastal dunes, sandspits, boulderbanks, gravel beaches, rocky islets and riverbeds, but some nest solitarily on coastal rock stacks and headlands, near mountain tarns up to 1500 m asl, and sometimes on roofs of city buildings. Numbers of birds at colonies start building up in late July, and nest-building commences almost immediately. The nest is built mainly by the male. It is a substantial mound of dry grass, seaweed, twigs, feathers and tidal flotsam, measuring about 20 cm in diameter, with a small but deep depression in the centre.

Most eggs are laid between mid-October and late November, with a peak in early November, but some repeat clutches are laid through to late January. The clutch is of 1–2–3–5 eggs, but the rare clutches of over 3 eggs may be laid by two females. The eggs (69 x 47 mm, 80 g) are greyish green in ground colour with brown spots and blotches, but there is usually considerable variation in the ground colour within a clutch. Eggs are laid 2–3 days apart, at any time of day, and egg size declines through a clutch. Both sexes incubate for 23–27–30 days and brood the nestlings for 2–3 days. The chicks then leave the nest for increasingly long periods. Until the chicks fledge at c. 50 days old, they are usually guarded by one of the parents. They remain with their parents for a couple of months after fledging, and juveniles up to 6 months old are seen begging for food. Some 2-year-old birds start displaying at colonies, but most probably do not start breeding until at least 4 years old. Annual survivorship of adults is about 93%, giving a life expectancy of about 14 years, but the oldest Black-backed Gull recorded in New Zealand lived over 28 years.

Behaviour: Generally gregarious; nesting in colonies, roosting in large flocks and often feeding in loose flocks. When breeding, they vigorously defend a small patch around their nest site and attack other birds or people entering the area. Young non-breeding birds normally form 'clubs' near the colony during the breeding season. Black-backed Gulls have a large variety of calls, but the most charac-teristic calls are a contagious 'long call' heard especially in breeding colonies or in feeding flocks, described as 'uh, uh, eeah-ha-ha-ha-ha-ha' or 'kaloo-kaloo-kloo-kloo-kloo-kloo', and a non-contagious 'gorah gorah' call mainly from breeding adults.

Feeding: Black-backed Gulls are opportunists, taking a wide variety of food, including offal, refuse, carrion, marine invertebrates and shellfish, fish, eggs, frogs, lizards, birds, mammals and even small fruit and other plant material. They are often seen feeding on offal and refuse at rubbish tips, sewer outfalls, along the shoreline or behind boats. At sea, they feed on algae and plunge-dive for small fish and marine invertebrates. Along the coast, they can be seen carrying shellfish aloft and dropping them to break open the shells. During bad weather, Black-backed Gulls often head inland to feed on worms and insects forced to the surface in wet pasture or playing fields. They also congregate in lambing paddocks to feed on placentas and dead lambs, and will occasionally attack live lambs and sick or cast sheep. Undigested food items are regurgitated as pellets at roosts and breeding colonies.

In the hand: Males are larger than females, but measurements overlap, e.g. wing 400–**427**–440 mm cf. 373–**404**–428 mm; and bill 49–**54**–59 mm cf. 44.5–**49**–53 mm. Males have a positive score from the equation 0.126 x head length + 0.289 x bill depth - 19.707, and females have a negative score.

Reading: Fordham, R.A. 1964. *Notornis* 11: 3–34; 110–126. Fordham, R.A. 1968. *Proc NZ Ecol Soc* 15: 40–50. Fordham, R.A. 1970. *J Anim Ecol* 39: 13–27. Kinsky, F.C. 1963. *Rec Dom Mus* 4: 149–219. Nugent, G. 1982. *Notornis* 29: 37–40. Powlesland, R.G. & Powlesland, M.H. 1994. *Notornis* 41: 117–132. Powlesland, R.G. & Robertson, H.A. 1987. *Notornis* 34: 327–338.

234. RED-BILLED GULL *Larus novaehollandiae* Plate 54

Other names: Tarapunga, Silver Gull (Australia)
Size: 37 cm; males 300 g, females 260 g
Geographical variation: Four subspecies: *hartlaubii* breeds in South Africa, *novaehollandiae* in Australia, *forsteri* in the southwestern Pacific from Torres Strait to New Caledonia, and *scopulinus* in New Zealand.
Distribution: Breed on coasts and offshore islands of South Africa, Australia and New Zealand, and on islands in Melanesia. In New Zealand, they breed in about 80 colonies on the mainland coasts and offshore islands, and on the Three Kings, Chatham, The Snares, Auckland and Campbell Islands. They are stragglers to the Kermadecs and are strangely absent from the Bounty Islands and the Antipodes. There is an inland colony in the North Island at Lake Rotorua, where they nest with, and rarely hybridise with, Black-billed Gulls. Red-billed Gulls frequent estuaries, harbours and open coastlines, and parks of coastal cities. They sometimes venture inland onto wet paddocks, sportsfields and freshly ploughed farmland, and a few use lakes in the central North Island.

They are moderately mobile; most birds abandon the breeding colony in autumn, and many individuals undertake regular seasonal movements of several hundred kilometres between breeding sites and their traditional wintering sites, e.g. between Kaikoura and Wellington Harbour. Most birds remain within 400 km of their breeding colony, but birds banded at Kaikoura have been seen in Auckland and in Invercargill. Individuals commute 20 km or more each day between roosting or breeding sites and offshore feeding sites. At sea, they are mainly in coastal waters; however, they occasionally follow ships out into pelagic waters.

Population: Widespread and locally common. The three largest colonies, each with 5000+ breeding pairs, are at the Three Kings Islands, Mokohinau Island and at Kaikoura. The New Zealand population has increased substantially since European settlement, but may now be stable or declining, as the important winter food supplies of offal and sewage discharged into the sea have been greatly reduced since 1970.

Conservation: Protected native. Red-billed Gulls have benefited from human settlement in New Zealand, especially with the creation of readily available winter food supplies from meatworks, fish processors, fishing boats, sewer outfalls and scraps discarded in city parks.

Breeding: Red-billed Gulls nest in large, densely packed colonies of up to 6000 pairs on sandspits, boulderbanks, shellbanks, gravel beaches, rocky headlands and rocky islets, usually near marine upwellings. Numbers of birds at colonies start building up in mid-July, but nesting sites are not occupied until early August. Pairs usually remain together year after year, but their nesting site changes within the colony. Both birds help to build the nest, but the male does most of the work. The nest is a small mound of dry grass, seaweed, twigs, feathers and tidal flotsam, measuring about 15 cm in diameter, with a shallow depression in the centre.

On the mainland, most eggs are laid from early October to late December, but on the subantarctic islands the season is about a month later. Older birds lay earlier in the season than younger ones. The clutch is of 1–**2**–5 brownish-ochre eggs (52.5 x 37.5 mm) with purple or brown spots and blotches. Clutches of 4 or 5 are laid by two females. Egg size declines through a clutch and through the season. Both sexes incubate for 24–**25**–27 days and then brood and feed the nestlings. The chicks remain close to the nest and are usually guarded by one of the parents. The fledging period is c. 37 days, and the fledglings remain dependent on their parents for a further 3 weeks. A few males start breeding at 1 year old, but most do not start nesting until 3–4, about a year younger than females. Females have a higher annual survival rate (89%) than males (84%), with corresponding life expectancies of 9 and 6 years, respectively. The oldest bird recorded lived at least 28 years.

Behaviour: Highly gregarious; nesting in large colonies, roosting in large flocks and often feeding in flocks of thousands of birds at locally abundant food. When breeding, they vigorously defend a small area around their nest and attack other birds or people entering the area. Young non-breeding birds normally form 'clubs' near the colony during the breeding season. Red-billed Gulls have a variety of breeding calls, but the most characteristic call heard through the year is a strident and discordant scream.

Feeding: During the breeding season, Red-billed Gulls feed mainly in inshore waters on the planktonic euphausiid *Nyctiphanes australis*, although some other marine invertebrates, small fish, terrestrial insects and earthworms are also taken. A few birds specialise in stealing eggs from other Red-billed Gulls or White-fronted Terns. In autumn and winter, the diet is much more varied and they feed on offal, refuse, carrion, marine invertebrates, shellfish and fish. They are usually seen feeding on offal from fishing boats, fish-processing plants or meatworks, at sewer outfalls, along the shoreline, at rubbish tips or on scraps in city parks. During bad weather, they often head inland to feed on worms and insects forced to the surface in wet pastures or sportsfields.

In the hand: Males are larger than females, but measurements overlap. Bill measurements provide a good discrimination between sexes; males have a positive score from the equation 0.26 x bill length + bill depth at gonys (deepest part) -22.875, and females have a negative score.

Reading: Gurr, L. 1967. *Ibis* 109: 552–555. Gurr, L. & Kinsky, F.C. 1965. *Notornis* 12: 223–240. Mills, J.A. 1969. *Notornis* 16: 180–186. Mills, J.A. 1971. *NZ J Mar Fresh Res* 5: 326–328. Mills, J.A. 1973. *J Anim Ecol* 42: 147–162. Mills, J.A. 1979. *Ibis* 121: 53–67. Mills, J.A. 1989. In Newton, I. (ed.). *Lifetime Reproduction in Birds*. London: Academic Press. Powlesland, R.G. & Powlesland, M.H. 1994. *Notornis* 41: 117–132.

235. BLACK-BILLED GULL *Larus bulleri* Plate 54

Size: 37 cm; males 300 g, females 250 g
Distribution: New Zealand only. Breed mainly on braided riverbeds of the South Island from Marlborough to Southland, but some nest on Hawke's Bay and Wairarapa riverbeds, and there are also a few colonies on the North Island coast (Manukau Harbour, Bay of Plenty, Gisborne, Wairoa, Clive and Porangahau) and a colony at Lake Rotorua, where they nest with, and rarely hybridise with, Red-billed Gulls. In spring and summer, Black-billed Gulls are mainly inland on the larger rivers and lakes of the South Island and on nearby arable farmland where they are often seen following the plough. In winter, they are mainly coastal, frequenting estuaries, harbours, open coastlines and parks of coastal towns, often in association with Red-billed

Gulls. In bad weather, they head inland to feed on flooded pasture and wet sportsfields. A few inhabit lakes in the central North Island. They are moderately mobile, with many South Island birds moving to the southern North Island in winter; some birds reach Stewart Island and vagrants appear at The Snares.

Population: c. 50,000 pairs in 1996. For some unknown reason, numbers of Black-billed Gulls have crashed in the South Island since the 1970s. For instance, the number nesting on the Oreti River, Southland, declined from 85,000 pairs in 1974 to 15,000 pairs in 1997 and there were only 33,500 pairs in Southland in 1996. However, they are slowly increasing in numbers and range in the North Island. Before 1970, the only known regular breeding colony in the North Island was at Lake Rotorua, but several coastal and riverbed colonies have been established recently.

Conservation: Protected endemic. Although Black-billed Gulls are less parasitic on man than are the other gulls, they have probably benefited from human settlement in New Zealand, especially with the creation of arable farmland near their South Island riverbed breeding sites. The cause of the recent declines in Southland are unknown, but possibly due to introduced predators, weed encroachment and human disturbance of colonies.

Breeding: Black-billed Gulls nest in large, densely packed colonies of up to 1000 pairs on open shingle margins or islands in braided riverbeds, or on the coast on sandspits, boulderbanks or shellbanks. Most birds form pairs in their winter flocks. On South Island rivers, birds return in September to the general area of their previous colony, but with changes in riverbed patterns and in vegetation growth, they rarely use the same site for more than a few years. Once a site has been chosen, they quickly build their nests and start laying, but further nest material is added as incubation proceeds. The nest is a small mound of dry grass and twigs of driftwood, measuring about 15 cm in diameter, with a shallow depression in the centre. Nests are c. 50 cm apart in the centre of colonies, further apart towards the edge.

Laying is from from late September to December; later clutches are generally replacements after a colony has been destroyed by floods or predators, or deserted if food supplies dwindle in the early stages of the nesting cycle. Within each colony, most birds start laying within a few days, and usually within a fortnight of occupying the site, although some late arrivals lay near the edge of the colony well after the majority are incubating. They lay 1–2–4 pale olive-green to pale grey eggs (55 x 37 mm) with sparse light and dark brown blotches. Both sexes incubate for 20–24 days. The chicks are capable of walking within 24 hours of hatching, and 1–2 days after the final chick hatches, the family abandons its nest site and becomes nomadic within the vicinity of the colony, though both parents continue to brood, feed and guard the young. The young chicks are fed by regurgitating onto the ground, but older chicks feed from their parents' bills. From about 2 weeks old the chicks are capable of swimming, and at about this age the chicks tend to congregate in loose crèches guarded by a few adults. These are usually near the water's edge, and if a ground predator approaches, the chicks swim out in a tightly packed raft, with the adults mobbing the predator by swooping and calling noisily. The chicks fledge at c. 26 days. They first breed at 2 years old and can live for over 18 years.

Behaviour: Highly gregarious; nesting in large colonies, roosting in large flocks and often feeding in flocks of hundreds of birds at locally abundant food. When breeding, they defend a small patch around their nest site, attack other birds entering the area and mob predators and people approaching the colony. Black-billed Gulls have a large variety of breeding calls, but the most characteristic call heard through the year is a loud and discordant screech.

Feeding: Inland-breeding Black-billed Gulls usually feed in flocks on unpredictable but temporarily rich food supplies such as invertebrates (especially earthworms and grass-grub adults and larvae) exposed by ploughing or brought to the surface by irrigation or rains, and shoals of small fish such as whitebait and young flatfish. They are also adept at hawking above flowing water for aquatic invertebrates on the wing. In winter, their diet is more varied and includes marine and freshwater invertebrates and shellfish, small fish, scraps in city parks, and worms and insects forced to the surface in wet pastures or sportsfields.

Reading: Beer, C.G. 1965. *Auk* 82: 1–18. Beer, C.G. 1966. *Ibis* 108: 394–410. Black, M.S. 1955. *Notornis* 6: 167–170. Dawson, E. W. 1958. *Notornis* 8: 1–7. Evans, R.M. 1982. *Ibis* 124: 491–501. Gurr, L. 1967. *Ibis* 109: 552–555. Powlesland, R.G. & Powlesland, M.H. 1994. *Notornis* 41: 117–132.

236. WHISKERED TERN *Chlidonias hybrida* Plate 56

Size: 26 cm, 90 g
Geographical variation: Three subspecies: *hybrida* breeds in Europe and Asia, *delalandi* in Africa, and *javanicus* in Australia.
Distribution: Breed in widely separated populations, in the marshes of southern Europe and Asia; in southeastern Africa and Madagascar; and in inland Australia, mainly in the southeast. Australian birds migrate north after breeding into New Guinea, Indonesia and southeastern Asia. The few birds seen in New Zealand come from Australia, judging by the timing of plumage changes: Lake Horowhenua (1977, 1978), lower Waikato River (1978), Pukekohe (1980) and Lake Rotorua (1987).

Behaviour: Breeding and feeding habits are very like those of White-winged Black Terns. Their flight is buoyant, typical of marsh terns, flying upwind over fresh or brackish water, then dropping downwind to start again. They sometimes patrol and feed over the same stretch of still, inland water and use the same roosting places for months.

Reading: Heather, B.D. & Jones, E.B. 1979. *Notornis* 26: 185–195.

237. WHITE-WINGED BLACK TERN *Chlidonias leucopterus* Plate 56

Other name: White-winged Tern
Size: 23 cm, 65 g
Distribution: Breeding in marshes from eastern Europe to Siberia, in eastern China, Mongolia and Manchuria. They migrate to winter in Africa, southern and southeastern Asia, and in Australasia. They are a regular migrant to New Zealand, from the harbours of Northland to the lagoons and estuaries of Southland, but especially around the Auckland isthmus and in coastal Canterbury. A pair bred among Black-fronted Terns at the mouth of the Opihi River, South Canterbury, in 1973–74.
Population: Usually fewer than 10 reach New Zealand each year, except for occasional small influxes, e.g. 13 at Ahuriri Estuary (1972). A few overwinter in some years.

Behaviour: In New Zealand, some birds have a reversed plumage sequence, that of the Southern Hemisphere, and stay as though to breed. In the South Island, single birds often associate with colonies of Black-fronted Terns, and a pair attempted to breed twice in 1973–74. Normally the nest is a rough mass of vegetation, floating or moored in fresh water.
Feeding: Gregarious; overseas they forage in noisy flocks, but in New Zealand they are usually singles, beating into the wind and contact-dipping (i.e. submerging the bill only) to pick insects from the water surface.

Reading: Pierce, R.J. 1974. *Notornis* 21: 129–134.

238. GULL-BILLED TERN *Gelochelidon nilotica* Plate 54

Size: 43 cm, 230 g
Geographical variation: Of the six subspecies, *macrotarsa* of Australia and New Guinea is one most likely to reach New Zealand. The Asian subspecies *affinis*, recorded near Darwin, is possible.
Distribution: Almost cosmopolitan, breeding in the Americas, Africa, across temperate

Europe and Asia to China, Indonesia, New Guinea and inland Australia, mainly in the southeast. They are common on most Australian coasts but rare in Tasmania. In New Zealand, a few vagrants have been seen in most years since they were first recorded at Invercargill in 1955. They are occasionally seen in small flocks, e.g. eight at Manukau Harbour (1976) and six at Tapora (2001), and some birds remain in a district for several years.

Behaviour: Most New Zealand records have been at estuaries or coastal lagoons and marshes, but they are as likely to feed over grassland and ploughed fields. They fly low and swoop from time to time to snatch invertebrates or small fish from the surface.

Reading: McKenzie, H.R. 1955. *Notornis* 6: 163–164.

239.   BLACK-FRONTED TERN   *Sterna albostriata*   Plate 56

Other name: Tarapiroe

Size: 29 cm, 90 g

Distribution: New Zealand only. Black-fronted Terns breed on the shingle riverbeds of the eastern South Island from Marlborough to Southland, and on the upper Motueka and Buller Rivers in southern Nelson. They feed over the rivers and nearby fields. In late summer and autumn, they disperse north, occasionally reaching Northland, and south to waters off Stewart Island, and once to The Snares (1998); however most feed at sea within 10 km of the eastern South Island and in Cook Strait north to the Waikanae Estuary and west to Farewell Spit. Autumn and winter flocks of 100–300 birds are regularly seen at Farewell Spit, Lake Grassmere, Kaikoura Peninsula, Hurunui, Ashley, Ashburton and Opihi River mouths, and at Aramoana. Smaller wintering flocks of 20–50 birds regularly appear in the North Island at the Bay of Plenty, Hawke's Bay and at Lake Onoke, Palliser Bay. In the non-breeding season, they sometimes feed over coastal fields or lagoons, and come ashore to roost in the middle of the day, often near roosting flocks of White-fronted Terns.

Population: c. 5000 birds.

Conservation: Protected rare endemic. Black-fronted Terns are declining in number throughout their breeding range. Their colonies are easily disturbed by predators and people, and many of their riverbed nesting sites have been invaded by exotic plants such as willows and lupins. The development of farmland beside their nesting sites may have created feeding opportunities, as they often follow the plough to catch insects and worms that are exposed.

Breeding: They nest in small colonies of up to 50 pairs, some on riverbeds near the coast, but most are well inland, often near colonies of Black-billed Gulls. The nests, scrapes in the shingle, are spaced well apart. Eggs are laid from early October to late November, sometimes into January. They lay 1–2–4 dark stone eggs (40 x 29 mm, 18 g) with brown blotches. Both sexes incubate for 22–23–26 days. The eggs hatch a day or two apart. The young fledge at c. 30 days old.

Behaviour: Black-fronted Terns attack intruders at their colonies, by diving, calling harshly, and often striking the intruder's head with their feet. The usual call is a repetitive 'kit'; they usually feed silently.

Feeding: While breeding, they feed in flocks over rivers and nearby fields. They work their way up rapidly flowing rivers and return repeatedly to their starting point. They contact-dip from about 2 m above the water (i.e. dipping to touch the surface with the bill only) to take mainly emergent nymph and subimago mayflies and stoneflies. They sometimes plunge-dive to take small fish, such as upland bullies. On farmland, their main food is earthworms and grass-grub larvae. After breeding, most move to the coast for the autumn and winter, taking mostly planktonic crustaceans from the sea, as well as earthworms from wet coastal pasture.

Reading: Latham, P.C.M. 1981. *Notornis* 28: 221–239. Lalas, C. 1977. Unpubl MSc thesis, Univ Otago. Lalas, C. & Heather, B.D. 1980. *Notornis* 27: 45–68.

240. CASPIAN TERN   *Sterna caspia*   Plate 54

Other name: Taranui
Size: 51 cm, 700 g
Distribution: Almost cosmopolitan, breeding locally in temperate parts of all continents but South America. They breed in Central and North America north to the Great Lakes, in Africa, from Europe across central Asia to China, and Australasia. In New Zealand, they breed on both main islands, usually coastal but small numbers sometimes inland, especially near Rotorua and on Canterbury rivers. A rare vagrant to the Kermadec and Chatham Islands. The main colonies are on estuarine shellbanks or sandspits: Rangaunu, Whangarei, Kaipara, Whangapoua and Kawhia Harbours; Mangawhai Estuary; Bowentown, Tauranga Harbour; Matakana Island; Ohope Spit; Lake Onoke Spit, Palliser Bay; Farewell Spit, Waimea Estuary, Vernon Lagoon, Lake Ellesmere and Invercargill Estuary. Single pairs and small colonies breed on sandy beaches and at many harbours and estuaries, sometimes in association with colonies of Black-backed Gulls, less often with Red-billed or Black-billed Gulls.

After breeding, North Island birds tend to stay within 100 km of their breeding places; birds banded in Northland feed and roost on such harbours as the Kaipara, Manukau and the Firth of Thames, but some birds move much further south. South Island birds tend to move north in autumn, and adults return to breed again in spring. Birds banded near Invercargill travel in stages to wintering places at the Avon–Heathcote Estuary and Lake Ellesmere, some reaching southern North Island estuaries, and one even reached the Manukau Harbour. Most Caspian Terns stay on or near the coast, but single birds may be seen working rivers well inland, e.g. to Palmerston North, Masterton and Upper Hutt, and a few visit inland lakes such as Taupo.
Population: c. 3000 birds; colony sizes and locations are quite variable from year to year but rarely exceed 100 pairs.
Conservation: Protected rare native. Caspian Terns may be a quite recent colonist of New Zealand, as they were not recorded by early

naturalists until about 1860. They were scarce until about the 1930s but became increasingly common to the 1970s. Since then, the population may have slipped back, as several major colonies have been disturbed by increased human activity and planting pine trees and marram on the favoured bare sandspits. Some colonies are now fenced off to prevent damage from off-road vehicles and from people and dogs.
Breeding: Most Caspian Terns nest in large, loose colonies. The nest is a shallow, unlined scrape in the sand or other substrate. Laying is from late September to early December. They lay 1–2–3 light stone eggs (64 x 45 mm, 75 g), evenly sprinkled with dark brown spots and blotches. Both adults incubate for 26–29 days, and brood the chicks for the first 5–10 days. The chicks hatch over several days, and, when food is in short supply, the youngest starve. The chicks fledge at 33–38 days old and continue to be fed for several months. They accompany their parents to wintering sites, usually staying there until they return to the colony to breed at 3–5 years old. The oldest banded bird in New Zealand lived over 24 years.
Behaviour: Gregarious; many breed in loose colonies of up to 100 pairs, up to 350 pairs at the South Kaipara Head colony in the 1970s. They roost in small flocks between feeding bouts at estuaries and on sandy beaches, but they usually feed alone.

Caspian Terns are often heard first, the usual call in flight being a loud, harsh 'kaaa', or a repetitive variant of it; there are other, less frequent calls. Juveniles are very audible, uttering a persistent high-pitched mewing call.
Feeding: Diet is mainly small surface-swimming fish such as yellow-eyed mullet, smelt and piper; also stargazers and small flounders, which are caught by plunging into the water at a steep angle, often fully submerging. Inland, they catch smelt, whitebait, bullies, trout and small eels. Juveniles dip-feed while standing in shallow water at the tide's edge, taking worms and small flounders.
Reading: Pierce, R.J. 1984. *Notornis* 31: 185–190. Sibson, R.B. 1992. *Notornis* 39: 87–93.

241. WHITE-FRONTED TERN *Sterna striata* Plate 55

Other name: Tara
Size: 42 cm, 160 g
Distribution: New Zealand only, apart from a few that have bred on islands of Bass Strait, Australia, since 1979. White-fronted Terns breed abundantly from Northland to Southland, especially on the eastern coast and on offshore islands. They are also abundant at the Chatham and Auckland Islands, and breed around the coast of Stewart Island. An occasional visitor to The Snares and Campbell Island. Colonies are ephemeral, a site used successfully one year may be abandoned and a new site used. In autumn, large numbers of young birds and some adults migrate to the southeastern coast of Australia, mostly May–November in New South Wales, Victoria and Tasmania, some ranging west to South Australia and north to Queensland. However, many adults stay on New Zealand coasts throughout the winter. They are rarely recorded inland but have visited Lakes Taupo and Rotorua.
Population: 15–20,000 pairs in 1997. By far the commonest tern on the New Zealand shore and in coastal waters. Some colonies contain thousands of pairs, but usually 50–200 pairs. Some birds nest alone or in groups of only a few pairs.
Conservation: Protected native. For unknown reasons, the number of birds seems to be declining rapidly, but the capriciousness of colonies makes them difficult to monitor.

Large numbers persist despite severe predation of breeding adults by cats, and of eggs and chicks by mustelids, rats and cats.
Breeding: Large colonies are generally on sandy beaches, low-lying sandspits, shingle- or shellbanks and rocky islets, and smaller colonies are usually on rock stacks, steep cliffs and offshore islands. White-fronted Terns often nest close to Red-billed Gull colonies. Laying is from mid-October to January, during which several replacement clutches are laid if eggs or chicks are lost to predators or storm surges. They lay **1**–2 eggs (46 x 33 mm) on the mainland of New Zealand, but 1–2–3 eggs (46 x 32 mm) on the Chathams. Eggs vary from pale green-blue to light brown with an array of spots. The first egg is larger than the second, and birds over 6 years old lay on average larger eggs than younger birds. Both adults incubate for c. 24 days and then brood the chicks for several days; the chicks then join others in a crèche. Each pair usually rears only one chick to fledging at 29–35 days old. The adults continue to feed their young up to 3 months after leaving the colony. Young birds can start breeding at 3 years old, but most start when at least 7 years old. The oldest banded bird lived over 26 years.
Behaviour: Gregarious. Most breed in large, tightly packed colonies with less than a metre between nests. White-fronted Terns feed in coastal waters in large flocks, forming great 'swirls' over shoaling fish, in company with

Fluttering and Flesh-footed Shearwaters, Australasian Gannets and Red-billed and Black-backed Gulls. They roost in tight flocks of up to 2000 birds on beaches, on shellbanks and at the mouths of estuaries. The usual call is a single high-pitched note: 'siet', repeated at intervals and given particularly in flight by day or night.

Feeding: Diet is mainly small surface-shoaling fish such as smelt and pilchards, caught by shallow plunge-diving. They often work shoals that kahawai and kingfish have driven to the surface. They are often pursued by skuas, which force them to disgorge and drop the fish they have caught.

Reading: Mills, J.A. & Shaw, P.W. *NZ J Zool* 7: 147–153.

242. SOOTY TERN *Sterna fuscata* Plate 58

Other name: Wideawake Tern
Size: 45 cm, 210 g
Geographical variation: Many subspecies of doubtful validity, of which *serrata* of the southwestern Pacific is the one that breeds at the Kermadecs.
Distribution: Widespread in tropical and subtropical parts of the Atlantic, Indian and South Pacific Oceans, from the Great Barrier Reef and Norfolk Island east to Samoa and Tonga. They breed throughout the Kermadecs but now mainly at Macauley and Curtis Islands and in the Herald Group (North and South Meyer, and Dayrell Islands). After breeding, they become much more pelagic and are rarely seen at the Kermadecs between late April and August. Occasional vagrants reach the North Island, usually after autumn and winter gales. The sighting of at least 13 birds in two flocks at Pakiri Beach in July 1986 was exceptional.
Population: c. 22,000 pairs in 1990: Macauley 10,000 pairs, Curtis 5500 pairs, Herald Group 4000 pairs, Raoul 2000 pairs.
Conservation: Protected native. The current population estimate is well down from the 1966–67 minimum of 80,000 pairs in two colonies on Raoul Island alone. The Denham Bay and Hutchinson Bluff colonies on Raoul Island have been virtually wiped out by Norway rats (taking eggs and chicks) and feral cats (taking adults and young). The improved habitat and less disturbance on Macauley Island since the eradication of goats has probably helped to offset some of the loss.
Breeding: Much more seasonal in the Kermadecs than in the tropics, where breeding can be continuous on a nine-month cycle. Laying at the Kermadecs is in October–December and is remarkably synchronised within large colonies, most eggs being laid over a few days. The nest is an unlined scrape in sand and low vegetation at the top of the beach. They lay 1 cream egg (53 x 36 mm), spotted and blotched dark brown and black. Both adults incubate for c. 28 days. The fledging period is c. 30 days, but the young stay at the colony for several months, sometimes forming a crèche. A chick banded at the Kermadecs was found breeding in the Indian Ocean at Aride Island, Seychelles, aged 33.5 years old.
Behaviour: Gregarious during breeding; their colonies are noisy, day and night, both from their harsh 'wideawake' calls and from their incessant nocturnal activity. The calls are also heard among feeding flocks.
Feeding: Diet is mainly squid, small fish and crustaceans, caught mostly at night by surface-dipping. Sooty Terns feed far out to sea, and so regurgitate to feed their young, whereas other terns that feed close to shore give whole undigested fish to their young.

Reading: Cossee, R.O. 1995. *Notornis* 42: 280.

243.   ANTARCTIC TERN   *Sterna vittata*   Plate 55

Size: 36 cm, 140 g

Geographical variation: Of several sub-species, *bethunei* breeds in the New Zealand region.

Distribution: Circumpolar in the Southern Hemisphere, breeding on the Antarctic Peninsula south of Argentina, on islands of the South Atlantic and South Indian Oceans, and on subantarctic islands of Australia and New Zealand. In the New Zealand region, they breed on islands off Stewart Island (islands in Port Pegasus, and Stage, Solomon and Moggy Islands), The Snares, Auckland, Campbell, Antipodes and Bounty Islands. At the northern breeding sites, adults and young stay in nearby coastal waters all year, but further south they are absent in April–October, apparently in the southern oceans, as the only Antarctic Tern recorded north of Foveaux Strait was at the Chathams in 1997.

Population: c. 1000 breeding pairs in New Zealand, fairly evenly spread through the subantarctic.

Conservation: Protected native. Populations in the subantarctic appear to be secure as long as rats and cats do not reach their breeding grounds.

Breeding: Colonial whenever possible but usually in small groups. On The Snares, they are mostly solitary on cliff ledges overlooking the sea; on the Auckland and Campbell Islands they nest on rocks close to the sea and in areas of scrub well inland. Laying is prolonged and varies from island to island: September–March on The Snares, October–February on Campbell Island, December–March on Antipodes Island, and November–February on the Auckland Islands. The nest is a scrape or a depression on the ground or on a ledge. They lay 1–2 buff-olive eggs (46 x 32 mm, 25 g) with brown and black blotches. Both adults incubate for 24–25 days. In 2-egg clutches, the eggs hatch 2–3 days apart, or the second egg does not hatch. The fledging period is 27–32 days. Young can first breed at 3 years old. The oldest bird recorded in New Zealand lived at least 14 years.

Behaviour: Gregarious; feeding and roosting in small flocks of up to 100 birds.

Feeding: Antarctic Terns feed close inshore, taking fish and crustaceans. Their feeding methods vary depending on the prey type and sea conditions. In calm seas, they feed on crustaceans by contact-dipping (i.e. submerging the bill only) or take fish by plunge-diving to become completely or partially submerged. As seas become rough, they mainly contact-dip to take crustaceans and small fish, but may also partially plunge for crustaceans and plunge for fish.

Reading: Robertson, C.J.R. & Bell, B.D. 1984. In Croxall, J.P. *et al.* (eds). *Status and Conservation of the World's Seabirds*. Cambridge: ICBP. Sadleir, R.M.F.S. *et al.* 1986. *Notornis* 33: 264–265. Sagar, P.M. 1978. *Notornis* 25: 59–70. Sagar, P.M. & Sagar, J.L. 1989. *Notornis* 36: 171–182.

244.   FAIRY TERN   *Sterna nereis*   Plate 57

Size: 25 cm, 70 g

Geographical variation: Three subspecies: *nereis* breeds in southern and western Australia, *exsul* in New Caledonia, and the New Zealand Fairy Tern *davisae* in New Zealand.

Distribution: Fairy Terns are the smallest and rarest of the terns that breed in New Zealand. Up to the early 1900s, they were apparently widespread and bred on the coasts of the North Island and inland on the riverbeds of the South Island. By the 1950s, about 18 pairs were confined to Northland, breeding in the east from Skull Creek (Whangarei Harbour) in the north to Pakiri in the south, including Ruakaka, Waipu, Mangawhai and Te Arai. Some were discovered breeding on the west coast at Papakanui Spit (South Kaipara Head) in 1969. Fairy Terns are now largely confined to Northland and the Kaipara Harbour, and since 1985 have bred at three sites only: Waipu Estuary (maximum of three pairs), Manga-whai Heads (maximum of five pairs), and Papakanui Spit, South Kaipara Heads (two or three pairs). The eastern birds form flocks at or near the breeding places from late December to the end of March, and then move to the Kaipara Harbour for the winter, although a few single birds have been seen as far afield as Sulphur Point, Tauranga. Flocks of 8–18 birds are regularly seen from late February to July on the Kaipara Harbour, mostly at Tapora, or at Papakanui Spit, where breeding birds probably stay all year. In July, flocks disband and birds return to their eastern coast breeding places.

Population: The New Zealand total in 2001 was c. 30 birds, comprising 13 breeding birds and 17 immatures.

Conservation: Protected native; the endemic subspecies is critically endangered. The decline of New Zealand Fairy Terns was largely a result of degradation of the breeding habitat, disturbance by people during the breeding season and probably predation by gulls and introduced mammals. Fairy Terns nest in exposed areas of mobile sand, and so their habitat is degraded when sand is stabilised by plantings of marram, lupins and pines, or levelled for housing development. Fairy Terns nest on beaches used by people and frequented by gulls, cats, mustelids and dogs. Protection by trapping mammals, erecting temporary fences and signs, and regular patrols by wardens resulted in the population increasing from three pairs in 1983 to nine pairs in 1994. Rescued eggs are hatched at Auckland Zoo and the juveniles subsequently liberated.

Breeding: Fairy Terns nest solitarily. Nests are on low-lying sand and shell, mostly above the reach of spring tides but exposed to storm surges. First clutches are laid from mid-November to early December, but they may re-lay through to mid-January if earlier clutches are lost. They lay 1–2 buff eggs (35 x 25 mm, 13 g), spotted and blotched dark brown. Both adults incubate for 23–25 days. Young fly at 22–23 days old. The oldest Fairy Tern recorded in New Zealand lived at least 11 years.

Behaviour: Solitary when breeding, but several pairs may inhabit the same sandspit. They flock shortly after breeding and stay in small feeding and roosting flocks through the winter. Fairy Terns are generally silent in flight.

Feeding: Diet is mainly small fish, caught inside the estuaries and at sea just beyond the breaking waves. When feeding, they flutter, hover, and then plunge-dive to catch their prey.

Reading: Parrish, G.R. & Pulham, G.A. 1995. *Tane* 35: 161–173; 175–181.

245. LITTLE TERN   *Sterna albifrons*   Plate 57

Size: 25 cm, 50 g

Geographical variation: Several subspecies, of which the Eastern Little Tern *sinensis* breeds from southeastern Asia to Australia, and reaches New Zealand.

Distribution: Breed worldwide in North America, Africa, Europe, Asia and Australasia. Eastern Little Terns *sinensis* breed on the eastern and southern coasts of Australia south to Tasmania, as well as in Japan, Korea, China, Taiwan, the Lesser Sunda Islands, New Guinea and the Solomon Islands. The arrival in September of Little Terns in Australasia, including a tern banded as a nestling in Japan and recovered in New Guinea, shows that many eastern Asian birds head south in the northern winter. Some of these Asian birds reach New Zealand as annual migrants, arriving in October–November and gaining breeding plumage in February–April as they are about to leave. They favour the large harbours of Northland and South Auckland, especially Rangaunu and Kaipara Harbours, and some visit estuaries and coastal lagoons south to Stewart Island, and at Chatham Island (1997–98). A few overwinter.

Population: In New Zealand, the summer total is probably 150–200 birds.

Behaviour: Gregarious; at high tide, Little Terns may roost loosely together near wader flocks, such as Bar-tailed Godwits and Knots, but they may feed over high tide and so, appearing only when the tide is falling, can easily be missed. Their foods and feeding behaviour is similar to the Fairy Tern, except Little Terns chatter while hovering to feed.

246. ARCTIC TERN   *Sterna paradisaea*   Plate 55

Size: 34 cm, 110 g

Distribution: Circumpolar, breeding in arctic and subarctic regions of the Northern Hemisphere; Greenland, northern Europe, Siberia and North America. Arctic Terns migrate well south to the edge of the pack ice of the southern oceans, taking two routes, down the eastern sides of the Pacific and Atlantic Oceans; return routes are less clearly defined. They are a rare but annual visitor to New Zealand as they pass by on their way to and from Antarctic waters. Most records are of single birds on beaches and at river mouths from Northland to Southland, also at the Chathams. They are quite regular visitors to Auckland and Campbell Islands. A few subadults may overwinter.

Behaviour: Gregarious; often joining roosting flocks of White-fronted Terns, in which they are easily overlooked.

Reading: Latham, P.C.M. 1979. *Notornis* 26: 63–67.

247. COMMON TERN   *Sterna hirundo*   Plate 55

Size: 36 cm, 120 g

Geographical variation: Three or four subspecies, some probably clinal rather than subspecies: *hirundo* breeds in North America and Europe, *minussensis* in central and southern Siberia, *tibetana* in central Asia, and *longipennis* in eastern Asia and is the form most likely to reach New Zealand, although *hirundo* has also been recorded in Australia.

Distribution: Breed in eastern North America and across temperate Europe and Asia. Eastern Common Terns *longipennis* breed in northern Asia eastwards from Lake Baikal. They winter from eastern India to Australasia. Since the 1960s, they have become commonplace in northern and eastern Australia and New Guinea each summer, where flocks come ashore to roost. In New Zealand, one was recorded at Lake Horowhenua (1977), but the first positive sighting was of an adult in breeding plumage with White-fronted Terns at the mouth of the Rangitaiki River, Bay of Plenty (1984). Singles have subsequently been seen almost annually, mainly in the Bay of Plenty and on the Kapiti/Horowhenua coast.

Behaviour: Gregarious; often joining roosting flocks of White-fronted Terns, in which they are easily overlooked.

Reading: Latham, P.C.M. 1986. *Notornis* 33: 69–76.

248. CRESTED TERN   *Sterna bergii*   Plate 54

Other name: Swift Tern

Size: 47 cm, 350 g

Geographical variation: Of four subspecies, probably *cristata* of New Guinea, Australia and the tropical South Pacific east to French Polynesia reaches New Zealand.

Distribution: Breed in South Africa, islands and coasts of the Indian Ocean, Australia and islands of the tropical South Pacific. Rare vagrants have been seen in New Zealand twelve times: Raoul Island, Kermadecs (1910), Spirits Bay (1951), Farewell Spit (1960), Firth of Thames (1974), Napier (1981), Wellington Harbour and Kapiti Coast (1981–88), Kaikoura (1985), Pukerua Bay (1992), Manawatu Estuary (1995), Waikanae Estuary (1995), Washdyke (1995), Kaipara (1996) and New Plymouth (1996–97).

Behaviour: Adults in breeding and non-breeding plumage and immatures have all been seen, often roosting with White-fronted Terns. One bird apparently remained on, or regularly visited, the Wellington coast for eight (possibly 15) years.

249. BRIDLED TERN   *Sterna anaethetus*   Plate 58

Other name: Brown-winged Tern
Size: 41 cm, 120 g
Geographical variation: Of several sub-species, *anaethetus* breeding in New Guinea and northern Australia is most likely to reach New Zealand.
Distribution: Widespread across all tropical seas but seldom straying to temperate waters. One record in New Zealand, a beach-wrecked bird at New Brighton, Canterbury (November 1987).

Reading: Hulsman, K. & Langham, N.P.E. 1985. *Emu* 85: 240–249. Tunnicliffe, G.A. & Langlands, P.A. 1990. *Notornis* 37: 131–139.

250. COMMON NODDY   *Anous stolidus*   Plate 58

Other name: Brown Noddy
Size: 39 cm, 200 g
Geographical variation: Of the five sub-species, *pileatus* breeds on islands in the Indian Ocean and in the tropical South Pacific Ocean, including the Kermadecs.
Distribution: Tropical and subtropical islands of the Atlantic, Indian and Pacific Oceans. In the South Pacific, they breed on many tropical islands from the northern Great Barrier Reef east to French Polynesia, but also in the subtropics at Norfolk and Lord Howe Islands, and at Curtis Island in the southern Kermadecs. There were two New Zealand records in the 1800s, then in 1989 they were discovered breeding on cliff ledges at Curtis Island. Subsequently, beach-wrecked birds have been found on Muriwai Beach (June 1992) and at Waitara (June 2002).
Population: c. 25 pairs nesting on Curtis Island in 1989.
Conservation: Protected native. This common species has recently established as a breeding species in the New Zealand region.
Breeding: In some tropical places they breed year-round, but in the South Pacific they breed in spring and early summer. Eggs are laid on Curtis Island in September–November. The nest is usually an untidy heap of sticks and seaweed, cemented by guano, in trees, scrub and sometimes on the ground; at the Kermadecs all nests are on cliff ledges and steep slopes. They lay 1 creamy-white egg (53 x 36 mm, 36 g), blotched reddish brown. Both adults incubate for 32–35 days and care for the white downy young.
Behaviour: Gregarious; in New Guinea and Australia they breed in large colonies, often with Sooty Terns, but at Curtis Island they nest alone. After breeding, Common Noddies disperse and may be seen hundreds of kilometres from land, where huge feeding flocks are likened to smoke on the horizon.

251. WHITE-CAPPED NODDY   *Anous tenuirostris*   Plate 58

Other names: Lesser/Black Noddy
Size: 37 cm, 100 g
Geographical variation: Of several sub-species, the White-capped Noddy *minutus* breeds in the southwestern Pacific Ocean, including the Kermadecs. Some taxonomists separate the Lesser Noddy *tenuirostris* of the Indian Ocean from the White-capped Noddy of the Pacific and Atlantic Oceans.
Distribution: Breed on tropical and sub-tropical islands of the Atlantic, Indian and Pacific Oceans. The White-capped Noddy breeds widely in the tropical Pacific from the Great Barrier Reef to French Polynesia, and in the subtropics at the Norfolk and Kermadec Islands. They breed on North and South Meyer Islets in the Herald Group off Raoul Island, and at Macauley, Curtis and Cheeseman Islands and L'Esperance Rock in the southern Kermadecs. Fourteen records of single birds from the New Zealand mainland, some appearing after northerly gales: Kaipara Harbour (1953, 1964), Farewell Spit (1961), Spirits Bay (1965), Whangarei (1965, 1997),

345

Houhora Harbour (1975), Taieri Estuary (1977), Karikari Bay (1986), Muriwai (1986), Three Kings (1989), Rangaunu (1990) and Waikato (1997), Rapahoe (2000).

Population: c. 1100 pairs: Meyer Islets 1000 pairs, Macauley Island 50 pairs, Curtis Island 40 pairs, Cheeseman Island 20 pairs, and a few pairs on L'Esperance Rock.

Conservation: Protected native. They formerly bred on Raoul Island, but rats and cats have eliminated them. Moves to eradicate these predators could see White-capped Noddies become re-established there.

Breeding: The breeding season varies from year to year at the Kermadecs; eggs are laid in August–January, mostly October–November. The nest is usually an untidy heap of sticks and seaweed, cemented by guano, in trees and scrub. Sometimes, such as on Macauley Island, where there are no trees, the nest is on a rock ledge or in a cave. They lay 1 creamy-white egg (44 x 31 mm), blotched reddish brown. Both adults incubate for c. 36 days and care for the black downy young. The fledging period is 50–55 days.

Behaviour: Like the Common Noddy, except that after breeding they stay at or near the islands, feeding at sea during the day and roosting in the colonies at night.

Feeding: At sea, they hover and dip at the surface mainly for fish, also plankton.

252. GREY TERNLET   *Procelsterna cerulea*   Plate 57

Other names: Blue-grey/Grey Noddy
Size: 28 cm, 75 g
Geographical variation: Several subspecies, of which *albivittata* breeds in northern New Zealand and northeastern Australia.

Distribution: Breed on islands of the tropical and subtropical Pacific Ocean from New Zealand and Norfolk Island north to Hawai'i and east to islands off Chile. Breed on all islands of the Kermadecs, but mainly on Macauley and Curtis Islands. Known only as an occasional vagrant to the New Zealand mainland before the summer of 1969–70, mostly single birds off the coast of Northland between Cape Maria van Diemen and Waipu. That summer many frequented the waters off eastern Northland and the Bay of Plenty, and c. 1000 apparently bred at the Volkner Rocks off White Island; they were seen also at Sugarloaf Rock in the Aldermen Islands. Small groups have since bred irregularly at West Island, Three Kings Islands; Sugarloaf Rock, Poor Knights Islands; and Cathedral Rocks, Mokohinau Islands and at Volkner Rocks. One South Island record, at Banks Peninsula, following the *Wahine* storm of mid-April 1968. One was seen at Lake Taupo (1994).

Population: c. 17,000 pairs: Macauley 10,000 pairs, Curtis 5000 pairs, Raoul Island and Herald Group several thousand pairs, and L'Esperance Rock several hundred pairs. The number breeding on islands off the north-eastern North Island has not been determined but is probably fewer than 50 pairs.

Conservation: Protected native. Numbers breeding on Raoul Island have decreased in the last 30 years, but the removal of goats from Macauley Island has probably helped to increase productivity there.

Breeding: Eggs are laid in August–December at the Kermadecs. They are laid on a bare rocky surface sheltered from the sun, in cavities and crevices, on cliff ledges, under clumps of vegetation along cliff tops and in the shade of boulders on the beach. They lay 1 creamy-white egg (42 x 28 mm) with small dark and light brown blotches. Both sexes incubate for c. 32 days. The fledging period is c. 35 days.

Behaviour: Gregarious; breeding in loose colonies and feeding in flocks. Sometimes these flocks are immense and include 5000+ birds. Grey Ternlets are mainly sedentary; some disperse after breeding, but most stay within 20 km of their breeding site, and a few come ashore during the non-breeding period. Their flight is graceful, floating and unhurried.

Feeding: Flocks work into the wind, hovering and fluttering over the water, repeatedly dipping down to pick up plankton from the surface, sometimes skipping on the surface like a storm petrel, getting bill and feet wet only. As they run out of the feeding area, they veer away to the side, circle round to rejoin the rear of the flock and start working their way forward again. Their main food is plankton, but they also take small fish. Chicks are fed by regurgitation, not whole small fish like most terns. They peck at first at the webs of the adult's feet, not at the bill as is usual.

Reading: Falla, R.A. 1970. *Notornis* 17: 83–86.
Soper, M.F. 1969. *Notornis* 16: 75–80.

253. WHITE TERN *Gygis alba* Plate 57

Other names: White Noddy, Fairy Tern
Size: 31 cm, 110 g
Geographical variation: Of the six subspecies, *royana* breeds in Australasia, including at the Kermadecs.
Distribution: Breed on tropical and some subtropical islands of the Atlantic, Indian and Pacific Oceans. The subspecies *royana* breed in large numbers on Norfolk Island and in small numbers on Lord Howe Island and on Raoul Island, Kermadecs. During breeding, they are usually seen at sea within 100 km of the main breeding islands. For several months after fledging, young birds feed with their parents during the day and return to their breeding trees to roost at night. In autumn and winter, they become more pelagic and are absent from Raoul Island in April–August. Vagrants occasionally reach the North Island of New Zealand: Waipu (1883), Bethells Beach (1960), Pakotai, inland Northland (1964), Palmerston North (1972), Otaki Beach (1986), Te Horo Beach (1988), Dargaville Beach (1990), Muriwai Beach (1990) and Taupiri, Waikato (1998). Recorded only once in the South Island: Ettrick, Otago (1945). These White Terns were recorded mainly in March–July, mostly May.
Population: Probably fewer than 10 pairs breed annually on Raoul Island.
Conservation: Protected native. The popula-

tion on Raoul Island is in a very precarious state, as birds suffer from predation by cats and perhaps rats. Moves by the Department of Conservation to eradicate these pests from Raoul Island may help to prevent the extinction of the White Tern as a breeding species in New Zealand.
Breeding: At Raoul Island, White Terns return to their breeding trees in September and eggs are laid in October–December. They particularly favour pohutukawa and Norfolk pines as breeding trees on Raoul Island, laying their single egg in a depression, slight hollow or irregularity on a bare, horizontal branch, often many metres above the ground. They lay **1** white egg (44 x 33 mm), heavily marked with brown and grey blotches. Both adults incubate for c. 28 days and, unlike other noddies, feed their chick on whole fish. The chick, which takes 60–75 days to fly, clings to the bark tenaciously with its long, sharp claws.
Behaviour: White Terns seldom associate with other noddies and terns. Their flight is fluttering and ethereal. Inquisitive and tame, they hover in front of a human intruder's face, uttering strange wheezing and twanging sounds.
Feeding: They flutter over the water surface and catch tiny fish from near the surface without submerging themselves.

PIGEONS and DOVES

Columbidae

About 290 species worldwide; 1 is endemic to New Zealand and 3 have been introduced.

Usually the larger members of the family are called pigeons, and the smaller ones, doves.

Pigeons and doves have plump bodies with short legs and necks, small heads and short, straight bills. The plumage is soft, dense and loose, and some have brilliant or iridescent colouring. They feed mainly on vegetable matter and can be split into two groups: grain-eaters and fruit-eaters. Both groups supplement their diet with foliage, buds and flowers. Pigeons and doves have a large crop for storing grain or fruit. The fruit-eating pigeons play an important ecological role in forest regeneration, transporting intact seeds of trees and shrubs and depositing them at a new site.

Unlike most birds, pigeons can drink without raising their heads to swallow. They are strong fliers and have aerial displays in which the bird stalls and dives with wings and tail held stiffly, and they also clap their wings together above their backs during display flight.

The nest is rudimentary, usually a flat basket of interwoven twigs in a tree or on the ledge of a cliff or an artificial structure. All species lay only one or two small eggs; most granivorous species lay two eggs, and most fruit pigeons lay only one. The total clutch weight, at on average 9% of female body weight, is the lightest of all bird groups. The breeding season is usually determined by suitable food being available, and normally several broods are reared each year. This is helped by having very short incubation and fledging periods, and the young usually fledge well below adult weight. Clutches are sometimes overlapped, eggs being incubated in one nest while chicks are still being fed in another.

Apart from Emperor Penguins and flamingoes, pigeons and doves are the only birds to produce food for their chicks. They feed their chicks (sometimes called squabs) crop-milk, a protein-rich, cottage-cheese-like secretion from the crop wall. At first, crop-milk is the only food, but as the chicks grow, regurgitated foods form an increasingly large part of the diet.

Reading: Goodwin, D. 1970. *Pigeons and Doves of the World.* London: British Museum. Robertson, H.A. 1988. *J Zool* (Lond) 215: 217–229.

254. NEW ZEALAND PIGEON

Hemiphaga novaeseelandiae **Plate 59**

Other names: Kereru, Kukupa (northern North Island), Parea (Chathams), Woodpigeon
Size: 51 cm, 650 g (NZ); 55 cm, 800 g (Chathams)
Geographical variation: Two subspecies: the Kereru or Kukupa *novaeseelandiae* breeds on the North, South and Stewart Islands and on many forested offshore islands; the Parea *chathamensis* breeds on the Chatham Islands.
Distribution: New Zealand only, although they were on Norfolk Island (subspecies *spadicea*) until the early 1800s. New Zealand Pigeons are found throughout the North, South, Stewart and Chatham Islands, and until the mid-1800s on Raoul Island, Kermadecs. They are also on many forested offshore islands. On the mainland, they are most common in Northland, the King Country, Nelson and the West Coast. They favour native lowland forests dominated by podocarps, tawa, taraire and puriri, bush patches on farmland, gardens, and parks of cities. Their breeding and wintering distributions are similar, but birds move long distances (100 km) to good sources of fruit or foliage outside the breeding season.

On the Chathams, they are mainly in the forests of southern Chatham Island, especially around the Tuku River, but a few are seen elsewhere on Chatham Island, and on Pitt and South East Islands.
Population: Kereru are widespread and locally common, but in serious decline in

many places; Parea: c. 150 in 1994.

Conservation: Protected threatened endemic. In the early 1900s, the New Zealand Pigeon was in serious decline from overhunting and clearance of lowland forest, but with protection since 1921, and perhaps the planting of food plants such as tree lucerne and willows, it increased. Although still widespread and locally common, Kereru are now threatened because in many places adult mortality (from illegal hunting, predation, starvation) exceeds breeding productivity, which is low because of loss of eggs and chicks to rats, stoats and possums, and competition for fruit by possums may reduce breeding attempts. Experimental control of predators has improved breeding on the mainland, and Kereru have increased greatly on Kapiti Island in the decade since possums were eradicated.

The Parea is endangered but now increasing. They were common in the 1870s, but by 1990 the population had declined to as few as 40 birds. Predator control and fencing in and around the Tuku Valley has led to improved breeding and rapid population growth. Birds are now venturing into parts of Chatham Island where they have not been seen for many years.

The conservation of New Zealand Pigeons is particularly important because they play a key ecological role in the regeneration of native forests by dispersing the seeds of large-fruited trees and shrubs, some of which (e.g. miro, tawa, taraire, puriri and karaka) are too large to be dispersed by other birds.

Breeding: The timing of breeding is closely linked to certain fruits being available; they can lay at any time of the year, but also some or all pairs fail to breed in years when fruit is in poor supply. Kereru lay mainly in September–February, and Parea mainly June–October. During the season, each pair can lay 2–3 clutches, which can be overlapping, birds incubating while still feeding a chick in another nest. Pairs usually occupy the same area each breeding season. The nest is a platform of sticks on a horizontal fork or in a tangle of vines 2–15 m above the ground, and the egg or chick can often be seen through the nest.

They lay **1** white egg (48 x 33 mm, 30 g).

Both adults incubate for 27–30 days (Kereru) or 27–29 days (Parea); females incubate from late afternoon to mid-morning, males through the middle of the day. Both adults brood the chick. It is at first fed just crop-milk, a protein-rich secretion from the crop wall of the adults, but as it grows, regurgitated fruits form an increasingly large part of the diet. The chick fledges at 30–45 days old (Kereru) or 36–53 days old (Parea), well below adult weight and with a conspicuously short tail. The chick is fed by regurgitation for several weeks after fledging. The first chick raised is evicted when its parents renest, but the last chick raised stays close to its natal territory for at least 2–3 months. First breeding can be at less than 12 months old, but is usually at 1–2 years old. The oldest banded bird in the wild lived at least 6 years, but some are likely to live 10 or more.

Behaviour: The most conspicuous breeding display is the display dive; a bird flaps upward from a perch, stalls, and then dives on stiffly held wings. This display is done by both sexes, but particularly by males, close to the time of egg-laying, often, but not always, close to the nesting area. Other breeding displays include close chases, head-and neck-bobbing, and a display where the male bounces up and down on a branch while posturing and calling. Incubating or brooding birds defend their nest with grunts and wing-flicking.

Feeding: Herbivorous; fruits are preferred and in some parts of the country are the sole diet. The preferred fruits eaten by Kereru are of miro, tawa, taraire, puriri and pigeonwood; other main fruits are of kahikatea, coprosma, titoki, nikau, karaka, privet, elder and plums. Supplejack and cabbage-tree fruits are also eaten but are much less preferred. On the Chathams, the main fruits eaten by Parea are of matipo, hoho, mahoe and karamu. When fruit is in short supply, New Zealand Pigeons feed on foliage, especially old leaves of kowhai, tree lucerne, broom and clover, leaves of coprosma, hoheria and *Parsonsia*, and young leaves or buds of willow, elm and poplar. Flowers of kowhai, tree lucerne, broom and laburnum also form an important seasonal part of their diet.

Reading: Clout *et al.* 1988. *Notornis* 35: 59–62. Clout *et al.* 1986. *Notornis* 33: 37–44. Clout *et al.* 1995. *Ibis* 137: 264–271. McEwen, W.M. 1978. *NZ J Ecol* 1: 99–108. Pierce, R.J. & Graham, P.J. 1995. S & R Series No. 91. Wellington: DoC. Powlesland, R.G. *et al.* 1994. S & R Series No. 66. Wellington: DoC.

255. ROCK PIGEON *Columba livia*   Plate 59

Other name: Feral Pigeon

Size: 33 cm, 400 g

Geographical variation: Over 200 varieties of dovecote or racing pigeons have been selected through thousands of years of domestication. Rock Pigeons in towns are continuously supplemented by lost dovecote or racing pigeons, and so have more variable plumages than rural birds, which are mainly like the original Rock Pigeon plumage type.

Distribution: Natural range is Europe, North Africa, western Asia and India. Domesticated birds were taken from Europe to most parts of the world. Early settlers brought birds to New Zealand, and they quickly reverted to the wild and established feral populations in the North and South Islands, but mainly in the cropping districts of Hawke's Bay, Marlborough, Canterbury and Otago, and in cities and large towns. City pigeons are sedentary, frequenting city parks and grain-handling and storage facilities, but rural birds often commute over 20 km between their roosting and breeding sites and their feeding grounds on newly sown crops or stubble.

Population: Widespread and locally common.

Breeding: Breed solitarily on buildings or under bridges, and the territory is defended all year, but they also nest in small colonies on cliffs high above a river or the sea, on offshore rock stacks or in sea caves, and rarely in a tall tree where a broken branch or old nest provides a flat platform. The nest is a simple platform of straw and twigs on a ledge. They can breed at any time of year, depending on food being available, but the peak is in spring and summer, and the low is late autumn. Rock Pigeons renest up to five times each season, sometimes while they are still feeding young in another nest. In a normal season, they probably raise 2–3 broods each year.

The clutch is 1–2–4 white eggs (39 x 29 mm; 19 g), but those of over 3 eggs are probably laid by more than one female. Both adults incubate for c. 17 days and brood the chicks for the first week. Chicks are at first fed just crop-milk, a protein-rich secretion from the crop wall of both adults, but as they grow, regurgitated food forms an increasingly large part of the diet. The chicks fledge at c. 30 days old at about 84% of adult weight and quickly become independent. The young are capable of breeding at 6 months old.

Behaviour: Rock Pigeons are usually seen feeding or roosting in loose flocks, and they commute in tight, fast-flying flocks between roosts and feeding places. In parks, birds can be seen displaying at any time of year, the male bowing and strutting around the female with his neck arched and chest puffed out. They also perform aerial displays where the male flies with slow, deliberate wingbeats interspersed with gliding with wings held stiffly upwards. Calls are variations on a rippling coo of three notes: 'oor-roo-cooo'.

Feeding: In towns, Rock Pigeons readily take scraps of food from people, and spilt grain. In rural areas, they feed on newly sown or stubble grain, peas, maize, beans, clover and weed seeds, supplemented with occasional invertebrates such as snails, worms and slugs. Rock Pigeons can cause serious damage to newly sown pea and bean crops, as a flock can work systematically through a crop day after day.

Reading: Dilks, P.J. 1975. *NZ J Ag Res* 18: 87–90. Dilks, P.J. 1975. *Notornis* 22: 295–301. Murton, R.K. *et al.* 1972. *J Appl Ecol* 9: 835–874. Robertson, H.A. 1988. *Ibis* 130: 261–267.

256. BARBARY DOVE *Streptopelia roseogrisea* Plate 59

Size: 28 cm, 140 g

Distribution: Natural range is across the Sahel zone of northern Africa from Senegal to Ethiopia, and into Arabia. Domesticated birds were taken to Europe and many other parts of the world. They were brought to New Zealand as cage birds but have become feral from time to time. A few established in Masterton in the 1970s, but this population did not last. Small feral populations are now established near Whangarei, in South Auckland, Rotorua, Whakatane, near Havelock North.

Population: The status of Barbary Doves in New Zealand is marginal, with probably fewer than 100 birds, mostly near Havelock North and near Whangarei.

Breeding: Breed solitarily in shrubs, hedges or trees. They can breed at any time of year if food is available, but the peak is in spring and summer, and the low is in late autumn. Barbary Doves renest several times each season. They lay **2** white eggs (29 x 23 mm, 8 g) on a simple platform of twigs. Both adults incubate for c. 15 days and brood the chicks for the first week. Chicks are at first fed just crop-milk, a protein-rich secretion from the crop wall of both adults, but as the chicks grow, regurgitated seeds form an increasingly large part of the diet. They fledge at c. 15 days old and quickly become independent.

Behaviour: Barbary Doves are usually seen alone or in pairs, occasionally in small flocks at good food sources. Calls are a mellow 'coo-crroo', the second note being lower and longer; also a high-pitched excitement cry: 'heh-heh-heh', sounding like a jeering laugh.

Feeding: In towns, they readily take scraps of food from people, and spilt grain. In rural areas, they feed on newly sown or stubble grain, and clover and weed seeds, supplemented with occasional invertebrates such as snails.

Reading: Stidolph, R.H.D. 1974. *Notornis* 21: 383–384.

257. SPOTTED DOVE *Streptopelia chinensis* Plate 59

Other names: Spotted Turtle-Dove, Malay Spotted Dove

Size: 30 cm, 130 g

Geographical variation: Five subspecies, of which *tigrina*, from Burma through south-eastern Asia to Indonesia, has been introduced to New Zealand.

Distribution: Natural range is Asia, from India and Sri Lanka to southern China, Taiwan and Timor. Introduced to Hawai'i, Australia and New Zealand as a cage bird. The Spotted Doves in the Auckland area, from Albany to Pukekohe, probably originated from escaped cage birds and from a substantial liberation at Mt Eden in the 1920s. They are mainly found in well-treed suburbs and city parks, and in rural areas around Howick, Whitford, Clevedon and Karaka; a few birds have been recorded as far south as Miranda on the Firth of Thames. Small populations have established recently in rural Bay of Plenty near Te Puke and Opotiki.

Population: Locally common in the Auckland area.

Breeding: Spotted Doves breed solitarily. The nest is a flimsy platform of twigs, well concealed in a large shrub, hedge or tree, up to 12 m above the ground. They can breed at any time of year if food is available, but the peak is in spring and summer, and the low is in late autumn. Spotted Doves renest several times each season. They lay **2** white eggs (27 x 21 mm, 7 g). Both sexes incubate for c. 16 days and brood the chicks for the first week. Chicks are at first fed just crop-milk, a protein-rich secretion from the crop wall of both adults, but as the chicks grow, regurgitated seeds form an increasingly large part of the diet. They fledge at c. 15 days old and quickly become independent.

Behaviour: Spotted Doves are secretive and more often heard than seen. When seen, they are normally alone or in pairs as they search for food on the ground; however, they sometimes form flocks where grain has been spilt or where weeds are seeding prolifically. A spectacular display is a steep upward flight and downward glide with wings and tail stiffly spread. Their calling reaches a peak in autumn and spring, 2–4 coo notes varying in rhythm and emphasis, e.g. 'croo-croo' or 'cu-cu-croo-crook'.

Feeding: In towns, they feed on grass and weed seeds in lawns and along paths, but in rural areas they feed on spilt grain, especially where horses and other livestock have been fed, around poultry yards and on grass, clover and weed seeds in short cover. Their diet is supplemented with occasional invertebrates such as snails.

COCKATOOS and PARROTS
Cacatuidae and Psittacidae

About 330 species worldwide; 10 breed in New Zealand. Five are endemic to New Zealand, 1 is native and 4 have been introduced.

Parrots are well known for their colourful plumage and are widely held in captivity.

All have a large head and eyes, a short neck, and a short, deep bill. Mainly herbivorous, although some also eat invertebrates. The upper mandible of the bill is strongly curved, sharply pointed, and hinged at the base so that the parrot can crack nuts or other

unyielding food. Parrots can use their bill as an extra limb, showing great agility at climbing. They have a large fleshy cere, surrounding the nostrils. Two toes are pointed forwards and two back, giving a strong grip. Parrots can hold food while shredding it and pass it to their mouth. Most parrots are gregarious, and many have loud, harsh voices. They mostly lay white eggs in holes in trees or in crevices in rocks.

Reading: Forshaw, J.M. & Cooper, W.T. 1978. *Parrots of the World*. Melbourne: Lansdowne.

258. SULPHUR-CRESTED COCKATOO   *Cacatua galerita*   Plate 60

Other name: White Cockatoo
Size: 50 cm, 900 g
Distribution: Natural range is northern, eastern and southeastern Australia and Tasmania, New Guinea and adjacent islands. They were introduced to New Zealand in the early 1900s and have become well established in the Waitakere Ranges and in the western Waikato, in the Turakina River catchment and in the Kapiti Coast/Hutt Valley/Wainuiomata area of Wellington. Small groups have established at scattered sites from Northland to Canterbury, and single stragglers (perhaps even from Australia) or cage escapees have been recorded widely, including on the West Coast.
Population: Probably fewer than 1000 birds, the main sites are: northwestern Waikato

c. 300, Turakina c. 300, Wellington c. 50.
Breeding: Breed in hollow limbs and trunks of tall podocarps, usually above 20 m. The nest is a hollowed-out funnel lined with wood chips. Eggs are laid in August–November. They lay 1–2–3 white eggs (48 x 33 mm). Both sexes incubate for c. 30 days and brood the young, which fledge at c. 40 days old.
Behaviour: Gregarious when not breeding. Small, widely dispersed flocks and pairs gather into large flocks (up to 100+ birds) at winter communal roosts. In spring, these large flocks split up as pairs begin nesting and non-breeders resume a more nomadic lifestyle. Sulphur-crested Cockatoos remain alert and are hard to approach. Birds perched high in trees while the flock feeds on the ground or in neighbouring trees scream at the approach

of an intruder, and the whole flock flies up.
Feeding: In New Zealand, they feed on the seeds of grasses, cereals and weeds (including thistles), fruit of podocarps, seeds of introduced conifers, walnuts, orchard fruit, and insect larvae dug out of rotting wood. Despite occasionally feeding on grain crops, they do not seem to cause major damage, probably because their populations are kept in check by people trapping adults and collecting chicks for the cage-bird trade.

259. GALAH *Cacatua roseicapilla*   Plate 60

Size: 36 cm, 325 g
Distribution: Native to Australia, where they are widespread except for the wet eastern coastal belt and Tasmania. Introduced to New Zealand as a cage bird. A group of smuggled birds that were released at sea off the Horowhenua coast in the 1970s failed to establish. However, cage escapees have recently established in the wild in South Auckland and the northern Waikato, including visiting Pakihi and Ponui Islands in the inner Hauraki Gulf. Most sighting are around Ponui Island/Hunua Ranges, Mangatawhiri, and Pukekohe/Port Waikato areas.
Population: Probably fewer than 150 birds; the largest flock recorded is 50 birds.

Breeding: Galahs have bred in the wild in New Zealand, but few details are available. Courtship and mating has been noted in August. In Australia, they lay 2–5 white eggs in a hollow tree.
Behaviour: Gregarious; they are often in small flocks and pairs during the summer and early autumn, but gather into larger flocks in the winter and early spring. The flocks are highly mobile and somewhat nomadic.
Feeding: In Australia, they feed mostly on the ground on seeds of grasses, cereals and weeds; they have been recorded feeding on maize stubble in New Zealand. As they are a major pest of grain crops in Australia, their increase and spread could also cause problems here.

260. KAKAPO *Strigops habroptilus*   Plate 60

Other name: Owl-parrot
Size: 63 cm; males 2.5 kg, females 2.0 kg
Distribution: New Zealand only. Subfossil and midden records show that Kakapo were throughout North, South and Stewart Islands before and during early Maori times. In the early 1800s, they were still in the central North Island and the forested parts of the South Island. Their range contracted rapidly when stoats were introduced in the 1880s, and by 1900 they remained common only in parts of the southern and western South Island. By the mid-1970s, only 18 males were known in remote parts of Fiordland, and they probably died out in the early 1990s.

In 1977, however, a population of about 100 birds was found living south and east of the Tin Range in southern Stewart Island. This population was also in serious decline because of predation by feral cats – there are no stoats or other mustelids on Stewart Island. The remaining 61 Kakapo were moved to several cat- and mustelid-free islands, but by 2005 they were mostly on Codfish Island (Whenua Hou).
Population: In 2005, the total was 83 birds.
Conservation: Protected critically endangered endemic. Kakapo evolved without mammalian predators, and although their nocturnal habits and camouflaged plumage were presumably effective against the avian predators of ancient New Zealand, they are particularly susceptible to mammalian predators, being large, flightless, relatively slow-moving, placid, and strong-scented. To make matters worse, they often roost and nest on the ground, and in a breeding year males congregate on traditional display grounds and boom loudly for 6–8 hours every night for 3–5 months. They also have a long breeding period (100+ days), during which the female leaves the eggs and chicks unattended for

long periods on most nights while she forages. Their productivity is naturally low and is dependent on an abundant supply of fruits being available, and much is removed by competing introduced herbivores such as possums, deer, goats and chamois, and introduced omnivores such as rats, pigs and introduced birds.

Recent conservation attempts have concentrated on clearing predators from suitable islands, and shifting Kakapo to these islands once predators have been eradicated. The fate of individual birds and all breeding attempts are closely monitored. Supplementary food (mainly fruit, nuts and formulated artificial pellets) is supplied in some years on these islands to try to stimulate breeding more frequently than once every 3–5 years in nature. Unlike some parrots, wild-raised adults have not been kept successfully in captivity.

Breeding: Successful breeding requires an abundant supply of high-quality food throughout the 8-month breeding cycle. This 'masting' seems to happen every 3–5 years, e.g. in Fiordland the seeds that have high protein value are of tussock grasses and beech trees, and on Stewart Island the key fruits are rimu and pink pine. With supplementary food, however, Kakapo may breed more often than every 3–5 years, e.g. two supplementary-fed females on Little Barrier laid eggs in consecutive years.

Kakapo are unique among New Zealand birds, parrots and flightless birds in having a lek, or arena mating system. In good fruiting years, males establish a miniature display territory that has no connection with feeding or nesting sites. The display area is a 'track and bowl' system consisting of a series of bowls, each a shallow depression about 50 cm across, connected by tracks 30–60 cm wide, mostly clustered within an 'arena' on a prominent vantage point, a ridge or hilltop with low-growing and sparse vegetation, where calls can be projected a long distance. Males remove encroaching vegetation from their track-and-bowl system. They give three major types of call during the booming season (December–March): non-directional, low-pitched 'booming', which is highly resonant and can carry several kilometres on a suitable

night; highly directional, high-pitched 'chinging', which may reveal to an approaching female the exact position of the male; and harsh 'skrarking', which is apparently related to territorial defence and aggression between neighbouring males. When booming, males inflate their thoracic air sacs hugely, and by holding their head low, the sacs act as a resonating chamber. They utter 20–50 booms at about 2-second intervals, then pause for 30–120 seconds between sequences. Booming continues throughout the night for 6–8 hours each night for 3–5 months. Females travel several kilometres to briefly visit the displaying males to mate. The dominant males mate with several females, and males take no part tending or defending the nest.

Nests on Stewart Island were in the decayed centre of fallen tree trunks, in the hollow centre of a standing stump, and under tussock clumps. They lay 2–3–4 white eggs (51 x 38 mm) at intervals of 3–5 days. The female alone incubates for c. 30 days, starting when the first egg is laid and so hatching may be staggered over many days. During the first 2 weeks of incubation, the female rarely leaves the nest, but later she leaves to feed for several hours. The chicks are usually brooded for the first 3–4 weeks all day, but for only part of the night, then she broods for less of the night, and finally, when the chicks are about 8 weeks old, she visits only once or twice a night and roosts elsewhere by day. The fledging period is 10–12 weeks, and the chicks associate with the female for a further 4 months. The young may first breed when 6–8 years old. Kakapo are long-lived, the oldest known bird in the wild is at least 35 years old, but some probably live to 100 years old.

Behaviour: Solitary, unlike other parrots. Kakapo are the heaviest parrot and are flightless. The keel on the sternum is rudimentary, but the broad wings are used to maintain balance when climbing and running, and they slow the bird's steep fall from low trees.

Feeding: Herbivorous. Kakapo eat a wide variety of fruits, seeds, leaves, stems and roots. The stout bill is used for grubbing and grinding; the inside of the upper mandible has a series of ridges that work with the tongue and the lower mandible to grind fibrous foods, acting as a kind of juice extractor. Tussock and other grass seed is removed by using the foot to pass stems through the bill from the base to the end. Foliage is browsed while attached to the plant, the fibrous material being ejected as tightly compressed, kidney-shaped 'chews', often still attached to the plant.

Reading: Butler, D. 1989. *Quest for the Kakapo.* Auckland: Heinemann Reed. Cemmick, D. & Veitch, D. 1987. *Kakapo Country.* Auckland: Hodder & Stoughton. Lloyd, B.D. & Powlesland, R.G. 1994. *Biol Cons* 69: 75–85. Merton, D. *et al.* 1984. *Ibis* 126: 277–283. Powlesland, R.G. *et al.* 1992. *Ibis* 134: 361–373. Powlesland, R.G. *et al.* 1995. *NZ J Zool* 22: 239–248. Williams, G.R. 1956. *Notornis* 7: 29–56.

261. KAKA *Nestor meridionalis* Plate 60

Size: 45 cm; males 475 g, females 425 g (North Island); males 575 g, females 500 g (South Island)

Geographical variation: Two subspecies: the North Island Kaka *septentrionalis*, and the South Island Kaka *meridionalis*.

Distribution: New Zealand only. Kaka were common as subfossils throughout both main islands and in middens throughout the North Island. They were abundant when Europeans arrived, but by the early 1900s they had declined to localised flocks. North Island Kaka are still in the large forest tracts from Coromandel Peninsula to the Aorangi Range in the southern Wairarapa. They are moderately common in the central North Island, especially in the Pureora and Whirinaki forests. They are most numerous on the larger offshore islands: Hen and Chickens, Great Barrier, Little Barrier, Mayor and Kapiti. Kaka commute freely between the northern islands and wander to mainland forests and towns, e.g. Northland, Auckland, Hamilton, Greytown, and to other offshore islands where they are not normally resident.

South Island Kaka are in the forested parts of the South and Stewart Islands and on some offshore islands, e.g. Chetwode, Codfish and Big South Cape, but are nowhere common. They are chiefly west of the Southern Alps and in Fiordland and southwestern Southland. They extend east of the alps into Canterbury at lower mountain passes. Birds wander occasionally to coastal Canterbury and Otago.

Population: Probably fewer than 10,000 birds, mostly on large offshore islands, especially Little Barrier, Kapiti and Codfish.

Conservation: Protected threatened endemic. The range and number of Kaka have been greatly reduced by the clearfelling and 'sustainable logging' of beech and mixed podocarp/hardwood lowland forests, competition with possums for fruit and nectar-bearing plants such as mistletoe, competition with wasps for beech honeydew in the South Island, and predation by introduced mammals. Numbers of Kaka have increased greatly on Kapiti Island in the decade since possums were eradicated. Island populations are reasonably secure, but reducing the numbers of possums, rats, stoats and wasps in mainland forest may safeguard mainland birds.

Short-term conservation measures on the mainland may be to reduce predators and provide supplementary food in a few enclaves where there are still enough potential breeders, and to provide predator-proof nest boxes and wasp-proof feeding stations.

Breeding: Nests are a shallow bowl of decayed wood dust in the bases of hollow trees or in hollow branches or trunks, and so Kaka need mature and dying trees to provide such sites. In September–January, they lay 1–4–5 white eggs (42 x 31 mm). The female alone incubates for 23–25 days. The eggs hatch over several days, and so at first the chicks vary in size. The male regurgitates food to the female during incubation and shares in caring for the chicks, which take 60–70 days to fledge and another 5 months to become fully independent of their parents.

They first breed from 4 years old. The oldest Kaka in the wild was still breeding at 14 years old, but in captivity they have lived to over 20 years old.

Behaviour: Kaka can be conspicuous when in a flock but cryptic when feeding alone, the sound of falling pieces of wood often betraying their presence. They delight in acrobatics and aerobatics, jumping through the trees and tumbling through the air for enjoyment. Their calls are a wide variety of liquid, whistling notes and harsh, grating calls.

Feeding: Diet is mainly fruit, nectar and insects. They use their powerful bill to tear off loose bark and break up decaying wood to extract the grubs of wood-boring beetles such as the kanuka longhorn beetle, and to tap into sap from the bark of beech, mountain totara, and especially southern rata trees. They eat many kinds of seed and succulent fruit, and use their delicate brush-tipped tongue to take honeydew, and nectar from flowers of flax and trees such as rata and pohutukawa.

Reading: Beggs, J.R. & Wilson, P.R. 1987. *NZ J Ecol* 10: 143–147. Beggs, J.R. & Wilson, P.R. 1991. *Biol Cons* 56: 23–38. Moorhouse, R.J. 1991. *Acta XX IOC*: 690–696. O'Donnell, C.F.J. 1993. *Notornis* 40: 79–80. O'Donnell, C.F.J. & Dilks, P.J. 1989. *Notornis* 36: 65–71.

262. KEA *Nestor notabilis* Plate 60

Size: 46 cm; males 1000 g, females 800 g

Distribution: South Island only. Kea are in high country from northwestern Nelson and Marlborough southward to Fiordland. They are mostly in high-altitude forest, the mountains, and high alpine basins and steep valleys; but they often come down to the lowland flats, mainly on the west of the Southern Alps, and have also been recorded as far afield as Farewell Spit lighthouse. Subfossils at one North Island site indicate a previously wider range, and odd records from the Tararua Range could be of birds crossing Cook Strait or cage escapees from nearby collections.

Population: Little known; probably c. 5000 birds.

Conservation: Protected rare endemic. Kea range widely, and so it is difficult to assess population trends. They have received wide publicity as sheep killers; while they certainly feed on dead sheep, and occasionally kill sick and injured sheep, only a few birds actually attack healthy sheep. Thousands of Kea were killed for a bounty until they were partially protected in 1970. They were fully protected in 1986.

Kea are playful and inquisitive, but are destructive, and soon make themselves unwelcome at ski-fields and subalpine carparks, on hut roofs and tents. The worst offending birds are caught and transferred to distant sites or taken into captivity.

Breeding: Males may often be polygamous, i.e. support more than one nesting female.

Kea nest in holes in the ground, under logs and in cavities among the jumbled boulders of old moraines overgrown with scrub and trees, usually in the upper forest. The nest comprises twigs, grasses, moss and lichens. In July–January, they lay 2–4 white eggs (44 x 33 mm). Females alone incubate for 23–24 days. The males feed the females while they are incubating and after hatching. The fledging period is 90–100 days. Young are probably over 3 years old before they breed. The oldest Kea recorded in the wild lived over 20 years.

Behaviour: Gregarious; flocks of mainly juvenile and subadult males gather at ski-field carparks and refuse dumps, and small groups of 5–15 birds are seen elsewhere. Their call is a ringing, far-carrying 'keee-aa', an evocative sound, especially when heard in the swirling mists of the alpine tops. They fly strongly and delight in tumbling in air currents.

Feeding: Mostly herbivorous, feeding on berries and shoots. Many have learnt to fossick through refuse dumps and eat carrion and food scraps. A few may specialise in using their bill to dig into the flesh of healthy sheep above the kidneys; the sheep may develop a large festering area above the kidneys or blood poisoning.

Reading: Bond, A.B. & Diamond, J. 1992. *Notornis* 39: 151–160. Clarke, C.M.H. 1970. *Notornis* 17: 105–114. Wilson, K.-J. 1990. *Forest & Bird* 21: 20–26.

263. CRIMSON ROSELLA *Platycercus elegans*   Plate 61

Size: 35 cm, 130 g
Distribution: Native to eastern Australia, from northern Queensland to eastern South Australia. Introduced to Norfolk Island and New Zealand. A rare cage escapee in New Zealand, a small number established near Dunedin about 1910 but died out by the 1950s. A few have become established in the wooded parks and suburbs in Wellington, most often seen in Central Park and the Botanical Gardens. A few birds, probably recent cage escapees, are seen elsewhere.
Population: Probably fewer than 20 birds in the wild.
Breeding: Not studied in New Zealand, but juveniles have been seen in October–March. In Australia, the nest is a shallow bowl of decayed wood dust in a hollow limb of a tree. In August–February, they lay 4–**5**–8 white eggs (29 x 24 mm). The female alone incubates for c. 21 days. The fledging period is c. 35 days. The young remain with their parents for several months after fledging.
Behaviour: In New Zealand, Crimson Rosellas are usually seen as singles or in small family groups, but in Australia immatures form small flocks in autumn and winter while adults remain in pairs or small parties. Their usual call is a low-pitched 'kweek-kweek-kweek', lower in tone than the similar Eastern Rosella call.
Feeding: Diet is mainly seeds of grasses, weeds and trees, and fruit.
Reading: Hamel, J. 1970. *Notornis* 17: 126–129.

264. EASTERN ROSELLA *Platycercus eximius*   Plate 61

Size: 32 cm, 110 g
Geographical variation: Of the three doubtfully distinct subspecies, *eximius* of southern New South Wales, Victoria and eastern South Australia was introduced to New Zealand.
Distribution: Native to southeastern Australia, from southern Queensland to eastern South Australia and Tasmania. Introduced to New Zealand as a cage bird, but escaped in Dunedin around 1910. They became well established and spread through southeastern Otago until about the 1940s, when they declined in range back to the Dunedin area. A separate population became established in Auckland before 1920; they spread northwards to reach Wellsford and Leigh in the early 1940s, and by 1970 had spread throughout Northland. They have also spread southwards into the Waikato and Taranaki in the west and to the Coromandel and Bay of Plenty in the east. Another population became established in the Wellington area in the 1960s, and they have since spread northwards along the foothills of the ranges into the Horowhenua and Manawatu in the west and to the Wairarapa and Hawke's Bay in the east. They favour open or lightly timbered country, such as farmland with scattered totara, and orchards, but may also occupy dense native forest.
Population: Common in many parts of the North Island, especially Northland, Auckland, Coromandel Peninsula, eastern Wairarapa and the Hutt Valley.
Breeding: No New Zealand study. In Australia, they nest mostly in cavities in trees, laying 4–**5**–9 white eggs (27 x 22 mm) in October–January. The female alone incubates for 22–24 days, and the fledging period is c. 30 days. The young remain with their parents for several months after fledging.
Behaviour: Gregarious when not breeding; often in small flocks of 5–25 birds. Their usual call, often uttered in flight, is a loud, ringing, bell-like 'kwink', reminiscent of a Bellbird call, sometimes a single note, but usually repeated two or three times. Other calls are a loud 'chitty-chew', and strident screech when alarmed. Their flight is undulating, steady wingbeats alternating with long glides, often ending in an upward swoop into a tree.
Feeding: Diet includes a wide range of seeds, fruits, flowers, buds, shoots and occasional insects, especially case moths. Seeds are often taken on or near the ground, e.g. Scotch thistles in paddocks. They have been reported

to cause some minor damage to citrus fruit and kiwifruit in Northland, and occasionally eat tomatoes, apples and other orchard fruit.

Reading: Fleming, C.A. 1944. *Notornis* 1: 60. Hamel, J. 1970. *Notornis* 17: 126–129. Woon, J.A. *et al.* 2002. *Notornis* 49: 91–94.

265. ANTIPODES ISLAND PARAKEET
Cyanoramphus unicolor   Plate 61

Size: Males 32 cm, females 29 cm; 130 g
Distribution: Only at Antipodes Island and associated islets, including Bollons Island. They are most numerous in tall, dense tussocks and sedges, especially on lower parts of the islands, on steep slopes and along watercourses.
Population: An estimate of 2000–3000 birds in 1978.
Conservation: Protected endemic. At present there are no threats, but, with a very restricted natural range, they remain vulnerable to rats, should that predator ever get to the Antipodes. They adapt readily to captivity and are widely held in collections.
Breeding: They nest in well-drained burrows in fibrous peat beneath vegetation, or in the thick, matted bases of tall tussocks. The burrow is often over a metre deep. Eggs are laid in October–January. In captivity, they lay 5–6 white eggs (27 x 23 mm), but in the wild only 1–3 newly fledged young are usually seen, and so the clutch may be smaller. The female alone incubates for c. 28 days. The male helps by feeding the female and chicks by regurgitation. The young probably start breeding at 1 year old. They are probably quite long-lived; of 38 birds banded on Antipodes Island in 1969, two were recaptured 10 years later.
Behaviour: Solitary or in family groups. They are sedentary and, although they can fly well, prefer to walk and climb through the vegetation, especially when feeding. With care, they can be approached closely. Their calls are similar to those of their ancestor, the Red-crowned Parakeet, but are lower-pitched.
Feeding: They feed mainly on tussock and sedge leaves, holding them in one foot and chewing towards the tip, extracting the juices. They also eat seeds, berries and flowers, and fossick round the colonies of Rockhopper and Erect-crested Penguins for scraps of fat left on skua-killed penguin and petrel carcasses, and for remains of broken eggs.

Reading: Taylor, R.H. 1975. *Notornis* 22: 110–121. Warham, J. & Bell, B.D. 1979. *Notornis* 26: 121–169.

266. RED-CROWNED PARAKEET
Cyanoramphus novaezelandiae   Plate 61

Other name: Kakariki
Size: Males 28 cm, 80 g; females 25 cm, 70 g
Geographical variation: Of eight subspecies, two are extinct (*subflavescens* of Lord Howe Island and *erythrotis* of Macquarie Island). The Green Parrot *cookii* breeds on Norfolk Island, the New Caledonian Red-crowned Parakeet *saisseti* breeds in the forested mountains of New Caledonia, and the other four subspecies are in New Zealand: the Red-crowned Parakeet *novaezelandiae* breeds on the main islands, many offshore islands, and at the Auckland Islands; the Kermadec Parakeet *cyanurus* breeds in the Kermadec Islands: the Chatham Island Red-crowned Parakeet *chathamensis* breeds in the Chatham Islands; and Reischek's Parakeet *hochstetteri* breeds at the Antipodes Islands.
Distribution: Common on the Herald Islets and occasionally visit nearby Raoul Island; abundant on Macauley. On the North and South Islands, they mixed with Yellow-crowned Parakeets and were an occasional serious pest of crops, orchards and gardens in the 1870s and 1880s, but with the introduction of feral cats, ship rats and stoats they became rare. In the North Island, a few are now found in heavy forest of western

Northland, the central North Island and the Ruahine Range, and vagrants visit bush patches along the eastern coast of Northland from nearby islands; they are common on many offshore islands from the Three Kings, through the Hauraki Gulf to the Bay of Plenty, and on Kapiti Island. Now largely gone from the South Island, although some may persist in Nelson, the Catlins and South Westland. Widespread on Stewart Island and its outliers; vagrant to The Snares. Common at the Auckland Islands except for Auckland Island itself. A few Chatham Island Red-crowned Parakeets are on Chatham and Pitt Islands, but they are numerous on Mangere, Little Mangere and South East Islands. Reischek's Parakeet is on Antipodes, Bollons and smaller islands; most common on the more open parts of the central plateau and in coastal places.

Population: Common to abundant on many islands free of mammalian predators. Very rare on the mainland.

Conservation: Protected native. Red-crowned Parakeets are particularly susceptible to mammalian predators (especially cats, stoats and ship rats) because they often feed on the ground and nest in holes close to the ground. They are secure on many island reserves; however the Macauley Island population of Kermadec Parakeet fell from c. 20,000 to less than 2000 between September and November 1988, probably due to a drought, but had recovered to c. 9000 by 2002.

Breeding: Red-crowned Parakeets favour holes in branches and trunks of trees, particularly decaying trees, but they also use crevices in cliffs or among rocks, burrows in the ground or densely matted vegetation. Most eggs are laid in October–December, but re-laying can continue through to March. They lay 4–7–9 white eggs (26 x 21 mm, 6 g), which the female incubates for c. 23 days. During incubation, the male calls the female off the nest and feeds her by regurgitation. Both sexes feed the chicks, but the male usually transfers the food to the female, which then feeds the chicks. The fledging period is 40–50 days, but sometimes the chicks leave the nest earlier and are fed on the ground before they can fly. In captivity, the young first breed at less than a year old, but they probably breed later in the wild. Occasionally they interbreed with the Yellow-crowned Parakeet.

Behaviour: Usually solitary or in pairs, but in autumn and winter they form small flocks. Non-migratory, though they may fly long distances to get to good sources of food or fresh water. In flight, they make a loud, rapid chatter: 'ki-ki-ki-ki-ki'. Silent or chatter and babble when feeding.

Feeding: Mainly herbivorous. Diet varies seasonally and includes seeds of many kinds (particularly flax, beech, sedges, grasses, tussocks, *Mariscus* and *Muehlenbeckia*), fruits (particularly *Coprosma*, ngaio and *Solanum*) flower buds, flowers, nectar, leaves, shoots; also invertebrates and carrion. They often feed on the ground rather than in the canopy.

Reading: Bellingham, M. 1987. *Notornis* 34: 234–236. Dawe, M.R. 1979. Unpubl MSc thesis. Univ Auckland. Greene, T.C. 1988. Unpubl MSc thesis. Univ Auckland. Nixon, A.J. 1994. *Notornis* 41(S): 5–18. Sagar, P.M. 1988. *Notornis* 35: 1–8. Taylor, R.H. 1975. *Notornis* 22: 110–121. Taylor, R.H. 1985. Pp. 195–211. *In* Moors, P.J. (ed.) *ICBP Technical Publication No. 3*. Cambridge: ICBP.

267. YELLOW-CROWNED PARAKEET

Cyanoramphus auriceps Plate 61

Other name: Kakariki

Size: Males 25 cm, 50 g; females 23 cm, 40 g

Geographical variation: Two subspecies: the Yellow-crowned Parakeet *auriceps* on the New Zealand mainland, offshore islands and at the Auckland Islands; and Forbes' Parakeet *forbesi* on the Chatham Islands. The Orange-fronted Parakeet (*C. malherbi*), recently thought to be a colour phase of the Yellow-crowned Parakeet, is again recognised as a distinct species. It is known mainly from inland North Canterbury and in the Nelson region.

Distribution: New Zealand only, breeding in the North, South, Stewart, Chatham and

Auckland Islands, and on some offshore islands. They favour podocarp forest and beech forest on the mainland and taller forest and scrub on offshore islands. Mixed flocks with Red-crowned Parakeets were an occasional serious pest of crops, orchards and gardens in the 1870s and 1880s; but with the introduction of feral cats, ship rats and stoats they became uncommon. In the North Island, they are now mainly in forested areas across the centre from Taranaki through the King Country and the Urewera to the Raukumara Range, and in the Tararua and Rimutaka Ranges; also on some offshore islands, including the Three Kings, Hen and Chickens, Little Barrier, Great Barrier and Kapiti, but in much lower numbers than Red-crowned Parakeets. In the South Island, they are widespread: western Marlborough (including the Chetwode and Titi Islands), Nelson, Westland, inland North Canterbury, western Otago, the Catlins and Fiordland. They are on Codfish Island, and Stewart Island and its outliers. In the Auckland Islands, they are common on main Auckland Island but outnumbered by the Red-crowned Parakeet on the other islands. On the Chathams, Forbes' Parakeet is uncommon on Mangere and Little Mangere Islands, and a few have been seen on Chatham Island.

Population: The Yellow-crowned Parakeet is widespread and uncommon throughout. On the Chathams, the total number of Forbes' Parakeets in the 1970s was 56 pure birds, mostly on Little Mangere Island.

Conservation: Protected native; Forbes' Parakeet is threatened. Yellow-crowned Parakeets are susceptible to mammalian predators (especially cats, stoats and ship rats) because they sometimes feed on the ground and nest in holes, but have probably survived better on the mainland than Red-crowned Parakeets because they generally have more arboreal feeding and nesting sites. They are probably secure on island reserves, but they are nowhere common and well outnumbered by Red-crowned Parakeets.

Between the early 1900s and late 1960s, Forbes' Parakeets were virtually confined to Little Mangere Island. With the removal of stock and the resultant flush of rank grass, Mangere Island was colonised by Forbes' Parakeets, but much larger numbers of Chatham Island Red-crowned Parakeets, and in this artificial environment these two species hybridised. Since the 1970s, conservation effort has concentrated on removing hybrids and the more common Red-crowned Parakeets, and this will have to continue until the habitat improves to allow the usual habitat segregation between these species.

Breeding: Yellow-crowned Parakeets favour holes in branches and trunks of trees, particularly holes in mature or old trees. Eggs can be laid at almost any time of year, but mostly in October–December. They lay 2–5–6–9 white eggs (24 x 19 mm). The female alone incubates for 15–20 days starting mid-way through the clutch. She is called from the nest and is fed by the male. The fledging period is 37–45 days. Both sexes feed the chicks by regurgitation.

Behaviour: Usually solitary or in pairs, but in autumn and winter they form small flocks. In flight, they make a rapid high-pitched chatter: 'ki-ki-ki-ki-ki'. Silent or chatter and babble when feeding. On Little Barrier, a frequent call of males, perhaps territorial, is a loud 'err-e-e'.

Feeding: Diet varies seasonally but is dominated for most of the year by invertebrates (particularly scale insects, leaf miners and aphids), flower buds and flowers (especially of kanuka, rata and beech) and seeds (especially beech). Leaves, shoots and fruits are also taken as they become seasonally available. They feed in the canopy rather than on the ground, and often follow mixed feeding flocks led by Whiteheads in the North Island and Yellowheads in the South Island.

Reading: Elliott, G.P. *et al.* 1996. *NZ J Zool* 23: 249–265. Greene, T.C. 1988. Unpubl MSc thesis. Univ Auckland. Kearvell, J.C. *et al.* 2003. *Notornis* 50: 27–35. Nixon, A.J. 1981. *Notornis* 28: 292–300. Nixon, A.J. 1994. *Notornis* 41 (S): 5–18. Taylor, R.H. *et al.* 1986. *Notornis* 33: 17–22.

CUCKOOS   Cuculidae

About 120 species worldwide; 2 breed in New Zealand and 4 are vagrants.

Most cuckoos are parasitic, laying their eggs in nests of other insectivorous bird species and then letting the host rear the young, fledging often well after it is capable of flying well. Cuckoos lay their eggs while the host's clutch is being formed, or a day or two after completion of that clutch. The cuckoo removes one of the host's eggs and replaces it with its own. The cuckoo egg develops very rapidly and usually hatches first. The cuckoo chick then ejects all other eggs and chicks from the nest, or simply dominates the smaller chicks and they starve to death. Young cuckoos make persistent, high-pitched begging calls even after leaving the nest, and this stimulates its foster parents and other birds of the same or different species to feed it, thus causing confusion about the true identity of the foster parents.

Cuckoos are strong fliers, and most migrate between temperate and tropical regions. During the breeding season, they are conspicuously vocal, but at other times they remain silent and cryptic.

268. ORIENTAL CUCKOO *Cuculus saturatus*   Plate 62

Size: 33 cm, 100 g

Distribution: Breeds in central and eastern Asia from the Himalayas and Siberia to Japan, parasitising nests of warblers and flycatchers. In September, they migrate south to winter from southern India eastwards to the Philippines, New Guinea, the Solomon Islands and northern and eastern Australia. A few birds straggle to New Zealand, with a total of about 25 records from the Far North to The Snares, in October–April.

Behaviour: Oriental Cuckoos are usually seen in open areas with trees, such in willows along riverbanks, trees around farmhouses, or near a forest edge. They typically perch on a branch or post and make repeated forays to catch insects and earthworms from the ground nearby. They are generally silent in New Zealand, but a bird on Little Barrier Island uttered a quiet, regular 'tsoo-tsoo-tsoo' about a dozen times at 1 second intervals.

269. PALLID CUCKOO *Cuculus pallidus*   Plate 62

Size: 30 cm, 85 g

Distribution: Breeds in southwestern, southern and eastern Australia, including Tasmania, parasitising open-nesting species such as honeyeaters and flycatchers. After breeding, they move northwards to central and northern Australia, New Guinea and the western parts of Indonesia. A rare vagrant to New Zealand with only six records: Craig Flat, Otago (one bird seen in May–October 1939, 1940 and 1941), Okarito (December 1941), Greymouth (March 1942), Wairarapa (1977), Omarama, Otago (January 1990), Riverton (1998).

Behaviour: In New Zealand, Pallid Cuckoos have usually been seen perched on power poles or fenceposts in open country, then gliding down to the ground to catch insects and earthworms. The first bird recorded in New Zealand appeared on the same farm for three years in a row during the non-breeding season. The distinctive call of the male is a monotonously repeated phrase, consisting of an ascending and accelerating series of melancholy notes: 'too too . . . too too'. The female utters a hoarse 'kheer'.

Reading: Marples, B.J. 1942. *Notornis* 2: 10–11.

270. FAN-TAILED CUCKOO *Cacomantis flabelliformis* Plate 62

Size: 26 cm, 50 g

Distribution: Breeds in Australia and Tasmania, New Guinea, Solomons, Vanuatu, New Caledonia and Fiji, parasitising mainly dome-nesting species but also some cup-nesting ones. After breeding, some Australian birds migrate northwards, but many remain sedentary or become nomadic. Very rare vagrant to New Zealand from Australia (subspecies *flabelliformis*) with only five records, including a small invasion in 1991: Lyttelton Harbour (subadult female killed by a cat in June 1960), Wanaka (September 1991), Haast (October 1991), Whangarei (October 1991) and Culverden (December 1999).

Behaviour: Fan-tailed Cuckoos often perch on low branches, power poles or fenceposts in open country or open forest, then glide down to the ground to hop around in search of insects and earthworms. On landing on a perch, they typically cock and fan their tail. Their call is a repeated phrase consisting of a rapid descending trill.

271. SHINING CUCKOO *Chrysococcyx lucidus* Plate 62

Size: 16 cm, 25 g

Other name: Pipiwharauroa

Geographical variation: Four subspecies are currently recognised, of which the nominate *lucidus* occurs in New Zealand.

Distribution: Breeds in southwestern and eastern Australia (including Tasmania), Vanuatu, New Caledonia and New Zealand. In New Zealand, they breed throughout the mainland and offshore islands, mainly in scrub and forest habitats (to about 1200 m asl) where Grey Warblers, their main host species, lives, but they are also heard in suburban gardens. A few Shining Cuckoos reach the Chathams each summer, and stragglers have reached the Kermadecs, The Snares, Auckland Islands and Rarotonga. In March, they migrate north to winter in western Indonesia, New Guinea and the Bismark Archipelago (New Britain, New Ireland and Bougainville) and the Solomons. It is believed that many New Zealand birds migrate through eastern Australia to or from their wintering grounds in the Bismark Archipelago and the Solomons, but many are recorded on passage at Lord Howe Island, which suggests that some take a more direct route. A few birds overwinter in New Zealand, especially in the northern North Island, but they remain quiet and inconspicuous in winter. Shining Cuckoos return to New Zealand in late September and early October, and adults return to the same site year after year.

Population: Widespread and locally common, especially conspicuous in late spring and early summer.

Conservation: Protected native. Numbers appears to be moderately stable, as their main host, the Grey Warbler, has adapted well to human settlement in New Zealand. However, continuing clearance of large tracts of subtropical rainforest at the wintering grounds of Shining Cuckoos could have a severe impact.

Breeding: Like other cuckoos, Shining Cuckoos parasitise other breeding birds by laying in nests of other species, and so take no part in the incubation of their eggs or in raising their young. Despite anecdotal reports of Shining Cuckoos laying eggs in the nests of a wide variety of birds, the only good evidence is that Grey Warblers are the host species on the mainland, and the Chatham Island Warbler is the host on the Chathams. Shining Cuckoos return to the same general area each year and establish a territory that encompasses several Grey Warbler territories. The male frequently feeds his partner during the spring, and the birds are often seen together. Exactly how Shining Cuckoos lay their eggs in the dome-shaped nest of Grey Warblers has not been observed, but the nest is not damaged in the process. One of the host's eggs is removed and replaced with a single cuckoo egg, usually laid a couple of days either side of the host clutch being completed and incubation starting.

Eggs are laid from mid-October to mid-January, usually into the second or replacement clutches of Grey Warblers, whose first clutch is usually laid in September before Shining Cuckoos arrive back from their wintering grounds. The olive-green egg (18.5 x 12.5 mm, 1.8 g), which is slightly larger than those of the Grey Warbler and stands out clearly by its different colour, hatches after 14–15–17 days, c. 4 days faster than those of the host. When the cuckoo chick is 3–4–7 days old, it evicts the other Grey Warbler eggs or chicks in the nest and is then raised alone. Fledging period is 19–21 days, and the fledgling begs incessantly – 'eee-eee-eee' – and is fed by both Grey Warblers for at least 4 weeks, before becoming independent. Juvenile Shining Cuckoos migrate to winter in the tropics, and they possibly remain there until 2 years old, when they have been recorded back in their natal area.

Behaviour: The arrival of Shining Cuckoos in spring is often heralded by clear, descending 'tsee-ew' calls heard at night as birds fly overhead. They advertise their territory in spring with a loud and far-carrying, highly distinctive song: 'coo-ee coo-ee . . . coo-ee', usually repeated 10–20 times, followed by one or two descending notes: 'tsee-ew'. They become silent after December, their continued presence known only from occasional sightings and as a relatively common casualty from flying into windows. Although usually a solitary bird, small groups sometimes gather in spring and summer to display excitedly with wing-flicking and uttering trilling notes and the descending 'tsee-ew' notes from the territorial song. Large pre-migratory flocks of several hundred birds have been reported in autumn.

Feeding: Diet is mainly invertebrates, especially the small green caterpillars that feed on kowhai leaves and the black hairy caterpillars of the Magpie Moth – Shining Cuckoos are often killed by cats among the cinerarias.

Reading: Gill, B.J. 1982. *Notornis* 29: 215–227. Gill, B.J. 1983. *Ibis* 125: 40–55. Gill, B.J. 1983. *NZ J Zool* 10: 371–381.

272.   LONG-TAILED CUCKOO   *Eudynamys taitensis*   Plate 62

Size: 40 cm, 125 g
Other names: Koekoea, Long-tailed Koel (Australia)
Distribution: Breeds in New Zealand only. Long-tailed Cuckoos are found throughout forests of the mainland, and on forested offshore islands such as Little Barrier, Kapiti, Codfish and Stewart. Stragglers have reached the Chathams, The Snares and Auckland Islands. In January–April, they migrate to winter in the tropical Pacific in an arc from the Bismark Archipelago and Micronesia in the west to the Marquesas and Tuamotu Islands of French Polynesia in the east, but mainly to the east of Fiji. Some migrate through the Kermadecs and Lord Howe Island, and a few pass through Norfolk Island and the east coast of Australia on their northward passage. Adults probably migrate before the juveniles. A few adults appear in the Cook Islands in mid-January, but most do not arrive until March. It seems that yearlings remain in the wintering grounds during their first summer.

In New Zealand, the breeding distribution is governed by the distribution of the host species, the Whitehead in the North Island, and the Yellowhead and Brown Creeper in the South Island; however, during migration, birds are heard well away from the range of these species (e.g. Northland and Manawatu). A few birds overwinter in New Zealand, especially in the northern North Island, but they remain quiet and inconspicuous in winter. Adult Long-tailed Cuckoos return to New Zealand in early October, and adults return to the same site year after year.

Population: Widespread and sometimes moderately common, especially conspicuous in late spring and early summer.

Conservation: Protected endemic. The numbers of Long-tailed Cuckoos in New Zealand are probably declining in line with the decline of the host species (especially

Yellowheads) on the mainland. Clearance of subtropical rainforest in parts of their wintering range could have an impact on the numbers of Long-tailed Cuckoos visiting New Zealand.

Breeding: Like other cuckoos, Long-tailed Cuckoos parasitise other breeding birds by laying their eggs in nests of other species, and so take no part in the incubation of their eggs or in raising their young. Despite anecdotal reports of Long-tailed Cuckoos laying eggs in the nests of a wide variety of birds, including Robins, Fantails, Silvereyes and Tomtits, clearly the main host species are the Whitehead in the North Island, Yellowhead in the South Island, and the Brown Creeper on the South, Codfish and Stewart Islands. Banding has shown that Long-tailed Cuckoos return to the same general area each year. Little is known of the social behaviour of Long-tailed Cuckoos, but they may have a lek-type breeding system, because groups of adults (possibly males) gather to call and Long-tailed Cuckoos are not encountered in simple pairs.

Laying is from mid-November to mid-December. They lay a single creamy-white or very pale pink egg (23 x 17 mm) covered in brownish blotches. It is noticeably larger than those of the host but is usually accepted. The incubation period is estimated to be c. 16 days. The cuckoo chick evicts the host's eggs and chicks and is then raised alone. The fledging period is estimated to be c. 21 days, and the fledgling begs incessantly and is then fed by both foster parents and their helpers for at least 4 weeks, before the young becomes independent. Juvenile Long-tailed Cuckoos migrate to winter in the tropics and probably remain there until at least 2 years old.

Behaviour: The arrival of Long-tailed Cuckoos in late spring is often heralded by their harsh, piercing, long-drawn-out shriek: 'zzwheesht', heard at night as birds migrate southward. This is also the typical daytime call during the breeding season, but they also give a loud, rapid, ringing chatter: 'zip, zip, zip, zip', or 'rrrp pe-pe-pe-pe-pe'. When calling, they usually sit on a high perch in the canopy. When giving the shriek call in combination with the chatter call, they often display by fanning their tail, slowly flapping their wings and adopting a hunched posture. Several birds (possibly males) gather in a tight group only a few metres apart as they display, and others (possibly females) watch from 20–30 m away. Long-tailed Cuckoos continue to call into January and February, well after breeding has finished, and they are also vocal during their northward migration. They are a relatively common casualty from flying into windows.

Feeding: Diet is mainly large invertebrates such as weta, stick insects, spiders, beetles and bugs. Skinks, geckos, small birds, eggs, nestlings, berries and fruit are also taken.
Reading: McLean, I.G. 1988. *Notornis* 35: 89–98.

273. CHANNEL-BILLED CUCKOO
Scythrops novaehollandiae   **Plate 62**

Size: 61 cm, 700 g
Distribution: Breeds in northern and eastern Australia, parasitising nests of magpies, crows and currawongs. After breeding, they migrate north to winter in eastern Indonesia, New Guinea and the Bismark Archipelago. Rare vagrant to New Zealand; with a minor influx in spring 1996; six records: Invercargill (December 1924), Aupouri Peninsula, Northland (October 1986 to January 1987), Raglan (October 1996), Pukerua Bay (November 1996) and Mangawhai (October 2002).
Behaviour: Channel-billed Cuckoos are usually found in open country with scattered trees. In Australia, they fly with slowly flapping wings in small noisy groups and are often harassed by corvids. They have a loud, melodious, trumpet call.

TYPICAL OWLS   Strigidae

About 130 species; 1 extinct species was endemic to New Zealand, 1 is native and 1 is introduced.

Owls are mainly nocturnal birds of prey, although overseas some species hunt by day. They have a large head and very flexible neck, so that the whole of the head can be rotated through 270° to look for prey at the side or the rear. The large eyes, directed forward, give good binocular vision in low-intensity light. The yellow eyes are set in a brown circular disc of feathers. This facial disc helps to direct sound to the large ear openings. The bill is short and hooked. Legs are well feathered, except for the bare powerful feet with needle-sharp talons. As their plumage is soft and wing feathers have softened edges, the flight of typical owls is silent. They specialise in catching rodents, small birds and large insects. Prey is usually eaten whole, and the indigestible parts are regurgitated in a sausage-shaped pellet lined with bones and hard pieces and coated with fur and feathers. Their eggs are white and usually laid in a hollow.

Reading: Burton, J.A. 1973. *Owls of the World: Their Evolution, Structure and Ecology*. Netherlands: Lowe. Hollands, D. 1991. *Birds of the Night: Owls, Frogmouths and Nightjars*. Balgowlah, NSW: Reed.

274. MOREPORK *Ninox novaeseelandiae*   Plate 63

Other names: Ruru, Boobook (Australia)
Size: 29 cm, 175 g
Geographical variation: Three subspecies, if the Southern Boobook *N. boobook* of Australia and its various subspecies is treated as a separate species. The subspecies *albaria* formerly bred on Lord Howe Island, *undulata* breeds on Norfolk Island, and *novaeseelandiae* breeds in New Zealand.
Distribution: Throughout forested areas of the North, South and Stewart Islands from sea level to the upper bushline, and on most larger forested offshore islands from Three Kings to Codfish Island. Vagrants have reached The Snares. Widespread but sparingly distributed in drier eastern areas. They live in native and exotic forest and in open country with clumps of mature trees for shelter and nesting.
Population: Widespread and moderately common.
Conservation: Protected native. The subfossil and midden records of Moreporks are all within the last 1000 years, perhaps indicating that they were scarce before human settlement of New Zealand. Although much forest was cleared by Maori and then by European settlers, their food supply may have been increased with the introduction of small mammals – the Pacific rat, brought by Maori,
and then mice, ship rats and Norway rats brought by Europeans.
Breeding: The nest site is usually in a hollow tree or branch, but sometimes in a clump of epiphytes, in a cabbage tree, in a pile of pine needles in a tree fork, or on the ground in the shelter of a rock, in a petrel burrow or among the roots of pohutukawa. Laying is in September–February, mainly October–November. They lay 1–**2**–3 white eggs (38 x 34 mm). The female alone incubates for 20–30 days but is called from the nest and fed by the male. The fledging period is c. 35 days.
Behaviour: Moreporks roost in trees, preferably in gullies, with plenty of shelter overhead, but they may be found and mobbed by small birds. Their usual call is a clear 'morepork', the final syllable sometimes repeated and prolonged. Other calls include a monotonous, deep, repeated 'more-more-more- . . .', and a repeated 'cree' when hunting. They rarely call during daylight, usually starting from dusk.
Feeding: Diet is mainly large insects such as weta and cicadas, and night-flying insects such as moths and huhu beetles, including those attracted to lights, which they catch with their talons or bill; also spiders, mice, young rats and small birds. When eating large

prey, they hold it in one foot or stand on it with both feet and tear off pieces. Pellets of indigestible material are cast beneath their daytime perches.

Reading: Imboden, C. 1975. *Notornis* 22: 221–230. Lindsay, C.J. & Ordish, R.G. 1964. *Notornis* 11: 154–158.

275. LAUGHING OWL *Sceloglaux albifacies* Plate 74

Other name: Whekau
Size: 38 cm, 600 g
Geographical variation: Two subspecies: *rufifacies* of the North Island, and *albifacies* of the South Island and Stewart Island.
Distribution: Subfossil remains of the North Island subspecies are found at numerous sites, including swamps, caves, dunes and a few middens. There were only four records since European settlement: skins collected on Mt Taranaki (1854) and in the Wairarapa (1868), and sightings near Gisborne (1889) and near Porirua (before 1892). The southern subspecies is also widespread as subfossils, including a few midden records from the South and Stewart Islands. In the mid-1800s, Laughing Owls were fairly common and reported widely from Nelson, Canterbury, Otago and Fiordland, and skins came from Stewart Island in about 1880. They seemed to prefer forest and scrub edges and rocky places in open country, such as limestone outcrops. They declined rapidly and were rare by 1880. The last known bird was found dead at Bluecliffs, South Canterbury, in 1914.

Likely causes of extinction: The rapid decline suggests introduced avian diseases as a possible cause; however, the introduction of mustelids for controlling rabbits in the habitats used by Laughing Owls, the decline of the Pacific rat and the collection of museum specimens can not be ruled out as contributing factors.
Breeding: A few nests, lined with dry grass, were found in deep, dry, crevices among rocks, mostly with such narrow entrances that birds had to be smoked out. The usual clutch was 2 white eggs (48 x 40 mm).
Behaviour: The calls of the Laughing Owl were described as 'a loud cry made up of a series of dismal shrieks frequently repeated' and 'a peculiar barking noise . . . just like the yelping of a young dog'.
Feeding: Cave deposits indicate their diet was mainly birds, geckos, bats and rodents. Earthworms and insects such as beetles were also eaten.

Reading: Holdaway, R.N. & Worthy, T.H. 1996. *J Zool (Lond)* 239: 545–572. Williams, G.R. & Harrison, M. 1972. *Notornis* 19: 4–19.

276. LITTLE OWL *Athene noctua* Plate 63

Other name: German Owl
Size: 23 cm, 180 g
Geographical variation: Twelve subspecies, of which *vidalii* of Germany, was introduced to New Zealand; this was the subspecies introduced to Britain in the late 1800s.
Distribution: Natural range is continental Europe, northern Africa and western Asia. In an endeavour to control the numbers of small introduced birds, the Otago Acclimatis-ation Society imported 219 Little Owls from Germany between 1906 and 1910, and others were liberated in Canterbury about the same time. They are now widespread in farmland and towns in Nelson, Marlborough, Canter-

bury, Otago and Southland. A few are seen in Westland and Fiordland. No recent con-firmed records from Stewart Island or the North Island. They live in hedgerows, haysheds, old farm buildings, clumps of trees; in daylight they often sun themselves on fenceposts, hedges, tree branches, roof ridges, and telegraph poles near old farm buildings.
Population: Widespread and locally common, especially in drier coastal areas of the eastern South Island.
Breeding: The usual nesting sites are holes in trees, old farm buildings, haystacks, stacks of hay bales, rabbit burrows, and banks, e.g. disused quarry walls. Most eggs are laid in

October–November. They lay 2–**3**–**4**–5 white eggs (35 x 29 mm), which the female alone incubates for c. 28 days. The fledging period is 30–35 days. The age of first breeding is 1 year, though not all breed then. The oldest bird banded in Britain lived to at least 10 years old. **Behaviour:** Solitary. They are usually seen in the late afternoon sunning themselves rather than looking for food, or are disturbed from roosts in farm buildings or hedgerows. Their usual call, heard mostly in autumn and winter, is a clear, high-pitched 'kiew'. They bob up and down when alarmed. Their flight is undulating.

Feeding: Although introduced to control small birds that had become pests in orchards and cereal crops, their diet in New Zealand is mainly insects (caterpillars, beetles and earwigs), spiders and earthworms. They also take a few small birds, frogs, lizards, mice and rabbits. Little Owls often feed on the ground, walking and running freely, sometimes by day as well as at night.

Reading: Marples, B.J. 1942. *Trans Proc Roy Soc NZ* 72: 237–254.

BARN OWLS   Tytonidae

10 species; 1 is a rare vagrant to New Zealand.

The barn owls are mainly nocturnal birds of prey. They have a large head and very flexible neck, so that the whole of the head can be rotated to look for prey at the side or the rear. The large eyes, directed forward, give good binocular vision in low-intensity light. The dark eyes are set in a white, heart-shaped disc of short feathers. This facial disc helps to direct sound to the large ear openings. The bill is short and hooked. Legs are well feathered, except for the bare powerful feet with needle-sharp talons. Unlike typical owls, the inner toe is as long as the middle toe, and the claw of the middle toe has comb-like serrations. As their plumage is soft and wing feathers have softened edges, the flight of barn owls is silent. They specialise in catching rodents, small birds and large insects. Prey is usually eaten whole, and the indigestible parts are regurgitated in a sausage-shaped pellet lined with bones and hard pieces and coated with fur and feathers. Their eggs are white and usually laid in a hollow.

Reading: Burton, J.A. 1973. *Owls of the World: Their Evolution, Structure and Ecology.* Netherlands: Lowe. Hollands, D. 1991. *Birds of the Night: Owls, Frogmouths and Nightjars.* Balgowlah, NSW: Reed.

277. BARN OWL   *Tyto alba*   Plate 63

Size: 34 cm, 350 g
Geographical variation: More than 30 subspecies, of which *delicatula* of Australia and the Solomon Islands reaches New Zealand as a vagrant.
Distribution: The most widely distributed landbird, being found almost worldwide. They are widespread in mainland Australia but rare in Tasmania. Vagrants naturally reach New Zealand: Barrytown (1947), Haast River mouth (1955), Runanga (1960), South Kaipara Head (1986) and New Plymouth (1990). Others are believed to have come from Australia as stowaways in aircraft undercarriage: live birds at Papatoetoe, near Auckland Airport (1983), and at Whenuapai RNZAF Base (1992); probably the same bird was seen six weeks later on Little Barrier Island (1992).
Behaviour: At night, Barn Owls are seen sitting upright on fenceposts or branches, or are caught in car headlight beams like a buoyant white ghost. Their call is a menacing, long-drawn-out, rasping screech 'skiirrr'.
Reading: Gill, B.J. & Turbott, E.G. 1984. *Notornis* 31: 177–179.

SWIFTS   Apodidae

71 species; 2 are stragglers to New Zealand.

The swifts are somewhat swallow-like in appearance and behaviour, but are larger and have very long narrow scythe-like wings and short tails. They are the most aerial of all birds, some only landing at their nest sites. They fly rapidly and wheel in broad arcs. In fine weather, they fly high and so easily escape notice, but at dusk and in poor weather they often fly low over open water or around headlands, hilltops or stands of tall trees. They have short, broad bills that open extremely wide for catching aerial insects. Their feet are tiny and their toes point forward, so swifts rest by clinging to the sides of trees, rocks or walls, not on branches or the ground.

278. SPINE-TAILED SWIFT *Hirundapus caudacutus*   Plate 64

Other names: White-throated Needletail (Australia), Needle-tailed Swift
Size: 20 cm, 90 g
Geographical variation: Three subspecies, of which *caudacutus* of northeastern Asia and Japan is a straggler to New Zealand.
Distribution: Breed in eastern Asia from Siberia to Korea and Japan, and south to Taiwan, Burma and the Himalayas. The subspecies *caudacutus* migrates south through China and the Philippines to winter in New Guinea, Australia and Tasmania from October to April. In most years, a few overshoot their normal wintering grounds or are carried ahead of storm-fronts to reach New Zealand. There are over 60 records dating back to 1888, mainly from the North Island, but as far south as The Snares. Most records are from mid-November to March, but a few have been seen as late as May. From time to time, invasions are considerable, the most notable being in 1942–43, when birds were reported from Northland to Stewart Island and flocks appeared in Westland, in 1968–69, and in February 1979, when a flock of 60+ birds was seen in southern Otago.
Behaviour: Usually gregarious; small flocks circle hilltops, cliff tops or stands of trees. Swifts fly rapidly and wheel around in sweeping glides as they catch insects in mid-air. They feed high in fine, calm weather, but in windy or stormy weather, or at dusk, they feed close to the ground and so are more easily seen.
Reading: McCaskill, L.W. 1943. *Notornis* 1: 38–40.

279. FORK-TAILED SWIFT *Apus pacificus*   Plate 64

Size: 18 cm, 35 g
Geographical variation: Four subspecies, of which *pacificus* of northeastern Asia and Japan is a straggler to New Zealand.
Distribution: Breed in eastern Asia from Siberia to Korea and Japan, and from north India to Malaysia. The subspecies *pacificus* migrates south through China and the Philippines to winter in New Guinea, Australia and Tasmania from October to April. They occasionally reach New Zealand, probably carried along ahead of storm-fronts. Since the first record of four birds in Taranaki in 1884, there have been about 15 records of Fork-tailed Swifts in New Zealand, from Northland to the Antipodes (2002), and at Pitt Island, Chathams (1991). Mostly single birds or small flocks in October–February, but others have been seen unexpectedly in May–September, when they are usually breeding in the Northern Hemisphere.
Behaviour: Usually seen alone or in small flocks circling hilltops or clifftops. Swifts fly rapidly and wheel around in sweeping glides as they catch insects in mid-air. They feed high in fine, calm weather, but in windy or stormy weather they feed close to the ground and so are more easily seen. They are usually quite vocal, with a shrill whistle or excited chattering.
Reading: Turbott, E.G. 1964. *Notornis* 11: 107–109.

KINGFISHERS   Alcedinidae

About 86 species worldwide; 1 is native to New Zealand, and 1 is introduced and also possibly a vagrant.

The kingfishers are brightly coloured birds with a plump body, short legs, tail and neck, a large head and a long, broad and dagger-like bill. Their flight is fast and direct. They often perch on posts, branches and powerlines and dart down to the ground, or dive into water, to catch their prey. Despite their name, kingfishers do not necessarily eat fish; some species are entirely terrestrial.

They nest in tree hollows or earth banks, which they excavate by repeatedly flying at the vertical surface and spearing with their bill; the skull has special shock-absorbing structures.

280. KOOKABURRA *Dacelo novaeguineae*   Plate 63

Other names: Laughing Kookaburra, Laughing Jackass
Size: 45 cm, 350 g
Geographical variation: Two subspecies: *minor* of Cape York Peninsula, and the more common *novaeguineae*, which is the subspecies in New Zealand.
Distribution: Despite the scientific name, this species is native to Australia, not New Guinea. Kookaburras are common in eastern and southeastern Australia, and have been successfully introduced to southwestern Australia, Tasmania and New Zealand. Sir George Grey introduced them to Kawau Island in the Hauraki Gulf in the early 1860s. Introductions to Wellington, Nelson and Otago in the 1860s and 1870s did not establish. They are now found in open country and on forest margins from near Whangarei in the north to the northern Waitakere Range in the south. The main places where they are reported include: Glenbervie, Whangateau, Dome Valley, Warkworth, Kaukapakapa, Puhoi, Wenderholm and Waiwera. Reports of single birds elsewhere, from Waikato and Gisborne to Westland and Otago, are vagrants from Northland or, more likely, Australia.
Population: Scarce and with a limited distribution in New Zealand; probably fewer than 500 birds.

Breeding: Little New Zealand information. Pairs remain on territory all year; their young stay with them as helpers. The nest is in a tunnel bored in a rotten tree trunk, e.g. in a Phoenix palm at Wenderholm, or in a natural cavity in a pohutukawa. Eggs are laid in November–February. They lay 2–**3**–4 white eggs (44 x 33 mm). The incubation period is c. 23 days, and the fledging period is 33–39 days. Chicks may be fed for several weeks after fledging. Kookaburras are long-lived, the oldest known in Australia lived over 13 years, but some probably live much longer.
Behaviour: Family groups roost and breed together. The common call is a loud, bois-terous 'koo-hoo-hoo-hoo . . . hoo-hoo-ha-ha-ha-ha-ha', often uttered in undisciplined chorus by a family group. It is heard all year, mostly at dawn and dusk, and both advertises the territory and keeps the family together.
Feeding: Kookaburras sit rigidly on a pro-minent branch or post, bill pointing down, and suddenly swoop to the ground or into shallow water. They catch mainly earth-worms, snails, insects, freshwater crayfish, frogs, lizards, rats, mice and small birds.

Reading: Parry, V.A. 1970. *Kookaburras*. Melbourne: Lansdowne Press. Parry, V.A. 1973. *Emu* 73: 81–100.

281.   KINGFISHER   *Halcyon sancta*   Plate 63

Other names: Kotare, Sacred Kingfisher,
New Zealand Kingfisher
Size: 24 cm, 65 g
Geographical variation: Of eight subspecies
in Australia, New Caledonia, the Loyalty, Lord
Howe, Norfolk and Kermadec Islands and
New Zealand, the New Zealand subspecies
is *vagans*.
Distribution: Widespread on the Kermadecs,
North, South and Stewart Islands and most
offshore islands, but not the Chathams or
subantarctic islands. Uncommon well inland
and in the southern South Island. They occupy
many habitats, especially bush patches near
the coast, in tidal estuaries, and in mangrove
swamps in the north. They also live in
developed farmland with scattered trees, and
breed inland along river and stream edges
or by lake shores, along forest margins and
well into forests, both native and exotic. In
winter, most birds that breed at high altitude
or in forests move to lowland farms and the
coasts.
Population: Common and widespread,
especially in coastal districts and lowlands
in winter.
Conservation: Protected native. Although
Kingfishers occasionally live well into forests,
they have probably benefited from the
clearance of forest and the creation of forest-
edge habitats and riparian margins of willows
and poplars along rivers and near lakes.
Artificial structures such as powerlines and
posts in estuaries are excellent elevated
perches to hunt from.
Breeding: Kingfishers nest in rotten tree
trunks, knotholes or hollow branches, in the
soil held by the roots of blown-over trees, in
riverbanks, roadside cuttings, heads of slips,

and coastal cliffs. The nest is in a chamber at
the end of a short tunnel that slopes slightly
upwards. To start a tunnel, they sit on a branch
slightly above and several metres from the
site and fly straight at it, neck outstretched
and uttering a peculiar whirring call, and
strike it forcefully with the bill tip. They
continue until the hole is big enough to perch
in, and the rest is pecked and scooped out.
Eggs are laid in October–January. They lay
3–5–7 white eggs (29 x 24 mm), which the
female mostly incubates for 20–21 days. The
chicks fledge at 26–27 days old.
Behaviour: Usually solitary or in pairs, spaced
widely apart when breeding and when
perching on posts or powerlines between
feeding flights. Their usual call is a loud,
penetrating 'kek-kek-kek-kek'.
Feeding: On tidal mudflats, diet is mainly
small crabs, especially *Helice crassa*; in fresh
water, tadpoles, freshwater crayfish and small
fish; in open country and forest, earthworms,
large insects such as cicadas, weta, stick
insects, dragonflies, chafers, wasps and
beetles, spiders, lizards, mice and small birds,
especially Silvereyes. They often perch for
long periods on any elevated object such as
a rock, post, powerline, driftwood or bare
branch, especially those that overlook pasture
or tidal mudflats. When a bird sees prey, it
suddenly darts with a direct, descending
flight, snatches its victim and immediately
returns to its perch, carrying the food
crosswise in its bill. Larger animals may be
battered against the perch. They regurgitate
pellets of indigestible material below their
perch and nest hole.

Reading: Fitzgerald, B.M. *et al.* 1986. *Notornis* 33:
23–32. Hayes, L.M. 1989. *Notornis* 36: 107–113.

ROLLERS   Coraciidae

16 species worldwide; 1 reaches New Zealand.

Rollers are colourful birds with a large head, plump body, short neck and legs, long wings and a wide, short, slightly hooked bill. They spend a lot of time perched high on bare tree branches, making harsh noises. They feed mainly early morning or late afternoon, diving from their perch to take large insects on the wing, often with aerobatic twisting and turning, and then circling back to their perch with an upward swoop.

282. DOLLARBIRD *Eurystomus orientalis*   Plate 65

Other name: Eastern Broad-billed Roller
Size: 29 cm, 130 g
Geographical variation: About a dozen subspecies, of which *pacificus* breeds in northern and eastern Australia and then migrates to winter in Indonesia and New Guinea.
Distribution: Asia and Australasia. Dollarbirds arrive in Australia from late September to November, and the adults leave in February–April, soon after the young have fledged, and the young follow about a month later. A few Dollarbirds reach New Zealand in most years. Some sightings are of adults in October–December, but most are of young birds caught up by adverse winds when on northward passage in March–May. There are many records of single birds or small groups, mostly from the western coasts of both main islands from Northland to Southland.

NEW ZEALAND WRENS   Acanthisittidae

All 4 species; family endemic to New Zealand; 1 (the Stephens Island Wren *Traversia lyalli*) became extinct in 1894, 1 is probably extinct, and 2 remain.

The New Zealand wrens are an ancient family of tiny birds with no close affinity to other groups of birds. They have short, rounded wings and a very short tail. Females are larger than males.

283. RIFLEMAN *Acanthisitta chloris*   Plate 66

Other name: Titipounamu
Size: 8 cm; males 6 g, females 7 g
Geographical variation: Two subspecies: the North Island Rifleman *granti* on the North Island, Great and Little Barrier Islands; and the South Island Rifleman *chloris* on the South Island, Stewart Island and its outliers.
Distribution: New Zealand only. Subfossil remains are scarce, but Riflemen were apparently widespread at the time of European settlement, then declined with the loss of lowland forest. In the North Island, apart from a small remnant in kauri forest at Warawara in Northland, they are now absent north of the Waikato and the Coromandel Peninsula. Elsewhere, they are widely but patchily distributed in forests and older stands of scrub. They are common on Little Barrier Island, and some are on Great Barrier Island. In the South Island, they are widely distributed through forests and scrubland from Marlborough and northwestern Nelson to Fiordland. They are common in forest on D'Urville Island, Stewart Island and its outliers, including Codfish Island. Throughout New Zealand, best numbers are in high-

altitude beech forest and in lowland podocarp forest, and they like mature tawa forest in the North Island, and manuka/kanuka and hakea scrub in the eastern South Island. They also use some older exotic forests, especially those with a dense understorey of native shrubs and with trees left in gullies, but are uncommon in young stands of pine, kahikatea and scrub where nest-holes are rare.

Population: Widespread and locally common, especially so in beech forest and older stands of tawa and podocarp forest.

Conservation: Protected endemic. Riflemen seem to have a stable distribution, but their poor dispersal across water or open habitats has led to a fragmented distribution in some parts of the country, and there are small isolated pockets in Northland and the eastern Hawke's Bay and Wairarapa hill country.

Breeding: Pairs remain on their territory all year. Some pairs have one or more helpers attending their nests. The male starts building several nests before the female finally joins in. The usual tree-hole nest is completely enclosed except for a small side entrance tunnel, and is well lined with leaf skeletons, fern roots, twigs and feathers. It is placed from near the ground to about 18 m (usually 3–6 m), but occasionally they use a small crevice in a bank or a disused rabbit burrow. They readily use a 15 cm square nest box with a 2 cm diameter entrance hole, especially where natural holes are scarce.

First clutches are laid in late September to early October, with replacement clutches and some second clutches being laid to the end of December. Courtship feeding is common early in the breeding season from about 12 days before laying to the completion of the clutch. They lay 2–4–5 white eggs (16 x 12.5 mm, 1.3 g) at 48-hour intervals. Both sexes incubate for 19–20 days, males incubate about 50% more during daylight hours than females. Chicks hatch about the same time. Both parents brood them for the first 10–12 days and feed them (mainly the male and occasionally helpers) until they fledge at 21–24–27 days old. After fledging, the chicks continue to be fed for 4–5 weeks, when they become fully independent. Riflemen often start building a second nest while still feeding chicks in the first nest and start incubating while still feeding fledglings. Most pairs lay replacement clutches if their first nest fails, and about 50% of pairs lay a second clutch after successfully raising a brood. Pairs remain together year after year. Young females sometimes pair up with a regular male helper on independence, and young of both sexes can start breeding at c. 9 months old. Annual survival of adult Riflemen near Kaikoura was c. 73% for males and 53% for females, giving life expectancies of 3.2 and 1.6 years respectively, but two banded males are known to have lived at least 6 years.

Behaviour: Pairs remain on territory all year, but helpers assist in raising young, especially late in the breeding season. Regular helpers are mainly unpaired males, some of which subsequently pair with one of the offspring raised. Casual helpers occasionally feed chicks in one or more broods; they are sometimes unpaired adults, but most are chicks from the first brood helping with their parents' second brood. Males are very protective of their female early in the season and remain close to her until she lays, but later in the season they allow unpaired males to assist in raising their broods. The main call of Riflemen is a very high-pitched, sharp 'zipt-zipt-zipt-zipt', often uttered by a pair as they feed a few metres apart. The call is so high-pitched that many older people can not hear it.

Feeding: Diet is almost entirely invertebrates; beetles, spiders, small weta, flies, moths and caterpillars are the most important food, with bugs, snails and lacewings also recorded. Some ripe fruit is taken. Riflemen glean most of their food from small crevices and epiphytic mosses and lichens on the trunks and large branches of trees at almost any level of the forest, although they only rarely feed on the forest floor.

Reading: Gaze, P.D. 1978. *Notornis* 25: 244. Gray, R.S. 1969. *Notornis* 16: 5–22. Moeed, A. & Fitzgerald, B.M. 1982. *NZ J Zool* 9: 391–403. Sherley, G.H. 1990. *Behaviour* 112: 1–22. Sherley, G.H. 1993. *NZ J Zool* 20: 211–217. Sherley, G. 1994. *Notornis* 41: 71–81.

284. BUSH WREN *Xenicus longipes* Plate 74

Other name: Matuhi
Size: 9 cm, 16 g
Geographical variation: Three subspecies: the North Island Bush Wren *stokesii* of the North Island, the South Island Bush Wren *longipes* of the South Island, and Stead's Bush Wren *variabilis* of Stewart Island and its outliers.
Distribution: New Zealand only. Subfossil remains are scarce, but Bush Wrens were apparently widely distributed before European settlement. The North Island Bush Wren was probably absent from Northland but otherwise widespread in forests until the late 1800s, though not as common as the Rifleman. In the 1900s, the only authentic records are from the southern Rimutaka Range (1918) and the Urewera Ranges (several records up to a sighting in the Aniwaniwa Valley in 1955).

The South Island Bush Wren was reported as common throughout forested mountain country, especially high-altitude beech forest, from northwestern Nelson and the Richmond Range south on both sides of the Southern Alps to Fiordland. By the early 1900s, they were declining rapidly, and by the 1950s they were recorded only sporadically, and mainly in Fiordland; however, the last two authentic records are from the Little Wainihinihi River, Arthur's Pass (1966), and Moss Pass, Nelson Lakes National Park (1968). Subsequently there have been a few rumours of birds in the Nelson Lakes area and Fiordland.

Stead's Bush Wren was common in forest on Stewart Island and in coastal 'muttonbird' scrub of *Olearia* and *Hebe* on several outlying islands. They survived on Stewart Island up to 1951, on Kotiwhenua (Solomon) Island to the early 1960s and on Big South Cape Island to 1965. In 1964, ship rats invaded Big South Cape, and six birds were transferred to Kaimohu Island, where they persisted until the last sighting in 1972.
Population: Probably extinct. Some hope stems from the recent rediscovery of Riflemen in dense forest in Northland, where they were long thought to have been extinct. The most likely places that a few birds could persist are in the Urewera, northwestern Nelson,

Nelson Lakes area, Fiordland or Stewart Island.
Conservation: Protected probably extinct endemic. The Bush Wren declined about the time of European settlement with the loss of much lowland forest, and then disappeared from most of the country in the late 1800s with the arrival of ship rats and mustelids. The extinction of Stead's Bush Wren is directly attributable to the arrival of ship rats at Kotiwhenua and Big South Cape Islands in the early 1960s. The attempt to relocate six birds to a predator-free island failed, probably because of chance events in such a small founder population.
Breeding: The nest was often built low to the ground among the roots of standing or fallen trees, in a low hole or fork of a tree, among clumps of fern or in petrel burrows. It was spherical with a small side entrance near the top; built of moss, fern rootlets and leaves, and lined with feathers. Eggs were found in November–December. They laid 2–3 white eggs (20 x 14.5 mm). Incubation and fledging periods were not known, but both parents incubated and fed nestlings. One bird transferred from Big South Cape to Kaimohu Island was at least 7 years old when last seen.
Behaviour: Pairs were territorial during the breeding season, but at other times of the year single birds, pairs or small family parties were recorded. The common call was a 'subdued trill' or a loud 'seep', sometimes rapidly repeated like the 'whirring' call of the Rock Wren.
Feeding: Diet was almost entirely invertebrates, with moths, flies and spiders recorded being fed to chicks. On the South Island, Bush Wrens fed by running along outer branches of trees, and not close to the trunk like the Rifleman; however, on the 'muttonbird' islands they often fed on or close to the ground, which probably made them especially vulnerable to mammalian predators. They moved swiftly and furtively while searching for prey on branches, among plants on the forest floor or around the bases of trees, with a characteristic hopping or bobbing movement.

Reading: Blackburn, A. 1965. *Notornis* 12: 191–207. Creswell, R.A. 1968. *Notornis* 15: 168. Guthrie-Smith, H. 1925. *Bird Life on Island and Shore.* Edinburgh: Blackwood. Stead, E.F. 1936. *Trans Roy Soc NZ* 66: 313–314.

285. ROCK WREN *Xenicus gilviventris* Plate 66

Size: 10 cm; males 16 g, females 20 g

Geographical variation: At one time a subspecies, *rineyi*, was proposed for greener birds found in Fiordland; however, they are now considered to be just a colour phase. Birds in northwestern Nelson are green, those in the central South Island are distinctly browner, whereas those in Westland and Fiordland are again much greener and the sexes are very distinct.

Distribution: South Island only, although subfossil remains have also been found in the North Island. Rock Wrens are patchily distributed in alpine and subalpine habitats of the Tasman Mountains of northwestern Nelson and the Victoria Range of northern Westland, down both sides of the Southern Alps and on some side ranges to the east, to Fiordland. They are apparently sedentary and do not move altitudinally with season.

Population: Widespread and locally common, especially near the Homer Tunnel, near Mt Aspiring and in the Murchison Mountains. They are commonest close to the treeline, especially where screes or rockfalls are interspersed with stable areas of low scrub, fellfield and cushion vegetation.

Conservation: Protected endemic. Rock Wrens disappeared from the North Island before European settlement, but in the South Island their range has changed little since European settlement; however, the distribution has become patchy and numbers have probably declined in some areas. Fires and introduced mammalian predators, especially stoats and mice, are major reasons for their decline. Being a high-altitude species, they are susceptible to long-term climate changes affecting their habitat, overwinter survival and timing of breeding.

Breeding: Contrary to popular speculation, pairs remain on their territory all year and do not migrate to low altitudes in winter. The female selects the nest site, but both birds work together to excavate a hollow in a bank or rocky crevice, or use a soil-covered ledge for the nest. The large enclosed nest has an entrance tunnel in the side. It is made of tussocks, grasses and sedges, and is lined with feathers. During the week of nest-building and the next 5 days before eggs are laid, the female is frequently fed by the male. Most first clutches are laid from mid-October to mid-November, but replacement clutches are laid until late December. They lay 1–3–5 creamy eggs (20 x 15.5 mm, 2.5 g). Both sexes incubate equally for 18–20–22 days. The chicks, which hatch over 1–3 days, are brooded throughout the fledging period of 21–24–26 days. Towards fledging, they are only brooded about 40% of daylight hours by both parents, but all night by the female. Both parents feed the chicks until they disperse 2–4 weeks after fledging. Many juveniles form pairs in the summer they are hatched and then breed when 11 months old. The oldest bird recorded lived at least 8 years.

Behaviour: Pairs remain on territory all year and, unlike the Rifleman, there is no indication that they have helpers at their nests. They have quite weak flight and bob their body on alighting. A conspicuous display involves bobbing and wing flicking. The main calls are a high-pitched and far-carrying three-note call, with the first note being accentuated, and a 'whirring' call. Pairs sometimes duet.

Feeding: Diet is mainly invertebrates, especially beetles, spiders, centipedes, caterpillars, flies and larvae of moths and caddisflies, but *Coprosma* and *Gaultheria* fruit and grass seeds are also eaten.

Reading: Heath, S. 1986. In *Flora & Fauna of Alpine Australasia*. Melbourne: CSIRO. Michelsen Heath, S. 1989. MSc thesis, Univ Otago. Soper, M.F. 1961. *Notornis* 9: 158–161.

LARKS
Alaudidae

76 species worldwide except South America; 1 has been introduced to New Zealand.

The larks are small songbirds of open country, especially rough grassland and undeveloped tussockland. They have long legs and toes, and an especially long hind toe and claw. Their bill is usually stout, and they feed on a mix of invertebrates and seeds. Although larks have erectile crown feathers that can form a short crest, their plumage is otherwise drab to provide camouflage on the ground. The territorial song is a beautiful torrent of trills and runs, often delivered while hovering high overhead.

286. SKYLARK *Alauda arvensis*
Plate 67

Size: 18 cm, 38 g

Distribution: Natural breeding range is Europe, North Africa, the Middle East and northern Asia to China; migrating south to India and northern Africa. At least 1000 birds were introduced into New Zealand by Acclimatisation Societies for sentimental reasons, and widely released between 1864 and 1875. They quickly became well established and spread throughout the country.

The Skylark is now very common in all types of open country, such as sand dunes, farmland and tussock grassland, from North Cape to Stewart Island and on offshore islands, and from sea level to subalpine herbfields at 1900 m; it avoids forest and other thick stands of vegetation. They are common on the Chatham Islands and vagrants have reached the Kermadecs, The Snares, Antipodes, Auckland and Campbell Islands. In their natural range, most birds migrate south in winter, but in New Zealand most seem to be sedentary or make local movements to flock at good food sources; however, some northward migration from Farewell Spit has been noted in late autumn.

Population: Widespread and locally abundant in open country, especially in drier parts east of the Main Divide, in sand-dune country and on the Chathams.

Breeding: Some pairs remain on territory all year and breed together year after year. Other birds, perhaps mainly juveniles, form loose flocks in autumn and winter. Singing by males increases from May, but eggs are not laid until September–January, during which pairs lay 2–3 clutches. The female builds the nest and then lays 2–**3**–**4**–5 eggs (23 x 17 mm), greyish white to creamy buff, thickly speckled brown, frequently with a darker zone at the broader end. The nest is a neat grass-lined cup in a small depression in the ground, especially a hoofprint, and often concealed by an overhanging clump of grass, rush or tussock. The female alone incubates for c. 11 days, but both parents feed the nestlings, which leave the nest at 9–10 days old, but do not fly until c. 20 days old. Young breed at 1 year old. Few birds have been banded in New Zealand, but in Europe a Skylark lived at least 8 years.

Behaviour: Pairs are strongly territorial during the breeding season, but some form winter flocks, and some migrate within New Zealand. The territorial song of the male, heard mainly in August–January and rarely from mid-February to mid-April, is a vigorous torrent of variable trills and runs, sustained for up to 5 minutes while the bird soars steeply, hovers at 30–100 m facing into the breeze and as it drops slowly earthwards. They occasionally sing from a post or on the ground. The call note is a liquid 'chirrup', often given in flight.

Feeding: Diet is mainly seeds of grass, cereals, sedges, clover and various weeds, supplemented with moderate quantities of invertebrates such as beetles, flies, spiders, bugs and larvae of flies, beetles and moths. All food is taken from the ground. Skylarks can cause considerable economic damage to crops by eating sown grain and seeds, and by pulling out or defoliating seedlings of tomatoes, cabbages, wheat and peas.

In the hand: Males have longer wings (105–**110**–116 mm) than females (95–**100**–104 mm).

Reading: Delius, J.D. 1965. *Ibis* 107: 466–492.

Garrick, A.S. 1981. *NZ J Ecol* 4: 106–114. Hamel, J. 1972. *Notornis* 19: 20–25. Moeed, A. 1975. *Notornis* 22: 135–142. Niethammer, G. 1971. *J f Orn* 112: 202–206.

SWALLOWS and MARTINS   Hirundinidae

74 species worldwide; 1 is a recently self-introduced native, and 2 are vagrants to New Zealand.

Swallows are usually larger than martins, but the two terms are interchangeable and follow no taxonomic differences. They are generally small, graceful, dark blue and white birds, with variable amounts of rusty red on their head and breast. They have a streamlined body with short neck and long, pointed wings with 9 primaries. Most have a deeply forked tail, but some have a square tail. Their flight is graceful and rapid as they wheel and dart to catch aerial insects in their short, wide bill. They are birds of open country, especially hunting over lakes, rivers and grassland; on warm, calm days they often fly high, but in poor weather they hunt close to the ground or water surface where flying insects are concentrated. Their feet are very small, and they shuffle about when they rarely land on the ground; they usually perch between feeding bouts on posts and on powerlines. Swallows and martins build distinctive mud nests, formerly mainly in trees or in cliff overhangs, but now often under bridges or culverts or under the eaves of buildings.

287. WELCOME SWALLOW   *Hirundo tahitica*   Plate 64

Other names: House Swallow (Asia), Pacific Swallow (Pacific)
Size: 15 cm, 14 g
Geographical variation: Several subspecies, of which *neoxena* breeds in Australia, Tasmania, Lord Howe Island and New Zealand.
Distribution: Breeds in southern Asia from India to Malaysia, in Australasia and the western Pacific. They have only recently colonised New Zealand, with breeding first recorded in 1958. Before then, they had been only a rare vagrant: Northland (1920), Auckland Islands (1943), Awhitu Peninsula (1944), Lake Ellesmere (1953), Stewart Island (1953) and Farewell Spit (1955). There were probably several invasions in the late 1950s and early 1960s. They were first recorded breeding at Awanui, near Kaitaia, in 1958, and by 1965 were well established throughout Northland. They bred at Lake Ellesmere in Canterbury in 1961, in Hawke's Bay and Manawatu in 1962, and in Wairarapa in 1964.

The spread of the Welcome Swallow has been spectacular, and they are now common in open country of lowland parts of the North and South Islands, except Otago and Southland, where they are uncommon. They are still scarce but expanding into high country of the Volcanic Plateau and the Mackenzie Country and Central Otago. Vagrants have reached the Kermadec, The Snares, Auckland and Campbell Islands. Breeding on the Chathams since about 1976.

In Australia, they are partial migrants, with some birds moving north in winter, but many remaining in the south. Welcome Swallows are probably also partial migrants in New Zealand, as they are quite often recorded at sea north of New Zealand in autumn and regularly appear at Norfolk Island in winter. Some birds have been seen leaving Farewell Spit for the North Island in late autumn; however, a southwards movement has been recorded in coastal Otago in autumn, and each winter moderate numbers of birds appear in Southland, where few breed.

Population: Widespread and locally common, especially in lowland farmland with numerous small streams or drains, and in wetlands.

Conservation: Protected self-introduced native. Welcome Swallows sometimes cause a minor nuisance by building their nests on houses, and so fouling doorways and patios, but generally live up to their name and are regarded as a welcome addition to our birdlife.

Breeding: Pairs begin prospecting for suitable nest sites in August, and several days are spent courting, including courtship feeding, before nest-building commences. Both birds help to build the half-cup mud nest, which is strengthened with dry grass. It is lined with dry grass, rootlets, hair, wool and a layer of feathers. The nest is attached to a rough vertical surface, usually within 15 cm of the top, normally under a small bridge or culvert, under eaves of houses, sheds and garages, inside water tanks, under jetties and in boats.

Some nests are built in natural sites such as caves, rock outcrops or under overhanging banks.

Eggs are laid in August–February, during which they raise up to 3 broods, sometimes in the same nest. The female lays 2–**4**–7 pale pink eggs (18 x 13 mm, 1.6 g), variably flecked reddish brown. Clutches of up to 10 eggs are probably laid by two females, or a fresh clutch has been laid in an abandoned nest. Clutch size is higher in New Zealand (4.1) than in eastern Australia (3.7) or western Australia (3.2), but seems to have declined as they have become well established. The second clutch of the season (4.7) is larger than the first (3.8) or third (3.3). Eggs are laid daily, usually about an hour after sunrise. The female alone incubates in spells of c. 8 minutes, with 4-minute feeding spells, for 15–**17**–19 days. The eggs hatch over 48 hours in the order they were laid. The female broods the young, but both birds feed them during the fledging period of 18–**21**–23 days. For several days after first flying, the young return to the nest to roost. They continue to be fed for c. 3 weeks, even though renesting may have begun. Welcome Swallows probably breed at 1 year old. The oldest bird recorded in New Zealand lived 6 years.

Behaviour: Welcome Swallows maintain a small territory around their nest and sometimes tolerate other pairs nesting in the same culvert, as close as a metre away, but usually there is just one pair to each site. During the breeding season, juveniles form summer flocks, and from late December adults start to join them; however, some pairs remain close to their breeding site all year. Flocks of up to 500 birds congregate in autumn and winter at good feeding sites such as over sewage ponds, lakes, rivers, sand dunes and root crops. Temporary roosting flocks often form during the day on powerlines, especially in a sheltered spot, but at night they often roost in huge aggregations of several thousand birds in raupo swamps. In the breeding season, pairs indulge in high-level chasing flights or slow, almost hovering flights accompanied by tail-fanning; the male quite often follows the female in these flights. The pair often sit together on a perch and twitter quietly, occasionally rubbing bills. The main call is a twittering 'twsit'.

Feeding: Diet is entirely invertebrates such as flies, including midges and blowflies, small beetles and moths. They catch most of their prey by hawking with their characteristic dipping, diving, darting flight. Sometimes they catch insects from the surface.

Reading: Crouchley, G. & Crouchley, D. 1979. *Notornis* 26: 309–310. Edgar, A.T. 1966. *Notornis* 13: 27–60. Michie, R. 1959. *Notornis* 8: 61–62. Park, P. 1981. *Corella* 5: 85–90. Tarburton, M.K. 1993. *Emu* 93: 34–43. Tunnicliffe, G.A. 1968. *Notornis* 15: 228–233. Turbott, E.G. 1965. *Notornis* 12: 241–244.

288. AUSTRALIAN TREE MARTIN *Hirundo nigricans* Plate 64

Size: 13 cm

Geographical variation: Three subspecies, of which *nigricans*, which breeds in eastern Australia and migrates north to northern Queensland, New Guinea and the Solomon Islands in winter, visits New Zealand.

Distribution: Breeds in Australasia; southern populations migrate northwards in winter and regularly reach the Solomons. A few vagrants reach New Zealand, with more than 25 records of single birds or flocks of up to 30–35 birds (East Cape, April 1974) since 1851. They have been reported from Miranda to The Snares (1968–69) and Chatham Island (November 1988). Some of the early records, including newspaper reports of their breeding in a mill near Oamaru in 1892–93, may have referred to Welcome Swallows. Tree Martins have been recorded in New Zealand in all months, but usually in autumn and early winter when birds are migrating northwards in eastern Australia. Some birds have stayed in one locality for several years or regularly returned to one site over several years, but breeding has not yet been confirmed.

Behaviour: In Australia, Tree Martins nest in mud-lined holes in trees or cliffs, but sometimes nest in buildings. They form large flocks in open country in late summer to winter, often resting on powerlines by day. When migrating, they wheel high as a large flock and then head off. They hawk insects on the wing as Welcome Swallows do, but their flight appears slower and more direct.

Reading: Henley, J.C. 1974. *Notornis* 21: 266–267. Nevill, A. 1984. *Notornis* 31: 173–175.

289. FAIRY MARTIN *Hirundo ariel* Plate 64

Size: 12 cm
Distribution: Endemic to mainland Australia but only a straggler to Tasmania. Birds breeding in southern states migrate north in winter and stragglers reach New Guinea, whereas vagrants reach Lord Howe Island and New Zealand. Fairy Martins were first recorded in New Zealand in December 1978, when two unusual bottle-shaped nests were found in a pumping shed near Lake Wairarapa. No birds were seen, but the nests had been built in 1977 or 1978. Subsequently seen at Farewell Spit (November 1982), Totaranui (possibly 5 in February 1983), Taieri (2 in February–March 1983 and 1 in December 1983), Cape Reinga (November 1983), Leigh (November 1984), Papakura (January 1985), Kawerau (January 1998), near Cape Reinga (August 2001) and Rahotu (4 in September 2001).

Behaviour: In Australia, Fairy Martins nest in colonies and construct distinctive large bottle-shaped nests of mud pellets against the wall or ceiling of a cave, culvert, building or cliff. They form large flocks in open country in late summer to winter, often resting on powerlines by day. They hawk insects on the wing as Welcome Swallows do, but tend to glide more.

Reading: Bell, B.D. 1984. *Notornis* 31: 172–173. Nevill, A. 1984. *Notornis* 31: 173–175.

PIPITS Motacillidae

43 species worldwide; 1 is native to New Zealand.

The pipits are small birds of open country, especially rough grassland, undeveloped tussockland, beaches and rivers. They resemble larks in having drab plumage to provide camouflage on the ground, and like the larks they have long legs and toes, and an exceptionally long hind toe and claw. Their most notable feature is a long tail, which is wagged up and down. Their bill is slender, and they feed mainly on invertebrates caught on the ground. Their calls are loud and unmusical.

290. NEW ZEALAND PIPIT *Anthus novaeseelandiae* Plate 67

Other names: Pihoihoi, Richard's Pipit (overseas)
Size: 19 cm, 40 g
Geographical variation: The species has a wide distribution with many subspecies, four of which are only in New Zealand; the New Zealand Pipit *novaeseelandiae* of the North, South and Stewart Islands, and offshore islands; the Chatham Island Pipit *chathamensis* of the Chatham Islands; the Antipodes Island Pipit *steindachneri* of the Antipodes Islands; and the Auckland Island Pipit *aucklandicus* of the Auckland and Campbell Islands. Recent genetic research suggests that populations on the various outlying islands are quite similar, and should be treated as a separate species to that on the mainland of New Zealand, perhaps indicating a double invasion of the New Zealand region by pipits.
Distribution: Breeds from central and eastern

Africa across central and southern Europe and Asia to Australasia. They are winter vagrants to western Europe, including Britain. In New Zealand, they are widely but patchily distributed in open habitats such as beaches, riverbeds, gravel roads and road verges, rough pasture and tussock grassland, and from sea level to subalpine tussock and herbfields at 1900 m. They are scarce in very dry parts of the South Island and in intensive agricultural districts such as Auckland, Waikato, Bay of Plenty, Taranaki, Manawatu, Canterbury and Southland. They are abundant on the Chatham Islands and common on the Antipodes and Auckland Islands, but are restricted to offshore stacks in the Campbell Islands. Stragglers have reached the Kermadecs and The Snares. In Europe and Asia, they are migratory, but there is no evidence of long-distance movement in New Zealand.

Population: Widespread and locally common in open country, especially in Northland, central North Island, eastern hill country from East Cape to Cape Palliser, Nelson, northern Westland, eastern foothills of the Southern Alps, Stewart Island, Chatham Islands, and some offshore islands.

Conservation: Protected native. At first, Pipits probably benefited from the clearance of forests and the creation of open habitats, but as pasture improved, pesticides were used and mammalian predators and magpies were introduced. Pipits declined locally and disappeared from some arable districts. Some people think that the Skylark has ousted them, but there is little overlap in diet and both species can be abundant in rough open country, such as on the Chathams.

Breeding: Some pairs remain on territory all year and breed year after year. The female builds the nest, which is a deep cup in a bulky structure of dry grass, well hidden at the base of a clump of grass, tussock, bracken fern, manuka bush, or occasionally under a fallen log or in a hollow on a bank or road cutting. Each pair has 2–3 clutches between August and February. They lay 2–**3**–**4**–5 cream eggs (23 x 17 mm), heavily blotched brown with a darker zone at the broader end. The incubation period is 14–15 days. Both parents feed the nestlings, which fledge at 14–16 days old. When visiting the nest, the adults usually alight 5–10 m away and walk to it, but they fly directly from the nest.

Behaviour: Pairs are strongly territorial during the breeding season, but some birds, perhaps mainly juveniles, form loose flocks in autumn and winter. The territorial song of the male, heard mainly in August–February, is a repeated, high-pitched and slurred 'pip-it' and a musical trill given from a prominent perch. The common call throughout the year is a shrill 'scree' or drawn-out 'zwee'.

Feeding: Diet is mainly invertebrates, especially beetles (including grass grubs), wasps, flies, spiders, crickets, moths and bugs, and insect larvae and pupae. On beaches, they eat sandhoppers. Seeds of grasses, clover and weeds make up a small part of the diet. Most food is taken from the ground, but some insects are caught on the wing.

Reading: Foggo, M.N. 1984. *Notornis* 31: 1–5. Foggo, *et al.* 1997. *Ibis* 139: 366–373. Garrick, A.S. 1981. *NZ J Ecol* 4: 106–114. Hamel, J. 1972. *Notornis* 19: 20–25. Moeed, A. 1975. *Notornis* 22: 135–142.

CUCKOO-SHRIKES and TRILLERS
Campephagidae

72 species in Africa and Asia; 2 vagrants reach New Zealand.

This family superficially resembles cuckoos by plumage colouring and slender silhouette, and shrikes by their bill shape, but they have no direct connection with either. Their plumage is usually mostly grey and black or, in trillers, black and white. The bill is short, stout and decurved near the tip, and they eat mainly insects. Their flight is undulating like that of a cuckoo.

291. BLACK-FACED CUCKOO-SHRIKE
Coracina novaehollandiae   **Plate 65**

Size: 33 cm
Distribution: Breeds in the Lesser Sunda Islands, New Guinea, Australia and the Solomon Islands. Birds in southern Australia migrate northwards to winter in the tropics, and some juveniles and a few adults get caught up in bad weather and stray to New Zealand, mostly in autumn and spring. About 15 records, mostly sight records on or near western coasts: Motueka (1869), Invercargill (1870 and 1976), Westport (c. 1895 and 1931), Lake Ellesmere (1904), Greymouth (1914), Okato, Taranaki (1914), Poutu, North Kaipara Heads (1953), Himatangi, Manawatu (1955),

Feilding (1965), Okuru, south of Haast (1966), Rotorua (1987), Tarras, Central Otago (1990) and Stewart Island (2001).
Behaviour: They feed on insects and fruit in the outer foliage of trees, dart from a prominent perch to catch flying insects, or take earthworms and insects on the ground. Their flight is strong and undulating, distinctly closing their wings at the top of each wave. They repeatedly shuffle their wings when they land on a perch. The main call is a croaky purr.

Reading: Smith, M.H. 1978. *Notornis* 25: 159–160.

292. WHITE-WINGED TRILLER   *Lalage tricolor*   **Plate 65**

Size: 18 cm
Distribution: In Australia, they breed only on the mainland. Some migrate to southern areas in spring to breed and then head north in autumn, reaching New Guinea. They are summer vagrants in Tasmania. There is one New Zealand record, of a male, seen in February–June 1969 at Macandrew Bay, Otago Peninsula.

Behaviour: Trillers feed on insects in the outer foliage of trees, hover close to the ground or alight on the ground to feed on insects. They fly rapidly with slight undulations. The call, heard mostly at dawn and dusk in New Zealand, was 'rather liquid, descending and with a similar pattern to the first part of a Chaffinch's song'.
Reading: McPherson, B. 1973. *Notornis* 20: 46–48.

BULBULS
Pycnonotidae

118 species in Africa and southern Asia; 1 introduced to New Zealand.

Bulbuls are lively birds with cheerful and attractive songs, and so are common cage birds. Their plumage is mainly a dull brown-green or grey, but with bright patches of red, white and/or yellow. Their most notable feature is a patch of hair-like feathers on the nape that sometimes form a distinct crest.

293. RED-VENTED BULBUL   *Pycnonotus cafer*   **Plate 73**

Size: 20 cm
Distribution: Natural breeding range is the Indian subcontinent, Sri Lanka, Nepal, Burma and southwestern China. Successfully introduced to Fiji, New Caledonia, Samoa, Tonga, Tahiti and Hawai'i. Birds of the subspecies

bengalensis (originally from northern India and the eastern Himalayas, but a popular cage bird in ports of Asia) were liberated in Auckland (probably from a ship) in 1952. They bred well, and by 1954 the population in well-treed suburbs of central Auckland (Takapuna,

Mt Eden and Remuera) was as high as 50 birds. The Department of Agriculture moved to exterminate them before they firmly established and spread from Auckland. All the birds were apparently killed by 1955; however, since about 1984 a few birds have been seen in the Auckland suburbs of North Shore and Mt Eden, and so some may have survived, or again escaped or have been released from captivity.

Breeding: Only one nest has been recorded in New Zealand; this contained 3 pinkish eggs (23.5 x 16 mm), closely spotted and blotched with reddish brown, in December. The nest was a compact and relatively shallow cup of fibres and twigs, lined with fine fibres,

hanging from branchlets near the tip of a pine branch about 3 m from the ground.

Behaviour: The common call note of the Red-vented Bulbul is a cheerful and attractive 'be-care-ful', with the last note stressed. The main note heard in Auckland was a low, scratchy, double croak: 'cark-cark', but single notes of a more musical quality were sometimes uttered.

Feeding: Diet is a mixture of invertebrates and fruits, and they can inflict serious damage to fruit and flower crops. Stomachs of New Zealand birds contained native burrowing bees, wasps and some fruit.

Reading: Turbott, E.G. 1956. *Notornis* 6: 185–193. Watling, D. 1978. *Notornis* 25: 109–117.

ACCENTORS

Prunellidae

13 species in Europe, North Africa and Asia; 1 introduced to New Zealand.

These small, rather drab brown birds resemble sparrows but have a fine, pointed bill for catching insects.

294. DUNNOCK *Prunella modularis*

Plate 67

Other name: Hedge Sparrow
Size: 14 cm, 21 g
Distribution: Natural breeding range is Europe and western Asia, some migrate south to winter around the Mediterranean and in North Africa. Several hundred birds were introduced into New Zealand by Acclimatisation Societies and private individuals in 1867–82. They were released in both islands and spread quickly, although some parts of the country, especially Auckland and Northland, were not colonised until the 1930s. The species now breeds throughout New Zealand, including the Chathams, Antipodes, Auckland and Campbell Islands, and is a vagrant to The Snares. They are found in a variety of habitats from sea level to subalpine scrub at 1600 m, including suburban gardens, orchards, exotic plantations, scrub and forest. Uncommon on well-forested offshore islands such as Little Barrier and Kapiti Islands. In Eurasia, they migrate, but there is no evidence

of long-distance movement in New Zealand.
Population: Widespread and locally common in scrub, orchards, parks and suburban gardens, places where there is a mix of dense cover and open spaces. They are inconspicuous and so are little known by the public.
Breeding: In England, Dunnocks have a variety of mating arrangements, including simple pairs, a male with several females, a female with several males, or even several males with several females (usually the surplus birds are helpers at the nest of the main pair). This has not been studied in New Zealand, but most seem to be in simple pairs. Eggs are laid in August–January, during which time 2–3 broods are raised. The female takes c. 5 days to build the nest, and she is sometimes helped by the male. The nest is usually well concealed in thick undergrowth or a hedge, and normally less than 2 m above the ground. It is a neat bowl of twigs, grass and moss, lined with hair, wool, feathers, tree

fern scales and moss. After a gap of c. 4 days after the nest is complete, the female lays 2–4–5 clear deep blue eggs (20 x 14.5 mm) at daily intervals. Incubation is by the female alone, and takes 11–12–14 days. Both parents feed the young during the fledging period of 10–12–14 days. The oldest Dunnock recorded in New Zealand lived over 6 years.
Behaviour: In England, many territories contain a main pair plus other birds that help to defend the territory and to feed the nestlings. In New Zealand, birds seem to remain on territory all year and do not migrate. The territorial song of the male, heard mainly in April–January, is a hurried warble, faster and stronger than that of a Grey Warbler, and rendered 'weeso, sissy-weeso, sissy-weeso, sissy-wee'; this lasts a few seconds but is repeated several times in rapid succession. The male often sits high in a tree or on top of a bush to sing. The main call is a sharp, insistent 'tseep'.
Feeding: Diet is mainly small invertebrates, such as beetles, spiders, flies, aphids, ants and worms. Some small fruits and seeds are also eaten. Most food is taken from the ground, usually not far away from cover.

In the hand: Males and females are virtually identical, with the male tending to be more grey on the chin, throat and breast. During breeding, the female has a brood patch and the male has a large bulbous cloacal protuberance. In autumn, adults have a reddish-brown eye, black bill and are often in wing-moult, while juveniles have a dull or greyish-brown eye, dark brown bill and are not moulting wing feathers.

Reading: Birkhead, M.E. 1981. *Ibis* 123: 75–84. Mauersberger, G. 1977. *Zool Abh Mus Tierk Dresden* 34: 101–126. Moeed, A. & Fitzgerald, B.M. 1982. *NZ J Zool* 9: 391–403.

THRUSHES   Muscicapidae

304 species worldwide; 2 introduced to New Zealand.

A big group of plump songbirds, mostly with brown or black plumage, but sometimes offset with spots and bright colours. Many have musical songs and harsh, staccato alarm calls. They often catch insects and earthworms on the ground, but also eat fruit from trees.

295. BLACKBIRD *Turdus merula*   Plate 67

Size: 25 cm, 90 g
Distribution: Natural breeding range is Europe and northwestern Africa, the Middle East, and Asia south to India and Sri Lanka and east to southern China. About 1000 birds were introduced into New Zealand by Acclimatisation Societies for sentimental reasons in 1862–75. They were liberated in both islands and established quickly, so that by 1900 they were distributed widely on the mainland and had colonised the Chatham and Auckland Islands. The species is now abundant throughout the mainland and offshore islands, and well established on the Kermadecs, Chathams, The Snares, Auckland and Campbell Islands, and vagrants have reached the Antipodes Islands.

Blackbirds are common in suburban gardens, parks, orchards, paddocks surrounded by hedges, exotic plantations, scrub and native forest, reaching at least 1500 m. The only places they are uncommon are on offshore islands with intact native bird and forest communities, such as on Little Barrier and Kapiti. In Eurasia, some birds migrate, but there is no evidence of regular long-distance movement in New Zealand; the maximum movement of a banded bird is only 90 km, from the Orongorongo Valley to Levin.
Population: Probably the most widespread

species within New Zealand, and especially abundant in parks, suburban gardens, orchards and farmland hedgerows where there is a mix of dense cover and open spaces.

Breeding: Males establish territories in April; usually the same territory is used by the same pair year after year. Most eggs are laid from late August to late December, but occasionally as early as June or as late as February. Pairs quickly replace nests that fail, and so most pairs nest 2–5 times each year and raise 2–3 broods, sometimes in the same nest. The female takes over a week to build the nest at the start of the season, but as little as 3 days later in the season. The nest is a substantial cup of twigs, grass, roots and moss, bound together with mud, and roughly lined with grass and leaf skeletons. It is usually built in the fork of a shrub or hedge 1–10 m above the ground, but occasionally nests are built on a ledge on a bank or in a shed.

They lay 2–**3**–**4**–6 eggs (28 x 21 mm, 6.5 g) at daily intervals. The eggs are bluish green to greenish brown, and are densely freckled with reddish brown. The female starts incubating before the clutch is completed, and incubation takes 13–14 days. Both parents feed the nestlings, which fledge at 13–15 days old. The young remain near the parents and are occasionally fed for several weeks after fledging. Young can breed at 9 months old. The oldest Blackbird recorded in New Zealand lived 15 years, but in Europe the record is over 20 years.

Behaviour: Blackbirds defend their territory for 8 months from April to January, but during the autumn moult they often congregate (but do not flock) at good sources of food such as orchards or mast-fruiting kahikatea forests. The territorial song of the male, heard mainly in July–January and delivered from an elevated perch, is loud, fluent and mellow, with notes running into each other. In late summer and early autumn, Blackbirds may sing a soft, warbling subsong while remaining hidden in a shrub or hedge. Alarm notes are an anxious, repeated 'tchook', especially given when a bird is flushed from cover, and a persistent, repeated 'tchink' when a predator is being mobbed.

Feeding: Diet is a mixture of invertebrates and fruits. The main invertebrates eaten include worms, beetles, amphipods, caterpillars, millipedes and spiders. Small fruits of native and introduced shrubs and weeds are eaten whole, but flesh of larger fruits is pecked from ripe fruit in trees or from fallen fruit. Blackbirds can cause considerable damage to commercial crops of berryfruits, grapes, pipfruit and stonefruit, and tomatoes. They also spread weed seeds into native forests and crops, but in some native forests they help to disperse seeds of fleshy-fruited understorey plants.

Most food is taken on the ground, especially close to cover or from closely mown lawns. When they are searching for insects, leaves are flicked aside with the bill and occasionally scratched away by the feet, but when hunting worms the bird usually takes a few hops, and then stops with head cocked before moving a step or two to catch the worm and pull it from the ground.

In the hand: Adults can be sexed in the field, but juveniles are difficult; young males tend to have brownish-black upperparts, not olive-tinged as in young females. In autumn, adults moult wing and tail feathers, and so have feathers missing or have fresh feathers, whereas young birds do not moult their primaries until over a year old, and so have very worn primaries by the next breeding season. In the first winter male, the worn, brown primaries contrast with the black body feathers acquired in a partial moult in the autumn.

Reading: Bull, P.C. 1946. *Emu* 46: 198–208. Bull, P.C. 1953. *Notornis* 5: 149–156. Flux, J.E.C. 1966. *Notornis* 13: 142–149. Gurr, L. 1954. *Ibis* 96: 225–261.

296. SONG THRUSH *Turdus philomelos* Plate 67

Size: 23 cm, 70 g

Distribution: Natural breeding range is Europe, western and central Asia. Several hundred birds were introduced into New Zealand by Acclimatisation Societies in 1862–78. They were released in both main islands and spread quickly, so that by 1900 they were well established. Now they are found throughout the mainland and offshore islands, and have colonised the Kermadecs, Chathams, Antipodes (breeding not confirmed), The Snares, Auckland and Campbell Islands, and have also reached Lord Howe, Norfolk and Macquarie Islands.

Song Thrushes are found in a variety of habitats from sea level to subalpine scrub at 1600 m, including suburban gardens, orchards, exotic plantations, scrub and forest, although they are scarce in virgin native forest and on islands such as Little Barrier and Kapiti where original forest and bird communities are largely intact. In Eurasia, some migrate, but there is no evidence of regular long-distance movement in New Zealand.

Population: Widespread and one of the most common birds in New Zealand; especially abundant in farmland hedgerows, orchards, parks and suburban gardens.

Breeding: Males establish territories from April; often the same territory is used by the same pair year after year. Most eggs are laid from early August to late December, but occasionally nests are found as early as May, or as late as February. Pairs quickly replace nests that fail and so most pairs nest 2–5 times each year, and raise 2–3 broods, rarely in the same nest. The female takes 1–2 weeks to build the nest, and then it is often left for a few days before she lays 2–**3–4**–6 eggs (27 x 20.5 mm, 6 g) at daily intervals. The eggs are a clear greenish blue with small black spots. The nest is a substantial cup of twigs, grass, roots and moss, bound together with mud and smoothly lined with mud or a mixture of rotten wood and saliva. It is usually built in the fork of a shrub or hedge 1–5 m above the ground. The female starts incubating when the clutch is complete, and incubation takes 12–13 days. Both parents feed the nestlings, which fledge at 13–15 days old. The young remain with the parents and are occasionally fed for several weeks after fledging. Young can breed at 9 months old. The oldest Song Thrush recorded in New Zealand lived over 10.5 years, but in Europe the record is over 13 years.

Behaviour: Song Thrushes defend their territory for 9 months from April to January, but during the autumn moult they become secretive and inconspicuous. The territorial song of the male, heard mainly in April–December and delivered from an elevated perch, is an energetic, bold and varied string of repeated musical phrases, each of which is clear-cut with a brief pause between phrases: 'chitty-choo chitty-choo, oo-eee oo-eee . . .' Sometimes Song Thrushes are mimics, incorporating phrases borrowed from other species. The alarm note is a rapidly repeated 'chuk' or 'chip', and the flight call is a thin, high-pitched 'seep'.

Feeding: Diet is a mixture of invertebrates and fruits. The main invertebrates eaten include snails (garden, mud, marine, flax and native landsnails), insects, worms, amphipods, millipedes and spiders. Small fruits of native and introduced shrubs and weeds are eaten whole, but flesh of larger fruits is pecked from ripe fruit in trees or from fallen fruit. They can cause damage to commercial crops of berryfruits, grapes, pipfruit and stonefruit, and tomatoes. They also spread weed seeds into native forests and crops. Most food is taken on the ground, especially close to cover or from closely mown lawns. When feeding on snails, they carry the animal to a favourite rock and then bash the snail against the rock with a flick of the head until the shell breaks and the animal comes free; such 'anvils' can be surrounded by the remains of 20+ snails. When hunting worms, the bird usually runs a few paces or takes a few hops, and then stops with head cocked before moving a step or two to catch the worm and pull it from the ground.

In the hand: Adults can be sexed reliably only in the breeding season, when the female has a brood patch. Song Thrushes have a conspicuous yellow gape, even as adults, and so this cannot be used to age birds. In autumn, adults moult their complete wing and tail feathers, but first-year birds moult only some of the smaller wing feathers, and so in winter there is a contrast between the large triangular buff tips of the 5 outer greater coverts and the smaller tips of the 5 freshly moulted inner ones. The tail feathers of adults have blunter ends than in first-year birds, and in adults the primary coverts have less contrast between the tip and the outer webs. In spring, the primaries of first-year birds are more worn than in adults and the contrast in the greater coverts is still clear.

Reading: Bull, P.C. 1946. *Emu* 46: 198–208. Flux, J.E.C. 1966. *Notornis* 13: 142–149. Nye, P.A. 1975. *Notornis* 22: 248–249.

OLD WORLD WARBLERS　　Sylviidae

339 species worldwide; the Fernbird is endemic to New Zealand. The closely related, but much larger, Chatham Island Fernbird B. *rufescens* is believed to have become extinct in about 1900, and so is excluded from this book.

A large and diverse group of small songbirds. Most have a small, thin bill, and they move actively through vegetation as they search for insects. Their song is usually musical and loud, although the Fernbird is an exception.

297.　FERNBIRD　*Bowdleria punctata*　　Plate 68

Other name: Matata
Size: 18 cm, 35 g
Geographical variation: Five subspecies, each restricted to a single island and its outliers: North Island Fernbird *vealeae*, South Island Fernbird *punctata*, Stewart Island Fernbird *stewartiana*, Codfish Island Fernbird *wilsoni*, and Snares Islands Fernbird *caudata*.
Distribution: New Zealand only. In the North Island, they are widely but patchily distributed north of a line from the Manawatu Estuary to Porangahau, and on Great Barrier and Aldermen Islands. In the South Island, they are common west of the Southern Alps from Farewell Spit and Nelson to the Hollyford Valley, including the Open Bay Islands. They are found along the eastern edge of the Fiordland mountains to Southland and eastward to about Dunedin. Fernbirds are on Stewart Island and many outliers, Codfish Island and on The Snares. Their main habitats are low, dense ground vegetation interspersed with emergent shrubs in swamps, pakahi, rush and tussock-covered frost flats and saltmarsh, low manuka scrub and some young pine plantations, from sea level to c. 1000 m. On The Snares, they are on the forest floor in open *Olearia* and *Senecio* forests. After becoming independent, juveniles roam away from their natal territory and can turn up in small scrub patches and wetlands 20+ km away from the nearest breeding birds.
Population: Widespread and locally common on the mainland, especially in Northland and parts of the Volcanic Plateau, the northern and western South Island, and coastal Southland and Otago. The island populations are moderately abundant, except on Codfish Island. The population on Main Island,

The Snares, was estimated to be c. 1750 pairs in 1972.

Conservation: Protected endemic. The Fernbird declined about the time of European settlement with the loss of much wetland and fernland through agricultural development, the introduction of mammalian predators, and periodic burning of wetland and scrub habitats. Fernbirds disappeared from most of the southern North Island and most of the eastern South Island by the late 1800s. They seem to have stabilised in their current distribution, mainly on poorer land unsuitable for farming, and have colonised some young stands of exotic forest in the central North Island and Hawke's Bay.

Breeding: Most Fernbirds stay in pairs or small groups all year, and many pairs stay in or near their breeding territory. In spring, territorial disputes and call rates increase. Both birds work together to make the nest, which takes about 3 days to build. It is a neatly woven deep cup of dry grass, sedge and rushes, generally lined with feathers. It is usually placed deep in cutty grass, rushes or tussock 15–75 cm above the ground or water level, but occasionally in a small shrub up to 2 m off the ground. On the mainland, Stewart Island and Codfish Island, eggs are laid from late August to January, but on The Snares they are laid from mid-October to late February. Probably two or three clutches are laid each year on the mainland, but on The Snares they normally raise only one brood. Clutch size in the North Island is 2–**3**–4 eggs (19.5 x 14.5 mm), in the South Island 1–**3**–5 eggs (20.5 x 15 mm), on Stewart and Codfish Islands 2–**3** eggs (22.5 x 15.5 mm), and on The Snares 1–**2**–3 eggs (23 x 16.5 mm). The eggs, which are laid daily, are pale pink, heavily flecked with purplish brown, especially towards the large end, but the amount of flecking decreases with successive eggs in a clutch. Both adults incubate for 12–**13**–15 days on the mainland, but for 15–**16**–19 days on The Snares. Both parents feed the chicks during a fledging period of 15–**17** days on the mainland and 20–21 days on The Snares. Young can breed at 9 months old. The oldest Fernbird recorded in New Zealand lived 6.5 years.

Behaviour: Fernbirds are usually territorial and sedentary, and their flight is weak. Their calls often reveal their presence in a swamp or scrub. They are secretive, but sometimes an inquisitive bird appears out of a tangle of vegetation for a moment or two, and equally quickly disappears. They are reluctant to leave cover, but when forced to, they fly low, with their tail hanging down. Territory defence breaks down during the autumn moult and in the early winter, but territorial calls increase in early spring. The main calls are a mechanical double call consisting of a low and a sharp metallic note: 'uu-tick', either given by the male alone or in duet with his mate, who responds very rapidly with the 'tick' portion. Other calls include 'tchip', 'tcheong' and 'zrup' notes, and a series of rapid clicks, or 'chittering' and, rarely, a melodic warble.

Feeding: Diet is mainly invertebrates, especially caterpillars, spiders, grubs, beetles, flies and moths. They feed in low vegetation or on the ground. On The Snares, Fernbirds eat maggots and flies around dead penguins, and they often perch on the back of a fur seal or sea lion to catch flies.

Reading: Barlow, M. 1983. *Notornis* 30: 199–216. Best, H.A. 1973. Unpubl MSc thesis, Univ Canterbury. Best, H.A. 1979. *Notornis* 26: 279–287. Best, H.A. 1979. *NZ J Zool* 6: 481–488.

WHISTLERS and allies   Pachycephalidae

28 species confined to Southeast Asia, Australasia and the southwestern Pacific; 3 endemic species in New Zealand.

These small, robust forest and scrub birds have relatively large rounded heads and short stout bills for catching insects amongst foliage and from crevices on branches and trunks. Most species have loud and varied calls, usually melodious but sometimes harsh and scolding.

298. WHITEHEAD   *Mohoua albicilla*   Plate 68

Other name: Popokatea
Size: 15 cm; males 18.5 g, females 14.5 g
Distribution: The North Island and some offshore islands only. Subfossil remains of Whiteheads have been found throughout the North Island, and they were still widespread at the time of European settlement. However, they disappeared from Northland in the 1870s, from the Auckland area in the 1880s, and from Great Barrier and Arid (Rakitu) Islands since the 1950s. They are now widely but patchily distributed in native forests, some older exotic plantations and older stands of scrub on the mainland south of a line from Te Aroha to Mt Pirongia. They remain abundant on Little Barrier and Kapiti Islands, and have been successfully introduced to Tiritiri Matangi Island, and Mokoia Island in Lake Rotorua.

Population: Widespread and locally common on the North Island, abundant on Little Barrier and Kapiti Islands.

Conservation: Protected endemic. Whiteheads declined about the time of European settlement with the loss of much lowland forest, and disappeared from the northern North Island in the late 1800s. They seem to have stabilised in their current distribution and have colonised exotic pine plantations in the central North Island, especially stands with a dense understorey of native shrubs.

Breeding: In late winter, family groups of Whiteheads start to defend a territory. The group consist of a breeding pair, or sometimes two breeding females, with 0–6 surviving young from previous years. Nest-building starts in early September. The nest is built by the main female in each group in 4–7 days. It is a compact, deep cup of twigs, dry grass, leaves and leaf skeletons, rootlets, strips of bark, moss and lichen, bound with cobwebs and lined with tree-fern fibres, feathers and wool. It is placed in the canopy of the forest or sometimes in a shrub or low tree 1–15 m above the ground. During nest-building and the following 2–3 days before eggs are laid, the male closely guards the female. Laying is from late September to late December, mostly between mid-October and mid-November. Usually only one brood is raised each year and most late nests are replacement clutches, but a few true second clutches are laid while helpers feed the fledglings from the first nest.

They lay 2–**3**–4 eggs (20 x 15 mm, 2.5 g), at 24-hour intervals. The eggs are white, variably speckled orange-brown. Only the main female incubates for 17–**18**–19 days, and broods. The male and any helpers help to feed the chicks during the fledging period of 16–**17**–19 days and after they have flown. The chicks start feeding themselves c. 10 days after fledging, but still beg and are fed at up to 9 months old. Young are capable of breeding at 1 year old in low-density populations, but at high densities, such as on Little Barrier Island, breeding is delayed for several years, and most young birds act as helpers instead. Adult survivorship on Little Barrier Island averaged 82%, giving a life expectancy of 5 years, but the oldest bird lived over 16 years.

Whiteheads are the host of the Long-tailed Cuckoo, and family groups can sometimes be seen in summer feeding a cuckoo chick many times larger than themselves.

Behaviour: Gregarious; in small flocks all year. Whiteheads often join feeding parakeets, Saddlebacks or Silvereyes to catch the insects they dislodge. In the breeding season, the strictly territorial groups are usually a main pair and their progeny from previous years, especially young males. In autumn and winter, each group has a larger home range centred on its territory, but home ranges overlap and sometimes groups coalesce to form flocks of up to 30 birds. Whiteheads are vocal all day and all year, except during the late summer moult. Territorial song peaks in spring. Calls help to maintain contact within flocks and to proclaim territories. Only males give the loud territorial calls, usually from a prominent perch. These calls are varied, based on a phrase starting with several chirps, followed by a string of clear canary-like chimes or 'peek-o, peek-o, peek-o' calls and descending slurs and finishing with a chuckle. The contact call in flocks is a single harsh 'cheert', which forms a constant chatter in the distance, and the alarm calls are an excited, loud 'chirrt' and a ringing 'chee-chee-chee'.

Feeding: Diet is mainly invertebrates but includes some fruit. Main prey are spiders, beetles, caterpillars and moths, gleaned from leaves, twigs and branches in the canopy and understorey, sometimes by hanging upside down. They feed on invertebrates dislodged by other feeding birds, and occasionally on insects under loose bark on trunks and large branches; rarely feed on the ground. They eat some fruit of native shrubs, especially mahoe, matipo, coprosma and hangehange.

In the hand: Adult males have an almost pure white head and shiny black legs, but the crown and nape is shaded brown in adult females and juveniles of both sexes. Males are larger and heavier than females, but most birds can be sexed from a combination of wing and weight, even though throughout the North Island there is some overlap: wing 67–**71.5**–77 cf. 62–**66**–70 mm, and weight 16–**18.5**–21 cf. 12–**14.5**–19.5 g. Juvenile females in their first winter can be separated from adult females by having fleshy rictal flanges and pale grey (not dark grey) legs.

Reading: Gill, B.J. 1993. *Notornis* 40: 141–143. Gill, B.J. & McLean, I.G. 1986. *NZ J Zool* 13: 267–271. Gill, B.J. & McLean, I.G. 1992. *Condor* 94: 628–635. Gill, B.J. & Veitch, C.R. 1990. *Notornis* 37: 141–145. McLean, I.G. & Gill, B.J. 1988. *Emu* 88: 177–182. Moeed, A. & Fitzgerald, B.M. 1982. *NZ J Zool* 9: 391–403. Robertson, H.A. et al. 1983. *NZ J Zool* 10: 87–98.

299. YELLOWHEAD *Mohoua ochrocephala* Plate 68

Other names: Mohua, Bush Canary
Size: 15 cm; males 30 g, females 25 g
Distribution: South Island only. In the 1800s, Yellowheads were abundant and conspicuous in the beech forests, particularly red beech, from Nelson and Marlborough to Southland, and in the podocarp-hardwood forests of the West Coast and Stewart Island. They declined throughout the South Island in the late 1800s and disappeared from Banks Peninsula. However, the dramatic decline of Yellowheads began in c. 1890 after ship rats and mustelids were introduced. By 1930, they had disappeared from Stewart Island and the podocarp forests of the West Coast, and subsequently have gone from northwestern Nelson, Nelson Lakes National Park, Lewis Pass, Paparoa Range and many South Island beech forests, including northern and central Westland. They have now gone from nearly 85% of their former range and are well established only in Fiordland and Mount Aspiring National Parks, extending east to the Dart Valley. Moderate pockets remain in and near Arthur's Pass National Park (especially in the South Hurunui); Catlins, Blue Mountains and the Landsborough Valley. Small, isolated groups remain in the Rowallan, Takitimu, Longwood and Waikaia forests. Introduced to Breaksea Centre, Pigeon, Nukuwaiata and Ulva Islands.
Population: Several thousand birds, mainly in Fiordland and adjacent forests.
Conservation: Protected threatened endemic. Forest clearance and selective logging of mature trees removed most of their prime habitat: lowland red beech on fertile river terraces. Stoat and rat predation are probably the main cause of Yellowhead decline. Numbers of rodents explode after beech has flowered and seeded profusely, about every 5 years, and the number of stoats also explodes following this boom in their main prey. Yellowheads often feed noisily on or close to the ground, and females incubate and oversee nestlings for long periods in their nest holes; this results in a periodic population crash and a disproportionately high loss of females. Competition with introduced ves-pulid wasps since the 1940s may have contributed to the dramatic decline of Yellowheads in the northern half of the South Island. The aims of conservation management are to control stoats and rats around the best remaining breeding sites, and to transfer birds to predator-free islands and to captivity.

Breeding: Yellowheads breed as pairs or in small groups with one or more helpers. They nest in holes high in mature or rotting trees, usually beech trees. The female builds a cup-shaped nest of moss, rootlets, twigs and spiders' webs, lined with fine grass; this is unusual for a hole-nesting bird. Laying is from early October to late January, with peaks in early November and late December corresponding to the two clutches usually laid by each pair in good habitats; however, in places where the habitat is poor, most pairs probably lay just one clutch per year.

They lay 1–**3**–5 pink eggs (23.5 x 18 mm), faintly freckled pale reddish brown. The female alone incubates for c. 20 days, and broods. The male and any helpers help to feed the chicks during the c. 22-day fledging period and after they have flown. The chicks still beg and get fed right through their first winter. The young usually breed first at 2 years old. Adult Yellowheads at Knobs Flat, Eglinton Valley, had an annual survivorship of 83% and life expectancy of 5 years, but the oldest bird lived to at least 16 years old.

Yellowheads and Brown Creepers are the hosts of the Long-tailed Cuckoo, and in late summer Yellowheads can sometimes be seen feeding a cuckoo chick many times larger than themselves.

Behaviour: Gregarious when not breeding. From mid-summer to the end of winter, family parties coalesce into roaming feeding flocks of up to 25 Yellowheads; the bigger the flock, the noisier. They often lead mixed-species feeding flocks, and especially join parakeets to feed on insects they have disturbed. They are vocal all day and all year, except during the late summer moult. Territorial song peaks in late spring. Only males give the loud territorial song: musical, canary-like whistles and trills. Other calls are loud and varied, mainly a rapid staccato chatter, musical whistles and slurs, and the female only sometimes utters a buzzing call.

Feeding: Diet is mainly invertebrates but includes some fruit. They search vigorously for insects and spiders, often upside down, in or just under the canopy in the leaves, twigs, cracks and crevices of branches and trunks, pressing with their tail feathers until these

are so worn down that they look like spines. Yellowheads sometimes come to ground but prefer to scratch through the leaf litter that accumulates in tree forks.

Reading: Elliott, G.P. 1990. Unpubl PhD thesis, Victoria Univ, Wellington. Gaze, P.D. 1985. *Notornis* 32: 261–269. O'Donnell, C. 1993. *Mohua/ Yellowhead Recovery Plan.* Wellington: DoC. Read, A.F. 1987. *Notornis* 34: 11–18. Read, A.F. & O'Donnell, C.F.J. 1987. *Notornis* 34: 307–315.

300. BROWN CREEPER   *Mohoua novaeseelandiae*   Plate 68

Other name: Pipipi
Size: 13 cm; males 13.5 g, females 11 g
Distribution: South Island, Stewart Island and some offshore islands only. Although widespread at the time of European settlement, Brown Creepers have declined with the loss of lowland forest and the introduction of mammalian predators. They are now widely but patchily distributed in native forests, exotic plantations and scrub from sea level to the treeline on the South Island mainland, mostly to the north and west of the Southern Alps, in beech forest on river flats to the east of the alps, in Fiordland and on Stewart Island and some of its outliers. They are also in dry scrub of Marlborough and Banks Peninsula, in pine forests of Nelson and Otago, and in native forests in the Catlins and around Dunedin.
Population: Widespread and locally common on the South Island mainland and Stewart Island, abundant on Codfish Island.
Conservation: Protected endemic. Brown Creepers declined about the time of European settlement with the loss of much lowland forest and the introduction of rats, cats and mustelids. Little is known of population trends, but they seem to have stabilised in their current distribution.
Breeding: Pairs defend their territory all year. From early September, females start building the nest, taking 5–**10**–17 days. The nest is a compact deep cup of strips of bark, small twigs, grasses, moss, leaves and leaf skeletons and lichen, bound with cobwebs and lined with dried grasses, feathers and wool. It is

placed in a dense patch of vegetation in the canopy of the forest or sometimes in a shrub or low tree 1–10 m above the ground. During nest-building, the following 2–3 days before eggs are laid and the first part of the laying period, the male closely guards the female. Laying is from late September to late January, with peaks in early October and late November representing successive clutches.

They lay 2–**3**–4 eggs (18.5 x 14 mm, 2.0 g) at 24-hour intervals. The eggs are white to dark pink, variably speckled reddish brown. The female alone incubates for 17–**19**–21 days, and broods. Both sexes feed the young, which fledge at 18–**20**–22 days old. The chicks are mainly fed by the male when the female renests, but some non-breeding birds also help to feed chicks. The chicks are occasionally fed to the end of winter. The young stay as a group once they have become independent and often coalesce with other juvenile groups to form autumn and winter flocks of up to 50 birds. Brown Creepers are capable of breeding at 1 year old. At Kaikoura, adult survival was over 82%, giving a life expectancy of 5 years.

Brown Creepers are the main host of the Long-tailed Cuckoo in the South and Stewart Islands, and a pair can sometimes be seen in summer feeding a cuckoo chick many times larger than themselves.
Behaviour: Adults are normally strongly territorial all year, but some that breed at high altitude move downhill and form flocks in winter. Brown Creepers often associate with other feeding forest birds, especially Silver-

eyes, parakeets, Grey Warblers and Fantails. They are vocal all day and all year, except during the late summer moult. Territorial song peaks in spring. Only males give the loud territorial song, which varies from bird to bird, and is a phrase including slurs, musical whistles and harsh notes, described as 'chi-roh-ree-roh-ree-ree'. Females sing a rapid sequence of brief notes, the last being high-pitched and prolonged, often in a duet with the male. A wide variety of 'chi's, chatters, trills and harsh 'zick's are given.

Feeding: Diet is mainly invertebrates but includes some fruit. Main prey are beetles, spiders, flies, moths and caterpillars, gleaned from leaves and especially from small branches in the canopy, sometimes by hanging upside down. Brown Creepers occasionally feed on insects under loose bark on trunks and large branches, and only rarely feed on the ground. Some ripe fruit of native shrubs such as coprosmas are eaten, especially in autumn.

In the hand: Males are larger and heavier than females. Wing length and weight showed no over-lap in a sample of 26 males and 18 females at Kaikoura: 59.5–**61**–64 cf. 54.5–**57**–58.5 mm and 12–**13.4**–15 cf. 10.5–**11.0**–12 g respectively. Before May, juveniles could be distinguished by their yellow bill flanges and dark brown (not light brown) legs and feet.

Reading: Cunningham, J.B. 1984. *Notornis* 31: 19–22. Cunningham, J.B. 1985. Unpubl PhD thesis, Univ Canterbury. Gill, B.J. *et al.* 1980. *Notornis* 27: 129–132.

AUSTRALASIAN WARBLERS   Acanthizidae

59 species in Southeast Asia, Australasia and the southwestern Pacific; 2 endemic species in New Zealand.

A diverse group of very small or small forest and scrub birds. Many, like the thornbills and warblers, have short, fine bills for gleaning insects in foliage, or more distinctively, by hovering and picking insects from leaves. Most species have a distinctive, loud and beautiful song.

301. GREY WARBLER   *Gerygone igata*   Plate 66

Other name: Riroriro
Size: 10 cm, 6.5 g
Distribution: New Zealand only. Subfossil remains are scarce, but Grey Warblers were apparently widespread historically. They are one of the few native passerines to have benefited from human modification of the landscape. They are common through many forest, scrub, rural and city habitats from sea level to the subalpine zone on the main islands and most offshore islands, but absent from the outlying islands, except for the vagrants at The Snares. Scarce on Little Barrier and Kapiti Islands, where forest-bird communities are relatively intact.
Population: Widespread and abundant. They are especially common in manuka, kanuka and gorse scrub.
Conservation: Protected endemic. The Grey Warbler is common and widespread, and no specific conservation management is necessary.
Breeding: Grey Warblers establish their territories in late July and August. The female takes up to 27 days to build the enclosed nest with a 3 cm diameter hole in the side. About half the nests are pensile (hanging freely from an attachment at the top), and the rest are also secured elsewhere. It is made of rootlets, moss, lichen, leaves, bark, tree-fern scales and fibres, twigs, cobwebs, spider egg-cases, wool, hair and feathers, and is lined with a thick layer of feathers, downy seeds and tree-fern scales. Nests are 1–10 m above the ground,

usually in the lower half of the forest. Eggs are laid in August–December; usually two broods are raised each year with peaks of laying in September and November.

They lay 2–4–5 white eggs (17 x 12 mm, 1.5 g) with reddish-brown speckling concentrated near the larger end. Eggs are laid at 2-day intervals, and incubation starts once the final egg is laid. The female alone incubates for 17–19.5–21 days, and broods the chicks for the first 10 days. The chicks are fed by both parents during the 15–17–19-day fledging period and for up to 35 days after leaving the nest. The male does most of the later care of the first brood as the female prepares to lay the second clutch. Once independent, the young become mobile and disperse several kilometres from their natal territory. First breeding is probably at 1 year old. Pairs are monogamous and persist all year and between years. At Kowhai Bush, adult survivorship was at least 82% and life expectancy was 5 years. The oldest recorded lived 5.8 years, but some are likely to live to 10+ years old.

The Grey Warbler is the only host to the Shining Cuckoo on the New Zealand mainland. First clutches escape parasitism because they are laid before the cuckoos arrive, but often Shining Cuckoos replace an egg in the second clutch with one of their own, and eventually the bigger and faster-growing

cuckoo chick expels all other eggs or chicks.

Behaviour: Males defend their breeding territory with long chases interspersed with bouts of loud and prolonged singing; females join in the chases, especially when the intruder approaches a nest. The territories expand into overlapping home ranges between the breeding seasons, and flocks of up to 25 birds form in the winter. Grey Warblers occasionally join flocks of other insectivorous birds such as Silvereyes, Brown Creepers and White-heads.

Feeding: Diet is almost entirely invertebrates, especially spiders, caterpillars, flies, beetles and bugs, but also includes a few small fruits. Grey Warblers take most of their food by gleaning from leaves, but they often feed in a highly distinctive way by catching prey near the ends of branches while hovering in mid-air.

In the hand: Sexes are indistinguishable for most of the year, but only females develop a brood patch; sexes are best distinguished by the behaviour of birds during the breeding season. Juveniles have brown, not red, eyes, and their legs are dull grey, not black, and some have a pale yellow eye-ring. Juveniles moult into adult plumage in January–March, at about the same time that adults moult.

Reading: Gill, B.J. 1982. *Ibis* 124: 123–147. Gill, B.J. 1982. *Emu* 82: 177–181. Gill, B.J. 1983. *Notornis* 30: 137–165.

302. CHATHAM ISLAND WARBLER *Gerygone albofrontata* Plate 66

Size: 12 cm; male 10 g, female 8.5 g

Distribution: Chatham Islands only. Subfossil remains and records in the first half of the 1900s indicate that they used to be throughout all of the Chatham Islands. They are now confined to the forested areas of the southern half of Chatham Island, Pitt, Mangere, Little Mangere and South East Islands, and the Star Keys.

Population: Locally common, and abundant on South East and Mangere Islands.

Conservation: Protected endemic. Chatham Island Warblers do not seem to have adapted to human-modified habitats as well as Grey Warblers have done on the New Zealand

mainland. Those on Chatham Island have declined during this century and have disappeared from the northern half of the island, but they remain the commonest native bird in the southern forests and scrub. On predator-free offshore islands, such as South East and Mangere, they are abundant in native forest and scrub, and their future seems assured so long as these islands remain free of rats and cats. Chatham Island Warblers are sometimes parasitised by Shining Cuckoos, and so they were used to host broods of Black Robins in the early stages of the recovery of that critically endangered species. However, although able to successfully hatch Black Robin eggs and raise the Black Robin chicks through the first couple of weeks, they were unable to fledge them successfully.

Breeding: Pairs establish territories in August, and the female takes up to 13 days to build the enclosed hanging nest. It has a 3 cm diameter hole in the side and is made of rootlets, mosses, lichens, leaves, bark, twigs, grass stems, flowers, cobwebs, spider egg-cases and feathers, and is lined with a thick layer of feathers. On Chatham Island, most nests hang in the open, often on terminal branches of *Dracophyllum arboreum* about 6 m above the ground. On offshore islands, however, they are only 2–3 m above the ground and in dense foliage, presumably to protect them from damage from petrels landing at night. Most eggs are laid in September–December, and only one brood is raised each year, but some replacement clutches are laid late in the season.

They lay 2–**3**–4 white eggs (18 x 13 mm; 1.8 g) with reddish speckling concentrated near the larger end. Eggs are laid at 2-day intervals. The female alone incubates for 17–**19.5**–21 days and broods the chicks, but both parents feed the chicks. The fledging period is 19–**20**–23 days, and chicks are fed by their parents for up to 24 days after leaving the nest; normally the male and female split their brood and care for one or two chicks each. When the population density is high, small juvenile flocks form late in the breeding season. First breeding is probably at 2 years old, because 1-year-old birds are in subadult plumage and are non-territorial in the following breeding season. The oldest bird recorded in the wild lived over 7 years.

Some nests late in the season are parasitised by Shining Cuckoos.

Behaviour: Males defend their territory with long chases interspersed with bouts of loud and prolonged singing; females occasionally join in the chases but have only a weak subsong.

Feeding: Diet is entirely invertebrates, especially spiders, caterpillars, flies, beetles and bugs. They glean most of their food from leaves and from crevices in trunks and branches. Unlike the Grey Warbler, they seldom hover to catch food, but quite often feed on the ground in the leaf litter.

In the hand: Sexes are told by colour and size, the adult male having white underparts and a prominent white face with contrasting dark eyestripe, and the adult female having grey-white underparts and a face with a yellow tinge, especially on the throat. Only females develop a brood patch. Males are larger in all measurements, with little overlap in wing length: 60–**64**–67 mm cf. 57–**60**–62 mm. Juveniles are like females, but their upperparts have an olive-grey tone rather than brownish olive, underparts are yellower, outer webs of primaries are green-yellow not buff-yellow, and their iris is brown, not red. Juveniles moult into adult plumage in November–January, while adults probably do not moult until January–March, several weeks after breeding.

Reading: Dennison, M.D. *et al.* 1984. *Notornis* 31: 97–105. Robertson, H.A. & Dennison, M.D. 1984. *Emu* 84: 103–107.

MONARCH FLYCATCHERS Monarchidae

About 170 species from Africa through southern Asia and Australasia to the South Pacific islands; 1 native species and 1 vagrant in New Zealand.

A varied group of insectivorous forest birds with proportionately large heads and short, broad bills with abundant bristles at the base. Most hawk insects in the air with short flights, but some glean insects from the foliage.

303. SATIN FLYCATCHER *Myiagra cyanoleuca* Plate 65

Size: 16 cm
Distribution: Breeds in eastern Australia from Cape York to Tasmania. They migrate from the southern part of their range to northern Queensland and New Guinea, leaving in late February and March and returning in Septem-

ber. Three New Zealand records: a female seen in Gisborne (June 1963), a male found dead at Motueka Sandspit (December 1988) and one at Okarito (March 1992).

Reading: Blackburn, A. 1963. *Notornis* 10: 262–265.

304. FANTAIL *Rhipidura fuliginosa* Plate 68

Other names: Piwakawaka, Grey Fantail (Australia)
Size: 16 cm (including 8 cm of exposed tail); 8 g
Geographical variation: About 10 subspecies, three in New Zealand: North Island Fantail *placabilis*, South Island Fantail *fuliginosa*, and Chatham Island Fantail *penitus*. The South Island subspecies has two colour forms, pied phase and black phase, with black phases making up 12–25% of the population, and with highest percentages in native forest and at higher altitudes. Black phase birds make up less than 0.1% of North Island birds but are recorded mainly around Wellington, indicating some gene flow across Cook Strait.
Distribution: Breeds widely in Australia and Tasmania, Lord Howe Island, the southern Solomons, Vanuatu, New Caledonia, Norfolk Island and New Zealand. The Fantail breeds throughout the North, South and Stewart Islands and their offshore islands, and on the Chathams and The Snares. They have not been recorded on any of the other subantarctic islands or on the Kermadecs. Fantails are common in forest, scrub, farmland where there are scattered trees, farm gardens, orchards and suburban gardens from sea level to 1500 m, but they are scarce in the dry open country of inland Marlborough, the Mackenzie Basin and Central Otago, which are prone to severe frosts and snow in winter. Some adults are sedentary, but others seem to wander and form loose flocks in winter and early spring. Independent juveniles disperse away from their natal territory.
Population: Widespread and locally abundant, especially on forest edges and second-growth scrub habitats. Fantails are one of the

most common and widely distributed native birds on the New Zealand mainland.
Conservation: Protected native. The Fantail is one of the few native forest birds to have benefited from the large-scale clearance of forest and the creation of forest edge and scrub habitats. Fantail populations undergo major fluctuations from year to year, especially caused by prolonged or severe winter and spring storms. These fluctuations can lead to brief local extinctions on islands (e.g. on South East Island, Chathams), but as their annual productivity is high and juveniles (and possibly some adults) disperse, they quickly recolonise temporarily vacated areas.
Breeding: Fantails remain in pairs all year. Males retain the same territory in successive years, but high mortality means that few pairs remain together in successive seasons. Territorial defence becomes obvious in August, and first nests are built in about a fortnight in late August. In the North Island Fantail, the female apparently builds the nest alone, but in the South Island Fantail the male helps, especially early in the season when not looking after dependent fledglings. The nest is a neat cup of dried grass, strips of bark, moss and cobwebs, lined with fine fern fibres, hair and feathers, and with a tail of nest material hanging about 10 cm down from the bottom of the nest. It is usually built about 2–3 m above the ground in a slender fork of an understorey shrub, or on the frond of a tree fern, and is often protected from above by overhanging vegetation and is normally above a gap in the shrub layer. On the New Zealand mainland, eggs are laid from late August to February, during which they raise 2–5 broods; one pair raised 15 young from

16 eggs laid in 5 clutches in a season. Island populations (including the Chathams) have a shorter season, with a later start and earlier finish, and raise up to 2 broods per year.

They lay 2–**3**–**4**–5 white eggs speckled with light brown spots (16 x 12 mm). Clutches of 3 eggs are most common at the start and end of the season, whereas clutches of 4 are common in November–December. On the mainland, incubation starts with the final egg, but on the Chathams it begins with the laying of the penultimate egg. Both birds incubate for 13–**14**–16 days and brood and feed the nestlings during the fledging period of 11–**13**–16 days. After leaving the nest, the chicks often remain close together and are fed by both parents, but when the female starts building the next nest, the male looks after the fledglings. Some juveniles may breed at c. 2 months old, but most breed the next season at c. 9 months old. Juvenile and adult mortality is high in New Zealand, and the oldest bird recorded lived only 3 years; however, in Australia they have reached 10 years old.

Behaviour: Fantails are strongly territorial while breeding, but territories break down in autumn. Loose flocks and communal roosts of up to 10–20 birds are sometimes seen in winter. Calls of Fantails are simple, with the main territorial call of the male being a harsh rhythmical 'saw-like' song: 'tweet-a-tweet-a-tweet-a-tweet . . .' The usual contact call is a penetrating, sweet-sounding 'cheet'. Birds regularly call from near the nest during incubation and brooding change-overs and when waiting to feed nestlings. Males are more vocal than females throughout the day, and in the early morning only males sing from song-posts.

Feeding: Diet is mainly invertebrates, occasionally supplemented with fruit. Main prey are moths, flies, wasps, beetles and spiders, taken while fly-catching in the understorey, along tracks, in forest clearings and river flats, and sometimes above the canopy. They are very manœuverable and use their fanned tail to stop in mid-air and to change direction when hawking and fly-catching. Fantails also hop around upside down along tree-fern fronds or among foliage to pick prey from the underside of leaves, or more often to catch insects that fall, and they occasionally hover to pick prey from the undersides of leaves. They rarely feed on the ground, except on predator-free offshore islands. Fantails often associate with feeding Silvereyes, Whiteheads, parakeets or Saddlebacks and feed on insects dislodged by feeding birds.

In the hand: Males and females are alike. Juveniles have a tawny, not white, eyestripe, and secondary coverts have large fawn tips, the black throat band is absent and the legs are pale grey, not black.

Reading: Blackburn, A. 1965. *Notornis* 12: 127–137. Blackburn, A. 1966. *Notornis* 13: 189–196. Dennison, T.C. *et al.* 1979. *Notornis* 26: 392–395. McLean, I.G. 1984. *Notornis* 31: 279–283. McLean, I.G. & Jenkins, P.F. 1980. *Notornis* 27: 105–113. McLean, I.G. & Jenkins, P.F. 1980. *Ibis* 122: 98–102. Moeed, A. & Fitzgerald, B.M. 1982. *NZ J Zool* 9: 391–403. Powlesland, M.H. 1982. *Notornis* 29: 181–195.

AUSTRALASIAN ROBINS — Eopsaltriidae

About 44 species in Australasia; 3 endemic to New Zealand.

Australasian robins are small, robust, confiding forest birds with short necks and large heads, and an upright stance on moderately long, thin legs. Their bill is short, broad at the base and surrounded with abundant bristles. Males are mostly black, grey and white with patches of red or yellow, whereas females have a duller basic colour and lack bright colours. Although superficially similar, this group is not closely related to the European Robin *Erithacus rubecula*, which belongs to the thrushes (Muscicapidae).

305. TOMTIT *Petroica macrocephala* Plate 69

Other names: Miromiro, Pied Tit (North Island); Ngiru-ngiru, Yellow-breasted Tit (South Island); Black Tit (The Snares)
Size: 13 cm, 11 g; 20 g (The Snares)
Geographical variation: Five subspecies, each restricted to an island and its outliers: North Island Tomtit *toitoi*, South Island Tomtit *macrocephala*, Chatham Island Tomtit *chathamensis*, Snares Island Tomtit *dannefaerdi*, and Auckland Island Tomtit *marrineri*.
Distribution: New Zealand only. Subfossil, midden and historical records show that Tomtits were throughout the mainland of New Zealand at the time of European settlement. In the North Island, they are widespread and locally common from Kaitaia to Cape Palliser, although they are scarce between Whangarei and the southern Waikato, sparsely distributed in the lowlands and coastal hill country of the east coast from East Cape to southern Wairarapa, and absent from agricultural districts in the lowlands of Rangitikei, Manawatu and Horowhenua. Moderate numbers on the Hen and Chickens, Little Barrier and Kapiti Islands, and a few persist on Great Barrier Island. Introduced to Tiritiri Matangi in 2004.

The South Island Tomtit is common to the west of and in the Southern Alps from Farewell Spit and the western part of the Marlborough Sounds to Fiordland, and on Banks Peninsula, in Southland and the Catlins; throughout Stewart Island and its outliers, and on the Solanders Group.

The Chatham Island Tomtit was common throughout the group in the 1800s but disappeared from Chatham Island in the 1970s and was removed from Little Mangere and Mangere Islands in 1976 so that they would not compete with the critically endangered Black Robin, leaving it only on Pitt and South East Islands; but subsequently reintroduced to Mangere Island. The Snares Island Tomtit is throughout the group, and the Auckland Island Tomtit is on Auckland, Adams, Ocean, Rose, Ewing and Enderby Islands.

Throughout New Zealand, Tomtits are in mature native forests, especially open beech forest, in second-growth manuka/kanuka scrub, and in some districts they use older stands of exotic plantations. On The Snares and the Auckland Islands, they feed in tussock grassland with scattered shrubs, and out onto coastal rocks and even floating kelp.

Population: Widespread and locally common, especially in beech forests of the central North Island and the South Island. The Snares Tomtit numbered c. 500 pairs in 1987.

Conservation: Protected endemic. Tomtits declined with the clearance of much lowland forest and the introduction of mammalian predators, but they have adapted well to the changed conditions, and their populations have probably stabilised. The Chatham Island Tomtit has declined through the 1900s to have a restricted distribution on some predator-free islands.

Breeding: Tomtits have been studied on the mainland, the Chathams and The Snares. They maintain their territory all year, and usually keep the same partner year after year. From July onwards, males start to sing their territorial song, and territorial defence and singing increase markedly in August. The female takes about 4 days to build its bulky cup nest of twigs, bark, fibres and moss, bound together with cobwebs and lined with tree-fern scales, moss, fine grasses and occasionally with feathers or wool. It is 1–10 m (usually 2–4 m) off the ground in a sheltered cavity in a tree where a branch has broken off and rotted out, in a fork, attached to the trunk of a tree fern or in a thick tangle of vines such as *Muehlenbeckia* or bush lawyer.

North and South Island Tomtits lay in September–January, during which each pair raises up to three broods, but if their nests fail, they re-lay up to six times in a season. They lay 3–4–6 cream eggs (18 x 15 mm) with yellowish-purple spots at the larger end. Eggs are laid daily, usually shortly after sunrise. The female incubates for 15–16–17 days, and broods the chicks. She is regularly fed near the nest by the male, and both parents feed the nestlings. The fledging period is 17–18–20 days. Fledglings are fed by both birds, but once the female starts renesting, the male takes full care of them. Juveniles start foraging at

c. 28 days old, but continue to be fed until c. 35 days old. Once independent, they soon disperse from their natal territory.

Chatham Island Tomtits lay from late September to mid-December and raise two broods. They lay 2–**3**–4 eggs (19 x 15 mm). The female incubates for 17–18 days, and the chicks fledge at 16–21 days old.

Snares Island Tomtits have similar breeding behaviour, but most nests are within a metre of the ground in hollows in logs or stumps, or among roots of wind-thrown trees. They lay from mid-October to mid-December and usually raise only one brood each year, but in 'El Niño' years, which are exceptionally windy and wet on The Snares, they may not breed at all. They lay 2–**3** eggs (20 x 15.5 mm). The female incubates for 18–20 days, and the chicks fledge at 17–22 days old.

Tomtits start breeding at 1 year old. The oldest Tomtit recorded to date lived just 3 years, but some probably live 10+ years.

Behaviour: Adult Tomtits remain on their territory all year, but only actively defend it from about July to February, when the male patrols his patch and sings from prominent perches. The main territorial song of the male is a loud and clear burst: 'ti oly oly oly oh', often answered by a neighbouring male; a much softer version of this song is sometimes sung by the female. Tomtits have a variety of other calls, the main ones being a simple, short, high-pitched 'swee' used by males and a reedy 'seet' used by females as a contact call. In aggressive encounters between birds, they raise their crown feathers, but in encounters with other species, including humans, all but Snares Tomtits flash the white frontal spot in the centre of their forehead.

Feeding: Diet is mainly invertebrates, supplemented with small fruits in autumn and winter. Main prey are spiders, beetles, caterpillars, moths, weta, earthworms, flies and wasps. On the mainland and at the Chathams, the main search method is 'watch and wait' – perching and scanning an area, and then flying to catch the prey, usually on a nearby trunk or branch. They also glean insects from leaves and small branches, occasionally hover and only rarely catch insects on the wing. On The Snares, Tomtits often forage on the ground and hop about in the leaf litter, as Robins do elsewhere. They also feed on flies that abound in penguin colonies, and perch on seals and sea lions to catch associated blowflies.

Reading: Best, H.A. 1975. *Wildlife – A Review* 6: 32–37. Fleming, C.A. 1950. *Trans Roy Soc NZ* 78: 14–47; 127–160. Kearton, J.M. 1979. Unpubl. MSc thesis, Univ Canterbury. McLean, I.G. & Miskelly, C.M. 1988. *NZ Natural Sciences* 15: 51–59. Miskelly, C.M. 1990. *Emu* 90: 24–27.

306. NEW ZEALAND ROBIN *Petroica australis* Plate 69

Other name: Toutouwai
Size: 18 cm, 30 g
Geographical variation: Three subspecies, each restricted to one of the main islands and its outliers: North Island Robin *longipes*, South Island Robin *australis*, and Stewart Island Robin *rakiura*.
Distribution: New Zealand only. Subfossil, midden and historical records show that Robins were widespread through the mainland of New Zealand at the time of European settlement. In the North Island, they disappeared from northern and southern parts in the early 1900s, and, apart from strong populations on Little Barrier and Kapiti Islands, they are now restricted to a band across the central North Island from Taranaki (but not Mt Taranaki) to the Bay of Plenty and Te Urewera National Park. Introduced to Mokoia Island, Lake Rotorua (1991) and Karori Sanctuary, Wellington (2001).

In the South Island, they are quite common north of Arthur's Pass National Park, in Buller, Nelson and coastal Marlborough, but south of Arthur's Pass they are patchily distributed, with strongholds in Okarito Forest, the eastern foothills of Fiordland, the Umbrella Mountains of northern Southland, and around Dunedin. The Stewart Island Robin is moderately common on Stewart Island and on some outliers.

Robins are found mainly in mature native

forests, but in some districts they use older stands of exotic plantations and scrub.

Population: Widespread and locally common; abundant on Little Barrier and Kapiti Islands and in some parts of the northern South Island.

Conservation: Protected endemic. Robins have declined since European settlement as a result of clearance of much prime lowland forest and the introduction of mammalian predators. The current distribution of Robins is puzzling, as they are common or even locally abundant in parts of the northern South Island, yet generally rare and patchily distributed elsewhere on the mainland, despite no obvious difference in habitat modification or introduced predators present. At Kowhai Bush, near Kaikoura, a colour-banded population declined from 94 to 16 adults in the space of 10 years, probably as a result of predation of adult birds by mustelids and/or rats. Robin numbers on Kapiti Island increased rapidly in the decade after the eradication of possums in the 1980s, thus showing that possums may be a serious predator or somehow alter the habitat to the detriment of Robins. On the mainland, Robins are generally in decline as a result of ongoing predation and habitat changes.

Breeding: Robins keep their territory all year, and usually keep the same partner year after year. From March to July, the main song is a downscale, but in August–December males mainly sing their full territorial song. From July, they start courtship feeding. The female takes about 5 days to build its nest, a bulky cup of twigs, bark, fibres and moss, bound together with cobwebs and lined with tree-fern scales, moss, fine grasses and occasionally with feathers or wool. It is usually 1–4–11 m up in the fork of a tree trunk or fork between large branches, and quite often the nest is built in an old nest of a Robin, Song Thrush, Blackbird or Bellbird. Laying is in July–January, during which time each pair may raise up to four broods, but if their nests fail, they can re-lay up to six times in a season.

They lay 2–3–4 eggs; first clutches are mainly of 2 eggs, and later clutches mainly of 3. The eggs are cream with purplish-brown spots (25 x 18.5 mm, 4.5 g) and are laid daily,

usually shortly after sunrise. The female incubates for 17–18–19 days and broods the chicks. She is called off the nest and fed 20–50 m away by the male 2–3 times an hour while incubating, and both birds feed the nestlings. The fledging period is 19–21–22 days. Single fledglings are looked after by the male, but if there are two or more, the parents divide care of the brood. This division continues until the female starts renesting and then the male feeds all juveniles. They start foraging c. 2 weeks after leaving the nest, but continue to be fed by their parents for 25–50 days before being ousted from the territory. Robins start breeding at 1 year old. The average annual survivorship of adult Robins at Kowhai Bush, during a period when they were stable, was about 70%, giving a mean life expectancy of c. 3 years; however, the oldest Robin recorded lived over 16 years.

Behaviour: Robins are territorial all year but especially so in the breeding season, when the male patrols his patch and sings from prominent perches. The main territorial song of the male is loud and clear, and consists of a variety of simple notes strung together and sometimes sustained for half an hour, broken only by short pauses. Robins also give a short 'chirp' as a contact call. In aggressive encounters between birds, they raise their crown feathers, but in encounters with other species, including humans, they often flash the white frontal spot in the centre of their forehead. In some areas, Robins are shy and secretive, but elsewhere they are bold and can be induced to come near by clearing a patch of leaf litter and then sitting quietly nearby.

Feeding: Diet is mainly invertebrates, supplemented with small fruits in summer and autumn. Main prey are earthworms, spiders, amphipods, beetles, moths and caterpillars, weta, cicadas, stick insects, snails and slugs. Most are caught on the forest floor. Robins often perch on a low branch, supplejack or trunk of a sapling, scanning the ground before flying down to grab their prey. When on the forest floor, they sometimes tremble one foot as a means of inducing prey to move in response to the vibrations caused. They sometimes glean insects from leaves or under bark on a branch or trunk, and occasionally take insects or fruit from a tree while hovering, but only rarely catch flying insects on the wing.

Reading: Flack, J.A.D. 1975. *Notornis* 23: 90–105.

Fleming, C.A. 1950. *Trans Roy Soc NZ* 78: 14–47; 127–160. Powlesland, R.G. 1981. *Notornis* 28: 89–102. Powlesland, R.G. 1981. *NZ J Ecol* 4: 98–105. Powlesland, R.G. 1983. *Notornis* 30: 265–282. Powlesland, R.G. 1983. *NZ J Zool* 10: 225–232.

307. BLACK ROBIN *Petroica traversi* Plate 69

Size: 15 cm; males 25 g, females 22 g
Distribution: Chatham Islands only. Subfossil and midden records show that Black Robins were once widespread through the Chathams group, but by the 1870s they had become restricted to Mangere and Little Mangere Islands. They disappeared from Mangere about 1880, but a few persisted on Little Mangere. In 1976–77, all seven Black Robins were shifted from Little Mangere Island to Mangere, and in the early 1980s some were taken to South East Island, where they subsequently became established. They are now found throughout forest and scrub on Mangere and South East Islands.
Population: 155 birds in autumn 1994: Mangere Island 40, South East Island 115.
Conservation: Protected threatened endemic. The intensive management of the Black Robin, by the Wildlife Service and then the Department of Conservation, is one of the world's outstanding conservation success stories. When rediscovered on Little Mangere Island in 1938, there were 20–35 pairs. Over the years, the habitat deteriorated and the population had declined to just seven birds in 1976. These five males and two females were transferred to a small forest patch on nearby Mangere Island, which was clear of the cats that had caused their disappearance from the island in the 1880s. The Black Robins continued to decline, and by 1979 there were only five birds left, including just one productive pair.

In 1979–88, the Wildlife Service carried out intensive management, which included supplementary feeding to boost breeding, protection of nests from seabirds and starlings, and, in 1980, the cross-fostering of eggs and chicks to Chatham Island Warblers; however, the warblers were unable to raise Black Robin chicks to fledging age. In 1981, female 'Old Blue' laid three clutches. Two clutches of three

eggs were fostered to Tomtit nests on South East Island, and the three resultant chicks were reintroduced to Mangere Island, taking the population to 12 birds. Since then, cross-fostering eggs and chicks to Tomtits, to boost Black Robin productivity, became an essential part of the recovery programme. Black Robins were permanently introduced to South East Island in 1983. With cross-fostering, the population reached 100 birds by autumn 1989, and since then Black Robins have continued to increase without further intervention to 150+ birds.

Breeding: Black Robins maintain their territory all year, and usually keep the same partner year after year. From June onwards, males start to sing their territorial song, and from September they start courtship feeding. The female normally builds 2–3 nests, but only one is completed. It is a neat open cup of twigs, bark, leaves and moss, held together with spider webs, and thickly lined with moss and feathers. They usually build in a shallow cavity; a hollow branch or rotten stump, sometimes among rocks, and occasionally in an old Blackbird nest in a tangle of vines. They readily use nest boxes. Most eggs are laid in October–November, and each pair usually raises only one brood a year; however, they re-lay if they lose a clutch, and this behaviour was used to induce Black Robins to lay up to three clutches in a season through to January.

They lay 1–**2**–3 cream eggs (22 x 17 mm) with purplish-brown blotches and spots. The eggs are laid at 24-hour intervals, normally in the morning. The female incubates for 17–**18**–19 days and broods the chicks. Both parents feed the chicks during their fledging period of 20–**22**–23 days. Young are capable of breeding at 1 year old, but most do not start until 2 years old. The average annual survivorship of Black Robins from 1980 to 1991 was 78%, giving a mean life expectancy of c. 4 years; however, the key female 'Old Blue' lived for 12+ years.

Behaviour: Black Robins are territorial all year, but especially so in the breeding season, when the male patrols his territory and sings from prominent perches. The main territorial song of the male is a clear, simple and sustained phrase of 5–7 notes. Females sometimes sing brief phrases but never the full song. They also have a high-pitched, single-note contact call.

Feeding: Diet is entirely invertebrates such as caterpillars, spiders, beetles, aphids, fly larvae and weta, mostly taken from the forest floor or from low branches. Black Robins generally hop when feeding and only rarely hawk for insects.

Reading: Butler, D. & Merton, D. 1992. *The Black Robin: Saving the World's Most Endangered Bird.* Auckland: OUP. Merton, D.V. 1990. *Forest & Bird* 21: 14–19. Merton, D.V. 1993. *NZ J Ecol* 16: 65–68.

WHITE-EYES   Zosteropidae

85 species in Africa, southern Asia, Australasia and the southwestern Pacific; 1 native to New Zealand.
Small, mainly olive-green forest birds, most with white rings around the eyes. They have a fine, tapered bill and a brush-tipped tongue for drinking nectar, but they also feed extensively on insects and fruit.

308. SILVEREYE *Zosterops lateralis*   Plate 66

Other names: Tauhou, Waxeye, White-eye
Size: 12 cm, 13 g
Geographical variation: This species has complex racial variation in Australasia and the southwestern Pacific. Up to six subspecies are recognised in Australia alone: one breeding in the west, one confined to islands of the Great Barrier Reef, three breeding in the east between South Australia and Queensland, and one breeding in Tasmania. The Tasmanian subspecies *lateralis* migrates to eastern states of the Australian mainland in winter, and it is this form that colonised New Zealand.
Distribution: Breeds in Australia, Norfolk Island, New Caledonia, Vanuatu, Loyalty Group, Banks Island, Fiji and New Zealand. Silvereyes were recorded in New Zealand as early as 1832, and may have established on Stewart Island and in Southland, but it was not until 1856 that they apparently arrived in large numbers in many parts of the country and colonised permanently. The Maori name 'tauhou' means 'stranger', thus implying that Silvereyes were a new bird to New Zealand. It is now among the most abundant of New Zealand birds, being found in native forest and scrub from sea level to the treeline, in exotic plantations, orchards and suburban gardens. Since colonising the mainland of New Zealand, they have spread to all offshore islands, the Kermadecs, Chathams, Antipodes, The Snares, Auckland and Campbell Islands, and possibly provided birds that colonised Norfolk Island in 1904.

There is considerable local movement of small flocks in autumn and winter, mainly seeking fruit or nectar, and banded individuals are often recorded in the same town gardens, or other wintering site, year after year. The pattern of regular seasonal movements is sometimes disrupted by irregular variations in food supply, such as the periodic intense flowering of rata, or in years when there is very good fruiting of kahikatea, when several thousand birds can occupy a forest patch for several weeks or months.

Flocks of Silvereyes have been reported flying northwards up the South Island at night in autumn and winter, and at Farewell Spit flocks have been seen on clear, calm mornings flying very high towards the northeast, and heading for southern Taranaki; however, movement across Cook Strait has not yet been supported by band recoveries.

Population: Widespread and locally abundant. Silvereyes are especially common in podocarp forests and some orchards and vineyards when fruit is available in autumn and winter, and in town gardens in the winter when food (fat, fruit or sugar water) is provided for them in the winter. The only places where Silvereyes are relatively scarce are in open habitats such as tussockland and grassland, and on some offshore islands where the forest and native forest bird communities are relatively intact, e.g. the Poor Knights, Little Barrier and Kapiti Islands.

Conservation: Partially protected native. Because the Silvereye colonised New Zealand naturally (although possibly helped by sailing ships), it has been classified as a native species. It is likely that Silvereyes have had a significant impact on native forest habitats by changing the pattern of seed dispersal and by competing with other animals for fruit, nectar and invertebrates, because the biomass of Silvereyes in some forests, especially in autumn and winter, exceeds that of any other bird species. Silvereyes can cause considerable economic damage to grapes and other fruit crops, especially cherries, apricots and figs; although they often feed from fruit already damaged by other birds.

Breeding: Established pairs remain together in winter flocks, but in late winter they leave to set up territories and first-year birds pair up. The nest is a delicate cup suspended like a hammock from twigs and foliage. The nest is woven strongly from fine grasses, rootlets and fibres, with fragments of moss, spider web, lichen and thistledown, which provide camouflage. Nests are from 1–**2**–**3**–15 m above the ground, usually towards the outermost branches of a tree, shrub or tree fern.

Eggs are laid from September to February, during which pairs can raise 2 or 3 broods. Each clutch is of 2–**3**–5 pale blue eggs (17.5 x 13 mm), laid at 24-hour intervals. Incubation starts after the second egg is laid and is shared by both parents during the 10–**11**–12-day incubation period. Both parents brood and feed nestlings during the fledging period of 9–**10**–11 days. The family stays together for 2–3 weeks after the chicks leave the nest, but the young then become independent. The interval between successive clutches has been recorded as 47–60 days. Young breed at 9 months old, and pairs remain together year after year. The oldest banded bird recorded in New Zealand lived at least 11.5 years.

Behaviour: Pairs are strongly territorial during the breeding season, but Silvereyes form winter flocks. Within flocks, there are dominance hierarchies, and birds are often seen fluttering their wings aggressively at another bird. The flocking call, often heard in flight, is an excited chirping 'cli-cli-cli', and single birds often give a plaintive 'cree' call. The song of males in the breeding season is similar to that of the Dunnock but is a less powerful and more melodious mix of warbles, trills and slurs, interspersed with occasional high-pitched plaintive notes; it is usually given from a song-post within a tree or shrub, not from the top like a Dunnock. Also, in autumn they also give a Blackbird-like warbling subsong from dense cover.

Feeding: Diet is varied, mainly comprising invertebrates, fruit and nectar, although some birds rely on fat, cooked meat, bread and sugar water provided at bird tables in winter. The main invertebrates eaten include caterpillars, spiders, bugs, flies and beetles. In the early phase of their colonisation of New Zealand, Silvereyes were known as 'Blightbirds' because they fed on woolly aphids that infested apple trees. They feed on a variety of fruit, including commercial fruit and grape crops, but most fruit eaten is taken from native trees and shrubs, such as kahikatea, rimu, *Coprosma*, fuchsia, broadleaf, hangehange and kiekie. They eagerly take nectar from native plants such as rata, fuchsia, kowhai, rewarewa, kiekie and puriri, and from introduced species such as gums and banksias, but they are often excluded by local Tui and Bellbirds. Their specially modified tongue, with bristles, allows them to lap up nectar.

Reading: Dennison, M.D. *et al.* 1981. *Notornis* 28: 119–120. Fleming, C.A. 1943. *Emu* 42: 193–217. Kikkawa, J. 1961. *Ibis* 103A: 428–442. Kikkawa, J. 1962. *Notornis* 9: 280–291. Kikkawa, J. 1963. *Emu* 63: 32–34. Marples, B.J. 1944. *NZ Bird Notes* 1: 41–48. Moeed, A. & Fitzgerald, B.M. 1982. *NZ J Zool* 9: 391–403. Stead, E.F. 1932. *The Life Histories of New Zealand Birds*. London: Search.

HONEYEATERS

Meliphagidae

About 170 species in Australasia and the islands of the Pacific, to the Bonin Islands and Hawai'i; 3 endemic species in New Zealand. The Red Wattlebird *Anthochaera carunculata* **was twice recorded in New Zealand as a vagrant in the 1800s, but is not covered here.**

Honeyeaters are medium-to-large forest birds with a slightly decurved bill and a protrusile brush-tipped tongue, which is divided at the tip and has its edges frayed. It is used to reach deeply into flowers and drink nectar, or to extract sugar secretions from cracks in bark. Despite their name, all three New Zealand honeyeaters feed on a mixture of nectar, fruits and insects. They follow the seasonal flowering of certain plant species and play an important ecological role in pollinating the flowers of many native trees and shrubs, and dispersing the seeds of mainly small-fruited plants.

309. STITCHBIRD *Notiomystis cincta* Plate 70

Other name: Hihi
Size: 18 cm; males 40 g, females 30 g
Distribution: North Island only. Subfossil and midden remains and historical records show that Stitchbirds were throughout the North Island and on offshore islands such as Great Barrier, Little Barrier and Kapiti up to the 1840s. They have never been reported from the South Island. Up to the early 1870s, they were comparatively common in southern parts of the North Island, as far north as the Waikato. They then declined rapidly, and by 1885 had vanished from the mainland, Great Barrier and Kapiti Islands. They survived only on Little Barrier Island from 1885 to 1980, since when birds have been transferred to Hen, Cuvier, Kapiti, Tiritiri Matangi and Mokoia Islands, and to Karori Sanctuary, Wellington. A few are in captivity at Mt Bruce. They breed on all islands, but the Hen, Cuvier and Mokoia Islands releases have been unsuccessful; but the Kapiti, Tiritiri Matangi and Karori populations are maintained through supplementary feeding.
Population: Several thousand are probably now on Little Barrier Island and fewer than 200 at the other sites.
Conservation: Protected threatened endemic. The cause of the rapid decline in the late 1800s is not known but may be due to avian disease (perhaps introduced with European passerines) or, more likely, the spread of tree-climbing ship rats, stoats and feral cats. The extermination of cats (by 1980) and kiore (by 2004) on Little Barrier Island should allow that population to increase and be more secure. Management aims to establish self-sustaining populations of Stitchbirds on several islands, in case ship rats or stoats get to Little Barrier Island. The other islands tried to date, although lacking ship rats and stoats, may not have enough variety of nectar- and fruit-producing plants, especially since the more aggressive Tui and Bellbirds dominate the best nectar and fruit sources. Although Kapiti Island is large (2000 ha) and the habitat is improving with the eradication of possums (by 1985) and rats (by 1997), it is still short of nectar- and fruit-producing plants and, for some time yet, may not be self-sustaining without the supply of artificial nectar from feeders.
Breeding: Although Stitchbirds are apparently monogamous on Little Barrier, which is their one remaining natural habitat, on Kapiti Island, where there may be a shortage of suitable tree holes for nests and a lack of food plants, they are polygynandrous, i.e. many males and females breeding in the same nest; this is rare among passerines. The Stitchbird is one of only two honeyeaters known to nest in tree holes; they are usually high, in live, mature trees. On Little Barrier, these are mainly in pohutukawa, tawa and puriri; on Kapiti, in pukatea, rata, kamahi and hinau. Nests are usually level with or above the entrance holes, often on top of previous nests. The nest is a platform of sticks

with a cup on top made of tree-fern rhizomes, lined with tree-fern scales and feathers. Eggs are laid in September–March, and several broods are raised each year. They lay 3–4–5 white eggs (19x15 mm), which females incubate for c. 15 days. Both sexes feed the nestlings, and the young take 28–34 days to fledge. The oldest Stitchbird recorded lived almost 7 years.

Behaviour: Stitchbirds are quite nomadic, travelling several kilometres in a day between good feeding sites. During their first winter, the young may form loose flocks with an adult male. The adult male has a loud, explosive whistle: 'wee-a-wee' or 'see-si-ip', a territorial call given near the nest and when feeding. Both sexes give the familiar, loud 'stitch' note – the probable origin of the name stitchbird. It is also given as a warning call whenever

birds are worried, e.g. by intruding humans. Among other calls is a penetrating alarm call: 'yeng, yeng, yeng', like a Bellbird's but higher-pitched.

Feeding: Diet is a wide variety of nectar and fruits whenever available, also invertebrates gleaned from foliage and bark. Normally, whenever Tui and Bellbirds are present, Stitchbirds tend to feed in the lower strata of the forest, taking low-grade sources of nectar; however, when nectar is abundant they feed in the canopy with the other two honeyeaters.

Reading: Boyd, S. 1994. *Recovery Plan for the Stitchbird*. Wellington: DoC. Gravatt, D.J. 1970. *Notornis* 17: 96–101. Rasch, G. 1989. *Notornis* 36: 27–36. Rasch, G. & Craig, J.L. 1988. *NZ J Zool* 15: 185–190.

310. BELLBIRD *Anthornis melanura* Plate 70

Other names: Korimako, Makomako
Size: 20 cm; males 34 g, females 26 g
Geographical variation: Four subspecies; the Bellbird *melanura* shows clinal variation in plumage colour from Northland to Stewart and Auckland Islands; the Three Kings Bellbird *obscura* is confined to the Three Kings Islands; and the Poor Knights Bellbird *oneho* breeds only on the Poor Knights but occasionally visits the nearby mainland of eastern Northland; and the Chatham Island Bellbird *melanocephala* was confined to the Chathams but became extinct about 1906.

Distribution: New Zealand only. Present and often common in forest and scrub areas on the North, South, Stewart and Auckland Islands and many offshore islands. In the South Island they have expanded into settled districts and large exotic plantations, and are common in orchards, gardens, parks and farm shelterbelts, and on river margins. On the mainland north of the Waikato, they became extinct in the 1860s, although, in winter, a few males fly to eastern Northland, e.g. to Tutukaka from the Poor Knights Islands, to Whangarei Heads from the Hen and Chicken Islands, to Leigh from Little Barrier Island,

and to Whangaparaoa Peninsula from Tiritiri Matangi Island. Females, however, seldom fly to the mainland, and so Bellbirds have not re-established, except that juveniles, together with a female feeding them, were seen at Shakespear Regional Park on Whangaparaoa Peninsula in November 1993.

Population: Common in many parts of the South Island and in some forested parts and offshore islands of the North Island.

Conservation: Protected endemic. The cause of the rapid decline of the Bellbird from Northland and around Auckland in the 1860s may have been caused by some disease, because island populations offshore were not affected and Bellbird survive well elsewhere on the mainland in the presence of the same array of introduced mammalian predators.

Breeding: Bellbirds maintain the same breeding territory year after year. Mainland Bellbirds lay in September–January, rarely to March, during which they commonly raise two broods. On the Poor Knights Islands, the laying period is from late September to late November, and usually only one brood is raised. The female makes the nest, which is loosely built of twigs and fibres with a deep

cup lined with feathers and fine grass. Most nests are in dense cover in a fork, but on islands with nesting petrels many are sheltered in a rock or trunk cavity. At daily intervals, they lay **3–4**–5 pinkish-white eggs (23 x 16 mm, 3.1 g) with reddish-brown spots and blotches, densest at the larger end; 2–**3**–4 eggs on the Poor Knights. The female incubates, from laying the last egg, for c. 14 days. Both parents feed the chicks, which fledge at c. 14 days old. Mainland birds can breed at 1 year old. The oldest Bellbird recorded lived 8+ years.

Behaviour: Bellbirds are territorial in the breeding season but may leave the territory to feed at a nearby nectar source. After breeding, they become nomadic and are usually solitary; even though several may be feeding simultaneously in a tree, they defend a feeding territory within the tree.

The famous bell notes are impressive only when given by many birds at once, mostly at dawn and dusk in places of high density and few other species.

Feeding: Diet is mainly nectar from many native and introduced plants, and in late summer and autumn, when flowers are not common, they take fruit. They also eat many insects and spiders by gleaning trunks, branches and leaves; also by hawking. Female Bellbirds take more insects and less nectar than males do, probably because the more aggressive males exclude them from nectar plants. The chicks are almost entirely fed insects.

Reading: Bartle, J.A. & Sagar, P.M. 1987. *Notornis* 34: 253–306. Craig, J.L. & Douglas, M.E. 1984. *Notornis* 31: 82–86. Gaze, P.D. & Clout, M.N. 1983. *NZ J Ecol* 6: 33–38. Sagar, P.M. 1985. *NZ J Zool* 12: 643–648.

311. TUI *Prosthemadera novaeseelandiae*   Plate 70

Other name: Parson Bird
Size: 30 cm; males 120 g, females 90 g (mainland); males 150 g, females 110 g (Chathams)
Geographical variation: Two subspecies; the Chatham Island Tui *chathamensis* breeds on the Chathams only, the nominate race *novaeseelandiae* breeds elsewhere in New Zealand.
Distribution: New Zealand only. Throughout forests and towns in the North, South and Stewart Islands and many offshore islands. They have spread north to the Kermadec Islands, east to the Chatham Islands and south to the Auckland Islands. They are abundant in subfossil and midden deposits in both North and South Islands, being the main passerine found in middens. Tui are mainly forest and scrub birds; however, outside the breeding season they become partially nomadic and travel to towns and rural gardens and forest patches in search of good sources of nectar or fruit. Some birds regularly occupy each year a summer breeding and winter feeding territories that are 20+ km apart.
Population: Common on the Kermadec and Auckland Islands, and locally common in the main islands, but scarce east of the Southern Alps. Chatham Island Tui are now rare on Chatham Island, in moderate numbers on Pitt Island, and common on South East Island.
Conservation: Protected endemic. Tui have adapted well to human changes in New Zealand. Even though much prime lowland forest has been cleared, the widespread planting of flowering plants (especially gums, banksias, kowhai, flax and puriri) in town and rural areas has probably provided them with a regular year-round food supply. Tui play an important ecological role as pollinators of many native trees, and, being highly mobile, they are one of the main dispersers of seeds of plants with medium-sized fruits.
Breeding: Tui establish their territories in September–October and sing from high perches, especially in the early morning and late afternoon. The female alone builds the nest. It is a bulky structure of twigs and sticks, lined with fine grasses, in a fork or an outer branch in the canopy or subcanopy. Eggs are laid in September–January, mainly November–December. They lay 2–3–4 eggs (29 x 21 mm), which are white or pale pink with reddish-brown spots and blotches, especially at the larger end. The female alone incubates for c. 14 days. The young are at first fed by the female, then by both adults, and take c. 21 days to fledge. The oldest Tui recorded lived 12+ years.
Behaviour: Tui are usually solitary, but when travelling long distances between feeding sites they usually wheel upwards calling others, and then travel in small loose flocks. In winter, they sometimes form loose communal roosts. Even though several birds may feed simultaneously in the same tree, they have clearly defined feeding territories. Tui are the dominant honeyeater in New Zealand; they are aggressive and pugnacious, particularly near the nest or a prominent food source. They vigorously chase other Tui and other birds from their feeding territory, and chase other Tui from breeding territories in the forest at great speed and with noisy, whirring wings. The notch in the 8th primary, particularly of males, makes the wingtips flutter, which produces a noise in flight.

They also soar above the canopy and then make a noisy, near-vertical dive back into the forest. The song dialect varies in each district. It consists of rich, fluid, melodious notes intermixed with croaks, coughs, clicks, grunts, wheezes and chuckles. An energetic, high-pitched subsong is only partly audible close up.
Feeding: Preferred diet is nectar, honeydew, fruit and invertebrates. When breeding, they often commute 10+ km in a day to visit a prime nectar source, such as a stand of kowhai, fuchsia, rewarewa, flax, pohutukawa or rata. Outside of the breeding season, they will shift 20+ km to gain regular access to winter-flowering gums, puriri or kowhai, or to good crops of kahikatea fruit. When breeding, they hawk large flying insects, and jump around beating the outside branches of shrubs and trees to disturb stick insects, cicadas and other large insects. They

feed nestlings at first on small insects and nectar, and later also on berries and larger insects, spiders and moths.

In the hand: Juveniles are at first browner (except on wings and tail) and lack the throat tufts for c. 6 weeks. Juveniles and first-year birds may be told by the lack of a notch in the 8th primary until their first complete moult in their second autumn.

Adult males are larger than adult females, and the sexes can be told apart by a combination of wing length, head and bill length, and weight.

Reading: Bergquist, C.A.L. 1985. *NZ J Zool* 12: 569–571. Craig, J.L. 1984. *NZ J Zool* 11: 195–200. Craig, J.L. 1985. *NZ J Zool* 12: 589–597. Craig, J.L. *et al.* 1981. *NZ J Zool* 8: 87–91. Onley, D.J. 1986. *Notornis* 33: 45–49. Stewart, A.M. & Craig, J.L. 1985. *NZ J Zool* 12: 649–666.

BUNTINGS, CARDINALS and TANAGERS
Emberizidae

552 species worldwide, except Australasia; 2 species introduced to New Zealand.
Small birds of open country, with short, robust, conical bills adapted for husking and crushing seeds. The lower bill is hinged at the base to allow large seeds to be swallowed.

312. YELLOWHAMMER *Emberiza citrinella*

Plate 72

Size: 16 cm, 27 g
Distribution: Natural breeding range is Eurasia from Britain to Siberia; many migrate south to winter in North Africa, the Middle East and southern Asia. About 500 Yellow-hammers were introduced into New Zealand by Acclimatisation Societies between 1862 and the early 1870s. They were released in both islands and spread quickly so that by 1900 they were well established throughout the mainland. Now they are found throughout the North, South and Stewart Islands and many offshore islands, and have colonised the Kermadecs and the Chathams, although they remain uncommon on Chatham Island. There is no clear evidence of migration within New Zealand, but vagrants have reached The Snares, Campbell and Lord Howe Islands. Yellowhammers are in farmland, orchards and open tussockland from sea level to subalpine herbfields at 1600 m.
Population: Widespread and locally common.
Breeding: Males start territorial singing in late August. Laying is from October to mid-February, during which two broods are normally raised. The nest is usually built on or very close to the ground in gorse, black-berry, bracken, long grass or other clump of thick vegetation on a bank or other ungrazed ground. A few nests are built above 1 m in a tree, and some have even been built in old Song Thrush nests. The nest is a cup of dry grass, lined with rootlets, moss, hair, wool and feathers. They lay 3–4–5 whitish-pink eggs (21 x 16 mm) covered in fine scribbling of dark brown lines. The female does most incubation during the incubation period of 12–13–14 days. Both parents share the feeding of the young during the fledging period of 12–13 days. The oldest Yellowhammer recorded in New Zealand lived 9+ years, but in Europe one lived 11+ years.
Behaviour: Yellowhammers are territorial during breeding, but in autumn and winter they form flocks of up to 200–300 birds at good food sources such as spilt grain or where stockfood or hay is being fed out. Male Yellowhammers have a distinctive and monotonous song, usually delivered from a conspicuous perch, and rendered 'chitty-chitty . . . sweee' or 'a little bit of bread and no cheese', the 'swee' or 'cheese' is omitted at the start (August) and end (February) of the singing season. The call-note is a ringing 'tink' or 'chip'; a single 'twick' is the usual flight call, and a liquid 'twitup'

is characteristic of winter flocks.

Feeding: Diet is a mix of seeds and invertebrates. Seeds are from a variety of introduced weeds, grasses, clover and cereals. Invertebrates include caterpillars, beetles, flies, bugs and spiders. They feed mainly on the ground, and hop as they search for food in short grass or on bare ground. Yellowhammers sometimes eat newly sown seeds, but generally they are regarded as a colourful addition to open landscapes rather than as a serious pest.

In the hand: Males are larger than females, but their measurements overlap (wing 82–**87**–97 mm

cf. 78–**82**–86 mm). Adult males are much brighter yellow than females or juveniles, and can be reliably told by having over half of each crown feather yellow with a greyish-green tip and a tiny black spot or streak on the feather shaft near the tip. Adult females and first-year males have broad greyish-brown tips to their crown feathers, a narrow central yellow portion and broad black base, and a narrow black shaft streak, while first-year (and rarely adult) females have little yellow on the crown feathers and a prominent black shaft streak. In autumn, adults moult wing and tail feathers, whereas juveniles do not; and so in winter adults have fresh rounded feathers, whereas first-year birds have worn feathers.

Reading: Harrison, J.M. 1955. *Notornis* 6: 176–177.

313. CIRL BUNTING *Emberiza cirlus* Plate 72

Size: 16 cm, 25 g

Distribution: An uncommon and declining sedentary species of southern Europe, North Africa and Turkey, which has its northern limit in southern England. Records indicate that only a few Cirl Buntings were introduced to New Zealand by Acclimatisation Societies: seven were liberated in Otago in 1871, and four in Wellington in 1880 (possibly from Otago stock). Cirl Buntings spread widely but are the rarest of the introduced birds, although easily overlooked. They are found in open country from Northland to southern Otago, but mainly in drier pastoral country with scattered trees or hedgerows, or rough grassland with patches of gorse, briar and matagouri, east of the Main Divide from Gisborne to Otago (especially in Marlborough and Central Otago) and near Nelson. There is some local or nomadic movement and winter flocking into suitable coastal grassland and saltmarsh habitats.

Population: Rare (perhaps 2000–5000 birds), but locally common in Marlborough and Central Otago, and small winter flocks are recorded each year at coastal sites in Tasman Bay.

Conservation: Unprotected introduced species. Cirl Buntings have declined significantly in their natural range, especially in Britain (where the population declined from c. 300 pairs in 1970 to 167 in 1982), probably

because of changes to agricultural practices. Continued persecution of small birds in southern Europe makes their status in Europe tenuous, and so the New Zealand population could become internationally important.

Breeding: Males start territorial singing in late August. Laying is in October–January, during which two broods are probably raised. The nest is built in thick vegetation in a gorse bush, matagouri, briar or macrocarpa 1–5 m from the ground. It is a cup of dry grass and moss, lined with fine grass, hair and wool, sometimes placed in the old nest of another species. They lay 2–**3**–4 bluish-green eggs (21 x 16 mm) covered in black streaks and hairlines. The female incubates for 11–13 days and is fed on the nest by the male. Both parents feed the young during the fledging period of 11–13 days.

Behaviour: Cirl Buntings are territorial during breeding, and some seem to remain on territory all year. In February–August, some birds form flocks of 5–15 birds, mainly in coastal wasteland but also recorded in Central Otago, or join winter flocks of Yellowhammers. The territorial call of the male is heard in the early morning and late afternoon from about mid-August and regularly from October. It is a monotonous, metallic, rattling buzz, resembling a black cricket, delivered up to nine times per minute from a high perch in a tree or powerline. Call notes are a thin 'zit' or 'see', sometimes run together in flight to form a strident 'sissi-sissi-sip'.

Feeding: Diet has not been studied in detail in New Zealand, but they have been seen feeding on seeds of barley grass and weeds, and adults feed their young caterpillars and moths.

In the hand: Males are larger than females, but measurements overlap (wing 77–**80**–83 mm cf. 76–

78–79 mm). Males have a greyish-black throat and chin rather than dull yellowish, spotted darker, in females. First-year males can be similar to bright adult females, but in January–March adults moult wing and tail feathers, while juveniles moult only a few central tail feathers. In winter, adults therefore have fresh rounded feathers, whereas first-year birds have worn feathers, except for fresh central tail feathers.

Reading: Taylor, T.J. 1978. *Notornis* 25: 249–251.

FINCHES Fringillidae

153 species worldwide, except Australasia; 4 introduced to New Zealand.

Small, often colourful birds of open country with short, stout, conical bills and powerful gizzards for breaking up seeds. They have 9 instead of the usual 10 primary flight feathers. Most have small, neat, cup-shaped nests. Their songs are varied and musical.

Reading: Newton, I. 1972. *Finches*. London: Collins.

314. CHAFFINCH *Fringilla coelebs* Plate 71

Size: 15 cm; male 22 g, female 21 g

Distribution: Natural range is Europe, North Atlantic islands, North Africa, the Middle East and western and central Asia; introduced to South Africa and New Zealand. Several hundred birds were liberated in New Zealand by various Acclimatisation Societies in 1862–80. They were slow to establish, but spread widely in the late 1800s and were well established throughout the country by 1920. Now abundant throughout the mainland and offshore islands, and breeding on the Chathams, The Snares, Auckland and Campbell Islands. Vagrants have been recorded from the Kermadecs, Antipodes and Lord Howe Island. They are in farmland, orchards, gardens, exotic plantations and native forest, from sea level to subalpine scrub at 1400 m. Although northern populations in Europe are migratory, there is no evidence of regular migration here; however, Chaffinches flock in winter and congregate in orchards and on stubble and where grain is being fed to stock.

Population: Abundant throughout New Zealand.

Breeding: Pairs form in early spring as winter flocks break up, and males start singing in late July. The female builds the nest over a period of 1–2 weeks. It is a neat cup of dry grass and moss, camouflaged with lichen and lined with hair, feathers and wool, and is usually firmly placed in a fork of a branch or between the trunk and a side branch 1–**3**–18 m above the ground. Manuka, matagouri, gorse, pine and willow are commonly used sites. Laying is from mid-September to late January, with a peak in October–November. They lay 3–**4**–6 greyish-blue (occasionally pink) eggs (20 x 14 mm) with purplish blotches. The female alone incubates for 11–**13**–15 days, and the eggs hatch over 1–3 days. The chicks are brooded by the female and are frequently fed whole invertebrates by both parents. They continue to be fed by both parents for c. 3 weeks after the fledging period of 10–**14**–16 days. The oldest Chaffinch recorded in New Zealand lived almost 10 years, but in Europe the record is 13+ years.

Behaviour: Gregarious in autumn and winter, forming flocks of several hundred birds, often mixed in with other finches. Flocks are sometimes just of one sex. From late July to January, males advertise their territory with a distinctive and loud territorial song – a series of short notes ending in a terminal flourish, and rendered 'chip chip chip tell tell tell cherry-erry-erry tissi cheweeo'. This song is repeated persistently from a high perch. Each male has a slightly different call, and regional song dialects have established through New Zealand. The ordinary call note is a metallic 'pink' or 'chwink-chwink', and the flight call is a soft 'tsip'.

Feeding: Diet is a mix of seeds, invertebrates and fruits. The main seeds eaten are cereals and brassicas, weeds such as redroot and fat hen, and pine seeds from the ground or pulled from newly opened cones. Invertebrates, such as spiders, caterpillars, moths, flies and aphids, are most important in the breeding season, and chicks are fed mainly caterpillars. Small fruits of native shrubs and trees are eaten. They sometimes cause minor damage to newly sown cereal crops and to fruit buds, but rarely damage commercial fruit crops. Chaffinches mainly feed on the ground, walking about with short quick steps. They are sometimes seen hawking for insects above streams and riverbeds, or on the outer parts of conifers.

In the hand: Sexes are easily told by head and breast colours, and males are larger than females: wing 78–**86**–92 mm cf. 76–**81**–88 mm. Only adults moult primaries and tail feathers in autumn. First-winter males have dark grey alula, primary coverts and occasional greater coverts contrasting with the black inner greater coverts. In females, the contrast is less obvious. Adults of both sexes have more rounded outer tail feathers than juveniles, and often have a black centre near the tip of the central tail feathers.

Reading: Jenkins, P.F. & Baker, A.J. 1984. *Ibis* 126: 510–524. Sibson, R.B. 1983. *Notornis* 30: 70–72.

315. GREENFINCH *Carduelis chloris* Plate 72

Size: 15 cm, 28 g

Distribution: Natural range is Europe, North Africa, the Middle East and western Asia; introduced to the Azores, southeastern Australia and New Zealand. Fewer than 100 Greenfinches were liberated in New Zealand by various Acclimatisation Societies in 1862–68. Despite the modest size of the recorded liberations, they soon became numerous and widespread through farmland of the whole country, and reached the Chathams before 1920. Now they are common through North, South and Stewart Islands and offshore islands. Uncommon on the Chatham Islands, and vagrants have reached the Kermadecs, The Snares and Campbell Island. They have colonised Norfolk Island. Greenfinches favour farmland shelterbelts, edges of pine plant-ations, orchards and large gardens. There is no evidence of regular internal migration, although a bird banded in Upper Hutt moved to Christchurch. There is considerable local movement of flocks in winter, ranging over open paddocks and to the seashore.

Population: Widespread and locally common.

Breeding: Pairs form in early spring as winter flocks break up, and males start singing in September. Sometimes Greenfinches nest in loose colonies, with several pairs nesting within a few metres. The nest is 1–**2.5**–11 m off the ground, near the tip of a spreading branch of a large conifer or oak, or in a fork towards the top of a gorse bush, matagouri, boxthorn or other small shrub or tree. It is bulky and untidy, built of twigs, dry grass, moss, rootlets and wool, and lined with finer material and wool. Most eggs are laid between mid-October and early February, with peaks in late October and early January in the North Island, and in late November and mid-January in the South Island, corresponding with the two clutches per year. They lay 3–**5**–6 pale blue eggs (22 x 14.5 mm) with scattered brown spots and blotches. The female alone incubates for 11–**13**–15 days and is fed on the nest by the male. Both parents infrequently feed the young by regurgitation during the fledging period of 13–**16**–17 days. The oldest Greenfinch recorded in New Zealand lived over 7.5 years, but in Europe the record is over 12 years.

Behaviour: Gregarious in autumn and winter; flocks of 1000+ birds have been recorded. They often join House Sparrows at grain crops or stubble, or Goldfinches at paddocks full of weed or brassica seeds. Early in the breeding season, males have a characteristic butterfly-like display flight. The distinctive breeding season call of the male is a persistently repeated, harsh, drawn-out 'dzwee', reminiscent of a Long-tailed Cuckoo call. A common call, delivered from a prominent perch or in flight, is a pleasant twittering song: 'chichichi-chichit-teu-teu-teu-teu'. Sometimes they simply repeat the 'teu' notes or utter a sweet 'tsooeet' call.

Feeding: Diet is mainly seeds, supplemented with fruit buds and a few invertebrates. The main seeds eaten are maize, cereals, oilseed rape and other seeding brassicas, linseed, sunflowers, fodder radish, peas and hops, and weeds such as redroot, chickweed, storksbill and thistles, and they also eat pine seeds. Greenfinches are a minor pest, as they occasionally attack fruit buds of commercial crops such as apricots, peaches, nectarines and apples, but rarely cause serious damage.

They also eat small fruits of boxthorn and some native shrubs and trees (e.g. kahikatea). Insects such as beetles, flies and wasps are regularly eaten but never form a large part of the diet.

In the hand: Males are larger than females, e.g. wing 82–**87**–92 mm cf. 80–**84**–90 mm. Males have yellow outer webs of the three longest primaries (6–8), and the yellow on the inner (broad) webs of three outermost tail feathers clearly reaches to the black shaft, whereas in females a grey wash separates the yellowish-white inner vane from the shaft. Adult females have a brood patch in the breeding season. Adult males have mainly yellow outer webs of the alula, whereas this is mainly brownish-grey green in first-year males. Females are more difficult to age, but adults have green outer webs to their grey-tipped primary coverts, whereas these feathers are usually olive in first-winter birds. First-year birds often have incomplete moult of tail feathers or wing coverts, and so have contrast between old 'juvenile' feathers and new 'adult' feathers.

Reading: Gillespie, G.D. 1982. *NZ J Zool* 9: 481–486. McLennan, J.A. & MacMillan, B.W.H. 1985. *Notornis* 32: 95–100. MacMillan, B.W.H. 1981. *NZ J Zool* 8: 93–104. MacMillan, B.W.H. 1985. *Notornis* 32: 85–93.

316. GOLDFINCH *Carduelis carduelis* Plate 71

Size: 13 cm; male 16 g, female 15 g

Distribution: Natural range is Europe, North Africa, the Middle East and western Asia; introduced to Argentina, Bermuda, Australia and New Zealand. About 500 Goldfinches were liberated in New Zealand by various Acclimatisation Societies in 1862–83. They quickly established and were widespread by 1900. They are now common throughout the mainland and offshore islands, and have been recorded on the Kermadecs, Chathams, Antipodes, The Snares, Auckland and Campbell Islands, although possibly not established on the Kermadecs, Antipodes, The Snares and Campbell Islands. Recorded breeding on Norfolk Island, and vagrants from New Zealand or Australia have reached Lord Howe and Macquarie Islands. Goldfinches are in farmland, orchards and gardens from sea level to c. 500 m asl. There is no evidence of regular

migration in New Zealand, but there is some local movement and flocking in winter.

Population: Common and widespread at lower altitudes.

Breeding: Pairs form in spring after winter flocks break up, and males start singing in late September. The female builds the nest, a delicate cup of dry grass, fine twigs, moss, wool and cobwebs, lined with thistle down and wool. It is usually in the fork of a branch near the top or outside of a shrub 1–2–6 m from the ground. Many tree species are used, but peach, apple and conifer trees and grape vines are the most common sites. Laying is from mid-October to mid-February, during which some pairs raise two broods. They lay 2–**4**–5–6 pale blue eggs (17 x 12 mm) with reddish-brown spots and streaks. The female alone incubates for 11–**12**–13 days and is fed on the nest by the male. The chicks are brooded by the female for the first week, and at first the male feeds the female, who in turn feeds the chicks. Later, both parents infrequently feed the chicks by regurgitation during the fledging period of 12–**14**–17 days and for 2–3 weeks after leaving the nest. Young can breed at 1 year old. The oldest Goldfinch recorded in New Zealand lived nearly 8 years.

Behaviour: Gregarious in autumn and winter, forming flocks of several hundred birds, often mixed in with other finches. In the breeding season, they defend a small area around the nest but do not maintain an exclusive territory. From late September to early February, males sing from a perch near their nest a pleasant, liquid, twittering 'tswitt-witt-witt', which can be elaborated into a vibrant, canary-like song. The call note is a shrill 'pee-yu', and the flight call is a soft, rambling version of the full song.

Feeding: Diet is mainly weed seeds, supplemented with invertebrates. The main seeds eaten are from weeds such as winged thistles and Scotch thistles in late spring and summer, redroot in autumn and winter, storksbill and meadowgrass in spring. They sometimes damage strawberries when they peck seeds from the outside of ripening fruit, but they cause little damage compared with other introduced birds. Invertebrates such as aphids, bugs, flies, caterpillars and spiders are eaten in small quantities all year, but are more important in spring and are an important part of the diet of young nestlings. When feeding on tall weeds and thistles, birds flutter from plant to plant and hang upside down to extract the seeds.

In the hand: Males are larger than females: wing 72–**77**–82 mm cf. 70–**74**–78 mm. Males have more extensive red on the throat and head, especially above and behind the eye. The nasal bristles of adult males are black, whereas they are grey to blackish grey in adult females. Most first-year males also have black nasal bristles, and most first-year females have light grey bristles, but some intermediate juveniles are not possible to sex. In autumn, adults moult wing and tail feathers, whereas juveniles have slightly worn and distinctly pointed outer tail feathers, and at least some of the greater coverts are not moulted and so are tipped buffish white rather than yellow or white as in adults.

Reading: Campbell, P.O. 1972. Unpubl MSc thesis, Massey Univ. Middleton, A.L.A. 1970. *Emu* 70: 159–167. Niethammer, G. 1970. *Notornis* 17: 214–222.

317. REDPOLL *Carduelis flammea* Plate 71

Size: 12 cm, 12 g

Distribution: Natural range is northern parts of North America, Europe and Asia; many migrate south to winter in lower latitudes in the United States, around the Mediterranean and in southern Asia. About 500 Redpolls were liberated in New Zealand by the various Acclimatisation Societies in 1862–75, including over 200 near Auckland in 1872. They quickly established and were widespread by 1900. They are now throughout the mainland and offshore islands, although much more common in the South Island than in the North Island. They have colonised the Kermadecs, Chathams, Antipodes, The Snares, Auckland and Campbell Islands, and also Macquarie Island. Vagrants have been recorded on Lord Howe Island. Redpolls are in farmland, orchards, tussock-land, coastal dunes, forest and scrub margins, and subalpine scrub and herbfields from sea level to 1750 m, more common at higher altitudes and in less intensively developed areas. There is no evidence of regular migration in New Zealand, but there is some local movement and flocking in winter.

Population: Common, especially in higher and drier parts of the South Island.

Breeding: Pairs form in flocks in late winter, and males establish territories and start singing in September. The female builds the nest, which is a small, neat cup of dry grass, fine twigs, moss, wool and cobwebs, lined with feathers, willow catkins, wool and hair. It is usually placed in a fork in a low shrub such as gorse, matagouri, briar or lupin, 0.2–**2**–7 m from the ground. Laying is from mid-October to early February, during which most pairs probably raise two broods. They lay 3–4–6 bluish-green eggs (15 x 11.5 mm) with light brown spots and streaks. The female incubates for 10–11–15 days and is fed on the nest by the male. The chicks are fed infrequently by regurgitation by both parents and fledge at 12–13–15 days old. They continue to be fed for 1–2 weeks after leaving the nest. The oldest Redpoll recorded in New Zealand lived c. 8 years.

Behaviour: Gregarious in autumn and winter, sometimes forming huge flocks of several thousand birds. One flock in the King Country was estimated to be of 100,000+ birds. In the breeding season, they defend a small area around the nest, and sometimes they form loose colonies where breeding sites are limited. From late September to early February, males sing from a perch near their nest a short, rippling trill. The most common and distinctive call is the harsh, rattling flight call: 'chich-chich-chich', sometimes followed by a 'bizzzz'. The alarm note is a plaintive, 'questioning' 'tsooeet'.

Feeding: Diet is mainly small weed and grass seeds, supplemented with invertebrates and

fruit buds; unlike most birds, Redpoll chicks are fed only seeds. The preferred seeds are grasses, sedges, clovers, brassicas, dock, red-root, fat hen, thistles and evening primrose. Redpolls sometimes cause serious economic damage by destroying fruit buds of apricots and peaches during a brief period in spring, and also damage strawberries when they peck seeds from the outside of ripening fruit.

In the hand: Males are slightly larger than females: wing 64–**69.5**–75 mm cf. 62–**67.5**–72 mm. In autumn and winter, adult males have pinkish-red breast, flanks, rump and sides of head, whereas adult females have pinkish red on the head only. In spring and summer, females develop a brood patch, and birds with pinkish-red breast and flanks are adult males, but birds lacking these pink markings, and without a brood patch, cannot be sexed. Adult males and females can have similar head markings. In autumn, adults moult all wing and tail feathers, while juveniles may moult only a few tail feathers, and so in winter juveniles have distinctly worn wing and tail feathers.

Reading: Fennell, J. et al. 1985. *Notornis* 32: 245–253. Fennell, J. & Sagar, P.M. 1985. *Notornis* 32: 254–256. Stenhouse, D. 1962. *Notornis* 10: 61–67.

SPARROWS and WEAVERS   Ploceidae

143 species in Africa, Europe and Asia; 1 species introduced to New Zealand.
Small birds of open country with heavy conical bills for eating seeds. Most build untidy domed nests, or nest in holes. Calls are simple and unmusical.

318. HOUSE SPARROW   *Passer domesticus*   Plate 71

Size: 14 cm, 30 g
Distribution: Natural range is Europe, North Africa, the Middle East and Asia, except for the southeast; introduced to North America, South America, southern Africa, Java, Australia, New Zealand and various islands including Mauritius, New Caledonia and Hawai'i. Over 100 House Sparrows were liberated in New Zealand by various Acclimatisation Societies in 1866–71. They quickly became established and were widespread by 1880, at about which time they colonised the

Chatham Islands. Now common throughout the mainland and inhabited offshore islands, and the Chathams and Norfolk Island, and recorded from the Antipodes, The Snares, Auckland and Campbell Islands. They are mainly in arable farmland, rural and suburban gardens, town streets and around grain-storage or grain-handling facilities. House Sparrows are generally sedentary, but a few long movements have been recorded in New Zealand: 300 km from Upper Hutt to Reporoa,

85 km from Hawera to Raetihi and 65 km from Ward to Picton.

Population: Abundant, especially in arable farmland and in towns.

Breeding: Pairs form in flocks in late winter, and males establish territories in September. The male spends about a week building a bulky, domed nest with a side entrance. It is usually in a hole in a tree, building, cliff or nest box, or near the tops of tall conifers or gums, and occasionally on an abandoned Blackbird or Song Thrush nest in a low shrub. Laying is from late September to January, during which time 3–4 broods are raised. They lay 1–**4**–6 greyish-white eggs (22 x 15.5 mm, 2.9 g) marked with brown spots and streaks. Eggs are laid daily, shortly after dawn. Both the birds incubate, from the laying of the penultimate egg, for 10–**12**–15 days. The chicks are fed by both parents and fledge at 11–**15**–19 days old. House Sparrows breed at 1 year old. The oldest bird recorded in New Zealand lived over 15 years.

Behaviour: Gregarious, feeding in flocks of hundreds of birds and roosting in their thousands in dense conifers and bamboo stands or in buildings in the autumn and winter. In the breeding season, they defend a small area around the nest, and sometimes form loose colonies where breeding habitat is limited. From late September to January, males call from a perch near their nest a series of unmusical chirps. At roosts, the chirping of many birds creates a loud chattering.

Feeding: Diet is mainly cereal, grass and weed seeds, supplemented with invertebrates, fruit and nectar. The main seeds eaten are standing or stubble wheat and barley, maize, grasses (especially toetoe), fat hen, redroot and matt amaranth. Invertebrates are rarely eaten by adults but form the most important part of the diet of young nestlings. Main invertebrates eaten are beetles, caterpillars, leafhoppers, grasshoppers, flies and spiders. In late summer, they frequently chase and catch cicadas. House Sparrows are probably the most economically important bird pest in New Zealand, by causing serious damage to wheat, barley and maize crops, and lesser damage to oats and seedling peas and brassicas. They also attack grapes, cherries and other ripening fruit, and feed on grain products being fed to livestock and poultry.

In the hand: Males are slightly larger than females: wing 71–**78**–84 mm cf. 70–**75**–80 mm. In summer, recently fledged juveniles resemble adult females but have fresh wing and tail feathers. Juvenile males usually have a dusky throat patch, rather like the adult female, while juvenile females have a grey throat. In autumn, all birds moult wing and tail feathers, and so after moult is complete, ages are impossible to determine; however, during moult the unmoulted wing feathers of adults are very worn compared with those of juveniles.

Reading: Baker, A.J. 1980. *Evolution* 34: 638–653. Dawson, D.G. 1970. *NZ J Ag Res* 13: 681–688. MacMillan, B.W.H. 1981. *NZ J Zool* 8: 93–104. MacMillan, B.W.H. & Pollock, B.J. 1985. *NZ J Zool* 12: 307–317. Summer-Smith, J.D. 1963. *The House Sparrow*. London: Collins.

STARLINGS and MYNAS — Sturnidae

106 species in Africa, Europe and Asia; 2 introduced to New Zealand.

Medium-sized birds of open country and forest. Most species are dark, sometimes with a glossy sheen of purple or green. The bill is straight and slender, and they are generally omnivorous. Most nest in holes. Their calls are highly varied, and they often mimic other species.

319. STARLING *Sturnus vulgaris* Plate 73

Size: 21 cm, 85 g

Distribution: Natural breeding range is northern and central Europe, the Balkans, the northern Middle East and in Russia east to the Urals; many migrate south to winter on the Iberian Peninsula, the Mediterranean, North Africa, southern Middle East and Asia Minor east to India. Widely introduced around the world and now established in North America, South Africa, Australia, New Zealand and on some oceanic islands. About 1000 birds were introduced to New Zealand by Acclimatisation Societies and private individuals in 1862–83. Most introductions were successful, and Starlings soon spread throughout the country. Now abundant throughout the mainland, suitable offshore islands and the Chathams in farmland, orchards, gardens and forest edges, but rarely deep in forests. They breed on the Kermadec, Bounty, Antipodes, The Snares, Auckland and Campbell Islands; in these more remote sites they feed along sandy and rocky shores or in grassland, and nest in tree hollows or rock crevices. They have also spread to Tonga, southern Fiji, Lord Howe, Norfolk and Macquarie Islands. There is no evidence of migration within New Zealand. In winter, large flocks are often seen flying purposefully as they converge on favoured roosts; these flocks can travel 30+ km between their roosting and feeding site each day. Favoured roosts are in isolated stands of tall trees (especially macrocarpas) and on cliffs or islands.

Population: Locally abundant and probably one of the most numerous species in New Zealand. Starlings were extremely common up to the 1940s but then declined, probably because of the widespread use of DDT to kill pasture pests. Since that insecticide has been banned, numbers have increased again.

Breeding: Males visit their nest site in the early morning all year, but it is not until August–September that they stay nearby all day and defend the site from other males. The nest is a cup of dry grass, twigs and leaves, usually in the hole of a tree, cliff or building, but sometimes they will nest in the

base of a toetoe, pampas or flax, in tight-growing cypresses or in a thick tangle of vegetation in a pine tree. Starlings readily use 18 x 18 x 30 cm deep nest boxes with a 6 cm diameter entrance, especially if raised 2–3 m off the ground in an open situation. Laying is highly synchronised; in most parts of the country first eggs are laid in the second or third week of October. First breeders usually start a little later, and lost clutches are replaced, producing a second peak in early November. Second clutches are laid by 30–50% of successful breeders, and so there is a third peak from late November to the first week of December. Clutches are of 1–**4–5**–9 eggs, but those of over 6 eggs are usually laid by more than one female. First clutches and those laid by experienced pairs are usually larger than replacement or second clutches, or those laid by new pairs.

The clear pale blue eggs (30 x 21 mm) are laid daily in the early morning. Incubation begins with the laying of the last egg and is shared by both parents during the day, but by the female alone at night, for 11–**12**–13 days. Both parents feed the nestlings during the fledging period of 18–**20**–24 days. The young are often fed for 1–2 weeks after their leaving the nest. Many young females breed at 1–2 years old, but males rarely breed until 2–3 years old. In New Zealand, adult survivorship is at least 72%, giving a life expectancy of just over 3 years; however, the oldest banded bird lived 14+ years, and in Europe the record is 23 years.

Behaviour: Gregarious in autumn and winter, forming feeding flocks of up to 1000 birds, and they form even larger flocks as they head towards their evening roost. They often stop at staging points before moving on to the final night-time roost, which can include 1 million+ birds. In the breeding season, non-breeders form small flocks of up to 50 birds, and juveniles also form small flocks or join non-breeders shortly after becoming independent. During breeding, Starlings do not defend a feeding area but vigorously defend their nest site. The territorial song, usually delivered from a high perch near the nest, with bill pointed upwards and half-opened wings flapping stiffly, is a lively, rambling medley of throaty warbling, clicking and gargling notes interspersed with musical whistles and imitations of other species or mechanical noises. The two birds most often imitated are Pukeko and California Quail. At large roosts, Starlings maintain a twittering chorus, often late into the night.

Feeding: Diet is a mix of invertebrates and fruit, supplemented with nectar from flowers such as flax and pohutukawa (when their forehead becomes covered in orange-red pollen). Starlings mainly eat small invertebrates, such as grass grubs and porina moth caterpillars, worms, snails and spiders, caught by probing in short pasture or grain stubble, occasionally on beaches or mudflats. Starlings sometimes hawk for insects, especially in calm, warm weather. Fallen fruits are eaten in orchards, but Starlings can cause severe localised damage to grapes and other commercial orchard fruit. In autumn, flocks of Starlings sometimes descend on bush patches where kahikatea is fruiting well and strip the trees of fruit in weeks, thus depriving Kereru, Tui and Bellbirds of a good supply of food through the winter.

In the hand: The sex of most Starlings can be told from eye and bill colours; males have uniformly dark brown or liver-coloured eyes, whereas females have brown eyes with a narrow inner and/or outer margin of yellow or orange. In May–December, when the bill is yellow, the rami of the lower bill of males is bluish, whereas it is pink or yellowish in females. Adults moult in December–February, about a month earlier than juveniles. After autumn, adult and first-year birds that have been sexed can be recognised by the length of the iridescent portion of their throat hackles: adult males >12 mm, first-year males <10 mm; adult females >7 mm, first-year females <6 mm. In addition, first-year birds rarely have yellow on the tongue, and the tail feathers are rounded, not slightly pointed as in adults.

Reading: Coleman, J.D. 1973. *Notornis* 20: 324–329. Coleman, J.D. 1977. *Proc NZ Ecol Soc* 24: 94–109. East, R. & Pottinger, R.P. 1975. *NZ J Ag Res* 18: 417–452. Flux, J.E.C. & Flux, M.M. 1981. *NZ J Ecol* 4: 65–72. Moeed, A. 1980. *NZ J Zool* 7: 247–256.

320. MYNA *Acridotheres tristis*　　　　　Plate 73

Size: 24 cm, 125 g

Distribution: Natural breeding range is from Afghanistan east through India and Sri Lanka to Bangladesh, but either through introductions or natural range extension in the 1900s they have reached much of Southeast Asia. They have been widely introduced around the world and are established in South Africa, Australia, New Zealand, Solomons, New Caledonia, Fiji, Western Samoa, Cook Islands, Hawai'i and some other oceanic islands. Several hundred birds were introduced to New Zealand, mainly to the South Island, by Acclimatisation Societies and private individuals between 1870 and 1877.

Mynas persisted in the South Island (Nelson, Christchurch and Dunedin) until about 1890, but they fared better in the North Island and by the 1930s they were split into two populations: one in the east from Waipukurau to East Cape, and the other in the west from Wanganui to the Waikato. From about 1940, they spread quickly to colonise the Volcanic Plateau and reached Auckland by about 1947, Tauranga and Rotorua about 1950, the Bay of Islands 1960 and Kaitaia 1965. At the same time, they were disappearing from the southern North Island. They were once numerous in Wellington, Masterton and Palmerston North, but apart from a small population based on the Masterton Refuse Tip, and odd other birds, the southern limit is a line from Wanganui to Waipukurau, and this is still shifting slowly northwards. Mynas are locally abundant in the northern North Island in farmland, orchards and suburban gardens, and have colonised some offshore islands such as Poor Knights, Waiheke, Kawau and Great Barrier. They rarely venture far into forests, but can be common on the forest edge.

There is no evidence of migration within New Zealand. In winter, large flocks are often seen flying purposefully as they converge on favoured roosts; these flocks can travel 10+ km between their roosting and feeding sites each day. Favoured roosts are in isolated stands of tall trees.

Population: Locally abundant in northern New Zealand.

Breeding: Pairs stay together year after year and keep the same territory in successive years. The nest is a cup of dry grass, twigs and leaves, usually in the hole of a tree, cliff, building or other structure, but sometimes they will nest in a thick tangle of vegetation. Mynas readily use 20 x 20 x 30 cm deep nest boxes with an 8 cm diameter entrance, especially if raised 2–3 m off the ground in an open situation. Laying is from mid-October to early March, mostly in November and January. Each pair usually raises two broods a year.

They lay 1–**3**–**4**–6 greenish-blue eggs (29 x 22 mm, 7.5 g) daily in the early morning. Incubation starts with the laying of the last egg and is mainly by the female during the day, but by the female alone at night, for 13–**14** days. Both parents feed the nestlings during the 20–**25**–32-day fledging period and for c. 3 weeks after leaving the nest. Juveniles form small flocks when they become independent. Many young form pairs when 9 months old, but only a few females attempt to breed in their first year. In Hawke's Bay, some colour-banded Mynas lived over 12 years.

Behaviour: In the breeding season, they are strongly territorial, and neighbouring pairs often fight furiously; however, in autumn and winter they often feed in flocks of 5–20 birds.

Except for incubating females, Mynas spend the night at communal roosts, some of which are of 1000+ birds. Territorial birds normally have a bout of intense calling for 5–15 minutes when they arrive in their territories in the early morning. Males call more often than females, and pairs sometimes duet. The territorial call is a rowdy medley of notes, raucous, gurgling, chattering, even bell-like, in rapid sequence. Adults with young utter a harsh 'skwark', and the call of flying young is a noisy, persistent 'chi-chi-chi'. At their communal roosts, Mynas maintain a noisy chattering even well after nightfall and before dawn.

Feeding: Diet is a mix of invertebrates and fruits, scraps found at rubbish tips, on roads and from places where stock and poultry are fed. They also eat eggs, chicks and lizards. The main invertebrates eaten include beetle larvae and adults, bugs, caterpillars, worms, flies, snails and spiders, mainly taken from the ground and especially along roads, where many insects are killed by cars. They also feed by pecking prey from the surface in short pasture and grain stubble. In Hawke's Bay, the main fruit eaten was black nightshade and fallen fruits in orchards, but they occasionally inflict damage to grape and other fruit crops.

In the hand: Males are larger than females: wing 131–**142**–150 mm cf. 127–**135**–145 mm.

Reading: Councilman, J.J. 1974. *Notornis* 21: 318–333. Cunningham, J.M. 1948. *Notornis* 3: 57–64. Moeed, A. 1976. *Notornis* 23: 246–249. Wilson, P.R. 1973. Unpubl PhD thesis, Victoria Univ.

WATTLEBIRDS

Callaeidae

3 species, all endemic to New Zealand.

The origin of the wattlebirds and their relationship with other perching birds are obscure and ancient. They have colourful fleshy wattles at the gape, short, rounded wings, limited flight and prefer to progress with leaps and bounds on strong legs. The tail is long and drooping. The bill size and shape is highly variable within the group, but all feed on forest invertebrates and fruits. Their calls are loud and varied.

321. KOKAKO *Callaeas cinerea*

Plate 70

Size: 38 cm, 230 g

Geographical variation: Two subspecies: the North Island Kokako *wilsoni* of the North Island and some offshore islands, and the South Island Kokako *cinerea* of the South and Stewart Islands.

Distribution: At the time of European settlement, the North Island Kokako were widespread in the forests of the North Island and Great Barrier Island. They have gone from forests in Hawke's Bay, the Wanganui hinterland, the Ruahine, Tararua and Rimutaka Ranges, and the Wairarapa. The few that survived at the north end of Great Barrier Island have been transferred to Little Barrier. They are now in low numbers in the much-reduced native forests of Northland (Puketi, Raetea, Waipoua, Mataraua and Waima), Hunua Ranges and in southern Waikato and northern Taranaki. Their main strongholds are tall, mixed lowland forest of podocarp and hardwood in parts of the Bay of Plenty (Mamaku, Horohoro and Rotoehu Forests), the Pureora and Mapara Forests of the King Country, and the northern Urewera Ranges of East Cape. Kokako prefer tall, mixed lowland forest of podocarp and hardwood that has a high diversity of plant species. They have been successfully transferred to Little Barrier and Kapiti Islands. Some are held in captivity at the National Wildlife Centre at Mt Bruce, and at Otorohanga.

At the time of European settlement, South Island Kokako were in the western part of the South Island from northwestern Nelson to Fiordland, also Banks Peninsula and, probably, large areas of beech forest east of the Southern Alps. They were also in forest and scrub on Stewart Island. They probably died out on the South Island about 1960, and only a few, if any, remain on Stewart Island.

Population: North Island, c. 1400 birds, mainly in the northern Urewera.

Conservation: Protected threatened endemic. The decline of Kokako probably has many causes. In the North Island, the clearance and fragmentation of tall lowland forest has turned prime Kokako habitat into isolated pockets. Logging, including 'selective logging', removes many of their main food plants. Predation of eggs, chicks and adults by introduced mammals, especially ship rats and possums, and by Australasian Harriers, and the destruction of understorey food plants by the browsing of goats, deer and possums have limited their breeding success. Experimental control of introduced mammals has increased the number of Kokako at Kaharoa and especially at Mapara, and is being tried elsewhere on the mainland. Birds have been shifted from the mainland to predator-free islands with the aim of improving the total to over 2500 birds, in at least four groups, by the year 2010.

Breeding: Kokako remain in territorial pairs all year. The female builds the nest over several days in dense foliage or beneath the cover of the canopy, 3–**16**–30 m above ground. It is always well concealed from above, and the birds approach from below. Nests are a twig base on which is woven a cup of long stems of epiphytic orchid, filmy fern, rata vine and lycopod, often lined with tree-fern scales, moss, lichen or rotten wood, or they are built directly in a clump of epiphyte. Eggs are usually laid in October–December, but in years when there is a good supply of fruit they may continue laying until March and raise two, exceptionally three, broods.

They lay 2–**3** eggs (37 x 26.5 mm), pinkish grey with brown and mauve spots and splotches. The female incubates for c. 20 days and both parents feed the chicks during the c. 31-day fledging period. The young stay in the adults' territory and are fed by them for up to 12 months, but they are usually independent after 4 months. Females are known to breed in their first year. The oldest Kokako recorded lived at least 11 years, but some probably live to 20+ years.

Behaviour: Pairs or solitary birds (probably mainly males) hold their territory all year and for many years. They sing loudly and for prolonged periods, mainly about dawn, rarely during the rest of the day. Pairs sing delightful organ- or flute-like duets of long, melodic syllables, short clucks and buzzes. The main call is a slow, rich 'ko-ka-ko-o-o-o',

tailing off at the end. The singing bird flaps its wings as it calls. Kokako prefer to bound along branches and from branch to branch rather than fly. Flights are usually short and seldom sustained for more than 50 metres.
Feeding: Diet is mainly foliage and fruit, supplemented with invertebrates. All year, they feed on leaves at all levels of the forest. When available, they feed on the fruits of podocarp and hardwood trees and on berries from a variety of shrubs, epiphytes and

vines. They take insects during summer and autumn, especially when feeding chicks.

Reading: Clout, M.N. & Hay, J.R. 1981. *Notornis* 28: 256–259. Innes J. 1999. *Recovery Plan for North Island Kokako*. Wellington DoC. Innes, J. & Hay, R. 1995. *Notornis* 42: 79–93. Innes J. *et al.* 1999. *Biol Cons* 87: 201–214. Lavers, R.B. 1987. *Notornis* 25: 165–185. MacMillan, B.W.H. & McClure, B.R. 1990. *Notornis* 37: 107–119. Meenken, D.S. *et al.* 1994. *Notornis* 41: 109–115.

322. SADDLEBACK *Philesturnus carunculatus* Plate 70

Other names: Tieke, Jackbird (South Island juvenile)
Size: 25 cm; males 80 g, females 70 g
Geographical variation: Two subspecies: the North Island Saddleback *rufusater* of the North Island and offshore islands, and the South Island Saddleback *carunculatus* of the South and Stewart Islands and offshore islands.
Distribution: Subfossil and midden records show a wide distribution in the North, South and Stewart Islands. At the time of European settlement, Saddlebacks were plentiful and widely distributed in the forests of the main islands and on many offshore islands. They declined during the 1800s after the spread of Norway rats and feral cats, and by 1870 they had largely gone from north of the Waikato. The decline accelerated late in the century as ship rats and mustelids spread, and they had gone from the rest of the North Island and all but one offshore island by 1910. About 500 North Island Saddlebacks survived on Hen Island. Since 1964, they have been successfully transferred to nine islands: Whatupuke (1964), Red Mercury (1966), Cuvier (1968), Lady Alice (1971), Stanley (1977), Kapiti (six releases 1981–89), Little Barrier (four releases 1984–88), Tiritiri Matangi (1984) and Mokoia in Lake Rotorua (1992). Coppermine Island in the Chickens Group was colonised when birds flew the 150 m gap from neighbouring Whatupuke Island. Transfers to Motukawanui Island in the Cavalli group (1983, 1984) failed when a stoat invaded in 1986, and transfers to Fanal Island in the Mokohinau group (1968, 1985) failed for unknown reasons.

South Island Saddlebacks disappeared from the main islands somewhat later than *rufusater* in the North Island. However, they survived on Big South Cape Island (930 ha) and two adjacent islets, Pukeweka (2 ha) and Solomon (25 ha), off the southwest corner of Stewart Island, until the accidental arrival of the ship rat in 1963. In 1964, 36 were shifted successfully to nearby Big and Kaimohu Islands, and in 1965, 30 were shifted unsuccessfully to the Inner Chetwode Islands, Marlborough Sounds. Since 1965, they have been transferred to many islands off Stewart Island, to Breaksea (1992) and South Passage (2001) Islands in Fiordland (1992), and in Marlborough Sounds, to the Inner Chetwodes again (1969; unsuccessful), to Maud Island (1980, 1982; unsuccessful) and to Motuara Island (1994).
Population: c. 5000 North Island Saddlebacks, but only c. 650 South Island Saddlebacks in 1992.
Conservation: Protected threatened endemic. The decline of Saddlebacks seems to have been linked to the spread of rats, cats and mustelids. Although they can survive in tall forest in the presence of Pacific rats, numbers increased dramatically in young forest on Red Mercury Island in the three years after the Pacific Rats were eradicated. Because of island transfers, provision of nest boxes, and better rodent control, and plans to eradicate rodents from many island reserves, both subspecies are now secure.
Breeding: Saddlebacks nest in tree holes, rock crevices, tree-fern crowns and dense

epiphytes, usually close to the ground. They make their nests of rootlets, leaves and twigs, lined with fine grasses, bark fibres and tree fern scales. Eggs are usually laid in October–January, and one brood is raised, but at recently colonised sites where resources are unlimited they can breed from August to May and raise up to 4 broods. They lay 1–**2**–**3**–4 grey or white eggs (30 x 22 mm) with dark blotches and streaks, mainly at the larger end. Females alone incubate for c. 18 days (North Island) or c. 20 days (South Island). Both adults feed the young, which fledge at c. 26 days old. The oldest bird lived at least 17.5 years. **Behaviour:** Pairs hold their territory all year and defend it loudly. The main call is a loud, far-carrying 'cheet, te-te-te-te'; the long, steady, introductory note is followed by up to 30 short notes. Saddlebacks are active and inquisitive. They prefer to bound along branches, from branch to branch and across the forest floor rather than fly. Flights are noisy, rapid and usually short, seldom sustained for more than 50 metres. Saddlebacks roost in cavities that are often on or near the ground, under overhanging stream banks or several metres up in tree holes or beneath epiphytes.

Feeding: Diet is mainly invertebrates, but in season they also take a wide variety of fruits and nectar. They take invertebrates from the forest floor to the canopy. On the forest floor, they rummage in the litter and dig into rotting logs with their strong, chisel-shaped bills. On trunks and branches, they examine crevices, sometimes inserting one mandible only, or forcibly open their bills to prise off bark or to unroll dead, curled leaves. This feeding is vigorous and noisy, often attracting Fantails or Whiteheads, which feed on insects that have been disturbed. They hold large insects such as weta with one foot and pull them apart with the bill.

In the hand: Males have longer tarsi, with little overlap: 40–**41.8**–44 cf. 36.5–**38.8**–40.5 mm.

Reading: Blackburn, A. 1965. *Notornis* 12: 191–207. Jenkins, P.F. 1978. *Anim Behav* 26: 50–78. Jenkins, P.F. & Veitch, C.R. 1991. *NZ J Zool* 18: 445–450. Lovegrove, T.G. 1996. *Biol Cons* 77: 151–157. Lovegrove, T.G. 1996. *Notornis* 43: 91–112. Merton, D.V. 1965. *Notornis* 12: 208–212. Merton, D.V. 1965. *Notornis* 12: 213–222. Rasch, G. & McClelland, P. 1993. *Notornis* 40: 229–231. Roberts, A. 1994. *South Island Saddleback Recovery Plan*. Wellington: DoC.

323. HUIA *Heteralocha acutirostris*   Plate 74

Size: Males 45 cm (bill 60 mm), females 48 cm (bill 104 mm)
Distribution: Extinct; formerly North Island only. Subfossil and midden remains have been found from North Cape to Wellington. Huia were recorded after European settlement only from forests from the Raukumara Range and the Turakina River south to the Wairarapa and the Rimutaka Range, near Wellington. The last accepted record was of three birds seen by W.W. Smith in 1907, but quite credible reports were made up to c. 1920.
Likely causes of extinction: A long period of Polynesian settlement, during which the birds' range shrank markedly, followed by extensive destruction of prime habitat of lowland forest after European settlement, especially in the Manawatu, the southern Hawke's Bay and the Wairarapa. Introduced predators, especially ship rats, cats and

mustelids, probably killed many birds. The final demise of Huia may have been brought by the collection of many specimens for museum skins; e.g. 646 skins were collected from the southern Hawke's Bay in a month in 1888.
Breeding: Little is known. The nest was a large structure of sticks and twigs with finer material lining the cup. The clutch was 2–4 (45 x 30 mm) eggs, greyish with brown and purplish markings.
Behaviour: Huia were almost always in pairs, readily attracted and easily caught or shot. They travelled on the ground or in the canopy in long leaps and bounds, flying only short distances on their rounded wings. Their alarm call was a shrill whistle, which was easily imitated, bringing them to investigate.
Feeding: Huia were one of the few birds in the world whose sexes differed in bill shape.

The male had a short, chiselling bill and concentrated on the outer surfaces of wood; it had a special ability to insert its bill into rotting wood and then force it open to split the wood. The female probed its long, decurved bill deeply so as to retrieve insects unobtainable to the male. They were seen to take huhu grubs and weta, and took other insects, spiders and berries.

Reading: Medway, D.G. 1968. *Notornis* 15: 177–192. Phillipps, W.J. 1963. *The Book of the Huia.* Christchurch: Whitcombe & Tombs.

WOODSWALLOWS — Artamidae

10 species in Australasia; 2 are vagrants to New Zealand, although 1 of them bred once.

Woodswallows are not closely related to the swallows (Hirundinidae) and are probably related most closely to the bell magpies (Cracticidae). They are accomplished fliers, soaring and gliding gracefully on long, curved wings as they catch insects with their short, stout bill with a strongly decurved upper surface. They also feed on the ground and take nectar and pollen. Woodswallows build a flimsy platform nest of fine twigs in a tree fork. They are gregarious, often roosting huddled in tight bunches.

324. MASKED WOODSWALLOW *Artamus personatus* Plate 65

Size: 19 cm
Distribution: Breed in mainland Australia only. They are migratory and nomadic in Australia, and a pair once reached New Zealand. The birds were seen at Naseby, Central Otago, from January 1972 to August 1973, and although a nest was not seen, they are believed to have reared two chicks in an exotic pine plantation in the summer of 1972–73.
Breeding: In Australia, most nests are within several metres of the ground. They lay 2–3 pale greyish-white eggs (21 x 17 mm), which are profusely marked with brown blotches and smudges, especially at the larger end. Both adults incubate and feed the young. Flying but apparently dependent young were first seen at Naseby in early March 1973.
Behaviour: A persistent twittering and chattering kept the Naseby birds in contact. They often roosted huddled together on a wire or branch.

Reading: Child, P. 1974. *Notornis* 21: 85–87. Child, P. 1975. *Notornis* 22: 67–68. Darby, J.T. 1972. *Notornis* 19: 114–117.

325. WHITE-BROWED WOODSWALLOW *Artamus superciliosus* Plate 65

Size: 19 cm
Distribution: Breed in mainland Australia only, especially in eastern states. They are migratory and nomadic, and vagrants have reached New Zealand. Four males were seen at Naseby Forest, Central Otago, between December 1971 and July 1973, associating with a pair of Masked Woodswallows that apparently bred there. On 21 September 1991, a single male appeared on the site of the limeworks at Miranda, Firth of Thames.

Reading: Child, P. 1974. *Notornis* 21: 85–87. Child, P. 1975. *Notornis* 22: 67–68. Darby, J.T. 1972. *Notornis* 19: 114–117.

BELL MAGPIES

Cracticidae

10 species in Australasia; 1 introduced to New Zealand.

Medium-to-large crow-like songbirds. They are mostly black, grey and white, and have large, powerful, straight bills. They are omnivorous and feed mainly on the ground in open or lightly wooded country. They have loud, often tuneful calls.

326. AUSTRALIAN MAGPIE *Gymnorhina tibicen* Plate 73

Size: 41 cm, 350 g

Geographical variation: Two subspecies were brought to New Zealand: the White-backed Magpie *hypoleuca* of southeastern Australia and Tasmania, and the Black-backed Magpie *tibicen* of northern Australia and New Guinea. The two subspecies interbreed where they meet in Australia. In New Zealand, they also interbreed, but the White-backed Magpie clearly predominates except in Hawke's Bay and in North Canterbury, where up to 95% of birds are of the Black-backed form.

Distribution: Natural range is Australia and southern New Guinea. Over 1000 Magpies were introduced into New Zealand by Acclimatisation Societies in 1864–74, with the main releases being on Kawau Island and in Hawke's Bay, Wellington, Canterbury and Otago. The Otago liberation failed, but the others were successful, and Magpies spread slowly so that by 1945 there were three discrete populations: from the Bay of Islands to South Auckland, the southern North Island, and the eastern South Island from Kaikoura to near Dunedin. The spread has continued, and Magpies are now in open pasture, forest patches and suburban areas throughout the North Island and on suitable offshore islands, and through the eastern South Island from Blenheim to Southland, and on the West Coast around Hokitika, the Grey and Inangahua Valleys. Magpies are scarce but increasing in inland Marlborough, Nelson, Buller and South Westland.

Population: Locally common in hill country and arable farmland with shelterbelts of pines, macrocarpas or gums.

Breeding: The social organisation of Magpies is complex: pairs, family groups of 2–10 birds and unrelated groups of 2–10 birds defend territories all year. There are also non-territorial flocks of up to 80 birds, mainly yearlings and subadults. In each defended territory, there is normally only one breeding pair, but sometimes two females have separate nests within the territory, each attended by a different male. The breeding birds do not receive help at the nest from the other birds in the territory, and breeding success of groups is no better than for pairs. Nest-building begins in June. The nest is a platform of twigs with a cup lined with small twigs, leaves, grass and wool. It is usually high in tall trees such as pines, macrocarpas or eucalypts, but sometimes on powerpoles and in low hedges if tall trees are absent. Laying is in July–November; later nests are mostly replacement clutches but some are true second clutches.

They lay 2–**3**–**4**–5 pale bluish-green eggs (39 x 28 mm) with olive blotches. The female alone incubates for 20–21 days. Chicks are fed by both parents and fledge at c. 28 days old. A few females breed at 1 year old, but most Magpies are at least 3 years old when they start breeding. In the Manawatu, survivorship of adults averaged 85%, giving a life expectancy of 6 years. In Australia, the oldest banded Magpie lived 19+ years.

Behaviour: Many Magpies are territorial all year, some in pairs but others in groups of related or unrelated birds. During the breeding season, some individuals become fiercely territorial and attack people and other animals approaching the nest. Many yearlings and some subadults remain in non-territorial flocks throughout the year, and, although sometimes termed 'nomadic', these flocks are usually found in the same area year after year. The territorial song is a beautiful, flute-like carolling, described by the poet Denis Glover as 'quardle oodle ardle wardle doodle', and is most often heard in the early morning and at dusk when birds are going to roost.

Feeding: Diet is mainly invertebrates, supplemented with some seeds and occasional vertebrates and carrion. Magpies were introduced to New Zealand to control pasture pests and were protected until 1951. They eat many harmful pests including grass grubs, weevils, porina and army worm caterpillars, but probably do not keep these pests under control. They also eat worms, spiders, ants, flies, crickets and snails. Plant material includes seeds and grain. Occasional small birds, eggs, chicks, lizards, mice and sick or dead sheep and lambs are also eaten. Magpies usually feed in open pasture or on ploughed paddocks, and peck prey from the surface, although they can probe quite deeply.

Reading: McCaskill, L.W. 1945. *Notornis* 1: 86–104. Veltman, C.J. 1989. *Ibis* 131: 601–608. Veltman, C.J. & Hickson, R.E. 1989. *Aust J Ecol* 14: 319–326.

BIRDS-OF-PARADISE, BOWERBIRDS and PIOPIO — Paradisaeidae

62 species in Australasia; 1 endemic species is probably extinct.

Until recently, Piopio were considered part of an endemic family (Turnagridae), but now they are treated as part of the birds-of-paradise and bowerbird assemblage, perhaps most closely related to the catbirds (a bowerbird) of eastern Australia. These medium-to-large forest birds are renowned for their often bright plumages and/or complex displays, and many varied calls. They eat mainly fruit and insects.

327. PIOPIO *Turnagra capensis* — Plate 74

Other name: New Zealand Thrush
Size: 26 cm
Geographical variation: Two subspecies: the North Island Piopio *tanagra* of the North Island, and the South Island Piopio *capensis* of the South Island, Stephens Island and probably Stewart Island.
Distribution: Probably extinct. Subfossil and midden records are widely distributed from Northland to Stewart Island. Piopio were widespread in forest at the time of European settlement, especially in the southern North Island and most of the South Island, also Stephens Island. In some districts, they were at first common but had all but disappeared by 1900. The last confirmed specimen in the North Island was shot at Ohura, southern King Country, in 1902. Reports of sightings, mainly in the Urewera Ranges and inland Wanganui/Taranaki up to the 1950s, could not be confirmed. Few birds were seen in the South Island after the 1880s, but unconfirmed sight records persisted in western Nelson and Fiordland to 1963.
Likely causes of extinction: The Piopio's rapid decline suggests introduced predators or avian disease as possible causes, because much forest habitat remained. The spread of introduced mammals, particularly cats, Norway rats, ship rats and mustelids, probably contributed significantly to their demise.
Breeding: The nest was a cup built of twigs and moss, lined with grasses, tree-fern scales or other fine material, in a tree fork usually c. 2 m high. The usual clutch was **2** white or pinkish-white eggs (35 x 25 mm) with scattered black or brown spots.
Behaviour: Piopio lived in forest and scrub from the coast to the mountains. They were very tame and readily came around people camping, where they were easily killed by dogs; Sir James Hector on one occasion counted 40 by his camp on the West Coast. They had a variety of song and calls.
Feeding: Diet included invertebrates, often from the forest floor, plus fruits, seeds and foliage.

Reading: Mead, W.P. 1950. *Notornis* 4: 3–6. Medway, D.G. 1968. *Notornis* 15: 177–192. Olson, S.L. et al. 1983. *Notornis* 30: 319–336.

CROWS and JAYS

Corvidae

About 105 species worldwide; 1 introduced to New Zealand.

Medium-to-large mainly black birds with large, powerful, straight bills. They are omnivorous and feed mainly on the ground in open or lightly wooded country. They have loud, simple, often harsh calls.

328. ROOK *Corvus frugilegus*

Plate 73

Size: 45 cm; male 425 g, female 375 g
Distribution: Natural breeding range is Europe and Asia, east to Siberia and Mongolia; many migrate south to winter around the Mediterranean, in Iran and the northern part of the Indian subcontinent. Several hundred birds were introduced into New Zealand by Acclimatisation Societies in 1862–74. Liberations in Nelson and Auckland failed, even though some Auckland birds persisted to 1905; however, liberations in Hawke's Bay and Canterbury were successful, even if they spread very slowly at first. In the first 50 years to 1920, Rooks in Hawke's Bay had spread only 30 km. Although colonies established near Feilding in the 1920s and near Pirinoa, southern Wairarapa, in 1930, the spread was very slow until numbers built up to pest levels in Hawke's Bay, leading to shooting and poisoning in the 1960s and 1970s. Displaced Rooks then spread rapidly and established colonies near Miranda (Firth of Thames), Tolaga Bay (Gisborne) and Waitotara (Taranaki) in the 1960s; in southern Hawke's Bay and at Aokautere (Manawatu) in the 1970s; in southern Waikato in the 1980s; and in the Pohangina Valley and Taihape area in the 1990s. Rooks in Canterbury spread less than 50 km in the first 100 years, except for the establishment of a colony near Middlemarch (North Otago). Rooks are capable of dispersing widely, with mainly juveniles seen in Northland, Wellington, Southland and on Chatham and Stewart Islands.
Population: Locally common in hill country and arable farmland in Hawke's Bay and formerly around Banks Peninsula. The total population in 1978 was just under 30,000 birds, of which c. 25,000 were in Hawke's Bay and 2500 in Canterbury. Since then, pest-control operations have greatly reduced populations, especially in Canterbury.

Breeding: Occasionally a pair of Rooks nest in isolation, but they usually nest in colonies of 20–100 pairs, and of up to 900 pairs. Even though most birds roost away from their colony in winter, they usually visit the colony each day, in the early morning and sometimes again in the late afternoon. Nest-building begins in August. The nest is a large untidy platform of twigs and lined with small twigs and leaves, in the top of a tall tree such as a pine, macrocarpa or gum. Laying is from late August to mid-November; most late nests are replacement clutches.

They lay 1–**3–4**–7 pale greenish-blue eggs (39 x 28 mm, 16 g) with brown blotches. The female alone incubates for 15–**17**–19 days and broods the nestlings, but the male feeds both the chicks and the female. The fledging period is 26–**33**–38 days, shorter for smaller broods. Some Rooks breed at 1 year old, especially in establishing colonies or in colonies recently reduced by poisoning, but usually they do not start nesting until 2–3 years old. Two Rooks banded in Hawke's Bay as adults were killed when at least 11 years old, and in Europe the oldest Rook lived at least 19 years.
Behaviour: Gregarious all year; breeding in colonies and roosting in 'parishes' (large communal roosts of up to 5000 birds from several colonies) and feeding in flocks. They are extremely wary, especially after being persecuted, and birds quickly take to the wing as danger approaches, and utter their characteristic 'caw' or 'kaah'; an occasional higher-pitched 'kiow' is uttered as the birds circle overhead. The 'caw' call is the usual contact call as Rooks fly in loose flocks.
Feeding: Diet is a mix of invertebrates and vegetable matter. The main prey are beetles (especially grass grubs), flies, caterpillars (especially porina), earthworms, spiders and wasps. When feeding on grass grubs, they

uproot infested damaged pasture in their search. Plant matter eaten includes walnuts, acorns, maize, cereals, pumpkins, seeds of peas and beans, stock feed, and occasional leaves of clover and grasses. In autumn, Rooks store walnuts by burying them in a tuft of grass or in a crevice between clods of ploughed soil, and then in late autumn and winter they search for and recover stored nuts. Birds feeding on newly sown crops methodically work their way along rows, extracting each seed in turn. They sometimes also damage ripening peas, and because of this Rooks in Hawke's Bay were declared a 'pest of local importance' in 1971 and 35,000+ birds were poisoned or shot in the next 6 years. The damage was much reduced on the Heretaunga Plains, but this control caused the rapid expansion in range of the species.

In the hand: Males are larger than females: wing 300–**319**–337 mm cf. 284–**301**–333 mm; bill 56–**60**–68 mm cf. 46–**56**–64 mm. The brood patch of the female in the breeding season is the only consistently reliable feature. Adults have a bare face, whereas juveniles have cheeks and chin covered in black feathers until about August, and nostrils covered in black feathers until about 1 year old. In spring and summer, juveniles have very worn blackish-brown wing feathers, whereas adults have glossy black wings.

Reading: Bull, P.C. 1957. *Notornis* 7: 137–161. Bull, P.C. & Porter, R.E.R. 1975. *NZ J Zool* 2: 63–92. Coleman, J.D. 1971. *NZ J Sci* 14: 494–506. Coleman, J.D. 1972. *Notornis* 19: 118–139. Langham, N.P.E. & Porter, R.E.R. 1991. *NZ J Zool* 18: 389–397. McLennan, J.A. & MacMillan, B.W.H. 1983. *NZ J Agr Res* 26: 139–145. Porter, R.E.R. 1979. *NZ J Zool* 6: 329–337. Purchas, T.P.G. 1979. *NZ J Zool* 6: 321–327. Purchas, T.P.G. 1980. *NZ J Zool* 7: 557–578.

ADDENDUM

Since 1996, the following 11 species were accepted by the Rare Birds Committee of the Ornithological Society of New Zealand as having been reliably recorded for the first time in the New Zealand region. All appeared as single vagrants or stragglers, and none of the species has settled to breed.

LAYSAN ALBATROSS *Diomedea immutabilis*

Size: 80 cm

Description: Similar to adult NZ Black-browed Mollymawk, but slightly smaller, *the bill is pink, tipped black,* and the dark eye patch is usually larger, especially below the eye. Whole body white, except for eye patch, giving a frowning appearance. Upperwings and back, black; tail dark grey; underwings white with broad black edges and coverts, though the latter can be white streaked with black.

Distribution: Breeds on islands in the Hawaiian Chain in the North Pacific Ocean, and on Bonin Island to the south of Japan. Scatters widely across temperate and tropical waters of the North Pacific, but a few stray to the Southern Hemisphere. Recorded from Australia, Norfolk Island and once in New Zealand waters: a bird seen on the Lachlan Banks about 30 km off Cape Kidnappers, Hawkes Bay (December 1995).

BULWER'S PETREL *Bulweria bulwerii*

Size: 27 cm, 100 g

Description: Dainty prion-sized all-dark petrel, except for pale diagonal streak across the base of the upper upperwing, with *very long wings, exceptionally long tail* and small head. The tail is wedge-shaped, but usually appears pointed. Completely dark sooty brown, except for a slightly paler chin and face, and grey diagonal bar across coverts on inner part of the upper wing. Bill black with large nail at tip. Legs pink with grey and pink feet. Flight erratic and often zig-zagging with rapid flapping interspersed with long glides; appears bouyant like a tern or noddy, although rarely rises more than 5 m from the surface.

Distribution: Breeds on islands in the tropical and warm temperate parts of the North Pacific Ocean from off China to Hawaii, Phoenix and Marquesas Islands, and in the North Atlantic Ocean. After breeding, remain in tropical waters across the Pacific, but many Pacific birds migrate to the tropical Indian Ocean. Often recorded off northwestern Australia, and occasionally in the Tasman Sea as far south as Victoria. One New Zealand record: Waikanae Beach (January 1998).

NEWELL'S SHEARWATER   *Puffinus newelli*

Size: 33 cm
Description: A small black and white shearwater in the Fluttering/Hutton's/Manx Shearweater group, but separable from these species by its *black* upper surface, white underwings, and *extensive black feathering on the undertail coverts.*

Distribution: Breeds in Hawaii, especially on Kauai, from late April to October. The wintering grounds are not known, some wander south to tropical or temperate waters of the Southern Hemisphere. One bird caught in American Samoa (January 1993) and a single New Zealand record: a dead female found on Dargaville Beach (November 1994),

Reading: Taylor, G.A. 1996: *Notornis* 43: 187–196.

CAPE GANNET   *Morus capensis*

Size: 90 cm, 2.6 kg
Description: Very similar to Australasian Gannet, but at close quarters it can be seen that its gular (throat) stripe is 3–4 times as long, running from the base of the bill to the foreneck rather than to the chin, the eye is a paler pearly white, and the black face mask is slightly larger. At sea, the tail is usually completely black, but about 10% have white outer tail feathers, like Australasian Gannet. Juveniles and immatures have a great variety of black, brown and white mottled plumages and are indistinguishable from Australasian Gannets at sea.

Distribution: Breeds mainly on islands off South Africa and Namibia, and disperses to coastal waters of southern Africa from the Gulf of Guinea to Mozambique. A few reach islands in the Indian Ocean and off Australia, but since the early 1980s a few have nested with Australasian Gannets in Bass Strait. One New Zealand record, a bird at the Australasian Gannet colony at Cape Kidnappers, Hawke's Bay, between 1997 and 2002.

NORTHERN PINTAIL   *Anas acuta*

Size: 60 cm, excluding 10 cm tail streamers in adult male; 800 g
Description: Large slender duck with *long slim neck and long pointed tail.* Breeding male distinctive with chocolate brown head and neck, except for a white streak down the side of the nape from eye level; lower neck, flanks and upperparts pale grey-brown, breast, underparts and conspicuous patch on thigh, white. Long thin central pair of tail feathers project 10 cm beyond rest of tail. Bill pale grey marked black, legs and feet grey, speculum green. Eclipse male, female and juvenile are brown with pale buff edges to feathers on body and finely streaked buff on neck and head. *Bill, legs and feet grey with black webs,* speculum brown.

Distribution: Breed in the Arctic from northern Scandinavia to Siberia, and in Alaska and northern Canada. They migrate south to winter mainly between 40°N and the equator, but some overshoot to reach Australia, New Guinea, Micronesia and Polynesia. One New Zealand record: a male in breeding plumage at Farewell Spit, October 1997.

Reading: Petyt, C. 1999. *Notornis* 46: 298–299.

LONG-TOED STINT   *Calidris subminuta*

Size: 15 cm, 25 g
Description: Similar to Red-necked Stint, but the colouration is reminiscent of a Sharp-tailed Sandpiper, with its bold rufous markings on cap, back and mantle; slightly smaller with a finer head and neck and a short rear-end, and with longer and *pale greenish yellow legs*. Compared with other pale-legged stints, the Long-toed Stint has bolder colouration, a pale V on the mantle and the long toes, especially the middle one, give the foot an awkward appearance. The middle toe is longer than the bill or the tarsus. The mantle is *streaked* with black and rufous, whereas in the Least Stint it is scalloped.
Distribution: Breeds in the low Asian Arctic from Kazakhstan to Siberia, and most winter in South East Asia and the Philippines, but they regularly reach Australia, especially in the west and north. One New Zealand record, at Lake Ellesmere in August–September 1997.
Reading: Petch, S. *et al.* 2002. *Notornis* 49: 185–186.

STILT SANDPIPER   *Micropalma himantopus*

Size: 21 cm, 50 g
Description: Non-breeding birds are similar to Curlew Sandpiper but longer neck and much longer legs make it look larger, and reminiscent of a small Marsh Sandpiper. Similar in flight to Curlew Sandpiper with a bold white rump, but there is no clear wingbar. The bill is heavier, slightly longer and straighter than that of a Curlew Sandpiper, and the legs are *greenish or yellowish*. Often feeds in belly-deep water by probing vertically.
Distribution: Breeds in Arctic regions of Alaska and Canada, and migrates to southern South America. A few vagrants have reached Australia, and two New Zealand records; both at Lake Ellesmere, in September to November 1998 and in December 2000.

FRANKLIN'S GULL   *Larus pipixcan*

Size: 35 cm, 280 g
Description: Like a very *dark grey* Black-billed Gull or Red-billed Gull with *extensive black on the head, especially from the eye to the hind crown* in all plumages, and a contrasting white crescent around the back of the eye. Back, scapulars and wing coverts slate grey, separated from the black hood, hind crown and upper neck by a white lower neck. Bill black, turning red in breeding plumage; legs and feet black. Flight graceful, almost tern-like, the wings appearing long and narrow. In flight, the *upperwing is grey with a broad white trailing edge*, white wing tips with broad black subterminal band separated from grey upperwing by a white band. Immatures have a black subterminal bar across the entire tail and less distinct wing markings except for the broad white trailing edge.
Distribution: Breeds in inland North America, especially in the prairies, and migrates to the Gulf Coast, Mexico and the western coast of South America. Vagrants have reached Australia, and the one New Zealand record was of a bird in full breeding plumage in July 2002 at Tomahawk Lagoon, Dunedin.

Reading: Onley, D.J. & Schweigman, P. 2004. *Notornis* 51: 49–50.

COMMON KOEL   *Eudynamys scolopacea*

Size: 41 cm, 250 g
Description: A large long-tailed cuckoo similar in shape and sometime appearance to the Long-tailed Cuckoo. The *male is glossy black* with a red eye, grey feet and off-white bill, but immature males have some barring on wings and tail, and sometime on the abdomen. The *female is highly variable, but all have a white or cream streak (moustache) broadening as it runs from the base of the bill,*

under the eye, to the upper breast. Many birds have a head that is black or dark brown, streaked buff. Chin dark or streaked brown. The upperparts are dark brown, boldly spotted white. Underparts white to buff, with fine dark barring or mottling; underwing and undertail dark grey with narrow white barring. Eye red, feet grey, bill off-white. Juveniles are like females, but more heavily mottled with bars rather than spots on the upperparts, eye brown. Like the Long-tailed Cuckoo, the Common Koel calls loudly by day and night in the breeding season; a far-carrying 'koo-well' or 'coo-ee', a rising 'wurra wurra wurra wurra', or a piping, screeching 'keek keek keek'.

Distribution: Southern Asia from Iran to China and the Philippines, and Australasia from Indonesia to eastern Australia. A regular summer breeding migrant to northern and eastern Australia, mainly east of the Great Dividing Range, but rarely south of Sydney. Arrives to parasitise nests of friarbirds, Figbirds, Magpie-larks and large honeyeaters in August or September; departs for wintering grounds in Indonesia in April and May. One New Zealand record: a female was killed when it flew into a window in Lees Valley, Banks Peninsula (March 1997).

BLACK-FACED MONARCH   *Monarcha melanopsis*

Size: 17 cm, 25 g
Description: A slim bird with a rather long tail which often sallies into the air in pursuit of insects. Pale grey upperparts, wings, tail, head and chest, with a sharp border on the lower chest to rufous underparts and undertail. Adults have a large black patch on the forehead, throat, and upper breast, but the black does not reach the eye. Bill blue-grey. Calls varied, but mainly variations on a loud clear 'why-you, wichye-oo', or a mellow descending 'why you'.

Distribution: Breeds in coastal eastern Australia from Cape York to Victoria, especially in the tropics. They migrate from the southern part of their range to northern Queensland and New Guinea, leaving in February to April, and returning in August and September. One New Zealand record: a juvenile male killed by a cat at Stratford (April 1996).

Reading: Tennyson, A. 1997. *Notornis* 44: 267–269.

WILLIE WAGTAIL   *Rhipidura leucophrys*

Size: 20 cm
Description: Distinctive *black and white* flycatcher, similar in shape to a large Fantail, but with the *extremely long tail moved constantly from side to side*. Black head, neck, upperparts, wings and tail, relieved only by a white eyebrow. Lower chest and underparts white. Short black bill and black legs. Immature birds similar, but with brownish tips to feathers on the wing and upperparts. Frequents most habitats, and feeds mainly on the wing in short flights from a perch like a Fantail, but also hops on the ground. The call is a scolding 'chick-a-chick-a-chick' and they also have a brief musical Fantail-like song.

Distribution: Breeds in New Guinea, the Molluccas, Bismark Archipelago, the Solomons and throughout mainland Australia and on many of its offshore islands, but is rarely recorded in Tasmania. It is a partial migrant, with many birds breeding in Victoria and New South Wales moving north to overwinter in Queensland. One New Zealand record, a first-year bird at Mangere Island, Chatham Islands, in October 1999.

Reading: Gummer, H. 2002. *Notornis* 49: 186-188.

WHERE TO SEE BIRDS IN NEW ZEALAND

By international standards, New Zealand has a small number of species (the record seen in 24 hours is 98 species), but what it lacks in diversity, it makes up in uniqueness. The 12 sites listed here are not necessarily the best birding places in New Zealand, but they provide a wide geographical spread of good birding sites, often in spectacular or interesting settings. The sites are easily accessible, cover a range of habitat types, and should allow you to see or hear a good variety of native and endemic species during a visit. Many species (e.g. *Australasian Harrier*, *Pukeko*, *Variable Oystercatcher*, *NZ Pigeon* and *Fantail*) can be seen almost anywhere and so they are not included in the lists of notable native species you are likely to see at each site. Others are sufficiently rare that the chances of seeing them on a site visit are so low that it would be misleading to raise your hopes too much. Even if you manage to visit all 12 sites, many native species will still be missed, either because they have a limited distribution that doesn't include these sites, or because they were not apparent during your particular visit. The distribution and conspicuousness of birds can vary through the year and so you should bear this in mind when planning a visit to a particular site.

We have included information about sites that was accurate in 2005, but site conditions, operators, charges, contact information and schedules will change over time.

Aroha Island, Bay of Islands

This 12 ha 'island' in the Bay of Islands is owned by the Queen Elizabeth II National Trust and is the site of the Aroha Island Ecological Centre. The island is actually connected to the mainland by a causeway, and is situated about 10 km north-east of the Kerikeri Stone Store (one of the oldest buildings in New Zealand). Access is via Landing, Kapiro, Redcliffs, Rangitane and Kurapari Roads. The island is open to the general public 0930 to 1730 Tuesday to Sunday, except for July and August, with entry by donation; however, various forms of accommodation (self-catering cottage, bed & breakfast, and camping/campervan sites) are available on the island all year round. The Ecological Centre has good educational displays, including material on the star attraction of the site, the *Brown Kiwi*. An overnight stay is necessary to hear or possibly see them on the island; guided night walks are available from the manager of the centre by arrangement @ $60 for 1–4 people. A wide range of bush, wetland and estuarine birds, are also seen here, including *Reef Heron*, *Banded Rail* and *Morepork*. Contact: Aroha Island Ecological Centre 09 407 5243, fax: 09 407 5246, e-mail: kiwi@aroha.net.nz

Tiritiri Matangi Island

This 220 ha island is an open sanctuary run by the Department of Conservation. It lies 3.5 km off the tip of the Whangaparaoa Peninsula and 25 km from downtown Auckland. The Department of Conservation and Supporters of Tiritiri Matangi Inc. are restoring the island from mainly farmland back to a forest haven for birds, and so apart from several valleys of mature forest, most vegetation is less than 20 years old. Because all mammalian predators have been eradicated, and many species re-introduced, the island has a particularly abundant and diverse birdlife. Gulf Harbour Ferries (09 367 9111, e-mail: enquiries@fullers.co.nz) depart Auckland and Gulf Harbour (near the tip of the Whangaparaoa Peninsula) on

Thursdays, Saturdays and Sundays (extra days from October to April), and the Adventure Cruising Co. (09 444 9342, e-mail: adventure_cruise@clear.net.nz) call at the island during 3-day bird cruises between October and March. On the journey from Auckland you may see: *Flesh-footed Shearwater, Buller's Shearwater, Fluttering Shearwater, Common Diving Petrel, Australasian Gannet, Pied Shag* and *Arctic Skua*. The resident rangers will welcome you to the island and explain about its history and the restoration work; they will be able to advise you about the best birding sites on the island. A day visit should reveal *Blue Penguin* (in nesting and roosting boxes along the shore from the wharf), *Brown Teal, Takahe, Red-crowned Parakeet, Whitehead, NZ Robin, Tui, Bellbird, Stitchbird, Saddleback* and *Kokako. Spotless Crake* are heard occasionally in swampy areas, especially in Wattle Valley.

Miranda

The Firth of Thames, 50 km south-east of Auckland, is one of the best and most accessible wader sites in the country. The area is approached from Auckland by a scenic but winding route via Takanini or Papakura and Clevedon on the Blue Pacific Highway (watch for *Pied Shag* and *Spotted Shag* along the coast), or more directly from either north or south from SH2 or SH25. The major roosts are on the western coast between Kaiaua and Miranda, and these shellbanks and freshwater pools are easily accessible. The only bird observatory in New Zealand is situated 2 km north of Miranda and 6.5 km south of Kaiaua (famed for its excellent fish & chips) and is run by the Miranda Naturalists' Trust. The observatory (phone/fax 09 232 2781, e-mail: shorebird@xtra.co.nz) has comfortable accommodation and self-catering facilities at $17.50/person, or $50/couple for the use of a self-contained flat in the observatory. The resident manager can advise day visitors or overnight guests about the best places to see particular species, and a blackboard lists the species seen recently in the area. A high tide visit to Access Bay (just south of the observatory) at

any time of year should reveal: *Pied Oystercatcher, NZ Dotterel, Banded Dotterel, Wrybill* and *Black-billed Gull*, along with numerous Arctic waders from October to March, especially *Bar-tailed Godwit, Lesser Knot, Turnstone, Whimbrel, Red-necked Stint, Terek Sandpiper, Sharp-tailed Sandpiper, Curlew Sandpiper* and *Pacific Golden Plover*. Many Arctic migrants overwinter, but the diversity is usually not so great. In summer, a few *Eastern Curlew* sometimes roost near the old limeworks site near Miranda or on the shellbanks at Access Bay, and *Little Tern* are regular visitors to the area.

Rotorua

The Rotorua area is famed for its impressive geothermal attractions of geysers, boiling mud and hot pools, and it also has displays of Maori culture, New Zealand agriculture, and trout. *Brown Kiwi* are displayed in nocturnal houses at Rainbow Springs Nature Park and at the NZ Maori Arts & Crafts Institute. Lake Rotorua has a wide variety of waterfowl, and the best place to see them is at Sulphur Bay, a wildlife refuge, on the edge of downtown Rotorua. A walkway follows the shoreline from Rotorua City Lakefront Reserve east to Motutara Point and then along the western edge of Sulphur Bay to the Polynesian Spa. The peaceful Government Gardens and active thermal vents provide a unique backdrop to bird-watching. In spring and summer, *Pied Stilt, Spur-winged Plover, Banded Dotterel, Red-billed Gull* and *Black-billed Gull* nest on the silica flats in Sulphur Bay. *NZ Dabchick, Little Shag, Little Black Shag, Black Shag* and *NZ Scaup* nest in willows along the shoreline or on the island at Motutara Point. Other resident waterfowl include *Black Swan, Paradise Shelduck, Grey Duck, Grey Teal* and *Australasian Shoveler*.

Manawatu Estuary / Lake Horowhenua

A visit to the mouth of the Manawatu River at Foxton Beach provides a good opportunity to see a wide range of waders and other wetland birds. Turn west off SH1 at Foxton and a couple of kilometres into Foxton Beach township turn left at crossroads where the main road turns right. Follow signs to the motor camp and turn left into a track through tall trees as though to go to the motor camp, but then drive past the motor camp and park near the edge of the trees. The main high tide roost is on a sandspit extending eastward from the pines. Species likely to be seen at roost, or feeding on mudflats either side of high tide include *Pied Oystercatcher, Banded Dotterel, Wrybill* (January to July), and a variety of Arctic waders, especially *Bar-tailed Godwit, Lesser Knot, Pacific Golden Plover* and *Sharp-tailed Sandpiper*. A variety of terns often call in during the summer and autumn, and *Royal Spoonbill* often feed on the mudflats about 1 km upstream from the high tide roost. About 15 km to the south is Lake Horowhenua, a good site to see waterfowl. In Levin, turn west off SH1 into Queen Street West at the traffic lights opposite to where SH57 joins. Follow the road 2.5 km to the domain, where *NZ Dabchick, Australasian Shoveler, Grey Teal* and *Paradise Shelduck* are found around the northern shore of the lake. A few *Black-billed Gull* roost at the domain in winter.

Kapiti Island

This 1965 ha island has New Zealand's premier nature reserve and some private land. The island has been cleared of all mammalian pests, and a large range of forest birds abound. The nature reserve is run by the Department of Conservation and strict conditions apply to visitors to maintain the quality of the reserve. A maximum of 86 people are permitted to visit the island each day and up to 16 are allowed to stay overnight on the private land at the Kapiti Island Alive bunkhouse (06 364 8618; fax: 06 364 5828, e-mail: john@kapitiislandalive.co.nz) for $140–180 per night, including a guided walk looking for *Little Spotted Kiwi*.

A permit ($9/adult and $4.50/child) is required to enter the Nature Reserve, and is obtained from the Department of Conservation, PO Box 5086, Wellington (04 472 7356, fax: 04 471 2075, e-mail: kapiti.island@doc.govt.nz). Bookings are accepted up to 3 months in advance of the travel date, and it is recommended that you book early. You will be advised how to contact the concessionaires who run the boat trips to the island from Paraparaumu Beach. The tariff is $30/person. Trips depart at 0900 and return at 1530 to 1600. Your bags will be inspected to ensure that you aren't accidentally carrying any rodents, and you will be given a short talk about the island on your arrival. One-hour guided walks are available for $15/person, but visitors are allowed to wander the various tracks. Most birds can be seen within 500 m of the landing site at Rangatira Point, but many visitors still climb to the summit (521 m) where spectacular views of the Cook Strait region can be had on a fine day. It is recommended that people going to the summit climb the Trig Track and return down the more gently-graded Wilkinson Track. Birds likely to be seen during a day trip at any time of year include: *Fluttering Shearwater, Blue Penguin, Weka, Takahe, Kaka, Red-crowned Parakeet, NZ Pipit, Whitehead, Tomtit, NZ Robin, Stitchbird, Bellbird, Tui, Kokako* (scarce) and *Saddleback*.

Kaikoura

This small seaside township lies about halfway between Picton and Christchurch, and is overlooked by the majestic Seaward Kaikoura Mountains, nesting site of the rare *Hutton's Shearwater*. A deep marine canyon lies just offshore and upwellings of cold nutrient-rich water make this a highly productive feeding ground for seabirds and marine mammals. Kaikoura is best known for its whale watching (mainly sperm whale) and opportunities to watch or swim with dusky dolphins and NZ fur seals. Weather permitting, Ocean Wings (03 319 6777, fax: 03 319 6534, e-mail: info@oceanwings.co.nz) run three specialist pelagic seabird cruises per day, each lasting 2–3 hours @ $70/adult or $40/child. These trips run all year, but May-September are the most productive months. The following species are regularly seen: *Wandering Albatross, Royal Albatross, Black-browed Mollymawk, Shy Mollymawk, Buller's Mollymawk, Flesh-footed Shearwater, Sooty Shearwater, Fluttering Shearwater, Hutton's*

Shearwater, Common Diving Petrel, Westland Petrel, White-chinned Petrel, Grey-faced Petrel, Cape Pigeon, Southern Giant Petrel, Northern Giant Petrel, Fairy Prion and *Grey-backed Storm Petrel*. On shore, the tip of the peninsula has huge colonies of *Red-billed Gull* and *White-fronted Tern*, and *Turnstone* and the occasional *Wandering Tattler* feed on the wave platforms amongst the NZ fur seals. A good range of accommodation is available in Kaikoura. Contact Kaikoura Information and Tourism (03 319 5641, fax: 03 319 6819, e-mail: info@kaikoura.co.nz), but the Kaikoura Youth Hostel (03 319 5931) and neighbouring Panorama Motel (03 319 5053, fax: 03 319 6605, e-mail: panorama.motel@xtra.co.nz) on The Esplanade both have stunning views across the sea to the mountains.

Arthur's Pass

This alpine pass is on the main road (SH73) and trans-alpine railway from Christchurch to the West Coast. A variety of accommodation is available in Arthur's Pass village. A stop at the Department of Conservation Visitor Centre is recommended to get advice about the various walks available in the National Park and around the village, and for the latest information on particular species. Approaching from Christchurch, look for *Australasian Crested Grebe* on Lake Pearson to the right of the main road about 25 km past Porters Pass (8 km before Cass) and Black-fronted Tern on the Waimakariri River. At night, *Great Spotted Kiwi* are often heard calling from the hills around the village, however, they are unlikely to be seen. Daytime bush walks should reveal *Rifleman, Brown Creeper, Tomtit, NZ Robin* and *Bellbird*. *Kea* are heard and occasionally seen around the village, but some usually hang out at the Otira Gorge lookout. *Blue Duck, Kaka* and *Tui* are best seen in the Otira Valley on the West Coast side of the pass. In summer and autumn, *Rock Wren* are sometimes seen above the bushline in Temple Basin, a 500 m (2 hour) climb through beech forest.

Eglinton Valley / Milford Sound

The very scenic drive from Te Anau to Milford Sound, via the Eglinton and upper Hollyford Valleys, passes through several very good bird-watching spots, which offer chances to see a wide range of native birds. In summer, *Black-fronted Tern* nest on the Eglinton River. *Blue Duck* are sometimes seen in Monkey Creek, Falls Creek or the main Hollyford River and NZ Scaup are on most lakes. Bush birds include: *NZ Falcon, Kaka, Yellow-crowned Parakeet, Long-tailed Cuckoo, Rifleman, Brown Creeper, Tomtit, NZ Robin, Bellbird* and *Tui*; the best places to stop to look for them are Smithy Creek, Lake Gunn nature walk, north of the Deer Flat camping area, and at Lake Lochie near 'The Divide'. *Kea* are also found at the latter, around the Homer tunnel, and at 'The Chasm' on the Milford side. By following the Gertrude Saddle Track a short distance up the Gertrude Valley from the Homer Huts (1.5 km east of the Homer tunnel), you should come across *Rock Wren*; they are occasionally seen on the nature trail near the eastern portal to the Homer tunnel. At Milford Sound, cruise boats run 10 day trips (October-April) or 3 day trips (May-September) down the spectacular fiord to near the Tasman Sea, and some cruises stop at an underwater observatory in Harrison Cove where surprisingly colourful corals, sponges, anemones and fish can be viewed from 12 m under the surface. During the $1^3/_4$–$2^1/_2$ hour round trip ($48–75/adult, $12–22/child), *Fiordland Crested Penguin* are often seen on the northern shores of the fiord – contact: Milford Sound Red Boat Cruises (03 441 1137, fax: 03 441 1197, e-mail: redboats@milford.co.nz).

Otago Peninsula

Dunedin is known as the 'Wildlife Capital of New Zealand' because of its wide range of wildlife and natural habitats close to the city. The Otago Peninsula is the jewel in the crown, and a number of ecotourism operators conduct general wildlife tours (contact Dunedin Visitor Information Centre 03 474 3300, fax: 03 474 3311, e-mail: visitor.centre@doc.govt.nz). The Otago Peninsula Trust (03 478 0499, fax: 03 478 0575,

e-mail: reservations@albatross.org.nz) operate a specialist observatory to view the
unique *Northern Royal Albatross* colony at
Taiaroa Head, where birds come and go all
year round. Entry can be gained through
one of the land-based tours or at the centre
itself; however, in summer and at weekends
bookings should be made in advance.
Nearby, Southlight Wildlife (03 478 0287, fax:
03 478 0089) and Penguin Place (03 478
0286), both on Harington Point Road, offer
good opportunities to get excellent views of
Yellow-eyed Penguin and *Blue Penguin*. Monarch Wildlife Cruises (03 477 4276, fax: 03
477 4275) operate wildlife cruises from
Dunedin City and Wellers Rock wharf, near
Taiaroa Head, to give close views of the albatross colony, cliff-nesting *Spotted Shag* and
Stewart Island Shag, penguins and other
wildlife.

Stewart Island

The southernmost of the three main islands
of New Zealand is reached by light aircraft
(Southern Air Ltd, 03 218 9129, fax: 03 214
4681), or by fast ferry across Foveaux Strait
from Bluff (Stewart Island Experience, 03
212 7660, fax: 03 212 8377). A wide range of
seabirds can sometimes be seen on this
crossing, but the ferries usually travel too
fast for good bird-watching. Halfmoon Bay
is a delightful fishing village of about 400
people, nestled into the bush surrounding
Halfmoon and Horseshoe Bays. A wide variety of accommodation is available, ranging
from backpackers to luxury lodges (contact
the Stewart Island Visitor Centre, P.O. Box
3, Stewart Island, 03 219 0002, fax: 03 219
0003 or e-mail: stewartislandfc@doc.govt.nz
for details). Bush birds such as *Weka, Kaka,
Red-crowned Parakeet, Yellow-crowned Parakeet, Morepork, Brown Creeper, Tomtit, Bellbird*
and *Tui* abound around the village or on
nearby Ulva Island. From the tip of Akers
Point (a 1 km walk from the village centre)
a good range of seabirds can be seen, including *Black-browed Mollymawk, Shy Mollymawk,
Southern Buller's Mollymawk, Sooty Shearwater, Common Diving Petrel, Cape Pigeon,
Southern Giant Petrel, Northern Giant Petrel,
Fairy Prion, Broad-billed Prion, Yellow-eyed*

Penguin, Blue Penguin, Spotted Shag and
Stewart Island Shag, and the occasional *Antarctic Tern*; however, a boat charter should
give you a better chance to get amongst
these seabirds and add to this list of
species that abound around the Muttonbird
Islands, the mouth of Paterson Inlet and the
east coast of the island. Bravo Adventure
Cruises (phone/fax: 03 219 1144, e-mail:
philldismith@xtra.co.nz) run such cruises
and also an excellent 4 hour evening visit
for $60/person on alternate nights for mod-
erately fit people to view free-living *Brown
Kiwi (Tokoeka)* feeding on invertebrates
amongst the tidal wrack on a remote beach
– flash photography is not permitted. A trip
to Mason Bay via a water taxi to Freshwater Landing and a 4 hour (sometimes
muddy) walk to Mason Bay Hut, and then
a 20 minute walk to the beach down Duck
Creek is a must for seabird enthusiasts.
Seabirds are often wrecked on this wild,
west-facing sandy beach, especially in the 3
km section south of Duck Creek. Species
often found include albatrosses and
mollymawks, *Sooty Shearwater, Common Diving Petrel, Fairy Prion, Broad-billed Prion,
Mottled Petrel, Snares Crested Penguin* and
*Fiordland Crested Penguin. Brown Kiwi
(Tokoeka)* are often seen at night or even in
daylight near Mason Bay hut and *NZ Dotterel* and other waders sometimes roost on
sandflats 200 m due south of the first creek
crossing below the hut. Charter aircraft from
Southern Air Ltd or the Southland Aero
Club (03 218 6170) can land on the beach at
Mason Bay at low tide.

Chatham Island

This small cluster of islands, lying about 800
km east of Christchurch has many rare endemic birds, but some are inaccessible on
small island nature reserves. Main Chatham
Island, with a population of about 700 people is reached by 5 weekly flights from
Auckland (1), Wellington (3) or Christchurch (1) – contact Air Chathams (03 305
0209 or 04 388 9737). Visitors can hire vehicles from Chatham Motors (03 305 0093),
and a range of accommodation is available:
motel (03 305 0003), hotel (03 305 0048) and

lodge (03 305 0196).

Weka and *NZ Pipit* abound throughout the island, and *Grey Duck* are moderately common. *Chatham Island Shag* and *Pitt Island Shag* are common around the coast and a mixed colony is found on cliffs at Matarakau Point on the northern coast. *Chatham Island Oystercatcher* nest on many parts of the coast, especially on low rocky headlands and stream mouths on the northern coast, especially at Cape Pattison, Maunganui Beach and at Taupeka Point. *Banded Dotterel*, a variety of Arctic waders, and numerous *Black Swan* are found on the north-eastern shore of Te Whanga Lagoon between Hapupu and Ocean Mail. Forest birds such as *Chatham Island Pigeon, Red-crowned Parakeet* and *Chatham Island Warbler* are best seen at the Tuku Nature Reserve in the south-western corner of Chatham Island. A permit is required from the Department of Conservation (PO Box 114, Waitangi, Chatham Island; 03 305 0098, fax: 03 305 0376) to enter the Nature Reserve, and permission to cross private land must be obtained from Bruce and Liz Tuanui who live south of the Awatotara valley on the Tuku Road, and all gates on the road must be left as they are found. Seawatching or, better still, a boat charter from Waitangi or Owenga to Pitt Strait, should offer views of some of the numerous species of seabird that breed in the group, especially *Northern Royal Albatross, Northern Buller's Mollymawk, Chatham Island Mollymawk, Sooty Shearwater, Common Diving Petrel, Northern Giant Petrel, Broad-billed Prion, Grey-backed Storm Petrel, White-faced Storm Petrel* and *Blue Penguin*. A visit close to the shore of South East (Rangatira) Island would permit views of *Chatham Island Oystercatcher, Shore Plover* and *Brown Skua* on the wave platforms, but landing is not permitted.

INDEX

Numerals in **bold type** refer
to the plate number and its
facing text, those in plain
type refer to page numbers
in the handbook section.

Acanthisitta chloris, **66**, 371
Acanthisittidae, 371
Acanthizidae, 391
Accentors, 382
Accipitridae, 274
Acridotheres tristis, **73**, 415
Alauda arvensis, **67**, 375
Alaudidae, 375
Albatross, Black-footed, 175
 Laysan, 424
 Light-mantled Sooty,
  6, 183
 Northern Royal, **3**, 177
 Royal, **3**, 177
 Snowy, 176
 Sooty, **6**, 184
 Southern Royal, **3**, 177
 Wandering, **3**, 176
Albatrosses, 175
Alcedinidae, 369
Alectoris chukar, **35**, 280
 rufa, **35**, 280
Amokura, **21**, 236
Anarhynchus frontalis, **45**, 307
Anas acuta, 425
 aucklandica, **32**, 270
 castanea, **32**, 269
 clypeata, **31**, 272
 gracilis, **32**, 269
 platyrhynchos, **31**, 266
 rhynchotis, **31**, 271
 superciliosa, **31**, 268
Anatidae, 258
Anhinga melanogaster, **23**, 248
Anhingidae, 248
Anous stolidus, **58**, 345
 tenuirostris, **58**, 345
Anser anser, **29**, 262
Anthochaera carunculata, 402
Anthornis melanura, **70**, 403
Anthus novaeseelandiae,
 67, 379

Apodidae, 368
Aptenodytes forsteri, **18**, 226
 patagonicus, **18**, 227
Apterygidae, 167
Apteryx australis, **1**, 168
 haastii, **1**, 170
 owenii, **1**, 169
Apus pacificus, **64**, 368
Ardea novaehollandiae, **26**, 250
 pacifica, **27**, 251
Ardeidae, 250
Arenaria interpres, **45**, 311
Artamidae, 420
Artamus personatus, **65**, 420
 superciliosus, **65**, 420
Athene noctua, **63**, 366
Avocet, Australian Red-
 necked, **39**, 299
Avocets, 297
Aythya australis, **32**, 273
 novaeseelandiae, **32**, 273

Bartramia longicauda, **42**, 323
Bellbird, **70**, 403
Bird of Providence, 217
Bird, Parson, 405
Birds-of-Paradise, 422
Bittern, Australasian, **26**, 255
 Little, **26**, 256
 New Zealand Little,
  250, 256
Bitterns, 250
Blackbird, **67**, 383
Boobies, 237
Boobook, 365
Booby, Blue-faced, 239
 Brown, **22**, 239
 Masked, **22**, 239
Botaurus poiciloptilus, **26**, 255
Bowdleria punctata, **68**, 386
 rufescens, 386
Bowerbirds, 422
Branta canadensis, **29**, 261
Brolga, **27**, 292
Bubulcus ibis, **25**, 253
Bulbul, Red-vented, **73**, 381
Bulbuls, 381
Bulweria bulwerii, 424
Bunting, Cirl, **72**, 407
Buntings, 406

Cacatua galerita, **60**, 352
 roseicapilla, **60**, 353
Cacatuidae, 352
Cacomantis flabelliformis,
 62, 362
Calidris acuminata, **46**, 317
 alba, **45**, 316
 alpina, **44**, 316
 bairdii, **46**, 317
 canutus, **44**, 314
 ferruginea, **44**, 316
 fuscicollis, **44**, 318
 mauri, **47**, 319
 melanotos, **46**, 317
 minuta, **47**, 318
 minutilla, **47**, 318
 ruficollis, **47**, 318
 subminuta, 426
 tenuirostris, **44**, 315
Callaeas cinerea, **70**, 417
Callaeidae, 416
Callipepla californica, **35**, 279
Calonectris diomedea, **7**, 186
Campephagidae, 380
Canary, Bush, 389
Cardinals, 406
Carduelis carduelis, **71**, 410
 chloris, **72**, 409
 flammea, **71**, 411
Catharacta lonnbergi, 327
 maccormicki, **53**, 329
 skua, **53**, 327
Cereopsis novaehollandiae,
 29, 262
Chaffinch, **71**, 408
Charadriidae, 300
Charadrius bicinctus, **40**, 302
 hiaticula, **41**, 304
 leschenaultii, **40**, 304
 melanops, **41**, 303
 mongolus, **40**, 305
 obscurus, **40**, 300
 ruficapillus, **41**, 303
 veredus, **42**, 305
Chenonetta jubata, **30**, 265
Chlidonias hybrida, **56**, 337
 leucopterus, **56**, 337
Chrysococcyx lucidus, **62**, 362
Chukar, 280
Chukor, **35**, 280

Circus approximans, **33**, 275
Coenocorypha aucklandica, **43**, 313
 pusilla, **43**, 314
Cockatoo, Sulphur-crested, **60**,
 352
 White, 352
Cockatoos, 352
Colinus virginianus, **35**, 280
Columba livia, **59**, 350
Columbidae, 348
Coot, Australian, **37**, 291
 Eurasian, 291
Coots, 283
Coraciidae, 371
Coracina novaehollandiae,
 65, 381
Cormorant, Black, 240
 Great, 240
 Little Black, 242
 Little Pied, 243
 Pied, 241
Corncrake, 283
Corvidae, 423
Corvus frugilegus, **73**, 423
Coturnix novaezelandiae, 279
Coursers, 299
Cracticidae, 421
Crake, Ballion's, 288
 Marsh, **36**, 288
 Spotless, **36**, 287
Crane, Blue, 250
Cranes, 292
Creeper, Brown, **68**, 390
Crex crex, 283
Crows, 423
Cuckoo, Channel-billed,
 62, 364
 Fan-tailed, **62**, 362
 Long-tailed, **62**, 363
 Oriental, **62**, 361
 Pallid, **62**, 361
 Shining, **62**, 362
Cuckoos, 361
Cuckoo-shrike, Black-faced, **65**,
 381
Cuckoo-shrikes, 380
Cuculidae, 361
Cuculus pallidus, **62**, 361
 saturatus, **62**, 361
Curlew, Bristle-thighed,
 48, 321
 Eastern, **48**, 320
 Far-eastern, 320
 Little, 321
Curlews, 312
Cyanoramphus auriceps, **61**, 359
 malherbi, 360
 novaezelandiae, **61**, 358
 unicolor, **61**, 358
Cygnus atratus, **29**, 260
 olor, **29**, 259

Dabchick, New Zealand, **2**, 173
Dacelo novaeguineae, **63**, 369
Daption capense, **11**, 202
Darter, **23**, 248
Darters, 248
Dendrocygna eytoni, **30**, 259
Diomedea bulleri, **5**, 182
 cauta, **4**, 180
 chlororhynchos, **4**, 182
 chrysostoma, **5**, 181
 epomophora, **3**, 177
 exulans, **3**, 176
 immutabilis, 424
 melanophrys, **5**, 178
 nigripes, 175
Diomedeidae, 175
Dollarbird, **65**, 371
Dotterel, Banded, **40**, 302
 Black-fronted, **41**, 303
 Large Sand, **40**, 304
 Mongolian, **40**, 305
 New Zealand, **40**, 300
 Northern New Zealand, **40**,
 300
 Oriental, **42**, 305
 Red-breasted, 300
 Red-capped, **41**, 303
 Red-kneed, **41**, 306
 Southern New Zealand, **40**,
 300
Dotterels, 300
Dove, Barbary, **59**, 351
 Malay Spotted, 351
 Spotted, **59**, 351
Doves, 348
Dowitcher, Asiatic, **49**, 320
Duck, Australian Wood,
 30, 265
 Blue, **30**, 265
 Grass Whistling, **30**, 259
 Grey, **31**, 268
 Maned, 265
 Mountain, 264
 Pacific Black, **30**, 265
 Pink-eared, **31**, 272
 Plumed Whistling, **30**, 259
 White-eyed, **32**, 273
Dunlin, **44**, 316
Dunnock, **67**, 382

Egret, Cattle, **25**, 253
 Eastern Reef, 252
 Great, 251
 Intermediate, **25**, 252
 Little, **25**, 252
 Plumed, 252
Egrets, 250
Egretta alba, **25**, 251
 garzetta, **25**, 252
 intermedia, **25**, 252
 sacra, **25**, **26**, 252

Emberiza cirlus, **72**, 407
 citrinella, **72**, 406
Emberizidae, 406
Eopsaltriidae, 395
Erithacus rubecula, 395
Erythrogonys cinctus, **41**, 306
Eudynamys scolopacea, 426
 taitensis, **62**, 363
Eudyptes chrysocome, **20**, 231
 chrysolophus, **20**, 232
 pachyrhynchus, **20**, 233
 robustus, **20**, 234
 sclateri, **20**, 235
Eudyptula minor, **19**, 230
Eurystomus orientalis,
 65, 371

Falco cenchroides, **33**, 278
 novaeseelandiae, **33**, 277
 subniger, **33**, 279
Falcon, Black, **33**, 279
 New Zealand, **33**, 277
Falconidae, 274
Fantail, **68**, 394
 Grey, 394
Fernbird, **68**, 386
 Chatham Island, 386
Finches, 408
Flycatcher, Satin, **65**, 394
Flycatchers, Monarch, 393
Fregata ariel, **21**, 249
 minor, **21**, 249
Fregatidae, 249
Fregetta grallaria, **17**, 224
 tropica, **17**, 224
Frigatebird, Great, 249
 Greater, **21**, 249
 Least, 249
 Lesser, **21**, 249
Frigatebirds, 249
Fringilla coelebs, **71**, 408
Fringillidae, 408
Fulica atra, **37**, 291
Fulmar, Antarctic, **11**, 203
 Silver-grey, 203
Fulmars, 184
Fulmarus glacialoides, **11**, 203

Galah, **60**, 353
Gallinago hardwickii, **43**, 314
 megala, 314
Gallinula tenebrosa, **37**, 289
 ventralis, **37**, 288
Gallinule, Purple, 289
Gallinules, 283
Gallirallus australis, **36**, 285
Gamebirds, 279
Gannet, Australasian, **22**,
 238
 Cape, 425
Gannets, 237

Gelochelidon nilotica, **54**, 337
Gerygone albofrontata, **66**, 392
  igata, **66**, 391
Glareola maldivarum, **51**, 300
Glareolidae, 299
Godwit, Bar-tailed, **49**, 321
  Black-tailed, **49**, 323
  Hudsonian, **49**, 323
Godwits, 312
Goldfinch, **71**, 410
Goose, Canada, **29**, 261
  Cape Barren, **29**, 262
  Domestic, 262
  Feral, **29**, 262
  Greylag, 262
  Maned, 265
Grebe, Australasian, 174
  Australasian Crested,
    2, 172
  Australasian Little, **2**, 174
  Great Crested, 172
  Hoary-headed, **2**, 174
  Southern Crested, 172
Grebes, 171
Greenfinch, **72**, 409
Greenshank, **50**, 324
  Common, 324
Gruidae, 292
Grus rubicundus, **27**, 292
Guineafowl, Helmeted, 283
  Tufted, **34**, 283
Gull, Black-backed, **53**, 332
  Black-billed, **54**, 335
  Dominican, 332
  Franklin's, 426
  Kelp, 332
  Red-billed, **54**, 334
  Silver, 334
  Southern Black-backed, 332
Gulls, 332
Gygis alba, **57**, 347
Gymnorhina tibicen, **73**, 421

Haematopodidae, 293
Haematopus chathamensis,
    38, 296
  ostralegus, **38**, 293
  unicolor, **38**, 295
Hakawai, **43**, 313
Hakoakoa, **53**, 327
Halcyon sancta, **63**, 370
Halobaena caerulea, **11**, 210
Hardhead, 273
Harpogornis moorei, 275
Harrier, Australasian, **33**, 275
  Swamp, 275
Hawk, 275
  Bush, 277
  Sparrow, 277
Hemiphaga novaeseelandiae, **59**,
    348

Heron, Blue, 250
  Great White, 251
  Nankeen Night, **27**, 254
  Pacific, 251
  Reef, **25**, **26**, 252
  Rufous Night, 254
  White, **25**, 251
  White-faced, **26**, 250
  White-necked, **27**, 251
Herons, 250
Heteralocha acutirostris,
    74, 419
Hihi, **70**, 402
Himantopus himantopus,
    39, 297
  novaezelandiae, **39**, 298
Hirundinidae, 376
Hirundapus caudacutus,
    64, 368
Hirundo ariel, **64**, 379
  nigricans, **64**, 378
  tahitica, **64**, 376
Hoiho, **19**, 227
Hokioi, 313
Honeyeaters, 402
Huahou, **44**, 314
Huia, **74**, 419
Hymenolaimus malacorhynchos,
    30, 265

Ibis, Australian White,
    28, 257
  Glossy, **28**, 256
Ibises, 256
Icthyophaga australis, 275
Ixobrychus minutus, **26**, 256
  novaezelandiae, 250, 256

Jackass, Laughing, 369
Jackbird, 418
Jays, 423

Kahu, **33**, 275
Kaka, **60**, 355
Kakapo, **60**, 353
Kakariki, **61**, 358, 359
Kaki, **39**, 298
Karakahia, 273
Karearea, **33**, 277
Karoro, **53**, 332
Karuhiruhi, **23**, 241
Kawau, **23**, 240
Kawaupaka, **23**, 243
Kea, **60**, 356
Kereru, **59**, 348
Kestrel, Australian, 278
  Nankeen, **33**, 278
Kingfisher, **63**, 370
  New Zealand, 370
  Sacred, 370
Kingfishers, 369

Kite, Black, **33**, 275
  Fork-tailed, 275
Kiwi, 167
  Brown, **1**, 168
  Great Spotted, **1**, 170
  Little Spotted, **1**, 169
Kiwi-pukupuku, 169
Knot, Great, **44**, 315
  Lesser, **44**, 314
  Red, 314
Koekoea, **62**, 363
Koel, Common, 426
  Long-tailed, 363
Koitareke, **36**, 288
Kokako, **70**, 417
  North Island, **70**, 417
  South Island, **70**, 417
Kookaburra, **63**, 369
  Laughing, 369
Korimako, **70**, 403
Korora, **19**, 230
Korure, **14**, 214
Kotare, **63**, 370
Kotuku, **25**, 251
Kotuku-ngutupapa, 257
Kuaka, **9**, 195, **49**, 321
Kukupa, **59**, 348
Kuruwhengi, **31**, 271

Lalage tricolor, **65**, 381
Lapwing, Masked, 309
Lapwings, 300
Laridae, 332
Larks, 375
Larus bulleri, **54**, 335
  dominicanus, **53**, 332
  novaehollandiae, **54**, 334
  pipixcan, 426
Leucocarbo campbelli, **24**, 246
  carunculatus, **24**, 244
  chalconotus, **24**, 244
  colensoi, **24**, 246
  onslowi, **24**, 245
  ranfurlyi, **24**, 246
Limicola falcinellus, **47**, 319
Limnodromus semipalmatus, **49**,
    320
Limosa haemastica, **49**, 323
  lapponica, **49**, 321
  limosa, **49**, 323
Lugensa brevirostris, **15**, 201

Macronectes giganteus, **6**, 204
  halli, **6**, 205
Magpie, Australian, **73**, 421
  Black-backed, **73**, 421
  White-backed, **73**, 421
Magpies, Bell, 421
Makomako, **70**, 403
Malacorhynchus membranaceus,
    31, 272

Mallard, **31**, 266
Martin, Australian Tree, **64**, 378
  Fairy, **64**, 379
Martins, 376
Matata, **68**, 386
Matuhi, 373
Matuku, **26**, 255
Matuku moana, **26**, 252
Megadyptes antipodes, **19**, 227
Meleagris gallopavo, **34**, 282
Meliphagidae, 402
Merganser, Auckland Island, **74**, 274
Mergus australis, **74**, 258, 274
Micropalma himantopus, 426
Milvus migrans, **33**, 275
Miromiro, **69**, 396
Moho, 290
Moho-pereru, **36**, 283
Mohoua albicilla, **68**, 387
  novaeseelandiae, **68**, 390
  ochrocephala, **68**, 389
Mohua, **68**, 389
Mollymawk, Atlantic Ocean Yellow-nosed, **4**, 182
  Black-browed, **5**, 178
  Buller's, **5**, 182
  Chatham Island, **4**, 180
  Grey-headed, **5**, 181
  Indian Ocean Yellow-nosed, **4**, 182
  New Zealand Black-browed, **5**, 178
  New Zealand White-capped, **4**, 180
  Northern Buller's, **5**, 182
  Salvin's, **4**, 180
  Shy, **4**, 180
  Southern Buller's, **5**, 182
  Subantarctic Black-browed, **5**, 178
  Yellow-nosed, **4**, 182
Monarch, Black-faced, 427
Monarcha melanopsis, 427
Monarchidae, 393
Moorhen, Dusky, **37**, 289
Morepork, **63**, 365
Morus capensis, 425
  serrator, **22**, 238
Motacillidae, 379
Muscicapidae, 383
Muttonbird, **8**, 189
  Northern, 217
  Tasmanian, 191
Myiagra cyanoleuca, **65**, 394
Myna, **73**, 415
Mynas, 413

Native-hen, Black-tailed, **37**, 288

Needletail, White-throated, 368
Nelly, **6**, 204, 205
Nestor meridionalis, **60**, 355
  notabilis, **60**, 356
Ngiru-ngiru, **69**, 396
Ngutuparore, 307
Ninox novaeseelandiae, **63**, 365
Noddies, 332
Noddy, Black, 345
  Blue-grey, 346
  Brown, 345
  Common, **58**, 345
  Grey, 346
  Lesser, **58**, 345
  White, 347
  White-capped, **58**, 345
Notiomystis cincta, **70**, 402
Notornis, **37**, 290
Numenius madagascariensis, **48**, 320
  minutus, **48**, 321
  phaeopus, **48**, 320
  tahitiensis, **48**, 321
Numida meleagris, **34**, 283
Nycticorax caledonicus, **27**, 254

Oceanites oceanicus, **17**, 221
  maorianus, 222
  nereis, **17**, 222
Oceanitidae, 220
Oceanodroma leucorhoa, **17**, 221
Oi, **15**, 217
Owl, Barn, **63**, 367
  German, 366
  Laughing, **74**, 366
  Little, **63**, 366
Owl-parrot, 353
Owls, Barn, 367
  Typical, 365
Oystercatcher, Black, 295
  Chatham Island, **38**, 296
  Pied, **38**, 293
  South Island Pied, 293
  Variable, **38**, 295
Oystercatchers, 293

Pachycephalidae, 387
Pachyptila belcheri, **12**, 207
  crassirostris, **12**, 207
  desolata, **12**, 208
  salvini, **12**, 208
  turtur, **12**, 205
  vittata, **12**, 209
Pagodroma nivea, **11**, 201
Pakaha, **9**, 192
Papango, **32**, 273
Paradisaeidae, 422
Parakeet, Antipodes Island, **61**, 358
  Orange-fronted, **61**, 360

  Red-crowned, **61**, 358
  Yellow-crowned, **61**, 359
Parara, **12**, 209
Parea, **59**, 348
Parekareka, **24**, 247
Parera, **31**, 268
Pari, 263
Parrots, 352
Partridge, Grey, **35**, 281
  Red-legged, **35**, 280
Passer domesticus, **71**, 412
Pateke, **32**, 270
Pavo cristatus, **34**, 282
Peafowl, **34**, 282
  Indian, 282
Pediunker, **10**, 197
Pelagodroma marina, **17**, 223
Pelecanoides georgicus, **9**, 196
  urinatrix, **9**, 195
Pelecanidae, 237
Pelecanus conspicillatus, **27**, 237
Pelican, Australian, **27**, 237
Pelicans, 237
Penguin, Adélie, **19**, 229
  Blue, **19**, 230
  Chinstrap, **19**, 230
  Eastern Rockhopper, **20**, 231
  Emperor, **18**, 226
  Erect-crested, **20**, 235
  Fairy, 230
  Fiordland Crested, **20**, 233
  Gentoo, **18**, 228
  King, **18**, 227
  Little Blue, 230
  Macaroni, **20**, 232
  Magellanic, **18**, 235
  Moseley's Rockhopper, **20**, 231
  Rockhopper, **20**, 231
  Royal, **20**, 232
  Snares Crested, **20**, 234
  Yellow-eyed, **19**, 227
Penguins, 225
Perdix perdix, **35**, 281
Petrel, Antarctic, **11**, 203
  Barau's, 215
  Black, **10**, 198
  Black-bellied Storm, **17**, 224
  Black-winged, **14**, 212
  Blue, **11**, 210
  Bulwer's, 424
  Chatham, **14**, 213
  Common Diving, **9**, 195
  Cook's, **13**, 211
  Frigate, 223
  Great-winged, 217
  Grey, **10**, 197
  Grey-faced, **15**, 217

Gould's, **13**, 211
Grey-backed Storm,
    17, 222
Herald, 216, 217, 218
Juan Fernandez, **14**, 215
Kerguelen, **15**, 201
Kermadec, **15**, **16**, 216
Leach's Storm, **17**, 221
Magenta, **16**, 218
Mottled, **14**, 214
New Zealand Storm, 222
Northern Giant, **6**, 205
Parkinson's, 198
Phoenix, **16**, 216
Pintado, 202
Providence, **15**, 217
Pycroft's, **13**, 210
Snow, **11**, 201
Soft-plumaged, **16**, 220
South Georgian Diving,
    9, 196
Southern Giant, **6**, 204
Stejneger's, **13**, 210
Sunday Island, 214
Tahiti, **16**, 200
Westland, **10**, 199
Westland Black, 199
White-bellied Storm,
    17, 224
White-chinned, **10**, 200
White-faced Storm, **17**, 223
White-headed, **15**, 219
White-naped, **14**, 214
White-necked, 214
Wilson's Storm, **17**, 221
Petrels, 184
    Storm, 220
Petroica australis, **69**, 397
    macrocephala, **69**, 396
    traversi, **69**, 399
Phaethon lepturus, **21**, 236
    rubricauda, **21**, 236
Phaethontidae, 236
Phalacrocoracidae, 240
Phalacrocorax carbo, **23**, 240
    melanoleucos, **23**, 243
    sulcirostris, **23**, 242
    varius, **23**, 241
Phalarope, Grey, **51**, 326
    Northern, 326
    Red, **51**, 326
    Red-necked, **51**, 326
    Wilson's, **51**, 327
Phalaropes, 326
Phalaropodidae, 326
Phalaropus fulicarius, **51**, 326
    lobatus, **51**, 326
    tricolor, **51**, 327
Phasianidae, 279
Phasianus colchicus, **34**, 282
Pheasant, **34**, 282

Common, 282
    Ring-necked, 282
Philesturnus carunculatus,
    70, 418
Philomachus pugnax, **46**, 319
Phoebetria fusca, **6**, 184
    palpebrata, **6**, 183
Pigeon, Cape, **11**, 202
    Chatham Island, **59**, 348
    Feral, **59**, 350
    New Zealand, **59**, 348
    Rock, **59**, 350
    Southern Cape, **11**, 202
    Snares Cape, **11**, 202
Pigeons, 348
Pihoihoi, **67**, 379
Piopio, **74**, 422
    North Island, **74**, 422
    South Island, **74**, 422
Pintail, Northern, 425
Pipipi, **68**, 390
Pipit, New Zealand, **67**,
    379
    Richard's, 379
Pipits, 379
Pipiwharauroa, **62**, 362
Piwakawaka, **68**, 394
Platalea flavipes, **28**, 258
    regia, **28**, 257
Platycercus elegans, **61**, 357
    eximius, **61**, 357
Plegadis falcinellus, **28**, 256
Ploceidae, 412
Plover, American Golden,
    42, 309
    Asiatic Golden, 308
    Black-bellied, 309
    Black-fronted, 303
    Double-banded, 302
    Eastern Golden, 308
    Greater Sand, 304
    Grey, **42**, 309
    Large Sand, 304
    Least Golden, 308
    Lesser Sand, 305
    Masked, 309
    Mongolian, 305
    Oriental, 305
    Pacific Golden, **42**, 308
    Red-capped, 303
    Ringed, **41**, 304
    Shore, **41**, 306
    Spur-winged, **38**, 309
    Wrybilled, 307
Plovers, 300
Pluvialis dominica, **42**, 309
    fulva, **42**, 308
    squatarola, **42**, 309
Poaka, **39**, 297
Podiceps cristatus, **2**, 172
Podicipedidae, 171

Pokotiwha, 233
Poliocephalus poliocephalus,
    2, 174
    rufopectus, **2**, 173
Popokatea, **68**, 387
Porphyrio mantelli, **37**, 290
    porphyrio, **37**, 289
Porzana pusilla, **36**, 288
    tabuensis, **36**, 287
Pratincole, Oriental, **51**, 300
Pratincoles, 299
Prion, Antarctic, **12**, 208
    Broad-billed, **12**, 209
    Fairy, **12**, 205
    Fulmar, **12**, 207
    Lesser Broad-billed, 208
    Narrow-billed, 207
    Salvin's, **12**, 208
    Slender-billed, 207
    Thin-billed, **12**, 207
Prions, 184
Procellaria aequinoctialis,
    10, 200
    cinerea, **10**, 197
    parkinsoni, **10**, 198
    westlandica, **10**, 199
Procellariidae, 184
Procelsterna cerulea, **57**, 346
Prosthemadera novaeseelandiae,
    70, 405
Prunella modularis, **67**, 382
Prunellidae, 382
Pseudobulweria rostrata, **16**, 200
Psittacidae, 352
Pterodroma alba, **16**, 216
    axillaris, **14**, 213
    baraui, 215
    cervicalis, **14**, 214
    cookii, **13**, 211
    externa, **14**, 215
    heraldica, 216, 217
    inexpectata, **14**, 214
    lessonii, **15**, 219
    leucoptera, **13**, 211
    longirostris, **13**, 210
    macroptera, **15**, 217
    magentae, **16**, 218
    mollis, **16**, 220
    neglecta, **15**, **16**, 216
    nigripennis, **14**, 212
    pycrofti, **13**, 210
    solandri, **15**, 217
Puffinus assimilis, **9**, 194
    bulleri, **7**, 188
    carneipes, **8**, 186
    creatopus, **7**, 186
    gavia, **9**, 192
    griseus, **8**, 189
    huttoni, **9**, 193
    nativitatis, **8**, 191
    newelli, 425

pacificus, **7**, **8**, 187
puffinus, **9**, 192
tenuirostris, **8**, 191
Pukeko, **37**, 289
Putangitangi, 263
Puteketeke, **2**, 172
Putoto, 287
Puweto, **36**, 287
Pycnonotidae, 381
Pycnonotus cafer, **73**, 381
Pygoscelis adeliae, **19**, 229
   antarctica, **19**, 230
   papua, **18**, 228

Quail, Brown, **35**, 281
Bobwhite, **35**, 280
California, **35**, 279
New Zealand, 279
Virginian, 280

Rail, Auckland Island,
   36, 284
Banded, **36**, 283
Buff-banded, 283
Chatham Island, 283
Lewin's, 284
Sooty, 287
Rails, 283
Rallidae, 283
Rallus modestus, 283
   pectoralis, **36**, 284
   philippensis, **36**, 283
Raptors, 274
Recurvirostra novaehollandiae,
   39, 299
Recurvirostridae, 297
Redpoll, **71**, 411
Reeve, **46**, 319
Rhipidura fuliginosa, **68**,
   394
   leucophrys, 427
Rifleman, **66**, 371
Riroriro, **66**, 391
Roa, **1**, 170
Robin, Black, **69**, 399
European, 395
New Zealand, **69**, 397
North Island, **69**, 397
South Island, **69**, 397
Robins, Australasian, 395
Roller, Eastern Broad-billed,
   371
Rollers, 371
Rook, **73**, 423
Rosella, Crimson, **61**, 357
Eastern, **61**, 357
Rostratula benghalensis,
   43, 292
Rostratulidae, 292
Ruff, **46**, 319
Ruru, **63**, 365

Saddleback, **70**, 418
North Island, **70**, 418
South Island, **70**, 418
Sanderling, **45**, 316
Sandpiper, Baird's, **46**, 317
Bartram's, 323
Broad-billed, **47**, 319
Common, **45**, 324
Curlew, **44**, 316
Least, **47**, 318
Marsh, **50**, 325
Pectoral, **46**, 317
Sharp-tailed, **46**, 317
Stilt, 426
Terek, **45**, 325
Upland, **42**, 323
Western, **47**, 319
White-rumped, **44**, 318
Sandpipers, 312
Scaup, New Zealand, **32**, 273
Sceloglaux albifacies, **74**, 366
Scolopacidae, 312
Scythrops novaehollandiae,
   62, 364
Shag, Auckland Island,
   24, 246
Black, **23**, 240
Blue, 247
Bounty Island, **24**, 246
Bronze, **24**, 244
Campbell Island, **24**, 246
Chatham Island, **24**, 245
Little, **23**, 243
Little Black, **23**, 242
King, **24**, 244
Pied, **23**, 241
Pitt Island, **24**, 248
Spotted, **24**, 247
Stewart Island, **24**, 244
Shags, 240
Shearwater, Allied, 194
Buller's, **7**, 188
Christmas Island, **8**, 191
Cory's, **7**, 186
Flesh-footed, **8**, 186
Fluttering, **9**, 192
Hutton's, **9**, 193
Little, **9**, 194
Manx, **9**, 192
New Zealand, 188
Newell's, 425
North Atlantic, 186
Pink-footed, **7**, 186
Short-tailed, **8**, 191
Sooty, **8**, 189
Subantarctic Little, **9**, 194
Wedge-tailed, **7**, **8**, 187
Shearwaters, 184
Shelduck, Australian, 264
Chestnut-breasted, **30**, 264
Paradise, **30**, 263

Shoemaker, **10**, 200
Shoveler, Australasian, **31**, 271
New Zealand, 271
Northern, **31**, 272
Silvereye, **66**, 400
SIPO, 293
Skua, Antarctic, 329
Arctic, **52**, 330
Brown, **53**, 327
Long-tailed, **52**, 331
MacCormick's, 329
Pomarine, **52**, 331
South Polar, **53**, 329
Southern, 327
Southern Great, 327
Subantarctic, 327
Skuas, 327
Skylark, **67**, 375
Snipe, 312
Chatham Island, **43**, 314
Japanese, **43**, 314
Latham's, 314
New Zealand, **43**, 313
Painted, **43**, 292
Swinhoe's, 314
Sparrow, Hedge, 382
House, **71**, 412
Sparrows, 412
Spheniscidae, 225
Spheniscus magellanicus,
   18, 235
Spoonbill, 271
Royal, **28**, 257
Yellow-billed, **28**, 258
Spoonbills, 256
Starling, **73**, 414
Starlings, 413
Stercorariidae, 327
Stercorarius longicaudus,
   52, 331
   parasiticus, **52**, 330
   pomarinus, **52**, 331
Sterna albifrons, **57**, 343
   albostriata, **56**, 338
   anaethetus, **58**, 345
   bergii, **54**, 344
   caspia, **54**, 339
   fuscata, **58**, 341
   hirundo, **55**, 344
   nereis, **57**, 342
   paradisaea, **55**, 344
   striata, **55**, 340
   vittata, **55**, 342
Stictocarbo featherstoni,
   24, 248
   punctatus, **24**, 247
Stilt, Black, **39**, 298
Black-winged, 297
Pied, **39**, 297
White-headed, 297
Stilts, 297

Stint, Little, **47**, 318
  Long-toed, 426
  Red-necked, **47**, 318
Stitchbird, **70**, 402
Streptopelia chinensis, **59**, 351
  roseogrisea, **59**, 351
Strigidae, 365
Strigops habroptilus, **60**, 353
Sturnidae, 413
Sturnus vulgaris, **73**, 414
Sula dactylatra, **22**, 239
  leucogaster, **22**, 239
Sulidae, 237
Swallow, House, 376
  Pacific, 376
  Welcome, **64**, 376
Swallows, 376
Swamphen, Purple, **37**, 289
Swan, Black, **29**, 260
  Mute, **29**, 259
Swift, Fork-tailed, **64**, 368
  Needle-tailed, 368
  Spine-tailed, **64**, 368
Swifts, 368
Sylviidae, 386
Synoicus ypsilophorus, **35**, 281

Tachybaptus novaehollandiae, **2**, 174
Tadorna tadornoides, **30**, 264
  variegata, **30**, 263
Taiko, **10**, 198
  Chatham Island, **16**, 218
Takahe, **37**, 290
Takahikare-moana, **17**, 223
Takapu, **22**, 238
Tanagers, 406
Tara, **55**, 340
Taranui, **54**, 339
Tarapiroe, **56**, 338
Tarapunga, **54**, 334
Tattler, Grey-tailed, **50**, 324
  Siberian, **50**, 324
  Wandering, **50**, 323
Tauhou, **66**, 400
Tawaki, **20**, 233
Teal, Black, 273
  Brown, **32**, 270
  Chestnut, **32**, 269
  Grey, **32**, 269
Tern, Antarctic, **55**, 342
  Arctic, **55**, 344
  Black-fronted, **56**, 338
  Bridled, **58**, 345
  Brown-winged, 345
  Caspian, **54**, 339
  Common, **55**, 344
  Crested, **54**, 344
  Fairy, **57**, 342, 347
  Gull-billed, **54**, 337
  Little, **57**, 343

Sooty, **58**, 341
Swift, 344
Whiskered, **56**, 337
White, **57**, 347
White-fronted, **55**, 340
White-winged, 337
White-winged Black, **56**, 337
Wideawake, 341
Ternlet, Grey **57**, 346
Terns, 332
Tete, **32**, 269
Thalassoica antarctica, **11**, 203
Thinornis novaeseelandiae, **41**, 306
Threskiornis molucca, **28**, 257
Threskiornithidae, 256
Thrush, New Zealand, 422
  Song, **67**, 384
Thrushes, 383
Tieke, **70**, 418
Tit, Black, 396
  Pied, 396
  Yellow-breasted, 396
Titi, **8**, 189, **13**, 211
Titi Wainui, **12**, 205
Titipounamu **66**, 371
Toanui, 186
Tokoeka, **1**, 168
Tomtit, **69**, 396
  North Island, **69**, 396
  Snares, **69**, 396
  South Island, **69**, 396
Torea, **38**, 293, 295
Toreapango, **38**, 295
Toroa, **3**, 176, 177
Toutouwai, **69**, 397
Traversia lyalli, 371
Triller, White-winged, **65**, 381
Trillers, 380
Tringa brevipes, **50**, 324
  flavipes, **50**, 325
  hypoleucos, **45**, 324
  incana, **50**, 323
  nebularia, **50**, 324
  stagnatilis, **50**, 325
  terek, **45**, 325
Tropicbird, Red-tailed, **21**, 236
  White-tailed, **21**, 236
Tropicbirds, 236
Tui, **70**, 405
Turdus merula, **67**, 383
  philomelos, **67**, 384
Turkey, Wild, **34**, 282
Turnagra capensis, **74**, 422
Turnstone, **45**, 311
  Ruddy, 311
Turtle-Dove, Spotted, 351
Tuturiwhatu, **40**, 300, 302

Tuturuatu, **41**, 306
Tyto alba, **63**, 367
Tytonidae, 367

Vanellus miles, **38**, 309

Wagtail, Willie, 427
Wanderer, 176
Warbler, Chatham Island, **66**, 392
  Grey, **66**, 391
Warblers, Australasian, 391
  Old World, 386
Waterfowl, 258
Wattlebird, Red, 402
Wattlebirds, 416
Waxeye, 400
Weavers, 412
Weka, **36**, 285
  Buff, 36, 285
  Western, **36**, 285
Weweia, **2**, 173
Whalebird, 209
Whekau, **74**, 366
Whimbrel, **48**, 320
  American, **48**, 320
  Asiatic, **48**, 320
  Little, **48**, 321
Whio, **30**, 265
Whistlers, 387
White-eye, 400
White-eyes, 400
Whitehead, **68**, 387
Woodhen, 285
Woodpigeon, 348
Woodswallow, Masked, **65**, 420
  White-browed, **65**, 420
Woodswallows, 420
Wren, Bush, **74**, 373
  Rock, **66**, 374
  Stephens Island, 371
Wrens, New Zealand, 371
Wrybill, **45**, 307

Xenicus gilviventris, **66**, 374
  longipes, **74**, 373

Yellowhammer, **72**, 406
Yellowhead, **68**, 389
Yellowlegs, Lesser, **50**, 325

Zosteropidae, 400
Zosterops lateralis, **66**, 400

Three Kings Is

North Cape
Parengarenga Harbour
Rangaunu Harbour
Ninety Mile
Beach
NORTHLAND
Kaitaia
Bay of Islands

Poor Knights Is

Hokianga Harbour
Whangarei

Hen and Chickens Is
Little Barrier I
Dargaville
Beach
Great Barrier I
Hauraki
Gulf
Tiritiri Matangi I
Kaipara Harbour

AUCKLAND
Mercury Is
Auckland
COROMANDEL
Manukau Harbour
Mayor I
Miranda
Firth of
Tauranga Harbour
Waikato River
Thames
Maketu Estuary
WAIKATO
Ohope Estuary
Raglan Harbour
Tauranga
East
Cape
Hamilton
BAY OF PLENTY
Raukumara Range
Kawhia Harbour
Rotorua
Rotorua
Lakes
KING
Urewera
POVERTY
COUNTRY
Taupo
BAY
New Plymouth
Lake
L Waikaremoana
Gisborne
Taupo
VOLCANIC
PLATEAU
Mahia
Mt Taranaki
Wairoa
Peninsula
Mt Ruapehu
Portland I
TARANAKI
Ahuriri Estuary
Napier
Waitotara Estuary
Hastings
Cape Kidnappers

Palmerston North
Ruahine Range
Manawatu Estuary
Porangahau Estuary
Levin
Mt Bruce
Cape Turnagain
Kapiti I
WAIRARAPA
Tararua Range
Mana I
Masterton
Wellington
L Wairarapa
Cook Strait
Cape Palliser